DANCING WITH SOPHIA

SUNY series in Integral Theory

Sean Esbjörn-Hargens, editor

DANCING WITH SOPHIA

INTEGRAL PHILOSOPHY ON THE VERGE

Edited by

Michael Schwartz and Sean Esbjörn-Hargens

SUNY PRESS

Cover image: Jennifer Baird, *Deep Time 5. Fallen Angel Feathers.* Painting—oil, acrylic, and silver-leaf on canvas. Reprinted with permission.

Published by State University of New York Press, Albany

Printed in the United States of America

For information, contact State University of New York Press, Albany, NY
www.sunypress.edu

Library of Congress Cataloging-in-Publication Data

Names: Schwartz, Michael, Ph.D., editor; Esbjörn-Hargens, Sean, editor
Title: Dancing with Sophia : integral philosophy on the verge / edited by Michael Schwartz and Sean Esbjörn-Hargens.
Description: Albany : State University of New York, 2019. | Series: SUNY series in integral theory | Includes bibliographical references and index.
Identifiers: LCCN 2018054475 | ISBN 9781438476551 (hardcover : alk. paper) | ISBN 9781438476544 (pbk. : alk. paper) | ISBN 9781438476568 (ebook)
Subjects: LCSH: Metatheory.
Classification: LCC B842 .D35 2019 | DDC 149—dc23
LC record available at https://lccn.loc.gov/2018054475

10 9 8 7 6 5 4 3 2 1

To my glorious family of origins—Ella, Len, and the late Lou and Ethel—with a heart of love and gratitude.

—Michael Schwartz

and

To Athena, my very own wisdom-dance partner—moving to the silent sound of your own owl's wings flapping.

—Sean Esbjörn-Hargens

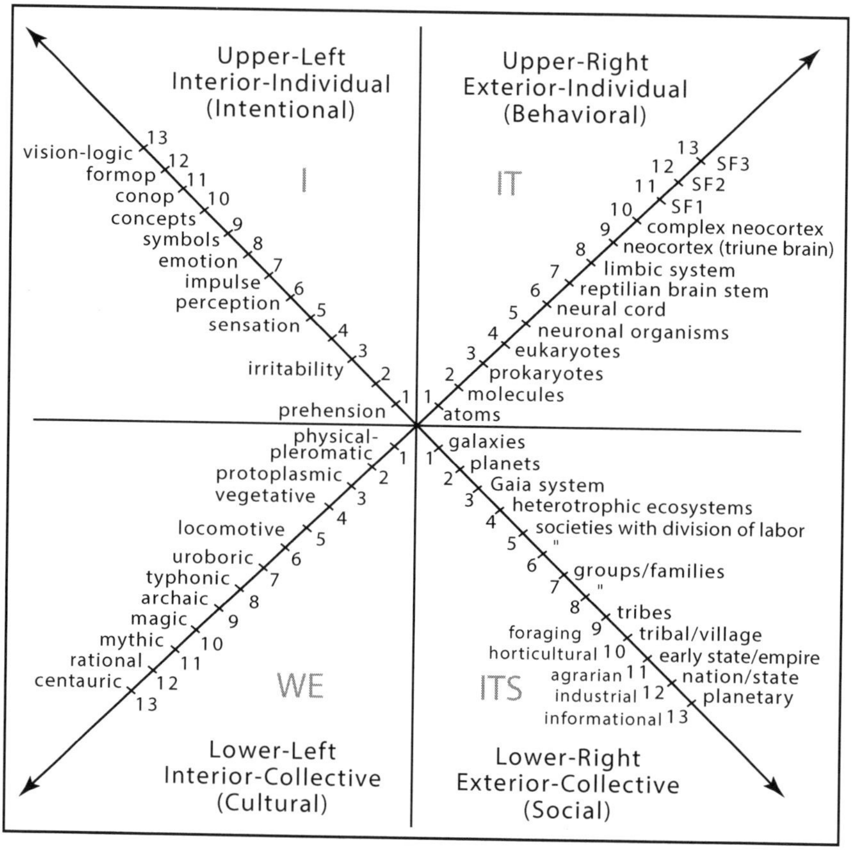

Wilber's iconic four quadrants. *Source:* Ken Wilber.

Contents

Part II: Wild Nature—Plural Touch

Part III: Limits and Critique

Part IV: Philosophy and Meta-Philosophy

Illustrations and Tables

Figures

Tables

Foreword

The Global-Historical Movement of Integral Thinking

Brian Schroeder

In a world perhaps more divisive and on edge than ever before, fraught with tensions and perils that just a couple of generations ago seemed practically unimaginable, what is called for is nothing less than a radically different way of thinking interrelationships. Rather than building fences of all types to shield oneself from the perceived threat of the other, withdrawing into reactive conservatism and xenophobic nationalism, the dangers we face—whether perceived or actual—must be met head-on lest retreat and fear take over as the dominant way of being in the world.

What binds us together is the shared place that we occupy in the world. This precarious life, as Judith Butler refers to it, is rife with uncertainty, suspicion, and fear. We exist in a historically unprecedented scenario: We are points in an evershifting intersection of "lines of flight," to use Gilles Deleuze and Félix Guattari's term, of multiple flows of information, forces, images, and representations that purport to communicate truth and meaning while simultaneously blurring exactly what that is. This goes beyond the age-old problem of competing interpretations; this is something new and different. We are witnessing the actualization of Orwellian doublespeak, of so-called alternative facts competing for equal footing on the field of what is demonstrably or evidentially true—or at least actual, if we can no longer rely on that vaunted word *truth.*

Modern Japan's first original philosopher, Nishida Kitarō, developed a "logic of place." This logic signifies the relation between two terms that are always determined in relation to a third term, namely, the place (場所 *basho*) wherein the relation occurs. In a nutshell, what Nishida attempted to do was give us a concept of the universal or the common. A remarkable figure in many respects, Nishida was thoroughly familiar with Western philosophy and employed its language, yet he always thought in relation to his culturally native Buddhism. So profound and influential was his thinking that it is today simply referred to as *Nishida tetsugaku*, which gave rise to the Kyoto School, the first genuinely world comparative philosophy. The universal place that Nishida invites us to enter is the Buddhist standpoint of *emptiness*, not the standard Western concept of being. For Nishida, emptiness, or what he preferred to call absolute nothingness (絶対無 *zettai mu*), affords us a place that is not restricted by preconceived ideas of boundary, limit, or truth. Instead, absolute nothingness, in its radical silence about such ideas, opens both thinking and relationships in an everflowing dialogical space that responds to difference and otherness—which, depending on one's perspective, are either the cornerstones or the stumbling blocks of community—in such a way as to make space for the silence that listens to the other rather than the silence that closes off communication.

The philosophy of one such as Nishida serves both as a model and an inspiration for precisely the type of thinking that occurs in Michael Schwartz and Sean Esbjörn-Hargens's rich and provocative coedited volume *Dancing with Sophia: Integral Philosophy on the Verge*. The project of integral theory is an effort to realize a new place for philosophy. Rethinking interrelationships is predicated on rethinking the place and the scope of thinking per se. Although the initial association of integral theory is with the work of Ken Wilber, the desire for a holistic theory extends back millennia. The Buddha's conception of codependent origination, Laozi's understanding of *dao* (道), Heracleitus's dynamic conception of the unity of φύσις and λόγος, the wisdom of the *Bhagavad Gītā*, Adi Shankara's *advaita vedānta*—these are but a few early moments in the history of ideas that prefigure integral theory, even if the contemporary scope of the term is much broader. The spirit of integral theory also emerged in the nineteenth century, beginning with the romantic era and in thinkers such as F.W.J. Schelling, G.W.F. Hegel, and even Friedrich Nietzsche, despite his great emphasis on the individual. In the twentieth century one can look to Henri Bergson, Alfred North Whitehead, and Justus Buchler, but also to Martin Heidegger and

Maurice Merleau-Ponty, and the already mentioned contributions of the Kyoto School, for integral tendencies and to the more recent thinking of Peter Sloterdijk, Deleuze, and Guattari. This is just to name a very few of the wide range of thinkers (and here only from the discipline of philosophy) who have helped to inform, if not shape, both the reception and place of integral theory.

To be sure, integral theory is a controversial standpoint among many academics today, as the editors of this volume, Schwartz and Esbjörn-Hargens, point out in their informative introduction. In part that controversy stems from integral theory being a genuinely comparative approach to thinking, which is, unfortunately, still all too often ignored or disregarded in the professional academic world. But despite the political orientation of some very large and influential players on the world stage, globalism is an indisputable fact and its scope extends beyond the mostly economic mask it has adopted until now, affecting societies and cultures across the planet in multivalent ways.

The essays contained in *Dancing with Sophia* gather the perspectives of a number of significant thinkers on a truly dazzling array of issues and themes. If a perceived weakness of integral theory is that it attempts to be, as Wilber writes, a theory of everything, this is also its strength. The impulse toward the metatheoretical is not a delusional desire to adopt a panoptical or divine perspective; rather, it is the inclination to reorient thinking past the narrow lenses of a predominantly egocentric stance that still tends to see the world in terms of a classical epistemological distinction between subject and object, thus perpetuating and reinforcing all the traditional valuative dualisms that emerge from such a perspective.

Integral theory is a bold and provocative endeavor. It challenges one to think past the norm, to sail beyond the horizon and risk encountering the Scylla and Charybdis of what is academically acceptable—or at least familiar—and what is possible, in ways that only are now beginning to dawn on both thinking and dwelling. If it is nothing else, integral theory is the movement beyond the purely intellectual into the lived experience. This is its "meta-" dimension properly understood. Zen master Hakuin Ekaku, in his famous *Zazen Wasan* (*Song in Praise of Zazen*), grasped the spirit of integral philosophy as reflected in the beautiful title of the present volume: "With form that is no-form, going and coming, we are never astray; with thought that is no-thought, even singing and dancing are the voice of the Dharma. How boundless and free is the sky of Samadhi! How bright the full moon of wisdom!"[1] May the reader of this unique collection put aside all preconceptions and join this splendid dance with Sophia, moving wondrously toward the verge of . . .

—Rochester, NY

Notes

1. "Hakuin Zenji's 'Song of Zazen,'" in Robert Aitken, *Taking the Path of Zen* (San Francisco: North Point Press, 1982), p. 113; translation modified slightly.

Introduction

Integral Philosophy on the Verge

Michael Schwartz and Sean Esbjörn-Hargens

The title of this volume, *Dancing with Sophia*, conjures the spirit of twentieth-century Russian philosopher, poet, and mystic Vladimir Solovyov, who wrote his first book, *The Philosophical Principles of Integral Knowledge* in 1874 when he was twenty-four-years old. It was published three years later in 1877. Solovyov (2000) was perhaps the first modern writer to use the phrase *integral philosophy* (p. 57), advancing a philosophically informed integral way of knowing and knowledge-formation that "must be free of any exclusiveness or one-sideness" (p. 71) in "answer[ing] to all the requirements of the human spirit" (p. 109). Solovyov was deeply inspired by visions he had of Sophia over the course of his life.[1] We ourselves are inspired by his fearless call for rigorous and critical inclusiveness—especially germane today for any philosophy to address the complexity of our planetary moment and its globalizing processes—and perhaps even more so by his bold invocation of Sophia as the guiding light of philosophy: Wisdom to retake her rightful seat as a core regulative principle of philosophy itself.

The subtitle, "Integral Philosophy on the Verge," echoes and honors contemporary American Continental philosopher John Sallis's *The Verge of Philosophy* (Sallis, 2008) and in its articulation of philosophy as always already at the limit, on the verge, never finished, always already underway and emergent (as in the twisting free of its metaphysical inheritance)—here adapted to the situation of contemporary integral theory on the verge of its own clarification *as* philosophical. Together the title and subtitle signal our sense that integral theory has a unique and important contribution to make to the contemporary philosophical landscape in its capacity to orient wise, skillful action for the well-being and flourishing of our hypercomplex planetary civilization.

What, then, is integral theory? It is an ironically self-titled "theory of everything."[2] More technically and centrally, it is an integrative metatheory that discerns and organizes the interrelationships among existing (first and second order) theories, methodologies, and epistemologies in a given discipline or across disciplines, as these are proper to and conditioned by differing regional ontologies. In this way, it invites and enacts meta-systemic to cross-paradigmatic modes of post-formal cognition in opening up interdisciplinary and transdisciplinary domains of inquiry and insight.[3] Its fruition in the present moment has been seeded by American Ken Wilber, author of over two dozen books translated into over twenty languages. Drawing on an impressive range of knowledge and research domains, Wilber has for the past four decades been developing a metatheory that has had a wide impact on fields as diverse as ecological studies, sustainability, leadership training, cognitive development, business management, psychology, psychiatry, contemplative Christianity, esoteric Buddhism, comparative religion, spiritual practice, and metatheorizing itself. Many prominent artists and musicians, such as Saul Williams, Alex Grey, Ed Kowalczyk, Lana and Lilly Wachowski, to name a few, have attested to being deeply influenced by Wilber's work.

Pointedly, Wilber is not an academic, nor has he ever held a university teaching position. His books are written purposely for a wider audience. As Clint Fuhs once reported,[4] early in his twenties Wilber decided that his life aims were soteriological, concerned with individual and collective emancipation; where a more direct writing style would reach a wider audience. When turning to his texts, some professional academics tend to complain about their populist, nonspecialist, and generalizing-sweeping tenor—the kinds of detailed argumentation, proper to academic conventions, not always at the forefront or even discernable by inference. Nonetheless, in our view, his vast corpus of published and unpublished texts, interviews, and talks contain, if sometimes in the margins of a footnote or in pith form, novel insights and formulations deserving of sustained academic attention and debate. He is, in the Heideggerian sense, an *orginary thinker*; or, to echo Deleuze and Guattari, an *inventor of concepts.*[5]

While Wilber has been the principle inaugurator of present-day integral theory, there has emerged over the past two decades a large and diverse international community of scholar-practitioners who are advancing integral in ever more novel ways. As of this writing, there have been four international integral theory conferences in San Francisco's Bay Area (2008, 2010, 2013, and 2015), each with presenters from all five continents. There is also a flourishing scholarly book series at SUNY Press (to which this volume belongs) and a peer-reviewed academic periodical—the *Journal of Integral Theory and Practice*—with nearly a decade of quarterly publications.[6] Slowly but surely, integral's entry into academic debate and scrutiny is taking shape; as in the recent and ongoing dialogue of integral theory with one of the other most important academic metatheories available, that of critical realism founded by the late Roy Bhaskar.[7]

Given the scope and ambition of integral theory, it has at times been referenced, if loosely, as a philosophy—in fact, some academic authors refer to Wilber in their own work as "an American philosopher." And, to be sure, Wilber has drawn upon and engaged a vast number of North Atlantic and Asian philosophers: from Plato to Foucault and from Nagarjuna to Aurobindo. Taking this topic up with directness, this volume explores the philosophical dimensions and implications of integral theory. It is, as the title announces, a dancing with Sophia, the movement of integral at its own (metatheoretical) limit, on the verge of its own philosophical emergence. Which invites the questions: What or when is philosophy?

While the term *philosophy* is used regularly in both professional and popular circles, there is no clear agreement in the academy on the delimitation of its meaning and sense—more so than in most academic fields once deemed part of the *Geisteswissenschaften*. To take up a purposely generic source of definition, this from a Wikipedia entry:

> *Philosophy is the study of general and fundamental problems, such as those connected with reality, existence, knowledge, values, reason, mind, and language. Philosophy is distinguished from other ways of addressing such problems by its critical, generally systematic approach and its reliance on rational argument.*[8]

Although from a Wikipedia entry, this definition draws upon several academic source texts. And, to be sure, it is a clear and fair characterization. Yet does it apply only to the *Fach* of philosophy? For instance, one can make the case that the system theorizing of Niklas Luhmann satisfies many of the basic points of this definition, where his monumental project incorporates or translates operations from philosophical streams like phenomenology and deconstruction into system theory terms.[9] Conversely, widely recognized philosophers might find themselves at odds with some or many aspects of the above definition. A number of prominent Continental philosophers of recent times would call into question the desirability or possibility of a philosophy that is "systematic" in orientation (raising the question of what such philosophers mean by "system" vis-à-vis the sense of system in a Luhmann). The characterization of philosophy's "reliance on rational argument" itself is complicated in certain circles, as one of the themes descending from strains of German Idealism is the question of the limits of rationality—the relation of reason and non-reason. The Nietzschean and Derridean thematic explorations and performance of philosophical metaphor are cases in point. John Sallis, in turn, sees philosophy as emerging in ancient Greece around the question of the relation between of being and logos. He goes on to develop a novel philosophy of the "logic of the imagination" that includes *both* rational non-contradictory as well as exorbitant logics—making room for a range of logoi that are rational and a-rational.[10] And the American pragmatist tradition has often looked to developmental psychology for clarification on matters of rational thought, where today a number of lines of leading-edge empirical research no longer posit analytic reason as the pinnacle of human cognition.

Centering on the life-practice of the philosopher herself, Michel Foucault, at the end of his life, posited that philosophy in its descent from the ancient Greeks bequeaths at least two distinct strains of inquiry that have complexly intersected and diverged over the centuries: 1) an analytics of truth, and 2) an ontology of who we are—the latter as philosophy a way of life, a bios replete with practices of self (Foucault here inspired by the scholarship of Pierre Hadot).[11] In the ancient world these two strains intersected in the figure of Socrates, giving rise to the philosopher as *parrhesiastes*—the one who tells the truth or incites truth-telling on behalf of obligations beyond the self, going so far as to risk his or her very life.

Other lines of recent philosophy have broached the theme of the other of modern and postmodern philosophy in terms to the side of that of transformational practices—the relation then of philosophy to non-philosophy. Jürgen Habermas sees philosophy in the modern university as having been decentered by the rise of specialized domains of inquiry, such that many of the themes and claims proper to premodern philosophy have become taken up by these disciplines with a new specialized methodological rigor, displacing philosophy's claim to superior knowledge: Philosophy assuming, then, a new role as placeholder of critical reflection (Habermas, 1993). For Bhaskar, philosophy has a special and crucial role as *underlaboring* for existing disciplines and domains of being, clarifying these disciplines while never standing above them, an interlocutor in mutual learning processes.

He also offers critical genealogies that go back to the ancient Greeks (e.g., Parmenides) and forward to the postmodern moment (e.g., Rorty); arguing further that the "non-philosophy" of historical-social conditions and everyday practices readily affect a given philosophy's character, pointing inquiry into what he terms the field of the "meta-philosophical" as required for a meta-critique of philosophical problems and their resolution.[12] As a kind of twist on this theme of philosophy and the social, the later Wittgenstein, according to some recent readings of his work, practiced philosophy as a kind of therapeutic of our language games, in instances examining seeming deep philosophical problems or puzzles, showing how these dissolve and clarify (and thereby "purify") a form of life already underway.[13]

From this brief sampling, it is clear that the Wikipedia definition, as fine as it is, cannot cover the range of what counts as philosophy today—which is not a fault, but a symptom of the overlapping-*cum*-diverging senses and practices of philosophy. While this is not to say that all views of what philosophy is are equally valid, it is to acknowledge that the professional practice and status of philosophy today is "singular plural." And this is even without turning to so-called non-Western philosophy and to the enterprise of comparative philosophy now underway, which countenances the validity of a view of the "Greek miracle" of the West as the origin of what can count as philosophy proper.[14]

Nonetheless, within this plurality of philosophical practice there are emergent trends of pregnant import that transverse the various philosophy lineages. Stepping back to look more broadly at the human and natural sciences, we see an upsurge in the call for interdisciplinary and transdisciplinary theoretical models and knowledge-integration. Rather than a mere fashion of the times—and despite the majority of this activity in the human sciences leaving much to be desired—this endeavor is well-intended to counter the fragmentation of ever-increasingly specialized disciplines (and even fragmentation within a given discipline) in generating higher order modes of insight that in their epistemic complexity and ontological nuance are better able to engage our planetary situation.[15] In philosophy too one can detect trends toward the more integrative and inclusive: the revival and theoretical reformulation (as responsive to modern and postmodern critiques) of what might count as systematic philosophies (e.g., Puntel, 2008), as synthetic philosophies (e.g., Zalamea, 2012), and even as meta-philosophies (e.g., Bhaskar, 2012a and 2012b). In cases, there is a conscious striving to retrieve and reintegrate discarded elements of prior philosophizing while honoring modern and postmodern philosophical insights and critiques, as with the effort to vindicate strong ontology and re-enliven the question of substance in strains of speculative realism and object-oriented ontology (e.g., Harman, 2010).

A symptom of this trend is the expanding use of the term *meta*: meta-metaphysics (e.g., Chalmers et al., 2009), metaontology (e.g., Berto, 2015), metaethics (e.g., van Roojen, 2015; Miller, 2013), and metaphilosophy (e.g., Overgaard et al., 2013). So while postmodern philosophers like Lyotard critiqued our inherited meta-narratives, it would seem that today all kinds of meta-views are making a comeback, albeit in more sophisticated philosophical forms—leaving behind what Mark Edwards (2009) calls "integrative monisms" (taken in a vulgar sense as closed, subsumptive without remainder, and naively totalizing) to explore "integrative pluralisms" (taken in one of many interrelated senses as open dynamic wholeness inclusive of tensions, singularities, absence, and the non-reduction of otherness). Integral theory, in its best moments, has gestured toward versions of the latter—even, as some of the authors in this volume contend, these latter approaches themselves entail philosophical complication and critique.

Having affinities with integral theory itself, Peter Sloterdijk has posited a philosophically motivated general disciplinics for the future that

> would integrally encompass the spectrum of ability systems composed of knowledge and practical acts. This spectrum extends from 1) acrobatics and aesthetics, including the system of art forms and genres—NB: in the post-university House of Knowledge, the *studium generale* consists of artistry, not philosophy—via 2) athletics (the general study of sporting forms) to 3) rhetoric or sophistry, then 4) therapeutics in all its specialized branches, 5) epistemics (including philosophy), 6) a general study of professions (including the 'applied arts,' which are assigned to the field of *arts et metiers*), and 7) the study of machinistic technologies. It also includes 8) administrativics, which constitutes both the static substructure of the political or governmental and the universe of legal systems, as well as 9) the encyclopedia of meditation systems in their dual role as self-techniques and not-self-techniques (the distinction between declared and undeclared meditations comes into play here), 10) ritualistics (as humans, according to Wittgenstein, are ceremonial animals and the ceremonies form trainable behavioral modules whose carriers appear as 'peoples'—which is why the linguistic sciences, like the theory

> of games and 'religions,' form a sub-discipline of ritualistics), 11) the study of sexual practices, 12) gastronomics, and finally 13) the open list of cultivatable activities, whose openness means the interminability of the discipline-forming and thus subjectification-enabling field itself.

He states that "ordinary philosophers restrict themselves to field 5, with occasional excursions to 8 or 3 and 1," a claim, to be sure, which is not beyond questioning—whereas, for Sloterdijk, Foucault was unusual in that his "interventions touch on fields 1, 3, 4, 5, 8, 10 and 11" (Sloterdijk, 2013, pp. 156–157).

Significantly, integral theory plays in more of these than does Foucault, opening spaces of inquiry into domain-interrelationships among virtually all the fields that Sloterdijk lists. And it does so in ways that often align with a number of the philosophical ventures and themes cited above, as various essays in this volume will make clear. What we can say, in light of the plurality of contemporary philosophical projects, is that integral theory has genuine philosophical dimensions and potencies, which the subsequent chapters venture forth. And that it is a certain rigorous openness and critical inclusiveness—what Wilber (2003, pp. 16–21) has called the principle of non-exclusion—which is perhaps a signal feature of any philosophy that might be called integral: An inclusiveness, moreover, that holds to an ethos that philosophy recognize and acknowledge its own allergies, blind spots, and reactivity, ready to adjust itself accordingly, as always already oriented toward individual and planetary well-being and flourishing. This radical critical openness and non-exlusiveness entails, in the philosophical register, a remarkable drawing together into dialogue and critique diverse voices, this volume's chapters including those of Derrida, Schelling, Dōgen, Heidegger, Nietzsche, Levinas, Whitehead, Habermas, Kierkegaard, Žižek, Buber, Dewey, Nancy, Kant, Irigaray, Serres, Latour, Hegel, Hume, Levi Bryant, Harman, Wittgenstein, among others.

Before we present an overview of each chapter in the volume, it is to be noted up front that all the authors in this volume are men. There are, to be sure, brilliant and active women scholar-practitioners in the integral worlds; many of them of outstanding philosophical acumen, such as Bonnitta Roy—who is cited in the volume—and who were invited to contribute. And yet despite the editors' sincerest efforts, including delaying the volume to secure at least one contribution from a woman writer, this did not come to pass for a variety of circumstantial reasons. We, as editors, painfully acknowledge this lacuna. And while we did make strong efforts in this regard—and from the start of the project titling the book wisdom as feminine (Sophia)—the fault for not securing a more balanced gender array of authors lies with us alone. We wonder too if this is not also a symptom of a decisive masculine imbalance in the integral worlds, perhaps (in echoing Freeman's chapter) that integral theory has been centered in embracing and performing a Lacanian-Žižekian masculine logic of the All over that of a feminine logic of the Non-All. Some of the chapters address this and related philosophical topics. The following overview of the volume proceeds in the order that chapters appear by each author listed.

Zachary Stein situates Wilber's integral theory within the tradition of American pragmatism and that lineage's commitments to: 1) philosophical psychology, 2) epistemic comprehensiveness, 3) action-oriented theorizing, 4) the integration of science and religion, 5) evolutionary metaphysics, and 6) social emancipation. For Stein, integral opens important vistas for the future of philosophy in its responding to the current moment of geo-historical planetization. Propounding a unique mode of meta-theorizing, which can be traced to earlier pragmatists like Peirce and Baldwin, integral organizes knowledge across many domains via principled distinctions with emancipatory aims, countering the modern research university's increasing bureaucratization and fragmentation of knowledge, which renders inquiry and knowledge formation incapable of addressing the complexity of contemporary planetary problematics.

Martin Beck Matuštík, who studied philosophy under Habermas, opens his contribution boldly: "Ken Wilber has articulated a remarkably robust postmetaphysical spiritualty after post/modernity at the same time Jürgen Habermas has been reconsidering some of his earlier dismissals of religious thinking." For Matuštík, integral is dangerous for the current age in its capacity and acumen for criticizing both dogmatic secularizing reason and religious belief retreating into premodern fundamentalist waves of development. In turn, Matuštík forwards a project of an *integral critical theory* (ICT) that with emancipatory care attends to three dimensions of human existence and need: material, sociopolitical, and spiritual. As regards the last or spiritual domain, integral theory has posited two discrete axises—*stages* and *states* of consciousness. Drawing on Kierkegaard, Matuštík posits a third axis transversing these first two (and with regard the Dustin DiPerna's spiritual developmental cube, also transvering its dimension of vantage points), what

he terms *modes of existence*; thus enabling linkage of individual existential and collective political-economic concerns, a theme earlier explored (if unsatisfactorily for the author) by Marcuse, Sartre, and Habermas himself—ICT will thus be able to advance a multidimensional view of redemptive hope.

Michael Schwartz takes up Levinasian insights about the call of the Good through the face of the other and reworks these in light of integral views of the quadrants and the elemental nature of perspectives. Given the integral view of a non-dual Kosmos and the twining of being and becoming, of stillness and dance, all is always already perfect, Goodness pervades all that is—even as the Good incessantly calls Being to be otherwise. Schwartz invites us to attune to the call of the Good as tetra-arising, as multi-perspectival: the always already calling of us into ever greater 1) freedom, 2) vitality, 3) responsibility, and 4) justice—where these four "hyper-goods" and their interrelationships help us see anew the moral orientations of a number of Continental philosophies.

For **Michael E. Zimmerman** integral theory "addresses the problem of nihilism that arose in modernity and that became even more pronounced in postmodernity," by moving us from the negative evaluations of modernity offered by Nietzsche and Heidegger to the critique-infused appreciation offered by Wilber. Rather than a deflationary narrative, as in Heidegger's history of being, Wilber cites evidence for a nuanced view of an evolving Kosmos in which humanity is always already situated and participates. This also separates Wilber's views from that of early Buddhism, which also sees history as decline. While agreeing with Heidegger that human being is a clearing, a nothing, no-thing, Wilber presses this non-dual insight in the direction of the spiritual saturation of all that arises, such that nothing *matters*—and matters profoundly for an evolving Kosmos, where the local outcome of humanity and earth is an open question, one worthy of our concern and energies.

David E. Storey sees the integral ecology of Sean Esbjörn-Hargens and Michael E. Zimmerman (both contributors to this volume as coeditor and author respectively) as a "sounder basis for a philosophy of nature than Heidegger's thought." Heidegger, especially in the earlier moment of the Dasein analytic, tries to steer a middle way through realist and constructivist views of nature; yet he does not account for how the domains of intentionality and causality relate. Later Heidegger offers first a repetition of the

Greek notion of *physis*—elemental earth—eventually forwarding an account of the fourfold of earth and sky, mortals and gods within the embrace of Godhead. For Storey, despite these efforts, the later Heidegger "does scant justice to the rich world being explored and charted by the biological and ecological sciences." While honoring Heidegger's various, often nuanced, approaches to nature and life, including his philosophical adapting of the notion of *Umwelt* (environment) from von Uexküll, Storey argues for the robustness of the senses of nature as forwarded in integral ecology.

Jason M. Wirth's chapter directly echoes the title of this volume by exploring the dance between *Naturphilosphie* and integral ecology. Wirth is particularly interested in how an "ecology of thinking" can be an expression of integral philosophy. Drawing on the figures of Schelling and Dōgen, Wirth (himself a leading Schelling scholar) explores integral ecology's distinction among "nature," "Nature," and "NATURE." This sets the stage for Wirth to consider the role of transrational practice in "thinking on the verge." (It is worth noting that Schelling is an important historical figure for any exploration of integral philosophy; Wilber evoking Schelling at crucial junctures in his 1995 study *Sex, Ecology, Spirituality: The Spirit of Evolution*, often considered the inaugural moment of contemporary integral theory.) Wirth's chapter is particularly valuable in the way it anchors an exploration of key philosophical distinctions within integral ecology where Western philosophy and Eastern contemplative practice move to the exquisite music of the rain dripping off pine needles as a crisp breeze passes.

Sam Mickey interprets integral theory as a philosophy of touch, with the integral approach able to honor, map, and coordinate varieties of Continental thought that entertain this theme—as with phenomenology, postmodernism, feminist theory, and speculative realism—integral is able to offer a rigorous and critical meta-philosophical overview of these philosophical theories. Yet integral, in its movement to coordinate a vast array of perspectives, need take up a *lightness of touch*. Thus, this study opens with an inquiry into what this lightness might be: which, paradoxically, integral in touching perspectives must also leave it all untouched—the withdrawal of sense in non-sense. Mickey drawing upon Jean-Luc Nancy, speculative realism, and other recent modes of philosophizing in articulating a philosophical lightness of touch.

Zayin Cabot challenges the coherence of classical integral theory's non-dual account of novelty and change. He draws on distinctions in process philosophy between novative-transformational and innovative-creative regimes of thought. He cites classic integral as falling for the most part into the novative-transformational camp, where what changes is theory superficial and hence less real than what does not change. He argues that in integral's case spirit sides toward a primacy of timeless spirit. If classic integral theory is, by its own account, process philosophy in a microgenetic sense, Cabot is pointing to a reformulation of integral theory. He seeks to bring together enlightenment and evolution in the context of a process thought that takes on a macrogenetic turn as it locates creativity as ontologically primary and particularly capable of addressing the dance of spirit and world.

Gregory Desilet considers the respective (and what for the author are incompatible) views on the nature of being in the philosophies of Ken Wilber and Jacques Derrida. Desilet opens his comparative commentary on what he diagnoses as Wilber's misreading of Derrida on the theme of the transcendental signifier/signified—Wilber positing spirit in a manner that in the end Derrida would consider baldly (and badly) metaphysical, despite the former's claim of advancing an integral "post-metaphysics." If there is a question of transcendence in Derrida, it is that of a radical atheism, where the call of justice-yet-to-come is less a metaphysical "substantive" in its timelessness and more a temporally displaced/displacing moral "regulative" as undeconstructable promise. While confessing to being divided in his loyalties to the respective positions and contributions of Wilber and Derrida, Desilet concludes that a Derridean "general economic metaphysic," rather than the more closed metaphysical economic of Wilber, is the philosophically more justifiable position.

For **Nicholas Hedlund** critical realism (CR) and integral theory (IT) are among the most comprehensive and sophisticated expressions of a still yet-to-be fully consolidated integral, post-postmodern philosophy. Both CR and IT explicitly situate themselves not only as alternatives to postmodernism, but claim to go beyond both positivism and social constructivism while integrating key aspects of those respective philosophical discourses. In the face of radicalized forms of post-Kantian skepticism and anti-realism characteristic of postmodernism, both approaches champion a return to ontology at a higher turn of the developmental spiral—a return to some form of realism that substantially integrates the epistemic advances of both positivism and social constructivism and thus is not a regression to a form of precritical, first philosophy (*prima philosophia*) or dogmatic metaphysics. In this chapter,

Hedlund explores the ontological and epistemological strengths and weaknesses of CR and IT, highlighting their key points of complementarity on the way to forging the outlines of a provisional synthesis of these two approaches to being and knowing, what the author calls critical realist integral theory (CRIT)—thus attempting to do with CR and IT what they each attempt to do with the philosophical discourse of modernity and postmodernity: Transcend and integrate them into an emergent intellectual formation.

Tom Murray is successful in drawing on the embodied philosophy of Mark Johnson and George Lakoff to explore issues of ontology and epistemology. Johnson and Lakoff's groundbreaking work into "metaphors we live by" and the resulting "philosophy in the flesh" are fertile soils for integral philosophies to explore how to anchor "vision-logic" in the centauric embodiment associated with integral thinking. A particularly important aspect of Murray's chapter is the ways in which he foregrounds the importance of integral philosophy being a self-critical philosophy that is not only embodied, but is self-reflexive and turns its integral lenses onto itself. This self-critical openness is one of the defining characteristics of integral philosophy on the verge.

Drawing on key figures such as Hegel, Schelling, Žižek, and Derrida, **Cameron Stewart Rees Freeman** explores the implications of Lacan's "Non-All" for Ken Wilber's post-metaphysics. In particular he cites the "Non-All" as a "feminine logic" in contrast to the totalizing impulse of Wilber's more (masculine) integral approach as a logic of the All. Freeman's deconstructive reading of integral philosophy places it on the verge of something perhaps even more integrative by allowing for the uncertainty and the non-totalizing expression of the Non-All. This chapter echoes others in the volume by making room in integral philosophy for what Roy Bhaskar calls absence, negativity, and non-identity in the latter's critique of the ontological monovalence of Western philosophical thought.[16] Thus, Freeman's contribution serves to help raise important questions around what is or can be integrated in an integral philosophy, what lies outside of that integration—and what is meant by "integration" itself.

For **Bruce Alderman** the four pronouns at the center of the integral model have yielded impressive explanatory and integrative power. While they are useful for classifying disciplines according to their primary epistemological orientations, they are not sufficient to account for or disclose the ontological views that inform our perspectives. After situating integral theory in a longer lineage of "pronoun philosophies," Alderman introduces an expanded set of grammatical lenses to complement integral's four fundamental perspectives. These lenses, based on six common parts of speech, can serve both metaphysical and meta-metaphysical ends, helping to identify the ontological views that inform our person perspectives, and providing an integrative architecture for correlating and interfacing various metaphysical systems and integrative meta-theories—advancing a meta-philosophical grammar of philosophies.

In addition to the volume's chapters, just summarized, we include as afterword a fresh piece by **Ken Wilber** himself, the principle inaugurator of integral theory—the written version of his keynote presentation at July 2015's Fourth International Integral Theory Conference in Sonoma County, California, titled "Realism and Idealism in Integral Theory," which extends his many previous discussions of the differences between and interwining of ontology and epistemology; on this occasion responding to the recent metatheory dialogues between critical realism and integral theory (mentioned above). We are grateful to be able to include this bonus in the volume.

In putting this volume together there are a number of questions that emerged for us. We offer some of these here as a way of setting the stage for the chapters you are about to read:

- Are there masculine and feminine modes of philosophy (cf. Nietzsche's Apollonian and Dionysian forces, or the Lacanian-Žižekian ontologies of the All and non-All)? If so, what would be their productive, dynamic, and wisest relationship?
- In what ways might the transformation of the philosopher transform his or her philosophizing, hence philosophy itself? What might be the dimensions—psychological, spiritual, emancipatory, etc.—of such capacity training and how might all this impact philosophical views and claims about themes like being and knowing?
- What might be the proper and productive relationship between philosophy and nonphilosophy? How can or should philosophy draw on and include nonphilosophical sources?
- What is one to make of the relationship between philosophy and expanding claims about "meta": metatheory, metaethics, metaphilosophy, etc.?

- What is the role of the history of philosophy—and more broadly, the role of sociocultural history itself—in the generation of an integral philosophy?
- In what ways can philosophy be responsive to and relevant for our evermore hyper-complex world?
- What are the historical threads and antecedents (e.g., Solovyov) of integral philosophy on the verge?
- Given the populist (and deeply compassionate) intent of Wilber's writings in seeding contemporary integral theory, how might certain entrenched integral phrasings, as these have been circulating outside of academic circles for over three to four decades, be reworked so to twist them free of their pre-philosophical and precritical resonances (as the latter senses have accrued through the diverse and populist uses of Wilber's generative concepts)?

As you engage the chapters in this volume, we invite you to dance with us exploring integral philosophy on the verge. Together we feel the authors in this volume are successful in naming and shining the light of wisdom on some of the key issues that an emerging integral philosophy is uniquely positioned to address.

Notes

1. See Kornblatt (2009) for a detailed exploration on the role of Solovyov's visions of Sophia and their influence on his poetry and philosophy.

2. Wilber (2001). Esbjörn-Hargens (2015) has re-envisioned integral metatheory as a "theory of anything." For an overview of integral theory, see Esbjörn-Hargens (2010).

3. On post-formal modes of cognition, see Cook-Greuter (2013) and also Fischer (1980). On the developmental demands for bringing forth actual, rather than so-called, interdisciplinary and transdisciplinary projects, see Stein (2007). On the question of metatheory itself (the nuanced debates about which are beyond the confines of this Introduction), see Bhaskar et al. (2015) and Hedlund and Esbjörn-Hargens (in press).

4. At the first Critical Realism and Integral Theory Symposium, John F. Kennedy University, September 2011.

5. Deleuze and Guattari (1994). For more on Wilber, see Visser (2003).

6. The *Journal of Integral Theory and Practice* was founded in 2006 and published approximately 400 pages of material each year for 9 consecutive years (2006–2015) for a total of approximately 4000 pages of academic peer-reviewed debate and discussion of integral theory applied in over 35 distinct disciplines by several hundred academics and professionals.

7. There have been four symposia bringing together leading practitioners in critical realism and in integral theory: in the Bay Area in 2011, 2013, and 2015; and at the University of London in 2014. Initially, this sparked a brief "exchange" between Bhaskar and Wilber (see Bhaskar, 2012a, 2012b, and Wilber, 2012). The more substantial outcome of these symposia is a two-volume collection of essays: Bhaskar et al. (2015) and Hedlund and Esbjörn-Hargens (in press).

8. See "Philosophy" (n.d.).

9. For example, Luhmann (1993). For commentary, see Moeller (2012).

10. See Sallis (2012). On stages of post-formal rationality, see Cook-Greuter (2013) and also Fischer (1980). For a critique of the limits of analytic reasoning in light of a Bhaskarean view of a four-stadia dialectic, see Laske (2008).

11. See Foucault (1984, 2001) and Hadot (1995). On the transformation of the contemporary philosopher, a study assuming a Foucaultian line of thought reworked through the integral theory distinction between transformation and translation (Schwartz, 2010).

12. On philosophy as underlabor, see Bhaskar (1987). On the meta-critique of the philosophical tradition, see Bhaskar (1993) and especially Bhaskar (1994).

13. Along these lines of a Wittgenstein interpretation, see Sloterdijk (2013).

14. On the "Greek miracle" of philosophy as innovatively re-articulated by Deleuze and Guattari, see Gasché (2014). And on the comparative enterprise itself, see the journal *Comparative and Continental Philosophy* (Maney Publishing: http://www.maneyonline.com/loi/ccp; retrieved February 27, 2015); the complementary book series of the same title (Northwestern University Press: http://www.nupress.northwestern.edu/series/comparative-and-continental-philosophy); and the Comparative and Continental Philosophy Circle's annual scholarly events (http://www.comcontphilosophy.org/).

15. This kind of integrative activity is already underway, in practice, as exemplified in the medical sciences, for example, through such approaches as systematic reviews (Gough et al., 2012). Rather than some precritical theoretical mistake, it has become essential for the advancement of knowledge on the one hand, and on the other has practical import in, for example, integrative approaches to the treatment of diseases like cancer, enhancing such treatment. With regard to ecological and sustainability studies, cf. Esbjörn-Hargens and Zimmerman (2009).

16. See Bhaskar (1993). Non-identity of the three depth of the Real is proper to the first moment of the four stadia proper to this dialectic scheme. Negativity and the reality of absence are proper to the second stadia. These are two of the

key components in Bhaskar's critique of ontological monovalence. For an argument that a Žižekian ontology of Non-All being must, in the end, be distinguished from and rejected in light of a robust Bhaskarean ontology (due to the former's lack of depth strata, hence falling toward the trap of what critical realism calls *actualism*), see Rutzou (2012). Rutzou's approach, couched as immanent critique, while a strong argument, seems by and large predetermined to defeat what is projected as a rival position rather than or in addition to engage in a mutual learning process—for example, what Žižekian ontology and philosophy might offer a critical realist dialectic, shedding light on what might be absences or edges in critical realism's own continuing maturation and unfolding.

References

Berto, Francesco, and Matteo Plebani. 2015. *Ontology and Metaontology: A Contemporary Guide*. London: Bloomsbury Academic.

Bhaskar, Roy. 1986. *Scientific Realism and Human Emancipation*. London: Verso.

Bhaskar, Roy. 1993. *Dialectic: The Pulse of Freedom*. London: Verso.

Bhaskar, Roy. 1994. *Plato Etc.: Problems of Philosophy and their Resolution*. London: Verso.

Bhaskar, Roy. 2012a. *The Philosophy of MetaReality: Creativity, Love and Freedom*. London: Routledge.

Bhaskar, Roy. 2012b. *Reflections on MetaReality: Transcendence, Emancipation and Everyday life*. London: Routledge.

Bhaskar, Roy. 2012c. "Considerations on 'Ken Wilber on Critical Realism,'" *Journal of Integral Theory and Practice* 7: 39–42.

Bhaskar, Roy, et al. 2015. *Metatheory for the Twenty-first Century: Critical Realism and Integral Theory in Dialogue*. London and New York: Routledge.

Cook-Greuter, Susanne. 2013. "Nine Levels of Increasing Embrace in Ego Development: A Full-Spectrum Theory of Vertical Growth and Meaning Making." http://www.cook-greuter.com/Cook-Greuter%209%20levels%20paper%20new%201.1%2714%2097p%5B1%5D.pdf. Retrieved February 25, 2015.

Chalmers, David J., David Manley, and Ryan Wasserman (eds.). 2009. *Metametaphysics: New Essays on the Foundations of Ontology*. New York: Oxford University Press.

Deleuze, Gilles, and Félix Guattari. 1994. *What is Philosophy?* trans. Hugh Tomlinson and Graham Burchell. New York: Columbia University Press.

Edwards, Mark. 2010. *Organisational Transformation for Sustainability: An Integral Metatheory*. London: Routledge.

Esbjörn-Hargens, Sean. 2010. "An Overview of Integral Theory: An All-inclusive Framework for the Twenty-First Century." In *Integral Theory in Action: Applied, Theoretical, and Constructive Perspectives on the AQAL Model*, ed. Sean Esbjörn-Hargens, 33–61. Albany, NY: SUNY Press.

Esbjörn-Hargens, Sean. 2015. "Developing a Complex Integral Realism for Global Response." In *Metatheory for the Twenty-First Century: Critical Realism and Integral Theory in Dialogue*, ed. Roy Bhaskar, et al., 99–139. London: Routledge.

Esbjörn-Hargens, Sean, and Michael E. Zimmerman. 2009. *Integral Ecology: Uniting Multiple Perspectives on the Natural World.* Boston: Integral Books.

Fischer, Kurt W. 1980. "A Theory of Cognitive Development: The Control and Construction of Hierarchies of Skills." *Psychological Review* 87: 477–531.

Foucault, Michel. 1984. "What is Enlightenment?" In *The Foucault Reader*, ed. Paul Rainbow, 32–50. New York: Pantheon.

Foucault, Michel. 2001. *Fearless Speech*, ed. Joseph Pearson. Los Angeles: Semiotext(e).

Gasché, Rodolphe. 2014. *Geophilosophy: On Gilles Deleuze and Félix Guattari's* What Is Philosophy? Evanston, IL: Northwestern University Press.

Gough, David, Sandy Oliver, and James Thomas. 2012. *An Introduction to Systematic Reviews.* London: Sage.

Habermas, Jürgen. 1993. *Postmetaphysical Thinking*, trans. W.M. Hohengarten. Cambridge, MA and London: MIT Press.

Hadot, Pierre. 1995. *Philosophy as a Way of Life: Spiritual Exercises from Socrates to Foucault*, ed. Arnold Davidson. Malden, MA: Blackwell.

Harman, Graham. 2010. *Towards Speculative Realism: Essays and Lectures.* UK: Zero Books.

Hedlund, Nick and Sean Esbjörn-Hargens. (in press). *Metatheory for the Anthropocene: Emancipatory Praxis for Planetary Flourishing.* London and New York: Routledge.

Kornblatt, Judith Deutsch. 2009. *Divine Sophia: The Wisdom writings of Vladimir Solovyov.* Ithaca, NY: Cornell University Press.

Laske, Otto. 2008. *Measuring Hidden Dimensions of Human Systems: Foundations of Requisite Organization (Vol. 2).* Medford, MA: Interdevelopmental Institute Press.

Luhmann, Niklas. 1993. "Deconstruction as Second-Order Observing." *New Literary History* 24: 763–782.

Miller, Alexander. 2013. *Contemporary Metaethics: An Introduction.* London: Polity

Moeller, Hans-Georg. 2012. *The Radical Luhmann.* New York: Columbia University Press.

Overgaard, Soren, Paul Gilbert, and Stephen Burwood. 2013. *An Introduction to Metaphilosophy.* Cambridge, UK: Cambridge University Press.

"Philosophy." (n.d.). http://en.wikipedia.org/wiki/Philosophy. Retrieved January 25, 2014.

Puntel, Lorenz B. 2008. *Structure and Being: A Theoretical Framework for a Systematic Philosophy*, trans. Alan White. University Park, PA: Pennsylvania State University Press.

Rutzou, Timothy. 2012. "The Monstrosity of Monovalence: Paradox or Progress?" *Journal of Critical Realism* 12: 377–399.

Sallis, John. 2008. *The Verge of Philosophy.* Chicago and London: University of Chicago Press.

Sallis, John. 2012. *Logic of the Imagination: The Expanse of the Elemental.* Bloomington and Indianapolis, IN: Indiana University Press.

Schwartz, Michael. 2010. "Introspection and Transformation in Philosophy Today." In *The Gift of Logos: Essays in Continental Philosophy*, ed. David Jones, Jason M. Wirth, and Michael Schwartz, 181–193. Newcastle upon Tyne (UK): Cambridge Scholars Publishing.

Solovyov, Vladimir. 2008. *The Philosophical Principles of Integral Knowledge*, trans. Valeria Z. Nollan. Grand Rapids, MI: Eerdmans.

Soterdijk, Peter. 2013. *You Must Change Your Life: On Anthropotechnics*, trans. Wieland Hoban. Malden, MA: Polity.

Stein, Zachary. 2007. "Modeling the Demands of Interdisciplinarity: Toward a Framework for Evaluating Interdisciplinary Endeavors." *Integral Review* 4: 92–107.

van Roojen, Mark. 2015. *Metaethics: A Contemporary Introduction.* New York: Routledge.

Visser, Frank. 2003. *Ken Wilber: Thought as Passion.* Albany, NY: SUNY Press.

Wilber, Ken. 1995. *Sex, Ecology, Spirituality: The Spirit of Evolution.* Boston: Shambhala.

Wilber, Ken. 2001. *A Theory of Everything: An Integral Vision for Business, Politics, Science, and Spirituality.* Boston: Shambhala.

Wilber, Ken. 2003. "Excerpt B: The Many Ways We Touch." Retrieved March 21, 2015, from http://www.kenwilber.com/Writings/PDF/ExcerptB_KOSMOS_2003.pdf.

Wilber, Ken. 2012. "In Defense of Integral Theory: A Response to Critical Realism. *Journal of Integral Theory and Practice* 7(4): 43–52.

Zalamea, Fernando. 2012. *Synthetic Philosophy of Contemporary Mathematics*, trans. Zachary Luke Fraser. New York: Sequence Press.

PART I

Criticality and Normative Orientation

Chapter 1

Integral Theory, Pragmatism, and the Future of Philosophy

Zachary Stein

> [I intend] to outline a philosophy so comprehensive that . . . the entire work of human reason . . . shall appear as the filling up of its details.
>
> —C.S. Peirce (in a letter to William James, 1888)

Considerations about the future of integral approaches to philosophy should be informed by an understanding of the various lineages contributing to its emergence. I have noted in several publications that many aspects of Ken Wilber's work land him squarely in the tradition of American Pragmatism (Stein, 2007, 2010a, in press). In this paper I elaborate on this claim, demonstrating the interpretive benefits and accuracy of characterizing Wilber as a Pragmatist, as well as the continued relevance of this approach to philosophy. I first clarify some confusion around what it means to be a Pragmatist, suggesting that it is a nonexclusive identity built around a complex set of overlapping commitments. That is, there are many ways to be a Pragmatist, and being one does not rule out being other things as well. I then discuss some of the similarities between Wilber's work and the work of key Pragmatists, specifically Peirce, James, and Dewey. I explore a constellation of six philosophical themes that both link Wilber to this lineage and display its continued relevance, namely: philosophical psychology, epistemic comprehensiveness, action-oriented theorizing, the integration of science and religion, evolutionary metaphysics, and social emancipation.

Solutions to Twenty-First-Century Problems in Nineteenth-Century Texts

> The distinctive office, problems, and subject matter of philosophy grow out of the stresses and strains of the community life in which a given form of philosophy arises. Its specific problems vary with the changes in human life that are always going on and that at times constitute a crisis and a turning point in human history. . . . The problems with which a philosophy relevant to the present must deal are those growing out of changes going on with ever increasing rapidity, over ever-increasing human-geographical range, and with ever-deepening intensity of penetration.
>
> —John Dewey (1920)

Philosophers work in socio-cultural contexts, under historically specific conditions, with access to certain communication technologies, libraries, and media. Wilber has been publishing books since 1971, producing a corpus that spans some 10,000 pages. He has worked with the changing times, from pen and paper to word processor, to the personal computer, and eventually to internet facilitated multimedia educational initiatives. Moreover, like the other Pragmatists discussed below, Wilber worked in response to a dynamically transforming American culture during a period of tremendous global change. At the risk of oversimplifying things, it could be said that the Classical American Pragmatists worked at the beginning of an epoch during which global techno-economic infrastructures were beginning a rapid transformation, while Wilber worked during the end of this epoch—in the twilight of America's global dominance, in a world newly integrated via networks of industrial, transportation, communications, and computer technologies. Thus, reflective critics have rightly suggested that it is as if the Pragmatists began a sentence about the human condition, and Wilber completed it (Carreira, 2007).

The subject of that sentence would be the new self-understanding of our species that is being created as the result of profound evolutionary transformations in our societies, cultures, and scientific technologies. When James and Peirce first convened the Metaphysical Club at Harvard 1871, they were aware that certain new ideas were ascending to prominence in the broader Zeitgeist, ideas big enough to signal a coming reorientation or repositioning of humanity's understanding of itself in the universe (Menand,

2001). Today, we reap the fruits of seeds sown in the century that followed those first meeting of the Pragmatists in Cambridge. These years saw psychology replace theology as the preferred language of self-understanding and interiority. The academy transformed with the birth of the modern research university, as the increasing bureaucratization and fragmentation of knowledge led to reflective appeals for more comprehensive epistemological approaches. Action-oriented theorizing supplanted pure research across many fields, as science—from physics to medicine—became wedded to technology. There were increasing conflicts between science and religion and calls for their integration, just as evolutionary theory replaced creationist myths for large segments of the population. Institutional innovation in the name of social emancipation proliferated as traditional forms of life disintegrated in the flux of cultural and economic modernization.

These six themes—philosophical psychology, epistemic comprehensiveness, action-oriented theorizing, the integration of science and religion, evolutionary metaphysics, and social emancipation—form the core of the discussion below. They link Wilber to the Pragmatist tradition and in turn link the Pragmatist tradition to certain fundamental geohistorical transformations that continue to shape the contemporary scene. These transformations are best grouped under the term *planetization*. This is process I have discussed before (Stein, in review), with reference to a variety of theorists who contrast economic processes of globalization (the homogenized, single-capitalist-path-to-flourishing approach), with the evolutionarily inevitable and predominantly cultural processes of planetization. This is the dialectic of global transformation, as economic structures expand to a vast planetary scale, bringing in their wake communication and information infrastructures, as well as large-scale migration and urbanization (Held, 2007). These trends have brought the birth of a truly global culture and consciousness as well as the possibility of the self-inflicted extinction of humanity. The polycentric global civilization that is emerging in the early decades of the twenty-first century is unprecedented in its complexity and scope.

Pragmatism is as much a reaction to this state of affairs as it is to any trends in academic philosophy or psychology. While Pragmatists tend to share a set of overlapping philosophical commitments—beyond those listed above, they also tend to posit the primacy of practice over theory, the radically social and processual nature of knowledge production processes, the centrality of language, and the epistemic value of first-person experiences (to name a few)—they also share a commitment to a unique and powerful form of *cosmopolitanism*. Peirce (Brent, 1998), James (Richardson, 2010), and Dewey (Westbrook, 1999) were self-consciously creating a worldview that could accommodate a variety of pressing global trends, including the ascension of science as an aspect of cultural meaning-making, the rapid transformation of socioeconomic life due to technology, and the emerging prospects of a perpetually mobilized military-industrial complex (Hook, 1939).

The typical characterization of Pragmatism as a distinctly American orientation is also misleading in so far as it overlooks the fact that key themes raised by Pragmatists were also raised during the same period by philosophers who are archetypally European, such as Marx, Heidegger, and Wittgenstein. This connection between Pragmatism and Continental philosophy has not gone unnoticed (Aboulafia et al., 2001). Habermas (1992), himself a declared Pragmatist, fondly considers the Classical Pragmatists as the American Young Hegelians. Standard treatments of the tradition overlook these confluences that lift Pragmatism from its parochial enclave of cowboys and behaviorism. More sophisticated recent treatments have drawn attention to the untold story of Pragmatism, which casts it as a preemptive solution to the problem of postmodernity (Brandom, 2011; Habermas, 1992). I endorse this view of Pragmatism, which positions contemporaries like Rorty on the fringes, takes Peirce's and James's metaphysics seriously, and seeks solutions to twenty-first-century problems prefigured in nineteenth-century texts.

These observations are the first word on the topic addressed here. Given limitations of space, I can offer only a suggestive discussion of the ways in which Wilber shares certain common orientations to the six themes listed above, and thus ultimately echoes and amplifies the Pragmatists. Using a method I have used elsewhere (Stein, 2010a), I am undertaking a partial and provisional *reconstruction* of a tradition and not attempting to detail the full complexity of the theorists and theories. I offer a story wherein the Pragmatists speak in unison and, along with Wilber, articulate a broad set of shared philosophical commitments that ultimately constitute an emergent worldview and a coherent response to the radical global transformations of our time. There are other stories, however, wherein the Pragmatists do not see eye to eye, nor share such a common voice. Likewise, given Wilber's scant use of texts by the Pragmatists, there are stories where they never really meet, let alone speak the same language. I do not pursue an account of the enlightening *discontinuities* that could be examined. My goal here is to focus on the continuities, unities, and harmonies that emerge if we try to cast Wilber as an heir to the great American philosophers who preceded him. The continued relevance of Pragmatism and the self-understanding of future integral approaches to philosophy are the overarching topic of my discussion. Below I take up each theme and explore how Wilber's approach reflects the approaches pioneered by the Pragmatists.

Wilber the Pragmatist; Pragmatism as an Integral Philosophy

> The meaning of a statement is the mode of its enactment.
>
> —Ken Wilber (2010)

> In order to ascertain the meaning of an intellectual conception one should consider what practical consequences might conceivably result by necessity from the truth of that conception; and the sum of these consequences will constitute the entire meaning of the conception.
>
> —C.S. Peirce (1887)

In a series of prior papers, I placed Wilber's writings in historical context by rationally reconstructing some of the thought-traditions that converge in his work. I've traced back a unique form of metatheorizing, from Wilber to Peirce and Baldwin (Stein, 2010a). This is a tradition of normatively oriented metatheorizing, where the theorist organizes knowledge across many domains according to a set of principled distinctions, as a means for directing future knowledge building toward certain aims. Metatheory in this tradition plays a discourse-regulative role, coordinating, integrating, and reflecting upon knowledge produced by the special disciplines, with an eye toward shaping future knowledge production processes in specific directions, e.g., toward more integral, comprehensive forms of knowledge. I have also explored Wilber's ties to traditions in developmental psychology, third wave or humanistic psychology, and the human potential movement (Stein and Hikkenin, 2008; Stein, in review). I've noted that Wilber's role of theoretical psychologist and East-West synthesizer has some precedence, beginning all the way back with Williams James. And more recently (Stein, in press), I've characterized Wilber as a philosopher with certain proclivities for popularity, cosmopolitanism, and soteriological (salvific/emancipatory) forms of knowledge production, which again align him with the Pragmatists. Here, I only explore six themes: philosophical psychology, epistemic comprehensiveness, action-oriented theorizing, the integration of science and religion, evolutionary metaphysics, and social emancipation.

Philosophical Psychology

William James (1890) is well known as the father of American psychology. His synthetic and speculative appropriation of the "new psychology" from Europe made the young science palatable to Americans still wedded to theology and "mental philosophy" (Richardson, 2007). John Dewey (1887) is also known as a psychologist, especially his work counteracting the reductionism of early experimentalists through his rigorous theoretical treatment of the reflex-arc concept. Less well know are Charles Peirce's contributions to psychology; yet he was, in fact, the first person to conduct psychological experiments on American soil and continued to make substantial contributions to theoretical psychology throughout his life (Cadwllader, 1975). Interestingly, aside from the subthemes to be considered below, these philosopher-psychologists also share with Wilber the distinction of *beginning* their careers as psychologists, while ending them as philosophers. And while Wilber did his experiments on the meditation cushion as a leading figure in trans-personal psychology, Pierce, James, and Dewey cut their teeth in the psychological laboratories of their day before branching out toward broader horizons. Like Wilber, their early concerns with psychology shaped their dealings with philosophy later in life. As I discuss in this section, all four—Pierce, James, Dewey, and Wilber—maintain at least three commitments with regards to psychology as a field. They all maintain that findings from psychology are relevant when considering philosophical questions. They all look beyond the bounds of given empirical findings in attempts to clarify the workings of the higher psychological functions. And they are all preoccupied with the psychology of religious experience in particular.

The Classical Pragmatists and Wilber share a meta-philosophical position that the findings of empirical psychology have relevance for traditional philosophical problems and inquiries. This is an important theme in the works of other twentieth-century psychologists, such as Jean Piaget (1970) and George Hebert Mead (1981), who likewise understood that the science of psychology had forever changed the nature of many philosophical problems, such as those about the nature of human knowledge and moral agency. Wilber, for example, has used findings from developmental psychology to structure his epistemological (e.g., Appendix II in Wilber, 2010) and ethical principles (e.g., the Basic Moral Imperative, per Wilber, 1995). James and Peirce adopted similar approaches in their treatments of many foundational philosophical issues. The principle of Pragmatism itself, as first articulated by Peirce, was heavily influenced by the psychological findings and theories of Alexander Bain (Brent, 1997).

But the idea that philosophy should be informed by psychology runs counter to many schools of philosophical thought that maintain the irrelevance of psychological data for philosophy (e.g., Frege, Russell, and most of the analytical movement). Moreover, the kind of appropriation of psychology undertaken by philosophers like James and Wilber also runs counter to the kinds of appropriations made by contemporary reductionists (e.g., Churchland and Dennet), who use psychology and neuroscience to *explain away* philosophical problems instead of creating novel action-orienting solutions. In the context of a global culture increasingly taken with scientific explanations, the Pragmatist were the first to model a strategy later adopted by Wilber: Using the human sciences to inform philosophical inquiries, while not limiting the conclusions of those inquires to the conclusions of any one discipline or experimental paradigm. They were all seeking a psychology capable of handling the whole person through a kind of methodological pluralism.

Relatedly, the Pragmatists and Wilber also share an interest in psychological theorizing about the so-called "higher psychological functions." This has always involved extrapolating beyond the data to characterize the upper reaches and outer limits of human experience and capability. Wilber's (1995, 1999, 2010) explorations of the limits of human consciousness, transformation, and development have yielded a broad framework for understanding the farther reaches of human nature. This quest for a map of the frontiers and boundaries of human thought and action was prefigured by Peirce, who was interested in the nature of the logical and mathematical norms that govern thought, including the human capability to build and test explicit theories and to reason about infinity and the tranfinite He hypothesized that there are natural structures and laws that channel the evolution of higher-order thought and constrain the architecture of reasonable theories. He did his best to relate these ideas to the crude neuroscience and psychology of his day and ended up positing processes that resemble very closely those posited by contemporary theories in neural network modeling and cognitive developmental psychology. Dewey, likewise, was after a psychology of the "higher-mental functions" that could characterize the difference between *sentience* and *sapience* and reveal the deeper structured order allowing for human reason, scientific inquiry, and social and aesthetic imagination (Sellars, 1950; Dewey, 1938). And of course, James is most famous for *The*

Varieties of Religious Experience (1902), which considers numerous cases of extraordinary sensory and physical abilities associated with mystical and religious experiences.

Varieties brings us to a yet another point of connection between Wilber and the Pragmatists: Their preoccupation with the psychology of religious experience. James is one of the most important figures in the psychology of religion and religious experience. Less well known are the concerns with the psychology of religiosity that run through the works of Dewey (1934) and Peirce (Brent, 1997). The Pragmatists, like Wilber, view religious experiences as both *explicable* in scientific terms, and as *inhabitable* as a practice or experience. The interanimation of third-person and first-person approaches to religion and religious experience again sets Wilber in camp with James and Pierce as a phenomenologist exploring the realities of mystical states, while also arguing for them with the psychology of the day. Importantly, these open-minded and exploratory stances reflect articulate commitments to forms of epistemic inclusiveness and comprehensiveness.

Epistemic Comprehensiveness

Along with the emergence of science as a dominant force in culture and industry came questions about the value of nonscientific forms of knowledge. Modernization involved the devaluation of a range of ways that humans had traditionally understood the world and themselves. Peirce, James, and Dewey worked in the wake of the first great scientific contributions to public welfare and knowledge and during the height of rhetoric for the "scientization" of everything. The Pragmatists accepted the importance and effectiveness of scientific knowledge, but worked to limit the epistemic exclusivity of the reductionist and empiricist ideologies that accompanied the ascendency of the sciences. Like Wilber, their criticisms are not anti-science, but rather, as Peirce (1898) so clearly explicated, they understand that the principles of science itself compel us beyond any given or current sense of what is or is not real, explainable, or inexplicable.

Peirce began his career arguing in favor of a kind of radical empiricism and materialism, but would later transcend and include his earlier views in the process of building a philosophical system capable of accounting for and "housing" a wide variety of validity claims and methodological approaches (Apel, 1995). James and Dewey were likewise both avidly scientific and yet epistemologically permissive, in that they admitted a wide variety of phenomena and data into the purview of scientific methods. A similar approach has been adopted by Habermas (1992), who explicitly links his theory of communicative rationality to the insights of Peirce and Dewey. And Wilber took from Habermas what Habermas had taken from Peirce: The idea of a comprehensive system for classifying forms of human knowledge that is built around the system of basic pronouns at the heart of every language: *I*, *We*, and *It*. Peirce had, of course, followed Kant in seeking the foundations for a philosophy that could extend epistemic legitimacy to the Good, the True, and the Beautiful. As I have argued elsewhere (Stein, 2010), a justified commitment to epistemic comprehensiveness is one of the principle virtues of integral theory and one of its greatest ties to the Pragmatist tradition.

Action-Oriented Theorizing

Importantly, analyzing the dynamics of interactions between the three primordial forms of reason lead Kant (second and third *Critiques*) to privilege the practical or actionable over the theoretical or speculative; that is, giving priority to questions about *what is good to do* over questions about *what is the case with the world*. This Kantian proclivity for action over theory was diverted through Hegel to Marx in Europe and through Hegel to Peirce and Dewey in America (Habermas, 1992). The central innovation in both Marxism and Pragmatism is an explicit reversal of the traditional theory-practice relation, a switching of the value and authority given to these respective orientations.

For the Pragmatists—although they express it differently and unpack different implication—*ideas and actions are symbiotically related*. Theory and practice are inseparable, and co-constitutive, with practice engendering new theory, which in turn engenders new practice. This dialectic plays out at multiple levels (from individuals to communities of inquiry) enabling both virtuous cycles of learning and viscous cycles of ideological self-replication (Bhaskar, 1993). The inter-animation of thought and action can be found in the specific and precise theory/practice constellation of an ongoing research program—where hypotheses are born from reflection on the results of prior experimental actions, only to be put to the test by future experimental actions that will, in turn, generate new hypotheses. The same broad notion also applies to the more vague and compelling ideas that populate our worldviews and identities, illuminating their genesis in our active social lives, and their inevitable result in actions and practices carried out by individuals and institutions.

According to this view, because ideas emerge from actions and actions emerge from ideas, *ideas cannot be evaluated apart from the forms of life they help to create*. This is not a commitment to a crude form of instrumentalism—where an idea is true because it has made something work—let alone a kind of placebo-ism, where it doesn't matter if it is true as long as it works. It is, rather, a commitment to bring about *the unity of theory and practice in practice*, if I can read a Marxist phrase as applicable to Peirce and Dewey (America's Young Hegelians). This means that ideas are more than the sum of what can be said, written, or thought, and their validity must be determined according to their *careers* in the world of action, both social and technical.

As Peirce (1884) used to say, *ideas are alive*, and they are progressively strengthened and weakened, growing or diminishing, according to the ways they sustain—and are sustained by—the complex ecologies of our practices and actions. That means if we want to test ideas or determine their validity, we must think in terms of wider criterion than are typically considered in epistemologies that divide theory from practice and thus limit the number and type of validity claims that are relevant. This brings us back to our earlier considerations about epistemic comprehensiveness. Wilber is aligned along multiple epistemic fronts with the Pragmatists, both in giving primacy to action and lived experience as an aspect of theory and abstract knowledge, and in crafting a system that inter-animates the epistemological and practical/moral domains.

Integration of Science and Religion

Perhaps one of the most important places where Wilber puts his action-oriented and epistemologically permissive theory of knowledge to work is in his arguments concerning the relationships between science and religion (Wilber, 1995; Esbjörn-Hargens and Wilber, 2006). Broadly speaking, this combination of a comprehensive epistemological framework with an overarching concern about the consequences and demonstrable results of practices, both scientific and religious, allows Wilber to place these reputedly "non-overlapping magisteria" into a common framework of shared meaning. Commonalities can be found between this approach and the approach of Peirce, who was likewise motivated to apply the tools from his philosophical system to the problem of integrating science and religion (Peirce, 1958). James, though less systematic, applied his talents to no less a degree in addressing the question, and like Peirce and Wilber, endorsed an epistemologically sophisticated and ultimately conciliatory view. The common thread between their positions is that religion and science are not opposites or antagonistic polarities, but rather complementary and continuous ways of understanding and dealing with the human condition.

Evolutionary Metaphysics

Importantly, all these views integrating science and religion involve, to a large degree, supplementary arguments concerning the evolution of humanity and the cosmos. It is no coincidence that since Darwin, discussions about the relations between religion and science have led to discussions about evolution and the position of humanity in the universe. The Pragmatists were all thoroughgoing evolutionary thinkers and all embraced some form of evolutionary cosmology or metaphysics (Wiener, 1949). Peirce articulated the most complex vision of cosmic evolution by far, even more so than Wilber, as toward the end of his life (starving to death in rural Pennsylvania) he offered one of the most complex evolutionary panpsychist-pansemiotic metaphysical systems ever created. Interestingly, one of the few places Wilber mentions Peirce is during a discussion of his own evolutionary metaphysics, specifically with reference to the idea of Kosmic Habits (Wilber, 2005). The idea that the universe evolves from flux to order through the establishment of habits, fields, or patterns of emergent and then continually regenerated structures is found in contemporary chaos and complexity theory; but it was first articulated by Peirce in the 1880s (Peirce, 1884, 1888; Popper, 1972). Importantly, both Wilber and Peirce go where the majority of chaos theorists will not and suggest that the norms humans create and the ways we organize our social lives create patterns that literally structure the future of evolution on the planet.

Social Emancipation

Both Peirce and Wilber evoke Kant when they discuss the implications of the Kosmic Habit theory for humanity. One articulation of the categorical imperative, the ethical principle at the heart of Kant's entire philosophical system, states that we should act only according to norms that we could endorse as future laws of nature. This means, in essence, that we should consider ourselves as co-creators of the future of nature, both organic and human, and act as if we were laying down groves for the future to follow. This unpacks as an obligation to act in coherent and reasonable ways and to consider the implications of our action and their ramifications for the future of human nature and social relations. It also compels one to honor humanity and the fullness of human potential. Wilber is, among other things, a theorist of human potential. He has consistently used psychological research as a framework for considering how to improve and liberate human capability.

Similarly, Peirce, James, and Dewey were vocal in their dissatisfaction with the psychology of their day, because it failed to address the developmental and normative aspects of human thought. Dewey (1929), the educationist, was asking for a psychological science that could inform a broader science of human transformation and learning, a science of education capable of liberating the entirety of society's human potential. Peirce (1868) was asking for a psychology capable of explaining and prescribing logical and mathematical norms in order to build an applied science dedicated to the improvement of human thought and inquiry. Peirce was looking to position this ameliorative psychology as a means for catalyzing social transformation toward his envisioned ideal of *a communication community coterminous with the cosmos*—an ideal that is the condition for the possibility of scientific truth and inquiry, according to Peirce's philosophy (Apel, 1995). We are thus brought back to where we began, with considerations of the geohistorical social transformation that informed the action-orienting self-understanding of the pragmatists, and that has also shaped the contours of integral theory.

Conclusion: Planetization and the Future of Philosophy

Since the end of World War II, there has been an acceleration of technological innovation and a related expansion of international economic and legal structures, all of unprecedented size and scope. This has created trends that have touched the lives of every person on the planet, weaving all of humanity into the fabric of a common history for the first time (McCarthy, 1978). The beginning of this remarkable era involved the liberation of science and industry from the normative texture of the lifeworld, as war mobilization efforts placed them on independent developmental trajectories (Nobel, 1979). The unchecked proliferation of industrial and communications technologies that resulted would transform the planet, radically increasing the complexity and intensity of human life and ultimately endangering the continued existence of the species. Simultaneously, there has been a deepening of human knowledge and experience, as wide swaths of humanity are being drawn into a fragile new global culture of remarkable diversity and scope. The specter of a homogenizing and oppressive globalization haunts the actual and necessary processes of planetization that are currently being played out. Those inhabiting the planetary civilization of the future will live in structures built in the half-light of our immature world-centric philosophies. As crises of global scope continue to occur more frequently, we will grope for global frameworks to organize the increasing complexity and fragmentation of our experience. The six themes discussed above represent a constellation of issues near the heart of our emerging global crisis and indicate the kind of philosophical response that is needed.

Technology-enabled advances in the human sciences are already continually transforming the languages we use to understand ourselves. Brain science and psychology are adapted to explain a wide variety of controversial social norms, such as greed, infidelity, and narcissism. The cognitive and brain sciences are also being used to *explain away* a variety of more "spooky" human abilities, like empathy, mystical union, and morality. These passing pop-sci headlines betray a deeper uncertainty about who and what we are. What will be the accumulated impacts of this culture based on a transient and continually reexplained sense of human nature? We face the possibility of a species-wide identity crisis resulting from the fracturing and "disenchantment" of our action-orienting self-understandings (Habermas, 2003; Stein, 2010, in press). A philosophy is needed that can translate the results of the psychological sciences into languages that addresses our self-understandings and the social and cultural realities of the lifeworld (Habermas, 1990; Wilber, 1999). Pragmatism represents a tradition that has positioned psychology in terms of a broader set of philosophical commitments and is thus capable of appropriately negotiating between the claims of the lifeworld and those special sciences for the self-understanding of the species. Integral approaches to philosophy must likewise take up the challenge of,—as Habermas (1990) has put it—serving as a stand-in-interpreter or integrative translator, between the ever-advancing human sciences and the self-understanding of a species that is, for the first time, self-consciously united in a single planetary narrative.

Our understanding of this emerging geohistorical metanarrative is also obscured by the fragmentation and irrelevance of knowledge production in the contemporary academy (Menand, 2010; Stein, 2010a). As noted above, the Pragmatists worked at the beginning of an era that was to be dominated by the ascendancy of science as a form of inquiry and the related depreciation of traditional, non- or extra-scientific, and value-landed knowledge claims. The Pragmatists' commitments to epistemological comprehensiveness and their arguments for action-oriented approaches to theory and research were attempts to counteract a newly formed techno-science-industry complex that was beginning to enshrine reductionist and ontologically-monovalent metatheories of knowledge in the large-scale research universities being built at the dawn of the twentieth century. This has lead us to today, a time when universities are privatizing, profiting, and proliferating under the banner of tech-enabled educational equity and student loan speculations.

Contemporary integrally-oriented philosophers must now carry out a problem-focused transdisciplinary integration of diverse and fragmented academic knowledge production processes. Peirce came to believe that in order to do truly integrative interdisciplinary or transdisciplinary work it is often necessary to build a new layer on top of the existing educational system. The graduate school and medieval doctoral certification system were imported to America from Germany during Peirce's time at Harvard and Johns Hopkins, and he was a vocal supporter of the *ideal* of the university they implied—cosmopolitan, trans-political, humanistic, philanthropic, and scientific. He never landed in the universities of his time, in part because of his allegiance to this *ideal* of the university. This same ideal compels integral philosophers to undertake projects in epistemic comprehensiveness—integral knowledge production and application—beyond the university system as it currently exists. This involves transcending, but including, the twentieth century's disciplinary fragmentation in the structure of a twenty-first-century problem-focused research and development complex.

Moreover, the institutionalization of epistemologically comprehensive forms of action-oriented research ought to be guided by the pursuit of innovations that will liberate human potential and result in the emancipation of humanity on a planetary scale. Beyond the aforementioned species-wide identity crises, there are also the impending crises accompanying the exhaustion of biological tolerance for the global industrial infrastructure. Efforts made by midwives of the coming postindustrial global ecocommons must be guided by profound sensitivities to the forms of social life engendered by future "world saving" technologies, be they biological, computational, or geoarchitectonic. Social emancipation is different from mere survival. Survival is a physical precondition for emancipation, which amounts to much more than physical *sustainability*. Emancipation occurs in social structures that allow individuals the freedom to take up reflectively chosen life-projects and conceptions of the good. Some life-projects and goods are to be preferred over others, and although they can't be mandated, they can be encouraged through skillful design. Integral philosophers will be quick to point out that there are some conceptions of the good life that include forms of emancipation typically described as religious or spiritual. Of course, these kinds of religious social structures and personality systems are at the center of the current global problematic.

Contemporary global philosophies are turning to address the dynamic, powerful, and indelible religiosity of humanity. The Pragmatists, like Wilber, are looking to articulate a coherent cosmopolitan identity, consistent with science, and yet inclusive of religion and religious experience. Their broader reflections about the possibility for integrating science and religion, and for reconciling religious intolerance in the global public sphere, are the result of experiences with lived traditions (Peirce, Wilber) and with noninstitutionalized, spontaneous religious experience (Dewey, James). The Pragmatists' vocal shared embrace of an evolutionary worldview eased the tensions between religious traditions and scientific innovations and opened the public's social imagination concerning religious forms. With Vivekananda's appearance at the Chicago World's Fair in 1893 and James's subsequent introduction of Eastern philosophy to Harvard (echoing Emerson, who had done so before), there emerged in America a fascinating proliferation of religious organizations and forms of teacherly and doctrinal authority (Stein, 2011).

Today, translineage, postconventional religious formations are emerging to foster global peace coalitions, many claiming James in their East-West lineage. However, their "world saving" dharma is not immune from the risk of creating unacceptably distorted social forms and identity structures. Integral philosophy must not shy away from considerations about the future of global religious configurations, nor from articulating preferable possibilities for the future of religion. James's ([1910] 1982) dictums about our needing to find a moral/religious equivalent to war ring more true now than ever, especially in our age of perpetual wars involving military operations of enormous scope and cost. Tremendous energy would be rechanneled in the event of a global religious revival-through-unity, as for millennia economies have been restructured around intentional communities of religious or spiritual vocation. Transgovernmental religious organizations will have the opportunity to spawn vast educational configurations in the coming decades, as lifeworlds will continue being decentered via the relentless push of planetization, creating fervent and widespread searching for certainty, liberation, and hope.

I have discussed six themes—philosophical psychology, epistemic comprehensiveness, action-oriented theorizing, the integration of science and religion, evolutionary metaphysics, and social emancipation. These themes link Wilber to the Pragmatist tradition and in turn link the Pragmatist tradition to certain fundamental geohistorical transformations that continue to shape the contemporary scene. These transformations are best grouped under the term *planetization*. This is the dialectic of global transformation, as economic structures expand to a vast planetary scale, bringing in their wake communication and information infrastructures, as well as large-scale migration and urbanization. These trends have brought the birth of a truly global culture and consciousness, as well as the possibility of the self-inflicted extinction of humanity. The polycentric global civilization that is emerging in the early decades of the twenty-first century is unprecedented in it complexity and scope. I have argued that Pragmatism is as much a reaction to this state of affairs as it is to any trends in academic philosophy or psychology. The Pragmatists were self-consciously creating a worldview that could accommodate a variety of pressing global trends, including the ascension of science as an aspect of cultural meaning-making, the rapid transformation of socioeconomic life due to technology, and the emerging prospects of a perpetually mobilized military-industrial complex. The overarching point here has been that integral philosophy should understand itself as continuous with this tradition. We therefore ought to continue work toward the accomplishment of the goals set out by the Pragmatists, who would have us reconstruct society in light of a reconstructed philosophy, an integral philosophy—comprehensive, action-oriented, evolutionary, and hopeful.

References

Aboulafia, Mitchell, Myra Bookman, and Catherine Kemp (eds.). 2002. *Habermas and Pragmatism*. New York: Routledge.

Apel, Karl-Otto. 1995. *Charles S. Peirce: From Pragmatism to Pragmaticism*, trans. John Michael Krois. London: Humanities Press.

Bhaskar, Roy. 1993. *Dialectic: The Pulse of Freedom*. New York: Verso.

Brandom, Robert. 2011. *Perspectives on Pragmatism: Classical, Recent, Contemporary*. Cambridge, MA: Harvard University Press.

Brent, Joseph. 1997. *Charles Sanders Peirce: A Life*. Bloomington, IN: Indiana University Press

Cadwllader, T.C. 1975. "Peirce as an Experimental psychologist." *Transactions of the Charles S. Peirce Society* 11: 167–186.

Carreira, J. Personal correspondence, August, 2006.

Dewey, John. 1916. *Democracy and Education*. New York: Macmillan.

Dewey, John. 1920. *Reconstructions in Philosophy*. Boston: Beacon Press.

Dewey, John. 1938. *Logic: The Theory of Inquiry*. Carbondale, IL: Southern Ilinois University Press.

Dewey, John. ([1887], 1975). *Psychology*. Edwardsville, IL: Southern Illinois University Press.

Esbjörn-Hargens, Sean, and Ken Wilber. 2006. "Towards a Comprehensive Integration of Science and Religion: A Post-metaphysical Approach." In *The Oxford Handbook of Science and Religion*, 523–546. Oxford, UK: Oxford University Press.

Habermas, Jürgen. 1990. *Moral Consciousness and Communicative Action*, trans. Christian Lenhardt and Shierry Weber Nicholsen. Cambridge, MA: MIT Press.

Habermas, Jürgen. 1992. *Postmetaphysical Thinking: Philosophical Essays*, trans. William Mark Hohengarten. Cambridge, MA: MIT Press.

Habermas, Jürgen. 2003. *The Future of Human Nature*. Cambridge, UK: Polity Press.

Hook, Sidney. 1939. *John Dewey: An Intellectual Portrait*. New York: Prometheus Books.

McGrew, Andrew, and David Held. 2007. *Globalization Theory: Approaches and Controversies*. New York: Wiley.

James, William. 1902/1920. *The Varieties of Religious Experience*. New York: Viking Press.

James, William. 1910/1982. *Essays in Religion and Morality*. Cambridge, MA: Harvard Univerity Press.

James, William. 1890/1950. *The Principles of Psychology* (volumes 1 and 2). Dover Publications, Inc.

McCarthy, Thomas. 1978. *The Critical Theory of Jürgen Habermas*. Cambridge, MA: MIT Press.

Mead, G.H. 1981. *Selected Writings*. Chicago: University of Chicago Press.

Menand, Louis. 2001. *The Metaphysical Club: A Story of American Ideas*. New York: Farrar, Straus and Giroux.

Menand, Louis. 2010. *The Marketplace of Ideas: Reform and Resistance in the American Academy*. New York: Norton.

Nobel, David F. 1977. *America by Design: Science, Technology, and the Rise of Corporate Capitalism*. New York: Knopf.

Peirce, Charles S. 1984. "Questions Concerning Certain Faculties Claimed for Man." In *Writings of Charles S. Peirce: A Chronological Edition (Vol. 2: 1867–1871)*, ed. Edward C. Moore, 193–211. Bloomington, IN: Indiana University Press.

Peirce, Charles S. 1986. "How to Make Our Ideas Clear." In *Writings of Charles S. Peirce: A Chronological Edition (Vol. 3, 1872–1878)*, ed. Christian J.W. Kloesel, 257–276. Bloomington, IN: Indiana University Press.

Peirce, Charles S. 1989. "Design and Chance." In *Writings of Charles S. Peirce: A Chronological Edition (Vol. 4, 1879–1884)*, ed. Christian J.W. Kloesel, 544–554. Bloomington, IN: Indiana University Press.

Peirce, Charles S. 2000. "A Guess at the Riddle." In *Writings of Charles S. Peirce: A Chronological Edition (Vol. 6, 1886–1890)*, ed. Peirce Edition Project, 166–203. Bloomington, IN: Indiana University Press.

Peirce, Charles S. 1898. *Reasoning and the Logic of Things: The Cambridge Conference Lectures of 1898*. Cambridge, MA: Harvard.

Peirce, Charles S. 1958. *Collected Papers of Charles S. Peirce, Vol. II*, ed. Burks. Cambridge, MA: Harvard University Press.

Piaget, Jean. 1970. *The Place of the Sciences of Man in the System of Sciences.* New York: Harper & Row.

Popper, Karl. 1972. *Objective Knowledge.* New York: Cambridge University Press.

Richardson, Robert D. 2006. *William James: In the Maelstrom of American Modernity.* New York: Houghton Mifflin.

Sellars, W. 1950. "Language, Rules, and Behavior." In *John Dewey: Philosopher of Science and Freedom*, ed. Sidney Hook. New York: Dial Press.

Stein, Zachary. 2007. "Modeling the Demands of Interdisciplinarity." *Integral Review* 4: 91–107.

Stein, Zachary, and Katie Hiekkinen. 2008. "On Operationalizing Aspects of Altitude: An Introduction to the Lectical Assessment System for Integral Researchers." *Journal of Integral Theory and Practice* 3(1).

Stein, Zachary, and Katie Hiekkinen. 2010. "On the Difference Between Designing Children and Raising Them: Ethics and the Use of Educationally Oriented Biotechnologies." *Mind, Brain, and Education* 4(2): 53–67.

Stein, Zachary, and Katie Hiekkinen. 2010a. "On the Normative Function of Meta-theoretical Endeavors." *Integral Review* 6(3).

Stein, Zachary, and Katie Hiekkinen. 2012. "On Spiritual Teachers and Teachings." *Journal of Integral Theory and Practice* 6(1).

Stein, Zachary, and Katie Hiekkinen. (in review). "Between Philosophy and Prophecy." In *True but Partial: Essential Criticisms of Integral Theory*, ed. Sean Esbjörn-Hargens. Forthcoming, SUNY Press.

Stein, Zachary, and Katie Hiekkinen. (in press). "On the Use of the Term Integral." *Journal of Integral Theory and Practice* 9(2).

Westbrook, Robert B. 1991. *John Dewey and American Democracy*. Ithaca, NY: Cornell University Press.

Wiener, Philip P. 1949. *Evolution and the Founders of Pragmatism*. Cambridge, MA: Harvard Univerity Press.

Wilber, Ken. 1999. *Integral Psychology: Consciousness, Spirit, Psychology, Therapy.* Boston: Shambhala.

Wilber, Ken. 2005. Excepts from Volume 2 of the *Kosmos Trilogy*. Integral Institute. Retrieved from http://wilber.shambhala.com/index.cfm/.

Wilber, Ken. 1995. *Sex, Ecology, Spirituality: The Spirit of Evolution*. Boston: Shambhala Publications.

Wilber, Ken. 2006. *Integral Spirituality: A Startling New Role for Religion in the Modern and Postmodern World.* Boston: Shambhala Publications.

Chapter 2

Stages, States, and Modes of Existence in Integral Critical Theory

Martin Beck Matuštík

Spirituality, to survive in the present and future world, is and must be post-metaphysical.

—Ken Wilber (2006)

Communicative reason does not make its appearance in an aestheticized theory of the colorless negative of religion that provides consolation. It neither announces the absence of consolation in a world forsaken by God, not does it take upon itself to provide any consolation.

—Jűrgen Habermas (1992)

What Questions Should Critical Theory Ask Today?

Ken Wilber (2006) has articulated a remarkably robust postmetaphysical spirituality *after* postmodernity at the time Jürgen Habermas (1984, 1987, 1992) has been reconsidering some of his earlier dismissals of religious thinking. Even if Habermas will have never studied or met Wilber, or vice versa, our post-secular condition would be ripe for inventing an encounter staged between secularizing understanding that leaves no room for sacred languages and post-formal understanding that articulates transpersonal, post-rational states of spiritual awareness. By the time of writing this essay, Habermas has made a decisive postsecular turn that leaves space open for a continuing dialogue between reflective faith and postmetaphysical thinking (Habermas 2008, 2017, Mendieta 2019). This counterfactual thought of opening a dialogue between secularizing reflection and post-formal stages of understanding strikes one at first as odd: How can secular thinkers detect in recognizable inflections those grammars that can be heard in the transpersonal emptiness of spiritual languages? How can spiritual thinkers communicate post-rational states of awareness into publicly accessible semantic contents without losing something of the spiritual connotations in the translation? Secularizing reflection must revise its summary bias against spiritual languages as contents tied to the archaic forms of understanding and unquestioned semantics of traditions. Spiritual thinkers for the twenty-first century must learn to articulate transpersonal, post-rational states of awareness, as well as semantic resources of wisdom traditions in post-formal forms of understanding. This dual requirement provides a groundwork for integral critical theory (ICT).

Habermas (1992) has neither become emphatically religious, nor has he articulated the postmodern languages of religion without religion (Matuštík, 2006b). Yet since 2001 he has been pleading for a communicative dialogue between secularizing reflection and the life-enhancing, semantic, and imaginative resources of the great wisdom traditions (Habermas 2008, 2017, 2019, Matuštík 2019, and Mendieta 2019). One aspect of the earlier contention between the sacred and profane has been settled under the locution of "postsecular," which Habermas and Wilber seem to share with critical theorists, sociologists of religion, as well as religious pluralists (Matuštík 2019).

A dawning realization of the twenty-first century brings to one table the Enlightenment secularists, syncretic postmodernists, traditionalists, and new age spiritualists who may not be recognizably religious: Religions and interreligious conflicts are here to stay and coexist with planetary secularization and its global systems rationality in the service of efficiently functioning technology and markets. Contrary to the intuitions of Nietzsche, Marx, Freud, and the early critical theorists, the return of the religious is an incontrovertible sign of the twenty-first century. The important question for our times is not this or that future of religions—and we know from Horkheimer (1974) as much as Freud (1989) that both religions and atheisms have their tyrants and martyrs—but rather whether and how reflectively mature *spiritual thinking* may become a dialogic partner with receptively open *postmetaphysical thinking*.

This way of posing the question calls for an ICT. By *integral* in the context of critical theory, I mean a theory that includes the three basic, yet non-mutually-reducible (or orthogonal) dimensions of human existence: material, sociopolitical, and spiritual needs (Table 2.1). ICT endeavors to bring together the personal or existential freedom with sociopolitical liberation and spiritual self-transformation. Critical theory is a theory with practical intent to address modes of material, sociopolitical, and spiritual needs.

While there have been schools of thought in other disciplines that chart various integral perspectives on human development, there have not been new or fully successful attempts in philosophy that meaningfully connect the methodologies that focus on personal or existential freedom with those pertaining to sociopolitical liberation. And the relationship between socio-political liberation and spiritual self-transformation is even more contested territory. We have become familiar with various developmental schemes from biological evolution (Darwin) to psychological growth (Piaget, Freud, Kohlberg) to social evolution (Hegel, Marx, Weber, Durkheim, Habermas). These evolutionary frameworks gradually gave birth to the nineteenth century historical consciousness and the twentieth century linguistic turn in our understanding of human cultures. Because Western modernity is closely tied with the secularization thesis according which the growth in rationalization of lifeworlds reduces the deficit of the sacred and yields to the secular, spiritual perspectives on human and social development were not mainstream modern possibilities. The spiritual needs should be met

Table 2.1. Dimensions, Fields, and Ideals of Integral Critical Theory

Field of Needs	*Dimension of Critique*	*Regulative Ideal or Possibility Sought*
material needs	critique of political economy	social justice: economic redistribution of resources
social and cultural needs	critique of society	deliberative democracy: political and cultural recognition
spiritual needs	critique of religions	redemptive hope: spiritual liberation and existential self-transformation

by the rational Enlightenment, democracy, and either capitalist markets or socialist markets. That evolution of spiritual perspectives would continue, rather than vanish, with rationalization of consciousness and the secularization of cultures, is an unexpected fruit of postmetaphysical thinking. That very evolution of postsecular spiritualities is a previously undetected ur-origin of Homo Sapiens shared with postmetaphysical thinking in engendering the Anthropocene. This century is rapidly reaching singularity when the convergence of biotech and infotech transforms Sapiens into a self-designing species (Harari 2016, Matuštík, 2019).

First, I want to reconstruct the outlines of the steps that would bring a critical theorist and an integral theorist to this juncture in conversation. I begin with a brief review of the six phases of critical theory. Second, I propose that ICT offers a seventh phase. As an example, I imagine a hypothetical encounter between the developmental models delineated by Wilber and Habermas. Third, I rearticulate my earlier existential rejoinders to Habermas in order to introduce a transversal existential axis into integral critical theory. In conclusion, I rephrase the initial question of how spiritual thinking could coexist with postmetaphysical thinking. I end with a question whether or not critical theory whose practical intent is social liberation must not ask about transformative hope. ICT embodies in its transversal existential axis conditions of possibility for counter/redemptive critique.

The Lineage(s) of Critical Theory

My most immediate motivating impulse for thinking through a possibility of ICT came from engagement with Ken Wilber's thought in 2006. Because I discovered Wilber rather late in my professional career, I brought a certain independence of thinking on this topic from other contexts. The possibility of ICT opens several novel question areas: How do we come to terms with economic, political, and religious conflicts in the context of their globalization? In response to their global character, how do we integrate the fields of the economy, politics, and spirituality? Answering these questions is a matter of planetary survival and some preparatory work is in order. In taking such a propaedeutic step in the direction that integral questioning opens for us, we encounter distinct and yet interrelated fields of needs and their historical modes of scarcity. These are traditionally named as economic, political, and spiritual needs. ICT requires us to rethink the fault lines of conflict not as so many clashes of civilization, but rather as collisions of frameworks among material, political, and spiritual levels of development within each civilization and increasingly globally.

In my 2001 biography of Habermas, I describe six phases of theory on the way to becoming "critical." In my recent engagement with Wilber and other integral thinkers, I began to work toward the seventh, integral Phase of critical theory. At the same junction, I introduced a transversal existential axis that would be able to complement the Wilber-Combs lattice, which shows the possible intersections of stages of consciousness with states of consciousness, mapping how the stages structures are an animating schema for interpreting and making sense of expanded states like non-dual awareness and witnessing. My model of ICT would be three-pronged: Stages and states of the Wilber-Combs lattice, combined with a third axis of modes of existence. After a brief account of the phases of critical theory, I will say why the transversal existential axis is a distinct dimension present in both Habermasian and Wilberian models of rationalization in human development. By reconstructing six phases of critical theory and arriving at the threshold of a seventh stage, we will have reconstructed stages of Western development from a moment in which we have to risk ahead.

First, I begin in the Euro-American Western modernity that in many areas of late industrial society has become our dominant planetary condition: The Kantian critique of the conditions of possible experience gives us a priori structures of reason. These conditions define possible formal perspectives. Wilber would rejoin to Kant's formal schematism of human understanding that perspectives as such are never experienced directly. One *is* a perspective, a window that is a world. Perspectives set limits to rational thinking. Going beyond one's perspective opens at least two possibilities: One: There are dangers of transcendental illusions that cannot be instantiated in experience (there is no space-time intuition that allows for the idea to *exist*, and in this sense G-d does not exist for rational judgment, but can only be postulated as a moral need). Two: One's perspective evolves to a new stage that can be thought. Kant would insist that one cannot take a sabbatical from one's world, and for this reason even G-d about whom one could speak cannot be on such a sabbatical for the understanding. I drag the perspective I am to the beach, shopping mall, the temple. Perspective is the Archimedean point from where one raises the world.

Let us not think of this modern Enlightenment insight as a prison for the self or knowledge. Let us call this insight a revolutionary achievement of theory that has become critical. Indeed, we call Kant's turn to the self a Copernican revolution. This turn accounts for itself, otherwise it could not be called critical, but would have to be unmasked as either biased or authoritarian. Perspectives are critical because they not only open the formal worlds through which we apprehend substantive reality, but they also protect understanding from illusions and contradictions. To be and remain rational, one ought not to think beyond what is possible for human experience. One can immediately detect that religion, G-d, self, spirit are categories that are in trouble, as there is nothing in rational conditions that can account for our experience of these intangibles. This too signals the death of uncritical religions, and Wilber would say this is a necessary good. He rejoins Kant in needing to inhabit a post-conventional perspective on the future of G-d and spirituality.

The second phase in theory arrives with Hegel, who had an impact on Darwin and nineteenth century historical consciousness. After the Copernican turn to the self, now one comes to also inhabit as window onto reality a historical revolution that must think truth and evolution in the same breath. Many still cannot do so, because if truth is evolving, how can it be true at any given moment? One should not, then, teach about this stage of critical window on reality in our schools. But this stage taught us that all formal structures or perspectives are themselves developmental. And so, while staircases of perspectives are also never experienced as such, they can be grasped retrospectively as distinct forms of life and forms of understanding. The process G-d, who is within our perspectives and who is our fellow sufferer, may be worthy of meditation as much as the immutable One. Modernity joins with Buddhism and the quantum leap of the sciences to recognize the impermanence of all perspectives. There is no place for "God" in Buddhism any more than there is a God-place within perspectives through which we open windows onto spiritual reality. With Kant and Kierkegaard, "God" does not *exist*; with Hegel and later Whitehead, "God" does not stay still. In Judaism, G-D cannot be written, spoken or represented. Integral thinking embraces these achievements and finds in them support for postmodern spiritual life that has grown up along with traditions that preceded our time.

The third phase can be named with the help of Marx's discovery that forms or perspectives of understanding are not just a priori or formal worlds. Our ways of seeing the worlds do not begin and end with developmental conditions of possible experience. Perspectives and developments are categories rooted in the material career of institutions and modes of economic life. Critical theory must not only think possibilities, it must emancipate concrete people and their lived possibilities. Wilber's four dimensions of speaking about everything (AQAL) include the changing individual and social perspectives (I, you, we), and they refer us to the systemic dimensions of material reality (it). These four dimensions open windows of the self as much as they name the faces of G-d, who is part of the evolving perspectives and their intensities of awareness states. G-d is not another reality outside of my perspectival stages and awareness states. Stages and states, the lattice of their intersection, write the kosmic address from which ultimate realities can be read.

The fourth phase is a nuance within the Frankfurt School of Critical Theory in the 1930s and then again after World War II: Western and Freudian Marxists, such as Herbert Marcuse, questioned the Soviet and other orthodox Marxists as to why some of the greatest critical deficits occurred in the context of revolutionary upheavals of the twentieth century. Why did Marxist revolutions, at least by name, not bring greater liberation, since that was Marx's pure critical intent? The question is unfair if asked only of these secular prophets. To be sure, every ideal of justice and heaven has had both their martyrs and their tyrants—and this thought is almost verbatim from Max Horkheimer, who was another critical theorist from Frankfurt. With Theodor Adorno, he wrote one of the darkest and most penetrating critiques of Enlightenment rationality, *Dialectic of Enlightenment*, albeit penned in the Santa Monica sunshine away from Nazi Germany. The early Frankfurt thinkers joined with Nietzsche and Freud in order to theorize the failure of Marx to attend to the depth (hidden, irrational, or deceptively willed) dimensions of human unfreedom. The early Frankfurt School thinkers—Benjamin, Marcuse, Adorno, and Horkheimer among them—learned as much from Western Marxists as from Max Weber. They rejected the vanguard hubris of the Soviet and Chinese Marxism. Yet they retained the emancipatory aims of critical theory. This is where Horkheimer's (1937/1972) classical differentiation of critical, emancipatory theory from traditional, disinterested theorizing belongs.

Fifth, critical theorists today are mostly secular post-Marxian thinkers—whom Anders Behring Breitvik, the Norwegian, white nationalist and terrorist of July 22, 2011, lumps together under the label of Cultural Marxists, in his 1,500-page-long verbiage manifesto about the downfall of the Christian West. Critical theorists—along with feminists and critical race theorists—get a lot of press in that violent complaint, because Western postmodernity can be easily blamed for the corruption of premodern European religious and moral traditions. Postmodern and literary critical theorists who read thinkers in the first four phases described above and also read thinkers associated with poststructuralism and deconstruction, find hospitality in cultural studies rather than in philosophy departments. By now, "critical theory" has its own special shelves in libraries. In sophisticated bookstores such as St. Mark's in New York City, the critical theory shelf is separated from the philosophy shelf. One finds books by Habermas in both places, next to J.L. Austin or next to M. Foucault. Integral thinkers are nowhere to be found on either shelf. But their brand is the most dangerous in being critical of the present age; integral thinkers diagnosing the plague of dogmatic secularizing reason and its mirror image in the religious retreat to tradition through the literalist reading of texts.

Sixth, in the late 1970s Habermas introduces a communicative model of critical rationality. He integrates perspectival formal elements of Kant with social evolution of Hegel and modes of material reproduction of Marx. He then reinscribes their achievements within the study of linguistic competences and stages of development. He envisions critical rationality best suited to our postmodern worlds as post-conventional, postmetaphysical, communicative, and secular. Wilber rejoins Habermas on the first three requirements of critical thought, and he begs to differ on the last as unwarranted by on grounds achieved by stages of theory becoming critical theory.

Postmetaphysical Thinking and the Post-secular Condition

The seventh phase is ICT. This articulation requires us to minimally bring Wilber and Habermas to the same discussion on the topic of postmetaphysical reason. ICT—as I want to shape it in this programmatic essay—adopts Habermas's (1984, 1987, 1992) linguistic-communicative turn and his postmetaphysical standpoint. Both represent a critical step of formal and discursive rationality. This is a step forward, insofar as Habermas's critical theory explains the a priori structures of understanding. In Habermas, the perspectives we encountered already in stage one become grammatical (performative) moves (speech acts) that take place nowhere if not within communicative interaction. When we are concerned about real concrete worlds and speak with one another, then a speaker (I) addresses a hearer (you, we) about something (it) in the world. The grammatical loci are our communicative perspectives, formal worlds. We detect contours of the integral model called AQAL in which formal perspectival structures are inhabited as subjective, intersubjective, objective, and interobjective wholes.

In my review of Habermas's newly noted interest in religions, I asked whether there has been a post-secular turn in his profane architectonic

(Matuštík, 2005: 9ff.). Habermas's (2001, 2003, 2005, 2008, 2017) discerningly original religious tonality—albeit he may call it "tone-deaf to religious connotations" (2001: 114)—emerges in his reflections on tolerance and religion after 9/11. Whether critical theorists need to be afraid that a great thinker has gone "softly" neo-religious (Pensky, 2005), one would be amiss to ignore a counter-monumental quality of Habermas's hope that propels his active critical work and public political witness (Matuštík, 2000, 2019).

Unlike Wilber, Habermas is partial to a secular version of postmetaphysical thinking. One cannot make spiritual speech acts in a fully postmetaphysical form insofar as one accepts Max Weber's reductive thesis about modern rationalization of religious and traditional worldviews. This thesis postulates a historical dissolution of spiritual content of traditions into one of the secularized validity spheres of culture. There are three such spheres identified early by Habermas in line leading from Kant's three critiques of reason; Hegel's philosophical newly attempted synthesis of tradition, religion and philosophical form; and Weber's value wars of gods and demons. These are cultural spheres of sciences, morality and law, and art or aesthetics. Spiritual needs are now rationally met through one of the cultural spheres, their translatable semantic resources, their resort experts, and their modes of validity claims. Science emphasizes truth claims, morality and law raise illocutionary performative claims to what is normatively right, and art becomes the primary domain of sincerity claims, truthfulness; perhaps with some aesthetically inflected religious tastes.

Habermas (1987, Fig. 28, *Forms of Mutual Understanding*, p. 192) introduces a very fine charting of the forms of understanding that accompany his reflections on the uncoupling of communicative structures of rationalized lifeworlds from the functional systems rationality of power and money. The table is framed by two sets of major categories. In the left column are four differentiations of validity spheres and at the top bar are two sacred (cultic practice and worldviews that steer practice) and two profane (communication and purposive activity) domains of action. The grid of four left-column and four top-bar categories yields sixteen spaces for forms of mutual understanding. We can read this grid as a Habermasian analogue to Wilber's perspectival stages running in each of the four quandrants in the AQAL model.

In Habermas's figure 28, the left column records the historical differentiations of initially confused spheres of validity (understanding) and effectiveness (systemic effectiveness, success). In Wilber's model, this would be the archaic to premodern magic to mythic stage. With fuller differentiation of specific validity claims, rationalized lifeworlds of modernity learn to differentiate I, you and we as communicative grammars and then distinguish these from the inter-objective systems of world coordination. The top bar in

Habermas's model separates sacred cults and sacred worldview from profane forms of communication and profane purposive action. Note that Wilber's model would not highlight the sacred-profane distinction as the main divider that emerges with modern and postmodern stages of understanding. Our present rationalization of lifeworlds, for Habermas, differentiates domains of normative communicative action from systems of administration steered by efficient power and economic imperatives.

Where would one find any space left for postmetaphysical spirituality or reflective faith? It could not be expected in Habermas's model in the two top right columns. One is unable to find modern analogues to ritual action and mythic steering at the level where one would have to combine profane forms of understanding with conflated domains of communication and effectiveness. Habermas leaves these two top right boxes empty, because globally we live increasingly under the disenchanted and linguistified conditions of postmodernity. But in his most recent turn, he revitalizes focus on the postsecular need for ritual as the ur-origin of postmetaphysical thinking (Mendieta, 2019). Fundamentalist forms of ritual and mythmaking would be some of the post-profane, willed attempts to fill in these blanks with uncritical claims to understanding or with a decisionist basis for action. While Habermas never articulates a space within his chart for open, reflective, and mature postmetaphysical spirituality, he is faithful to the structure of stages. At the bottom left, Habermas leaves two spaces in his table of forms of understanding uncannily blank. These bottom-left empty sets under sacred practices and worldviews correspond to the two empty sets at the top right under profane equivalents to ritual and myth. We must think and imagine what can inhabit these empty sets (Matuštík 2019).

In my happy disagreement with Habermas, I want to place the emergent possibility of postmetaphysical spiritualities precisely at the bottom left, where his secularizing critique projects blank vanishing points that ought to dissolve all sacred contents into profane communicative forms of understanding. That figure 28 is supposed to indicate that a reduction of all sacred contents into profane domains of validity claims has been achieved in principle with the Enlightenment and discursive rationality. Entering the two blank spots Habermas left in figure 28, this is one area where I would theorize an emergence of post-formal stages of understanding suited so well for postmetaphysical spiritual grammars and transpersonal states of awareness. Please let us write into the blank spaces of Habermas's chart our candidate: ICT.

Wilber adopted the Habermasian linguistic structure of three validity claims of truth, normative rightness, and sincerity with which we address one another about something in our lifeworld. Habermas distinguishes between system, or noncommunicative reason, and lifeworld. Wilber has a place for a distinct nonlinguistic rationality: What in Habermas comes under the rubric of systems theory or functionalist reason, we encounter as one of the four AQALs. Wilber speaks about holons as the wholes that are simultaneously parts of some other whole. There are four major perspectives an individual holon can take in the integral AQAL perspectival structure: subjective, intersubjective, objective, and interobjective.

- In this stage of our discussion it becomes recognizable how these holonic perspectives correspond roughly to Habermas's architectonic. There are three validity claims of communicative action: intentional or truthfulness speech claims
- cultural or normative speech claims
- behavioral or objective speech claims
- noncommunicative systems rationality
- social or interobjective, functional imperatives of markets and administrative power

At this juncture, Wilber and Habermas share all that comes under the sixth phase of postmetaphysical critical theory. The key to my thinking is not what Wilber takes over from Habermas, but rather what he impugns to him. Habermas's social evolutionary model stops with formal stage of communicative rationality. Habermas does not admit the possibility that there could be post-formal stages of consciousness in individual, social, and cultural development. In principle, he may have closed doors to that post-metaphysical understanding that is at home with post-formal consciousness and post-rational, transpersonal, non-dual awareness and witness. And yet Habermas (2017, 2019) deems it important that we do not forget how to access archaic ritual awareness in the present postsecular condition. Without ongoing living communities of reflective faith, all of us would lose access to untapped ritual resources for renewal of human solidarities and communicative interaction. Wilber shows that in order to access old as well as new spiritualities critically, postmetaphysical thinking and reflective faith must effect perspectival shifts to postformal understanding and trans-personal (postrational, nondual) awareness.

Habermas adopts Weber's reading of Kant's three critiques (reason, morality, and art) and Hegel's three spheres of culture (science, morality and law, and aesthetics). On that view, social rationalization of modern cultures resulted in disrupted, fragmented value spheres of expert knowledge (laboratory, jurisprudence, museum and aesthetic criticism). For a secularizing thinker, this evolution also resulted in a thorough reduction of the differential rationality deficit between sacred and profane domains. In brief, albeit in the last few years he has begun to focus on religious topics, Habermas's view of social evolution has ushered our age into a thorough postmodern disenchantment with all spiritual or religious claims about subjective, intersubjective, and social worlds. If there has been a critical and evolving line of religious or spiritual development, in the worlds of emphatic modernist secularizers, religions have gone—or should go—the way of dinosaurs. Religious perspectives, so it is argued, cannot evolve like other critical perspectives do. Religiously, one dies the "death of God" with the linguistification of religious claims to validity. Those very claims are now answered by the expert cultures and the formal worlds of (I, you, we). Unlike for integral critical theory, Habermas's formal validity claims do not inhabit perspectives of G-d, self, and world. Rather, validity claims are grammatically formal perspectives that speakers and hearers adopt vis-à-vis contents of worlds (it). "God" is replaced in Habermas's architectonic by the regulative ideal of all perspectives that hearers and speakers may adopt, given infinite time and space for open discussion.

It may be legitimate to ask whether and how grammatical perspectives (Habermas) and perspective-taking (Wilber) speak about the parallel communicative structures. Habermas would call perspectives formal grammatical presuppositions of human interactions about something in the world; Wilber would articulate in the perspective-taking the dimensions in which faces of G-d are structurally available to us. In AQAL, three grammatical perspectives stand for spiritual faces of G-d as I, G-d as you, and G-d as transpersonal we. Moses may not see G-d and live, because face-to-face with the divine never arrives for humans in a single, all-comprehensive, intra-worldly, monological and decisionistic grammatical perspective of a papal "we." Perspectival stages are ways of being in, reading of, and transforming the world.

Modes of Existence Move a Transversal Axis of Integral Critical Theory

The claim of Integral Post-Metaphysics is that you can indeed account for all the really necessary ingredients of metaphysics or a spiritual

> philosophy without metaphysical assumptions. These metaphysical assumptions are, quite simply, unnecessary and cumbersome baggage that hurts spirituality more than helps. Spirituality, to survive in the present and future world, is and must be post-metaphysical.
>
> —Ken Wilber (2006)

With the crispness of a calligrapher, Wilber addresses post-rational spirituality at the juncture that Habermas theorizes as an empty set. The locution "postmetaphysical thinking" occurs in Habermas's (1992, 2008; Mendieta 2019) work on Mead, Kierkegaard, and communicative ethics from 1988, and before him in Martin Heidegger's critique of Western metaphysics and before both in Friedrich Nietzsche's genealogy of values. Postmetaphysical thinking emerges from the merciless secularizing reflection of traditional forms of understanding. Habermas does not leave Western rationality off the hook, as we must learn from the double failures of great traditions and disenchanted modernity who did not deliver us to perpetual peace. Communicative ethics for Habermas ideally intervenes in the conflict among uncriticizable claims of sacred authorities and the warring claims of modern gods and demons. Wilber learns from the best features of modernist rationality and he also identifies with postmodern suspicions of instrumental reason and great historical narratives. And learning from both legacies of postmodernity, Wilber discerns this to be the right time for the emergence of post-rational forms of spirituality fit for our times. Habermas's form, emptied of contents, is not a cognate for religious form of emptiness pregnant with genesis. Rather, communicative interaction takes the place of "God" or the regulative ideal distilled from the evolving forms of understanding. Habermas follows the secularizing reflection of the West and increasingly global modernity to the vanishing point where the rationality differential between the sacred contents and profane forms has been reduced or translated into criticizable validity claims without any remainder. Wilber has filled that very disenchanted, linguistified empty set neither with hyperrationality nor with uncriticizable newly mythologized contents of archaic traditions.

Habermas, just like Wilber, integrates post-Darwinian, Piagetian, Kohlbergian, Hegelian models of human evolution. Wilber does not stop short of allowing for religious evolution after Weber's and critical theory's disenchantment with religion. Wilber's post-formal model of stages of human evolution is, like Habermas's, based on a reconstructive social science. Yet, unlike Habermas, who may be tone-deaf to these spiritual perspectives,

ICT theorizes experience and claims of individuals who already today develop stages and states of consciousness beyond formal rationality. This nuance inserts throws a monkey wrench into a fully reduced rationality deficit of the sacred and secular contents. ICT permits us to raise spiritual claims to existence after the postmodern disenchantment with religions. ICT welcomes certain atheism or the "death of God" as a path to post-formal stages of understanding spiritual languages and communicating non-dual claims.

I want to open my imagined encounter with two relevant impacts of Wilber's thought on my thinking about the possibility of integral critical theory. The first impact is registered in Wilber's (1997, 2001) occasional, yet significant, engagements with Habermas's discourse ethics and communication theory. Nothing in Habermas's communicative model of critical theory precludes, Wilber (2001) writes, discovering post-rational stages and states of consciousness. Indeed, the unfolding of new patterns of forms of understanding cannot be read off from social evolution in ways that would a priori close off this emergent possibility. And so, in responding to Habermas, Wilber boldly calls for a "critical spiritual theory." Habermas's theoretical structure warrants no rationally defensible rejection of valid spiritual forms of postmetaphysical thinking. Habermas argues that all forms of ultimate concern can become linguistically secularized without spiritual remainders. In their place, he envisions a regulative ideal of communicative rationality.

As his alternative, Wilber (2001) proposes to develop "a thoroughly post-metaphysical, post-Kantian spirituality." And he hopes that this can be accomplished, in part, within a Habermasian formal framework of reconstructive science, yet with a new set of evidence of spiritually inflected stages of post-rational development. This Wilberian reconstruction of forms of understanding allows for developmental competences and social evolution in the dimensions of postmetaphysical spirituality. With a Habermasian toolbox, Wilber (2001) broadens critical theory into domains of spirituality:

> A "critical theory" can be established in any major discipline—whether in art, morals, or science. It simply depends on whether one has an approach that one *claims* to be more authentic, or more comprehensive, or more accurate, or more valuable, or "more something." The Frankfurt School, for example, developed a critical social theory that they claimed offered more political and personal freedom. You can have a critical art theory, critical moral theory, critical spiritual theory, and so on. But all *critical*

> theories are *internally* bound to a series of normative claims that they then must *justify* as compelling and in some sense binding on others.

If we had a conversation in which Wilber would try to make Habermas find a legitimate space for ICT in his architectonic, this could sum up all seven stages leading up to the ICT. Let me have Wilber (2001, Part 1) make his most important statement about Habermas's research program in critical theory:

> I consider Habermas [to be] the world's greatest living philosopher. This does not mean, however, that I agree with all of what he has to say. But in very general terms I do find much agreement with his quasi-universalist approach; his developmental perspective; his dialogical methods; his three domains and three validity claims (art, morals, science—one version of the four quadrants); his championing of the lifeworld in addition to the systems world; his attempt at a reconstruction of the pragmatic history of embodied consciousness; his normative boldness; his blend of both transcendental and context-bound claims; and his critical stance. I respectfully disagree on many of the details of those broad programs, however; and I strongly part ways with Habermas on his treatment of both pre-linguistic and translinguistic realms. Habermas relates humans to both preverbal Nature and transverbal Spirit in ways that I believe are profoundly incorrect. A more integral (or "all-quadrants, all-levels, all-lines, all-states") approach allows us to handle a much larger view of the Kosmos than Habermas allows.

This brings me to the second area that had impact on my current thinking about ICT. The online exchange in which I conversed with Wilber was not an imagined encounter (Wilber and Matuštík, 2006). I brought into it what I have learned from Habermas, as well as my own reflections on existential phenomenology through which I developed my dialogue with Habermas. My encounter with Wilber focused on stages of understanding and states of awareness. In that conversation, I proposed something analogical to what I developed in my published work on Habermas and Kierkegaard. Yet there is this caveat: Wilber did not need me to bring spiritual dimensions into his postmetaphysical thinking.

With Wilber, I am thus able to move from a merely imagined conversation with Habermas one step further. What if we introduced an existential dimension into the Wilber-Combs Lattice (Wilber, 2006)? See Figure 2.1.

We would take the integral model of stages (perspectives and development that characterize seven stages of critical theory) and states (these are the missing dimensions of awareness and witnessing unaccounted for in Habermas's architectonic) and then draw a distinct transversal axis that would complement the vertical axis of stages (or forms of understanding) and the horizontal axis of awareness and witness states (see Table 2.3 on page 49).

I developed my proposal for a transversal axis of existential modes without any knowledge of Dustin DiPerna's (2014) thinking on a parallel track. He introduced the third axis of vantage points into the Wilber-Combs Lattice. DiPerna splits the Wilberian axis of states into the axis of states/realms (gross, subtle, causal) and the axis of vantage points (gross, subtle, causal, subtle, non-dual). See Figure 2.2.

DiPerna de facto articulated the modern epistemological split between the subjective and the objective dimensions of the states that do not realize

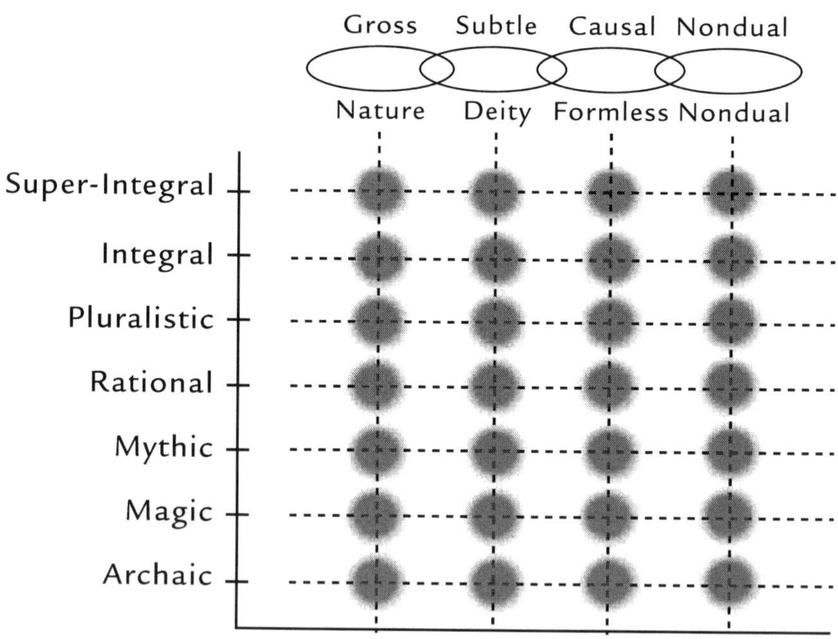

Figure 2.1. Wilber-Combs lattice. *Source:* Ken Wilber.

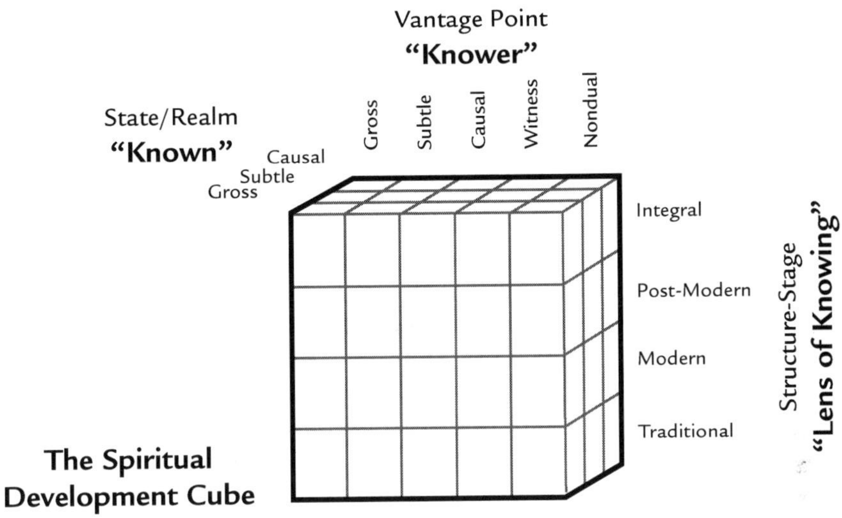

Figure 2.2. The spiritual developmental cube. *Source:* Dustin Diperna.

the non-dual awakened awareness in which the very split vanishes. DiPerna's three axes describe:

1. states and realms ("the known" or the objective lens of states)
2. vantage points ("knower" or the subjective lens of states)
3. structural stages ("knowing" or the interpretive lens of un understanding")

DiPerna singles out the structural developmental line of faith as the most important entry point for the study of religions. The main insights are that: The states have separable content and vantage point components; that moving into an experience of a subtle realm content can be done by a knower who does not need to be at a subtle level of identity, but at any number of (state) levels of vantage point. Furthermore, this combined experience of subject-object is always already interpreted within a level on the faith line.

DiPerna expands the Wilber-Combs Lattice by more fully articulating the modern epistemic lenses of the subject-object or the knower-known in their evolution (stage-structures) and transformations of knowing (states and vantage points) toward a non-dual, awakened awareness. I articulate the third axis as an existential mode or an integer of the self. My model considers the whole human person and articulates existential stages. Existential modes are not necessarily developmental (they are not structural stages or vantage points). And their transformations involve the entirety of human existence (existential stages are not reducible to states of awareness alone). Another way of characterizing the impact of existential stages on structural stages, states, and vantage points is to depict them as transcultural living biases, the musical keys that affect the entire tonal composition. That is why they function as integers and not just as lenses.

I think that the category of self, defined as spirit in a Kierkegaardian, rather than Hegelian parlance, is necessary if we want to account for the "how" of stages, vantage points, and states in the Wilber-Combs-DiPerna model. Kierkegaard (1982b) shows that the self is never a permanent or inherently existing entity. Its energetic, dynamic existence may be, however, defined as a three-pronged self-relation that relates itself to itself and in that self-relation relates to another. The interplay of self-other relations has impact on its structural perspectives, vantage points, and states of awareness and witness. Self, defined classically as a psycho-physical unity—or, in modern epistemology, as a mind-and-body unity—does not know itself strictly speaking as spirit self. In that technical sense, structural stages, vantage points, and states require the performative language of self in order to articulate the integer of existing spirit. This is Kierkegaard's main corrective to classical and modern ways of speaking about human knowing and being. The Wilber-Combs-DiPerna Cube lays out the structural and poststructural analysis of human understanding, language, consciousness, knowing, and awareness. My modest proposal that I offered to Habermas's communication theory (to articulate the how of grammatical positions through which speakers and hearers raise and evaluate validity claims about something in the world) is now to anchor the Spiritual Development Cube in existential phenomenology.

When Simone de Beauvoir suggests in her major work, *The Second Sex*, that one is not born a woman but becomes one, she adapts this insight from Kierkegaard, whose mantra has been that the self cannot be something given, but is a task. One is born Dan or American in this or that era, but to become self who is willing to be oneself free of despair, one must know oneself as spirit. Firstly, the structural stages of understanding define the developmental (social, moral, cognitive) *what* of perspectives in personal and social evolution. Furthermore, the vantage points (the subject-positions of the knower) are transformed in reduplications of the knower's knowing and known in existing. In other words, one is becoming human, as Kierkegaard's pseudonym (1992), Climacus says, by becoming a subjective thinker. That truth is subjectivity does not mean that it is relative (that would be an epistemic claim about truth), but rather that truth resides in the mode of its appropriation (reading, speaking, living). Thirdly, the states of awareness and witness are impacted by the *who* as the integer of self-relation. Thus, existential modes function as a particular bias that has impact on all other structures, vantage points, and states, and does so in a transcultural modality (i.e., not as this or that culture or religion or historical consciousness of an era).

Kierkegaard (1992) introduces a third category, *how*, which inflects the entire self- and other-relation, including language one uses. The third is the spirit self: The positive unity that brings the entire passive psychological and psychophysical unity to question. There is a need for such a third, transversal axis to complement states of awareness and stages of consciousness. One cannot teach spirit in direct didactic communication. G-d for Kierkegaard—not even the Christian incarnation that matters to him—cannot be reduced to a dogma. Divine presence is existence-communication available according to one's mode of existing. In this precise sense, G-d does not *exist* in modes of existing that cannot hear and speak spiritual vernaculars. Or, expressed paradoxically—as if in a koan, by one of his pseudonymous authors—that there is possibility is G-d (Kierkegaard, 1980a). Spirit is the relation in which one relates to oneself as thrown and posited in this or that perspective and awareness. This deep self is, ironically, available only indirectly. The self as spirit too does not exist in modes of existence in which oneself has not become a question. And when spirit self appears on stage, in the eyes of the worldly script, *spirit is no-self.* I believe that the Buddhist non-self and no-God perspectives, found in Keiji Nishitani (1982), invoke something analogical to Kierkegaard's spiritual spheres of existence.

There is a twofold background to my rejoinder to the Wilber-Combs-DiPerna Cube of states of awareness, vantage points, and structural stages: First, to resume from the previous discussion of stage six of critical theory, Habermas's analysis of social evolution gets us to an "orange altitude" (integral's phrase for formal operational and early post-formal schemas of cognition) as proper to modern and perhaps also to postmodern consciousness. Yet Habermas aims to reduce the rationality differential (gap) between sacred contents and secular forms. Until recently, Habermas (2008, 2017, 2019) has been requiring a thorough translation of spiritual faith-based mode of human development into the grammar of validity and cultural value domains of modernity. In this critical and secularizing translation of the religious value sphere and its semantic resources and forms, access to genuine spiritual awareness would drop out as a possibility for postmetaphysical thinking.

Second, Kierkegaard's study of existential spheres admits (with Hegel and, for us, also with Weber and Habermas) that there is no real existing religious culture in modernity. Just as there were virtually no genuine socialists among the leaders and ideologues of the so-called Marxist regimes of the twentieth century (Marcuse, for example, would argue this in his critical theory of Soviet Marxism); so Kierkegaard claims that, ironically, there have been no Christians in Christendom. We have had an era dominated by communism and we have had nationalist, herd-religious forms with many Christians willing to be Christians in despair. Something analogical can be developed in trying to articulate whether or not there can be any genuinely existing Muslims defined by the so-called Islamic regimes. The price of charicaturing Kierkegaard's uneven pants was, to be sure, much less to pay than saying anything even less controversial about Muslims in Muslimdoms today. Kierkegaard's critique of Christendom implies that what appears to be the most conservative, family-oriented, citizenship-promoting religion is, in fact, spiritually bankrupt. Hence, in real existing religious communities, one is wanting in finding living spirit.

To become spiritual in the existential sense, we are required to change the entirety of our sphere of existence. And this existence sphere cannot be identical with our birth culture; otherwise, to be born an American Christian slave owner in Frederick Douglass's time would be sufficient to being always already a decent American. But Douglass calls slave-owning Christianity of the American South a theft of heavens. I argued (2013) that Kierkegaard's transformation of individuals is required by the type of social evolution posited by Habermas. Otherwise, human selves fall into anomie and meaninglessness and remain too weak to resist fundamentalist and nationalist modes of individual and group formation (stages of postmodern consciousness fall back into a tribal-ethnocentric stage).

I agree with Wilber that individuals cannot jump developmental stages of consciousness (though collectives can). Habermas would agree with Hegel's and Marx's developmental theories that social evolution cannot run ahead of itself. For example, the so-called Arab Spring of the twenty-first century—even though it took place decades after the Prague Spring of 1968—did not spring from the social awareness generated by the French Revolution and the Enlightenment. The Velvet Revolution of 1989 discarded the Jacobin violence and interfaith or party warfare. The last time Muslims, Jews, and

Christians shared the remarkable levels of religious tolerance and understanding was during Golden Age Spain, before the New World discoveries. It is difficult to imagine how the gap in arrested shared social development between that early interreligious modernity and today's postmodernity can be closed any time soon. In this precise sense, structures of understanding and social evolution cannot run ahead of their achieved stages.

I also agree with Wilber, and here against Habermas, that the modern Enlightenment uncritically reduces all enlightenment to its particular stage of development, and so it now treats all religious states as ego- and ethnocentric, traditional, precritical, falsely requiring a full translation of the spiritual into the secular. And the fundamentalist forms of that archaic-cum-postmodern consciousness, then clash with the modernist critical view represented, e.g., by Habermas's formal rationality (Matuštík, 2006a). But I want to hold that we need, besides the vertical axis of stages and the horizontal axis of states also the transversal, or genuinely vertical-inward axis of existential self-transformation. It is true that one cannot jump stages or perspectives. Perspectives evolve with oneself and culture. Our senses of "God" evolve. "God" evolves with our perspectives through which G-d's faces become available to I, you, and we. The process understanding of G-d is a grammatical verb rather than a noun or even a dictionary definition. Even though a Buddhist awakening does not and Judaism cannot name G-d, still the refuge in Buddha, Dharma, and Sangha references the perspectives and states of those who take the refuge and the stages of understanding in which the refuge is articulated.

In a non-evolutionary sense, the spheres or modes of existence are available—like the awareness states—to everyone at every stage of consciousness and social evolution. How states are available to contemporaries is determined structurally by the stages of consciousness or forms of understanding. Yet the transversal existence spheres are not exactly the same as the intensity of states of consciousness. This is my rationale for articulating distinctness of stages, states, and modes of existence.

Kierkegaard criticized Hegel for confusing categories of transition with those of transformation. The evolutionary developmental structures are qualified by both-and: The later stages include and go beyond the earlier stages. This is the meaning of Hegelian logic of mediation or *Aufhebung*. The earlier forms of learning, the stages of spirit, are retained at ever-higher viewpoints of understanding. Most psychological, social, and moral models of evolution share this structural logic of both-and even when jumps, leaps, breaches, or depth dimensions of development are articulated.

Kierkegaard introduces the logic of either/or as distinct from Hegel, and by extension then also from Marx, Piaget, Kohlberg, and others. Existential transformative dialectic moves by disjunctions, through repelling, by discontinuous leaps. Existential modes are not developmental stages. Hence, the logic of either/or in modes is contrasted with the logic of both-and in stages. Modes of existence do retain elements of other modes, but transformations are never accounted for in an evolutionary manner. Rather, one always needs to speak of creation ex nihilo, genesis, difficult beginnings; and in modes, one begins in every generation at the beginning. There is no accumulated learning of existential modes in the sense of historical learning, progress, raising consciousness, or increasing probabilities.

To get at the transversal axis of ICT, we need to posit, in contrast to Hegel-Marx-Habermas-Piaget-Kohlberg-Gilligan and their evolutionary models, something akin to Kierkegaard's existential spheres of existence (see Table 2.2 for spheres or modes of aesthetic, ethical, ethico-religious, generic religious, and higher-level religiousness or spirituality). Modes define a motivational-inward prerequisite for the very possibility (condition of possibility) of evolutionary changes. Even though awareness and witness states when repeated may become new stable traits—and so take on structures of more permanent stages in some cases; still, we must notice that states and vantage points are not of themselves conditions for the possibility of emergence of structural or perspectival stages. And we cannot speak of spheres or modes of existence simply in terms of states either. My model of ICT assumes that we introduce into Wilber-Combs-DiPerna's *three-pronged lattice* (with structural or perspectival stages of consciousness and social evolution, vantage points of the knower, and states of non-dual awakened awareness) a fourth transversal axis of spheres or modes of existence (Table 3—or 3-D Cube).

Viewing the Wilber-Combs–DiPerna Lattice in a 3-D cube, we can describe evolutionary enlightenment on a *vertically* temporal and historical axis. Along this trajectory (on a two-dimensional graph we discern a line leading from left bottom to left up), we read structural stages of conscious, social, and cultural evolution, and they lead to ever-fuller contents. Enlightenment intensifies *horizontally* along vantage points and states (on a two-dimensional graph this can be represented by a single horizontal bottom line from left to right that does not show DiPerna's differentiation between states and vantage points). In the Spiritual Development Cube, there are two horizontal lines: front to back (states) and left to right (vantage points). This dimension represents a contemporary axis available, in principle, at every stage of consciousness or forms of understanding. Non-dual states of

Table 2.2a. Kierkegaard's Modes of Existence: Aesthetical

Mode	*Dialectic*	*Social Relation*	*Self-Relation*	*Time and History*	*Language and Communication*	*Collision of the Stage*
A E S T H E T I C A L	**external either-or:** interesting-boring, fortune-misfortune self-choice has not been posited enjoyment and pleasure in spontaneity of the sensuous: fun and curiosity **the logic of either-or:** extensive and intensive variation of experience without axis (rotation method)	crowd, herd, mass identity: neither "I" nor "we" but uniformity social masks arbitrary relations either embraces status quo or disdains conventions, but has no self as basis for either	**no self, no inwardness** shallow 'I' body and soul are unqualified by the third: spirit fragmented external self-identification too much possibility (abstract flight)	disjointed moments (instants of linear vanishing time become mere momentary masks) dupe of external history pursuit of pleasure and avoidance of pain is fleeting and filled with anguish Memory: nostalgia and regret and longing about the passage of time	idle talk, chatter masked "no-self" of a seducer and babble that grasps or says nothing	anguish of choices that lack the original self-choice dupe of fortune vs. misfortune in all pursuit of relations (self- and social alienation) enjoyment without joy (suppression) spontaneity with fear of risk (repression) fun without ecstasy (addiction)

continued on next page

Table 2.2a. Continued.

Mode	*Dialectic*	*Social Relation*	*Self-Relation*	*Time and History*	*Language and Communication*	*Collision of the Stage*
		social forms of aesthetic life: collectivism, nationalism, empire-striving *religious forms of aesthetic life*: fundamentalism, "God" idea as a crutch	too much necessity (anguished finitude)	no infinite or eternal, only abstract reflection into the past present: discontinuity without self-coincidence or life-harmonization living-dead: disintegration of existence before one has begun		inability to stand alone or to love or to receive love (anxiety) does not take his or her pursuit of spontaneity and joy seriously (bondage that only appears free)

Table 2.2b. Kierkegaard's Modes of Existence: Ethical

Mode	*Dialectic*	*Social Relation*	*Self-Relation*	*Time and History*	*Language and Communication*	*Collision of the Stage*
E T H I C A L	**existential either/or:** *good or evil, guilty or not-guilty* Shall I win the whole world but lose my self? responsible self-choice of oneself as capable of raising questions of good and evil self-choice as the original choice that recognizes one's life under the mode of its eternal validity	face-to-face relations raise the ethical call to responsibility and commitment vocation and marriage struggle for equality and reciprocal recognition dialogue: "I" and "we"	**self-choice: self = the category of freedom** spontaneity of the hylomorphic unity (body and soul) is qualified by *spirit* ethical continuity of the self is gained by repeated commitments self as deepening recollection and appropriation and self-choice	ethical continuity is recollected in time time is an occasion for self-transformation of the aesthetical and the deepening of the ethical beginning of internal history is an intensification of the fleeting aesthetical moments through the true existential moment of inward decision to take one's anguish and despair	disclosure of self to another transparency of promise and commitment renewal of vows dialogue reciprocity ethical and democratic speech social ethics of family and civic	the heroic project of the will to good, true, beautiful and just shatters on the inability (weakness of the ethical will) to sustain freedom without falling prey to the illusion of power anguish about good and evil appears also in the secular discovery of motivated deception (Marx, Freud,

continued on next page

Table 2.2b. Continued.

Mode	*Dialectic*	*Social Relation*	*Self-Relation*	*Time and History*	*Language and Communication*	*Collision of the Stage*
	the logic of either/or: *self-responsible freedom or drift*	free will finds itself fulfilled in the universal values of family, society, the state, and the religious community	begins to stand alone in one's commitment balances possibility (freedom) and necessity (finitude) becoming concrete infinite is gathered in time (time is rescued) by repeated self-becoming as an ethical task ethical self-transparency before the other	and one's pursuit of joyous immediacy seriously	duty and religious values ethical existence approximates its ideality through the illocutionary force of social and communicative ethics, deliberative democracy and law	Nietzsche) radical finitude of all ethical, social, political and heroic achievements is standing alone or in dissent against social expectations and even ethical commitments a form of arrogance and deception? *idolatry* revealed both in aesthetic forms of social and religious life and in ethical heroic projects

Table 2.2c. Kierkegaard's Modes of Existence: Religious

Mode	*Dialectic*	*Social Relation*	*Self-Relation*	*Time and History*	*Language and Communication*	*Collision of the Stage*
RELIGIOUS	**either/or movement by virtue of the absurd:** *resignation or faith*	singular individual stands higher than the universal	faith cannot be mediated: anxiety, fear and trembling of ethical-social-universal self-justifications	faith: decisive moment when the infinite creates something out of nothing in time	silence of faith is not capricious, it comes out of awed ethical speech and is a form of speaking	can one sustain faith without knowing that in time one begins in untruth or in sin?
	Shall I win the whole world but lose my self?	transgression of ethical-social obligations to family, society, and state	self-becoming is not at one's power: one is a "stranger to oneself"	the wholly other singularity of absolutely new is revealed in the every face-to-face encounter	faith communicates indirectly the ground of a life in truth, rightness and sincerity	does one need a gift of communication to grasp one's despair?
	moment of faith = leap = existential immediacy is unlike spontaneous immediacy of the aesthetic	transgression of ethical norms of good and evil or guilty/not guilty	dying to the immediacy of conventional	internal history and ethical continuity are suspended only to be created anew	possibility of speaking is not at one's own will	to despair without having a name for it (Faustian intellectual quest for immediacy, Freudean discovery of neurosis and unconscious Nietzsche's will to power, Marx's exploitation as social sin)
	self-choice as the original choice that recognizes one's life under the mode of its eternal validity	from the side of ethics, faith appears mad, irresponsible, irrational	self-ascriptions and cultural and heroic projects of self as *causa sui* (ground of itself)	harmonization of ends (happiness) in personal and public history is not rooted in heroic immortality projects (virtue)	witness to the birth of speech when it has become	to despair before God (faith, compassion)
	the logic of either/or: *either teleological suspension of the*					

continued on next page

Table 2.2c. Continued.

Mode	*Dialectic*	*Social Relation*	*Self-Relation*	*Time and History*	*Language and Communication*	*Collision of the Stage*
	ethical or all faith becomes false ultimacy (fanaticism, idolatry)	dissent gains priority over consensus trembling of law and order "god" of culture and aesthetic religiosity is dead	death of desire to be god, death of self as author of one's life, death of "god" as one knows "him" or "proves" "him" balances possibility (freedom) and necessity (finitude) yielding of self-mastery and will to be absolute creator trembling of self external war on evil is idolatry of self	faith is not a postulate trembling of the narrative time of self and history	impossible trembling of ethical promises and value-positing	do not Christians in Christendom need to learn again what it means to exist as a human being?

Table 2.3. Stages, States, and Modes of Existence

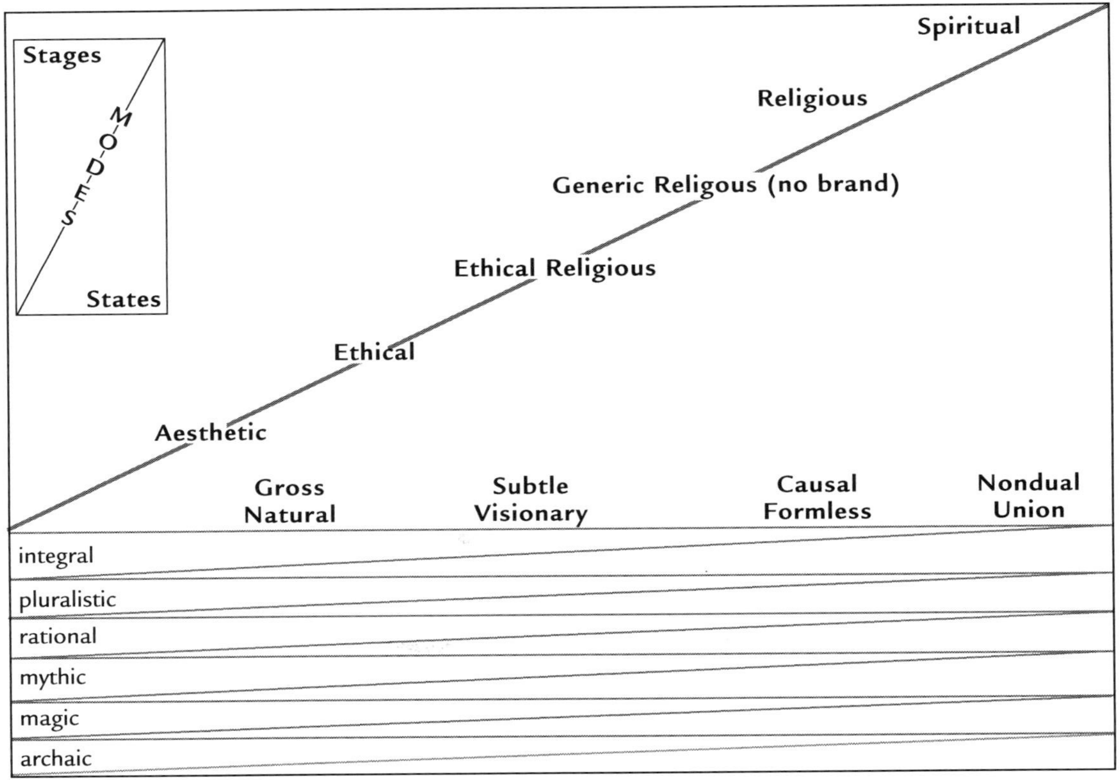

possible awareness and witnessing recede to the emptiness of form. Indeed, there are forms of witnessing and awareness that become placeholders for cultivation of new major areas of states.

Enlightenment moves *transversally* when existential spheres or modes transform the entirety of existence. This is represented by a third lattice line starting at bottom left and leading diagonally to the top right. Existential modes can be represented in a two-dimensional model as running from the zero point diagonally to the top right. In a 3-D model, the modes of existential integer must be envisioned by lines running diagonally between corners of the cube. The modal zero point in 3-D lies at the heart of the cube. Existential modes move neither historically, nor by vantage points or by states of intensity. They are akin to invisible dancers who lift up and land without ever leaving the spot. Their movements are accomplished as if without any effort, and yet they are characterized by an ever-deeper awakening of spirit in the understanding, aware and witness self. The transversal axis of sudden motion passes through spaceless extention and sudden nonchronological intensity of moment. Kierkegaard often calls this event at its most transparent modality a leap of faith, and dancers are appropriately dubbed as the knights of faith. One requires this level of modal analysis to anchor the developmental line of faith in actual practice of it.

Existential leaps, those transversal modalities, are akin to integers in math or musical keys in the tonal notations. They are like a Sabbath day that introduces *nothing* new in content of creation and yet gives the fullness of blessing through the emptiness of its form. The transversal emptiness is the divine rest that is nonetheless assumed by every exertion. Existential modes cannot be primarily driven by structural or perspectival or vantage points transitions or by shifts of conscious, social, cultural, and spiritual evolution. Structural stages and vantage points are shifts within spheres or modes of existence. Stages are akin to the epochs of creation. Yet transversal existential modes, unlike the mystical and non-dual awareness states or even witness states, are characterized by reflective awareness, acts of civil disobedience, posture of a gadfly or witness who is a dissident. Existential modes have a deliberative, reflective quality of self- and other-relations through which transformations take place (see Kierkegaard, 1995). Transversal axis of existential modes rides on the movement of radical self-choice of oneself as spirit who is an integer of stages and states, as well as an originator of contents and values. And yet this faithful self learns to will to be a self now free of despair. And so, as a non-self in the order of evolutionary stages and of awareness states, one rests transparently pouring its willing into that which integrates one's risk, novelty, faith.

Integral Critical Theory Becoming Counter-Redemptive

My thinking about an ICT of the present age has numerous theoretical and practical forerunners, and thus raises both old and new questions. While the notion that the political is personal and the personal is political echoes some of the more recent ferment of the 1960s, in the West we find much earlier ideas for integrating personal and social perspectives, both in the Judeo-Christian and philosophical writings. The Jewish Law, Torah, and the early Christian faith embody the communal forms of life that are at once socially and personally transformative. Plato's *Republic* offers a thorough examination of the intrinsic relationship between the twofold founding of justice, that of a just individual (psyche) and society (polis). The Middle Ages achieved an increasing synthesis of these classical perspectives: St. Augustine's *City of God* responds not just to Cicero, but mainly to the collapse of the ancient Roman civilization, and the "city" becomes the dominant metaphor of personal-political Ordo in its human and divine ordinances. St. Thomas Aquinas erects in his Summa an architectonic of a spiritually informed real-politics. And the Jewish, Christian, and Arabic scholars in the Golden Age in Spain; e.g., Maimonides, engage in a civilizing, philosophical dialogue among the three religions of the book.

The precursors to what I call integral critical theory are found much closer to our times. In his early essays from the 1930s, Marcuse attempted to integrate the existential ontology of Martin Heidegger with the newly discovered humanistic perspective of the young Marx. That attempt, initiated while Marcuse was writing his second doctorate under Heidegger, was cut short by the rise of Nazism. Marcuse joined the Frankfurt Institute of Social Research on its flight into exile and never resumed the project of phenomenological Marxism. It was not until the mid–twentieth century that Jean-Paul Sartre embarked upon a major effort to link in a single philosophical space of theory the existential (personal) together with the sociopolitical (public) perspectives on human development. The accent of the early Sartre in *Being and Nothingness* falls on the personal development; the accent of the late Sartre in *Critique of Dialectical Reason* falls on the social, political, and institutional analysis. These two perspectives, existential

Marxism, Marxist existentialism, are like the popular optical illusion showing, depending on one's figure or ground perspective, a duck or a rabbit, and so one can never quite see both at the same time. There were other parallel projects of phenomenological or dialectical Marxism proposed by the Yugoslav praxis philosophers, such as by Mihailo Markovic and Svetozar Stojanovic, and by the Czech philosopher Karel Kosík. The Yugoslav experiment in thought had its unreliable companion in Tito's authoritarian socialist regime that morphed after his death into ethnic warfare. Some of the former philosophers of existential praxis became the proponents of the new Serbian nationalism. The Czech idea of existential humanism was promulgated in practice by Alexander Dubček's socialism with the human face, only to be crushed by the invading Soviet army in 1968. What was left of this existential perspective emigrated into the theater of the absurd of Václav Havel, who performed it faithfully from his dissident years all the way into his Czechoslovak presidency after 1989.

In my earlier work (Matuštík, 2013, 2001), I took one small step in the direction abandoned by early Marcuse and unsuccessfully pursued by Sartre. I did so by articulating Habermas's theory of communicative or discourse ethics in conjunction with Kierkegaard's indirect communication underwriting his existential ethics. Kierkegaard is able to provide critical theory with an existential dimension of communication that critical theorists of the Frankfurt School tradition, for the most part, rejected on account of Heidegger's momentary lapse into Nazi activism and, more recently, also because of the lapse of the Yugoslav praxis philosophers into Serbian nationalism. Throwing out the baby of existential perspective with the dirty bathwater of nationalism left critical theory too weak to be able to confront the arising religious fundamentalism and white nationalism in the present age. Because with no space left for postmetaphysical stages of spirituality in their discourse, they were ill-equipped to critique pre-rational religious expressions otherwise than through some version of the Westernizing secularization thesis that valorizes achievements of postmodernity for its professed gradual reduction of the sacred-profane gap.

Whether or not one can begin to sketch a critical theory that would give justice to self-transformative and socially transformative perspectives without violence and reductionism, this is no longer an academic question. What is at stake is our ability to come to terms with globalization of socioeconomic, political, and religious conflicts. While social experiments in real existing socialism yielded at least as much suffering as they hoped to alleviate, the reigning neoliberal market ideologies deepen the wasteland left by the previous century. We must learn from their failures as much as achievements, but have we found yet an economic way of life that would not be self- and other-destructive, that would resemble in the material domain what many invoke in their Friday or Sunday prayers? Have we found a political and cultural way of life that would prevent even our best institutions from taking self- and other-destructive paths? Can we say with a clear conscience that more democracy has meant less war and exploitation? I pose these as questions, lest someone thinks I easily dismiss the levels of complexity seen in our age and the good efforts of humanity to meet them. These questions are not rhetorical points for a homily; asking them should not be judged as preaching either. The search for integral thinking and living in the fields of the economy, politics, and spirituality requires us transforming the very Athropocene.

What about hope addressed equally to redemptive waiting as to revolutionary urgency to act? Must not hope for us be always without a projected redemptive stasis, a heavenly practico-inert? Must not hope we imagine be counter-redemptive, never fully in our imaginary, prayers, or hands?

ICT addresses three non-reducible fields of human needs—material, social and cultural, and spiritual—developing three dimensions of critique and possibility: political economy of social justice, politics of recognition, and ultimate concerns for self-transformative and redemptive hope. Beginning with the seventh, integral phase of critical theory, let us imagine a triangle (see Table 1): At the base of the triangle are material needs (IT as represented by the objective behavior and body and inter-objective functional systems of markets and administration) and social-political needs (YOU/WE of intersubjective and cultural interaction); at the top are self-transformative or spiritual needs (I-I no longer as a metaphysical soul or transcendental ego, but as an existential integer within stages and states of consciousness). Speaking of needs and dimensions of ICT indicates that critical theory must operate in both incarnate and ideational modes. The needs represent the basic nourishment necessary for sustaining the very human existence. Each type of nourishment has its own field for growing and harvesting. Ideals become critical tools when we lack certain needs, and the time and place where one stands while envisioning what one lacks in the present condition is not a field but a projective dimension (utopos has no place or field, yet it exists in a dimension of ideal, hope, waiting, possibility). Any impetus for transformation of the field of needs thus comes from the recognition of the dissonance between the reality and the ideal; thus from the material, political and cultural, and spiritual dimensions of critique and possibility.

One field of ICT pertains to material needs and resources for their satisfaction. Its corresponding dimension encompasses critique of political economy, whereby it articulates vehicles for just economic distribution of material resources for the satisfaction of bodily needs. Another field concerns social and cultural needs for recognition and institutions for their expression. This dimension of ICT develops critique of society, whereby it seeks political vehicles for social integration, democratic participation, and cultural reproduction. The third field articulates ultimate concerns or hope—spiritual needs for self-transformation. The dimension of spiritual critique in this field is to unmask not only the secular, but also the religious idolatry of finite absolutes. In this triple approach, an ICT would promote ways of human self-transformation, practices aiming at spiritual liberation, and communicative channels to redemptive hope.

No one field of needs can be satisfied by another field (any such attempt would lead to suffering and violence); hence no dimension of critique can be overtaken by another dimension (any such attempt would lead to ideological reductionism). Material scarcity can be overcome by social justice, while the scarcity of recognition is met by reducing the democratic deficit in social, political, and cultural institutions. The scarcity of hope can be overcome neither by economic nor political means. Political economists, critical social theorists, and social activists presuppose hope for their work, but do not have access to its renewable resources. The ultimate concern or hope is not like addressing an inconvenient political truth about the climate and energy decline, e.g., by converting soybeans into biodiesel or switch grasses into ethanol.

Once again, what about hope still after the twentieth century horrors assigned to redemptive waiting and to secular action? Hope is not the same as hopes: One can have ultimate concern, hope (verb); yet one must not project one ultimate something, a hope (noun). As Rabbi David Cooper (1997) says, "God is a verb." No critical theory can get off the ground without hope in the verbal, active, performative sense, yet this dimension is recovered only within the seventh stage of critical theory that integrates material and sociopolitical hopes with redemptive hope. The scarcity of hope calls for a redemptive dimension of critical theory (Matuštík, 2008).

Beyond the skeptical postmodern claims, a new critical postmodern theorizing is at once normative and self-limiting (see Matuštík, 2001, 2008, part 1 on Derrida and Habermas). We are hoping against hope because we live in the crisis of the idolatrous ultimate or under the conditions of the "death of God." There is a growing worldwide community of thinkers and meditation practitioners; theorists of developmental studies and integral spirituality introduced models of stages and states of human development suited for understanding the inward dimension of global human flourishing. Beyond the post-secular claims of aesthetic religiosity and secular idolatry, integral spirituality introduces postmodern stages and states of consciousness that envision the divine as at once opening the doors to social justice, multicultural worlds, and the priority of one's inherence in spirit over the adherence to doctrines.

There is one astonishing implication of taking steps in the direction of ICT: What we are suffering in the twenty-first century is neither solely an economic class war, nor Huntington's (1998) *Clash of Civilizations*, e.g., between modern West and traditionalist Islam, nor simply religious wars. The revolutionary subject of true human needs, critique, and hoped-for ideals is not to be sought along one single trajectory: either economic or political class or orthodox religious brand names. ICT requires us to rethink the fault lines of conflict as collisions of frameworks among material, political, and spiritual levels of development. Such collisions arise both from disturbances within the frameworks and in hegemonic struggles among them. The economic analysts need to focus on models best suited to local and global justice. Political theorists and social critics cannot resolve market efficiency and distribution questions, but they must develop legal and political safeguards for deliberative practices and social recognition. Economists and political theorists, whether secular or religious, should in their domains hold their tongues about ultimate concerns. Marx was not the first, Trump is not the last who misspoke from left or right sides of their mouths on religion. It is always disastrous when politics cross-dresses in religious costumes, or when religion underwrites politics, or when economic welfare buys religious adherence.

References

Beaumont, Justin (ed.). 2019. *The Routledge Handbook of Postsecularity.* Kindle. New York: Routledge.

Cooper, David A. 1997. *God is a Verb: Kabbalah and the Practice of Mystical Judaism.* New York: Riverhead Books.

DiPerna, Dustin. 2014. *Streams of Wisdom: An Advanced Guide to Integral Spiritual Development.* Integral Publishing House.

Freud, Sigmund. 1989. *The Future of an Illusion.* New York: W. W. Norton.

Habermas, Jürgen. 1984. *The Theory of Communicative Action, Volume One: Reason and Rationalization of Society*, trans. Thomas McCarthy. Boston: Beacon Press.

Habermas, Jürgen. 1987. *The Theory of Communicative Action, Volume Two: Lifeworld and System: A Critique of Functionalist Reason,* trans. Thomas McCarthy. Boston: Beacon. Press.

Habermas, Jürgen. 1992. *Postmetaphysical Thinking: Philosophical Essays,* trans. William Mark Hohengarten. Cambridge, MA: MIT Press.

Habermas, Jürgen. 2001. "Faith and Knowledge." In *The Future of Human Nature,* trans. Hella Beister and Max Pensky, 101–115. Cambridge, MA: Polity Press.

Habermas, Jürgen. 2003. "Fundamentalism and Terror." In *Philosophy in a Time of Terror: Dialogues with Jürgen Habermas and Jacques Derrida*. Chicago: University of Chicago Press.

Habermas, Jürgen. 2005. *Religion and Rationality: Essays on Reason, God, and Modernity.* Cambridge, MA: Polity Press.

Habermas, Jürgen. 2008. *Between Naturalism and Religion: Philosophical Essays*, trans Ciaran Cronin. Cambridge: Polity Press.

Habermas, Jürgen. 2017. *Postmetaphysical Thinking II: Essays and Replies*. Cambridge, MA: Polity Press.

Habermas, Jürgen. 2019. *Auch eine Geschichte der Philosophie. Vol. 1. Die okzidentale Konstellation von Glauben und Wissen. Vol. 2. Vernüftige Freiheit. Spuren des Diskurses über Glauben und Wissen.* Suhrkamp Verlag: Frankfurt a/M.

Harari, Yuval Noah. 2016. *Homo Deus: A Brief History of Tomorrow.* New York: HarperCollins.

Horkheimer, Max. 1972. "Traditional and Critical Theory." In *Critical Theory*, trans. Matthew J. O'Connell, 188–243. New York: Herder and Herder.

Horkheimer, Max. 1974. "Theism and Atheism." In *Critique of Instrumental Reason*, trans. Matthew O'Connell, et al. Chapter 2. New York: Continuum.

Huntington, Samuel P. 1998. The *Clash of Civilizations and the Remaking of World Order*. New York: Touchstone Books.

Kierkegaard, Søren 1980a. *The Concept of Anxiety*, trans. Reidar Thomte in collaboration with Albert B. Anderson. Princeton, NJ: Princeton University Press.

Kierkegaard, Søren. 1980b. *The Sickness Unto Death*, trans. Howard V. Hong and Edna Hong. Princeton, NJ: Princeton University Press.

Kierkegaard, Søren. 1992. *Concluding Unscientific Postscript to* Philosophical Fragments, trans. Howard V. Hong and Edna H. Hong. Princeton, NJ: Princeton University Press.

Kierkegaard, Søren. 1995. *Works of Love*, trans. Howard V. Hong and Edna H. Hong. Princeton, NJ: Princeton University Press.

Matuštík, Martin Beck. 2013. *Postnational Identity: Critical Theory and Existential Philosophy in Habermas, Kierkegaard, and Havel.* Phoenix, AZ: New Critical Theory.

Matuštík, Martin Beck. 2000. "The Critical Theorist as Witness: Habermas and the Holocaust." In *Perspectives on Habermas*, ed. Lewis Edwin Hahn, 339–366. Chicago and La Salle, IL: Open Court.

Matuštík, Martin Beck. 2001. *Jürgen Habermas: A Philosophical-Political Profile*. Lanham, MD: Rowman & Littlefield.

Matuštík, Martin Beck. 2005. "Singular Existence and Critical Theory." *Radical Philosophy Review* 8(2): 211–223.

Matuštík, Martin Beck. 2006a. "Velvet Revolution in Iran?" *Logos: A Journal of Modern Society and Culture* 5(3). Retrieved from http://www.logosjournal.com/issue_5.3/matustik.htm.

Matuštík, Martin Beck. 2006b. "Between Hope and Terror: Derrida and Habermas Plead for the Impossible." In *The Derrida-Habermas Reader*, ed. Lasse A. Thomassen, 278–296. Edinburgh, UK: Edinburgh University Press.

Matuštík, Martin Beck. 2008. *Radical Evil and the Scarcity of Hope: Postsecular Meditations*. Bloomington, IN: Indiana University Press.

Matuštík, Martin Beck. 2019. "Dialectic of Rituals and Algorithms: Genealogy of Reflective Faith and Postmetaphysical Thinking." Special Issue of the *European Journal for Philosophy of Religion*, "Habermas on Religion." For Habermas's 90th birthday.

Mendieta, Eduardo. 2019. "The Postsecular Condition and the Genealogy of Postmetaphysical Thinking." In Beaumont 2019, chap. 4.

Nishitani, Keiji. 1982. "What Is Religion?" *Religion and Nothingness*, trans. Jan Van Bragt, 1–45. Berkeley, CA: University of California Press.

Pensky, Max. 2005. "Jürgen Habermas, Existential Hero?" *Radical Philosophy Review* 8(1): 192–209.

Schweickart, David. 2002. *After Capitalism*. Lanham, MD: Rowman & Littlefield.

Wilber, Ken. 1997. "An Integral Theory of Consciousness." *Journal of Consciousness Studies* 4(1): 71–92.

Wilber, Ken. 2001, August 6. "On the Nature of a Postmetaphysical Spirituality: Response to Habermas and Weis." http://wilber.shambhala.com/html/misc/habermas/index.cfm/.

Wilber, Ken. 2006. *Integral Spirituality: A Startling New Role for Religion in the Modern and Postmodern World*. Boston: Shambhala.

Wilber, Ken, and Martin Beck Matuštík. 2006. "Dialogue with Ken Wilber." Integral Spirituality Center; one hour online audio conversation on the topics ranging from my autobiography to social ethics, politics, interreligious dialogue, and the problem of violence (worldwide webcast, Boulder-Chicago, September 23).

Chapter 3

Tetra Call of the Good

MICHAEL SCHWARTZ

The World is perfect as it is, including my *desire to change it.*

—Ram Dass

Openings

In positing the "big three" of the True, the Good, and the Beautiful, integral theory's philosophical work has mostly been under the first category, that of the true, offering ontological maps and epistemic injunctions. It has, to be sure, also advanced important moral considerations: on 1) the three modes of value (ground, intrinsic, and extrinsic); 2) the holonic distribution of rights and responsibilities; 3) the Basic Moral Intuition (BMI); 4) the developmental line of moral stage-consciousness as researched by Kohlberg, Gilligan, and other scholars; 5) the ascending and descending currents of Love (Eros and Agape); and 6) the soteriological imperative (Buddhist-inspired) to awaken and liberate all sentient beings. And yet integral theory has yet to sustain direct philosophical focus on the Good, Goodness, and their interplay with Being.

In this essay, I inaugurate a moment in integral moral philosophy that focuses upon the latter nexus of philosophical themes. (Where likewise a ramified integral philosophy of beauty will be presented on another occasion.) I take my inspiration from the ethical thought of Emmanuel Levinas, who champions the Good beyond Being, such that one is always already called to responsibility through the face of the Other; this relationship of I to Other (for us, I to Thou) as always already asymmetrical and irreversible—one cannot escape the call through appeal to an intersubjective reversal of positions.[1] While taking my lead from Levinasian insights, I also critique this constellation of ethical thought (which includes Derrida on justice), questioning 1) making the I-Thou perspective primary, a move seen from an integral stance as a moment of perspective-fixation; 2) interpreting the Platonic trope of the Good beyond Being in a manner that hazards a dissociation between ontology and the moral call, the latter as a kind of radical transcending transcendental (as in the thought of Derrida on justice); 3) the lauding of the infinite character of the ethical call as "prior" to and over and beyond the more mundane and concrete calls of finite everyday social-cultural circumstances, in which we are always already situated; and 4) the subject so-called posited as finite only, hence always already stressed—"traumatized" is Critchley's term[2]—by the overwhelm of a finite being encountering this infinite call of the Good; downplaying the singularity of the situation that at any given moment can, more or less, wisely be addressed.

I open with a reconsideration of Being-and-Becoming and of Goodness-and-the-Good, incorporating the integral notions of perspectives and quadrants, attuning us to the post-foundational resounding of the *tetra call of the Good*.[3]

Core Paradox

One of the many strengths of integral theory is its starting point in a non-dual view; whereas so many meta-theories and philosophies either bypass serious consideration of expanded states and domains of Being, or take these up as supplements. Instead, an integral non-dual view embraces both the "absolute" and "relative," both non-dual realization and its embodiment, such that, following Saniel Bonder's singular articulation, we fall into the "core paradox" of existence in that non-duality and duality are "not two": We are at once boundless and finite, infinite and limited, impersonal no-Self and individuated unique (soulful) self, timeless and death bound.[4] In falling into and as this core paradox, realizing an embodied non-dual way of existence (fully inclusive of duality), all arises as natural perfection; nothing has ever happened, nothing needs to change or be different—as we directly and unmistakably recognize the inherent and radiant Goodness of all that is or could ever be. And at the same time, we are acutely sensitive to the limits of all forms, their impermanence—and, in cases, their brokenness—attuning to what Zen teachers have so long pointed to as the Great Sorrow of the world, the Divine and Beautiful Sadness of the Kosmos itself.

Existence as infinite and finite, boundless and soulfully incarnate; there is a rub igniting holy sparks between the sense of an inherent and all-pervasive Goodness and that of limits and brokenness—whence the silent murmur that there "ought to be something better, something more." This silent murmur, this incessant whisper, is the call of the Good—a call (in adapting Levinasian language) as otherwise than Being, the call of Being to be otherwise. This call is more properly and technically a *call-ing*, analogous to a verbal performative (if not reductively linguistic) exceeding, yet affecting Being.[5] The calling of the Good disturbs Being, inciting transformation and change in the direction of a limitless mode of perfection that finite forms, in their limitedness, can never achieve—what in deconstructive parlance is the "impossibility" of their being an adequate response to the vastness and always alreadyness of the moral call. Nevertheless—and this is what deconstructive lines of thinking tend to miss—Being's radical and chaotic-creative fecundity is incited and enticed by the call of the Good, and can lead to wise acts proper to the moment, generating "something better," as the moral call sounds a regulative orientation and direction within a given set of circumstances.[6]

Adapting terms that John Milbank has forwarded,[7] the deconstructive sense of the call of the Good, as with Derrida on justice, leans toward a "gnosticism" in dirempting the transcendental status of the moral call from the concreteness of our lives; whereas a more "incarnational" approach, to pick up Milbank's terms (if not the specifics of his argument), acknowledges on the one hand that the call can never be met in its infinitude, while on the other the call always references in resonance the specific circumstances that lights up in attention, the situation able to be met with requisite wisdom. The Good is always calling Being to be otherwise, a call at once infinite and finite, radically transcendental and impossible to meet while, at the same time, circumstantial and able to be met in comparatively wise ways.

And all the while everything is perfect as it is, nothing has ever happened, all shines as Beauty, an inherent Goodness permeating the dancing in-place of the revealing/concealing of What Is.

Inherent Goodness *and* the call of the Good—such is the paradox of living an embodied non-dual existence.

Perspectives

While we can train ourselves to attune to the Good directly (beyond Plato's claim, couched in visual language, that we can only catch a glimpse),[8] we most regularly do so, as the call of the Good reverberates and resounds through differing *perspectives*. Integral theory posits manifestation as perspectives prior to determinate subjects, objects, perceptions, and interpretations.[9] The quadrant model forwards four basic and very important perspectives based on the notion of a holon: the individual interior, the individual exterior, the collective interior, and the collective exterior. Each human being possesses these four basic perspectives, moment to moment, as dislosing one's "being in the world." Integral methodological pluralism multiples the number of basic perspectives from four to eight, dividing each of the quadrants into an outside view and an inside feel.[10] Going further, Clint Fuhs has shown through the method of integral math that as cognition develops into post-formal operational waves, the number of perspectives within a quadrant multiplies into the hundreds, perhaps the thousands, each quadrant associated with formally similar, yet differentiated perspectives.[11] As a heuristic opening, the approach in this essay takes the simplest of these avenues, exploring the four basic perspectives of the quadrant model as they resound the tetra call of the Good.[12]

To be clear, a perspective is a kind of Heideggerian clearing, a distinctive ontological space-time in the revealing/concealing of beings.[13] Each perspective discloses different kinds of beings: selves, bodies, systems. Any given perspective as an ontological clearing is aligned if non-coincident with a given modulation of the call of the Good—the calling to and within each of the four basic quadrant perspectives resounding in a distinctive manner. For the individual interior, the call is that of *freedom*. For the collective interior—in this essay's account, the relation to an irreducible Thou prior to any meta-subject or We—the call is that of an irreversible and unlimited *responsibility* for the sake and well-being of the Other. For the body (individual exterior) the call is that of *vitality* as power and health. And for systems and institutions (collective exterior), the call is that of *justice*.

Freedom, responsibility, vitality, and justice are the tetra-calling of the Good resounding in and through the four quadrants. Let us take a brief tour of each.

Freedom (UL)

The I of subjectivity is called to *freedom*. While there are any number of modalities of freedom that might be invoked, three are especially noteworthy: 1) *Freedom-from* as negative liberty, the lack of constraints and bounds; 2) *freedom-for* as positive liberty, grounded in the enacted achievement of self-integrity (not to be reduced to an unmediated self-presence of a subject); and 3) *freedom-as* as a mode of realized liberty, associated with various types or styles of non-duality in that boundless, wakeful mystery is non-other than manifestation. Our culture abounds in championing the first of these modes; is less clear about the second (involving a crisis in the valued status and enactment of integrity); and is increasingly embracing the third, if marginally so in a grassroots manner.[14]

Responsibility (LL)

Within the perspective of the lower left or "intersubjective" quadrant, subjectivity is called to responsibility by and for the Other in his/her radical thouness—a formulation echoing, in part, Levinas's expounding of the ethical relation.[15] The ethical relation, as here forwarded, is "prior" to a We as the meta-subject of a common and shared intersubjectivity. The Other as Thou is *radically other*, sheer mystery, ungraspable, a transcendence that breaks into and disrupts any seamlessness proper to the radical immanence of non-duality. Self and the Other are not primordially the Same, since there is no common basis for the exchanging of my position for yours, your position for mine—this is the "transcendence" within the seamless immanence of the boundless non-dual.[16] The ethical relation is one-to-the-Other in an irreversible asymmetry. In this perspective frame any common We-ness is sensed as "founded" on the ethical relation.[17] Through the Face of the Other a mysterious Thou-ness calls one incessantly to responsibility—a call that is boundless and "infinitely demanding."[18]

Vitality (UR)

Our bodies—gross, subtle, and causal (as proper to the Vedanta-Vajrayana inspired view of integral theory)[19]—are called to *vitality*; where vitality has as its twin facets *power* and *health*. *Powe*r, like the term *force*, has received diverse explications in modern and contemporary philosophy. In our usage, *power* is associated in part with energy (as in bodily energies) and is the *force* to do something in the world. Power also involves skill, as the deployment of the energy-force in an effective manner. Power is the energized skills across the spectra of bodily being and capacities. *Health* on its terms is articulated effectively in integral theory's view of the development and operativity of holons.[20] Development can go astray, especially as beings become increasingly complex, such that there results imbalances and dissociations in the holonic constellations of parts/wholes. Power and health are distinct. One can have great, yet that energy can be out of balance and replete with pathological kinks of enactment; while one can have great health and integrative balance, but comparatively little power and capacity for accomplishment. Vitality is *power plus health*—always already calling to the three bodily frequencies of our being.[21]

Justice (LR)

Systems and institutions are called to *justice*; where systems and institutions possess meshworks of distributed *rights* (what is due the individual) and *obligations* (what the individual members owe to others and to the whole) as these are encoded as norms.[22] Justice is the call to rectify and intensify the sense of fairness proper to this distribution of rights and obligations in lieu of the effective operation of the system/institution. That is, the system/institution perspective discloses members as in relationship, such that distribution is always already in play.[23] There is no pre-given calculus for assessing any such moral balance proper to existing patterns of distribution.[24] Especially with increasing complexity, tensions readily exist among rights, obligations, and system imperatives—justice calling their interplay toward greater fairness. Nor is fairness inherently a flatland sense of evaluation animating our deliberations and reflections, which would be to one-sidedly hold forth what Wilber calls ground value, but includes ground value, intrinsic value, extrinsic value, functional efficiency, and more, in "fairing-out" the mesh of rights, obligations, and system/institutional efficiency.[25]

Through comparison, justice also calls into question the inherent fairness of a given system/institutional arrangement: Whether the comparison is to actual, envisioned, or intuited alternative arrangements. In this light, rather than escapist, utopian narratives, both literary and filmic (and especially those proper to the genre of science fiction), are today important artistic spurs for attuning us to the call of justice.[26]

Sadly, in politics today, the call of justice is readily ignored and muffled by hyper onto-theoretical discourses (or atrophied and pathological value-speak) that shield themselves from the force of this call—as if systems and institutions are natural kinds; hence, fixed in what they are, rather than human artifacts/constructs. Vulgar arguments that economic markets need to be endlessly deregulated cover over their own norms and the enacted values by tacitly positing a nature/culture binary of deregulation/regulation, the market as a natural kind that ought not be impinged upon by culture (regulation), rather than economic markets being proper to the noosphere (socioculture domain) and irreducible to the physio- and biospheres.[27] Today we have a series of entrenched theoretical and ontological fundamentalisms propounding a series of sound-bite justifications that mask the injustices and nexus of the valuations actually in play. As such, ideological critique is crucial for clearing the air for heeding the call of justice.[28]

Quadrivia

Hence, there are thus four basic reverberations of the Good as these resound through the quadrants. And, one not only possess the quadrants (as dimenions of Being-in-the-world), but also "sees through them," (as perspectives on Being-in-the-world) generating what in integral theory are called quadrivia: Allowing for the intuition and discernment that other humans—and other sentient beings—also possess the quadrants.[29] This multiplies the moral interplay of perspectives. Not only the call to my own freedom (quadrants), but the sense of my friend being likewise called (quadrivia); not only being called to further the justice of an economic system of which I am a member (quadrants), but also the sense of the justice/injustice of other economic systems of which I am not an immediate member (quadriva); not only the directness of my being called to irreversible responsibility for the Other (quadrants), but the understanding that others are also so called (quadriva). One's direct address by the tetra call of the Good is compounded by the sense that such callings resound for sentient beings throughout the entire Kosmos.

Chords, Types, Metaphors

The perspectivalism proper to integral theory entails a post-foundational pluralism.[30] First, perspectives are not simply pre-given, but are enacted as primordial "building blocks" of the Kosmos. Second, perspectives condition one another, often in manners that are dynamic, dancing, sliding. Third, perspectives readily assume nested interrelationships and holonic orders. Fourth, some perspectives are categorically more appropriate to be enacted in a given situation than are others (e.g., one's focus, in a time of jobs crisis, on the explicit LR challenge of improving the economic situation for all than upon the president's golf game). Fifth, no perspective array is ultimately foundational for or all-encompassing of all others. The integral theory of perspectives entails a pluralism that is dynamic and sliding, while equally inclusive of a holarchism of nested orders; releasing any absolute foundation, it does not fall into flatland relativism. All views are not equally valid in a given context (however dynamic the latter may be); while differentiating views, proper to a robust pluralism, are incommensurable rather than mutual exclusive or a prior incompatible.[31]

As the Good resounds differentially through the four quadrant perspectives, with these perspectives shifting and sliding in their enacted interrelations, *the tetra-call of the Good is not fixed and static, but plural and dancing without announcing an absolute moral foundation.* As such, there are two principle modes of attunement to the tetra call of the Good: 1) from the center of the quadrant matrix; or 2) from within one of the four quadrants.

Being oriented at center is conceptually most straightforward, if experientially the more challenging. One simultaneously hears the calls of freedom, responsibility, vitality, and justice. All four have a kind of equal weight or force, initially resulting in cacophony. This is not the mode of attunement most readily enacted, even if it is a fruitful avenue to travel and explore.

Rather, we tend to be oriented from within one the quadrants, attuning to the call proper to that perspective. The call reverberating in this quadrant can become the predominate note of a *moral chord*—that chord's center of gravity. One can attune only to the note resounding directly in that quadrant; but one can train to hear the moral chord more in full—as in Levinasian moral philosophy. Here, the LL quadrant of one's asymmetrical responsibility to the Other is primary, the three other callings of the Good regulated through this predominate note: One's body and its vitality in service to and for the Other; freedom coming "later" than and "activated" by responsibility; while justice and politics, through the appearance of other Others, are "founded" on (and complicate) the ethical relation.

When the UL is primary in our listening to the tetra call of the Good, we have a moral orientation that is *authentic* or *existential*; when the LL is primary, the orientation is *ethical*; when the UR is central, the orientation is *vitalistic*; and when the LR is principle, the orientation is *political.* No one of these stances has an a priori priority—there is no moral orientation from one of the quadrants that must precede or predominate over the others. Yet they "overlay" each other in their respective chordal soundings. And while no chord is the foundation of the others, the chords share the same basic notes. They are incommensurable, rather than mutually exclusive or externally relativistic.

Many philosophies heed and enact the tetra-call of the Good through a certain moral center of gravity. Levinas, as we have seen, stands in the LL of the primacy of the ethical relation. Foucault most often stands in the UL and the primacy of various modes of freedom. Nietzsche, in certain key texts, affirms life and power as oriented from the UR and its primacy of vital embodiment. And Derrida, at moments, seems to stand in the LR and its primacy of justice as what is beyond deconstruction (Derrida, 1992). These are complex and nuanced philosophers, and the point is not to be reductive with regard to one or another of the quadrants, but rather to obtain some bearings on the respective moral orientations of a given thinker as an aid in comparing and contrasting such moral valences.

That someone gravitates toward one or another of the four calls of the Good over and beyond others points to the hypothesis that there might be *moral types* in line with the notion of psychological types. Rather than a problem, the diversity of moral types enriches collective moral life and deliberation. Even as I enact my typological orientation toward the tetra call (quadrants), I can also come to sense how my interlocutor does so in her case (quadriva), enabling reflexive thematization of our respective orientations, folding this understanding into our being here together, enhancing the mutual openness of the moral communication.

Further, the moral call proper to a quadrant domain can be transposed to another, generating *moral metaphors*. For example, we speak of the "health" of a system (LR), which borrows its terminological force from status of the body (UR). Rather than category mistakes or slippages, moral metaphors fine-tune the differential callings of the Good.

Self, Love, Wisdom

The Good goes to the heart of identity. Simon Critchley (2007, 19–23) has made the case that 1) "the self shapes itself through its relation to whatever it determines as good"; while going further to claim that 2) "this demand of the goods *founds* the self; or, better, that the demand of the good is the fundamental principle of the subject's articulation." For us, where ontology and the moral call are on more intimate terms than in Critchley's often Levinasian-inspired formulations, the self-sense can be said to be *co-constituted* through the play of perspectives and the ways one engages the Good.[32]

One can be stuck in a delimited constellation of perspective taking and therefore only attune to certain notes in a chordal sounding of the tetra-call. Or one can attune more fully to the tetra-call but ignore, shun, deny, rather than approve, this call. Or one can attune and approve the call and yet not respond in timely and effective action. There are three moments of engagement: 1) *attuning* to the call (in degrees of greater or lesser fullness); 2) *approving* (inclining and leaning toward) what one has attuned to; and 3) attending in wise act.[33]

We can train up in all three of these moments. As regards the first, we can open to becoming fuller and fluid in attuning to the various chordal soundings of the tetra-call. The second moment becomes empowered through the currents of love. And the third moment, also motivated by love, increases through the coming forward of practical wisdom.

According to integral theory, there are two vertical currents of Love, both primordial drives of the non-dual Kosmos, Eros and Agape.[34] Eros is the evolutionary impulse that drives transformation and development; while Agape is the embracing impulse of healing and integrating what already is.[35] One can develop into being an ever-deepening and expansive conduit of these impersonal/transpersonal currents, coming to feel that IAM in "substance" love itself—this formulation pointing to a direct experience and realization born of the fruits of profound practice. In brief, the more the Erotic and Agapic currents of love animate one's being in the world, the more likely will be the inclination to approve and respond to the call of the Good.

And yet one's response can be motivated by intense love and turn out to be unwise and ineffective. Love is necessary, but not always sufficient for acting wisely. Love can be deaf and blind if devoid of wisdom. The question of wisdom is well beyond the scope of the present study;[36] as "wisdom" encompasses various terms in the religious, philosophical, and spiritual lineages, referring to differing capacities and competences: *phronesis*, moral know-how, discriminating intelligence, heart-mind, etc. Nevertheless, as attested by the evidence of these same traditions, accessing some modality of wisdom can profoundly enhance affective responsiveness. Love and wisdom are the two wings needed for balanced response action to the callings of the Good.

Whether or not, and how, one attunes, approves, and responds to the moral call constellates the ongoing and always shifting sense of self.[37]

In/finitude

Critchley (2007), in an important Levinasian inspired formulation, posits the demand of the Other as infinite and the one who is to respond as finite, such that the finite subject is perpetually "traumatized" by the vastness of the call. Alain Badiou, in a public response to his friend's book, agrees, while going on to say:

> Yes, we have the utmost difficulty in accepting our limitedness and so on. But if there exists something like the possibility of an infinite demand, there is something infinite in human nature. And maybe the problem sometimes is not at all to accept our finitude, but to accept our infinite dimension . . . Yes, we have much tragedy because of our non-recognition of our finitude, but we have also another sort of tragedy, which is our inability to recognize our infinity. To recognize not only the infinite demand, but the possibility of something infinite in human creation. (2009, 156)

Reinscribing this view within Bonder's of the non-dual core paradox, we can say that one's response to the moral call can entail both finite and infinite dimensions of our being. The Levinasian and Derridean stress on the finiteness of human resources to respond is a "tragedy" indeed, as it shortchanges the possibility of the development of various kinds of responsive capacities on the one hand, and on the other is blind to the boundlessness proper to non-dual realization. Our capacities to respond are both developmentally finite and mysteriously boundless.

And too the call itself is not only infinite. An elderly woman needs some help crossing the street; with kindness one steps forward to help her cross. While this specific need of the woman by no means exhausts the call of the Good in that moment, her need can be met in a finite and specific responsive act. Rather than being merely derivative or secondary as a founded effect, this finite act is called for in and along with the infinite and plural call of the Good itself. There are universal and concrete singularities[38] proper to the situation of the incessant tetra-callings of the

Good. Parallel to the ontological-ontic distinction, where in certain (vulgar) uptakes of this Heideggerian framing of the ontological difference the concrete ontic is given lip service at best,[39] there is a danger with regard to the moral call that the infinite and general call of the Good is stressed, while the concrete situation as disclosed via the perspective array in that very moment is relegated to a secondary status or even neglected; this move generating a series of splits—between the infinite and the finite, Being and the Good, universal and the singular—rather than opening to the always already infinite singularity of the moment.[40] The tetra-call of the Good is at once infinite and finite, incessantly calling manifestation toward a kind of perfection it can never achieve in its limitedness, and also calling one to respond to the situation at hand as disclosed by the enacted perspectives. The call is both impossible to fulfill and, in cases, possible—the latter in the sense of "adequate," "okay," or "wise enough."

Dwelling as the non-dual core paradox of human existence, Goodness pervades each and all, while the Good incessantly disturbs and affects Being to be otherwise. The Good resounds through the four basic perspectives of the quadrant matrix as the tetra-calling of freedom, responsibility, vitality, and justice—that tetra-call itself assuming differing chordal soundings depending on one's moral type and stance within the four quadrants. As such, there are three moments of engaging the Good: attuning, approving, and attending. Each can be trained up; where the ways one engages the Good constellate the self-sense. Finally, the call of the Good and our capacities to respond are at once finite and infinite, limited and limitless—such are some of the basic lineaments of a ramified integral moral philosophy yet to come.

Theodor Adorno wrote in *Negative Dialectics* that: "The need to give voice to suffering is the condition of all truth" (1973, 17–18). For Adorno, the very impetus to know what is true, however unconscious or muted the motive may be, is always already in address to the pain and suffering proper to the limits of existence—whether this impetus is enacted via egocentric contraction focused on oneself alone, or enacted via compassionate expansive concern for the well-being of all sentient beings in the Kosmos—Our games of truth, so suggest Adorno, are always already called forth by the Good.

> *. . . and all the while everything arises as inherently perfect, Goodness pervades, nothing has ever happened, nothing needs to be done. . . .* Goodness *and* the Good, endlessly so.

Notes

1. On Levinas and integral, see Schwartz (2010), 232.

2. Critchley (2007).

3. The third term of the Big Three, the Beautiful, has likewise been undertheorized in integral circles, but must await another occasion for extended consideration. For a related study to this chapter, written after this one but published earlier, see Schwartz (2015).

4. For an introductory teaching, see Bonder (2004).

5. On the linguistic-like, performative sense of Levinas's notion of the ethical Saying (*le Dire*) of the propositional-constative Said (*le Dit*), see Critchley (1992).

6. "Regulative orientation" echoing notions like those of the Kantian regulative ideas of reason and the Derridean promises. On the latter, see Derrida (1992).

7. Milbank (2010).

8. On the glimpse of the Good in Plato, see Sallis (2008), 50–52.

9. For a discussion of perspectives in integral theory, see Esbjörn-Hargens and Zimmerman (2009), Chapter 2.

10. On integral methodological pluralism, see Wilber (2006), Chapter 1.

11. Fuhs (2010).

12. Cf. Wilber (2010a), Chapter 7, where he argues for a differentiation of validity claims as proper to the quadrants: truthfulness (UL), rightness (LL), truth (UR), and functional fit (LR).

13. This formulation of revealing/concealing is Heideggerian, even as it is it absent from integral theorizing about perspectives. In general, integral theory has not thematized the philosophical issue of negativity (and if advancing a positive philosophy, as with the mature period of Schelling, does not thematize the issue of positivity-contra-negativity). The Heideggerian construal, moving out of Husserl's notion of absent profiles, is negativity as abysmal reserve in the ontological even-ting of *Ereignis*. Bhaskar's dialectical critical realism (Bhaskar, 1993) posits modes of the negative as more or less determined absences such that nonbeing exists. Many of the Kyoto School philosophers explore what Nishida called *absolute nothingness*, which in their view cuts through the Western predilection for the priority of the beingness of being and nonbeing (see Shizuteru, 2011). Consideration of the Good's relation/proximity to these ontological themes of determinate-indeterminate negativity and absolute nothingness exceeds the present study.

14. On the grassroots character of more and more people tasting in direct experience modes of non-duality, see Forman (2004) and Ardagh (2005).

15. See Levinas (1969) and ibid. (1981). For excellent explications (and criticisms) of these two major texts, see Critchley (1992) and ibid. (2007). And on Levinasian ethics with regard to the LL quadrant, see Schwartz (2010), 232.

16. The terms of *transcendence* and *immanence* are terribly tricky—let alone when referenced to non-duality. That said, radical immanence is the boundless non-duality of impersonal consciousness and life-energy-matter, close in its sense to that of Deleuze (2001), a radical immanence that includes the manifest and (felt vastness of) the unmanifest. Yet unlike Deleuze, I suggest a transcendence that ruptures or breaks into radical non-dual immanence: A radical Thouness as Otherness that opens the sense of a "hole" within the seamless if open unbounded whole. Here the view presented differs from Levinas in that this rupture or puncture of Otherness is both ethical and ontological.

17. Levinas's complex formulations perhaps enable a twin reading of the ethical relation as at once founding the political (via the appearance of the third person) and co-emergent with the political (in that the third person arises with[in]/through the Other). See further Schwartz (2010), 249, note 5.

18. Echoing the title of Critchley (2007).

19. On bodies, see Wilber (2002) and Senzon (2007).

20. Wilber (2000b), 30–32. My reframing is that "health" is fundamentally an UR term that in holonic metatheory is applied to all four quadrants—the legitimate sliding of a moral category from one quadrant to another, a point to which we return later in this essay.

21. Cf. the notion of biopower as developed by Foucault (1978) as a historically constellated instantiation of practices and regimes of life stressing the gross body's sexuality (one aspect of one of the three vital bodies) and this body's health in functional service to systems oriented toward sufficient collective labor and military growth. On sexuality in modernity, see Wilber (2000b), 499–506.

22. Technically, in the context of the LR qudrant, these rights and obligations are exterior exchanges within system positions proper to the LR; but can be readily extended here to include symbolic contents proper to zones 3 and 4 intersubjective flows, exchanges, and patterns of meaning and mutual recognition. Here I adapt aspects of Wilber's notion of holonic ecology (2000b), 543–547.

23. Milbank (2010).

24. This formulation in part echoes that of Wilber's Basic Moral Intuition. See Wilber (2000b), 640–643, note 23 and 761–765, note 13, and (for a quick definition) Wilber (2007), 195–196: "to protect and promote the greatest depth for the greatest span . . ." where "depth" and "span" refer to the Kosmic evolutionary nesting of individual holons. I add that issues of pluralism and the status of social holons productively complicate the enactment of the BMI as it was initially formulated.

25. On ground value, intrinsic value, and extrinsic (instrumental) value proper to a holonic ecology, see Wilber (2000b), 544–546. On value proper to the Good, cf. Lonergan (1992): an ". . . aspect of the good, which is value . . . emerges on the level of reflection and judgment, on deliberation and choice." (620).

26. No one writing in English today has explored this facet of art more importantly and provocatively than Fredric Jameson.

27. On the nesting of the physiosphere, biosphere, and noosphere, see Wilber (2000b); Esbjörn-Hargens and Zimmerman (2009).

28. Often in play in enacting justice is the discernment of practices and systems that marginalize. Here, one is wise to take note of Girard (1996) and his important and cautionary theorizing about the status of the victim in its relation to cultural mechanisms like sacrifice and scapegoating.

29. Wilber (2006), 253–254; Esbjörn-Hargens and Zimmerman, 57–59.

30. These issues require a much more robust unpacking and unfolding than is possible in the present essay. For important remarks on these topics, see Esbjörn-Hargens and Zimmerman (2009), 63–64; and Esbjörn-Hargens (2010a). Wilber (2006) plays on the complexity of these issues, evoking both Buddhist and Western philosophical concerns and concepts: "And that makes everything **absolutely relative** to everything else. There is no ground, there is no metaphysics, there is no myth of the give; all that is solid melts into air, all that is foundational evaporates—and yet we can still generate all of the essentials of the great metaphysical systems but without their thoroughly discredited metaphysical baggage . . ." (254). In other words: No absolute foundation, yet better and worse local-comparative foundations or places on which at any (relative) moment to stand (or better, a wave to surf).

31. On incommensurability as entailing neither mutual exclusion nor necessary incompatibility, see Bernstein (1985).

32. To be sure, with regard to an integral view of being in the world, the self-sense (inclusive of "identity" as no-self), is or can be an all-quadrant affair and not confined to the I of subjectivity restricted to the UL quadrant. See Schwartz (2010), 236.

33. Cf. Critchley (2007), Chapter 1, on the twofold distinction between the demand (the call) and approval.

34. Wilber (2000b).

35. Agape as drive is also capable of bringing forward novel capacities. Whereas the emergence of novel capacities via erotic ascent in integral theory is called *transformation*, let us call such novel emergence via agapic descent *transfiguration* (a term the use of which here I owe in different ways to Saniel Bonder and to Nicholas Hedlund-de Witt).

36. Roger Walsh is currently writing a volume on the topic of wisdom for the Integral Theory Book Series (SUNY Press).

37. For example, living a Vedenta-type realization of identity as no-self or radical IAM witnessing consciousness will tend to incline toward freedom over the other three primary calls, and where the pervasiveness of Big Love does not so readily lead to affective responsiveness to the immediate situation, since manifestation in the end is a kind of empty illusion, unreal, *maya*.

38. On universality and the concrete singular, see Bhaskar (1993).

39. Cf. Milbank (2010).

40. This incorporates Levinasian emphases on the boundless call of the Good with Lonergan that "What is good, is always concrete" (1971), 27.

References

Adorno, Theodor 1973. *Negative Dialectics*, trans. E.B. Ashton. New York: Continuum.

Ardagh, Arjuna 2005. *The Translucent Revolution: How People Just Like You Are Waking Up and Changing the World*. Novato, CA: New World Library.

Badiou, Alain. 2009. "On Simon Critchley's *Infinitely Demanding*: Ethics of Commitment, Politics of Resistance." *Critical Horizons: A Journal of Philosophy and Social Theory* 10(2): 154–162.

Bernstein, Richard J. 1985. *Beyond Objectivism and Relativism: Science, Hermeneutics, and Praxis*. Philadelphia, PA: University of Pennsylvania Press.

Bhaskar, Roy. 1993. *Dialectic: The Pulse of Freedom*. London and New York: Verso.

Bonder, Saniel. 2004. *Great Relief: Nine Sacred Secrets Your Body Wants You to Know About Freedom, Love, Trust, and the Core Wound of Your Life*. San Rafael, CA: Mt. Tam Empowerments.

Critchley, Simon. 1992. *The Ethics of Deconstruction: Derrida and Levinas*. Oxford, UK and Cambridge, MA: Blackwell.

Crtichley, Simon. 2007. *Infinitely Demanding: Ethics of Commitment, Politics of Resistance*. London and New York: Verso.

Deleuze, Gilles. 2001. *Pure Immanence: Essays on A Life*, trans. Anne Boyman. New York: Zone Books.

Derrida, Jacques. 1992. "Force of Law: The Mystical Foundation of Authority," trans. Mary Quaintance. In *Deconstruction and the Possibility of Justice*, ed. Drucilla Cornell, et al., 3–67. New York: Routledge.

Esbjörn-Hargens, Sean, and Michael E. Zimmerman. 2009. *Integral Ecology: Uniting Multiple Perspectives on the Natural World*. Boston, MA and London: Integral Books.

Esbjörn-Hargens, Sean, and Michael E. Zimmerman. 2010a. "An Ontology of Climate Change: Integral Pluralism and the Enactment of Multiple Objects." *Journal of Integral Theory and Practice* 5(1): 143–174.

Esbjörn-Hargens, Sean, and Michael E. Zimmerman. 2010b. *Integral Theory in Action*. Albany, NY: SUNY Press.

Forman, Robert K.C. 2004. *Grassroots Spirituality: What It Is, Why It Is Here, Where It Is Going*. Exeter, UK: Imprint Academic.

Foucault, Michael. 1979. *The History of Sexuality, Volume 1: An Introduction*, trans. Robert Hurley. New York: Random House.

Fuhs, Clint. 2010. "An Integral Map of Perspective-Taking." In *Integral Theory in Action*, ed. Sean Esbjörn-Hargens, 273–302. Albany, NY: SUNY Press.

Girard, René. 1996. *The Girard Reader*, ed. James G. Williams. New York: Crossroad.

Levinas, Emmanuel. 1969. *Totality and Infinity: An Essay on Exteriority*, trans. Alphonso Lingis. Pittsburgh, PA: Duquesne University Press.

Levinas, Emmanuel. 1981. *Otherwise Than Being or Beyond Essence*, trans. Alphonso Lingis. The Hague, NL, Boston, MA, and London: Martinus Nijhoff.

Lonergan, Bernard. 1971. *Method in Theology*. Toronto: University of Toronto Press.

Lonergan, Bernard. 1992. "Insight: A Study of Human Understanding." In *Collected Works of Bernard Lonergan, Vol. 3*, ed. Frederick E. Crowe and Robert M. Doran. Toronto: University of Toronto Press.

Milbank, John. 2010. "Paul Beyond Biopolitics." In *Paul's New Moment: Continental Philosophy and the Future of Christian Theology*, ed. John Milbank, Slavoj Žižek, and Creston Davis. Grand Rapids, MI: Brazos Press.

Sallis, John. 2008. *The Verge of Philosophy*. Chicago: University of Chicago Press.

Schwartz, Michael. 2010. "Frames of AQAL, Integral Critical Theory, and the Emerging Integral Arts." In *Integral Theory in Action*, ed. Sean Esbjörn-Hargens, 229–252. Albany, NY: SUNY Press.

Schwartz, Michael. 2015. "MetaReality and the Dynamic Calling of the Good." *Journal of Critical Realism* 14(4): 381–396.

Senzon, Simon A. 2007. "Subtle Energies Viewed From Four Quadrants." *Journal of Integral Theory and Practice 2*(4): 134–136.

Shizuteru, Ueda. 2011. "Contributions to Dialogue with the Kyoto School." In *Japanese and Continental Philosophy: Conversations with the Kyoto School*, ed. Bret W. Davis, Brian Schroeder, and Jason W. Wirth. Bloomington and Indianapolis, IN: Indiana University Press.

Wilber, Ken. 2000a. *A Brief History of Everything*. Boston: Shambhala.

Wilber, Ken. 2000b. *Sex, Ecology, Spirituality: The Spirit of Evolution*. Boston: Shambhala.

Wilber, Ken. 2002. "Excerpt G: Toward a Comprehensive Theory of Subtle Energies." http://wilber.shambhala.com/html/books/kosmos/excerptG/part1.cfm/.

Wilber, Ken. 2006. *Integral Spirituality: A Startling New Role for Religion in the Modern and Postmodern World*. Boston, MA and London: Integral Books.

Chapter 4

Nothing Matters vs. Nothing *Matters*

How Integral Theory Addresses Nihilism

Michael E. Zimmerman

On many occasions, after noting my interest in integral theory, someone will ask me this question: What is it about? Sometimes I say it's about the idea that evolutionary development is a universal cosmic principle, or that all phenomena manifest themselves in several different ways. At other times, I answer that integral theory explores the possibility of a credible, postmodern spirituality. Lately, however, I have come to the conclusion that while partially true, none of these answers is adequate. Today, I would answer that what integral theory *addresses is the problem of the nihilism that arose in modernity and that became even more pronounced in postmodernity.*[1] Derived from the Latin word *nihil*—nothing—nihilism is the worldview according to which human life and the cosmos lack inherent value, meaning, and purpose.[2] As Friedrich Nietzsche famously put it, the death of God—that is, the collapse of the Christian-Platonic table of values—removed the goal that had justified European civilization for centuries. Gradually, Nietzsche forecast, people will conclude that *nothing matters*. Put in another way, no thing will matter more than any other thing. The ensuing nihilism will lead to world wars and even the collapse of Western civilization, so Nietzsche presciently predicted, while Europeans seek a new goal that would restore significance to their lives. For Nietzsche, of course, this goal was to be the Overman, a new kind of humanity that has been interpreted in many different ways. Recently, some have associated the Overman with the Buddha, while others associate it with transhumanism.[3] In what follows, I sketch how my concern about nihilism led me from Nietzsche and Heidegger and then to Ken Wilber, whose integral theory has attempted to counter modern and postmodern nihilism.

A caveat: In this wide-ranging essay, coverage of vast topics such as nihilism, modernity, postmodernity, cosmic evolution, and so on will be conducted from a high altitude. Inevitably, then, I will overlook important distinctions and counterexamples to my own argument. This is done in order to gain a particular kind of view of the issues that I feel is valuable, and it is done knowing other views are needed to complement and nuance my presentation.

Late nineteenth- and early twentieth-century conservatism, especially the kind advanced by Nietzsche, influenced Heidegger's views on nihilism. Born in a German village in 1889, Martin Heidegger lived through two world wars that featured ever-more destructive industrial technology. Like Nietzsche, he believed that such technology and constitutional democracy were not the culmination of the self-realization of reason, as Hegel claimed, but instead were symptoms of the West's long decline into nihilism. According to Heidegger, humans had in effect become little more than clever animals capable of encountering things—including human beings—only one-dimensionally, or in an ontologically flattened way: As raw material for enhancing power. Things can manifest themselves and in this sense "be" only within the temporal-historical clearing opened up through human Dasein (there-being). So constricted has become the human clearing in modern times, however, that many aspects of beings can no longer reveal or manifest themselves. The reduction of all beings to standing reserve for enhancing the Will to Power is a profound symptom of the nihilism afflicting late-modern Western civilization.

Heidegger and Nietzsche, along with postmodern thinkers influenced by them, attempted to pull the foundational props out from under modern ideologies, including capitalism and socialism. Modern "grand narratives" were to be read as quasi-religious, just-so stories needed to legitimate socio-political formations, whose real aim was increasing power for its own sake. Heidegger read Nietzsche's Will to Power as essentially a Will to Will, an endless and ultimately meaningless drive that animated a pointless cosmos.[4] Far from making possible human freedom, so Heidegger maintained, modern ideologies invented technologies of *control* over nature and human society. As events such as World War II, industrialized death camps, and ecological destruction eroded the credibility of the emancipatory goals of modernity, cynicism and irony became rampant in postmodern circles.

Wilber's view of nihilism was shaped in a very different sociocultural context than Heidegger's. Wilber was raised in post–World War II America, whose ascent to economic and political supremacy had been built on its commitment first to constitutional democracy and a corresponding market economy, and later to industrial technology, much of which grew out of research for military purposes. For Heidegger, America represented one of the most egregious expressions of modern nihilism. Wilber agrees that Western modernity has serious flaws, especially its flatland ontology, which reduces all phenomena to the status of commodities, material particles, and/or strands in the terrestrial system.[5] Such an ontology allows no place for interior or depth domains, such as consciousness and culture, much less for the spiritual domain, the mere mention of which prevents one from being taken seriously in respectable academic circles. A flatland (industrial) ontology that cannot account for depth, according to Wilber, is consistent with nihilism. Overcoming nihilism requires transcending the modern worldview, but not at the cost of jettisoning the noble achievements of modernity. Not unlike Jürgen Habermas, Wilber offers a critical affirmation of important aspects of the Enlightenment project, while simultaneously investigating the possibility of a constructive *post*modernism to surpass the limits of that project. Rather than adopting Heidegger's narrative of the devolutionary "history of being" that ends in techno-industrial nihilism, Wilber befriends earlier German thinkers, particularly the idealists Friedrich Schelling and G.W.F. Hegel, who offered developmental views of human and cosmic history.

Despite significant differences, Heidegger and Wilber share an important idea: Consciousness is neither a thing, nor an attribute of the human subject, but rather the nothingness, emptiness, clearing, or openness within which phenomena—subjective and objective, interior and exterior—can appear.[6] Whereas nihilists maintain that nothing matters, Heidegger and Wilber would say that nothing *does* matter. In other words, we shift from *nothing* matters to nothing *matters*! Heidegger and Wilber, then, propose that inquiring ever more deeply into nothingness is the way to recover from nihilism as customarily understood. As we will see, however, there are important differences in the approach taken by their inquiries.

Nietzsche and Heidegger: Antimodernism and Nihilism

Raised with seven siblings in Ohio by educated and relatively prosperous parents, I was strongly influenced—for good and ill—by my Catholic upbringing. As a child, I identified with what seemed to me like "wild nature" on the edge of my small town. I spent countless hours exploring many paths, creeks, glacial cliffs, woods, and fields. In the early 1960s, while in high school, prior to knowing anything about philosophy, I experienced an awakening to social justice in the form of the civil rights movement. In certain respects, identification with oppressed people was a sign of moral development. The midwest child of educated and prosperous white parents had expanded his identification beyond family and race. Years later, I came to see that the thirst for justice had mixed motives. I wanted to help alleviate serious wrongs, but doing so also gave me the chance to vent resentment and hostility toward the contemporary world and thus toward my parents.

Nihilism became a concern for me as an undergraduate. Which, if any of the values with which I had been raised, had any validity? At the time, I was studying philosophy: the "love of wisdom." Western philosophy has generated multiple and often conflicting interpretations of humankind and its place in the cosmos. This wide range of opinions, each of which has been aptly defended by brilliant thinkers, proved both fascinating and unsettling. Instead of providing the answer I wanted, philosophy seemed to generate even more questions. Indeed, studying the history of philosophy—with its interminable disputes and lack of agreement—was like journeying on what Hegel called the "highway of despair." Particularly disturbing for me was the modern scientific worldview, according to which everything can be reduced to matter in motion; that is what is "real" are atoms and their underlying structures. I was strongly attracted to the work of Alfred North Whitehead, in part because he made clear that such a reductionistic worldview was untenable.

Discounting for a decade Christianity's answer to the question "What is it all about?" I pursued the secular humanism that helped to inspire the civil rights movement. That movement, however, was also profoundly influenced by Jewish and Christian ideals that cannot be translated without loss into modern ideals. According to the liberal version of secular humanism, the major goals of life include improving one's well-being through individual effort, affirming democratic institutions and public policies that protect human rights; renouncing otherworldly beliefs and aspirations, while affirming insights provided by natural and social science. There is still much to be said in favor of such humanism, despite its various limitations.

In graduate school, I gravitated toward two thinkers who made the problem of nihilism a central topic: Nietzsche and Heidegger. Initially, both thinkers had been profoundly influenced by Christianity, but ultimately concluded that it had indirectly contributed to the rise of modern nihilism, rather than overcoming it. Both thinkers were sharply critical of secular modernity. Nietzsche maintained that modernity had been infected with attitudes, derived from Christianity, which undermined the Will to Power necessary for individual and cultural vitality. Nietzsche wrote that nihilism, "this uncanniest of guests," stood at the door of modern Europe.[7] Deprived of religious and metaphysical comforts that had once justified life, late–nineteenth century Europeans were already manifesting the symptoms of what Nietzsche called *passive* nihilism: disorientation, depression, and pessimism. So-called progressive movements, far from overcoming nihilism, were, in fact, hastening the decline and degeneration of the West. Paradoxically, Nietzsche approved of such movements, insofar as they played the role of instruments promoting *active* nihilism; that is, activity aimed at finishing off decadent European traditions as soon as possible. Only after having hit bottom would Europeans consider adopting a truly worthy goal: The intentional production of great individuals—even the Overman—who would provide a *this-worldly* justification for human existence.

Looking back from "two centuries in the future," Nietzsche predicted that world wars would be fought to gain mastery over the planet. Such industrial warfare would reduce humanity to what Ernst Jünger would later call the gestalt of the totally mobilized worker-soldier.[8] The revolt of the masses and the corresponding extirpation of individuality were merely symptoms of nihilism. Nietzsche believed that non-Europeans, who supposedly had more immediate access to instinctual energy, threatened a degenerate Europe. Disillusioned and nihilistic moderns (of course, Nietzsche had to include himself in these ranks) would be tempted to engage in the practices of "self-narcotization." Among these practices, he lists the following, some of which were recommended by his erstwhile intellectual and spiritual hero, Arthur Schopenhauer. We will return to this passage later on.

> Attempt to work blindly as an instrument of science; opening one's eyes to the many small enjoyments; e.g., also in the quest of knowledge (modesty toward oneself); resignation to generalizing about oneself, a pathos; mysticism, the voluptuous enjoyment of eternal emptiness; art "for its own sake" ("*le fait*") and "pure knowledge" as narcotic states of disgust with oneself; some kind or another of continual work, or some stupid little fanaticism; a medley of all means, sickness owing to general immoderation (debauchery kills enjoyment).[9] (WP, 29)

Although sharing many of Nietzsche's anti-modernist sentiments, Heidegger argued in *Being and Time* (1927) that human beings are ontologically structured to care about things. The being (*Sein*) of human Dasein is care. To be human means that things, people, and our projects *matter* to us.[10] The dynamically interrelated dimensions of temporality, past, present, and future articulate the structure of human care. Entities can manifest themselves—and thereby can "be"—only within those temporal-historical horizons. Those horizons are not entities, but the condition needed for entities to appear *as* entities. Human Dasein does not "own" its temporal openness, but instead is "thrown" into it at birth. Presencing (the being or the showing-up of entities) occurs within absencing (the clearing constituted by temporality). Within this primordial absencing, nothingness, or clearing arise the contents of consciousness, including thoughts, feelings, memories, emotions, intentions, and so on. Within the temporal clearing both subjective and objective, interior and exterior contents manifest themselves.

Heidegger's claim in *Being and Time* that human beings inevitably care about things would seem to counter Nietzsche's assertion that nihilism was engulfing European civilization. Soon enough, however, Heidegger showed that he largely agreed with Nietzsche's assessment of the historical situation. Being, understood as how entities can show up or manifest themselves, has a history—and that history involves a decline from its great beginning in ancient Greek. Back then, Dasein allowed entities to manifest themselves more primordially than today, in art, music, literature, philosophy, religion, rhetoric, and contests of all sorts. This allegedly grander era ended, as human openness began to grow constricted. The temporal clearing changes from one historical epoch to the next. Western history has been in decline for 2500 years, because entities show up for us in increasingly limited ways. In the era of techno-industrial modernity, everything—including humans—has been reduced to an instrument for human interest. The distinguishing feature of human Dasein—existing as the clearing in which things can "be"—has been eclipsed by modern fascination with studying, acquiring, and dominating the things that appeared within that clearing. Heidegger cited approvingly the words that Nietzsche put in Zarathustra's mouth: "The wasteland grows."[11]

Heidegger contested Nietzsche's claim that nihilism results from the collapse of values. Rather, value is itself a modern concept, symptomatic of modernity's slide into nihilism. Nietzsche maintained that values are *perspectives* posited to enhance human power and security. Calling on evolutionary thinking to expand Aristotle's notion human being as the "rational animal" (*zoon logon echon*), Nietzsche conceived of the human as a clever animal striving not merely to survive, but instead to increase its power. Gradually, as the techno-industrial system became planetary in reach, human subjects were themselves becoming the most valuable resources in the system's drive for power for its own sake. In effect, Heidegger agreed with Max Horkheimer and Theodor Adorno that this totalizing system is the unanticipated outcome of the Enlightenment.[12] Despite his many philosophical achievements, Nietzsche lacked understanding of the interplay between being and time, presencing and absencing, appearing and temporal-historical horizon. Heidegger writes:

> But where is the real nihilism at work? Where one clings to current beings and believes it is enough too take beings, as before, just as the beings that they are. But with this, one rejects the question of being [*die Seinsfrage*] and treats being [*Sein*] as a nothing (*nihil*), which in a certain way it even "is," insofar as it essentially unfolds [historically]. Merely to chase after beings in the midst of the oblivion of being—that is nihilism. Nihilism thus understood is the *ground* for the nihilation that Nietzsche exposed in the first book of *The Will to Power*.[13]

Although agreeing with Nietzsche that the West would have to undergo several centuries of nihilism, Heidegger prophesized that eventually the human openness to being would undergo a change. Human Dasein would recall its obligation to "let things be," by existing so as to let show up not merely as objects—or worse, as raw material—but rather in ways consistent with their own modes of being. For this to occur, human Dasein would somehow have to transcend the willing/not-willing dichotomy.[14] Heidegger did not provide a satisfying answer to how this transcendence would occur. In an interview published upon his death in 1976, he claimed that "only a god can save us" from the condition of nihilism.[15]

During the 1960s, translations of Heidegger's works resonated with a number of American academics, particularly those who regarded modernity with a jaundiced eye after two world wars, the death camps, the Gulag, the Vietnam War, continued oppression of minorities, and the philistinism of American culture. In 1964 key aspects of Heidegger's critique of techno-industrial modernity appeared in *One-Dimensional Man*, written by Heidegger's student, Herbert Marcuse, a leading figure in the 1960s counterculture.[16] Counterculturalists denounced the faceless modern "system," which was implicated in the Vietnam War, the nuclear arms race, environmental destruction, oppression of non-whites, women, gays and lesbians, animals, and other minorities. The late twentieth century witnessed the rise of postmodern Green sensibility, which regarded traditional liberalism and even the New Left with suspicion. Countercultural Greens were often angry with their parents, but also with their parents' society, even though—or perhaps even because—it had provided so many economic and personal advantages to the protesting young.

This was the context in which I became attracted to radical environmentalism, especially deep ecology. Like many, though not all, deep ecologists, I concluded that the environmental crisis stemmed from a modernity that was superficially anthropocentric, but ultimately nihilistic. For technological modernity, in effect, even humankind was merely the most important raw material needed to attain power for its own sake. Perhaps, so I thought in the late 1970s, I could bring together at least some of my competing commitments by reading Heidegger as a forerunner of deep ecology. The appreciation showed both by deep ecologists and Heidegger for premodern, nature-friendly sociocultural formations resonated with my own love for wild nature. Reading environmentalism as a liberation movement gave expression to my appreciation of modernity's emancipatory aims.

My proposal to read Heidegger's motto of letting things be as consistent with the aims of deep ecology showed early promise, but eventually ran into problems.[17] For one thing, Heidegger—unlike most deep ecologists—was no biocentrist. For him, only human Dasein holds open the clearing in which things can show up in the first place. Most of my deep ecology friends regarded this view as just another version of the anthropocentrism that justified the modern domination of nature. Another major obstacle to enlisting Heidegger as a deep ecologist was that he rejected all efforts to interpret human existence in terms of terrestrial evolution. Humans, he insisted, are not animals.

Given my intellectual debt to Heidegger, it was difficult for me to digest the fact that his affiliation with National Socialism was no mere political miscalculation.[18] Instead, he *agreed with* Nazism's anti-modernism, including its views that the West had been in decline since Greek and Roman antiquity, and that the modern individualism was a symptom of decadence and nihilism. Heidegger regarded as symptoms of nihilism the very ideals of liberty and equality that continue to inspire billions of people. Eventually, he concluded that "really existing" National Socialism, especially in its embrace of industrial technology, was as problematic as Soviet Marxism and American capitalism. Still, he never renounced his appreciation of the "inner truth and greatness" of the National Socialist movement.[19] Coming to terms with Heidegger's undeniable complicity with Nazism made me suspicious of deep ecology's anti-modernism. I realized that a number of deep ecologists also regarded modern ideals with disdain, because those ideals encouraged the modern scientific, technological, and economic systems that exploited nature.

Wilber and Heidegger on No-thingness

Despite my long flirtation with anti-modernism, I never abandoned my commitment to many of the ideals of modernity. My intellectual and psychological tension grew: How was I ever going to reconcile my competing intuitions of modernity as wrong and modernity as right? Here, Ken Wilber's work proved to be very instructive. In the early 1980s, I read his *Up From Eden: A Transpersonal View of Human Evolution*.[20] This audacious effort to reconcile spirituality with science, evolution, and modern political ideals offered a possible way of reconciling my critique of some aspects of modernity with my appreciation for other aspects of it. Another reason that Wilber's work proved so attractive was that he, like Heidegger, interpreted consciousness not in terms of its contents, but rather as the nothingness, openness, or emptiness within which such contents arise and fall.

There is not time here to rehearse the differing approaches that led both Heidegger and Wilber to emphasize nothingness/emptiness as central to human existence. For both thinkers, insight into and acting from one's own openness or no-thingness are consistent with what spiritual traditions describe as non-duality.[21] Existing non-dualistically allows one not to cling to or grasp onto any particular meaning, direction, purpose, or foundation. Non-dual existence is rare. Most people operate within dualistic frameworks, including those characterized by the dichotomies of self and other, subject and object. We become attached to what we think we are—body, ego, soul, desires, memories, aspirations, fears, relationships, beliefs, ideologies, traditions. On occasion and unbidden, anxiety (*Angst*) may arise to reveal that our very egoic structure, that with which we so closely identify, is itself thing-like and thus transient like all other phenomena. Undergoing what anxiety can reveal is at first like a death experience, but may turn into an expansive realization: I am not a self or thing, but instead a clearing, an opening within which experiences occur. From this perspective, nihilism amounts to assigning ultimate significance to any *thing*, while being oblivious to the *nihil*, that is, the no-thingness/openness necessary for that thing to show up in the first place.

Theistic traditions describe such assignment as idolatry. If humans are made in God's image, as Genesis states, perhaps this means that humans are both mortals (creatures, entities) and divine (creative, open, not things). Wilber speaks of Spirit as the all-encompassing nothingness, the infinite context of contexts, in which all phenomena have emerged. Analogously, humans are openness/nothingness within which things can reveal themselves *as* things, and within which wholly new kinds of things can be created. Human creativity is linked to divine creativity. "I and the Father are one," as Jesus of Nazareth put it (John 10:30). In experiencing the nothingness that one always already *is*, one may experience a key feature of divinity. In a somewhat different way, Buddhism also emphasizes that all phenomena are empty of self or substance. Form is not other than emptiness; emptiness is not other than form. Existing as and from this non-duality gives "one taste" to all phenomena, which are always already "perfect." There is no need to cling to anything, and there is nothing to which one can cling anyway. One already *is* timeless emptiness, nothingness, and openness.

Integral Theory's Developmental Interpretation of Cosmic, Terrestrial, and Human History

Where Wilber and other integral theorists part company with Heidegger and Buddhism is in regard to the fact that history—including human history—exhibits evolutionary development. Heidegger and traditional Buddhism regard history as a long decline from a noble beginning. In contrast with this, Wilber posits a *developmental* view of cosmic, terrestrial, and human history.[22] Such a view draws on findings from a host of inquiries, including natural science, cosmology, developmental psychology, and comparative religion and philosophy. According to the view, sometimes called the "new cosmic narrative," the universe began with the Big Bang and then, during an awe-inspiring twelve-billion-year process, gave rise to matter, life, and conscious life.[23] Cosmic history involves a tetra-evolutionary process involving first-person, second-person, and third-person phenomena. Time has a direction; the cosmos moves from simplicity to growing complexity and differentiation. Siding with Hegel, rather than with Heidegger, Wilber regards history as a move "up from Eden," rather than as a great Fall. That is, history is the process by which humankind has evolved from relatively simple modes of subjectivity, culture, and social organization, to ever-more complex and demanding modes. Like Hegel, moreover, Wilber acknowledges that this process is often no joyride. Each developmental stage or wave in human history is important, but also transient. Disorientation, despair, and nihilism often follow from experiencing the displacement and relative dissolution of one's worldview. Many Westerners underwent such experiences in the nineteenth and twentieth centuries, as traditional theism became increasingly untenable to many in the face of modern scientific claims, including evolutionary theory and mechanistic materialism.

Secular moderns attempted to overcome nihilism by translating otherworldly aspirations into this-worldly schemes. The New Jerusalem would not be reached by divine salvation in a supernatural world, but instead by applying scientific knowledge to pacify internal (human) nature and to gain control over external nature. While such control greatly improves the human condition, much is lost as well. As Nietzsche observed, natural science has undermined humanity's former sense of specialness by depicting humans as accidentally evolved animals in cosmos so vast that planet Earth itself loses significance. Indeed, cosmos and history are both *inherently meaningless.* Values are merely temporary *human* conventions, the aims of which are to enhance power and security of the human animal. Because consciousness cannot be easily accounted for in terms of material particles and forces, it has no place in the modern worldview, even though modern revolutions were motivated by the ideals of freedom and equality of rational persons. In the twentieth century, as the natural scientific worldview gained ever-greater prominence, the objectifying third-person perspectives reigned supreme.

Philosophically active during the heyday of such scientific positivism and reductionism, Heidegger had little confidence that an interpretation of human existence could benefit from natural science. Hence, he offers no account of how or why in Greek antiquity human existence was appropriated as the clearing or openness in which beings could show up. In *Being and Time*, he states that when seeking to understand the being of entities, including the human, he has no interest in "telling a story;" that is, "determining beings as beings by tracing them back in their origins to another being—as if being had the character of a possible being."[24] Tracing beings back to a foundation such as the Biblical God, for example, is not what he had in mind by ontology. Likewise, he had no confidence that tracing entities—especially human entities—to their molecular and atomic foundations would provide insight into their being. A scientific universe story that failed to understand the primacy of the interplay of being and no-thingness, presencing and absencing, did not attract him.

Some commentators claim that Heidegger ascribed to a kind of Cartesian dualism, with human Dasein on the one side and with all other beings on the other. In fact, he described humans and animals as separated by an abyss. For at least a time in the 1920s, he was more open to the possibility that humans and animals shared something important; namely, having a "world" (*Welt*). Heidegger derived one of his key concepts, Being-in-the-world (*In-der-welt-sein)*, from biologist Jakob von Uexküll's idea of the environing-world (*Umwelt*) of animal organisms.[25] According to von Uexküll, animals open up a proto-temporal world within which things that matter to them can show up. In a field in summer, various animals—including insects—encounters things only insofar as they are pertinent to their survival needs.[26] In lectures given in 1929 and 1930, Heidegger described animals as "world-poor" in comparison with "world-rich" human Dasein.[27] After 1930, however, Heidegger did not pursue the relationship between animal world and human world. (For an extensive discussion of the relationship between Heidegger and the philosophy of biology, see D. Storey; this volume.) He denied that evolutionary theory could explain what is distinctive about humankind: Namely, that human existence constitutes the temporal-historical clearing within which things can manifest themselves *as* things.

While agreeing with Heidegger's contention that natural science's objectifying disclosure of entities is inappropriate for studying human interiority and depth (first- and second-person domains), Wilber contends that natural science can provide important insight into the origins and character of the human. Drawing on scientific findings unavailable to Heidegger, Wilber maintains that human interiority, including conscious experience, is correlated with (but not reducible to) brain states, and is dependent as well on cultural and social structures. Moreover, interiority is not restricted to humans, or even to animals, but arguably goes all the way down. What we call consciousness has "tetra-evolved" with other phenomena over billions of years. Crucial here is that the openness that makes experience possible is not a late and bizarre arrival in cosmic history, but rather is somehow ingredient in things from the start. The human world does transcend the limits of the animal world, but with animals we share both physical world-space and emotional world-space. People are not separated by an *abyss* from animals; rather, humans are animals *plus*.

Some critics argue that Heidegger depicted human Dasein as so different from other life forms because he was a modern Gnostic. [28] Wilber explains the rise of Gnosticism and its influence on medieval/premodern Christianity in part as revulsion against and dissociation from an earlier psycho-cultural stage, largely governed by sexual desire and other bodily cravings. According to integral theory, people need to *integrate* what is of value in prior stages of development—whether psychological or cultural—rather than *dissociating* themselves from those stages. Unfortunately, rather than rethinking and then reintegrating the Ascent tradition so important to medieval premoderns, many moderns dissociated themselves from it, thereby throwing out the baby with the bathwater. Faced with the power and influence of dogmatic Christianity, many moderns believed that atheism was needed to extirpate traces of religiosity that had resisted the rise of modern ideals, practices, and institutions. By adopting a dissociative position, rather than one that merely *differentiated* itself from premodern religious views, modernity could not find an adequate account for humankind's place in the cosmos. Growing perception of the cosmic absurdity of human existence manifested itself in Nietzsche's works and beyond.

As noted above Wilber attempts to overcome modern nihilism—nothing *matters*—with a very different claim—*nothing* matters. He speaks of Spirit as the infinite context of all contexts, the context that *is not itself a thing, but no-thingness, the condition necessary for thinghood.* Within that infinite context, cosmic evolution continues. (Wilber prefers to use the Greek term *Kosmos*, in order to emphasize that he uses the word as a signifier for both the exterior and interior aspects of reality.) The drama of cosmic evolution is the process by which cosmic emptiness continually manifests itself in form, some of which evolve into self-conscious life that can then have some access to this interplay of emptiness and form.

Wilber describes cosmic nothingness—Spirit as infinite context—as exhibiting a feature that Plato and, to some extent, Aristotle attribute to divinity: Eros. Put in contemporary parlance, Eros constitutes the strange attractor luring entities to continually transcend themselves in the evolutionary process. There are, of course, problems with this idea, however appealing it may be. First, assigning Eros to divine emptiness runs the risk of turning Spirit into a super-entity with attributes, such as Eros, love, and so on. Mystical theism, particularly well articulated in Eastern Orthodoxy, addresses this problem in the following way: Godhead is distinguished from God; the former names absolute transcendence that cannot be characterized, whereas the latter names God's power as manifest in cosmic affairs. Wilber draws on contemporary science and employs the AQAL matrix to expand upon and to provide empirical support for theological assertions.

There is a second problem with conceiving spirit as the context in which all phenomena/entities appear. East Asian Buddhism, influenced by the Taoist tradition, interpreted the Mahayana concept of *sunyata* ("emptiness") as the void, womb, or matrix in which *tathata* ("suchness") can be manifest. *Sunyata* is to *tathata* as absencing/openness is to presencing/showing up.

The East Asian Buddhism/Heidegger parallel about *sunyata*/nothingness is perhaps the reason that there are *seven* Japanese translations of Heidegger's book, *Being and Time*. Within Buddhism, critics claim that conceiving of *sunyata* as analogous to a creative matrix errs by turning *sunyata* into a superior kind of entity or power, whereas the original meaning of *sunyata* is that all entities are devoid of substance or standing from their own side. Emptiness simply means that entities—even the dharmas that compose entities—*lack* permanence or substantiality.

Evidently, Wilber conceives of emptiness/nothingness in more than one way. Emptiness/nothingness refers to divine Spirit as infinite context in which all phenomena can arise. This context is not neutral, however, insofar as it allegedly lures beings to transcend their previous stages. Emptiness also refers, in a secondary sense, to the lack of substantiality/permanence on the part of all phenomena. In *samsara*, the cosmos as temporal-historical unfolding, all entities arise and then disappear. Wilber attempts to reconcile the other-worldly Ascent tradition with the this-worldly Descent tradition by saying that the One does not stand apart from the Many; that is, cosmic nothingness/emptiness is always already involved with the multiplicity of phenomena that arise and fall. Buddhist practitioners speak of the challenge involved in discerning the emptiness of all phenomena, while simultaneously engaging with and relying on those very phenomena. All spiritual adepts seek to be *in the world, but not of it*. Zen Buddhist aesthetic practices, especially haiku, explore the poignancy of beauty's transience. Life is always colored by death. How to affirm existence in the face of its finitude, when the latter so often brings with it affliction for all sentient beings and sorrow for humans?

Heidegger maintained that openness/emptiness is structured in terms of temporal dimensions and historical epochs. Mortal human Dasein opens up past, present, and future temporal *ek-stases* within which things can show up that concern us, matter to us, and thus mean something to us. Many other organisms too open up a more limited temporal horizon on which things important for survival can show up. Heidegger also claimed, more controversially, that the historical clearing constituting the Western encounter with entities has become ever more constricted over the centuries, until today entities generally reveal only those aspects of themselves consistent with being instruments or commodities. In other words, the meaning-content revealed by entities is gradually cut off. As a result, modern humans drift into boredom, coping with which has generated the entertainment industry, consumerism, and the massive popularity of digital devices. In Buddhism as well, one finds descriptions of how the three poisons—craving, aversion, and ignorance—close down or constrict the ways in which people and other entities can show up.[29]

In his early study of the role played by tragedy in ancient Greek culture, Nietzsche claimed that existence could be justified only as an aesthetic phenomenon. Hence, in the face of modern nihilism, he postulated that European humanity devote itself to a new meaning-giving and life-justifying goal, the creation of the glorious and awe-inspiring Overman, who would be as a god or gods to us. This goal would constitute a new *perspective* for reinvigorating an otherwise faltering human power. For Nietzsche, the need for perspectives is not limited to human life. All things require a perspective from which to take into account other things. Still more, those "things" that are taken into account do not preexist; instead, they are to some extent brought forth, constituted, or enacted by virtue of the perspective according to which they are interpreted. Likewise, the thing that is *being interpreted* is simultaneously *interpreting* the thing that is doing the interpreting from its own perspective. Nietzsche was, in effect, a pan-perspectivalist: For something to be—even an atom—means for it to operate as a perspective that interacts with other perspectives to enact a dynamic, ever-changing, participatory cosmos.

In an important but insufficiently appreciated move, Wilber has also emphasized the centrality of perspectives in articulating the openness/emptiness in which and *as which* all phenomena arise and fall. Openness/emptiness, in other words, is not undifferentiated, but instead occurs only in structured ways, in terms of first-person, second-person, and third-person perspectives. Wilber's perspectivalism is apparently influenced by Nietzsche's thought, which played a decisive role in postmodern theory's "critique of the given."[30] One motivation for Wilber's perspectival/postmodern turn was that assertions made by premoderns about Spirit lacked credibility, not only on the part of moderns for whom Spirit does not exist at all, but also on the part of postmoderns who reject the notion that Spirit is somehow preexisting and pre-given, ready for immediate apprehension by a properly prepared spiritual perceive. Urgently needed is an "integral post-metaphysics" capable of reconstructing "the premodern interpretations of Spirit in light of modern and postmodern developments, such that the enduring fundamentals of the premodern, modern, and postmodern forms of Spirit's own display can all be honored by trimming their absolutisms and acknowledging their true but partial natures."[31] Wilber writes:

> Although the premodern experiences of Spirit—by the great shamans, saints, and sages—were as authentic as authentic can get, the *interpretations* they gave those experiences were of necessity clothed in the fabric of their own time . . . The premodern interpretative frameworks all tended to be mythic, metaphysical, substance-oriented, and postulated a pantheon of *pre-existing ontological structures* (whether in the form of a Great Chain of Being or the form of a Great Web of Life)—which, ironically, is an interpretive framework that amounted to a type of higher, spiritual, transpersonal *myth of the given*—exactly the epistemology so effectively deconstructed by postmodernism—so that the typical new-paradigm approaches exalting such frameworks are actually advancing an epistemological prejudice no longer capable of generating respect.[32]

Postmodern/poststructuralist theory insists that *perspective is more fundamental than perception.* Great thinkers and sages from Buddha to Whitehead presupposed that consciousness somehow perceives or prehends pre-given phenomena. "[T]hese perceptions . . . are the 'building blocks' of a sentient, panpsychic world; the resulting network of perceptions is an Indra's Net of mutually perceiving and interdependent relationships."[33] To make these otherwise magnificent metaphysical systems credible in the eyes of postmoderns, Wilber maintains, perception must be replaced by perspective. "Subjects don't prehend objects anywhere in the universe; rather, first persons prehend second persons or third persons: perceptions are always within actual perspectives." To speak of "perception" emphasizes an abstract pre-given object, whereas to speak of "perspective" emphasizes the sentient being capable of holding that perspective.

> If all holons are sentient beings, then all perceptions are actually embedded in perspectives of, from, and between sentient beings, simplified as first-person, second-person, and third-person perspectives. Whenever the agency or intentionality of any holon—cell to ant to ape—is directed anywhere—and it is always directed somewhere—it is directed toward or within a world of other sentient holons, and this is why, if one atom bumps into another atom, then, from the point of view of that atom, a first person just encountered a second person, who in turn responded as first person to the second person of the first; if they influence

> each other in any way, that is a type of communication, and that communication is not merely a dynamic web but a third person, and so on. If the Kosmos contains sentient beings all the way down, then the Kosmos is composed not of feelings nor perceptions but perspectives, all the way down.[34]

In a passage cited earlier, Nietzsche wrote disparagingly of "mysticism, the voluptuous enjoyment of eternal emptiness." Here, he may seem like a typical modern, who celebrated this-worldly Descent, but the traumatizing experience of the death of God remained vivid for him. Nietzsche never lost his yearning for transcendence of the right sort. Skeptical of the otherworldly yearnings of major world religions, however, he sought transcendence compatible with Zarathustra's *desideratum* of remaining "faithful to the Earth." Perhaps Nietzsche could have brought his vision of transcendence to a measure of fulfillment if he had had access to twentieth century cosmological notions, which in effect generalize the evolutionary view of life: The whole cosmos is continually integrating and transcending previous stages of development.

Wilber's developmental narrative, which is most completely articulated in *Sex, Ecology, Spirituality*, but later revised in terms of integral postmetaphysics, interprets cosmic and human history as occurring within and as non-dual Spirit. In this narrative, which affirms both the Ascent and the Descent traditions, Wilber rethinks Nietzsche's pan-experiential perspectivalism as the ever-evolving, first-, second-, and third-person articulations of that no-thingness: The cosmic clearing for manifesting and concealing, for emerging and vanishing. Over enormous lengths of time, the dynamic interplay among perspective-constituting/constituted beings brings forth ever-greater depth and significance. The "value" we encounter in so many aspects of the cosmos—from the extraordinary complexity of a cell or the beauty of a landscape, to the interior magnificence of people whom we rightly admire—is not something *merely* "projected" by the evaluating subject. Rather, as philosopher Holmes Rolston III has so effectively argued, the cosmos developed depth and significance long before human beings evolved. Late expressions of this value-creating evolutionary process, humans both enact *and* appreciate the Goodness, Truth, and Beauty of the world.[35]

Some years ago I published a paper comparing Wilber's views with those of evolutionary theorist Stanley Salthe.[36] Despite holding similar views about many key issues, Wilber and Salthe come to very different conclusions about the point of cosmic development. For Wilber, moving from the Big

Bang to human consciousness and beyond is the way in which Spirit comes to self-recognition and, thus, to self-actualization in this particular cosmos. As Hegel maintained, human history plays an important role in the *enactment* of this complex process. For Salthe, in contrast, cosmic development is what happens to the cosmos when it is far from entropy, as in our case. Complex forms, including life, are drawn forth by the Second Law of Thermodynamics as effective ways in which to dissipate order. According to Salthe, an existential modernist, *we live in a universe that does not want to be.*[37] Discovery of the Second Law in the late nineteenth century is one reason for the despair and nihilism that was felt by many fin-de-siècle Europeans, including Nietzsche.

In contrast to Salthe's claim that the final cause of the cosmos is self-dissolution, Wilber affirms that the final cause of the Kosmos is continual self-transcendence toward ever more elaborate manifestations of the Good, the True, and the Beautiful. Wilber's pan-experientialist and perspectivalist metaphysics holds that Spirit both transcends *and* includes the cosmos. Non-dual Spirit may be spoken of as both no-thingness and as complete fullness. Spirit lures form into existence. Forms, in turn, yearn to unite with transcendent, non-dual Spirit, but finite forms cannot do so. Hence, the world of form is *samsara*. Yet, insofar as non-dual Spirit is also immanent in form, ingredient in the many, Spirit is not *other* than form. In Buddhism, the bodhisattva is said to have achieved the transcendent bliss of non-duality beyond the realms of form and formless, yet remains all the more compassionate toward the countless sentient beings that suffer. In Christian process theology, this idea is present in *kenosis*, according to which Christ entered fully into the world as a man, even while remaining transcendent Divinity. The God-man felt not only his own suffering, but also that of everyone else. Spirit is both eternal and ever-evolving with the cosmos.

Both Nietzsche and Heidegger knew of what mystics call "the dark night of the soul," those episodes when all seems black, pointless, and meaningless. For Nietzsche, nihilism arose from the death of God, whereas for Heidegger nihilism accompanied the self-concealment of the being of entities. Both thinkers yearned for an understanding of transcendence that would restore significance to human existence, but arguably neither succeeded in satisfying that yearning. In contrast, drawing upon the intellectual and existential struggles of Nietzsche and Heidegger, and supplementing their insights with those found in many spiritual traditions and evolutionary views of nature and human history, Wilber has developed a profound and well-grounded portrayal of humanity's place in the cosmos. To be sure, his understanding is tentative and incomplete; eventually, it will be transcended by a more adequate effort to make sense of it all. Nevertheless, Wilber has done a heroic job of reconciling major insights form science and spirituality, from practices that disclose the structures of the exterior domains and from practices that disclose the structures of the interior domains.[38] He has offered one way of overcoming the nihilism that remains such a problem for many moderns and postmoderns. This way will not satisfy everyone, of course. Here are a few possible critical observations:

First, how would Nietzsche assess Wilber's attempt to overcome nihilism? Even if impressed by the attempt's audacity and scope, would he conclude that it is nevertheless another exercise in providing "metaphysical comfort" for those afflicted by nihilism? Someone setting out to provide an adequate answer to this question would presumably need to engage in the enormous range of first-person, second-person, and third-person inquiries in which Wilber has engaged. At the end of that process, the person posing the question *may* have enacted a perspective sufficiently expansive to overcome many features of modern/postmodern nihilism. Such overcoming, however, does not mean that nihilism is either completely or permanently put at bay. Every *finite* perspective, however expansive, will be colored by uncertainty, doubt, and a measure of anxiety.

A cosmology that reconciles key features of science, spirituality, experience, cultural evolution, and so on may blunt the sharp edges of nihilism, but perhaps mainly for people operating at a relatively advanced developmental level. For many others, however, especially those without access to education and opportunity, the burdens imposed by life may provoke such suffering that death would seem a welcome deliverance. Nietzsche understood the enormously important compensatory role played by religious promises of otherworldly bliss, even though he also criticized religions for the damage they have done to humankind. Given that perhaps 80 percent of the human population remains at premodern levels of development, religious fundamentalism will continue to play a vital role in helping people to cope with living in a world that involves considerable suffering, not least from the deaths of those whom we love.

By postulating the Overman as a possible goal that would restore European vitality, Nietzsche may have engaged in a practice for which he criticized others: Namely, generating a narrative that provided metaphysical comfort at least for himself, and possibly for some others with his sensibility. Why use such a demeaning term as *metaphysical comfort*, however, to describe narratives that attempt to make sense of life through understanding its broader and deeper contexts? As Nietzsche made clear, life-affirming narratives (perspectives) are necessary for inspiring and guiding human individuals and cultures. Cynical postmodern theorists complain that grand narratives of all sorts provide metaphysical comfort, but what narratives do those postmoderns tell themselves to justify how they spend *their* time? Or do they engage in one or another of the above-mentioned self-narcotizing practices? And what does narcosis provide other than comfort?

Grand modern narratives may appear threadbare to many these days, but the ensuing metaphysical despair may lead people to compose alternatives. Wilber's grand narrative has inspired many readers, including the present author, even though it will eventually be transcended. Certain high-tech gurus, such as Ray Kurzweil and Hans Moravec, are writing controversial new narratives that look beyond merely *human* destiny.[39] These new narratives, which often cite the influence of Nietzsche's *Zarathustra*, call for creating artificially intelligent beings that are far more advanced in intelligence and in other ways than mere mortals.[40] Allegedly, these techno-post-humans who will be so magnificent that they will seem godlike to us, will eventually spread throughout the universe, and in the process will make the contents of the entire universe conscious. Needless to say, *this* is a grand narrative!

Let us turn to a second concern about Wilber's new narrative. It depends, to a large extent, on the validity of Big Bang cosmology. It is always dangerous to pin one's metaphysical scheme on a scientific hypothesis, as Christianity—long dependent on the theology of St. Thomas Aquinas—discovered in the face of the revolutionary discoveries of early modern science. Big Bang cosmology is undergoing significant challenges from a number of fronts. Even if the Big Bang theory remains credible, however, the increasingly influential multiverse hypothesis takes the luster off of efforts to find the unified field theory, expressible in an equation that ties everything together.[41] According to the multiverse hypothesis, there is not one cosmos; instead, there are zillions. Whatever "laws of nature" we happen to identify hold only for *our* cosmos, not for any of the others. One reason that the multiverse hypothesis has gained such a following is that it is consistent with the mathematics of string theory. Another reason is that the multiverse hypothesis does away with possible arguments in favor of intelligent design. Such arguments claim support from the remarkable fine-tuning of universal constants, without which life could not exist in our universe. But if those constants represent only *one possible ensemble* of constants among a virtual infinity of universes, the vast majority of which are incapable of bringing forth life, then our "Goldilocks's universe"—not too this, not too that, but just right—is a complete accident, without any significance whatsoever.[42]

Just at the moment when ennobling cosmic narratives have restored some broader significance to human life, as an expression of the *nisus* of universal evolution, physicists have pulled the rug out from under such narratives. The Big Bang universe has been out-contextualized; it now shows up not as the only game in town, but as a mere blip within countless and never-to-be-experienced others. Of course, this has happened before, when the Copernican revolution did away with the small-scale and comfortable medieval cosmology that located Earth at the center of Creation. Big Bang theory offered the basis for a cosmic evolutionary story that could be made consistent with a vision of Spirit as infinite context or generative no-thingness in which all phenomena—including far-off galaxies, as well as the Milky Way—can emerge. If Spirit is truly infinite, however, presumably it is capable of allowing countless alternative universes to arise, as well as our own. Needless to say, contemplating such possibilities makes my head swim. For the time being, I will focus my attention on the affirmative cosmic narrative that helps to make sense of the arrival of human life in *this* universe.

Notes

1. Nihilism, which has preoccupied me from the beginning of my professional career, figured in one my first publications, "Heidegger on Nihilism and Technique," *Man and World* VIII (November 1975): 399–414.

2. In his recent dissertation, *Nihilism, Nature, and Life in Heidegger and Nietzsche: Conceptual Foundations for an Environmental Ethic* (Fordham University Press, 2011), David E. Storey provides an excellent study of the history of modern nihilism, and an insightful critical examination of work by Heidegger and Nietzsche. In particular, Storey calls Heidegger to task for ignoring the extent to which natural science, including evolutionary theory and cosmology, can provide important insight into human existence. His book helped to inspire this essay.

3. See, for example, Robert G. Morrison, *Nietzsche and Buddhism: A Study in Nihilism and Ironic Affinities* (New York: Oxford University Press, 1997); Antoine Panaïoti, *Nietzsche and Buddhist Philosophy* (New York: Cambridge University Press, 2012); André van der Braak, *Nietzsche and Zen: Self-Overcoming without a Self* (Lanham, MD: Lexington Books, 2011). See also Michael E. Zimmerman, "Last Man or Overman? Transhuman Appropriations of a Nietzschean Theme," *The Hedgehog Review: Critical Reflections on Contemporary Culture*, vol. 13, no. 2 (Summer 2011): 31–44.

4. See Bret Davis, *Heidegger and the Will* (Evanston, IL: Northwestern University Press, 2007).

5. On flatland ontology, see Ken Wilber, *A Brief History of Everything* (Boston: Shambhala, 1996).

6. According to Nagarjuna, the great Buddhist thinker to whom Wilber often refers, emptiness is not different from form; form is not different from emptiness. Recognition of this amounts to the experience of non-duality.

7. Friedrich Nietzsche, *The Will to Power*, trans. Walter Kaufmann (New York: Vintage Books, 1968), section 1.

8. On Ernst Jünger and total mobilization, see Michael E. Zimmerman, *Heidegger's Confrontation with Modernity* (Bloomington, IN: Indiana University Press, 1990).

9. Nietzsche, *The Will to Power*, section 29.

10. Martin Heidegger, *Being and Time* (*Sein und Zeit*), trans. Joan Stambaugh (Albany, NY: SUNY Press, 1996).

11. Martin Heidegger, *What Is Called Thinking?* trans. J. Glenn Gray (New York: Harper Perennial, 1976), 46.

12. Max Horkheimer and Theodor Adorno, *Dialectic of Enlightenment*, trans. Edmund Jephcott (Stanford, CA: Stanford University Press, 2007).

13. Martin Heidegger, *An Introduction to Metaphysics*, trans. Gregory Fried and Richard Polt (New Haven, CT: Yale Nota Bene, 2000), 217.

14. John Sallis has used the term *twisting free* to describe the move away from the dichotomy of willing vs. not willing. See, for example, *Delimitations: Phenomenology and the End of Metaphysics* (Bloomington, IN: Indiana University Press), 160 ff.

15. Martin Heidegger, "*Nur noch ein Gott kann uns retten*," *Der Spiegel* 30 (May 1976): 193–219. Trans. by W. Richardson as "Only a God Can Save Us" in *Heidegger: The Man and the Thinker*, ed. Thomas Sheehan (Chicago: Precedent Publishing, 1981), 45–67. http://www.ditext.com/heidegger/interview.html.

In a provocative essay, Thomas J. Sheehan has argued that human Dasein can do no other than become absorbed in using, exploring, changing, and enhancing the entities that show up in the clearing opened up through human existence. The techno-industrial disclosure of being, in other words, is a more or less inevitable result of the way in which humans are ontologically constituted. See Sheehan, "Nihilism: Heidegger/ Juenger/Aristotle," in *Phenomenology: Japanese and American Perspectives*, ed. Burt C. Hopkins (Dordrecht, NL: Kluwer Academic Publishers, 1998), 273–316.

16. Herbert Marcuse, *One-Dimensional Man* (Boston: Beacon Press, 1964).

17. Michael E. Zimmerman, "Toward a Heideggerian *Ethos* for Radical Environmentalism," *Environmental Ethics* V (Summer 1983): 99–131.

18. See Zimmerman, *Heidegger's Confrontation with Modernity*.

19. Heidegger, *Introduction to Metaphysics*, 213.

20. Ken Wilber, *Up From Eden* (Wheaton, IL: Quest Books, 1983).

21. On this topic, see the excellent dissertation by Hans Gruenig, *Heidegger and Personal Transformation* (New Orleans: Tulane University Press, 2009).

22. See, for example, Steve McIntosh, *Integral Consciousness and the Future of Evolution* (New York: Paragon House, 2007) and *Evolution's Purpose* (New York: SelectBooks, 2012).

23. In his *Environmental Ethics* (Philadelphia: Temple University Press, 1988), Holmes Rolston, III provides an inspiring account of the universe story.

24. Heidegger, *Being and Time*, 5.

25. See Brett Buchanan, *Onto-ethologies: The Animal Environments of Uexküll, Heidegger, Merleau-Ponty, and Deleuze* (Albany, NY: SUNY Press, 2009).

26. Jakob von Uexküll, *A Foray into the Worlds of Animals and Humans: with a Theory of Meaning*, trans. Joseph D. O'Neil (Minneapolis, MN: University of Minnesota Press, 2010).

27. Martin Heidegger, *The Fundamental Concepts of Metaphysics: World, Finitude, Solitude*, trans. William McNeill and Nicholas Walker (Bloomington, IN: Indiana University Press, 2001). In section 48, p. 199 Heidegger writes: "If by world we understand beings in their accessibility in each case, if such accessibility of beings is a fundamental character of the concept of world, and if being a living being means having access to other beings, then the animal stands on the side of man. Man and animals have a world. On the other hand, if the intermediate thesis concerning the animal's poverty in world is justified and poverty represents deprivation and deprivation in turn means not having something, then the animal stands on the side of the stone. The animal thus reveals itself as a being which both has and does not have world."

28. As explained by Heidegger's famous student Hans Jonas, Heidegger came under the spell of Gnosticism while writing his masterpiece, *Being and Time*. (See Hans Jonas, "Gnosticism, Nihilism, and Existentialism," epilogue to *The Gnostic Religion: The Message of the Alien God and the Beginnings of Christianity* [Boston: Beacon Press, 1958]. See also Susan Anima Taubes, "The Gnostic Foundations of Heidegger's Nihilism," *The Journal of Religion*, XXXIV, no. 3, July 1954, 155–172.) Jonas too was fascinated by Gnosticism, a heretical and never fully eradicated form of Christianity. According to early Gnostics, Creation is the work of an incompetent and perhaps evil demigod, who is depicted in the Bible as God. The *true* God, however, is wholly Other than the Biblical God. The true God allowed his only Son to incarnate in order to provide the *gnosis* (wisdom) needed for human souls to leave the material world in order to return to their true home with God. Heidegger's claim in *Being and Time* that the human is "thrown" into the world, and his assertion that *Angst* (anxiety) reveals that we are fundamentally *not* of the world, reveal a Gnostic orientation. That same orientation led him to resists attempts to interpret humankind as a clever animal, thereby concealing humanity's non-worldly essence. Early Buddhism, with its rejection of *samsara* and its affirmation of an otherworldly nirvana, may also be plausibly read as a variant of such Gnosticism. Heidegger was

interested in Zen Buddhism, according to which enlightenment involves *becoming* the non-dual openness that we are always already.

Body-despising attitudes in early Buddhism and in some forms of neo-Platonic mysticism shed some light on why Wilber spent so much time in *Sex, Ecology, Spirituality* discussing Plotinus's critique of Gnosticism. According to Plotinus, Gnostics wrongly regarded material reality as inherently evil. Plotinus's version of the great chain of being affirmed that the material world was furthest from the One, but was not inherently evil. Wilber maintains that Mahayana Buddhism avoids the Gnostic tendencies of early Buddhism by insisting that nirvana is not other than *samsara*. Non-dual awakening reveals that all phenomena are empty of substance or self. Non-dual awareness involves the loving embrace of phenomena at all levels of development, while simultaneously recognizing that all phenomena are empty of inherent reality. Obviously, few individuals in world history have existed who made such non-duality their developmental center of gravity.

29. See, especially, Lama Thubten Yeshe, *Introduction to Tantra* (Somerville, MA: Wisdom Publications, 2001).

30. I say "apparently" because Wilber does not specifically mention Nietzsche in this context. Moreover, when I asked Wilber in an email whether his exploration of perspectives had links to Nietzsche's work, Wilber did not reply. Nevertheless, his views on perspectives and perspectivalism clearly parallel Nietzsche's views.

31. Ken Wilber, *Excerpt D: The Look of a Feeling: The Importance of Post/Structuralism*, part 1: Overview and Summary to Date. http://wilber.shambhala.com/html/books/kosmos/excerptD/part1.cfm/.

32. Ibid.

33. Ibid.

34. Ibid.

35. See Holmes Rolston, III's classic work, *Environmental Ethics* (Philadelphia: Temple University Press, 1988). In this book, Rolston developed many aspects of an integral approach to ecology years before the appearance of *Sex, Ecology, Spirituality* in 1995 or my own coauthored volume, *Integral Ecology*, in 2009. See Michael E. Zimmerman, "Integral Ecology's Debt to Holmes Rolston III," in *Integral Ecologies: Nature, Culture, and Knowledge in the Planetary Era*, ed. Sam Mickey, Sean Kelly, and Adam Robbert (Albany, NY: SUNY Press, 2017).

36. Michael E. Zimmerman, "The Final Cause of Cosmic Development: Divine Spirit, or the Second Law of Thermodynamics?" *Integral Theory in Action*, ed. Sean Esbjörn-Hargens (Albany, NY: SUNY Press, 2010), 203–228.

37. Stanley Salthe and Gary Fuhrman, "The Cosmic Bellows: The Big Bang and the Second Law." *Cosmos and History: The Journal of Natural and Social Philosophy*, vol. 1, no. 2 (2005): 295–317, 399. http://cosmosandhistory.org/index.php/journal/article/view/44/25.

38. See Ken Wilber, *The Marriage of Sense and Soul: Integrating Science and Religion* (New York: Three Rivers Press, 1999).

39. Ray Kurzweil, *The Singularity Is Near: When Humans Transcend Biology* (New York: Penguin, 2007); Hans Moravec, *Robot: Mere Machine to Transcendent Mind* (Oxford, UK: Oxford University Press, 2000). See my essay, "The Singularity: A Crucial Phase in Divine Self-Actualization?" *Cosmos and History: The Journal of Natural and Social Philosophy*, vol. 4, nos. 1–2 (2008): 347–370. Available as a PDF at: http://www.cosmosandhistory.org/index.php/journal/article/viewFile/107/213.

40. See my essay "Last Man or Overman? Transhuman Appropriations of a Nietzschean Theme," *Hedgehog Review* 13(2): 31–44.

41. See, for example, John Watson, "Top Ten Flaws in The Big Bang Theory," *The TechReader*, April 26, 2016, https://thetechreader.com/top-ten/top-ten-scientific-flaws-in-the-big-bang-theory/.

42. For an accessible survey of the psychological strains imposed on physicists by the multiverse hypothesis, see Alan P. Lightman, "The Accidental Universe: Science's Crisis of Faith," *Harper's* (December 2011), http://harpers.org/archive/2011/12/0083720. On cosmic fine-tuning, the multiverse, and many related issues, see Paul Davies's excellent study, *Cosmic Jackpot: Why Our Universe Is Just Right for Life* (Boston and New York: Houghton Mifflin Company, 2007).

PART II

Wild Nature—Plural Touch

Chapter 5

Heidegger and Integral Ecology

Toward an Intelligible Cosmos

David E. Storey

In this chapter I sketch the contours of integral ecology (IE) as put forth by Sean Esbjörn-Hargens and Michael Zimmerman, and I submit that it provides a sounder basis for a philosophy of nature than Heidegger's thought. First, I pose a common problem raised in different terms by Ted Toadvine, proponent of ecophenomenology, and Esbjörn-Hargens and Zimmerman, advocates of IE.[1] I will refer to this as the problem of alterity. Second, I briefly review Heidegger's early and later views on nature and explain how the challenge of an ecophenomenology is to overcome the problem posed in the first section. Third, I discuss Heidegger's brief, but intriguing foray into the philosophy of biology in the early 1920s and in his 1929 lecture course, *The Fundamental Concepts of Metaphysics*; here, he engages with biologist Jakob von Uexküll's views on animal environments. I argue that Heidegger would have done well to pursue this path in greater depth, and that his later view of nature encounters—and fails to resolve—the very problems pointed out by Toadvine, Zimmerman, and Esbjörn-Hargens. Fourth, I briefly sketch IE and show how it builds on the work of Heidegger and von Uexküll, and suggest that it charts a middle way between positivism and constructivism that overcomes the problem of alterity. I argue that we should see Heidegger's approach to nature as a halfway house in the shift away from scientific naturalism and toward a recovery of the traditional notion of nature as a cosmos. Furthermore, I contend that one of the great strengths of IE is that it seeks to integrate premodern, modern, and postmodern perspectives on the natural world without falling prey to their problems; specifically, IE embraces the premodern notion of a great chain of being, the modern discovery of evolution, and the postmodern emphasis on perspectivism.

The Problem of the Alterity of Nature

Recently, Toadvine, Esbjörn-Hargens, and Zimmerman have sketched, in slightly different terms, one of the most fundamental epistemological and ontological problems in the philosophy of nature. Toadvine refers to it as the problem of positivism vs. constructivism. "The positivist position," he writes "is that ontological and epistemological questions are either answerable by the natural sciences or are meaningless," and notes that it entails "the collapsing of the philosophy of nature into the philosophy of science and the abandonment of metaphysical inquiry into the being of nature."[2] The main problem with positivism, he notes, is that the account cannot account for the accountant: If all knowledge is caused by and reducible to local, particular factors, then an objective, universal view is not possible and there are no grounds for accepting one theory over another—including positivism. As C.S. Lewis put it, "If the whole universe has no meaning, we should never have found out that it has no meaning: just as, if there were no light in the universe and therefore no creatures with eyes, we should never know it was dark. Dark would be without meaning."[3]According to this view, the consequence of positivism is skepticism. This is the standard phenomenological critique of scientific naturalism. But what is scientific naturalism?

The term *naturalism* can mean many things. It could mean "methodological" naturalism, which eschews metaphysical claims and merely purports to study "empirical" phenomena, things that can be observed with the senses or the instrumental extension thereof. It could mean "metaphysical" naturalism, which makes the stronger claim that only empirical phenomena are real. According to Keith Campbell, "metaphysical naturalism affirms that the natural world is the only real one, and that the human race is not separate from it, but belongs to it as a part. The natural world is the world of space, time, matter, energy, and causality."[4] In a recent anthology devoted to the theme of naturalism, Mario De Caro and David Macarthur label this view "scientific naturalism" and develop it in detail: "scientific naturalists typically conceive nature as a causally closed spatio-temporal structure governed by efficient causal laws—where causes are thought of, paradigmatically, as mind-independent bringers-about of change or difference."[5] Despite the many varieties of scientific naturalism, they suggest that there are two main themes: One is ontological—"a commitment to an exclusively scientific conception of nature"—while the other is methodological—"a reconception of the traditional relation between philosophy and science according to which philosophical inquiry is conceived as continuous with science."[6] As the authors point out, scientific naturalists not only "claim that the conception of nature of the natural sciences is very likely to be true," but go further by insisting that "this is our only bona fide or unproblematic conception of nature."[7] In this way, scientific naturalism is one of the most entrenched default settings in contemporary philosophical and, as we'll see, environmental discourse.

The other extreme of Toadvine's problem is constructivism. "The constructivist view of nature," Toadvine writes, "holds that any 'access' to nature translates a certain function of discourse and ultimately our own self-reflections in the mirror of language, culture, and power."[8] For the constructivist, it is interpretation all the way down, and there is thus no view from nowhere, no standard to judge which interpretation is the most true; the consequence here too is skepticism. As far as nature goes, positivism gives us transcendence without meaning; constructivism gives us meaning without transcendence. One offers a vast, but alien country; the other, an embarrassment of maps. One ignores the constitutive role of subjectivity, while the other inflates it. But as Toadvine points out, the two views "share a common assumption, namely, that nature in its own right lacks a sense or a meaning that is open to human understanding."[9] So let's just hold that thought: The possibility of nature and natural beings having a meaning or sense "in themselves," accessible by, but not reducible to human experience and understanding.

Esbjörn-Hargens and Zimmerman discuss the same dilemma in terms of the "myth of the given" and the "myth of the framework." The former refers to the so-called "mirror of nature," the notion that there is an objective, pre-given, mind-independent world "out there" that our minds can more or less adequately represent; this is nature, according to scientific naturalism. Ecological historians, philosophers of science, and postmodern critics have pointed out, however, that what a particular observer or culture deems "nature" is deeply affected by a welter of social, economic, cultural, cognitive, and political factors. Moreover, as we saw with Toadvine, such a naturalism does not seem to have room for the minds that reflect upon it;

in the metaphor, it is we who are holding the mirror up to nature, but we are conspicuously missing from the image. This leads to so-called "social construction of nature" views, which hold that there is no nature "in itself" that we can speak of or access, only different interpretations of nature. There is no nature outside the text. Nature is as culture says. This leads to either a sort of linguistic idealism or to the view of nature as a kind of *Ding an sich* that completely transcends our frameworks of understanding. Esbjörn-Hargens and Zimmerman pinpoint the problems this causes for ecology: "Every definition of ecology is . . . the result of what part of reality ecologists look at [ontology], how ecologists look at that part of reality [methodology], and who they are as they look [epistemology]."[10] They add that we must "avoid postulating that ecological realities exist 'out there' in some sort of naïve empiricism that falls prey to the myth of the given. There is no such thing as a perceiver-free natural environment."[11] But once the constitutive role of interpretive frameworks is out of the bag, how can we avoid lapsing into the myth of the framework? Toadvine frames this as "the inherent paradox of any phenomenology of nature":

> [T]o the extent that phenomenology starts from experience, we seem constrained at the outset to reduce nature to the range of our perceptual faculties, to frame it in terms of our spatial and temporal scale, and to encounter it in anthropocentric terms, that is, to humanize it. Nature therefore confronts phenomenology with a problem of transcendence.[12]

Nature, in other words, poses a problem of alterity. The central problem is this: If we reject scientific naturalism, what are we to put in its place? How, in short, can we recover an intelligible vision of the natural world that is philosophically defensible and consistent with modern science without sliding into the kind of romanticism that often pervades environmental discourse, or the vagary that characterizes postmodern constructivism?

Esbjörn-Hargens and Zimmerman suggest that the problem stems from a facile culture/nature binary. Rather than see culture as a purely human domain of meaning, purpose, and intersubjectivity "stacked" on top of an indifferent nature (and as a radical rupture with and even corruption of that nature), they suggest a more complex relationship: "nonhuman nature is culturally inflected, whereas human culture is profoundly influenced by and affects nature. To pit nonhuman nature against human culture is to make a fundamental mistake with regard to humanity's relationship with the so-called natural world—not to mention that such a binary denies the existence of animal culture."[13] They advance a "post-naturalism" according to which "we live in a time in human history when nature and culture are so intermixed that we cannot rightly speak of the natural world without implicating ourselves in it. As opposed to reifying nature 'out there,' we champion a post-naturalism in which nature is intertwined with culture, culture is shot through with nature."[14] Note that culture is intertwined with nature here not just for contingent, historical reasons—namely, because humanity has come to inhabit, develop, or map virtually the entire earth—but for necessary, ontological ones. As Toadvine suggested with respect to meaning, Esbjörn-Hargens and Zimmerman propose that we push "culture"—in the sense of intersubjectivity or shared depth of meaning—beyond the human sphere, that it is not a peculiar capacity of human beings, but an intrinsic feature of all natural beings. As I explain in section four, they do this by elaborating on the work of von Uexküll and the integral framework of contemporary American philosopher Ken Wilber. But first, let us look at Heidegger's own confrontation with this problem.

Heidegger on Nature

Heidegger has long been regarded as a proto-ecological thinker, mainly for his rejection of scientific naturalism, his critical stance toward modern technology, his later poetic vision of nature, and his call for us to let beings be.[15] Here, I want to summarize the development of Heidegger's view of nature, point out the ways in which it prefigures IE, and argue that his view of nature is ultimately untenable, mainly because he falls prey to the myth of the framework.

Nature in *Being and Time*

In *Being and Time*, nature is considered almost exclusively from the perspective of human intentionality. Heidegger first analyzes how nature manifests from the pre-theoretical perspective of our "average everydayness," as conducive or resistant to our practical purposes, and then explains how it manifests from the theoretical perspective of the natural sciences, as the sum total of objective, simply present, value-neutral phenomena. Bruce Foltz and Hubert Dreyfus have provided the most comprehensive analyses of Heidegger's early views on nature, and have usefully categorized these two senses as "environing/

productive nature" and "objective nature" (Foltz), and as "available/unavailable" and "occurent" (Dreyfus).[16] Apart from the "existential categories" that the treatise is designed to divine, these two senses of nature correspond to the two main senses of being described in the text: readiness-to-hand and presence-at-hand. The former refers to how we encounter nature as our surrounding environment and perceptual and motile field; the latter refers to how we conceive nature once we have withdrawn from this field into the realm of abstraction.

It is important to point out that Heidegger is not saying that productive nature is a mere "projection" of human interests and concerns on to "mere nature," understood as a value-neutral realm of factual, purely given things. He claims that readiness to hand is the being "in itself" of productive nature, in the sense that it is just the normal way that nature shows itself to us: "this characteristic is not to be understood as merely a way of taking [these entities], as if we were talking such 'aspects' into the 'entities' which we proximally encounter, or as if some world-stuff which is proximally present-at-hand in itself were 'given subjective colouring' in this way."[17] The second sense of nature—objective nature—corresponds to the idea of nature operative in modern science, a realm of value-neutral, physical objects arranged in various positions in space-time and implicated in a system governed by efficient causality; it corresponds, in other words, to what we saw defined as "scientific naturalism" above. IE interprets this as a failure to recognize "interiority," the subjective and intersubjective dimensions of nature. Wilber refers to this view as "flatland": "it is industrialization that holds flatland in place, that holds the objective world of simple location as the primary reality, that colonizes and dominates the interiors and reduces them to instrumental strands in the great web of observable surfaces. That 'Nature alone is real'—that is the voice of the industrial grid."[18] And Whitehead, distilling the essence of what he called scientific materialism: "a dull affair, soundless, scentless, colourless; merely the hurrying of material, endlessly, meaninglessly."[19]

While Heidegger makes some cryptic remarks about a third sense of nature that transcends these utilitarian and scientific perspectives, such as that found in romanticism, his focus is mostly confined to these two "intra-worldly" senses. Since Heidegger's approach is phenomenological, he wants to claim that the present-at-hand is in some sense founded on and derivative of the ready-to-hand, because it has been shown as a horizon of meaning that arises only on the basis of what he calls "world," a totality of significance projected by Dasein and presupposed in all its practical and theoretical activities. The world, in other words, is not simply given, existing prior to our intending of it; it is enacted, brought forth, opened up by the constituting activity of Dasein. On this point, by embracing what is sometimes called the "enactive paradigm," Heidegger laid the groundwork for the perspectivism of IE. As Esbjörn-Hargens and Zimmerman explain:

> Perspectivalists maintain that mind—far from being a mirror that passively receives independent phenomena—plays an active role in co-constructing phenomena. Methodologies not only reveal, but also in some respects constitute the phenomena under investigation. What we call "facts," in other words, are not ready-made but emerge in a complex process of perceptual, emotional, and cognitive negotiation between knower and known. According to perspectivalism every assertion is made by a person occupying a viewpoint within a cultural worldspace.[20]

Despite the recognition of environing nature and the rejection of scientific naturalism, Heidegger's description of the third kind of being, existentiality, is almost entirely bereft of any reference to nature except for a few cursory references to Dasein's having a "bodily nature."[21] The questions of the "body," "life," and "natural history" are all bracketed in the existential analytic because these concepts are laden with unfounded meanings drawn from the interpretations of nature that stem from the philosophical tradition and the natural sciences. In *Being and Time*, then, natural being is treated primarily as a derivative concept ontologically distinct from human being, and this is so because of Heidegger's understanding of world as the basis of any and all senses of nature.

This poses a problem, however, regarding the relationship of ontological dependence between the two senses. Heidegger is in a difficult position here. On the one hand, by showing that the perspective of "knowing the world"—as an objective aggregate of present-at-hand entities ontologically distinct from and set over against a knowing subject—is a deficient mode of concern and is founded on the prior phenomenon of being-in-the-world, Heidegger has dethroned the objective sense of nature. On the other hand, he wants to say that productive or environing nature is not purely subjective—we do not just project purposes and usefulness onto natural entities, but they can be more or less conducive to those purposes. There really are *things there* whose being is not exhausted by their meaning for us or their factual properties, but we cannot say that they have meaning "in themselves" or that they do not. We can discover entities as appropriate or inappropriate, useful or useless, receptive or resistant to our practical purposes and theoretical understanding. We cannot say anything about them outside of the context of world; in this sense, they are like Kant's noumena. In short, Heidegger is trying to steer a middle way through realist and constructivist views of nature.

Hubert Dreyfus has engaged this problem by focusing on the following questions: "(1) Can Heidegger achieve his fundamental ontology, demonstrating that all modes of being, even the being of nature, can be made intelligible only in terms of Dasein's being, and not vice versa? (2) Can he still leave a place for ontic, causal, scientific explanation?"[22] Dreyfus is concerned about the relation of ontological priority between readiness-to-hand and presence-at-hand. If the existence of the present-at-hand is founded on Dasein's being, the legitimacy of scientific knowledge claims appears to be called into question. On the one hand, Dreyfus thinks, Heidegger does not want to reduce the objects of science to the projections and interests of human beings: "when theory decontextualizes, it does not *construct* the [present-at-hand], but . . . it reveals the [present-at-hand] which was already there in the [ready-to-hand]."[23] Dreyfus reiterates this view when he explains Heidegger's notion of occurrent nature: "Scientific observation can thus reveal a universe unrelated to human for-the-sake-of-which's. This is the nature whose causal powers underlie equipment and even Dasein itself insofar as it has a body."[24] Hence, it appears that the present-at-hand must be prior.

On the other hand, Dreyfus notes that Heidegger seems to maintain that the present-at-hand is founded on the ready-to-hand. The inspection or theoretical cognition of an entity is described as a "deficient mode of concern" and only arises when concern has been disrupted. And recall that Heidegger is adamant that when we take things as ready-to-hand, that is not just an interpretation we project onto the things.[25] This appears to contradict the view that Dreyfus imputes to Heidegger. In describing environing nature, Heidegger claims that "readiness to hand is the way in which entities as they are 'in themselves' are defined ontologico-categorially."[26] The trick is that Heidegger argues there is an "objective" or "real" aspect of the ready-to-hand (as Dreyfus puts it, "it seems that Dasein's self-interpreting everyday activity and [occurrent] nature codetermine what can be available for what"[27]) and that, conversely, there is a "subjective" or "ideal" aspect to the present-at-hand, which we usually take to be objective and mind-independent, but is actually encountered only through a modification of everyday concern. Here Heidegger shows us he is aware of the paradox: "Yet only by reason of something present-at-hand, 'is there' anything ready-to-hand. Does it follow, however, granting this thesis for the nonce, that readiness-to-hand is ontologically founded upon presence-at-hand?"[28] Moreover, both of these modes of being are founded on the existential structure of being-in-the-world. As he points out, "In Interpreting [present-at-hand and ready-to-hand] entities within-the-world . . . we have always 'presupposed' the world. Even if we join them together, we still do not get anything like the world as their sum."[29]

The point is that it does not seem possible to answer both of Dreyfus's above-mentioned questions in the affirmative: If all modes of being can be traced back to Dasein's being-in-the-world, then there seems to be no objective foundation for scientific explanations (question two); yet if there is such an objective foundation, then fundamental ontology cannot claim to ground all modes of being (question one). If the latter, then we are thrown back upon the Cartesian problems of interaction that fundamental ontology is intended to disarm: namely, how intentionality (consciousness) and causality (nature) are related. But Heidegger does not account for how the spheres of intentionality and causality relate to one another. If he maintains that while there can be no being or truth without Dasein, yet there can be beings without Dasein, then how are we to describe them if meaning and significance obtain only within the world? And if we are to maintain that there are indeed things, that there is a cosmos subtending and embracing human history, then how can it have no sense for us and why can we not say that it has its own distinctive temporality, intelligible structure, and way of being? The primordial sense of nature seems to be a kind of noumenal thing-in-itself that we cannot fail to acknowledge, yet cannot hope to comprehend. But this would appear to lead to a kind of idealism that Heidegger clearly wished to avoid. Heidegger's way around this is to claim that while there cannot be being—in the sense of meaning or significance—without Dasein, there can be beings. But this then begs the question: What is the ontological status of these "extra-worldly" beings? If philosophy cannot provide a register for addressing them—as opposed to the perspective of the environment of our pre-theoretical involvement and the "nature" of scientific naturalism—then they are sealed off into a noumenal realm of things in themselves that are resistant to human understanding; this lands us, bizarrely, back in the same dualistic position that Heidegger's approach was supposed to overcome: The ontological dissociation of the human and the world. This is what inspired early critiques from Hans Jonas and Karl Loewith of Heidegger as an anthropocentrist and instrumentalist with regard to nature. Heidegger's lectures from this time period contain scattered remarks about a "cosmos," yet he gives no sustained account of what this might mean. As I explain below, the problem stems in large part from Heidegger's refusal to recognize interiority in nonhuman beings and failure to furnish a robust philosophical biology.

Later Heidegger on Nature

Heidegger's later views on nature—his introduction of the notion of "earth" (*Erde*) in the mid-1930s, his increasing focus on *physis* (the Greek term for "nature"), his critiques of humanism and technology, his call for *Gelassenheit* ("letting be"), and his vision of the fourfold—are well known, so I will not discuss them in detail. But I do want to highlight three points. First, this later vision of nature is problematic, particularly as it relates to the other two senses and to Heidegger's phenomenology. Second, *physis* essentially becomes synonymous with being in Heidegger's later philosophy. Third, the opposition of the early, anthropocentric Heidegger and the later, eco-centric Heidegger is generally overdrawn: The 1929 lectures, hot on the heels of *Being and Time*, offer a sustained discussion of *physis* in the context of a critique of metaphysics and contain many of the mainsprings of his later work. Heidegger has already embraced the notion that all metaphysics has heretofore been merely "physics"—in the sense that its foundation, the physical, is not ontologically determined. The incompleteness of *Being and Time*, then, would seem to have much to do with a failure to articulate this third sense of nature as *Erde* and *physis*.

Primordial nature is a perplexing phenomenon, recalcitrant to analysis, because it does not show up within the world, and only that which shows up within the world can have a sense. A number of scholars have attempted to discern seeds of this later sense of nature in *Being and Time*. The main problem with these attempts is that in this text Heidegger had not yet introduced the notion of earth as the foil of world. Since this is an integral part of the primordial sense of nature, his vague references to the latter throughout the text are confusing, because Heidegger's methodology—the "ontic priority" of the question of being—restricts him to describing the intentional structure of human being-in-the-world. As Foltz points out, "The being of primordial nature lies neither in its presence-at-hand, nor in its readiness-to-hand. Moreover, it does not even belong to the being of nature as such to be within the world . . . [N]ature cannot be disclosed unless it is within the world."[30] Haar echoes this idea: "[For Heidegger,] although every being of nature that man encounters—including his own supposed naturality—is necessarily intra-worldly, 'intra-worldliness does not belong to the being of nature.' "[31] Taminiaux goes further, arguing that a primordial sense of nature, which Heidegger later renders as *physis*, is nowhere to be found in the existential analytic:

> [A] theme like nature is not worthy of much attention in fundamental ontology. *Physis*, therein is simply extant, available for manipulations; its Being is that of simple extantness or *Vorhandenheit*. No polemical tension is to be found in it. It is not the earth in conflicting relationship with the world, because the world according to fundamental ontology is not built upon *physis*. At this point in Heidegger's itinerary, *physis* is not at all an enigmatic source regulated by the tension of unconcealment and reserve. Instead, as soon as it appears, nature is *innerweltlich*, intraworldly.[32]

Otto Poggeler agrees, but takes a more critical angle in arguing that Heidegger's privative account of nature in *Being and Time* is "one-sided" because he begins from the perspective of the environment, and that, like objective nature, environing/productive nature *also* obscures the phenomenon of nature in its "inexhaustible otherness and alienness."[33] In his reading, *Being and Time* advances an instrumentalist view of nature on account of its point of departure: Dasein's average everydayness. Interestingly, this view is seconded by deep ecologist George Sessions. According to Zimmerman, "Sessions says that if Heidegger *had begun with the cosmos* and worked his way toward human beings, humans would have seemed less significant in his scheme. Yet by beginning with humans, he disclosed nature as ancillary to human concerns."[34]

"Beginning with the cosmos" is just what Heidegger attempted in his later work, starting in the mid-1930s, when he began to develop the concepts of *Erde* and *physis*. Heidegger's arcane invocations of the earth throughout his middle and later work, though music to the ears of some environmental philosophers, are motivated by several factors, and what we today refer to as the "ecological crisis" is not one of them. Heidegger is not concerned about the depletion of the ozone layer, the extinction of species, or other environmental problems and policy issues. The destruction of the earth that he laments is a more concrete-sounding locution for the same forgetfulness of being that he bemoans in *Being and Time*. The tragedy has to do with the progressive narrowing of the clearing through which being shines forth, not with increasing impediments to the flourishing of particular beings, the propagation of species, or the health of ecosystems. Even the consequences of the detonation of the atomic bomb itself, we are told, would pale in comparison to a total forgetfulness of being. As such, Heidegger's recollection of the earth should be approached with some skepticism by those looking to enlist him for environmental purposes.

With these caveats in place, let us examine Heidegger's account of the earth. Heidegger's introduction of the enigmatic notion of earth in the "Origin of the Work of Art" from 1935 initially seems out of place. One would expect the essay to be focused on aesthetics. However, when seen in the context of *Being and Time*, the simultaneous treatment of the earth and art make sense. Recall that in *Being and Time* Heidegger neglected to include a description of aesthetic judgment and experience in the existential analytic.[35] The art essay can be seen as Heidegger trying to tie up two "loose ends" from *Being and Time*: aesthetic experience and the third sense of nature. As he noted there, the first two senses of nature do not capture the so-called "Romanticist" sense of nature that we readily connect with aesthetic experience. As Haar notes, "It is fundamental that the concept of Earth—absent from *Being and Time* where nature is reduced to a 'subsistent being' . . . is elucidated for the first time in connection with the interpretation of the work of art."[36] Graham Parkes is more specific:

> Any impression that the proper attitude toward things is merely technological is quickly dispelled by this essay, a major concern of which is to describe a way of relating to things that is quite different from taking them as [ready-to-hand or present-at-hand]. The work of art, whose essential nature cannot be appreciated if it is taken as an implement or an object of scientific investigation, is to be seen here as a paradigm of things in general.[37]

Thus, it is no surprise that the inquiry into the ontological significance of art is at once an elaboration of the third sense of nature.

It is much easier to determine what the earth is not than to pin down what it is. First, we can clear away the popular senses. The earth is not the entity that came together some four billion years ago. It is not the planet that rotates around the sun and on its own axis, nor is it a planet among other planets. It is not an object or sum of objects. It is not any sort of "prime matter." The earth, in Heidegger's words, "is not to be associated with the idea of a mass of matter deposited somewhere, or with the merely astronomical idea of a planet."[38] Nor is it to be seen as a storehouse of energy for human purposes, a collection of "natural resources." Yet the earth also should not be construed as a gigantic ecosystem or biosphere comprising all organic and inorganic beings, since these are at least partially conceptual frames created by humans to make sense of nature. This is a popular frame for many ecological thinkers. A well-known example is James Lovelock's "Gaia Hypothesis," which construes the earth as a super-organism.

As Esbjörn-Hargens and Zimmerman report, Lovelock's interpretation of nature as a super-organism first arose toward the end of the nineteenth century, and underwent a number of metaphorical mutations, from "super-organism," to "economic machine," to "cybernetic web," to "chaos."[39] Yet as they point out, despite their differences, all of the four ecological metaphors "view 'nature' as a great interlocking order of exterior sensory data," and "all four definitions have been used to exploit the environment."[40] And as Bowler notes, both population ecology and systems ecology view nature in the economic terms of resources and raw material and both are correlated with the anthropocentric project of improving human management and control of natural processes, the former through free-market mechanisms, the latter through top-down technocratic interventions. The Gaia gestalt, often invoked by ecologists and environmentalists bent on combating an anthropocentric view of the earth, would seem to suggest a more holistic, interconnected view of the relationship between humanity and the earth. However, Heidegger would cry foul, since this still conceives the earth in objective terms as a system whose proper "balance" can be calculated and perhaps even engineered by human ingenuity. Bowler echoes this idea: "as far as systems ecology was concerned, the human economy was simply one aspect of the global network of resource utilization that science hoped to understand and control."[41] This resonates with Heidegger's notion of "Enframing" (*Gestell*), the way being appears in the modern age, in which nature is enacted as merely a standing reserve (*Bestand*) of energy. The so-called "holistic view" of nature as an integrated, self-regulating system that is touted as a paradigm shift by many contemporary ecological thinkers is actually the old view of nature as a super-organism, albeit garbed in green drag, an instance of what Heidegger calls "cybernetics" and what we might call "ecologism": The elevation of ecological concepts to ontological status.

For Heidegger, this way of thinking reduces humanity to, at best, an animal species, and at worst, a storehouse of energy, and thus glosses over its defining characteristic: Namely, its openness to being. Unsurprisingly, the earth escapes the intentional stances of the ready-to-hand and the present-at-hand. So long as we one-sidedly conceive of beings either as equipment or as objects—objects in themselves or in a system, atomism or holism—we pass over both their (and our) essential connection to the earth and the earth itself.

The earth refers, in Julian Young's phrase, to "the dark penumbra of unintelligibility that surrounds . . . our human existence."[42] It is illustrated through two examples in Heidegger's 1935 essay, *On the Origin of the Work of Art*: van Gogh's painting of a pair of shoes and a Greek temple. In the first example, Heidegger offers an interpretation of the world of the apparent owner of the shoes, a peasant woman. The point of his analysis is to show that the object (the shoes) implies a vast network of meaningful relations, what in *Being and Time* he called a "totality of significance"—in short, a world. The world does not appear as an object in the painting, but we can only understand and gain access to the painting at all because there is some degree of overlap between the scene depicted there and our own world. At first, this seems of a piece with the analysis of equipment in *Being and Time*, yet Heidegger includes something new: the earth. He claims that not just world, but earth is implicated in and thus partly constitutive of the "manifest content" of the painting:

> The equipmental being of the equipment consists in its usefulness. But this usefulness itself rests in the abundance of an essential Being of the equipment. We call it reliability [i.e., readiness-to-hand]. By virtue of this reliability the peasant woman is made privy to the silent call of the earth; by virtue of the reliability of the equipment she is sure of her world. World and earth exist for her, and for those who are with her in her mode of being, and only thus—in the equipment. . . . The reliability of the equipment first gives to the simple world its security and assures to the earth the freedom of its steady thrust.[43]

Despite the notorious obscurity of this passage, a few things are clear. First, the mention of "reliability" and its fragility reminds us of the discussion of equipmental breakdown in *Being and Time*. Natural materials resist our attempts to fashion them to our purposes, and our purposes only take form as over against such resistance. So the notion of earth is very much prefigured in the discussion of equipment in *Being and Time*, where Heidegger remarks that equipment refers to the natural material from whence it came.[44]

Second, world is associated with security, order, and stability, while earth connotes freedom, violence, and disruption. The latter call up the discussions of anxiety and freedom toward death in *Being and Time*, the total breakdown in the network of meaningful relations and the subsequent confrontation with the nothingness of both self and world. The following two quotations from both texts sharpen the similarity: "Earth shatters every attempt to penetrate it. It causes every merely calculating importunity upon it to turn into a destruction. This mastery and progress of technical-scientific objectification of nature . . . remains an impotence of will."[45] Yet in *Being and Time*, it is the world, not the earth, that fills the role of the void, the nothing, the nullity on which the self shipwrecks: "the world as such is that in the face of which one has anxiety."[46] In the earlier works, the breakdown of meaning is located much more on the self's experience of the nullity of the world; it is thus presented as a more subjective and worldly event. In the art essay and afterwards, however, it is construed less subjectively and as more extra-worldly. As Jacques Taminiaux notes, in *Being and Time*, *physis* "is not the earth in conflicting relationship with the world, because the world according to fundamental ontology is not built upon *physis*. At this point in Heidegger's itinerary, *physis* is not at all an enigmatic source regulated by the tension of unconcealment and reserve. Instead, as soon as it appears, nature is . . . intraworldly.[47] The analysis of equipment leads us to the notions of world and earth, and these can only become available to us, Heidegger thinks, through the medium of the work. This is why the artwork is granted such importance: "To be a work means to set up a world . . . The work holds open the open region of the world."[48] Here he invokes the example of the Greek temple:

> It is the temple-work that first fits together and at the same time gathers around itself the unity of those paths and relations in which birth and death, disaster and blessing, victory and disgrace, endurance and decline acquire the shape of destiny for human being. The all-governing expanse of this open relational context is the world of this historical people.[49]

The work raises a world in the sense that it erects and opens up and serves as the reference point for a horizon of meaning in which things can show up in their distinctness and in connection with each other. This horizon thus corresponds to the aspect of unconcealment, manifesting, and presencing proper to truth, an aspect Heidegger around this time begins to frequently refer to as *physis*. But this opening only occurs against the limiting background of earth: "The early Greeks called this emerging and rising in itself and in all things *physis*. It illuminates also that on which and in which man bases his dwelling . . . Earth is that whence the arising brings back and shelters everything that arises as such. In the things that arise, earth occurs essentially as the sheltering agent."[50] Heidegger is explicit about the connection between the artwork and the intimate relation between world and earth: "The setting up of a world and the setting forth of earth are two essential features in the work-being of the work."[51] This is why Heidegger wants to frame the artwork not purely in terms of aesthetics, but as "truth setting itself to work": Because there are revealing and concealing functions to it that are in perpetual tension with each other. As he says, "The world, in resting upon the earth, strives to surmount it. As self-opening it cannot endure anything closed. The earth, however, as sheltering and concealing, tends always to withdraw the world into itself and keep it there."[52] The work of art is, as it were, the portal through which the creative conflict of world and earth is manifested and the cradle in which it is preserved; in which the opaque and undifferentiated forms of the earth separate and congeal and form a world. But again, no mystical, exclusive importance need be attributed to artworks here; all that is meant is that, because they stand outside the contexts of utility and objectivity, aesthetic phenomena are more likely to "tip us off" and "clue us in" to what is always already going on with any phenomenon: Namely, its sheer coming to presence and withdrawal.

By stressing the intimate connection between world and earth, revealing and concealing, Heidegger is trying to counteract the assumption that the earth is purely unintelligible and chaotic, bereft of form, order, law and limit. Hence, he says that earth is "sheltered in its own law . . . Earth, bearing and jutting, endeavors to keep itself closed and to entrust everything to its law."[53] Creation is not the one-sided imposition of form on mere matter, but the development of latent potentials already nascent and lurking in the Earth. Heidegger appears to have developed this idea in his 1931 lectures on Aristotle's metaphysics, in which he analyzes Aristotle's concept of *dynamis* (potency or power).[54] Haar comments: "[the earth] is the reserve of possible forms to which manifestation would only give body . . . Earth is not chaos . . . Earth is for Heidegger a secret sketch of forms."[55] Thus art, for Heidegger, "is the disclosure in works of forms not yet sketched but secretly prefigured." He sums it up thus: "There lies hidden in nature a rift-design, a measure and a boundary and, tied to it, a capacity for bringing forth—that is, art."[56] So art is taken neither as the imitation of nature, nor as the superimposition of human forms and modes of perception onto it, but as furthering nature's own possibilities. Obviously, this points in the direction of a less exploitative relationship to beings. By remaining open to their own peculiar possibilities and letting them come forth just as they are, we can assist rather than stymie their unfolding and flourishing.[57]

While the earth tries to fill in a gap left by the treatment of nature in *Being and Time*, it only refers to the realm of concealment, an extra-worldy, semi-historical order that, though it cannot be simplistically regarded as chaos or abstractly taken as a reservoir of "prime matter," it does not canvass the realm of un-concealment that is worldly, yet is populated by animals, plants, and other life-forms. As soon as these beings fall within the ambit of language, world, and meaning (the realm of un-concealment) their essential, primordial natural being is covered up. "But," Haar observes, "nowhere does Heidegger consider that the very being of natural beings is exclusively derived from the world. From this point of view he is a 'realist.'"[58] It is just that we can never clarify the actual nature of these beings, and natural sciences such as biology and ecology fool themselves into thinking they can do so. Heidegger seems to regard all non-human beings as belonging to the earth. In the art essay, he says that "a stone is worldless. Plant and animal likewise have no world; but they belong to the covert throng of a surrounding into which they are linked."[59] Is this latter phrase synonymous with the earth? It seems so. Earth may correspond to the being of animals, plants, etc.—in short, to the being of life. It is a kind of limbo between the human world and the self-concealing dimension of being. Heidegger is forced into this position because he rejects an approach to natural entities based on sympathy or overlapping characteristics.

It is worth noting here that Heidegger must maintain a clear ontological line between world and earth, because he refuses to think of humans as animals, or as organic bodies. As he says in the *Letter on Humanism*, "the human being is essentially different from an animal organism.[60] However, he is not here denying that humans are embodied *in some way*. Hence, the important distinction, as Caputo points out, is not between human being and animal organism, but between lived body and organic body.[61] The point here is that there may be room to push world down beneath the human plane, and concede some sort of capacity for world-disclosure, language, and "culture"—some degree of interiority—for non-human beings; this is exactly the path taken by IE. And as I explain below, Heidegger flirted with such a non-reductive naturalism earlier in his oeuvre, but his paranoia about dragging humans down into the welter of animality and disregarding being stays his hand from situating humans along a common ontological continuum with non-human beings.

Heidegger has been praised by some environmental philosophers for his critiques of the positivist, naturalistic, and mechanistic view of nature enabled by Descartes and espoused by the natural sciences, as well as the technological mindset that underwrites this view. His later works especially attempt to convey a more poetic experience of nature in its alterity—rather than in the instrumental or scientific senses it has *for us*. They signal a turn away from the exploitative regime of modern technology, which is driven by the "will to will," the desire to master and control nature; as such, Heidegger calls us to overcome the posture of willing, and adopt a standpoint of letting-be.[62] For this reason, some have touted Heidegger as a non-anthropocentric figure and proto-environmentalist. In the early 1980s, Michael E. Zimmerman argued that Heidegger's critique of modern technology's reduction of nature to raw material or "standing reserve" (*Bestand*) purely for human purposes and his notion of *Gelassenheit* offered a way out of the domineering and exploitative attitudes and practices responsible for the ecological crisis.[63] In claiming Heidegger to be a biocentrist, Zimmerman and deep ecologists seized upon fixtures in his later philosophy, such as the elevation of poetic, meditative thinking over rational, calculative thinking, his affection for the pre-Socratics' view of *physis*, his critique of the enframing (*Gestell*) of modern technology, and his call for humans to learn how to dwell authentically in the fourfold of earth, sky, gods, and mortals.[64] Their optimistic outlook on a Heideggerean environmental philosophy and ethics was followed by a cluster of essays and books that were rather sanguine about the attempt to frame Heidegger as a deep ecologist or as a non-anthropocentric ecological thinker, grounding the project in his critique of humanism,[65] his reinterpretation of Aristotle,[66] his account of language,[67] or his unique understanding of dwelling on the earth.[68]

Despite these affinities, some scholars, including and especially Zimmerman himself, became suspicious of the compatibility of the two approaches.[69] These suspicions were bred in part by Heidegger's political entanglements, his espousal of a non-progressive understanding of history, his rejection (or at least circumvention) of Darwinism, his reservations about science, his ambiguous interpretation of animals, and his insistence that humanity is ontologically separate from nature. While Heidegger's final picture of nature—the so-called "fourfold" of mortals, gods, earth, and sky—may appear to offer a more holistic and less alienating alternative than both his earlier phenomenology and the modern view of nature, it does scant justice to the rich world being explored and charted by the biological and ecological sciences. While we may want to reject scientific naturalism and scientism with Heidegger, we still want to maintain that there is some connection between the order disclosed by science and the order of being, *physis*; we want to do this, that is, if we want to avoid lapsing into a dualistic view of a world of appearance (disclosed by the worker or scientist) and a world of reality (disclosed by the poet or nature-lover), the very metaphysical dualisms Heidegger is trying to overcome. In other words, we want to recover a sense of nature as a cosmos—a nature that we can speak (Logos) meaningfully about, and not in a merely poetic sense. Silence too can do as little—perhaps more—injustice to nature than anthropocentric speech. Heidegger's position seems to resemble that of the late, great evolutionary theorist Stephen Jay Gould: There is the realm of facts (science, the ontic) on the one hand, and the realm of meaning (religion, the ontological), on the other, and the two realms are simply incommensurable.[70] The posture of open-ness and *Gelassenheit* is supposed to allow things to manifest in their naked "that-ness," free from any human projections or categories; but the poetic articulation of this—the ontology from the view of *Gelassenheit*, the fourfold—appears to be an all-too human construction. Attempting to avoid the myth of the given, Heidegger, preoccupied with the hermeneutical perspective, appears to fall prey to the myth of the framework. Or, as Graham Harman puts it, Heidegger never quite twists free of the preoccupation with "access" to the world.[71] The larger point here is that the paranoid attempt to avoid anthropomorphism at all costs—reminiscent of Descartes's thought experiment of radical doubt—proves to be impossible. The poetic disclosure of being, bizarrely, ends up having nothing interesting to say about the "what-ness" of things; it has no thematic content because content has been "debunked" as a mentalistic, anthropocentric category. As I will discuss in the last section, a possible way around this issue is to stop seeing interpretation and meaning as purely human categories projected onto nature; interpretation goes all the way down, not in the sense of human understanding, but in the sense of an irreducible aspect of all natural entities' being-in-the-world. But first, we need to examine one more aspect of Heidegger's approach, because it will show us what is lacking in many ecophenomenological and Continental philosophies of nature, and what is needed to overcome the problem of alterity.

Heidegger's Confrontation with Biology in the 1920s

Heidegger's view of life is distinct from his view of animality. When he speaks about life, he is usually referring to "factical life" or human existence, a notion he believes must be clearly separated from any notion of animality. When Heidegger does discuss animality, he does so more in the spirit of the Aristotelian tradition (which sees living beings as "animated") than the modern tradition (which views them as mere physiological beings). Indeed, as David Farrell Krell notes, "animation . . . is Heidegger's principal preoccupation both before and after *Being and Time*, from the period of his hermeneutics of facticity [of 1921 onward] to that of his theoretical biology [in 1929–1930]."[72] There are roughly three phases to Heidegger's thinking about animals: 1) Pre–*Being and Time*, Heidegger weaves together elements from the biological works of Aristotle and Jakob von Uexküll into an ontology of life that ascribes disclosedness, being-in-the-world, being-with (*Mitsein*), and the capacity for signification to animals; 2) in *Being and Time* and *FCM*, he claims that they have an *Umwelt* but, as *FCM* puts it, are "world-poor," bound by their drives; 3) in *Introduction to Metaphysics* and after, he insists that animals have *neither* world *nor* environment, and generally seems to lose interest in the concept of the animal. All told, despite Heidegger's promising pre–*Being and Time* sketches for an ontology of life and his later occasional cryptic and intriguing comments to the contrary, his position roughly from *Being and Time* onward is that there is an essential, ontological separation between human and animal being, and one that should not primarily be regarded as a difference in "species." It may be "non-reductive," but it can no longer be called any kind of "naturalism."

In seizing on the peculiar movement of pre-reflective factical life, Heidegger believed he was uncovering a stratum of being long neglected by the tradition that had first been worked over by Aristotle, and his creative appropriation of this stratum would lead to his famed conception of being-in-the-world, which was developed in close concert with considerations on life and animality. While developing his conception of being-in-the-world over a series of early lecture courses that mainly deal with Aristotle,[73] Heidegger carries out sustained analyses of life and animal being. Here, he attributes much more to life and animal being than is generally done in both modern philosophy and biology and in his own later work. Heidegger's most direct engagement with Aristotle's writings on life and soul, especially the *De Anima*, is found in the 1926 lecture course, *Basic Concepts in Ancient Philosophy*, where he insists that Aristotle's key ontological innovation in the philosophy of nature is his understanding of *zoé* (life). Indeed, Heidegger here presents Aristotle's biology as the basis for understanding Dasein's way of being as a specific kind of living being. *Zoé*, he writes, has an "exemplary significance;" it is "the first-ever phenomenological grasp of life," and it "led to the interpretation of motion and made possible the radicalization of ontology."[74] Heidegger outlines Aristotle's *De Anima* by noting the different levels and essential features of life. Soul, he insists, should not be seen, as it commonly is in modern thought, as merely "psychological," but as pertaining to life as such. He interprets perception (*aisthesis*) in terms of world: "*aesthesis* . . . discloses the world, though indeed not in speech and assertion, not in showing and making disclosure intelligible. Fundamental concept of sensibility: letting a world be given and encountered by disclosing it."[75] The student transcription of the lecture fleshes this out further: "What is alive, and also stands in a determinate communication with something, is such that it has a world, as we would say today."[76] Heidegger points out that this interpretation of soul/life is the foundation for determining the being of Dasein, which Aristotle addresses in the *Ethics* and *Politics*; so while human being is distinct from animal being, the two are situated much more closely along a common continuum than in Heidegger's later writings.

The other major influence on Heidegger's early explorations of life is the biologist Jakob von Uexküll. Indeed, von Uexküll's insistence that the organism can only be understood in relation to and oriented toward its environment seems to have influenced his reading of Aristotle. Noting that Aristotle is assumed to be the father of the "theory of the soul as a substance," Heidegger asks:

> But what if [this assumption] rested on a fundamental misunderstanding of the sense and intention of the Aristotelian theory of the soul? There is so little of the soul as a substance, in the sense of a physical breath, housed for itself somewhere in the body and at death vanishing into the heavens, that it was precisely Aristotle who first placed the problem of the soul on its genuine ground.[77]

So rather than see the soul as something "in" the organism, Heidegger suggests that Aristotle, somewhat like von Uexküll, sees the soul as the power or potential for comportment toward a world, as a kind of intentionality.

Indeed, much like Aristotle, von Uexküll practiced biology primarily through field research, studying animal behavior in natural environments.[78] For von Uexküll, the implications of *Umwelt* research for understanding life were radical: The idea was that each animal inhabited a kind of soap bubble, an inner world, something like a first-person perspective. Von Uexküll means "inner" in the sense of inhabiting a horizon of meaning, not in the sense of locked within its own "mind" that represents a pre-given world.

As Brett Buchanan explains: "The *Umwelt* forms a figurative perimeter around the organism, 'inside' of which certain things are significant and meaningful, and 'outside' of which other things are as good as nonexistent insofar as they are 'hidden in infinity.'"[79] Animals enact and bring forth their environment; there is not just one region called the environment that is perceived differently by different organisms. As we will see below, this perspectival insight is central for the IE approach.

Von Uexküll's theory not only claimed a sphere of interiority for animals, but embraced what Buchanan calls an "intersubjective theory of nature."[80] For von Uexküll, animals do not merely perceive and react—they interpret and respond in a novel way to both their physical surroundings and other organisms. Buchanan notes how von Uexküll's ideas have been taken up by thinkers in the field of "biosemiotics." Jesper Hoffmeyer, for example, pushes intentionality all the way down, linking it to bodily movement and activity: "even amoeba, [Hoffmeyer] wants to say, anticipate their surroundings by interpreting cues and signs as meaningful, and thus suggest a kind of intentionality toward their *Umwelt*, no matter how primitive and rudimentary this may be."[81] Thus, organisms on this view must not be seen merely as passive objects in systems of causal interaction, but as interpreting subjects in networks of communication that can generate and register signs in their environment.[82] Something like this view is just what Heidegger embraced in the early 1920s, and IE regards interpretation and intersubjectivity as one of the four basic dimensions of every occasion in nature.

Drawing on his early sketches for a neo-Aristotelian ontology of life, Heidegger makes extended comments on life and animality that draw on examples from von Uexküll's research on animal *Umwelts*. For example, Heidegger concedes more to animal being in the 1924 lecture course, *Basic Concepts of Aristotelian Philosophy*, than perhaps anywhere else in his oeuvre. Here, animals are said to signal and indicate, to have *Mitsein* (being-with), and to possess world; he explicitly refers to "the being-in-the-world of animals."[83] Discussing Aristotle's treatment of "speaking" in the *Politics* and *Rhetoric*, Heidegger says of animals, "The being-possibility of animals has of itself reached this mode of being [i.e., "speaking-about"], having perception of what constitutes well-being and being-upset, being oriented toward this and indicating this to one another."[84] He specifies different kinds of animal indication a few pages later:

> Enticement and warning have, in themselves, the character of addressing itself to . . . Enticing means to bring another animal

> into the same disposition . . . [These] have in their ground being with one another. Enticing and warning already show that animals are with one another . . . Since animals indicate the threatening, or alarming, and so on, they signal, in this indicating of the being-there of the world.[85]

Granted, Heidegger will later see a deeper rift between *semantike* (meaning), which involves *nous* and Logos, and *phone* (sound), which does not, but here he nevertheless does ascribe a more robust semantic sphere to the animal.[86] Indeed, his language here sounds very similar to the "hierarchy of souls" view in the *De Anima*: there are, he says, "different gradations and levels" of world-disclosure between humans and animals.[87] It is exactly this *scala natura* language that Heidegger will eschew after *Being and Time*.

In a 1925 lecture on Dilthey, Heidegger makes some striking remarks about animal and living worlds:

> Life is that kind of reality which is in a world and indeed in such a way that it has a world. Every living creature has its environment not as something extant next to it but as something that is there for it as disclosed, uncovered. For a primitive animal, the world can be very simple. But life and its world are never two things side by side; rather, life has its world. Even in biology this kind of knowledge is slowly beginning to make headway. People are now reflecting on the fundamental structure of the animal. But we miss something essential if we don't see that the animal has a world.[88]

In a 1925–1926 lecture course, he even ventures that plants have a world in some sense, citing precedent and common ground in Aristotle and Karl von Baer:

> [E]specially in the 19th century, reference has been made to this structure [of being-in-the-world] . . . to the fact that animals above all, and plants in a certain sense, have a world. To my knowledge the first person to have run across these matters again (Aristotle had already seen them) was the biologist Karl von Baer.[89]

The upshot of his scattered remarks is that, prior to *Being and Time*, Heidegger appears decidedly open to the position that animals have world and that there is some sort of ontological continuity between human and nonhuman life. By situating Dasein in terms of Aristotle's "natural cosmos," rather than what he took to be the transcendental and anthropocentric categories of medieval and modern philosophy, Heidegger's pre–*Being and Time* writings arguably come closer to a non-reductive naturalism than anything else in the rest of his corpus.

We might be tempted to regard Heidegger's 1929–1930 lectures on biology, *Fundamental Concepts of Metaphysics*, as an idiosyncratic aside, a tangent divorced from the main currents of his philosophy. Yet he informs us that they are, in some sense, a continuation of the project of *Being and Time* because their point of departure is the concept of world. Whereas that work approached world from the perspective of humans' everyday understanding of world, in these works he explores the way that nonhuman entities are related to, or part of, or have world. When we couple this inattention to animals, plants, and material things with the bracketing of life and failure to articulate the third sense of nature, we can see that these lectures—as well as Heidegger's later musings on nature-related themes—are attempts to solve outstanding problems from *Being and Time*, especially the problem of the alterity of nature. And the key to that problem is philosophical biology.

He begins by positing that, at first glance, three theses seem self-evident: That humans are world-forming, that animals are world-poor, and that stones (material objects) are world-less. He focuses mainly on animals, since they are the ambiguous middle-case, and his analysis aims to pry apart the senses in which animals both do and do not have a world. In doing so, he draws on research in zoology and biology that seemed poised to trigger a paradigm shift in the understanding of life. He detects in the biology of his own day

> [A] fundamental tendency to restore autonomy to "life," as the specific manner of being pertaining to animal and plant, and to secure their autonomy for it. This suggests that within the totality of what we call natural science, contemporary biology is attempting to defend itself against the tyranny of physics and chemistry . . . The task confronting biology as a science is to develop an entirely new projection of the objects of its inquiry . . . [and] to liberate ourselves from the mechanistic conception of life.[90]

Heidegger points out both the importance and the difficulty of working out a "metaphysical interpretation of life," and alludes to the "inner unity of science and metaphysics."[91] This is all very tantalizing, but what I want to point out is that these lectures seem to be the closest Heidegger gets to carrying out such a project. His later works do not contain such a close collaboration with the science of his own day, an omission I consider a serious blow to his philosophy of nature; we do not see nearly the same degree of engagement with philosophical biology that we do in, say, Hans Jonas and Merleau-Ponty.[92]

In his interpretation of the organism, Heidegger proposes that we see organisms not as present-at-hand, but in terms of their potentiality. This is similar to his approach to human being, where we should approach the phenomenon in terms of its existence-possibilities, not its empirical actuality. The organism should not be divvied up into its organs and their functions and then patched back together as merely the sum of its parts; rather, the organs and parts should be seen as coordinated by its being as a whole. This is what distinguishes the organism from a machine: "Self-production in general, self-regulation and self-renewal are obviously aspects which characterize the organism over against the machine and which also illuminate the peculiar ways in which its capacity and capability . . . are directed."[93] He notes that behavior cannot be explained as immediate reactions, or the conditioned aggregate of immediate reactions, to environmental stimuli: "The regulation which always lies embedded in the capacity as such is thus a structure of instinctually organized anticipatory responses in each case which prescribes the sequence of movements."[94] This relates to the notion of drives, which have a futural aspect by which the animal is always driven away from itself toward its environment, a kind of "drive intentionality." Though the animal is driven beyond itself, it still remains within itself. Heidegger calls this behavior and captivation: "behavior is precisely an intrinsic retention and intrinsic absorption, although no reflection is involved."[95] Though the organism is more than its body, it cannot escape the closed circuit of its drives. Thus, the animal does not have genuine transcendence, like humans: It cannot recognize something *as* something. It lacks the capacities for understanding and interpretation. This is why it is world-poor, and why it is "separated from man by an abyss."[96]

Heidegger focuses on two innovations in biology: Hans Driesch's holistic view of the organism and von Üexkull's theory of animal *Umwelts*. While Driesch rescued the forest of the whole organism from the trees of its parts, he failed to see that it cannot be treated as an atomic unit in isolation from its environment. For Driesch, "the totality of the organism coincides as it were with the external surface of the animal's body."[97] Heidegger seems to think that this is what leads him, along with other vitalists, to mistakenly posit some force or entelechy internal to the organism that guides its behavior. To avoid both mechanism and a lapse into an untenable metaphysical biology, Heidegger, reiterating his ideas from the earlier Aristotle lectures, draws on von Uexküll's work to show that the organism must be seen not just as more than the sum of its parts, but as structurally coupled with its particular environment: "The organism is not something independent in its own right which then adapts itself. On the contrary, the organism adapts a particular environment *into* it in each case."[98] So the purposive behavior of the animal is grounded not in some mysterious élan vital, but in its dynamic relationship to its environment. So, much as human Dasein in *Being and Time* is reframed as always already outside of itself, entangled with the world, and not locked up in the "cabinet of consciousness," here animals are seen as constantly absorbed in their environments, driven out beyond themselves; suspended, as it were, between their body and its milieu.

Yet Heidegger ultimately resisted such a robust account of animals, denying them any kind of interiority, meaning, and intersubjectivity. But is this warranted? His phenomenological instincts make him wary of setting forth a full-blown ontology of nature without clarifying fundamental concepts, such as life and matter. Yet the momentum of his project of fundamental ontology in *Being and Time* leads to such questions, and after these 1929–1930 lectures, he never returns to them in adequate detail. What I am suggesting, then, is that his approach should have led him in the direction of a philosophy of nature that engaged the natural sciences. He seems to have been bedeviled by Toadvine's "inherent paradox of any phenomenology of nature" and the problem of alterity. He wants to avoid both positivism and anthropomorphism, but, as I have argued, in his later work he appeals to a notion of *physis* that is either a poetic construction or an unknowable thing it itself, a cosmos without a Logos; which is to say, not a cosmos at all. But this does scant justice to the spectrum of natural beings that we encounter, and the key to this, I think, is philosophical biology. Husserl avoided it, Heidegger flirted with it, but the task of integrating phenomeonology and biology would fall to Hans Jonas.

Jonas articulated what eluded Heidegger in the late 1920s: A metaphysical interpretation of life, or what he called "an existential interpretation of biological facts."[99] He seeks to show that aspects of Heidegger's account of human Dasein, such as transcendence, world, and care, can be attributed to living things as well. Life has transcendence both "outward" toward its environment, and "forward" toward its future. It is able and driven to reach out beyond itself to appropriate matter in its environment in order to sustain itself; thus it stands in a position of "needful freedom" toward a world. Philosophical biology is the place where the modern view of nature—scientific materialism—is overcome, and its replacement consists not in a sublime, chaotic, Kantian flux, but in a new understanding of intelligibility anchored in life's sense-making power. While he uses phenomenology to critique dualistic and materialist accounts of life, he rejects its metaphysical neutrality by positing what we might call a "Great Chain of Becoming," a robust vision of nature that has been called a synthesis of Aristotle, Hegel, and Darwin. It is in his neo-Aristotelian view of organisms and in his neo-Hegelian understanding of natural history that Jonas crosses over into metaphysics. For Jonas, the phenomenology of life is the gateway to a post-Kantian metaphysics of nature.

Jonas took a cue from Whitehead's view of nature as an immanently creative, self-transcending, evolving cosmos. What he finds attractive is that Whitehead's view is evolutionary through and through: "Whatever their success so far, all contemporary revisions of traditional ontology indeed start, almost axiomatically, from the conception of being as becoming, and in the phenomenon of cosmic evolution look for the key to a possible stand beyond the old alternatives."[100] This is exactly what Heidegger failed to see. The great challenge for ontology is to incorporate the notion of evolution without accepting its untenable materialist interpretation. As Jonas explains toward the outset of his masterwork:

> Aristotle read [the hierarchy of forms] in the given record of the organic realm with no resort to evolution . . . The terms on which his august example may be resumed in our time will be different from his, but the idea of stratification, of the progressive superposition of levels, with the dependence of each higher on the lower, the retention of all the lower in the higher, will still be found indispensible. One way of interpreting this scale is in terms of scope and directness of experience, of rising degrees of world perception which move toward the widest and freest objectification of the sum of being in individual percipients.[101]

Jonas's task was essentially to rewrite the *De Anima* after Darwin. Most of these concepts—the post-Kantian recasting of the Great Chain of Being, the rejection of the materialist view of evolution, the ascription of interiority to nonhumans, the correlation of increasing degrees of freedom with increasing complexity of organic form—are central to the integral approach.

We see a similar defection from classical phenomenology among another of Heidegger's (later) students: Graham Harman, inspired by Heidegger's ontology of tools, has recently developed what he calls an "object-oriented" ontology, breaking with the phenomenological preoccupation with "access" to the world and pursuing a critical realism. Harman identifies some key pivots that Continental thought needs to make: overcoming the preoccupation with "access," actually returning to things themselves ("carnal phenomenology"), and abandoning the pox on metaphysics. Harman provocatively claims that the crucial and shared prejudice of both analytic and Continental thought is that "their primary interest lies not in objects, but in human access to them. The so-called linguistic turn is still the dominant model for the philosophy of access."[102] Indeed, the obsession with methodological access is just what led Heidegger to reject a robust philosophical biology and embrace a poetic vision of nature. Harman's attempt to shift attention away from second-order questions of access to objects and the natural world is laudable. So too is his rejection of phenomenology's professed agnosticism over metaphysics: "Although phenomenology likes to disregard the dispute between realism and antirealism as both fruitless and passé, it is fully implicated in one side of this conflict—the wrong side, in fact."[103] Indeed, this is just why Heidegger falls prey to the "myth of the framework": By failing to take sides on metaphysical issues, the high ground will be seized by the scientific naturalist, who will deride all pretenders to the throne as caught in so much "poetic swooning"—precisely the dismissal with which Kant greeted Romantic biology.[104]

Despite these strengths, I think the central and serious error in Harman's approach is a failure to respect a key distinction that goes back to Aristotle (and is well heeded by Whitehead and Wilber), which we can represent in several ways: artifact vs. natural object, heap vs. whole, or machine vs. organism. Planes, trains, and automobiles—and even mountains, rivers, and rocks—are not proper individuals; they are heaps of wholes. If we do not heed this distinction and we seek to re-enchant the world, we are liable to project onto objects characteristics they do not warrant. This is exactly the error seen in some early attempts at ecophenomenology, such as David Abram's animism in *The Spell of the Sensuous*.[105] Indeed, such speculative projection is the danger against which naturalism is designed to defend. IE provides a hedge against such speculation by insisting that interiority belongs only to proper individuals, and in diminishing degrees with decreasing evolutionary complexity. Absent a robust philosophical biology, an ecophenomenology cannot build the bridge to metaphysics that Harman (correctly) desires.[106]

What if Heidegger extended his novel approach to humans to nonhuman beings? What if, after successfully critiquing the substance metaphysics that had pervaded and perverted the philosophical tradition—as well as its correlative conception of nature—Heidegger had forged a new conceptual scheme that restored not just our subjective experience of nature, but imbued subjectivity to all natural beings? If this were possible, then there would be a transition from fundamental ontology to cosmology; which is to say a conception of the being of nature that comprises humans and nonhumans. Again, while Heidegger is correct to combat the "tyranny of physics and chemistry" insofar as they reduce the phenomenon of life, this is not to say that they aren't genuine regions of being that need to be integrated in a complete account of nature. If we are to entertain pushing intentionality—albeit a very primitive mode—down to the level of amoebas, where do we stop? If we want to put forth a metaphysical or cosmological view of nature, then consistency would dictate that any being, no matter its formal complexity, possesses some degree of interiority. This is the direction taken by IE, and I turn now to summarizing some of its main points.

Integral Ecology

Integral ecology is largely based on the integral theory of American philosopher Ken Wilber. Here, I sketch some of its major conceptual innovations—especially its (meta)-methodology, value-theory, evolutionary theory, and cosmology—and suggest how it might address the problem of alterity sketched in the beginning and improve upon some of the shortcomings in Heidegger's approach.

The basic premise of integral theory is that there are four basic dimensions, or quadrants, to every occasion: There is an individual interior, an individual exterior, a collective interior, and a collective exterior. These can be referred to, respectively, as the subjective, intersubjective, objective, and interobjective domains or, more simply, as *I*, *We*, and *It/Its*.[107] Basically, the idea is that whatever phenomenon we are studying, we need to include all of these dimensions, and all of these dimensions co-arise equiprimordially. As is likely obvious, the myth of the given or positivist views of nature stem from the reduction of the interior quadrants to the exterior quadrants, and the myth of the framework or constructivist views reduce everything to the intersubjective quadrant. When it comes to ecology, Esbjörn-Hargens and Zimmerman contend that scientific ecologists and environmentalists tend to reduce the interior and objective quadrants to the interobjective quadrant, which looks at the physical systems of which organisms are a part, e.g., the energy and nutrient flows in an ecosystem. They refer to this move as "subtle reductionism," which I see as similar to what Heidegger calls *Gestell*, and what I referred to above as *ecologism*. The authors define ecology as "the mixed methods study of the subjective and objective aspects of organisms in relationship to their intersubjective and interobjective environments at all levels of depth and complexity."[108]

According to IE, it is crucial to keep in mind that as far as we know, humans are the only beings that can take up an ecological perspective, and that this should be seen as a developmental achievement. Even though all entities *possess* these basic dimensions, this does not mean that all entities can *take up* these perspectives. As the authors explain: "A human can encounter another organism 'from' and 'in' these perspectives. For example, a dog has third-person awareness (viewing objective phenomena via the five senses) but it cannot take a third-person perspective (viewing your perspective as wrong)."[109] On this basis, the authors distinguish between "quadrants" and "quadrivia." Quadrants refer to a thing's being (the perspectives it can inhabit), while *quadrivia* refer to epistemology (the perspectives *from which* something can be looked at): "in sum, quadrants highlight the four irreducible ontological dimensions that all organisms have, and quadrivia are the four fundamental epistemological perspectives that can be taken on any phenomena."[110] What emerges here is a threefold framework of observer, observation, and observed, which correlate with epistemology, methodology, and ontology: "Every definition of ecology is . . . the result of what part of reality ecologists look at, how ecologists look at that part of reality, and who they are as they look."[111] This is then translated into an ecological context, wherein the four quadrants become four ecological terrains: experience (subjective), behavior (objective), culture (intersubjective), and systems (interobjective).

For IE, the recognition of interiors is a necessary condition for holding a consistent position on values in the natural world. Here, Esbjorn-Hargens and Zimmerman identify what they call the

> fundamental paradox of environmentalism: Environmentalists value the natural world but typically subscribe to a conception of nature that either excludes value (subjective and intersubjective perspectives) or regards it as a conventional fiction useful for enhancing human survival . . . Yet if humans are merely strands in a complex state of affairs—the is—they are in no

> way capable of calling for alternative actions based on moral obligations—the ought.[112]

Like Heidegger, they pinpoint the contradiction in science's attempt to scrub the world free of intentionality; yet unlike Heidegger, they do not reject the concept of value tout court as an anthropocentric *projection* onto nature. Heidegger rejected value-theory because he saw it as inherently anthropocentric, as part and parcel of the modern project to master and conquer nature, of the vision of humans as the measure of all things. In this way, he prefigured the postmodern, non-judgmentalist, and anti-hierarchical position that characterizes much environmental thinking. IE offers a powerful critique of this way of thinking, and to understand how it does this, we need to look at its views on development and values.

For IE, it is not enough to recognize interiors; we must also acknowledge and track the ways that interiors develop. When they refer to "levels of depth and complexity," they are referring to both human psychological development and evolutionary development. Evolution, on this view, is not simply a matter of random mutation (changes in the organism, the exterior individual) and natural selection (factors in the environment, the exterior system) but also involves factors in the organism's subjective and intersubjective spaces. While different species have different degrees of interiority (an ape has more than an ant), there is considerable variation within humans. This has important consequences for how we approach ecology, because it shows how "interior development in humans determines in profound ways our relationship to the natural world."[113] How nature appears to us, and whether and in what ways it matters to us, will depend on our cognitive, emotional, and moral development; nature is not just a "social construct" but also a "psychic construct" (but never *merely* a construct). Thus, the authors draw on a large body of research in developmental psychology from Piaget, Jane Loevinger, Robert Kegan, Jean Gebser, and others in order to advance a stage-conception of the evolution of human consciousness (roughly, "archaic," "magic," "mythic," "rational," "pluralistic," and "integral"). They then plug this into the wider current of terrestrial evolution. Moreover, the authors adamantly resist historical declinist narratives of an "ecological fall from grace" that traffic in superficial denunciations of modernity and sanguine paeans to indigenous peoples. They claim that these accounts—like the vast majority of ecological discourse—are hamstrung by an ignorance of the developmental dynamics of individual and cultural psychology and a disregard for the inarguably progressive aspects of modernity—especially the birth of ecological consciousness! And this developmental, progressive vision informs IE's value-theory and distinguishes it from both Heidegger's and bioegalitarian accounts.

IE recognizes three kinds of value: ground, intrinsic, and extrinsic. Ground value is possessed equally by all organisms, and is rooted in their status as manifestations of "Spirit" (integral ecology espouses an ecotheology of "evolutionary panentheism"). Intrinsic value is based on an organism's depth of consciousness (e.g., an ape has more intrinsic value than an amoeba). Extrinsic value is based on how fundamental an organism is for others (e.g., a bacterium has more extrinsic value than a bear). This value scheme is based in part on Wilber's theory of "holarchy," which stipulates that all beings are "holons" or "whole/parts": Every being is a whole that is more than the sum of its parts, but these parts themselves are wholes comprising their own parts, and so on. A holarchy consists of vertical, hierarchical relationships *between* levels of organization, as well as horizontal, heterarchical relationships *at* all of its levels of organization. The capital distinction is between "growth" or "actualization" hierarchies, in which the senior, more encompassing holon embraces its juniors in a greater union, and "dominator" or "oppressor" hierarchies, in which the senior holon constricts the relative autonomy of its juniors. Much ecological and postmodern thought tosses out the baby of hierarchy with the bathwater of *unhealthy* hierarchy (indeed, one of Jonas's main problems with Heidegger's thought was his refusal to place humans in any *scala natura*), leading to deep confusion over values (and unconsciously smuggling in its own value-hierarchies and master narratives, since some kind of ranking and hierarchical thinking are, IE maintains, unavoidable).

IE entails a form of panpsychism and pan-semiotics, which correspond to the individual interior and collective interior quadrants. Since panpsychism is a notoriously complex issue, the authors make clear how they aim to avoid wildly implausible claims, quoting Wilber's view on the matter:

> [E]very major form of panpsychism equates "interiors" with a particular type of interior (such as feelings, awareness, soul, etc.), and then attempts to push that type all the way down to the fundamental units of the universe (quarks, atoms, strings, or some such), which I believe is unworkable . . . I am a pan-interiorist, not a pan-experientialist, pan-mentalist, pan-soulist. The forms of the interior show developmental unfolding: from fuzzy something-or-other to prehension to sensation to perception to

> impulse to image to concept to rules to rationality and so forth, but none of these go all the way down in one specific form.[114]

This approach is careful to avoid lapsing into a kind of animism that would ascribe agency or feeling to, e.g., mountains, rivers, etc., which is sometimes found in environmental literature; they *would* regard *this* as form of psychological projection, because these things are heaps, not wholes; assemblies, not entities. They do not make any heavy claims, for instance, about the precise nature of the interiority of a cell. But to be consistent, they suppose that interiority does indeed go all the way down.

As for pan-semiotics, the authors draw on the work of thinkers from Saussure to Charles Peirce to von Uexküll, to contemporary biosemiotics to propose an intersubjective theory of nature. As they write, "The universality of signaling indicates the cosmos is intelligible from the bottom up and that interiority is present from the bottom up . . . This position is a form of pansemiotics as described by Charles S. Peirce, which sees the universe as permeated with meaning at all levels of organization."[115] What they are proposing, in other words, is that the biosemiotic approach pioneered by von Uexküll and developed by others is a potential gateway for a new approach to cosmology; a fresh way to understand the intelligibility of nature, and, as such, a hedge against the black hole of alterity theory.

Indeed, one of the keys to IE is its careful parsing of the very word *nature*. One of the chief problems in ecological discourse, the authors suggest, is the ambiguous use of the term *nature*:

> [W]e offer three definitions, which we label as NATURE, Nature, and nature. NATURE includes the whole Kosmos in all its dimensions, including interiors and exteriors . . . Nature refers to the exterior domains of the Kosmos, the domains that are studied by the natural and some of the social sciences . . . Finally, nature means the empirical-sensory world in two different but related uses: the exterior world disclosed by the five senses (and their extentions), and the interior world disclosed by feelings . . . as contrasted with the rational mind and with culture.[116]

This threefold distinction is one of the hallmarks of the IE approach. This distinction exposes and dispels confusions riddling not only ecological discourse, but issues plaguing fields such as the philosophy of mind. For instance, Wilber notes that "nature is in the mind, but the brain is in Nature."[117] What Romantics and many ecophilosophers praise as somatic and emotional feelings of harmony and identification with the natural world—in contrast to purportedly dualistic, dissociative rationality—actually exist in "nature" (in prerational subjective awareness), but they often interpret this as though it indicates that humans are a part of "Nature" (the exterior objective world) and call it "holistic." In doing so, they are unwittingly ceding the terrain of interiority to the very mechanistic materialist view they are trying to transcend. According to IE, with the widespread emergence of rational-egoic consciousness—or the "noosphere"—in modernity, humans gradually began to approach nature merely in the second sense, giving birth to the scientific vision of nature as a mechanical system governed by laws of efficient causality. As Wilber notes,

> [O]nce we focus on Nature (or the entire sensory and empirical world), it becomes very hard to grasp how the noosphere transcends the biosphere, which transcends the physiosphere. For those distinctions rest in part on *interior* domains . . . When all interiors are reduced to exteriors, one can no longer recognize degrees of interior depth, and thus everything becomes equally a strand in the great interlocking web of valueless its. Everything is part of Nature.[118]

Desperate to supplant the old paradigm of mechanistic atomism, "holists" merely replace one substratum with another; instead of "atoms," we get "energy." Distributions or fields of energy now fill the role of serving as the "deep structure" of reality—in the form of food chains, quanta, biofeedback mechanisms, ecosystems, etc. All of this is motivated by a desire to reinsert the alienated subject and/organism back into "Nature." This approach is doomed from the outset, precisely because it fails to distinguish between interior subject and exterior organism. Wilber comments on the source of this mistake:

> The confusing part is that the exterior of the noosphere exists in Nature, but not in nature. And thus, the relation of the mind to the natural world depends on whether you mean nature or Nature . . . If you reduce all interiors to exteriors . . . it then appears that Nature includes everything, so of course the mind is just part of Nature . . . The brain exists in Nature. But the mind does not exist in Nature.[119]

Wilber's basic point is that as soon as we reduce the mind to the brain, or cultural meanings to social structures, we generate a slew of problems over how to integrate mind and body, or culture and nature. He connects this equivocation over nature to another semantic confusion: that over "inside" and "internal." The brain is very clearly *inside* the body, but the body is *internal* to the mind. Like Heidegger, IE's careful delineation of the multiple meanings of the term nature is intended to dethrone the dominant sense in modern discourse ("nature"); but, unlike Heidegger, it tries to restore a sense of the natural world as a tiered, evolving cosmos ("NATURE") that transcends and includes these partial senses of nature.

Lastly, I want to circle back to Heidegger. I mentioned that one of the flaws of his philosophy of nature is that it did not incorporate any account of evolution. Heidegger was obviously opposed to Darwinism, since it seemed to entail a scientific naturalism that phenomenology aims to critique. But this is not grounds to throw the baby of evolution out with the bathwater of Darwinism. There are other ways of conceiving evolution, and IE tries to do just this, setting forth an emergent view that takes into account causation in all four quadrants, not merely the exterior ones (which roughly correspond to random mutation in the physical organism [individual exterior] and successful adaption or functional fit with the exterior environment [collective exterior], as found in neo-Darwinism). As Esbjörn-Hargens and Zimmerman explain:

> [Our] evolutionary theory involves not only sexual selection and environmental pressures but organisms interpreting their environment and one another as well as experiencing themselves. So not only is it survival of the strongest and fittest but survival of the best interpreter and experiencer. Biosemiotics provides a powerful critique of neo-Darwinism's . . . emphasis by claiming that interpretation is the primary drive of evolution.[120]

They further explain how biosemiotics changes the game: "Biosemiotics emphasizes that sign production and interpretation are fundamental to organisms."[121] While this is certainly a controversial theory, I think it is a start for fashioning a theory of evolution that does justice to modern biology without reducing the sphere of sense and meaning addressed by Continental approaches such as Heidegger's.

To recap and sum up: I have suggested that Heidegger 1) fails to formulate a cosmology because he does not integrate his primordial and objective senses of nature and he neglects philosophical biology; 2) neglects to elaborate any notion of evolution because he thinks it necessarily entails naturalism, which fails to appreciate the significance of both being and human being; and 3) avoids panpsychism and value-theory because he thinks of them as forms of humanism, the projection of human categories onto nonhuman beings. I have argued that these aspects make integral ecology a more promising alternative than Heidegger's approach. I think that integral ecology points us in the right direction of recovering what we saw Toadvine allude to in the start as the lack common to positivist and constructivist views: Namely, a notion of nature and natural beings with a dimension of meaning or sense in themselves that is accessible by, but not reducible to, human understanding. We get *relative* alterity, but not *absolute* alterity. In such a view, we can be a part of nature without reducing ourselves to *mere* nature (in the objective sense), and nature (in the fuller sense of *physis* or cosmos) can have meaning independently of our own intentionality and interpretation. Moreover, we can incorporate the premodern view of nature as a Great Chain of Being (by converting static, eternal planes of being to creative, evolutionary emergents via Peirce's view of cosmic habits), the modern view of nature as driven by evolutionary pressures (by recognizing non-mechanistic dimensions), and the postmodern view of nature as conditioned by cultural matrices (by recognizing that interior perspectives extend beyond the human sphere and that they undergo stage-like development).

Notes

1. For a primer on eco-phenomenology, see Ted Toadvine, *Eco-Phenomenology: Back to the Earth Itself* (Albany, NY: SUNY Press, 2007). For the seminal work in IE, see Sean Esbjörn-Hargens and Michael Zimmerman, *Integral Ecology: Uniting Multiple Perspectives on the Natural World* (Boston: Integral Books, 2009). Hereafter I will abbreviate this work as IE. For the classical account of integral philosophy, see Ken Wilber, *Sex, Ecology, Spirituality: The Spirit of Evolution* (Boston: Shambhala Press, 2000).

2. Ted Toadvine, *Merleau-Ponty's Philosophy of Nature* (Chicago: Northwestern University Press, 2009), 5.

3. Lewis, 39.

4. Keith Campbell, 492–495, 492.

5. De Caro and Macarthur, 10.

6. Ibid., 3.

7. Ibid., 4.

8. Toadvine (2009), 13.
9. Ibid., 15.
10. *IE*, 170.
11. Ibid., 171.
12. Toadvine (2009), 52.
13. Ibid., 276.
14. Ibid., 272.
15. The most comprehensive account of Heidegger's philosophy of nature is Bruce V. Foltz, *Inhabiting the Earth: Heidegger, Environmental Ethics, and the Metaphysics of Nature* (Atlantic Highlands, NJ: Humanities Press, 1995).
16. See Hubert Dreyfus, *Being-in-the-World: A Commentary of Heidegger's* Being and Time, *Division I (*Cambridge, MA: MIT Press, 1991).
17. *Being and Time*, 101.
18. *IE*, 29. In section four, I expand on IE's semantics of the term nature.
19. Whitehead, 80.
20. *IE*, 35. I explain this view in more detail in section four.
21. Ibid., 143.
22. Ibid., 109.
23. Ibid., 120. Dreyfus illustrates this using the example of iron: "Dasein . . . appropriates iron into its referential whole. It can be used in hammer heads, nails, anvils . . . etc. Yet, of course, nature cannot be used in any way whatsoever. Occurrent [i.e., present-at-hand] nature sets limits as to what can be done with equipment. Given iron's causal powers and determinate properties, it cannot be used for fuel or a nourishing meal." (111).
24. Ibid., 111.
25. *Being and Time*, 101.
26. Ibid., 101.
27. Dreyfus, 110.
28. *Being and Time*, 101.
29. Ibid., 102.
30. Ibid., 42. Note the connection with Toadvine's inherent paradox of a phenomenology of nature mentioned above.
31. Haar, 10.
32. Taminiaux, 128.
33. Quoted by Foltz, 38.
34. Michael Zimmerman, *Contesting Earth's Future: Radical Ecology and Postmodernity* (Berkeley, CA: University of California Press, 1994), 119; my emphasis. I will return to the notion of cosmology as a promising prospect for environmental philosophy—and an option Heidegger unfortunately forgoes—in later chapters.
35. There is a curious parallel here with Kant's third critique: Kant left aesthetic judgment and a nonscientific conception of nature out of the transcendental analytic, much like Heidegger left them out of his existential analytic.

36. Haar, 6.

37. Parkes, 142, n. 26.

38. Martin Heidegger, "The Origin of the Work of Art," in *Heidegger: Basic Writings*, ed. David Farrell Krell (New York: HarperCollins, 1977), 168. Hereafter abbreviated "Origin."

39. *IE*, 164.

40. Ibid., 165.

41. Bowler, 540.

42. *IE*, 9.

43. "Origin," 160.

44. *Being and Time*, 100.

45. Ibid., 172.

46. *Being and Time*, 231.

47. Taminiaux, 128.

48. "*Origin*," 170.

49. Ibid., 167.

50. Ibid., 168.

51. Ibid., 173.

52. Ibid., 173.

53. Ibid., 188.

54. Martin Heidegger, *Aristotle's* Metaphysics *[Theta] 1–3: On the Essence and Actuality of Force*, trans. Walter Brogan and Peter Warnek (Bloomington, IN: Indiana University Press, 1995).

55. Haar, 108.

56. "*Origin*," 195.

57. It is strange, though, that Heidegger did not parlay this insight that "art completes nature" into a more biological notion that human beings are the continuation and extension of a process of life developing in and as nature.

58. Haar, 60.

59. Ibid., 170.

60. Martin Heidegger, "Letter on Humanism," in *Basic Writings*, 228.

61. Caputo, 126.

62. The seminal book on the concept of will in Heidegger's thought is Bret Davis, *Heidegger and the Will: On the Way Toward Gelassenheit* (Evanston, IL: Northwestern University Press, 2007).

63. Michael Zimmerman, "Toward a Heideggerian Ethos for Radical Environmentalism," *Environmental Ethics*, vol. 6, no. 2 (1983): 99–131; "Marx and Heidegger on the Technological Domination of Nature," *Philosophy Today* 23 (Summer 1979): 99–112; "Implications of Heidegger's Thought for Deep Ecology," in *The Modern Schoolman* 64 (November 1986): 19–43). See also Laura Westra, "Let It Be: Heidegger and Future Generations," *Environmental Ethics* 7, no. 4 (1985): 341–350, who makes a similar argument that Heidegger's non-hierarchical view of

nature and of humans as "freeing" things to exist in their own way offers a sounder basis than utilitarian or rights-based ethics for protecting future generations of humans and nonhumans.

64. Devall and Sessions, 98–100.

65. Tracy Colony, "Dwelling in the Biosphere? Heidegger's Critique of Humanism and Its Relevance for Ecological Thought," *International Studies in Philosophy* 31, no. 1 (1999): 37–45.

66. Nancy Holland, "Rethinking Ecology in the Western Philosophical Tradition: Heidegger and/on Aristotle," *Continental Philosophy Review* 32 (1999): 409–240.

67. Charles Taylor, "Heidegger, Language, and Ecology," in *Heidegger: A Critical Reader*, ed. Hubert Dreyfus (Cambridge, MA: Blackwell, 1992).

68. See the essays in Ladelle McWhorter, ed., *Heidegger and the Earth* (Kirksville, MO: Thomas Jefferson University Press, 1992).

69. See Michael Zimmerman, *Contesting Earth's Future* and "Rethinking the Heidegger–Deep Ecology Relationship," *Environmental Ethics* 15 (1993): 95–224; Foltz and DeLuca, cited above; Leslie Paul Thiele, "Nature and Freedom: A Heideggerian Critique of Biocentric and Sociocentric Environmentalism," *Environmental Ethics* 17, no. 2 (1995): 171–190; Stephen Avery, "The Misbegotten Child of Deep Ecology," *Environmental Values* 13, no. 1 (February 2004), 31–50; Daniel Dombrowski, "Heidegger's Anti-Anthropocentrism," *Between the Species*, vol. 10, no. 1–2 (1994): 26–38.

70. As I explain in section four, Wilber attempts in his integral theory to account for how this split between the interior and the exterior, or subjective and objective, or facts and interpretations, occurred, and how it can be healed.

71. See Graham Harman, *Guerrilla Metaphysics: Phenomenonology and the Carpentry of Things* (Chicago: Open Court, 2005). I return to Harman's view below.

72. Krell, 35.

73. Heidegger (1999, 2001, 2002, 2008, 2009).

74. Heidegger (2008), 153.

75. Ibid., 156.

76. Ibid., 228.

77. Ibid., 154.

78. Jakob von Uexküll, *A Foray into the Worlds of Animals and Humans: With a Theory of Meaning*, trans. Joseph A. O'Neil (Minneapolis, MN: University of Minnesota Press, 2010).

79. Buchanan, 23–24.

80. Ibid., 28.

81. Ibid., 35.

82. For an excellent article critiquing Heidegger for falling prey to the "prejudice of the lone animal," i.e., ignoring the intrinsically social dimension of animals, which draws on research in neuroscience and cognitive ethology, see Morris (2005). For a defense of animal minds on Heideggerian grounds, see James (2009).

83. Heidegger (2009), 39.

84. Ibid., 33.

85. Ibid., 39.

86. For a discussion of the human-animal distinction along these lines, see Elden, 280.

87. Heidegger (2009), 37.

88. Cited by Buchanan, 92–93. By "biology" Heidegger seems to be referring to anti-Darwinist trends led by von Uexküll.

89. Heidegger (2010), 215–16, my emphasis. Heidegger's dismissal of von Uexküll here is based on a facile distinction between "philosophy" and "biological research. As Buchanan demonstrates, von Uexküll's understanding of animal *Umwelt* was based on a creative application of Kant's first critique. See Buchanan, Chapter 1. Incidentally, Heidegger's dismissal of Darwinism may very well be a function of von Uexküll's uncharitable interpretation of Darwin.

90. *FCM*, 188–189.

91. Ibid., 189.

92. I discuss Jonas below. Merleau-Ponty also learned from von Uexküll. See his *Nature: Course Notes from the Collège de France* (Evanston, IL: Northwestern University Press, 2003).

93. *FCM*, 222.

94. Ibid., 229.

95. Ibid., 238.

96. Ibid., 264.

97. Ibid., 262.

98. Ibid., 264.

99. Hans Jonas, *The Phenomenon of Life* (Evanston, IL: Northwestern University Press, 2001), 1.

100. Ibid., 58.

101. Ibid., 2.

102. Harman, 1.

103. Ibid., 4.

104. For a magisterial history of biology in the Romantic age, see Robert J. Richards, *The Romantic Conception of Life: Science and Philosophy in the Age of Goethe* (Chicago: University of Chicago Press, 2002).

105. David Abram, *The Spell of the Sensuous: Perception and Language in a More-Than-Human World* (New York: Pantheon Books, 1996). Esbjörn-Hargens and Zimmerman expose the error in this way of thinking, which tries to enchant nature by criminalizing human innovations in language that purportedly robbed nature of its "voice": "[T]o claim that the artifact of the written alphabet served to remove us from nature is analogous to claiming that an anthill separates ants from nature. Imbedded in this thinking is the very dualism that the holistic approaches are trying to overcome. Language is in fact a development within Nature" (*Integral*

Ecology, 560n. 12).

106. This is precisely what Evan Thompson does attempt in his tour de force, *Mind in Life: Biology, Phenomenology, and the Sciences of Mind* (Cambridge, MA: Belknap Press, 2007). Like IE, Thompson embraces the enactive approach and extends it to nonhuman living things.

107. Interestingly, this also roughly echoes one of Heidegger's early formulations of being-in-the-world: a threefold phenomenon of *Selbstwelt* (self-world), *Mitwelt* (with-world), and *Umwelt* (around-world). However, IE places Heidegger's analysis as a first-personal, phenomenological perspective *on* the interior-individual, interior-collective, and exterior quadrants; it does not enjoy any sort of methodological priority.

108. *IE*, 11.

109. Ibid., 557.

110. Ibid., 58.

111. Ibid., 170.

112. Ibid., 11.

113. Ibid., 7.

114. Ibid., 545.

115. Ibid., 40.

116. Ibid., 25–26.

117. Ibid., 28.

118. *Sex, Ecology, Spirituality*, 455.

119. Ibid., 493.

120. *IE*, 570.

121. Ibid., 602.

References

Abram, David. 1996. *The Spell of the Sensuous*. New York: Pantheon Books.

Avery, Stephen. 2004. "The Misbegotten Child of Deep Ecology." *Environmental Values 13*(1): 31–50.

Bowler, Peter. 1992. *The Norton History of the Environmental Sciences*. New York: W.W. Norton.

Brown, Charles S., and Ted Toadvine (eds.). 2003. *Eco-phenomenology: Back to the Earth Itself.* Albany, NY: SUNY Press.

Buchanan, Brett. 2008. *Onto-ethologies: The Animal Environments of Uexküll, Heidegger, Merleau-Ponty, and Deleuze*. Albany, NY: SUNY Press.

Campbell, Keith. "Naturalism." 2005. In *Encyclopedia of Philosophy, Volume 6*, ed. Donald Borchert, 492–495. New York: Macmillan Reference.

Caputo, John D. 1993. *Demythologizing Heidegger*. Bloomington, IN: Indiana University Press.

Colony, Tracy. "Dwelling in the Biosphere? Heidegger's Critique of Humanism and Its Relevance for Ecological Thought." *International Studies in Philosophy* 31(1): 37–45.

Cooper, David. 2005. "Heidegger on Nature." *Environmental Values* 14(3): 339–351.

Davis, Bret W. 2007. *Heidegger and the Will: On the Way to Gelassenheit.* Evanston, IL: Northwestern University Press.

De Caro, Mario, and David Macarthur (eds.) 2004. *Naturalism in Question.* Cambridge, MA: Harvard University Press.

DeLuca, Kevin Michael. 2005. "Thinking with Heidegger: Rethinking Environmental Theory and Practice." *Ethics and the Environment* 10(1): 67–87.

Devall, Bill, and George Sessions. 1985. *Deep Ecology: Living as if Nature Mattered.* Salt Lake City, UT: Peregrine Smith Books.

Dreyfus, Hubert. 1991. *Being-in-the-World: A Commentary of Heidegger's* Being and Time, *Division I.* Cambridge, MA: MIT Press.

Elden, Stuart. 2006. "Heidegger's Animals." *Continental Philosophy Review* 39: 273–291.

Esbjörn-Hargens, Sean, and Michael Zimmerman. 2009. *Integral Ecology: Uniting Multiple Perspectives on the Natural World.* New York: Integral Books.

Foltz, Bruce V. 1995. *Inhabiting the Earth: Heidegger, Environmental Ethics, and the Metaphysics of Nature.* Atlantic Highlands, NJ: Humanities Press.

Haar, Michel. 1993. *The Song of the Earth: Heidegger and the Grounds of the History of Being.* Bloomington, IN: Indiana University Press.

Harman, Graham. 2005. *Guerrilla Metaphysics: Phenomenonology and the Carpentry of Things.* Chicago: Open Court.

Heidegger, Martin. 1995. *Aristotle's Metaphysics [Theta] 1–3: On the Essence and Actuality of Force,* trans. Walter Brogan and Peter Warnek. Bloomington, IN: Indiana University Press.

Heidegger, Martin. 2009. *Basic Concepts of Aristotelian Philosophy,* trans. Robert D. Metcalf and Mark B. Tanzer. Bloomington, IN: Indiana University Press.

Heidegger, Martin. 1977. *Basic Writings,* ed. David Farrell Krell. New York: Harper & Row.

Heidegger, Martin. 1962. *Being and Time,* trans. John Macquarrie and Edward Robinson. New York: Harper & Row.

Heidegger, Martin. 2001. *Phenomenological Interpretations of Aristotle,* trans. Richard Rojcewicz. Bloomington, IN: Indiana University Press.

Heidegger, Martin. 2001. *The Fundamental Concepts of Metaphysics,* trans. William McNeill. Bloomington, IN: Indiana University Press.

Heidegger, Martin. 1977. *The Question Concerning Technology and Other Essays,* trans. William Lovitt. New York: Harper & Row.

Holland, Nancy. 1999. "Rethinking Ecology in the Western Philosophical Tradition: Heidegger and/on Aristotle." *Continental Philosophy Review* 32: 409–420.

James, Simon. 2009. *The Presence of Nature: A Study in Phenomenology and Environmental Philosophy.* New York: Palgrave Macmillan.

Jonas, Hans. 1966. *The Phenomenon of Life.* New York: Harper & Row.

Kohak, Erazim. 1984. *The Embers and the Stars: A Philosophical Inquiry into the Moral Sense of Nature.* Chicago: University of Chicago Press.

Krell, David Farrell. 1992. *Daimon Life: Heidegger and Life-Philosophy.* Bloomington, IN: Indiana University Press.

Lewis, C.S. 1980. *Mere Christianity.* New York: HarperCollins.

McWhorter, Ladelle (ed.). 1992. *Heidegger and the Earth.* Kirksville, MO: Thomas Jefferson University Press.

Merleau-Ponty, Maurice. 2003. *Nature: Course Notes from the Collége de France.* Evanston, IL: Northwestern University Press.

Merleau-Ponty, Maurice. 1963. *The Structure of Behavior*, trans. Alden Fisher. Boston: Beacon Press

Parkes, Graham (ed.). 1987. *Heidegger and Asian Thought.* Honolulu, HI: University of Hawaii Press.

Richards, Robert J. 2002. *The Romantic Conception of Life: Science and Philosophy in the Age of Goethe.* Chicago: University of Chicago Press.

Taminiaux, Jacques. 1991. *Heidegger and the Project of Fundamental Ontology*, trans. Michael Gendre. Albany, NY: SUNY Press.

Taylor, Charles. 1992. "Heidegger, Language, and Ecology." In *Heidegger: A Critical Reader*, ed. Hubert Dreyfus, 246–259. Cambridge, MA: Blackwell.

Thiele, Leslie Paul. "Nature and Freedom: A Heideggerian Critique of Biocentric and Sociocentric Environmentalism." *Environmental Ethics* 17(2): 171–190.

Thompson, Evan. 2007. *Mind in Life: Biology, Phenomenology, and the Sciences of Mind.* Cambridge, MA: Harvard University Press.

Toadvine, Ted. 2009. *Merleau-Ponty's Philosophy of Nature.* Evanston, IL: Northwestern University Press.

von Uexküll, Jakob. 2010. *A Foray into the Worlds of Animals and Humans: With a Theory of Meaning*, trans. Joseph A. O'Neil. Minneapolis, MN: University of Minnesota Press.

Vogel, Steven. 1996. *Against Nature: the Concept of Nature in Critical Theory.* Albany, NY: SUNY Press.

Westra, Laura. "Let It Be: Heidegger and Future Generations." *Environmental Ethics* 7(4): 341–350.

Whitehead, Alfred North. 1997. *Science and the Modern World.* New York: Free Press.

Wilber, Ken. 2000. *Sex, Ecology, Spirituality: The Spirit of Evolution.* Boston: Shambhala.

Young, Julian. 2002. *Heidegger's Later Philosophy.* New York: Cambridge University Press.

Zimmerman, Michael E. 1994. *Contesting Earth's Future: Radical Ecology and Postmodernity.* Berkeley, CA: University of California Press.

Zimmerman, Michael E. 1990. *Heidegger's Confrontation with Modernity.* Bloomington, IN: Indiana University Press.

Zimmerman, Michael E. 1986. "Implications of Heidegger's Thought for Deep Ecology." *The Modern Schoolman* 64: 19–43.

Zimmerman, Michael E. 1979. "Marx and Heidegger on the Technological Domination of Nature." *Philosophy Today* 23: 99–112.

Zimmerman, Michael E. 1993. "Rethinking the Heidegger–Deep Ecology Relationship." *Environmental Ethics* 15: 95–224.

Zimmerman, Michael E. 1983. "Toward a Heideggerian Ethos for Radical Environmentalism." *Environmental Ethics* 6(2): 106.

Chapter 6

Dancing on the Verge

Schelling, Dōgen, and Integral Thinking

Jason M. Wirth

> Dancing fully and divine in every gesture of the universe, never really lost and never really found, but present from the start all along, a wink and a nod from the radiant Abyss.
>
> —Ken Wilber (2000, p. 516)

> What we call nature [NATURE] is a poem that lies locked in a mysterious, wondrous script. Yet the enigma could unveil itself if we would recognize the Odyssey of the spirit within it, which, in seeking itself, wondrously deceived, flees from itself.
>
> —F.W.J. Schelling (1992, p. 299)

This essay brings Schelling's *Naturphilosophie*—esteemed by Wilber—into dialogue with integral ecology by way of Dōgen Zenji's (1200–1253) transrational practices. I do so by taking the two figures evoked by the present book's title (philosophy on the verge and σοφία dancing) seriously enough to allow them the space to play themselves out.

Ecosophical integration—NATURE: Dancing fully and divine in every gesture of the universe! One need only think of Śiva, the *nataraja*, the lord of the dance, whose performance of the *tāṇḍava* is the blissful dance of the simultaneous creation, destruction, and preservation of the universe

(NATURE).[1] Immanuel Kant in a footnote in section 49 of the *Kritik der Urteilskraft* ("*Von den Vermögen des Gemüts*") also invoked an ancient tripartite articulation of NATURE by emphasizing its temporality: "Perhaps there has never been something more sublime said or a thought expressed more sublimely than that inscription over the Temple of Isis (of Mother Nature):[2] 'I am everything that there is, that there was, and that there will be, and no mortal has lifted my veil.' "[3] F.W.J. Schelling, in his unfinished opus, *The Ages of the World*, also echoed this ancient formulation:

> No consciousness whatsoever can be thought in an empty, abstract eternity. The consciousness of eternity can only be articulated in the phrase: "I am the one who was, who is, who will be." Or, more intimately, with the untranslatable word that the highest God gave to Moses and which in the original language expresses with the same word the various meanings: "I am the one who was, I was who I will be, I will be who I am." (I/8, 263–264)[4]

Such ancient language, however, even when reaffirmed by Schelling and Kant, still tends to strike me as irredeemably archaic and hopelessly quaint. This is still a time in which the Enlightenment decimation of NATURE into a "flatlined" scientific "Nature" and the Romantic yearning to escape the iron cage of Nature into "nature," still wreaks havoc, philosophically and ecologically, with NATURE.[5] It is also worth noting, however, that Wilber—in the opening passage that serves as one of my two epigraphs—is explicitly invoking Schelling, who attempted to preserve the question of NATURE from both its rationalistic overdetermination and the dissolution of rationality into fanaticism and the autocracy of communion-hungry affect. (This is not to deny the power of the analysis of the surfaces of Nature or the welcome respite of nature, but it is to take critical exception to the reduction or "flatlining" of NATURE to this consequent dualism.) As Wilber warned, "Once we focus on Nature . . . it becomes very hard to grasp how the noosphere transcends the biosphere, which transcends the physiosphere." (Wilber, p. 455)

Schelling did not engage in a reactionary response to the emergence of science, but rather fought *for* the heart of science and *against* the modern reduction of NATURE to Nature. Ironically, "natural science"—at least in its preeminent modern, positivistic version—is the loss of NATURE. Moreover, despite being considered a Romantic, Schelling also struggled against the Romantic yearning for an affective communion with "nature" as the proper response to the loss of NATURE symptomatic of the modern rise of Nature. In the 1809 *Freedom* essay, Schelling warned against the abdication of reason and thinking, dismissing it as the incapacity to find the "reconciling and mediating basis" without which one declines into the "gloomy and wild enthusiasm that breaks out in self-mutilation or, as with the priests of the Phrygian goddess, auto castration, which is achieved in Philosophy as the renunciation of reason and science" (I/7, 357). Schelling sought to navigate the Scylla and Charybdis of positivism (loss of the depths) and the worst excesses of Romanticism (the wholesale abandonment of reason in favor of a reactionary desire for the feeling of communion with lost Nature), while not abandoning the powerful insights and discoveries of either. The challenge for Schelling, and for integral ecology, is to think everything together without excluding anything and without collapsing into the destructiveness of any of the many prevailing monocultures of thinking. (Flatlining reduces the complexity of NATURE to one of its aspects and is, as such, not therefore wholly false, but it does suffer the unsustainability of any monoculture.) Schelling demonstrates this in his 1799 retrieval of the ancient question of NATURE within a context that does not reject what is powerful about the modern conception of Nature: "*Nature* as a mere *product* (*natura naturata*) we call Nature as *object* (with this alone all empiricism deals). *Nature as productivity* (*natura naturans*) we call *Nature as subject*" (I/3, 284).[6] Schelling's *Naturphilosophie* did more than try to retrieve what Wilber called the "interior" (SES, pp. 454–455) of NATURE (what Schelling here calls Nature as subject). It attempted to understand the latter as the inseparable belonging together and "indifference" (or we might say, to avoid misunderstanding, non-duality) of the subjective depths *and* its external products.[7] Moreover, it tried to understand their inseparable conjunction as the dynamic progressivity of their temporal force. NATURE is the unity of subjective and objective nature, *natura* as the non-duality of *naturans* and *naturata*. One can see here that Schelling repurposes Spinoza's distinction between the two valences of nature (*naturata* and *naturans*) to articulate the two dimensions of NATURE: nature as it has come to be (what can be seen and empirically studied) and Nature in its coming to be (the interior depth of nature as the productive abyss of nature whose future surfaces are always still to come).[8]

I would also like to reflect here on the problem of *Naturphilosophie* and integral ecology by taking the title of this volume seriously. It speaks of this ancient, but still contested, site by introducing the matter for thinking with two remarkable and evocative phrases. It speaks of *integral philosophy on the verge*, but on the verge of what? Of something new? For Schelling, thinking was paradoxically ever anew on the verge, despite its sublimation by modern philosophy, of the most ancient, of forces as old as the forces of time itself:

> How utterly modern this manner of representation is could be easily shown. For the entirety of our modern philosophy only dates as if it were from yesterday. For its originator, Descartes, completely rent the living interrelation with earlier developments and wanted to construct philosophy all over from the beginning, exclusively in accordance with the concepts of his time, as if no one before him had thought or philosophized. Since then, there is only a coherent and logically consistent further development of one and the same fundamental error which has spun itself forth into all of the various systems up to and including the most contemporary ones. It is in itself backwards to apply this utterly modern standard to what has broken itself from all interrelation to the past in order to reconnect oneself again with the truly ancient and the truly most ancient. (I/8, 270)

This is not a nostalgic urge for ancient and reactionary formulations, but rather the call to rearticulate as a living question, to be on the verge of, the most ancient of problems.

This phrase, *integral philosophy on the verge*, in turn elucidates the lead phrase *dancing with Sophia*. How does one engage in this most ancient dance? This dance itself assumes that σοφία is also dancing, but what does it mean to say that σοφία is dancing? This essay also seeks to develop these two phrases through the interrelated lenses of Schelling and Zen practice (especially Dōgen). These two reflections will be in the service of a broader question: *What does it mean to philosophize in an integral manner?* Or one can rephrase the question: *How is philosophy at its heart an ecology of thinking?* As Gregory Bateson warned, "There is an ecology of bad ideas, just as there is an ecology of weeds, and it is characteristic of the system that basic error propagates itself."[9] If we desire a healthy ecology of mind, we have to again ask one of philosophy's most pressing and difficult, but rarely posed, problems: Namely, *what is philosophy?* That one would feel compelled to ask about the possibilities of an integral philosophy assumes that philosophy is not (or has not been) necessarily integrated, that it can restrict its domain by fiat, acting as if what it does, precisely because it does it, is what it is to do philosophy. The founding violence of the arrogation of a certain moment of philosophy as the whole of philosophy is soon normalized and given the veneer of legitimacy by the habitual repetition of these normalized practices. Moreover, the implication of a reductionist and often politically impotent philosophy with the unprecedented degradation of the earth suggests that we have curtailed and restricted the range and resources of philosophy at our own—as well as the Earth's—peril.

In what follows, I will develop my dialogue between *Naturphilosophie* and integral ecology by allowing these two figures—philosophy on the verge and σοφία dancing—to shape my reflections

On the verge of the verge—I begin my development of these two phrases as a means of delineating an integral mode of philosophizing, not by tediously rehearsing the basic tenets of integral ecology, but rather by pursuing the latter as the reemergence of philosophy as something like what Arne Naess and Félix Guattari, each in their own respective fashions, called *ecosophy*. Guattari was especially adept and generous at extricating the ecosophical from its deflation in the "purely technological perspective" and returning it to its "three ecological registers (the environment, social relations and human subjectivity)" (TE, p. 28). As Guattari elsewhere poses the question:

> How do we change mentalities, how do we reinvent social practices that would give back to humanity—if it ever had it—a sense of responsibility, not only for its survival, but equally for the future of all life on the planet, for animal and vegetable species? Likewise for incorporeal species such as music, the arts, cinema, the relationship with time, love and compassion for others, the feeling of fusion at the heart of the cosmos?[10]

Ecosophical integration is another way of articulating what is at stake—everything!—in integral ecology and its "study of the subjective and objective aspects of organisms in relationship to their intersubjective and interobjective environments at all levels of depth and complexity" (IE, pp. 168–169).[11] Guattari's "three ecological registers," which includes the multiplicity of subjectivities and their intersubjective and interobjective relations, becomes integral ecology's quadrants (subjective, objective, intersubjective, and interobjective).[12]

These comprise the evolutionarily dynamic multiplicity of NATURE—"everything in the Kosmos" without the unwarranted reduction to the more limited planes of "Nature," i.e., all of the visible surfaces, and "nature," i.e., the affective and "nonrational experience of being away from our typical socio-cultural environment" (IE, p. 27). NATURE cannot be altogether flatlined to the allure of its surface (what Spinoza called *natura naturata* and what scientists study as an allegedly "objective" reality). The grind of the objective world, with its increasing agonized global dimensions, including the flattening of all values into global market values, makes "nature" a welcome respite, but its alterity is a mere phantom of NATURE. The former contests the routinization and mechanization of the so-called "objective world," but, as its alleged opposite, it is a mere alternative, not a fundamental challenge. It does not twist free from what Heidegger famously spoke of as the age of the *Gestell* and the diminishment of being to *Bestand* (the standing reserve). Although NATURE includes *natura naturata* (the objective surfaces of Nature and the spectral return of NATURE in a hike as "nature"), it includes the interiority of the earth, *natura naturans*, as well as the interiority of its participants, as well as the complex interaction between and among participants and a dependently co-originating earth. NATURE is spoken of as if it were one, but it has multiply singular points of access, forming the oneness (nothing excluded) of irreducible difference (the sharing of singularity). As Jean-Luc Nancy argued, the singular cannot be individual (it is what the community of the earth shares together) and hence we can speak of NATURE as being singular plural:

> But this circulation goes in all directions at once, in all the directions of all the space-times opened by presence to presence: all things, all beings, all entities, everything past and future, alive, dead, inanimate, stones, plants, nails, gods—and "humans," that is, those who expose sharing and circulation as such by saying "we," by saying we to themselves in all possible senses of that expression, and by saying we for the totality of all being.[13]

Ken Wilber, and following him, Esbjörn-Hargens and Zimmerman, locates one of the great battlegrounds for the idea of NATURE in the early Romantic period. Resisting the "flatlining" of NATURE into the ordered and mathematically calculable surfaces of Nature, many of the Romantics aspired to "participate in and express NATURE," but, alas, they tended to focus on "their feelings of awe and wonder" and hence "confusedly celebrated what amounted to ego-centric feelings . . . associated with childhood feelings" and ended up in a reactionary slide into "nature" (IE, p. 30). Contemporary worries about eco-fascism cannot be convincingly extricated from their implication in Romanticism's slide from a radical, libratory ecosophical revolution to a disturbingly nostalgic, reactionary, and doggedly (if often cryptically) conservative movement.

Schelling, whom Esbjörn-Hargens and Zimmerman call in passing "the great German idealist" (IE, p. 30), was a great exception to this tendency. Wilber's own defense of Schelling is as welcoming as it is effusive:

> And so, if you had to pick two philosophers who, after Plato, had the broadest impact on the Western mind, they might very well be Plotinus and then Schelling. For this reason alone: Plotinus gave the Great holarchy its fullest expression, and Schelling set the Great Holarchy afloat in developmental time, in evolution. And if there is one idea that dominates the modern and postmodern mind at large, it is evolution.
>
> And we are at the point, historically, that it is beginning to be understood that the Great Holarchy evolved over time. And standing at that crucial watershed is Schelling.[14]

As we have seen, Schelling was not the least bit dismissive of science, but rather fought to keep it from enabling the flatlining of NATURE to the dualism of Nature and nature. He argued powerfully that modern philosophy did not *value* NATURE, that it diminished it in order to trample all over it and exploit it. "The moralist desires to see nature not as living, but as dead, so that he can tread upon it with his feet" (I/7, 17). Modern philosophy is constituted by its drive for a dead system, not a living one (I/7, 356). Modern philosophy and science's representation of Nature, or, more precisely, its flatling of NATURE to the *representational domain* of Nature, is a kind of NATURE-cide: "Nature is not present to it" because modernity "lacks a living ground [*die Natur für sich nicht vorhanden ist, und daß es ihr am lebendigen Grunde fehlt*]" (I/7, 361). NATURE therefore becomes the lopsided abstraction of a dogmatic empiricism and its forces are reduced to mere repetitions of the same (natural laws, which, as such, are through and through recursive). Natural laws become Nature's unassailable operators, and NATURE becomes incapable of real progressivity; that is, bereft of creativity and productivity (*natura naturans*), so that it unsurprisingly repeats what it has always already been (*natura naturata*), "swiveling in the indifferent circle of sameness, which would not be progressive, but rather insensible and non-vital" (I/7, 345). Tomorrow Nature is just more of the same, leaving us to dream only of "nature" as a more palatable alternative to a home that has become intolerable. Nature has lost NATURE's force of the future.

Opposing "nature" to "Nature" not only ignores the powerful insights of the latter (science, the value of personal autonomy in the Kantian sense),[15] but it confuses the problem of NATURE with the return of the repressed. When there is only Nature, then and when the affective cult of nature confusedly attempts to commune with Nature, then NATURE returns as the opposite of what the Enlightenment extolled—namely, reason. Wilber, following Foucault's argument about the "blackmail of the Enlightenment," speaks of the "*repressive* side of the Enlightenment, the tendency of monological reason to marginalize everything that is not of its ilk" (SES, p. 466). When the marginalized returns, it only appears, however hauntingly, as the opposite of the flatland. The "Eco-camp," seeking a "self-abnegating *communion*" (SES, p. 469) with nature, rightly sensed the lost "unity, wholeness" and "harmony" that had been flatlined into Nature, but regressively attempted to compensate for this deficiency by trying to commune with Nature. "Under the intense gravitational pull of flatland, they reduced NATURE to Nature. And to Nature they pledged their undying allegiance" (SES, p. 470). Schelling, on the other hand, resorted neither to the monoculture of affect, nor to the alleged autonomy of reason, but rather to what he called, variously, "intellectual intuition," the "ecstasy of reason," and even "positive philosophy."[16] The cult of feeling and vague intuitions and dreams cannot retrieve what rationality has repressed. Reason and feeling turn on the same pivot, namely ego-consciousness. In Wilber's manner of speaking, NATURE "can only be grasped by an awareness that moves *beyond the rational-ego*" (SES, p. 470). The Eco-Romantic solution of "getting back to nature" ironically, in attempting to overcome the iron-cage of the positivism of Nature, ran back to it as a "lost paradise" (SES, p. 471), as if they were running away from it, armed not with reason, but feeling, confusing the "transrational" with the nonrational and even prerational (SES, p. 470). The *repression* of Nature became the Romantic *regression* to nature, convinced "that something had gone horribly wrong, that somebody or something had made a terrible mistake, that history was primarily the shadow of a great and heinous Crime, and that salvation, above, was the resurrection of the dead and dismembered Paradise Lost" (SES, p. 472).

From the get-go, Schelling sought to navigate between the Scylla and Charybdis of repression and regression. Yes, Schelling was highly critical of the modern cult of scientific positivism (Nature), but the way out of this trap was not through nostalgic yearning. The most ancient sense of NATURE could only be rearticulated anew by moving in and through science. If indeed NATURE dances, if it is progressive and auto-productive (*natura naturans*), then science appreciated in the right measure (as integral to NATURE and not as an imperious and pernicious monoculture) can and should be celebrated as a great gift. Regression, on the other hand, confuses modern philosophy with wholesale repression, and fails to see natural science's own unique—and uniquely valuable—mode of disclosure. One cannot avoid modernity, but one must move through it. To employ a phrase that often appears in Schelling's early writings, one must immerse oneself in something (x) so thoroughly and intimately that one can move *über x hinaus*, through x and thereby beyond x. "We must go through the form [*über die Form hinausgehen*] in order to gain it back as intelligible, alive, and as truly felt [*empfunden*]" (I/7, 299). Schelling sometimes called this movement *Depontenzierung*: To go through something in order to get beyond it (*über etwas hinaus*); to exhaust the possibilities of a given manner of thinking and therefore to delimit its potency; that is, arrive at the outer possibility of, in this case, what the scientific analysis of surfaces can do. In this sense, Wilber is right to affirm that Schelling "managed to unite Ego and Eco, Ascending and Descending, without sacrificing the gains of either" (SES, p. 516).

Despite the immense complexity of German Idealism and Romanticism, its reactionary regressions and its great breakthroughs, its central insight into the problem of an integral ecology, whether lost in the affective fanaticism of the demand for a return to a lost paradise or in Schelling's more rarefied attempt to reclaim NATURE through the transrational absorption of science, *rests of the stubborn difficulty of achieving a transrational standpoint*. The difficulty of this standpoint in part, I think, accounts for the proclivity of Romanticism to collapse into juvenile whining and exceedingly aggressive nostalgia. Where does one stand so that the transrational does not collapse into the nonrational? Despite some of their critical affinities, including a shared commitment to think developmentally and, in doing so, avoid the pitfalls of falling either into the ego or the eco camp, Hegel departed dramatically from Schelling on this immensely difficult, but utterly critical, problem. Hegel denigrated Schelling's intellectual intuition as the epistemic privilege of "Sunday's children." The transrational viewpoint (the intellectual intuition) is not universally demonstrable; that is, it is not directly born out of reason's internal and universalizable assessment of its own activity. Rather, the philosophy born of the intellectual intuition, as Hegel argued in *The Lectures on the History of Philosophy*, "gave the philosophy of Schelling the appearance of indicating that the presence of this intuition in individuals demanded a special talent, genius, or condition of mind of their own, or as though it were speaking of an accidental faculty which pertained to the specially favored few."[17] Hegel's account of spirit's peregrination to its own self-discovery attempts to remain wholly immanent to reason, demanding nothing external to it. This gave the Hegelian project an admirable internal coherence, but "when it began to unravel, which it did, it rather totally collapsed, whereas Schelling ended up planting numerous small time bombs that are still going off" (SES, p. 512).

Despite Hegel's disparaging comment that Schelling had conducted his education in public—he should have waited until he had an utterly coherent system in place—part of Schelling's power is the inability and unwillingness to prevent thinking from multiplying into divergent and autonomous standpoints, as if they were like Leibniz's monads, each reflecting the whole in its own unique way. Increasingly, Schelling could not separate the problem of a transrational standpoint from what he called *philosophical religion*. This is not to say that Schelling argued that philosophy can only issue from religious doctrine, but rather that there is something deeply *revelatory* at the heart of thinking. The revelatory, to use Schelling's felicitous neologism, is *das Unvordenkliche*, the unprethinkable, that which cannot be thought in advance; an eternal beginning to both NATURE's and thinking's productivity. The temporality of thinking, thinking's ecstatic relationship to its never-present, yet always recommencing ground, reveals thinking not so much as a method but as an ongoing practice, subject to the productivity of time. As William Blake's tenth proverb of hell from *The Marriage of Heaven and Hell* also proclaimed: "Eternity is in love with the productions of time."

Not only was thinking a practice for Schelling, I suspect that it was a part of his own life practices. That being said, not even Schelling advocates that the necessity of deepening philosophical activity depends on underlying transpersonal practices. For Wilber, in German Idealism there was "a failure to develop truly contemplative practices—that is, any true paradigms, any reproducible exemplars, any actual *transpersonal practice*. Put differently: no yoga, no meditative discipline, no experimental methodology to reproduce in consciousness the transpersonal insights and intuitions of its founders" (BHE, p. 333). And hence "the great Idealist systems" were "mistaken for metaphysics, or more of the same ole 'mere representation' philosophy" (BHE, p. 333).[18]

In transrational practice, we can more easily approach one of the most commendable and rare features of integral ecology: *To include everything and exclude nothing.* "We propose there is no single nature or environment" (IE, p. 170). This was also an imperative for Schelling's own practice, but to appreciate this, we have to differentiate this ambition from many of the great classical philosophical systems. They also attempt to offer an account of everything; that is, of NATURE, but they attempt to do so rationally, and hence always in terms of their own systems. To offer a rational account for why there is something, rather than nothing, is to reduce everything ultimately to philosophy and philosophy to a particular system of philosophy. To pick a more recent example, Schopenhauer reduces all that is to an explanatory fourfold root and, hence, he was right to begin his doctoral work (*On the Fourfold Root of the Principle of Sufficient Reason*) by claiming to follow Plato and Kant by ascribing everything to a principle of collection and division: "the law of *homogeneity* and the law of *specification*, should be equally observed, neither to the disadvantage of the other."[19] The former prescribes that we collect and gather things together into kinds "by observing their resemblances and correspondences [*Ähnlichkeiten und Übereinstimmungen*]." It begins with how "things" *are* fundamentally—that is, at the root, somehow the same, arriving at "the highest all comprehensive conception [*Alles umfassenden Begriff*]" (PSR, p. 1).

Homogeneity ("collection") does not, however, wash out all specificity by only generalizing to the greatest possible degree of homogeneity (the fourfold root of all beings). Specification demands that we properly differentiate the various kinds of being, specifying the ways in which what is ultimately the same is nonetheless also discernibly different. In a sense, specification differentiates different kinds of the same thing, a dual operation that Schopenhauer assures us that Plato claimed was "flung down from the seat of the gods with the Promethean fire" (PSR, p. 2). This classical move, despite his radically deflationary deployment of it (he tosses out many of our metaphysical ambition and comforts), allows Schopenhauer to reduce difference to differentiation (specifications of what is at the root the same and which, as such, explains everything). Although the young Nietzsche found Schopenhauer eye-opening and inspiring (his own peculiar awakening from a dogmatic slumber), it is the homogeneity of the principle of sufficient reason, including its manifestation in human motivation as the relentless and blind will to life, which helped open Nietzsche to a more radical thought of difference, a thought that homogeneity with its centralizing alliance with resemblances and correspondences represses. At the heart of NATURE there is not sameness, but a difference in itself that resists conceptual capture.[20]

> And Nietzsche's break with Schopenhauer rests on one precise point; it is a matter of knowing whether the will is unitary or multiple. Everything else flows from this. Indeed, if Schopenhauer is led to deny the will it is primarily because he believes in the unity of willing. Because the will, according to Schopenhauer, is essentially unitary, the executioner comes to understand that he is one with his own victim. The consciousness of the identity of the will in all of its manifestations leads the will to deny itself, to suppress itself in pity, morality and asceticism. Nietzsche discovers what seems to him the authentically Schopenhauerian mystification; when we posit the unity, the identity, of the will we must necessarily repudiate the will itself.[21]

If there is something unitary at the heart of NATURE, some discernable core reality that science and/or philosophy can represent to thinking, then who gets to be its spokesperson? This is the reactionary and authoritarian impulse that lies latent in a certain manner of conceiving deep ecology or neoromanticism. As Sean Esbjörn-Hargens and Michael Zimmerman pointedly ask: "Who will speak for the earth? And how will disagreements be dealt with? Who will help organize the ecologically ignorant masses? Who will decide which behaviors help and which hurt the Earth? Are we to believe that there are people endowed with special intuition about what the earth really needs" (IE, p. 114)? This had nothing do with Schelling's intellectual intuition, which was an intuition of the productive difference at the heart of NATURE, but this is a danger already latent in the capacity for regressive nostalgia in the eco-romantics: A revolutionary rejection of present life as a *complete* mistake and nature as an absolutely distinctive alternative. When Schelling endeavored to articulate a "system of freedom," there was no such thing as a final position or a standpoint that excludes every other possible standpoint. In a sense, the system of freedom was the standpoint within which the multiplicity of standpoints could flourish. We might call Schelling a nineteenth century prototype of the Eco-Sage (IE, p. 236) and the system was not the reduction of everything to one, just as Gaia is "not a single organism," but rather "as planetary collective or global ecosystem" (IE, p. 147). In the unprethinkability of NATURE, including its multiply singular interiorities, thinking finds itself never in front of, but always before, on the verge, of what is to be thought and what is to be done. In this sense, integral ecology is not just integral thinking on the verge of becoming philosophy and therefore, ironically, becoming less integral (collecting only that which resembles philosophy, whatever we decide the latter to be). It is an experience of thinking on the verge, a thinking of and from the verge. It is to this issue that we now turn.

Dancing with Sophia on the verge—There is no dance with σοφία that does not have an element of transrational practice. We begin speaking here of dancing with σοφία by remembering philosophy's ancient self-understanding not as the possessor of wisdom, but as the call to friendship with wisdom, to ally ourselves with wisdom even though the wise paradoxically know, as Socrates famously exemplified, that we are called to befriend what we can never properly own. This ancient vocation to friendship now reconfigures itself in integral thinking as a dance with a dynamically elusive partner, emphasizing that this relationship demands mutual movement, in a dance where neither partner can claim to be fully either leader or follower. The dance is closer to what the Buddha called *pratītyasamutpāda*, or dependent co-origination. As we study a juniper in the forest from its irreducibly multiple viewpoints (scientific, artistic, commercial, recreational, nonhuman, ecological, etc.), we can conclude that "there simply is no such thing as 'one tree' " (IE, p. 180). We cannot dance with σοφία if σοφία herself is not already dancing and as such, revealing to us that we too are already dancing, whether or not we know it. It is not a question of starting something anew, but of awakening to the dance that is always already underway, but since we have been sleeping through it, we have been dancing poorly.

The dance is, therefore, something like awakening to what the Buddha called the pure land or Dōgen called the "great earth." In the *Vimalakīrti Sutra*, the Buddha taught that "when the mind is pure, the Buddha land will be pure." A pure mind opens one to the pure land, just as the dancing mind opens one to the dance of σοφία. Śāriputra, ever the philosopher (his special gift was also wisdom), queried that if the world must be purified, then it must first be impure (and given that the Buddha's mind was pure, how could the world have been impure?). The Buddha responded, "Are the sun and the moon impure? Is that why the blind man fails to see them?"[22] Or as Dōgen learned from the *tenzo* (monastery chef) during his trip to China, the great earth is not hiding. That is not why we fail to see it. As Dōgen records the decisive words of the *tenzo* from whom he learned what is decisive in practice: "*henkai-fuzōzō*—everywhere, nothing hidden." Wilber makes this point in his own way, drawing on his own philosophical genealogy: "As Plotinus knew and Nāgārjuna taught: always and always, the other world is this world rightly seen" (SES, p. 536).

The dance involves practices by which we *wake up* to thinking always dancing on the verge of NATURE. As John Sallis has recently spoken with great eloquence of the verge:

> The verge itself is both the most definite and the least definite. On the one hand, it is the very source of definiteness; it defines the areas this side of and beyond the furthest verge and thereby bestow on each its definiteness. On the other hand, the verge not only is indeterminable but also is duplicitous in its relation to the side areas it delimits, belonging both to each and to neither . . . All originary determination is situated on the verge. All determination in and through which something is brought about that is entirely unprecedented takes place on the verge . . . Because philosophy would be the most radical such orientation, it must to the highest degree submit to the verge. The place at which philosophy comes to be established as such, the place from which it comes to be determined as such, is neither simply outside philosophy nor simply within it.[23]

Taking this a step further, we could say that integral ecology, on the verge of philosophy, is as such because—like philosophy—it must rigorously submit itself to the verge, to the liminal ambiguity that is the oneness of the noosphere. We can speak of it as one, not because it is any one thing, but because it excludes nothing and, in so doing, thinks from and of the verge in its unprethinkable productivity and inexhaustible singularities (irreducibly multiple interiorities in their interdependence). In so speaking, it is a question of transrational practice as the practice of opening the true Dharma eye. As such, it would be imprecise to speak of it as any particular philosophy, but rather as the verge of philosophy, as the dance in which philosophy remains open to the depths of philosophy. These depths, presupposed by any possible philosophy, remain at the verge of every single philosophy and, as such, are not in themselves philosophical, but rather the opening to philosophy. The depths of philosophy, like the depths of NATURE, are philosophy's relationship to what exceeds and precedes it. Philosophy is negotiated at the verge of nonphilosophy—no viewpoints can exhaust this standpoint and many viewpoints already comprise it. In their remarkable work, *What is Philosophy?*, Deleuze and Guattari argue that

> The plane of philosophy is prephilosophical insofar as we consider it in itself independently of the concepts that come to occupy it, but nonphilosophy is found where the plane confronts chaos. *Philosophy needs a nonphilosophy that comprehends it; it needs a nonphilosopical comprehension just as art needs nonart and science*

> *needs nonscience*. They do not need the No as beginning, or as the end in which they would be called upon to disappear by being realized, but at every moment of their becoming or their development.[24]

A plane of immanence is the possibility of moving from the nonphilosophical to the prephilosophical. The latter "does not mean something preexistent but rather something *that does not exist outside of philosophy*, although philosophy presupposes it. These are its internal conditions" and it "constitutes the absolute ground of philosophy, its earth." (WP, p. 41) One might even say that nonphilosophy, which at the verge is taken up ever anew as prephilosophy, is integral ecology as NATURE-philosophy (my proposed translation of Schelling's *Naturphilosophie*). The plane of immanence, the verge of philosophy, is "like a section of chaos," a prephilosophical slice of the utterly nonphilosophical, and it "acts like a sieve." (WP, p. 42) It is like a "desert that concepts populate without dividing up." (WP, p. 36) Working in tandem, concepts allow the prephilosophical ground of philosophy to appear in thinking. The prephilosophical plane of philosophical concept creation is not itself a phenomenon, but a *planomenon* (WP, p. 35) "the horizon of events, the reservoir or reserve of purely conceptual events." (WP, p. 36)

Where, we might now ask, is the moment when one is able to think the infinite speed of chaos in such a way that it yields a plane in which concepts can articulate it consistently "without losing anything of the infinite"? (WP, p. 42) How does one think the sectioning of the nonphilosophical so that it yields a plane in which it can be conceptually articulated? The planomenal negotiation of chaos is not in itself a concept, but rather the possibility of coordinated concept creation. It is, rather, "the image of thought, the image thought gives itself of what it means to think, to make use of thought, to find one's bearings in thought . . . The image of thought retains only what thought can claim by right" (WP, p. 37). In this sense, perhaps one can begin thinking about Dōgen's relationship to philosophy as an attempt to think and act from the verge, to express an imageless image of thought that allows one to think the image of thought as such. Let us attempt to be clear about this word "thought": For Dōgen, "thought" emerges in the "falling and casting away of body and mind [*shinjin datsuraku*]." It is not, therefore, a concept, nor is it the referent of a concept. "Thought" in this respect breaks through the duality of concept and thing conceived in the same manner that it no longer holds heaven and earth, ascent and descent, emptiness and form, as merely separate.

This being said, can one say that Dōgen or Schelling or integral ecology therefore expressed the "best" plane of immanence such that it remains unrivalled in expressing the infinity of chaos without surrendering it to the realm of concepts? Can one say that integral ecology has succeeded, or that Schelling's opening was the unparalleled proto-contemporary expression? I think that such claims are in bad taste. Our very language has always failed to think the "lifeworld of all holons" (IE, p. 149) and the problem with all maps is that "they leave out the mapmaker,' " ignoring "the fact that the mapmaker might itself bring something to the picture." (BHE, p. 106) Esbjörn-Hargens and Zimmerman confess, as did Wilber, that "even our map is a reduction of this complex and mysterious universe" (IE, p. 149)! Nonetheless, Deleuze and Guattari are right to insist: "We will say that THE plane of immanence is, at the same time, that which must be thought and that which cannot be thought. It is the nonthought within thought. It is the base of all planes, immanent to every thinkable plane" (WP, p. 59). This is not, however, to again lament the tribulations of finitude, but rather to unleash its forces. "Perhaps this is the supreme act of philosophy: not so much to think THE plane of immanence as to show that it is there, unthought in every plane" (WP, p. 59).

One finds this supreme act within Dōgen's practice of *shikantaza* (just sitting) as it cultivates the standpoint of mountains, rivers, the great earth (form, emptiness; that is, NATURE). It is also at the heart of Schelling's early experiments with *Naturphilosophie*, whose very idea is not to define Nature as a philosophical object, but rather to recover NATURE as "the *infinite* subject, i.e., the subject which can *never* stop being a subject, can never be lost in the object, become mere object, as it does for Spinoza."[25] As such, its translation as "the philosophy of nature," as if it were a philosophical account of a super-object called Nature or a romantic flight from it, is easily misleading. *Naturphilosophie*, in Schelling's sense, is more like doing philosophy in accordance with NATURE (not as an elective activity originating at the whim and command of the *res cogitans*). It is not, therefore, a kind of philosophy, or a topic within philosophy, but rather a gateway into the originating experience of philosophizing, of thinking dancing at the verge of NATURE's prodigal singularities. It is an early experiment with integral ecology as it dances with σοφία. "Wisdom," Schelling tells us, turning to one of the most ancient traditions, played from the beginning of time itself. "It *played*—not on the earth, for there was no earth yet—on *God's* earth, on what is ground and soil to God" (I/8, 197).

Notes

1. Wilber (2000b; henceforth SES), and, following him, Esbjörn-Hargens and Zimmerman (2009; henceforth IE), calls NATURE "the entire Kosmos, or the Great Holarchy of Being," (see, for example, SES, books one and two) the auto-poiesis of Being in its interior and co-originating depths and its exterior, co-originating expanses, or what Gary Snyder in the *Practice of the Wild* (1990) called the "wild." This is distinguished from Nature, the reduction of NATURE to its external dimensions, to the biosphere or "entire sensory and empirical world," and "nature" (SES, p. 471), that which opposes culture, ἄνθρωπος, the human originated world, or, to put the same point in Gary Snyder's terms, the wild understood as the opposite of the civilized. See Gary Snyder, *The Practice of the Wild* (San Francisco: North Point Press, 1990) (henceforth PW). Typically "wild" and "feral" (*ferus*), according to Snyder, are "largely defined in our dictionaries by what—from a human standpoint—it is not. It cannot be seen by this approach for what it *is*." (PW, p. 9) Hence, a wild animal is an animal that has not been trained to live in our house (undomesticated) and has not been successfully subjected to our rule (unruly); that is, it is the force of "nature" over and against our cultured, human fabricated ways. But what happens, Snyder asks, if we "turn it the other way"? What is the wild *to the wild*? Animals become "free agents, each with its own endowments, living within natural systems" (PW, p. 9). As Snyder further develops this turn, he gestures to the ways in which a renewed sense of the wild (as the fullness of NATURE) "comes very close to being how the Chinese define the term *Dao*, the *way* of Great Nature: eluding analysis, beyond categories, self-organizing, self-informing, playful, surprising, impermanent, insubstantial, independent, complete, orderly, unmediated . . ." (PW, 10). See also SES, pp. 454–455.

2. By "Mother Nature" we could again say NATURE in the sense developed above. It does not speak to the Romantic cult of feeling over and against rationality.

3. Kant (1990), 171.

4. Except where noted, all translations of Schelling are my own responsibility. Citations follow the standard pagination, which follows the original edition established after Schelling's death by his son, Karl. It lists the division, followed by the volume, followed by the page number. Hence (I/1, 1), would read *division one, volume one, page one*. It is preserved in Manfred Schröter's critical reorganization of this material. *Schellings Sämtliche Werke* (Stuttgart-Augsburg: J.G. Cotta, 1856–1861); *Schellings Werke: Nach der Originalausgabe in neuer Anordnung*, ed. Manfred Schröter (Munich: C.H. Beck, 1927). My translation of *Die Weltalter* originally appeared in Schelling (2000). For citations of this work I also cite the standard pagination and not the translation pagination, although the prior is embedded in the latter. Schelling's quote can be found at Exodus 3:14.

5. For a summary discussion of the three uses of "nature," see IE, 25–29.

6. F.W.J. Schelling, "Introduction to the Outline of a System of the Philosophy of Nature, or, On the Concept of Speculative Physics and the Internal Organization of a System of this Science," in (2004), 202.

7. Schelling is aware, of course, that the movement of his own thinking has exposed the highly problematic nature of subject and object, and Schelling endeavored to replace such language with a discourse of the *Ungrund*, the barbarian principle, freedom, etc. For more on this, see Jason Wirth with P. Burke (eds.), *The Barbarian Principle: Merleau-Ponty, Schelling, and the Question of Nature* (Albany, NY: SUNY Press, 2013).

8. The "within of things is *depth*, the without is *surface*" (SES, 117).

9. Gregory Bateson, *Steps to an Ecology of Mind* (New York: Ballantine, 1972), 484. See also Félix Guattari, *The Three Ecologies*, trans. Ian Pindar and Paul Sutton (London and New Brunswick, NJ: Athlone, 2000), 27; henceforth TE.

10. Félix Guattari, *Chaosmosis*, trans. Paul Bains and Julian Pefanis (Bloomington, IN: Indiana University Press, 1995), 119–120.

11. See also IE, 11.

12. See IE, 6.

13. Jean-Luc Nancy, *Being Singular Plural*, trans. Robert D. Richardson and Anne E. O'Byrne (Stanford, CA: Stanford University Press, 2000), 3.

14. Ken Wilber, *A Brief History of Everything*, in *The Collected Works of Ken Wilber, Volume 7* (Boston: Shambhala, 2000), 326. Henceforth BHE.

15. See the "Ego-positives" in SES, 456–461.

16. For more on the problem of intellectual intuition and direct experience, see Jason Wirth, *Conspiracy of Life: Meditations on Schelling and his Time* (Albany, NY: SUNY Press, 2003), Chapter 4.

17. See Dale E. Snow, "Genius: The 'Sunday's Children' Problem," in *Schelling and the End of Idealism* (Albany, NY: SUNY Press, 1996), 63.

18. See IE, Chapter 10, for its discussion of practices that awaken ecological awareness from its careless intellectual and emotional slumber.

19. Arthur Schopenhauer, *On the Fourfold Root of the Principle of Sufficient Reason*, trans. Karl Hillebrand (London: George Bell, 1907), 1;henceforth PSR.

20. Deleuze argued that there is no unitary being or thing at the ground of NATURE, but rather that such groundless ground is multiple, taken up again in differential repetition. Being is not the ONE. More recent thinkers have attempted to articulate even more clearly the non-unitary singularities at the heart of being. As we have seen above, Jean-Luc Nancy called this the "being-singular plural" of NATURE. John Sallis, in his "monstrological" articulation of the "upsurge into presence" of the image, speaks of this as presentation's elemental force (the meeting of earth and sky), beyond the unified field that recourse to Being as such inadvertently evokes. See Sallis (2000), Chapter 6. Alain Badiou speaks of this under the "proper name of the void" as pure multiples: "this infinity—once subtracted from the empire of

the one, and therefore in default of any ontology of Presence—proliferates beyond everything tolerated by representation." (2005), 149.

21. Gilles Deleuze, *Nietzsche and Philosophy*, trans. Hugh Tomlinson (New York: Columbia University Press, 1983), 7.

22. "Buddha Lands," in *The Vimalakīrti Sutra* (1997), 29.

23. John Sallis, *The Verge of Philosophy* (Chicago: University of Chicago Press, 2008), 3–4.

24. Gilles Deleuze and Félix Guattari, *What is Philosophy?* trans. Hugh Tomlinson and Graham Burchell (New York: Columbia University Press, 1994), 218; henceforth WP.

25. F.W.J. Schelling, *On the History of Modern Philosophy* (1827), trans. Andrew Bowie (Cambridge, UK: Cambridge University Press, 1994), 114. The early Schelling understood *die Naturphilosophie* as an attempt to think from Kant's "to us unknown root" without the duality of Kant's antinomian rendering of it and without thinking it dogmatically (the object called substance in Spinoza) or as a subject (Kant's autonomy, which remains, despite the radical overtures in the *Third Critique*, still a kind of object, a "thing in itself"). Schelling thought from the transrational standpoint that attempted to think these opposites in their underlying unity, despite Kant's misplaced denunciation of the intellectual intuition, despite the fact that his thinking ultimately presupposes it (I/2, 106).

References

Badiou, Alain. 2005. *Being and Event*, trans. Oliver Feltham. London and New York: Continuum.

Bateson, Gregory. 1972. *Steps to an Ecology of Mind.* New York: Ballantine.

Esbjörn-Hargens, Sean and Michael Zimmerman. 2009. *Integral Ecology: Uniting Multiple Perspectives on the Natural World.* Boston and London: Integral Books.

Deleuze, Gilles. 1983. *Nietzsche and Philosophy*, trans. Hugh Tomlinson. New York: Columbia University Press.

Deleuze, Gilles and Félix Guattari. 1994. *What is Philosophy?* trans. Hugh Tomlinson and Graham Burchell. New York: Columbia University Press.

Guattari, Félix. 1995. *Chaosmosis*, trans. Paul Bains and Julian Pefanis. Bloomington, IN: Indiana University Press.

Guattari, Félix. 2000. *The Three Ecologies*, trans. Ian Pindar and Paul Sutton. London and New Brunswick, NJ: Athlone.

Kant, Immanuel. 1990. *Kritik der Urteilskraft.* Hamburg, GER: Felix Meiner Verlag.

Nancy, Jean-Luc. 2000. *Being Singular Plural*, trans. Robert D. Richardson and Anne E. O'Byrne. Stanford, CA: Stanford University Press.

Sallis, John. 2000. *Force of Imagination: The Sense of the Elemental.* Bloomington, IN: Indiana University Press.

Sallis, John. 2008. *The Verge of Philosophy.* Chicago: University of Chicago Press.

Schelling, F.W.J. 1856–1861; 1927. *Schellings sämtliche werke.* Stuttgart-Augsburg: J. G. Cotta (1856–1861); *Schellings werke: Nach der originalausgabe in neuer anordnung*, ed. Manfred Schröter. Munich: C.H. Beck, 1927.

Schelling, F.W.J. 1992. *System des Transzendentalen Idealismus* (1800), ed. Horst D. Brandt and Peter Müller. Hamburg, GER: Felix Meiner Verlag, 1992.

Schelling, F.W.J. 1994. *On the History of Modern Philosophy* (1827), trans. Andrew Bowie. Cambridge, UK: Cambridge University Press.

Schelling, F.W.J. 2004. *First Outline of a System of the Philosophy of Nature*, trans. Keith R. Peterson. Albany, NY: SUNY Press.

Schelling, F.W.J. 2000. *The Ages of the World*, trans. and intro Jason. M. Wirth. Albany: SUNY Press.

Schopenhauer, Arthur. 1907. *On the Fourfold Root of the Principle of Sufficient Reason*, trans. Karl Hillebrand. London: George Bell.

Snow, Dale E. 1996. *Schelling and the End of Idealism.* Albany, NY: SUNY Press.

Snyder, Gary. 1990. *Practice of the Wild.* San Francisco: North Point Press.

The Vimalakīrti Sutra. 1997. trans. Burton Watson. New York: Columbia University Press.

Wilber, Ken. 2000a. *A Brief History of Everything.* In *The Collected Works of Ken Wilber, Volume 7.* Boston: Shambhala.

Wilber, Ken. 2000b. *Sex, Ecology, Spirituality: The Spirit of Evolution* (2nd rev. ed.). Boston: Shambhala.

Wirth, Jason M. 2003. *Conspiracy of Life: Meditations on Schelling and His Time.* Albany, NY: SUNY Press.

Wirth, Jason M. 2017. *Schelling's Practice of the Wild: Time, Art, Imagination.* Albany, NY: SUNY Press.

Wirth, Jason M. with Patrick Burke (eds.) 2013. *The Barbarian Principle: Merleau-Ponty, Schelling, and the Question of Nature.* Albany, NY: SUNY Press.

Chapter 7

An Integral Touch

Philosophies for Pluralism, Realism, and Embodiment

SAM MICKEY

Integral philosophy can be understood as a philosophy of touch, situated in relation to other philosophies of touch to emerge in recent decades, including many that work with varieties of Continental thought, such as phenomenology, postmodernism, feminist theory, and speculative realism. Each of those has unique contributions and limitations for articulating a philosophical sense of touch, and the integral approach stands out among them for its capacity to comprehensively map and coordinate a meta-philosophical perspective. Of course, all such senses of touch are important. Indeed, all senses are important, but there is something particularly moving and affective—particularly touching—about touch.

The importance of touch for integral philosophies is conveyed by the very meaning of *integra*l. Although it conventionally means "whole," "complete," or that which composes or is necessary for wholeness, the word *integral* is a touching word. It derives from the Latin *integer*, which—similar to the connotations of the English word *integer*—refers to a whole or complete entity. The *in-* prefix has a privative or negative force (like *un-*). The *-teg-* at the core of the word derives from *tag-*, which is the source of the Latin word *tangere* ("to touch") and English words like *tag*, *tact*, *contact*, *tangible*, and *tangent*. In light of its etymological derivation, the word *integral* could be defined as "untouched."

I elaborate on the importance of touch for integral philosophies by focusing on three topics: 1) a concept of touch implicit in Ken Wilber's integral theory; 2) concepts of touch and sense articulated in phenomenology, postmodernism, feminist theory, and speculative realism; and 3) the contributions of the aforementioned concepts to integral postmetaphysics (IPM) and other postmetaphysical philosophies, where *postmetaphysics* is defined in terms of commitments to *pluralism* (not a monism that erases differences), *realism* (not an idealism for which reality is given in human thought), and *embodiment* (instead of philosophy that divorces theory from practices, privileging the former over the latter). In this context, the task of integral approaches to philosophy can be understood as the task of developing theories and practices that tactfully touch the multiplicity of beings in the Kosmos.

A Touch of Wilber

For integral theory, the Kosmos is made up of perspectives—"I," "We," "It," and "Its"—all the way up and all the way down; from the highest spiritual levels to the lowest material levels of the Kosmos. This is an ontological and epistemological claim, as it implies that perspective is inherent in all beings (ontology) and thus all beings feel, experience, or know (epistemology). What and how an entity feels, experiences, or knows in any event depends upon its contextual situation; its "Kosmic address," which is determined by the evolutionary/developmental altitude (level) and the perspective (quadrant) of the entities involved in that event (Wilber, 2007, p. 69). "Everybody is right," or more specifically, every perspective is partially right ("true but partial") (Wilber, 2002b). This does not mean that integral theory affirms a vulgar relativism, where anything is as true as anything else. Nor does it mean that integral theory denies the possibility of comparing the truths of different perspectives. Everybody is partially true, and what one perspective discloses as true might be deeper or more complex than what appears true to another perspective.

As a love of wisdom (*sophia*), philosophy means, as Karl Jaspers puts it, "to be on the way" to wisdom, to be in "the search for truth" (Jaspers, 2003, p. 12). With the extremely ambitious aim of providing the most encompassing articulation of truth by including all perspectives at all levels, integral theory is a candidate for the most comprehensive approach to philosophy available today. Yet, it raises a serious question: How can integral philosophy search for the dazzling multiplicity of partial truths in the Kosmos without reducing some of those truths to oversimplifications or caricatures? Integral philosophy runs the risk of committing the straw man logical fallacy, accounting for other positions in a way that misrepresents those positions.[1]

To some extent, it is simply impossible to develop an integral philosophy that accounts for every partial truth in the Kosmos. Wilber himself acknowledges that all attempts at an integral "Theory of Everything" always "fall short," as they are "marked by the many ways in which they fail," not necessarily because of any deficiencies on the part of the theorist, but because "the task is inherently undoable" (2000a, p. xii). This is a fundamental problem of integral philosophy. It indicates that integral philosophy must undertake the awesome task of accounting for all the truths of the Kosmos, while also recognizing that those truths ultimately exceed the limits of even the most comprehensive philosophical inquiries.

Integral philosophy must attempt to embrace all truths while acknowledging that all truths are ultimately out of reach. How, then, can one embrace that which is out of reach, that which exceeds one's grasp? How can one touch that which is beyond one's touch? It is in response to this fundamental problem of integral philosophy that a concept of touch is needed. Such a concept is already implicit in integral philosophy, as is indicated by some of the ways in which Wilber deploys figures of touch in his writings. Examples from Wilber's latest writings draw out the meaning of an integral philosophical concept of touch.[2]

Wilber uses a metaphor of touch to describe the tone with which he wrote *Integral Spirituality*: "Lightness of touch is the wiser tone" (2007, p. ix). Too heavy of a touch does violence to what is touched, failing to respect its integrity. A light touch touches with tact, so that one touches while also honoring the extent to which whatever is touched remains out of reach, untouched, intact. In discussing this lightness of touch, Wilber implies that if one touches too lightly, touch can become a frivolous engagement, which is so superficial that just as much as a heavy touch, it fails to honor the untouched integrity of phenomena.

Wilber's discussion of this light touch is applied to the topic of spirituality, but taken more generally, it indicates that integral philosophy can include a concept of touch that attends to the limit where touch makes tactful contact, not touching too little or too much, but leaving intact the integrity of what is touched. *Only with a lightness of touch can integral philosophy undertake its ambitious project to coordinate the vast multiplicity of perspectives composing the Kosmos.*

Lightness is not the only feature of Wilber's concept of touch. More details are implicit in excerpt B from the second volume of Wilber's *Kosmos Trilogy*. According to the title of the excerpt, to practice an integral approach is to practice "the many ways we touch" (2002b). The practice of coordinating the multiple perspectives of the Kosmos is a practice of integrating the many ways we touch. Moreover, touch is used here as a metaphor that applies to any relationship and is not restricted to its conventional meaning as sensory perception, although it includes that meaning and, indeed, its conventional meaning helps support its function in a philosophical concept that avoids privileging theory over embodiment, practice, and concrete ways of feeling and looking.[3] In this context, touch extends to include all relationships, all the perspectives of all beings, which suggests that integral philosophy contains an implicit concept of touch that attends to the multiplicity of ways knowing and being—the many ways we touch.

Wilber (2002b) describes the integral framework as "an approach to any occasion that 'touches all the bases,' that refuses to leave some dimension untouched or ignored." Here Wilber does not mention a lightness of touch, but a diversity of touch; a diverse touch that reaches so far that nothing is left untouched. Wilber also uses the metaphor of touching bases in *Integral Spirituality*: "The important point about the Integral Approach," according to Wilber, "is that we want to touch bases with as many potentials as possible so as to miss nothing in terms of possible solutions, growth, and transformation" (2007, p. 17). In the same work, Wilber also invokes the figure of touching base to address the integration of masculine and feminine perspectives. "We are simply saying that, in either case, make sure you touch bases with both the masculine and feminine, however you view them" (p. 14).

Paradoxically, integral philosophy touches everything and leaves everything untouched. Touching base with everything, integral philosophy leaves nothing untouched, not even the intangible dimensions of reality. Touching lightly, integral philosophy leaves intact the many ways we touch, preserving their integrity and intangible mystery. True to the etymological derivation of the word, an integral philosophy can be understood as a philosophy of the untouched—a philosophy with a comprehensive and diverse reach extending to everything in the Kosmos, touched and untouched, tangible and intangible, aiming to honor and leave its integrity intact, untouched.

In this context, integral philosophy is a realist and embodied philosophy, facilitating inquiry that is situated in pragmatic contexts and attends to real beings, honoring the dimensions of their realities that infinitely exceed the grasp of any theory or practice. Furthermore, an integral touch supports a pluralistic philosophy of the many ways we touch. More specifically, insofar as the ways we touch implies the existence of things that are touching and touched, it supports what Sean Esbjörn-Hargens calls "integral pluralism"—a pluralism of ways of being and knowing, thus including "epistemological, methodological, and ontological" pluralisms (2010, p. 146). This integral touch and its postmetaphysical commitments (pluralism, realism, embodiment) can be further developed by making contact with other philosophies of touch, specifically phenomenology, postmodernism, feminism, and speculative realism. To facilitate such contact, I discuss concepts of touch and sense in thinkers whose work is indicative of some of the main contributions of those philosophies, with particular attention to the contemporary French philosopher Jean-Luc Nancy—the contemporary philosopher most committed to an explicit engagement with concepts of touch and sense.

A Sense of Philosophy

Focus on sense has been a prominent part of French philosophy since the 1960s, with the emergence of an influential school of thought that came to be called "postmodernism"—a contested term that is rarely, if ever, used by many of the most prominent philosophers considered to be among its adherents. Leonard Lawlor (2003) summarizes the postmodern school of thought as an attempt made by philosophers like Jacques Derrida, Gilles Deleuze, and Michel Foucault to get thought moving after millennia of metaphysics had made it stagnant. To get thought moving, these and other thinkers transformed "the metaphysical concept of essence (the transcendent)" into a more relational concept—a "concept of sense," which includes transcendent and immanent aspects and is grounded in a "non-sensical" structure opening up the mystery, the question at the heart of being (p. 142). Getting thought moving, participating in the nonsense of sense—this involves a transformation of the very meaning of what sense is, the very sense of sense.

Since Plato, philosophy has assimilated sense into a dualistic schema that sets the intelligible (*to noeton*) over against the sensible (*to aistheton*), such that the true world of ideal forms is opposed to the world of sense—the world of illusory appearances. With this opposition, the sensible and the intelligible become mutually exclusive (e.g., dualism), or one term is reduced to the other term (e.g., materialism and naive realism reduce the intelligible to the sensible, and idealism and social constructionism reduce the sensible to the intelligible). This opposition is at work in dualisms of transcendence and immanence, essence and manifestation, and subjectivity and objectivity, dualisms that propagate a "crisis of sense," which is affecting consciousness, cultures, and environments around the planet (Nancy, 2005, p. 161). The crisis of sense involves a proliferation of oppression, violence, and destruction that accompanies the dualistic logic colonizing the sense of the world, what the ecofeminist philosopher Karen Warren describes as the "the logic of domination," whereby dualistic hierarchies are used as justification for domination (e.g., sexism, classism, racism, ethnocentrism, speciesism) (2008, p. 37).

Philosophical concepts can enact a new sense, one that resists the logic of domination that partitions sense into oppressive dualisms. Nancy works toward enacting such a sense in *The Sense of the World*. For Nancy, the true world is not opposed to the world of sense. Rather, the true world is the world of sense. The phrase "the sense of the world" does not refer to a meaning or truth that the world has. The world does not *have* a sense, "but it *is* sense" (1997, p. 8). Nancy's account of sense shows multidimensional interrelations between the intelligible, perceptual, subjective, and objective. This is evident in the multivalent sense of the word *sense*, which can refer to an intelligible sense (meaning), as well as an aesthetic sense (perception), and also to subjectivity (sensing; apprehension) and to objectivity (sensed; apprehended). Nancy also mentions other connotations of the word *sense*: "the sense of the word *sense* traverses the five senses, the sense of direction, common sense, semantic sense, divinatory sense, sentiment, moral sense, practical sense, aesthetic sense, all the way to that which makes possible all these senses" (p. 15).

Nancy draws on many of the philosophies of sense that emerged throughout the twentieth century, including the aforementioned French postmodern philosophies, as well as phenomenological philosophies, which themselves are influential for postmodernism.[4] As Paul Ricoeur observes, phenomenology can be described as "a philosophy of 'sense'" (1967, p. 41). The phenomenologist most commonly associated with topics of sense, touch, perception, and embodiment is Maurice Merleau-Ponty, whose philosophy can be described as an "ontology of sense," where sense refers to the intertwining of intangible interiority and tangible exteriority at all levels of existence (Toadvine, 2004). Sense designates the fundamental crisscrossing structure ("chiasm") upon which all beings appear; which is to say, the fundamental framework of meaning (invisible sense) "co-functioning" with the visible and palpable sense of the world (Merleau-Ponty, 1968, p. 215).

Merleau-Ponty provides an "ontological rehabilitation of the sensible," wherein subjectivity and objectivity are expressions of one crisscrossing tissue or "intentional fabric"—the "flesh," which includes the "self-sensing" flesh of my body and the "sensible and not sentient" flesh of the cosmos (1964, p. 167; 1968, p. 250). Touch plays a prominent role in Merleau-Ponty's ontology of sense, with particular attention to the phenomenon of two hands touching. The chiastic structure of sense expresses a reversibility that unites the touching and the touched (identity), while also holding them apart (difference). When my right hand touches my left, my left hand feels touched, and if I try simultaneously to feel my left hand touching, then my right hand feels touched and no longer touching. The reversibility of touching and touched is "always imminent and never realized in fact. My left hand is always on the verge of touching my right hand touching" (p. 147). This reversibility can also appear in experiences with others, as in a handshake (p. 142). Touch exemplifies a reversibility present in all sense. Notwithstanding specific difference between sense organs and the complexities of the sensory system, every act of seeing, hearing, tasting, and smelling is done with a body that is in the world and open to its own exteriority as something that can be seen, heard, tasted, and smelled. In short, by accounting for the co-constitutive flesh composing touching/touched relations, Merleau-Ponty's ontology rehabilitates sense as the relational ground of terms often considered mutually exclusive throughout the history of philosophy (e.g., subjectivity/objectivity, meaning/matter, self/other, and identity/difference).

Following Merleau-Ponty, many philosophers have expressed concepts of sense and touch that draw on phenomenology, while also critiquing some of its shortcomings (e.g., its tendencies toward subjectivism, idealism, human-centeredness, and lack of engagement with sciences and abstract structures). For instance, Luce Irigaray draws on Merleau-Ponty's ontology of the flesh, while also opening it up to critical questioning as she develops concepts of sense and touch that are more explicitly oriented toward an ethics of difference, aiming to engender respectful engagements with the otherness (alterity) of other sexes, other bodies, and other ways of knowing and being (Irigaray, 2004, p. 127). As Judith Butler explains, Irigaray's thinking is dependent on Merleau-Ponty's theorization of relations of sense, yet Irigaray is also critical of Merleau-Ponty, "thinking against him within his terms," "attributing to him an arrested development, a maternal fixation, even an intrauterine fantasy" of being enwombed in flesh (2006, p. 108). Irigaray adapts Merleau-Ponty's ontology so as to enact a chiastic reversibility of its male-centered perspective, opening it up to the feminine and to an ethics of sexual difference. Moreover, Irigaray has a similar reading of Emmanuel Levinas's phenomenology of touch, which conceives of a "caress" that opens onto ethical engagements with the intangible alterity of the other (Irigaray, 2004, p. 153; Levinas, 1991, p. 258). Irigaray situates herself in alliance with the Levinasian ethics of alterity, while correcting its lack of attention to sexual difference.

Irigaray's emphasis on sexual difference and alterity is a shared commitment of many feminist philosophers, including Donna Haraway, who develops a concept of touch that follows feminist critiques of the dualistic logic of domination. For Haraway, touch is not just a sensory phenomenon, but is the performance of "naturalcultural contact zones"—"material-semiotic knots," whereby beings are entangled in mutually constitutive relations with "significant others" (i.e., "companion species"), whether human or nonhuman, male or female, natural or artificial (2008, pp. 4, 7). Postmodern philosophers of sense likewise share this affirmation of difference and its accompanying critique of dualisms, including the founder of deconstruction, Jacques Derrida, who wrote a book exploring concepts of touch throughout the history of philosophy, with particular attention to Nancy's work, which could be described as post-postmodernism or, more specifically, what Derrida calls "post-deconstructive realism" (2005, p. 46).[5] The postmodern thinker most well-known for a non-dualistic concept of sense is Gilles Deleuze, whose work is oriented toward emancipating the multifarious differences of existence from their imprisonment within dichotomies that dissociate subjects from objects or the heights of transcendence (ascent) from the depths of immanence (descent).[6] Deleuze's concept of sense aims to liberate the "pure event," "to liberate the singularities of the surface" where ascent meets descent and interior meets exterior (1990, p. 141). Singularities are different senses of sense, i.e., different distributions of matters and meaning. They are material-semiotic events, which emerge out of a non-dual creative process: nonsense. Deleuze is careful to note that nonsense is not an "absence of sense," but is a generative source that "enacts the donation of sense," such that nonsense and sense, like Merleau-Ponty's invisible and visible, are entangled in a co-functioning or "co-presence" (pp. 68, 71). That co-presence of (non)sense is the realm of the pure event, a non-dual process of "pure becoming" that "transcends affirmation and negation" (pp. 1–3, 123). This event is "the identity of form and void," such as is expressed in "the Zen arts." (Deleuze mentions drawing, gardening, flower arranging, tea ceremony, archery, and fencing as examples.) (pp. 136–137).

Nancy's post-deconstructive realism furthers the efforts of postmodernists, feminist theorists, and phenomenologists to develop concepts of sense and touch that overcome dualistic oppositions and affirm the intangible alterity of others (including other sexes, as indicated by Derrida's reflections on Nancy's touch, which account for sexual differences with specific reference to Irigaray's concept of touch) (Derrida, 2005, p. 164). Nancy articulates his philosophy of touch by drawing on Christianity—a "religion of touch"—with particular attention to the biblical scene where the recently resurrected Jesus tells Mary Magdalene, "Do not touch me" (Nancy, 2008, p. 14). That phrase is "the word and the instant of relation and revelation between two bodies" (p. 48). Mary's contact with the revelation of the resurrected Jesus leaves Jesus untouched. This scene makes a sensitive point about touch in general. To authentically relate to another being, to touch with tact, one must paradoxically leave that being untouched. One must open up to the "gap intrinsic to touch," to an "insurmountable edge-to-edge" relationship that unites while also separating (p. 13). That is the touch of love, the touch of truth. "Love and truth touch by pushing away: they force the retreat of those whom they reach, for their very onset reveals, in the touch itself, that they are out of reach. It is in being unattainable that they touch us, even seize us . . . you are unable to hold or retain anything, and that is precisely what you must love and know" (p. 37). The gap where touch contacts the untouched is the opening of the sense of the world, which is not only about the world as sense (ontology) or our sense of the world (epistemology). This opening is the space of tact. With tact, one participates in the opening that unites and differentiates the many ways we touch. Participating in this opening of sense is the task of ethics. Indeed, Nancy defines "*sense as ethos*," such that ethics becomes an embodied participation in practical situations and not merely a prescriptive schema or a system of rules derived from a theory (1996, p. 38).[7] This ethic supports the development of communities that bring the members together, while also honoring their differences, such that saying "we," according to Nancy, "expresses 'our' being divided and entangled" (2000, p. 65). "We" expresses the collective plurality of all singular beings. By learning ethical contact—tactful contact—we can "*say we for all being, that is, for every being, for all beings one by one, each time in the singular of their essential plural*" (p. 3).

Nancy could be considered as a proponent of the emerging movement of "speculative realism," although there have been relatively few efforts to explicitly bring his work together with speculative realism (O'Rourke, 2011,

p. 303). Beginning in 2007, the speculative realism movement includes diverse philosophical positions, which have at least two commitments in common: 1) realism, which overcomes the tendencies of philosophies to conceptualize reality only in terms of human access to reality, or some kind of "correlation" between subjective thinking and objective being; and 2) speculative metaphysics, which indicates that speculative realism is not a naive realism that focuses on what is given in immediate experience or scientific measurement, but is a "weird realism" that understands real beings in metaphysical terms (e.g., in terms of the meaning of being, the origin or end of the universe, the substance(s) underlying qualities and relations, the transcendental structure of nature, etc.) (Harman, 2010, pp. 1–2; Harman 2011, pp. 21–22).[8] It is important to mention that speculative realism, like integral philosophy, does not advocate a return to pre-Kantian or premodern metaphysics. Speculative realism advocates an approach to metaphysics that is thoroughly postmetaphysical, insofar as it discusses the metaphysical dimensions of the real world, while also including the insights of postmodern philosophies, which recognize that metaphysical descriptions are always enacted or constructed and thereby situated within a certain context, an opening of sense.

The branch of speculative realism most oriented toward touch is "object-oriented philosophy"—or object-oriented ontology (OOO)—which Graham Harman has been developing since 1999, almost a decade prior to the speculative realist movement of which it is a part (Harman, 2010, p. 93). Harman articulates an ontology of objects, where objects are not opposed to subjects but designate all beings, things, entities, in short, all "*integral units*" (2005, p. 118). Harman attempts to account for the reality of objects without "undermining" them (reducing them to their constituent parts or to an underlying process or continuum), or "overmining" them (reducing them to their appearances or relations to human consciousness) (2011, p. 24). Following Martin Heidegger's phenomenology, Harman affirms an untouched dimension of beings, an inexhaustible core that exceeds the reach of human contact, and in following Alfred North Whitehead's process philosophy, Harman claims that humans are different in degree (not in kind) to other actual entities, so that what Heidegger saw in humans can be said to occur in all beings (2010, pp. 95–101). In other words, beings withdraw from all contact, not just from human contact, such that "no substance ever comes in contact with another at all" (p. 119).

For example, when fire burns cotton, the fire does not directly touch the cotton itself. The real core of the cotton itself is an unfathomable depth that never becomes present. It only appears indirectly, as it is translated into the worldspace of other beings. The real cotton is touched indirectly as the fire enters into a relationship with the flammable qualities of the cotton (p. 124). Through this indirect touch, the cotton is consumed in flames without the flames ever touching the unfathomable core of the cotton. This means that all causality happens in such a way that things touch each other without touching at all, making contact while leaving one another intact. This is integral causality. Harman calls it "vicarious causation," according to which objects "touch without touching," interacting vicariously via one another's alluring qualities while leaving their real core untouched (2007, p. 220).[9]

Even during the act of lovemaking, the lover and the beloved do not directly touch, but touch in a way that respects the real core of the other and leaves it intact. Touching one another's real bodies, every touch, entwinement, and penetration leaves intact the inexhaustible core of the other. Touching without touching, every touch leaves the lovers wanting more, kiss after kiss, night after night. To touch without love is to touch in a way that hits or crashes into the other, effacing the inexhaustible and intangible reality of a thing by treating the thing as something merely present, something simply graspable or manipulable. When a compassionate gesture is said to be "touching," it is precisely because the gesture touched with tact, rather than hitting or crashing.

Along with phenomenology, postmodernism, and feminism, speculative realists such as Nancy and Harman provide concepts of touch that work to overcome the dualistic logic that opposes human subjects and nonhuman objects and to affirm the untouched alterity that lies at the core of reality. More than phenomenology and postmodernism, feminism and speculative realism talk about the real world in a way that is not focused exclusively on human access to the world, and they are more emphatically affirmative about the irreducible plurality of beings. Following the grain of these parallels between speculative realism and feminism, proposals for an object-oriented feminism are already underway (O'Rourke, 2011, p. 298). Nonetheless, although there are convergences and collaborations between these philosophies of touch, situating them in relation to integral philosophy can provide them with a map (AQAL) to further coordinate their efforts and to make their work more accessible and applicable to multiple perspectives, including other philosophical and nonphilosophical ways of being and knowing. Consider a few examples:

Touching levels: In conjunction with the integral map, these philosophies can engage with psycho-spiritual states and developmental levels that are not normally included in modern and postmodern philosophical inquiry. For instance, many postmodern philosophies fail to take religion seriously, or they take it seriously only in political or cultural contexts, with little or no appreciation for the realities of religious states and stages of consciousness, especially post-egoic, post-rational states/stages. Even though Deleuze draws from Zen, there are still many Deleuzians who ignore the spiritual aspect of his work. AQAL ensures that philosophies touch base with all levels, coordinating the continuities and differences between them (e.g., an infant's touch and a mystic's touch are both nonrational, yet the latter is generally post- and the former prerational). AQAL also enjoins philosophers to touch the levels lightly, leaving them intact and not simply assimilating them into one's own horizon of interpretation. Such tactful touch prevents the reduction of any being to its developmental level (developmental reductionism), and it prevents the sort of condescension where people in higher or meta-positions talk down to subjects expressing lower developmental levels.

Touching quadrants: By integrating multiple philosophies of touch, the integral map can broaden their horizons beyond the (inter)subjective values, experiences, and worldviews studied in the humanities ("I" and "We" quadrants), thus generating an integral philosophy of touch that interacts with those quadrants, along with the external world and the objects and systems studied in biophysical and social sciences ("It/s" quadrants), which are often neglected by the humanistic and literary emphases in Continental philosophy. For instance, phenomenological meditations on touch rarely mention the economics of touch (e.g., the commodified touch of a massage therapist) or the physics of touch (e.g., friction, force, quantum entanglement). Not only would AQAL facilitate engagements with all quadrants, it would also facilitate tactful touch between quadrants, such that no quadrant would be assimilated into the others, nor excluded. Tactfully drawn, the lines of distinction between the quadrants mark the entanglement and the difference between subjective/objective and individual/collective modes of being and knowing.

Touching lines: An integral philosophy of touch can expand philosophies of touch beyond cognitive ways of knowing to engage the developing lines of other intelligences (somatic, aesthetic, emotional, interpersonal, etc.). This does not just mean giving a cognitive account of multiple intelligences. It also entails practicing philosophy in a way that enacts multiple intelligences. For instance, even an embodied philosophy like Merleau-Ponty's is still a rather cognitive expression of embodied subjectivity. Integral philosophy enjoins us to embody our embodied philosophy. An integral philosophy of touch would include rational, verbal accounts of the intertwining of the flesh, and it would bring them into contact with somatic practices for embodying that philosophy and interpersonal exercises for realizing it in relationships with others. As with the levels and quadrants, an integral philosophy of touch would touch base with all lines of intelligence, and it would also facilitate a tactful touch that affirms the entanglements and differences marked by each line.

An integral philosophy of touch is one where the touching philosophies of sense developed throughout twentieth century schools of thought become radically comprehensive, coordinating with more fields of study and enacting more inclusive engagements with diverse modes of knowing and being. Furthermore, an integral philosophy of touch is one where the "all" of all-quadrant, all-level, all-line, etc., is a tactful "all." Sometimes when an integral scholar-practitioner says "all," people brace for an oncoming embrace. However, a tactful "all" is not a metaphysical meta-hug of death, not a process of dictatorial totalization or neocolonial assimilation. What exactly is it? Great care must be taken to articulate such a tactful "all." Saying too much or saying it too directly would compromise the openness of its sense, but saying too little or saying it too vaguely would fail to establish an integral sense of touch. To put it laconically, a tactful "all" does not come from a metaphysical system of hugs, but from postmetaphysical tactics.

Postmetaphysical Tactics

By bringing integral philosophy into integrative contact with philosophical concepts developed in phenomenology, postmodernism, feminism, and speculative realism, a compelling sense of touch emerges that can facilitate tactful contact with multiple ways of knowing and being. An integral philosophy of touch honors the integrity of everything it touches, including the mystery of the non-dual nonsense circulating in and beyond the multiple senses of sense. With tactics for tactful contact, an integral touch is postmetaphysical.

Wilber's proposal for integral postmetaphysics (IPM) draws on the "postmetaphysical thinking" of Jürgen Habermas (1992), which denotes the style of philosophical inquiry that takes place as philosophers learn to articulate their theories without taking metaphysical principles as givens (pp. 28–51).[10] Habermas argues that metaphysical thinking has dominated philosophy from Plato to Hegel and the modern philosophy of consciousness. Habermas enumerates three main principles that tend to accompany metaphysical thinking: 1) identity thinking, which posits a single, original identity that generates the multiplicity of appearances and differences; 2) idealism, which supposes that reality can be readily understood through an effort of intellectual apprehension; and 3) a strong concept of theory, according to which theory takes precedence over practices and over the ways of looking and feeling that enact theoretical inquiry (1992, pp. 29–34).

Integral philosophy would be metaphysical if it supposed that the different perspectives and levels of reality it coordinates actually designated the original structure of reality (identity thinking); if it supposed that the realms of reality designated by AQAL were constituted by an effort of the human intellect (idealism); or if it supposed that its theoretical significance supersedes practical engagements with the world (strong theory). Accordingly, instead of integral philosophy using AQAL to designate a pre-given ontological unity apprehended by an intellect detached from practice, Wilber holds that any ontological structures or levels of reality come about through engagements in practices. For Wilber, "the central contribution of an Integral Post-Metaphysics" is that "it does not itself contain metaphysics, but it can generate metaphysics as one possible AQAL Matrix configuration . . . but without relying on any pregiven archetypal, or independently existing ontological structures, levels, planes, etc." (Wilber, 2002a). By renewing metaphysical inquiry, while shedding some of the heavy baggage of metaphysical thinking, IPM facilitates "emancipation" in Habermas's sense of the term, where emancipation arises in dialogue that seeks mutual understanding for the sake of a more integrated relationship to one's practices in the world (1992, pp. xviii, pp. 184–199). An integral philosophy of touch facilitates emancipation by overcoming the identity thinking, idealism, and strong theory that characterize metaphysical thinking and replacing them with *pluralism*, *realism*, and *embodiment*.

Pluralism

Touch does not support a philosophy of simple oneness: For touching is different than touched, and touch is only one among many senses, such that concepts of touch generally support a *pluralism* that embraces the multiplicity of sense. Just as the philosophy of Irigaray (1985) supports a pluralism that embraces a "sex which is not one," we could say that her concept of touch embraces a sense which is not one. However, not all philosophies of touch are necessarily pluralistic. For instance, while phenomenology and postmodernism can be very affirmative of plurality and difference, their theories risk assimilating multiplicity into the unity of human experience (Merleau-Ponty) or the dynamic unity of a process of becoming (Deleuze). Nancy (2000) attempts to affirm the singularity and plurality of beings; yet, according to Harman, some of Nancy's writing still ends up undermining the plurality of beings by describing the specific differences between beings as an effect of an underlying unity, a "byproduct of a deeper primordial reality" (Harman, 2011, p. 23). In contrast, Harman's object-oriented philosophy considers the unique qualities of beings to belong to those beings themselves. Every being has its own specific ways of touching, being touched, and remaining intact. Harman staunchly defends a pluralistic position, affirming the diverse panoply of beings without falling into the identity thinking that has pervaded the history of metaphysics. OOO appears to be the most explicitly pluralist philosophy of touch.

Pluralism can be found in phenomenology, postmodernism, feminism, and OOO, yet it is particularly in the latter two that an integral philosophy finds support for the development of an "integral pluralism," such as that expressed by Sean Esbjörn-Hargens in his compelling proposal for an integral pluralism that includes integral epistemological pluralism (IEP), integral methodological pluralism (IMP), and integral ontological pluralism (IOP) (2010, p. 146). Of course, integral philosophy already includes an explicitly pluralistic commitment in the form of integral methodological pluralism (IMP). However, where IMP affirms a pluralism of methods and paradigms, a true affirmation of the many ways we touch must include many ways of knowing (methods), while also including a multiplicity of knowers (epistemology) and knowns (ontology). In other words, in order to include the vast array of ways of knowing and being, integral approaches to philosophy must be explicitly epistemological and ontological in their pluralism, as well as methodological. Integral pluralism includes the "who" (knower), "what" (known), and "how" (method) of the multiplicity of integral objects in the Kosmos. Esbjörn-Hargens mentions that while IMP has been explicitly developed in integral theory, IEP is largely implicit and IOP "is even less developed than the implicit notion of epistemological pluralism." Harman's ontology of touch would facilitate the further development of this ontological pluralism.

Interestingly, Esbjörn-Hargens draws on Harman's work to describe integral pluralism, specifically by pointing toward Harman's account of the philosophy of the contemporary French thinker Bruno Latour, who proposes a philosophy of actors (actor-network theory) that is similar to Harman's metaphysics of objects. According to Esbjörn-Hargens, "there is much in Latour's work that is relevant to an integral post-metaphysics" (p. 167). Indeed, Latour and Harman together have much to contribute to the pluralism, realism, and embodiment of IPM. However, Harman is perhaps better suited to ontological pluralism than Latour, for the latter defines actors primarily in terms of the networks of their complex relations, with the intact cores of the actors reduced to a single underlying substance. "Latour verges on acknowledging a single plasma-in-itself, not a plurality of distinct entities withdrawn from all relation" (Harman, 2009, p. 134). To put it briefly, the main difference between Latour and Harman is that Harman accounts for the untouched or withdrawn cores of objects, thereby making Harman more effective in elucidating the plurality of objects in ways that honor their depth, mystery, and alterity.

Realism

Integral philosophy, as a postmetaphysical philosophy of touch, is a pluralism that studies the many ways of touching, honoring every integral unit in the Kosmos in their difference and multiplicity. Along with pluralism, an integral philosophy of touch supports *realism*, overcoming the idealist tendencies found throughout the history of metaphysics, for which the real world is something readily given to human understanding. Realism suggests that questions of the real world are not merely questions of what is given to humans (whether in human rationality, thought, consciousness, experience, etc.). In other words, realism stands in contrast to "the myth of the given," which Habermas calls "the philosophy of consciousness," for it reduces reality to what is "simply given to me" or given to the subject or to consciousness (Wilber, 2007, p. 176).

Following Wilber's critique of the myth of the given, integral philosophy can be described as a postmetaphysical realism: Realism insofar as it affirms the existence of a real world, and postmetaphysical insofar as it that real world is never simply given, but appears differently from different perspectives and evolutionary/developmental levels. In short, there are real beings and their reality is situated in a "Kosmic address" that includes the perspective and level of the touching and touched beings (pp. 252–273). As Esbjörn-Hargens (2010) notices, integral theory bears many resemblances to "critical realism," which, not unlike speculative realism, integrates postmodern insights into the processes of translation and enactment through which beings appear, while going beyond postmodernism by recognizing that those processes involve real beings that are translated and enacted.[11]

Perhaps surprisingly, many philosophies of touch have various anti-realist tendencies. The history of Continental philosophy has been pervaded by anti-realism since Kant prohibited knowledge of things in themselves, with philosophers of idealism, existentialism, and phenomenology focusing exclusively on human experience and access to the world, and postmodernists and critical theorists (including Habermas!) analyzing structures of power, social constructs, texts, and discursive practices (Braver, 2007). Even feminist theory, which is generally realist in its attention to sexuality along with issues of materiality and embodiment, harbors tendencies to focus on discourse more than on the real world independent of its givenness to humans.[12] Moreover, Anglo-American philosophy (i.e., analytic philosophy) does not necessarily fare any better than Continental philosophy regarding realism, for it tends to focus on logic and linguistic analysis or scientific experimentation, still reducing reality to human access or given facts.

A postmetaphysical concept of touch must investigate the many ways we touch, while honoring realities that exceed the boundaries of what Derrida criticizes as "humanualism," which focuses only on what is accessible to human consciousness or able to be grasped by the human hand (2005, p. 182). The realist philosophies of Nancy and Harman provide such concepts of touch, particularly by expanding upon Heidegger's realism, which extended to the recognition that there is a real world for humans, but not for nonhumans. Instead of staying with Heidegger's human exceptionalism, for which nothing exists " 'in' the world" except humans, Nancy argues that even a stone touches the world and, indeed, "that it is world" (p. 62).

Like Nancy, Harman departs from Heidegger's anthropocentrism, while still appreciating Heidegger's contributions to an understanding of reality exceeding its presence to humans. Including insights from Whitehead, Harman claims that the relationship between humans and the real world is different only in degree from the relationships between any entities (Harman, 2010, p. 100). Just as human contact (theoretical and practical) never exhausts the profound being of real fire and cotton, "the fire and cotton also fail to make full contact with *each other* when they touch, despite their uniting in a bond of destruction . . . In other words, objects withdraw from each other and not just from humans" (p. 124).

While the realism of integral theory includes critical perspectives that overcome the myth of the given, integral philosophy can become more fully realist by touching base with the untouched dimensions of real beings as elucidated by the speculative realisms of Nancy's post-deconstructive philosophy and Harman's object-oriented philosophy. Adhering to postmetaphysical principles of pluralism and realism, integral philosophy touches base with everything, including the untouched and intangible cores of real beings.

Embodiment

To touch base with the diversity (pluralism) and intangible alterity (realism) of beings, postmetaphysical philosophies must touch lightly, tactfully, so as not to develop philosophical theories that are then unethically imposed on practical situations. An integral touch supports tactful theory, in contrast to the strong theory privileged throughout the history of metaphysics. In other words, an integral philosophy of touch must develop theories that emerge out of the openness of the pragmatics of sense—practices situated in concrete contexts; in short, *embodiment*. Integral theory already supports the development of theories grounded in concrete situations, as indicated by the methodological commitments of integral pluralism. Integral methodological pluralism not only affirms pluralism, but it also affirms the embodied practices, paradigms, ways of looking and feeling, whereby methods enact different truths. As Brad Reynolds notes, IMP implies that all methods of inquiry involve injunctions to practice: "*Engaging the injunction*, following the exemplar, exercising the practice—*doing the yoga*—is the actual method or methodology for disclosing new truths—but, the most important point is: *You have to do them*!" (2006, p. 229). Every truth is disclosed by an injunction, or "enaction" at a specific Kosmic address (Wilber 2007, p. 267).

Accordingly, integral pluralism can be considered a postmetaphysical philosophy of embodiment, a philosophy in which truth is always enacted in a pragmatic context. Integral pluralism grounds what Esbjörn-Hargens calls *integral enactment theory* (IET) (2010, p. 146). IET is "a post-metaphysical approach" that can be conceived as "a meta-field of Integral Theory," which is "anchored in Integral Theory" while "it reaches above and beyond Integral Theory to draw on other valuable enactive and integrative pluralistic approaches to articulate a sophisticated understanding of the complexities of enactment" (p. 168). Such enactive approaches appear in philosophies of touch, which recognize that all truths are enacted, embodied, situated amid practices of sense, such that no truth is pre-given and no theory privileged over the pragmatic context in which it arises. This attention to embodiment is shared by all of the philosophies of touch mentioned in this chapter. Indeed, this attention to embodiment is impossible to ignore, insofar as those philosophies define their concepts in terms of touch and sense, terms that presuppose contact zones—pragmatic contexts within which meanings and truths are generated.

With an emphasis on the ways in which all senses are generated out of a non-dual ground of nonsense, an integral philosophy of touch supports efforts to touch lightly—tactfully—so as to honor the intact core of embodiment—which is to say, the intangible alterity of other bodies; the irreducible differences of pragmatic contexts. To put it another way, integral philosophy can be defined in terms of tactics, where a tactic does not refer to another method that would fit within the AQAL framework (as the methods included in IMP), but to tactful strategies for contacting that which is untouched or untouchable by any philosophical theory or practice, that which withdraws from all enactment.[13] Integral tactics can get in touch with any nonsense that slips through the cracks of methods, models, and meta-theories. They can create surprising and unexpected openings where nonsense is free to make sense, openings where utterly novel and unpredictable perspectives can grow and develop. Integral tactics allow the pluralism and realism of integral philosophy to be embodied and embedded in tactful contact with the many perspectives composing the Kosmos.

Including the philosophies of touch in phenomenology, feminism, postmodernism, and speculative realism, integral philosophy becomes more postmetaphysical, thoroughly supporting pluralism, realism, and embodiment as guiding principles for philosophical inquiry. With an integral touch, philosophers can tactfully make contact with all beings, lightly touching base with the many ways we touch. Tactfully touching, that is, including without assimilating, integral philosophers can bring together and unite, while also allowing everything united to maintain its integrity—the irreducible uniqueness of its specific address in the Kosmos. By further developing concepts of touch and sense, integral approaches to philosophy can facilitate the development of effective tactics for engaging the depth, complexity, and mystery of a Kosmos made up of many ways of touching, being touched, and remaining intact.

Notes

1. The straw man fallacy can appear in many ways, e.g., broadening a position so that it appears to say more than it actually does, omitting aspects of a position by attending to only a few of its details (cherry-picking), and quoting a position without

accounting for the context or the intended meaning of the quotation (contextomy). One example of a straw man fallacy in integral philosophy comes from Wilber's misreading of the philosopher of deconstruction, Jacques Derrida (Desilet, 2007). Wilber recognizes that Derrida's philosophy is in agreement with integral theory insofar as both affirm the contextual conditions of all being and meaning. "Everything is always already *a* context *in* a context," such that "nothing is ever simply present" (Wilber, 2000b, p. 627). However, Wilber goes on to argue incorrectly that Derrida is also in agreement with integral theory in claiming that the world contains some signified reality beyond context (Derrida's "transcendental signified"). According to Wilber, Derrida "concedes" in an interview that "there are genuine transcendental signifieds" that make it possible to translate across languages and cultures (p. 629). Indeed, in that interview, Derrida (1981) says "no translation would be possible without it" (p. 20). However, the "it" in that sentence does not refer to a transcendental signified, but to the "opposition or difference" that contextualizes signifieds in relation to signifiers. Derrida denies precisely what Wilber claims he concedes.

2. To be sure, there are many uses of terms related to touching throughout Wilber's writings, including over twenty references to touch in his first book, *The Spectrum of Consciousness* (1977). The references to touch that appear throughout the earlier phases of Wilber's career have the same general orientation as those appearing in his more recent writings.

3. Touch in this context would include outside, as well as inside, views on every perspective, which correspond with what Wilber calls the look and the feel, respectively. "The outside view is how it looks, the inside view is how it feels" (2007, p. 154). Looking and feeling are two of the many ways we touch.

4. Nancy's philosophical project is paralleled in the United States by John Sallis, who likewise draws on phenomenology and postmodernism to articulate a postmetaphysical concept of sense (Sallis, 2000). Sallis has done much to facilitate the dissemination of Continental thought within the United States.

5. Along with Nancy, Derrida himself can be described as a post-deconstructive realist (Marder, 2009).

6. Although Deleuze frequently describes his philosophy in terms of "pure immanence," it is not an immanence opposed to transcendence, but a nondual plane or vitality irreducible to any such opposition (Deleuze, 2002).

7. The importance of touch for ethical and political engagements has been noted by many scholars, including: Stephen David Ross (1998) and Erin Manning (2007), who draw on postmodern philosophers (including French thinkers like Merleau-Ponty, Deleuze, Irigaray, Nancy, and many more) to articulate the ethics and politics of touch respectively. Also noteworthy is the work of Linda Holler (2002), who draws upon evolutionary biology, phenomenology, psychology, and Buddhist traditions to describe the important role that touch plays in the development of moral agency.

8. The commitment of speculative realists to a reality beyond human access is indicated in their adherence to the critique of "correlationism" expressed by

Quentin Meillassoux, one of the founding figures of speculative realism (along with Ray Brassier, Iain Hamilton Grant, and Graham Harman). Correlationism is Meillassoux's term for "the idea according to which we only ever have access to the correlation between thinking and being" (2008, p. 5).

9. Harman's vicarious causation draws from the causal theory in medieval Islamic and seventeenth century European philosophies of occasionalism, which posit God as an "occasional cause" that provides the mediating term through which any two things make contact (2010, pp. 119, 129, 157). Harman doubts the conceptual efficacy of God as a super-entity magically intervening in the world, and so he opts instead for "the more democratic solution of a local occasionalism," wherein real things contact one another vicariously through the alluring emanations of their intentionality or interiority (p. 206).

10. Wilber considers Habermas to be "the world's greatest living philosopher," which is not to say that he accepts all aspects of Habermas's philosophy; indeed, he strongly disagrees with Habermas on some points (e.g., Habermas's treatment of preverbal and transverbal dimensions of the Kosmos) (Wilber 2001).

11. Esbjörn-Hargens suggests that "critical realism is a viable integral alternative to Integral Theory" in "many respects" (2010, p. 167). Roy Bhaskar's critical realism even includes concepts that "echo Integral Theory's own all-quadrants, all-levels approach" (p. 166). For an introduction to critical realism, see Lopez and Potter (2005).

12. Judith Butler is a relevant example here. She is very concerned about real bodies and real life, recognizing that "life might be understood as precisely that which exceeds any account we may try to give of it" (2005, p. 43). Yet even though she recognizes that life and the body are not reducible to language, her account of the real world beyond human access always reverts to discussions of human experience and language. "Every time I try to write about the body, the writing ends up being about language" (2004, p. 198).

13. The French theorist Michel de Certeau differentiates tactics from methodologies or strategies that work with systems, models, or frameworks. Tactics work in cracks and gaps, where methods and strategies open onto anything other or irreducibly different. "The space of a tactic is the space of the other. Thus it must play on and with a terrain imposed on it and organized by the law of a foreign power . . . It must vigilantly make use of the cracks that particular conjunctions open in the surveillance of the proprietary powers. It poaches in them. It creates surprises in them. It can be where it is least expected" (1984, p. 37).

References

Braver, Lee. 2007. *A Thing of This World: A History of Continental Anti-Realism.* Evanston, IL: Northwestern University Press.

Butler, Judith. 2004. *Undoing Gender.* New York: Routledge.

Butler, Judith. 2005. *Giving an Account of Oneself.* New York: Fordham University Press.

Butler, Judith. 2006. "Sexual Difference as a Question of Ethics: Alterities of the Flesh in Irigaray and Merleau-Ponty." In *Feminist Interpretations of Maurice Merleau-Ponty*, ed. Dorothea Olkowski and Gail Weiss, 107–125. University Park, PA: Pennsylvania State University Press.

de Certeau, Michel. 1984. *The Practice of Everyday Life.* Berkeley, CA: University of California Press.

Deleuze, Gilles. 1990. *The Logic of Sense*, ed. Constantin V. Boundas; trans. Mark Lester with Charles Stivale. New York: Columbia University Press.

Deleuze, Gilles. 2002. *Pure Immanence: Essays on A Life*, trans. Anne Boyman. Cambridge, MA: MIT Press.

Derrida, Jacques. 1981. *Positions*, trans. Alan Bass. Chicago: University of Chicago Press.

Derrida, Jacques. 2005. *On Touching—Jean-Luc Nancy*, trans. Christine Irizarry Stanford, CA: Stanford University Press.

Desilet, Gregory. 2007. "Misunderstanding Derrida and Postmodernism: Ken Wilber and 'Post-Metaphysics' Integral Spirituality." Integral World.Net. http://www.integralworld.net/desilet.html. Retrieved July 7, 2011.

Esbjörn-Hargens, Sean. 2010. "An Ontology of Climate Change: Integral Pluralism and the Enactment of Multiple Objects." *Journal of Integral Theory and Practice* 5(1): 143–174.

Habermas, Jürgen. 1992. *Postmetaphysical Thinking: Philosophical Essays*, trans. W.M. Hohengarten. Cambridge, MA: MIT Press.

Haraway, Donna. 2008. *When Species Meet.* Minneapolis, MN: University of Minnesota Press.

Harman, Graham. 2005. *Guerilla Metaphysics: Phenomenology and the Carpentry of Things.* Chicago: Open Court.

Harman, Graham. 2007. "On Vicarious Causation." *Collapse* 2: 187–221.

Harman, Graham. 2009. *Prince of Networks: Bruno Latour and Metaphysics.* Melbourne, AU: re.press.

Harman, Graham. 2010. *Towards Speculative Realism: Essays and Lectures.* Winchester, UK: Zero Books.

Harman, Graham. 2011. "On the Undermining of Objects: Grant, Bruno, and Radical Philosophy." In *The Speculative Turn: Continental Materialism and Realism*, ed. Levi Bryant, Nick Srnicek, and Graham Harman, 21–40. Melbourne, AU: re.press.

Holler, Linda. 2002. *Erotic Morality: The Role of Touch in Moral Agency.* New Brunswick, NJ: Rutgers University Press.

Irigaray, Luce. 1985. *The Sex Which is Not One*, trans. Catherine Porter. Ithaca, NY: Cornell University Press.

Irigaray, Luce. 2004. *An Ethics of Sexual Difference*, trans. Carolyn Burke and Gillian C. Gill. London: Continuum.

Jaspers, Karl. 2003. *Way to Wisdom: An Introduction to Philosophy* (2d ed.), trans. Ralph Manheim. New Haven, CT: Yale University Press.

Lawlor, Leonard. 2003. *Thinking Through French Philosophy: The Being of the Question*. Bloomington, IN: Indiana University Press.

Levinas, Emmanuel. 1991. *Totality and Infinity: An Essay on Exteriority*, trans. Alphonso Lingis. Dordrecht, NL: Kluwer Academic Publishers.

Lopez, José and Garry Potter (eds.). 2005. *After Postmodernism: An Introduction to Critical Realism*. New York: Continuum Press.

Manning, Erin. 2007. *Politics of Touch: Sense, Movement, Sovereignty*. Minneapolis, MN: University of Minnesota Press.

Marder, Michael. 2009. *The Event of the Thing: Derrida's Post-Deconstructive Realism*. Toronto: Toronto University Press.

Meillassoux, Quentin. 2008. *After Finitude: An Essay on the Necessity of Contingency*, trans. Ray Brassier. New York: Continuum.

Merleau-Ponty, Maurice. 1964. *Signs*, trans. Richard C. McCleary. Evanston, IL: Northwestern University Press.

Merleau-Ponty, Maurice 1968. *The Visible and the Invisible*, trans. Alphonso Lingis. Evanston, IL: Northwestern University Press.

Nancy, Jean-Luc. 1996. *The Muses*, trans. Peggy Kamuf. Stanford, CA: Stanford University Press.

Nancy, Jean-Luc. 1997. *The Sense of the World*, trans. J. Librett. Minneapolis, MN: University of Minnesota Press.

Nancy, Jean-Luc. 2000. *Being Singular Plural*, trans. Robert Richardson and Anne O'Byrne. Stanford, CA: Stanford University Press.

Nancy, Jean-Luc. 2005. "Interview: The Future of Philosophy," trans. B.C. Hutchens. In *Jean-Luc Nancy and the Future of Philosophy*, 161–166. Chesham, UK: Acumen.

Nancy, Jean-Luc. 2008. *Noli Me Tangere: On the Raising of the Body*, trans. Sarah Clift, Pascale-Anne Brault, and Michael Naas. New York: Fordham University Press.

O'Rourke, M. (2011). " 'Girls Welcome!!!' Speculative Realism, Object-oriented Ontology, and Queer Theory." *Speculations* 2: 275–312.

Reynolds, Brad. 2006. *Where's Wilber At?: Ken Wilber's Integral Vision in the New Millennium*. St. Paul, MN: Paragon House.

Ricoeur, Paul. 1967. *Husserl: An Analysis of His Phenomenology*, trans. Edward G. Ballard and Lester E. Embree. Evanston, IL: Northwestern University Press.

Ross, Stephen David. 1998. *The Gift of Touch: Embodying the Good*. Albany, NY: SUNY Press.

Sallis, John. 2000. *Force of Imagination: The Sense of the Elemental*. Bloomington, IN: Indiana University Press.

Toadvine, Ted. 2004. "Singing the World in a New Key: Merleau-Ponty and the Ontology of Sense." *Janus Head* 7(2): 273–283.

Warren, Karen. 2008. "The Power and Promise of Ecological Feminism." In *Environmental Ethics: Readings in Theory and Application* (5th ed.), ed. Louis P. Pojman and Paul Pojman, 33–48. Belmont, CA: Thomson.

Wilber, Ken. 1977. *The Spectrum of Consciousness*. Wheaton, IL: Quest Books.

Wilber, Ken. 2000a. *A Theory of Everything: An Integral Vision for Business, Politics, Science, and Spirituality*. Boston: Shambhala.

Wilber, Ken. 2000b. *Sex, Ecology, Spirituality: The Spirit of Evolution* (2nd rev. ed.). Boston: Shambhala.

Wilber, Ken. 2001. "On the Nature of a Post-metaphysical Spirituality: Response to Habermas and Weis." 2 parts. Ken Wilber Online, http://wilber.shambhala.com/html/misc/habermas/index.cfm (accessed July 7, 2011).

Wilber, Ken. 2002a. "Introduction to Excerpts," from volume 2 of the *Kosmos Trilogy*. Ken Wilber Online, http://wilber.shambhala.com/html/books/kosmos/index.cfm (accessed July 7, 2011).

Wilber, Ken. 2002b. "Excerpt B: The Many Ways We Touch: Three Principles Helpful for any Integrative Approach." 3 parts. Ken Wilber Online, http://wilber.shambhala.com/html/books/kosmos/excerptB/part3.cfm (accessed July 7, 2011).

Wilber, Ken. 2007. *Integral Spirituality: A Startling New Role for Religion in the Modern and Postmodern World*. Boston: Integral Books.

PART III

Limits and Critique

Chapter 8

Toward an Integral Ontological Pluralism

A Process-Oriented Critique of Integral Theory's Evolutionary Cosmology

Zayin Cabot

In Appendix II of *Integral Spirituality*, Ken Wilber asks an important question that goes right to the heart of integral theory. How can we account for contemporary evolutionary theory and defend the possibility of Enlightenment with a capital *E*? Wilber (2006b, pp. 235–236) lays out the problem in the following way: First, if evolution does occur, and novelty does happen, then the Enlightenment is necessarily partial. If real novelty occurs, then the enlightenment of yesterday does not include the novelty of today. Enlightenment yesterday is not as "full" as enlightenment today. The typical response, says Wilber, among those who want to defend Enlightenment with a capital *E*, is to equate it with the Timeless, Eternal, and/or Unborn. The problem, again following Wilber, is that if you locate Spirit (that which is known through Enlightenment) as the timeless, unborn, and/or eternal, then you end up with a "massive duality." "[If] I revert to Enlightenment being defined only as a realization of the timeless and unborn," writes Wilber (2006b, p. 236), "and then I must deny that Spirit is also the world of manifest form." The key to an integral evolutionary cosmology must be articulated on this subtle point. Spirit cannot simply be timeless or eternal, or else it is distinct from the world of form. But if real novelty exists, how can one defend the existence of some ultimate Spirit?

Wilber assures the reader that his postmetaphysical integral spirituality is able to do just this—hence the *integral*—and does not fall into this dualist trap. The truth, I argue, is quite the opposite.

While Wilber has made valiant efforts to accommodate evolutionary theories into his cosmology, in the end I believe he maintains the exact same "massive duality" between Spirit and the evolving changing novelty prone world of form that his postmetaphysical stance sets out to avoid. Wilber's most recent work, what he terms his postmetaphysical stage, is still beholden to Jorge Ferrer's (2011, p. 15) characterization of Wilber's thought as a "peculiar hybrid of Buddhist emptiness and Advaita/Zen nondual embrace of the phenomenal world." This is because Wilber's postmetaphysics does exactly what it claims not to do. It offers a "sliding scale of Enlightenment," whereby Enlightenment can accommodate the changing of perspectives, but not the actuality of the one ultimate Perceiver. There is a sleight of hand at work here.

To assert something metaphysically, on Wilber's account, is to assert the existence of preexisting ontological structures. Wilber characterizes his later work as postmetaphysical, because he does not postulate such preexisting ontological structures. Rather, he asserts the existence of Spirit, which is able, if needed, to generate ontological structures like those established within traditional metaphysics (e.g., Platonic, Vedic, Buddhist, and Whiteheadian) (2006b, p. 42). Wilber's *Integral Post-Metaphysics*, on his account, "re-defines the manifest realm as the realm of perspectives not thing nor events nor structures nor process nor systems nor *vasanas* nor archetypes nor *dharmas*" (2006b, p. 42). These are all various perspectives of Spirit for Wilber, and in asserting Spirit he has not made a metaphysical claim. At least, this is his assertion. Rather, again according to Wilber, he has made a postmetaphysical claim. So what does Wilber's postmetaphysics amount to?

What were surface and deep structures (ontological givens) in his earlier work become probable perspectives, rather than ontologcial givens, in his later work. So Wilber is arguing against any simple assertion of static ontological structures, and in their place he is arguing for a theory of emergence whereby various structures, *vasanas*, *dharmas*, and systems are understood as emergent perspectives. The world of form and evolving perspectives is not presumed to be ontologically real; instead, Wilber's non-dual Spirit is ontologically given. Structures emerge from the various perspectives of Spirit. This is a strange kind of postmetaphysics in that it makes an obvious metaphysical claim (i.e., a strong idealist monism). As such, I find it hard to understand how this most recent iteration of Wilber's work can be seen as postmetaphysical. It is this curiosity that drives the rest of this chapter. As I show in detail throughout these pages, many integral theorists are well aware of this issue. As such, the rest of these pages are devoted to a defense of what Sean Esbjörn-Hargens (2010) has termed an *integral ontological pluralism*, a position that I am at some pains to develop by way of distinguishing it from the tendency toward ontological monism I see present in Wilber's own thought.

In the same appendix cited above, Wilber (2006b, p. 236) clarifies that an evolutionary theory must include "some sort of 'creative allure,' or what Whitehead called 'the creative advance into novelty.'" Through multiple readings of Wilber's work, it has become clear to me that he has not been able to accommodate the sort of radical creativity and novelty that Whitehead's philosophy argues for. And, more importantly, his postmetaphysical stance cannot accommodate the novelty that Darwin's evolutionary theory requires (see Ghiselin, below). Whiteheadian scholar Michel Weber has clarified what Whitehead means by "creative advance into novelty" by distinguishing between two sets of terms. He makes an important distinction between process-oriented thought that is *novative* and *trans-formative* (a continuity of becoming) and a more *innovative* and *creative* process-oriented thought that approaches the radical *becoming of continuity* that Whitehead's philosophy points us toward (Weber, 2006, p. 197; 2011, p. 95).

To this end, Whitehead (1978, p. 36) writes, "There is a becoming of continuity, but no continuity of becoming. The actual occasions are the creatures which become, and they constitute a continuously extensive world. In other words, extensiveness becomes, but 'becoming' is not itself extensive." This is different from Wilber's work, where Spirit is always already and the creatures are emergent. Creatures, for Whitehead, are the only real entities. "Apart from the experiences of subjects [not Subject]," writes Whitehead (1978, p. 167), "there is nothing, nothing, nothing, bare nothingness." The theoretical line of this chapter is drawn in parallel to these distinctions.

For Weber, novative and trans-formative thought assumes that change occurs within the context of an ontological unity or continuity, and so is superficial. This is in keeping with Wilber's notion of Spirit. If Spirit (Subject) is ultimately eternal or one, then any change is trivial. Novelty and change do not occur within the essential and timeless nature of Spirit, because Spirit cannot become more full. But Whitehead (1978, p. 36) tells us that "The ultimate metaphysical truth is atomism," not monism or any other expression of Being as continuity. If we follow this innovative and creative turn, then the ultimacy or continuity of Spirit must be called into question. Whitehead sees that for there to be real novelty, real freedom of decision, choice and enjoyment, then there can be no ultimate Continuity, Spirit or Being. Novelty, in relation to a Continuity, is relegated to surface changes that occur in superficial ways that do not affect an underlying essential unity. Whitehead sees this as an antiquated style of thought that is not in line with the very best of contemporary science. Innovation and creative process thought (i.e., Whitehead's mature process philosophy) point toward a far more radical atomicity. William Ernest Hocking, himself an important philosopher working at the beginning of the twentieth century, took a series of courses from Whitehead throughout the winter and summer of 1925. In one very important lecture of Whitehead's that occurred on April 7, Hocking records Whitehead as saying, "Science at present is asking for an atomic theory of time. Shall metaphysics say to science it can't have it?" (as cited in Ford, 1984, p. 281). The full thrust of Whitehead's mature work is born out these lectures as he sought to accommodate the radical novelty required by both the evolutionary theory and physics of his day. This is the same goal that Wilber has adopted for his own mature work, yet the possibility of accounting for the deep and radical change haunts integral theory to this day.

For Whitehead there is an underlying atomicity and pluralism that must take presidence over any assertions of continuity. The absolute (or Spirit) is not eternal; it is atomic and plural. Every absolute must perish, writes Whitehead (1978, p. 60), because if it is a coherent whole, there can be no real change that occurs at its essence. This would make it something wholly other. Any essentail change necessarily brings about something novel, which was not contained in the other absolute whole. This is not a problem for Whitehead, but it is a problem for anyone who wants to argue for both an innovative and creative novelty and a timeless spiritual Enlightenment.

To this end, Whitehead (1978, p. 84) warns us to be wary of the medieval tendency to overemphasize final causality (i.e., God, or in Wilber's case, Spirit), as well as the modern tendency to defend an overly mechanistic atomism that asserts nothing but efficient causality. Aristotle thought of change as trans-formative, a continuity of becoming that occurs in the context of the Kosmos. Neo-Darwinists have reduced all change to efficient causation and materialism, a monism predicated on Nature. Wilber defends his own nondual ontological unity, Spirit, which is a continuity in its own right. Following Whitehead, wherever we see a continuity we can be sure that change is trans-formative (i.e., superficial and not at the level of essence), rather than creative (i.e., essential). If we are going to rise to the challenge presented by contemporary evolutionary and physical theories, we will have to do better.

Whitehead's innovative/creative solution is to atomize the absolute essential subjectivity of becoming. He tells us that beyond autonomous atomic subjectivities there is "nothing, nothing, nothing, bare nothingness" (Whitehead, 1978, p. 167). Beyond atomic absolutes, there is no Absolute, no Spirit, no continuity that ties them all together. Whitehead argues that if we are truly up to the challenge of our contemporary sciences, we must assert some form of atomism and radical novelty. An ontological pluralism that asserts a diversity of what Whitehead has alternatively called subject-superjects, actual occasions, or moments of concrescence. Subject and object are intimately intertwined in a way that is different in kind from any traditional assertions that make either subject (e.g., Spirit) or object (e.g., Nature) primary. Ontological pluralism requires just that: pluralism and atomism at an ontological level.

Now it is important to understand that Wilber is well aware of this conversation, and more than open to considering Whitehead's process thought. He tells us, "The important point is that Whitehead was the first to spot the general features of the microgenetic holarchical nature of moment-to-moment existence, so we are more than glad to be Whiteheadians in this general area" (2006c, p. 10). Wilber sees the importance of what Whitehead is after, but he misunderstands Whitehead to be defending a microgenetic (novative-trans-formational) process philosophy as opposed to a macrogenetic (innovative-creative) process philosophy. Whitehead places Creativity as the answer to dualism and the disjointed nature of Spirit (*God*, to use Whitehead's word) and World (1978, p. 348). In mistaking Whitehead's assertion's regarding creativity, novelty, and change as microgenetic instead of macrogenetic, Wilber has misunderstood the distinction that I am making here between novative and innovate process thought.

In referencing Whitehead's work, Wilber writes, "Each moment is not a subject prehending an object; it is a perspective prehending a perspective" (2006b, p. 42). Here Wilber claims that Whitehead has a hidden "monological metaphysics," and that "Integral Post-Metaphysics can thus generate the essentials of Whitehead's view but without assuming Whitehead's hidden metaphysics" (2006b, p. 42). Here we are offered a clear view of where Wilber and Whitehead differ. Wilber takes Whitehead to be asserting a subject separate from an object. This subject is given, and has a perception of some object, and so Whitehead says he has given us an innovative process-oriented philosophy, but he has really slipped a subjective monism into his metaphysics.

Wilber addresses this by asserting that his work "replaces *perceptions* with *perspectives*," and as such solves the problem (2006b, p. 42). His integral postmetpahysics manages to generate all structures (as perspectives, rather than ontological givens), and so "generates [Whitehead and other traditional metaphysics] essential contours with assuming their extensive metaphysics" (2006b, p. 43). Remember Whitehead's assertion above. Extensiveness becomes, but becoming is not extensive. Wilber has misunderstood Whitehead's theory of prehensions to mean that a subject prehends an object, and as such the subject is somehow continuous or extensive. But for Whitehead, there is no continuous subject, nor any continuous object. There is only the act of prehension, predicated by a subject-superject. Whitehead's theory of prehension lies at the heart of his work and is too complex to fully outline here. But what is important to note is the subject and object become radically atomized as one moment of concresence. There is no subject, no object, and no continuity outside of this innovate process.

Trans-formative/novative process thought asserts a unity at the ontological level, and subjugates pluralism to a trivial surface that in its most extreme expression sees change as illusory. Creative innovative process thought asserts a true ontological pluralism, where 'becoming is not itself extensive,' and "the 'perpetual perishing' (cf. Locke, II, XIV, 1) of individual absoluteness is thus foredoomed" (Whitehead, 1978, p. 60). If integral theory is going to assert an evolutionary cosmology and an integral ontological pluralism that is predicated on real novelty, then it will likely have to adopt a process-oriented thought that is more *creative* and *innovative* that can align with Whitehead's challenge of ontological atomicity/pluralism. I clarify this important distinction in greater detail throughout the rest of this chapter.

Evolutionary Theory and Innovation

One of integral theory's great intellectual contributions to the academy is its defense of an evolutionary cosmology in the face of a critical turning away from such speculation. Yet it is my assertion here that the field has not faced the full philosophical ramifications of positing an evolutionary cosmology. The tendency to continue to assert the unity of Spirit as a given, in the face of evolutionary theories' emphasis on discontinuity and atomicity, offers one example of why such evolutionary theories have fallen out of favor. Herbert Spencer is an early example of this kind of lackadaisical cosmologizing that has given evolutionary thought a bad reputation.

Spencer conflated natural selection and survivability with his own notions of *goodness*. Jean Baptiste de Lamarck's work offers another example. He was an accomplished scientist, but not the best cosmologist. Like Wilber, Lamarck extrapolated a great-chain-of-being theory. But unlike Lamarck's idea of punctuated equilibrium (a precursor to the emphasis on atomicity and ontological pluralism defended here), the AQAL model as Wilber presents it continues to overemphasize an ontological monism. Following Whitehead, a similar point could be brought against neo-Darwinian thought, to the extent that it defends its own ontological monism in the form of Nature (see Cobb Jr, 2008; Nagel, 2012; Plantinga, 2012), but that is a point beyond the scope of this short chapter.

Wilber would, of course, push back at my insistence that his work is beholden to such a novative trans-formative monism. Yes, he would likely tell us, in *Sex, Ecology, Spirituality* (Wilber IV) there is an emphasis on Spirit, but there is also a distinction made between surface structures and deep structures that is tempered by an evolutionary-involutionary cosmology. Changes in surface structure are seen as superficial *translations*, while changes in deep structures are more innovative in nature. Instead of heaps, we get entirely new "wholes" that are created. This more creative change, which sounds close enough to Whitehead's creative process thought, is understood as *transformational* (2000, p. 68). Wilber is still privileging his deep ground-of-being over more superficial (and so trans-formative and novative) changes of perspective on the surface.

Wilber appears to agree with my basic point that innovative process is necessary, but to the extent that Wilber is still dealing with a nondual ontological continuity as his foundation (i.e., Spirit), his "transformational" changes are actually still translational (trans-fomational, not creative) because the essential nature of Spirit is not on the evolutionary table. Wilber approaches the need for an innovative form of process, but in the end he draws up short and does not attribute creative change and emergence to Spirit. He tells us, "There is no such holon [Spirit/Omega Point] anywhere in manifest existence" (2000, p. 85). The evolution of "Spirit-in-action" is seen as the movements and changes manifest "Form" of the Kosmos, which is understood as not distinct from the "Formless" or "pure Emptiness." This *nondual* or "not-two" reality is a "perfect expression of Spirit as Spirit" (2000, p. 317). While assuring the reader that this nonduality does not separate Form from Formlessness, he is also quick to quote Ramana Maharshi, who tells us that as these two merge into one, "Absolute consciousness alone reigns supreme" (2000, p. 317). A single unitary Absolute like this cannot really change today, or else—as Wilber pointed out at the very beginning of this chapter—how could it have also been Absolute yesterday? All change must be superficial in relation to this final nondual Spirit, and so is ultimately novative and trans-formational.

So Wilber IV is beholden to a form of trans-formational process thinking, but what about the more recent Wilber V? Wilber IV attempted to use the idea of involution to accommodate various important critical voices (transition of surfaces, transformation at the depths), while Wilber V lets go of this evolutionary-involutionary perennialist structuralism. In attempting to take heed of poststructuralist and postmetaphysical warnings against positing actual structures, Wilber V posits surface and deep probabilities in their stead (Wilber, 2006a, pp. 26–28. This still does not solve the problem that I am after, because this new "postmetaphysical" system is still founded on a monistic understanding of Spirit, wherein if Spirit is really the Absolute, then all change must be trans-formational and therefore superficial.

This point is crucial to my overall argument, and so it is worthwhile to take our time here. Wilber V posits nonduality as a "not-two" where "Spirit-in-Action" (Form) and "pure Emptiness" (Formlessness) are understood as not separate. This emphasis on nonduality is seen as offering a way toward honoring both that which changes and that which does not. This use of nonduality is supposed to solve the problem, because Form changes while Formlessness does not. If they are equal in their not-two-ness (nonduality), then both sides of this equation seem to have been included. I disagree with this use of the term, which leads directly to the heart of my own process-oriented critique.

Notice that right after offering this solution, Wilber turns toward Ramana Maharshi, and as he does this, he makes one side of the not-two/nondual primary; namely, the Absolute or Formlessness. I am arguing the exact opposite point: that we must make change and creativity primary (see Whitehead, 1978, p. 21). But not just change, as in the novative and, therefore, superficial trans-formational change that I have argued against. The change that must be made primary is innovative and creative, and ensures that no continuity (e.g., Spirit, Absolute, Formless) can be primary. Wilber sides with Ramana Maharshi and makes continuity primary within his use of the term *nondual.* This is a fairly traditional use of the term, and so when this same term is brought in to solve the desire to honor real novelty, change, and evolution, then I am more than a little suspect. Where Wilber and some integral theorists might find nonduality useful, I argue that it continues to bring with it traditional Vedic views regarding actuality that my process-oriented stance is directly opposed to.

It is important at this juncture to consider once again the problem of innovative novelty in relation to the assertion of an ontological unity like Wilber's (IV or V) Spirit. This style of thinking is a cosmological assertion that would later be obviated by Darwin's naturalistic observations with regard to the "tree of life." For this reason, much of the early evolutionary cosmologies lost favor. They were quickly shown to either not match the scientific theories of the day, or not to hold under careful philosophical examination. To this end, evolutionary biologist Michael T. Ghiselin (2005) writes: "To allow for change to be indefinite, and sufficient to permit the origin of new species, implies that we may need to rethink some of our fundamental metaphysical assumptions. Maybe species do not have essences" (p. 126). He juxtaposes this Darwinian insight over and against a "pre-Darwinian" understanding of change.

For pre-Darwinians, according to Ghiselin, change is understood as something trans-formative and superficial. Reality is something that preexisted in the mind of God. This is a different reality than Wilber's Spirit, and Ghiselin is primarily considering a Judeo-Christian context here, yet the point still holds that there is an assumed essential absolute quality to the world, an ontological ultimate, whereby change is novative and superficial in relation to this Absolute. Having been brought into existence by an act of God, or the imagination of Spirit, change is subsequently seen as the realization of something that already existed. There is continuity in this pre-Darwinian system that assumes all movement is the unfolding of a predetermined pattern (Wilber's own attempts to work out an evolutionary-involutionary cosmology seeks to address this issue, and is considered below).

Ghiselin understands Darwinian evolutionary theory as a pointed critique of ontological ultimates/monisms and trans-formative ways of thinking (including any recourse to a great-chain-of-being or spirit). Darwin's theory requires that something ontologically novel can come into being; innovation and ontological atomicity are required. We will need a creative, rather than a trans-formative, form of process thought to approach this challenge. While Ghiselin is defending the importance of novelty, it is also important to note that he is an adherent to a form of contemporary mechanism. "Teleology," writes Ghiselin (2005, p. 127), "is metaphysical delusion." At first, this appears to be the sort of mechanistic (flatland) thought that has motivated integral theory to search for better options. But this must be read in light of Ghiselin's understanding of teleology, wherein all purposefullness is associated with some ultimate Spirit/God/final causality. In contradistinction to such ultimates, the Darwinian evolutionary theory we have inherited requires a radical discontinuity and innovation, one that precludes some ontological given like Spirit.

To the extent that Ghiselin is correct here, an evolutionary theory and an ontological monism cannot go together. Wilber's project has to address this critical point. But this does not need to be the case. Against Ghiselin, we need not conflate teleology with some ultimate Telos-God-Brahman-Spirit. The teleology defended by creative/innovative process-thinkers, like Whitehead, is in keeping with the emphasis on innovation and atomism in Darwinian evolutionary theory and post-Enlightenment thought in general. By way of further defending my argument that Wilber's version of postmetaphysical spirituality rests too heavily on an ontological monism I consider the *right-wing* Hegelian influences on his thought in some detail.

Integral Theory, Hegelianism, and Aurobindo's Involution

Right-Wing Hegelianism and Integral Postmetaphysics

Daniel Gustav Anderson (2006) writes, "the influence of Aurobindo's idea of integration-as-synthesis cannot be overestimated in Integral studies" (p. 63). In order to understand Aurobindo's thought, it is useful to unpack the influences of what George R. Lucas, Jr. (1989, p. 27) has called a right-wing reading of Hegel's thought.[1] This right-wing exposition of Hegel's thought is a largely theological and politically conservative reading executed by various English interpreters like J.M.E. McTaggart (of Cambridge) and F.H. Bradley (of Oxford). Lucas (1989, p. 27) tells us that this right-wing Hegelianism retains Hegel's notions of "organism, teleology, and interconnectedness, while downplaying the more disturbing notions of finite freedom, novelty and creativity, contingency, temporal flux, and becoming." The upshot of such a theory is a very particular emphasis on what Bradley (1902) termed the Absolute. He writes that "the Absolute is one system, and . . . its contents are nothing but sentient experience. It will hence be a single and all-inclusive experience, which embraces every partial diversity in concord . . . no feeling or thought, of any kind, can fall outside its limits" (p. 100). This emphasis includes all feeling, thought, and experience within the "one system." This is similar to Wilber's own monism of Spirit and world of form and perspectives.

Within such a system, finite freedom, real novelty, contingency, and temporal flux are not only irrelevant, but problematic ideas. To put this simply, where ontological monism reigns, innovation and ontological pluralism have little or no relevance. If there is only one Absolute, there is no finite individuality? There is no real novelty in such a system, only perceived novelty. Flux requires change, and if there is change, then the idea of "one system" becomes hard to manage. This is as true for integral thinkers like Aurobindo and Teilhard de Chardin, as it is for integral theory's Wilberian nonduality.

For his part, Wilber offers his postmetaphysics as a solution to the problem of Wilfrid Sellar's "Myth of the Given," and so aims to bypass any association with idealist or monist philosophies. On the first page of Wilber's (2006b) chapter on "Integral Post-Metaphysics" he equates metaphysics to content or conception. On the following page, he writes that the "Great Chain of Being" has been the "official philosophy of the larger part of civilized humankind through most of its history" (p. 232). On the page after this Wilber continues: "These metaphysical assumptions are, quite simply, unnecessary and cumbersome baggage that hurts spirituality more than helps. . . . Theories such as the Great Holarchy of Being and Knowing . . . were simply ways that various philosophers and sages used to interpret their experience" (p. 233). What is real, he tells us, is Spirit and its perspectives, not content.

Wilber (2006b, p. 234) writes, "these structures of consciousness cannot be conceived as ones that are given eternally or timelessly—they are not archetypes, not eternal ideas in the mind of God . . . these post-metaphysical levels of being and knowing would have to be conceived as forms that have developed in time, evolution, and history." Metaphysics is about the ontological pluralism that happens in time. Postmetaphysics is the realization of this fact. This integral postmetaphysical turn is framed as postmodern and critical, but is really a return to an earlier ontological monism. Wilber goes on to write in the same chapter: "[I]f you think of a diagram of the 4 quadrants, the nondual or ultimate reality is the paper on which the diagram is written" (p. 288). And in a footnote on the same page: "[T]here is Absolute Subjectivity . . . which is actually Nonduality or pure perception . . . and then there is the manifest realm of relative subject and object" (p. 288). The real is Spirit and the manifest realm is simply made up of emergent perspectives. This means that the content, manifest realm, is relative, while the experiencer is absolute. Change is novative and trans-formative because there is always the Absolute Subjectivity that remains constant and continuous.

As much as Wilber and other integral theorists have argued otherwise, this iteration of integral theory's postmetaphysics adheres to an ontological monism. This does not have to be the case. Whitehead, for example, has in his own way been inspired by Bradley's thought, but there are important differences between his creative process thought and the trans-formative thought of Wilber. Leemon B. McHenry (1989) has written a foundational paper on the importance of Bradley to the history of process thought. In this paper he writes, "in one way or another Bradley, James, and Whitehead all agree upon the central place of 'immediate experience' or 'feeling' in their respective metaphysical systems . . . The rationality inherent in this flow of experience, however, takes on radically different interpretations in the monist and pluralist versions" (p. 153). McHenry continues: "but with the various attempts of these thinkers to construct a system from this basis, Bradley has denied that the flow of experience can be made up of genuine individuals and relations. The main challenge from the side of pluralism then is to show that relations are contained in immediate feeling" (p. 154). McHenry is outlining my line of critique with regard to integral theory. Within Bradley's system all individuals and relations, atomicity and pluralism, innovation and creative process, are subsumed in an idealist Absolute. Change is trans-formative for Bradley, not creative.

The question that I bring to Wilber is in regard to whether or not the emphasis on Spirit and nonduality in integral theory allows for real individual novelty. "The politically conservative reading of the Hegelian right wing," writes Lucas (1989, p. 27), "retained principally the notions of organism, teleology, and interconnectedness, while extensively downplaying the more disturbing notions of finite freedom, novelty and creativity, contingency, temporal flux, and becoming." Esbjörn-Hargens (2010) writes that there are instances of methodological and epistemological pluralism within the field of integral theory. He continues by writing that while an ontological pluralism is implied, it is surprisingly underdeveloped (pp. 145–146). Every integral thinker must deal with the problem of innovation and ontological pluralism in some way. A more in-depth inquiry into the idealist assumptions held within integral thought, might help to uncover this particular blind spot in the field. I now turn to the monistic assumptions inherited by Sri Aurobindo, and follow this with a consideration of the ontological monism in Bonnitta Roy's (2006a, 2006b) *Process Model of Integral Theory.*

Sri Aurobindo's Right-Wing Hegelianism

Aurobindo was studying at Cambridge when the Anglicized Hegelianism I am calling "right-wing" was in vogue. Anderson (2006) writes that though

Aurobindo had no real interest in Hegel's own writings, he received a very strong dose of Hegelianism (right-wing) through the work of A.C. Bradley. A.C. Bradley was a poet, more in keeping with Aurobindo's academic interests, and not to be confused with the philosopher F.H. Bradley mentioned above. It is important to note, however, that both of these authors were part of the same Anglo-Saxon Idealist school of thought.

Interestingly enough for the field of integral theory, the Absolute of F.H. Bradley is not that different from the Self of Advaita Vedanta. Frederic Fost (1998, p. 387) writes:

> T.R.V. Murti has claimed that any philosophy that distinguishes between an ultimately real, the Absolute, and a merely pragmatically real, the realm of ordinary experience (a view which Advaita Vedanta shares with Madhyamika Buddhism and the metaphysics of F. H. Bradley), inescapably gives rise to a doctrine of two truths and a theory of illusion. Eliot likewise argues that it is logically impossible to have the full reality of Brahman and the full reality of the world. "One must have either a limited God (subordinate in some sense to the world) or an unlimited Reality and an 'appearance-only' world." If Brahman is the sole Reality, then the cosmic manifold must be relegated to the status of mere Appearance. The world is designated as *Maya*—that creative power (*Sakti*) of Brahman that brings the illusory appearance of multiplicity into existence, analogous to the way a magician makes one thing appear as something else.

There are two important ideas in the quotation above that must not be missed. First, the views of Advaita, Madhyamika, and Bradley are not that different. We can include the ultimate of Aurobindo here, as well as the Spirit of Wilber. Secondly, if one asserts an unlimited Reality, like Wilber's non-dual Spirit, one is stuck with an appearance-only world, a world of perspectives.[2] This point can be clarified further by considering Roy's *Process Model of Integral Theory.*

Bonnitta Roy's Mind-Only Critique of Involution in Integral Theory

This problem can also be seen in the work of integral theorist Bonnitta Roy's (2006a, 2006b) own peculiar exposition of Dzogchen Buddhism. Her "process model of Integral Theory" begins to break down in her critique of Wilber's work, for the same reasons that any framework that starts with a dichotomy between the changing and the unchanging must do. Roy (2006b) writes that her process model can help our transformative practices by distinguishing between "useful ways of knowing about" and "paths of discovering or realizing being-as-suchness" (p. 133 n. 27). She makes the distinction between epistemological field and ontological ground throughout her work. She sees this distinction as a corrective for what she understands as Wilber's overemphasis on the epistemic field through his focus on the evolution of structures. This argument amounts to Roy's own idiosyncratic reading of Buddhism (Dzogchen and Yogacara, in particular) applied as a critique of Wilber's attempts to understand the evolution of consciousness outside such a particular Buddhist understanding of actuality. When Wilber tries to face the problem of real novelty and change, Roy sees this (rightly) as a betrayal of her (Buddhist) idealism.[3]

Aurobindo fully understood the issue that Roy seems to have overlooked when he introduces his theory of involution and supermind. An earlier Wilber IV (2000) similarly asserts involutionary structures to account for the problem of causality between his *One Taste* and the world of form. Aurobindo's solution is twofold. He begins with the idea of involution. Yes, there is only one Self, *Satchitananda*, but this one goes through a process of forgetting itself, called "involution." The world of form (that which evolves) is not separate or different from ultimate Reality (that which involves). This process of forgetting (involution) sets up a series of basic structures like Wilber's (2000, p. 61) "involutionary givens." This same Self can then engender a process of evolution, in affect remembering itself as Self, *Satchitananda*, through an "evolution" through those same structures.[4]

Wilber defends this theory in his early to middle work (Wilber I–IV). He writes, "the involutionary theories—from Plotinus to Hegel, from Asanga to Aurobindo, from Schelling to Shankara, from Abhninavagupta to the *Lankavatara Sutra*—are all attempts to take into account that the depths of the higher structural potentials are already present but not seen" (2000, p. 661). Wilber articulates a great chain of structures that have been laid down through some process of involution, and are now available to us through the return process of evolution. In this way, he has maintained the conservative idea of an Absolute, while seeming to account for freedom, novelty, and flux.

This becomes a very important issue for Whitehead. If there is one ultimate, then everything is internally related to this one, and there is no real freedom or change (only illusory perspectives of novelty). This is where the crux of my critique lies. I cannot see where Wilber has sufficiently dealt with this issue. As long as the "nondual or ultimate reality is the paper on which the diagram is written" (Wilber, 2006c, p. 288), there can be no innovation. Change is superficial and predicated on the assumption of an ontological continuity or monism. Perspectives can be written and rewritten, and to the extent that this is true, innovation is superficially interesting. But to the extent that innovation and novelty are only superficially efficacious, they remain novation or trans-formation. Aurobindo's *Satchitananda* does not change, is not ever truly surprised; but rather simply forgets. Similarly, Wilber's nondual Paper/Spirit, to the extent that it is ultimate, does not change and knows all, and so is neither changed nor surprised.

Wilber (2006b) and his integral postmetaphysics (Wilber V) makes a shift from structures of Spirit (ontological dualism) to "con-structures of the knowing subject" (epistemological dualism). In such a view the "manifest realm" or realm of form is understood to be a realm of perspectives, rather than perceptions. In this way, Wilber hopes to ride Kant's critical turn and not fall into the trap of mistaking the content of experience for perceptions (ontologically real), when they are actually perspectives (epistemologically relative). He sees the limitations of his early perennialist and structuralist stances (with some help by from the transpersonal community, e.g.,Ferrer, 2000, 2002; Rothberg and Kelly, 1998) and ventures to solve his early Aurobindian structuralist tendencies by taking up a critical ("post-Kantian post-metaphysical") stance of his own. But his critical solution is to retreat even further back into a conservative idealism, like that of Bradley and Advaita Vedanta, by defining metaphysics as the content of pre-conventional thinking. Evolutionary inheritances are enacted (postmodern, post-structuralist), while involutionary givens are simply that—givens. In the end, Wilber (V)'s integral postetaphysics and integral perspectivism and Roy's Process Model of Integral Theory are not all that different.

Rather, Wilber has already gone down a similar path as Roy's particular Dzogchen style of process thought, found a dead end (idealism generally does not allow for evolution/change), adopted Aurobindo's involutionary schemata, run into a post-structural dead end (where evolution follows the same pre-given path as involution), and has now given up all hope of speaking coherently about an evolutionary cosmology (where innovation, novelty, and ontological pluralism are real, and the problem of internal relatedness is taken seriously) by returning to Roy's basic Buddhist standpoint. Wilber (2006b, p. 288) continues in his ever-present dualism, Spirit is the paper—AQAL is the writing. A dualism that is not all that different from Roy's particular rendering of a dichotomy between Ontological View and Epistemological Fields. Roy's articles are not so much a critique of the basic integral postmetaphysics, but rather a helpful clarification with regard to the underlying metaphysical assumptions held within integral heory (whether in her Integral Process Model or in Wilber's postmetaphysics).

On Wilber's account, metaphysics is all about perspectives (the realm of form), and to miss this point is to have a failed View, to lack pure perception (*shunyata* or *nirvana*). Ferrer (2011) puts Wilber's position quite clearly when he writes: "I fail to see novelty in it because many contemplative traditions—such as Yogacara (Mind-Only) Buddhism or most Tibetan Buddhist schools—explicitly account for spiritual realms in terms of subtle dimensions of consciousness, not as external metaphysical levels of reality" (p. 12). In effect, Wilber has forgotten why Aurobindo labored so hard to create a theory of evolutionary and involutionary structures; all the while Roy has missed Aurobindo's lesson altogether and maintains a dichotomy between Real and relative. Wilber has missed (or conveniently forgotten) Deutsch's warning above, "one must have either a limited God (subordinate in some sense to the world) or an unlimited Reality and an 'appearance-only' world" (as cited in Fost, 1998, p. 387). In the context of this chapter, we could call this the predicament of trans-formative process thought with its emphasis on a single Kosmos or ultimate reality. Wilber wants to put forward a critical evolutionary cosmology, but he falls too far on the side of traditional cosmologies like those of Advaita Vedanta and Tibetan Buddhism to do so. Because of this he cannot fully account for novelty (finite freedom) and innovation.

Esbjörn-Hargens and Integral Ontological Pluralism

Esbjörn-Hargens (2010) wonders aloud: "Curiously, there is no mention of ontological pluralism within Integral Theory. Its absence is all the more striking given Integral Theory's post-metaphysical stance on enactment, which highlights that specific methodological practices bring phenomena into being" (p. 146). He goes on to write that integral theory does include both integral epistemological pluralism and integral methodological pluralism, but that to date the field of integral theory has largely assumed rather than argued overtly for a working theory of ontological pluralism. Following the argument laid out in this chapter so far, the reason for this seeming oversight appears clear enough.

Both an epistemological and a methodological pluralism fit rather nicely within the framework of integral perspectivism, as neither one appears to require overt ontological claims beyond the existence of a Whole/Spirit who is ultimately responsible for the diversity of perspectives available through the AQAL model. A real integral ontological pluralism is more than a little challenging to the underlying assumptions I have shown to lie at the heart of much integral theory. At times Wilber seems to allude to this pluralist stance; like when he places "perceptions" like Buddha-Nature, Nirguna Brahman and Godhead in the "metaphysical" upper-left hand quadrant of his AQAL model. If there is a possibility of multiple ultimates and distinct enlightenments, then a real ontological pluralism may be possible. There is a potential within integral theory that each of these ultimates is equally enacted or cocreated; yet it is hard to see this line of thought fully articulated. To this end, Esbjörn-Hargens's article could be a turning point within the field. But there is a problem.

In reading Esbjörn-Hargens writing on integral enactive theory, Wilber's basic integral perspectivism comes into focus. Esbjörn-Hargens uses the example of a soda bottle, where one bottle can be perceived in a variety of ways, making it a "multiple object." Esbjörn-Hargens (2010) alternatively writes of this soda bottle–multiple object as an "integral object: an ontologically distinct phenomenon that is a combination of first- , second- , and third-person dimensions" (p. 144). Here the bottle's ontological status is a distinct combination of *perspectives*. And here we find the real sticking point that haunts integral theory. Esbjörn-Hargens tells us that this bottle is independent in some way from the perceiver, while remaining "something constant." At the same time it is dependent upon social constructions, and thereby a "distinct ontological enactment."

In following the trajectory of integral theory through the history of process thought, Esbjörn-Hargens's integral enactive theory may be closest to the creative/innovative process thought that I suggest is necessary for a viable evolutionary cosmology, but there are important qualifiers. The first—and most important—hinges on what Esbjörn-Hargens means when he writes the words *something constant*. The innovative process-oriented realism defended in this chapter is committed to an ontological pluralism that is founded on contemporary logic's emphasis on atomism. According to Kevin Klement (2011), ontological pluralism:

> Endorse[s] both a metaphysical view . . . [This] metaphysical view amounts to the claim that the world consists of a plurality of independently existing things exhibiting qualities and standing in

> relations. According to logical atomism, all truths are ultimately dependent upon a layer of atomic facts, which consist either of a simple particular exhibiting a quality, or multiple simple particulars standing in a relation.

Esbjörn-Hargens's bottle is a "multiple object," something constant that is complexified by a dearth of *observations*. And here is the problem.

When Esbjörn-Hargens writes of "ontological perspectives" and equates "to see" with "to enact" he appears to be robbing ontological pluralism of its meaning, its metaphysical underpinning. If a constant is seen differently from different vantage points, then we have something akin to Wilber's integral perspectivism (2006b, p. 34), which in essence simply multiplies points of view, while maintaining the idealist assumption of Spirit. Pluralism is not ontological, as in the assertion of atomicity, but rather epistemological, as in integral epistemological pluralism. This point is drawn in sharp contrast when Esbjörn-Hargens (2010) continues to elaborate on integral theory's postmetaphysical turn in relation to ontological pluralism, ontological enactions, and something constant. If there is something constant, but it is not metaphysical, what is the nature of this/these constants in reality? Whitehead's ontological pluralism, following contemporary physics, requires atomicity or ontologically real and distinct constants. Esbjörn-Hargens (2010) writes, "The reality of the bottle . . . is not dependent on your viewpoint but rather on the social practice of interacting with the bottle" (p. 145). Here the use of the word *constant* seems to pointing to an atomicity and ontological pluralism not that different from Whitehead's.

This is good news for integral theory, but if it adopts this critical realism, it will have to face the same problems Whitehead and company have engaged (see Lucas, 1989). Esbjörn-Hargens (2010) writes, "So, if we are going to have epistemological pluralism (the Who) and methodological pluralism (the How), then we ought logically (or integrally) to have ontological pluralism (the What)" (p. 146). If the "Who" is given (Spirit) and the "What" are enacted, one of two problems arises. On one side, Wilber (2006b, p. 236) writes, "Emptiness is Freedom and Form is Fullness." Spirit is ultimately free, while the realm of forms is enacted, and though more or less free, not ultimately free. On this account there is no novelty in the creative innovative sense of the term being used here, because Spirit by virtue of being ultimate and internally related to all enactions, is ultimately responsible for all choice, and so change is actually superficial and novative/trans-formative. This is monism. If the Who (given) is ontologically distinct from the Whats (enacted) then the Who and the Whats cannot be inter-related.

Conclusion: Evolution and an Integral Ontological Pluralism

This is the point at which Whitehead's creative process thought becomes so important. He maintains an ontological pluralism and the possibility of internal relations by finding a way to make the Who and the What one and the same. Remember the subject-superject/actual occasion that I mentioned in the first section of this chapter. Instead of asserting the primacy of a Subject (Wilber's monism), or the primacy of objects (Nature-mechanism), or attempting to reunite the subject-object dualism of Descartes, Whitehead atomizes both the subject and the object, both the One and the Many. "Central to Whitehead's atomism," writes Michael Epperson (2004, p. 109), "is a repudiation not just of fundamental mechanistic materialism, but also of the Cartesian 'bifurcation of nature' that typically accompanies it." We can add to this list "the evolutionary monism of Hegel and of his derivative schools" (Whitehead, 1978, p. 210). As I have argued above, Wilber's integral thought can be included as one of these "derivative schools." Where Wilber continues to fall back on an "evolutionary monism," Whitehead's (1978, p. 309) creative and innovative process thought defends an ontological pluralism/atomism in service of what he terms an *organic realism*. As such, he has moved into conversation with twentieth and twenty-first century science. At the same time, he has managed to defend the importance of subjectivity and/or teleology without falling into flatland mechanism, Cartesian dualism, or the traditional idealism offered by Wilber.

In the end, I see integral theory as a field that continues to defend an indefensible position, an overly conservative idealism that posits a clear dualism between Spirit and AQAL, Reality and framework. The good news is that this problem has not gone unnoticed in the field. Wilber (2006b, p. 250) writes that his placement of certain ecosystems within his "turquoise" level of consciousness "is not subjective idealism." He is saying that these ecosystems are enacted (evolutionary inheritances), and hence they are not merely subjective perceptions. Another integral theorist, Sam Mickey (2008, 2010), does tend to use Wilber's terminology of Kosmos and nondualism, but at the same time offers interesting critique of this very same reductionism through his invoking of Félix Guattari and Gilles Deleuze, as well as Whitehead. Alternately, Michael Schwartz (2010) attempts to use the AQAL model to unfold a critical self-analysis of the overemphasis on what he calls the "philosophy of subject" (p. 232) and over privileging a "language of deep structures" (p. 237). Here he is attempting to root out the more extreme idealist-monist tendencies common in the field. In a somewhat similar vein, Michael Zimmerman (2010) pens a comparison of Stanley Salthe's "hierarchy theory" and Wilber's integral theory. This comparison is important in that it does not conflate Salthe's and Wilber's different final causes, and in fact opens the door for greater understanding with regard to each theory via their differences. Such comparisons and self-critical assessments need to continue to be highlighted within the field of integral studies, as they offer examples that can be modeled not only within the field, but within any number of other contemporary scholarly disciplines.

If integral theory means to articulate a critical evolutionary cosmology, it cannot continue its commitment to integral perspectivism and a non-duality that is somehow different from the world of enacted "multiple objects," form, and the AQAL map. Integral theory must own up to its ontological monism (i.e., Spirit), and continue the hard speculative work of Wilber's earlier writings. Wilber's postmetaphysics is a metaphysic in disguise, not all that different from Roy's Process Model of Integral Theory. It is my suggestion that one option available to integral theory is to consider the innovative and creative process thought I offer here. In so doing, I believe, it will find itself grasping on to a set of metaphysical assumptions that no longer serve it. This is a turning toward Esbjörn-Hargens's ontological pluralism with its realist discontinuities. If the field is to make the necessary critical turn, integral theory must loosen its grasp on Spirit (Esbjörn-Hargens's Who), recognizing in the process that the field has overcommitted itself to an overly abstract concept. Integral theory must consider some form of innovative evolutionary cosmology, one that honors radical creative novelty and innovation (e.g., Cabot, 2018),[5] and it is my assertion that the work of Whitehead and other process thinkers offers one very promising road toward this end.

Notes

1. It is important to note that for many contemporary scholars (Redding, 2010) this right-wing reading of Hegel is actually seen as the "traditional" reading. Lucas's *Naturphilosophie* reading of Hegel is a relatively new phenomenon, and often discounted in favor of seeing Hegel in light of the monisms of Bradley and Berkeley.

2. There is a subtle philosophical point expressed here that must not be missed. Deutsch is telling us that if you have an absolute unlimited reality, then the "world," the limited, must be appearance only. This is not always how the Vedic dictum is understood. Some might say that once you see past the illusion/appearance, the world and Brahman are both real, one and the same. This reading does not solve the problem of finite freedom and novelty, for if there are internal relations, and this is only One, the unlimited, then all other freedoms (individuality) are "appearance-only." This point will be made throughout the chapter in a variety of ways.

3. Roy looks to the work of Jason Brown (2000, 2002, 2005) to elucidate a process of microgenesis, whereby " 'waves' advance from an unarticulated core through discrete steps toward a more and more fully articulated cognition, then receding back to the core through the same steps" (Roy, 2006b, p. 138). Besides Brown, Roy has been reading author David Bohm, which brings some clarity to how she is imagining her process model might work. In maintaining her Ontological-Epistemological dichotomy (Bohm's Implicate and Explicate orders) Roy runs into the same problem that Wilber IV ran into, the same problem Aurobindo ran into, the same problem all dualisms and manifest-unmanifest dichotomies run into. The problem of how the One-the Implicate-the unarticulated-the Ontological-distinct subject is able to affect the many-the explicate-the articulated-the Epistemological-object.

4. In this chapter I argue that Aurobindo's thought was deeply influenced by English idealism. But we should also note, if only in passing, the deeper influence of Neoplatonist thought on both English idealism and on theosophy. Especially as the Mother, who worked so closely with Aurobindo, was a theosophist.

5. This work was originally written several years ago. As I read through it today, I realize that while it offers an important critique of integral theory, it does not offer a constructive alternative. For a more detailed consideration of my more recent work, please see Zayin Cabot, *Ecologies of Participation: Agents, Shamans, Mystics, and Diviners*.

References

Anderson, Daniel Gustav. 2006. "Of Synthesis and Surprises: Toward a Critical Integral Theory." *Integral Review* 3: 62–82.

Bradley, F.H. 1902. *Appearance and Reality: A Metaphysical Essay* (2d ed.). London: S. Sonnenschien & Co.

Brown, Jason W. 2000. *Mind and Nature: Essays on Time and Subjectivity*. London; Philadelphia: Whurr Publishers.

Brown, Jason W. 2002. *The Self-Embodying Mind: Process, Brain Dynamics and the Conscious Present*. Barrytown, NY: Barrytown/Station Hill Press.

Brown, Jason W. 2005. *Process and the Authentic life: Toward a Psychology of Value*. New Brunswick, NJ: Transaction.

Cobb, John B. Jr. 2008. *Back to Darwin: A Richer Account of Evolution.* Grand Rapids, MI: William B. Eerdmans.

Cabot, Zayin. Jr. 2018. *Ecologies of Participation: Agents, Shamans, Mystics, and Diviners.* Lanham, MD: Lexington.

Epperson, Michael. 2004. *Quantum Mechanics and the Philosophy of Alfred North Whitehead* (1st ed.). New York: Fordham University Press.

Esbjörn-Hargens, Sean. 2010. "An Ontology of Climate Change: Integral Pluralism and the Enactment of Multiple Objects." *Journal of Integral Theory and Practice* 5(1): 143–174.

Ferrer, J.N. 2011. "Participation, Metaphysics, and Enlightenment: Reflections on Ken Wilber's Recent Work. *Transpersonal Psycholgoy Review* 14(2): 3–24.

Ford, Lewis S. 1984. *The Emergence of Whitehead's Metaphysics, 1925–1929.* Albany, NY: SUNY Press.

Fost, Frederic F. 1998. "Playful Illusion: The Making of Worlds in Advaita Vedanta." *Philosophy East and West* 48(3): 387–405.

Ghiselin, Michael T. 2005. "The Darwinian Revolution as Viewed by a Philosophical Biologist." *Journal of the History of Biology* 38(1): 123–136.

Klement, Kevin. 2011. "Russell's Logical Atomism." In *The Stanford Encylopedia of Philosophy*, ed. E.N. Zalta. Retrieved May 11, 2014, from http://plato.stanford.edu/archives/win2011/entries/logical-atomism/%3E.

Lucas, George R. Jr. 1989. *The Rehabilitation of Whitehead: An Analytic and Historical Assessment of Process Philosophy.* Albany: SUNY Press.

McHenry, L.B. 1989. "Bradley, James, and Whitehead on Relations." *The Journal of Speculative Philosophy* 3(3): 149–169.

Mickey, Sam. 2008. "Cosmological Postmodernism in Whitehead, Deleuze, and Derrida." *Process Studies* 37(2): 24–44.

Mickey, Sam. 2010. "Rhizomatic Contributions to Integral Ecology in Deleuze and Guattari." In *Integral Theory in Action: Applied, Theoretical, and Constructive Perspectives on the AQAL Model*, ed. Sean Esbjörn-Hargens. Albany, NY: SUNY Press.

Nagel, Thomas. 2012. *Mind & Cosmos: Why the Materialist Neo-Darwinian Conception of Nature is Almost Certainly False.* New York: Oxford University Press.

Plantinga, Alvin. 2012. *Where the Conflict Really Lies: Science, Religion, and Naturalism.* New York: Oxford University Press.

Redding, P. 2010. "Georg Wilhelm Friedrich Hegel." *The Stanford Encylopedia of Philosophy.* Retrieved May 11, 2015, from http://plato.stanford.edu/archives/fall2010/entries/hegel/%3E.

Rothberg, David and Sean M. Kelly. 1998. *Ken Wilber in Dialogue: Conversations with Leading Transpersonal Thinkers* (1st Quest ed.). Wheaton, IL: Theosophical Publishing House.

Roy, Bonnitta. 2006a. "The Map, the Gap, and the Territory." *Integral Review* 3: 25–28.

Roy, Bonnitta. 2006b. "A Process Model of Integral Theory." *Integral Review* 3: 118–152.

Schwartz, M. 2010. "Frames of AQAL and the Emerging Integral Arts." In *Integral Theory in Action: Applied, Theoretical, and Constructive Perspectives on the AQAL Model*, ed. Sean Esbjörn-Hargens. Albany, NY: SUNY Press.

Weber, Michel. 2006. *Whitehead's Pancreativism: The Basics.* Piscataway, NJ: Transaction.

Weber, Michel. 2011. *Whitehead's Pancreativism: Jamesian Applications.* Piscataway, NJ: Transaction.

Whitehead, Alfred North. 1978. *Process and Reality: An Essay in Cosmology* (corrected ed.). New York: Free Press.

Wilber, Ken. 2000. *Sex, Ecology, Spirituality:The Spirit of Evolution* (2nd rev. ed.). Boston: Shambhala.

Wilber, Ken. 2006a. "Excerpt A: An Integral Age at the Leading Edge." Retrieved from http://www.kenwilber.com/Writings/PDF/ExcerptA_KOSMOS_2003.pdf.

Wilber, Ken. 2006b. *Integral Spirituality: A Startling New Role for Religion in the Modern and Postmodern world.* Boston and London: Integral Books.

Wilber, Ken. 2006c. "Note 26, Excerpt A: An Integral Age at the Leading Edge." Retrieved from http://wilber.shambhala.com/html/books/kosmos/excerptA/notes-3.cfm.

Zimmerman, M.E. 2010. "The Final Cause of Cosmic Development: Nondual Spirit or the Second Law of Thermodynamics?" In *Integral Theory in Action: Applied, Theoretical, and Constructive Perspectives on the AQAL Model*, ed. Sean Esbjörn-Hargens. Albany, NY: SUNY Press.

Chapter 9

Derrida and Wilber at the Crossroads of Metaphysics

Gregory Desilet

Over several decades, Ken Wilber has consistently addressed the task of modernizing and postmodernizing perennial philosophy. According to Wilber, advances in modern science and postmodern theory have been sufficiently validated to necessitate their inclusion in any scheme of understanding aimed at taking into account the full quality of human experience as currently measured among various world-class philosophers, theologians, and spiritual practitioners. Admiring science and its emphasis on methods of verification, Wilber wants to make a science of spiritual wisdom. And, following postmodern epistemological critique and twentieth century developments in science, he wants to upgrade that science to accord with current knowledge, including relativity theory in physics. Nevertheless, he wants to distance his views from certain aspects of postmodern theory—specifically all those views construing language as an endless play of signifiers untethered to anything outside the signifiers themselves. Wilber includes language theory among the many fields of theory in which he travels in his spiritual quest, because the problem of meaning is analogous to the problem of spirit. Issues of meaning and spirit involve the interior and intangible side of experience and these qualities have proven difficult to render unto science due to the difficulty they present to measurement. But Wilber's efforts of analysis and theory construction have enabled him to arrive at a philosophy of integral spirituality he believes overcomes the difficulties posed by the interior and the intangible, so that this realm now opens itself to access and management comparable to the tangible realm. And, if his work were indeed to accomplish such a task, it would be fair to say he has made it possible to pursue a science of spirituality.

This study argues, instead, that Wilber fails to formulate a science of spirituality consistent with his claims for the potential of such a science to relieve problems relating to confirmation and uncertainty. More specifically, it maintains that Wilber's claim to have ventured into the realm of postmetaphysical thinking overreaches, that his spiritual orientation remains grounded in classical metaphysics, and that his belief in the postmetaphysical nature of his spirituality and philosophy depends on questionable assumptions about both metaphysics and postmodernism.

Despite his dissatisfaction with the term *postmodern*, this analysis will use the late Jacques Derrida as the exemplary postmodernist and will center primarily on comparing and contrasting elements of Wilber's views with those of Derrida. The pairing of Wilber and Derrida is featured because Wilber offers a reading of Derrida and because, in my view, Derrida provides the most cogent lines of argument pertinent to a critical examination of Wilber's positions. This pairing is also featured because I have had the benefit of personal encounters with both Wilber and Derrida. Though I was able to spend considerably more time with Derrida than with Wilber, both of these encounters presented opportunities to ask questions relevant to the issues addressed in this essay.

A few words should be said about how critical commentary may be seen to square with an integral approach to doing philosophy and spiritual inquiry. It would seem consistent with the logic of "integral" that an integral approach to inquiry focus on integrating different views by way of a process Wilber describes as "transcend and include." However, when an integral philosopher such as Wilber includes and appropriates the views of another thinker such as Derrida into the framework of his (Wilber's) orientation, but does so on the basis of what appears to be an inadequate interpretation of those views, then critical commentary may be seen to be integrally beneficial in its effort to set the record straight. For, surely, integral theorists are not interested in building coherence out of misinterpretations of key philosophical works. And, if it should turn out to be the case that an illusory coherence were constructed on the basis of crucial misunderstandings of a philosophical position which, if adequately understood, challenged the metaphysical core of Wilber's spiritual vision, then it would be consistent with the integral desire for rigor and adequacy to throw open the door to this kind of critical commentary.

In the spirit of full disclosure, I confess I am divided in my loyalties on points where integral and postmodern philosophies may be seen to have fundamental differences. On the one hand, I side with Wilber on the issue of grand narratives. One of the things I most admire about Wilber is his steadfast attempt to fashion a "theory of everything." In pursuit of this ambition, the comprehensive interdisciplinary breadth of his reach into the archives of world knowledge and wisdom traditions has been remarkable and sets a standard few have been able to match. In my view, any philosophy claiming to be philosophy constitutes an attempt, explicit or otherwise, at grand narrative. Even when a philosophical position claims to be no more than, say, a philosophy of language or a philosophy of morality or a philosophy of whatever, it does not and cannot avoid including within itself default assumptions ushering in conclusions pertaining to metaphysics; conclusions about the nature of being that immediately trigger entanglement in a theory of everything. So, on the issue of meta-narratives, I do not side with Jean-François Lyotard insofar as postmodernism, as he defines it, avoids grand narratives. In my opinion, Derrida does not side with Lyotard on this issue either—a conclusion drawn from Derrida's statements that it is not possible to escape metaphysics.

On the other hand, when it comes to the question of the nature of being, I side with Derrida's postmodernism, rather than Wilber's integral philosophy. In principle, there can be no deeper level of critical analysis than the metaphysical level: the question of being. Therefore, a challenge at the level of being is one that affects every aspect of what rests above it. In challenging Wilber's metaphysics, then, no part of his approach to spirituality remains untouched, but only the primary aspects affected are discussed below. This postmodern deconstructive challenge to Wilber need not be seen as an attempt to demolish integral philosophy or spirituality. Instead, the reason for illuminating the contrasts between Derrida and Wilber will be to demonstrate that the deconstructive approach cannot be, as Wilber would have it, appropriated into the integral project as Wilber understands and practices it. As will be argued, an adequate understanding of Derrida's thinking about being and time precludes translating it into an orientation compatible at the deepest levels with integral post-metaphysics. Whether this incompatibility requires revisions of integral foundations to the point where the notion of "integral" no longer seems appropriate is a question remaining to be worked out in spiritual communities relevant to the question.

Seeing Derrida and Wilber as opposed in their respective views of the nature of being requires a fundamental characterization of both thinkers with regard to metaphysical positioning. Any such characterization amounts to interpretation—and interpretations, as will be argued herein, may always be significantly skewed from the mark of adequate textual and contextual understanding.

So, again, in the spirit of full disclosure, the reader should understand my descriptions of the views of Wilber and Derrida are offered in a spirit of provocative inquiry rather than a posture of authoritative insistence on the correctness of Derrida's views or the correctness of my interpretations of Derrida's or Wilber's views.

Constraints on length also necessitate limited engagement with many of the reasons and arguments for the positions taken by Wilber and Derrida. Nevertheless, I have attempted within the space limitations of an essay to cite key passages concerning the ideas expressed and thereby also to provide as much support as possible for the accuracy of my interpretations of Wilber and Derrida. In this respect, I only report on the main philosophically relevant maneuvers, while encouraging readers to explore for themselves in greater detail the sources provided.

My exchange with Wilber is a good place to begin, because it highlights a fundamental misreading of Derrida on Wilber's part. It is possible to view this particular instance of misreading as a minor lapse on Wilber's part, one not needing to be exploded into a major disjunction with the consequences I claim. However, I see this misreading as symptomatic of a very large difference between Wilber and Derrida running through the entire fabric of Wilber's thinking. Pulling on the thread of this difference results, I argue, in unraveling the fabric and rendering it into something substantially other than what Wilber intends and claims to offer. Wilber's misreading of Derrida is significant because it exposes a difference in their views with far-reaching consequences for any discussion of spirituality—especially any stance consistent with the deepest aspirations of the integral community and integral theorists. At bottom, this difference hinges, as already mentioned, on a difference in metaphysical positions, the most important consequence of which, as will be explored below, pertains to differences in the understanding of transcendence.

Analysis of Derrida's Remarks in *Positions*

I met Ken Wilber at his *Integral Spirituality* book signing in Boulder, Colorado in November 2006. Based on comments he made concerning

Derrida's views during the talk prior to the signing, I was most interested in his response to a particular question. When I approached him during the signing, I asked, "Do you believe Derrida errs by offering what amounts to a false critique of absolute transcendence?" Without hesitation, he answered "Yes." Derrida's approach, Wilber explained, contains a basic flaw most evident in his critique of transcendence, culminating in specious claims about transcendental signifiers and signifieds. He directed me to the footnote in *Integral Spirituality* where he describes how Derrida came to understand the overstatement of the relativism of language advanced by many postmodern theorists, including Derrida himself. Wilber claimed Derrida reversed himself by acknowledging the transcendental signifier/signified's necessary role in language. This reversal occurred specifically in relation to the issue of translation. Since the passage in Wilber's book is brief and important and repeats the substance of what he said to me at the book signing, it bears repeating here, since it can be cited and therefore verified by others:

> Although poststructualism has many important, enduring, and universal truths, its rabid denial of universal truths landed it in the first of many performative contradictions . . . But, in any event, that rather complete relativism ended with Derrida's admission, in *Positions*, of a transcendental signifier—there is a reality to which signifiers must refer in order [sic] get a conversation going. Without a transcendental signifier, Derrida said, we couldn't even translate languages—and there ended the extreme poststructualist stance. (Leaving behind its very important, but very partial, truths. Many of these partial truths of poststructualism—contextualism, constructivism, and aperspectivism—are fully incorporated in AQAL) . . . Overall, then, we might note that AQAL includes **signifiers** *and* **signifieds** *and* **referents**, including both their sliding (or relativistic, culturally specific) and their non-sliding (universal) aspects [emphasis in original]. (Wilber, 2006, pp. 155–156)

Derrida's admission, according to Wilber, marks a grudging capitulation to the necessity for grounding, some manner of overview or transcendence with respect to systems of meaning in order for such systems to be, in any genuine sense, meaningful. Wilber appears to have first introduced this reading of Derrida at a much earlier date than the *Integral Spirituality* text (e.g., Wilber, 2000, pp. 601–602). Several commentators (Meyerhoff, 2006,

2010; Desilet, 2007a; Hampson, 2007) have previously questioned Wilber's reading of Derrida. When I suggested to Wilber his insistence Derrida had "reversed" himself regarding the transcendental signifier was likely not accurate—based on my knowledge of Derrida—Wilber replied, "No, see for yourself. Look at what he says in *Positions*." Wilber continued, explaining that Derrida had finally realized the role of a transcendental signifier in language could not be eliminated without undermining a feature of language crucial to reliable communication. Not having the book in front of me and not sure what passage he might be referring to, I was unable to effectively contest the issue with him in the moment. Later that evening, I searched through my copy of *Positions* and found the passage in question. Before considering the broader philosophical implications of Wilber's claim regarding Derrida, it is worthwhile reviewing in detail what Derrida actually says in *Positions*.

The passage Wilber refers to opens by establishing the context for what follows as one wherein the possibility of a transcendental *signified* is questioned. In this questioning, Derrida begins by asserting that the possibility for any *signifier* to function as a transcendental signifier is fundamentally linked to the possibility for a clear separation between signifier and signified. This separation is complicated, in Derrida's view, by the fact that every signified also behaves as a signifier.[1] Since, for Derrida, the problems of the transcendental signifier and the transcendental signified are inextricable and interchangeable, in *Positions* he uses the phrase "transcendental signifier/signified." He then submits a two-part explanation for why the distinction between signifier and signified is problematic and must be undertaken with exceptional caution:

> a) it [the operation of clearly distinguishing between signifier and signified] must pass through the difficult deconstruction of the entire history of metaphysics which imposed, and never will cease to impose upon semiological science in its entirety this fundamental quest for a "transcendental signified" and a concept independent from language; this quest not being imposed from without by something like "philosophy," but rather by everything that links our language, our culture, our "system of thought" to the history and system of metaphysics. (Derrida, 1981, p. 20)

The "entire history of metaphysics" has never ceased to "impose upon semiological science" the quest for a "concept independent of language," because this is precisely what is needed in order to provide the metaphysical ground for a "science" of semiology, a "science" of language and meaning. Also, Derrida underscores the need for a transcendental role for the signified in order to create a clean separation of the roles of signified and signifier. He next points out, however, that the *inability* to mark a clean separation of signified and signifier does not thereby imply a complete merging of the roles of signified and signifier, since languages do, in fact, perform certain functions, including translation from one language to another:

> b) nor is it a question of confusing at every level, and in all simplicity, the signifier and the signified. That this opposition or difference cannot be radical or absolute does not prevent it from functioning, and even from being indispensable within certain limits—very wide limits. For example, no translation would be possible without it. (Derrida, 1981, p. 20)

This segment appears to be the source of Wilber's confusion. He reads the last sentence as Derrida's admission that translation would not be possible without the transcendental signifier/signified. In arriving at this misunderstanding, Wilber appears to do the following: In part b he reads the sentence—*For example, no translation would be possible without it*—such that the antecedent for the preposition *it* becomes the *transcendental signified* (which concept is featured in part a). But a careful reading shows that the antecedent for *it* in the previous sentence is *this opposition or difference*. And *this opposition or difference* is that between the signified and signifier—a difference remaining slippery and fundamentally problematic; a distinction not transparently clear, not "radical or absolute." Consequently, in this passage, Derrida is *only* acknowledging that the complication of the distinction between signified and signifier need not entail assuming the complete collapse of the distinction. He reinforces this point in the next sentences:

> In effect, the theme of a transcendental signified took shape within the horizon of an absolutely pure, transparent, and unequivocal translatability. In the limits to which it is possible, or at least *appears* possible, translation practices the difference between signified and signifier. But if this difference is never pure, no more so is translation, and for the notion of translation we would have to substitute a notion of *transformation*: a regulated transformation of one language by another, of one text by another. We will never have, and in fact have never had, to

> do with some "transport" of pure signifieds from one language to another, or within one and the same language, that the signifying instrument would leave virgin and untouched [emphasis in original]. (Derrida, 1981, p. 20)

When Derrida says *translation practices the difference between signified and signifier* he prefaces this with the crucial words: *In the limits to which it is possible, or at least* appears *possible.* And he notes further that "this difference is never pure," never clear to the point of being a difference calculable to the measure of "unequivocal transparency." Therefore, the difference between signifier and signified always remains problematic and, thereby, so also does translation.

When Derrida states, *In effect, the theme of a transcendental signified took shape within the horizon of an absolutely pure, transparent, and unequivocal translatability*, he describes the presuppositional landscape within which the transcendental signified is theorized as possible in traditional metaphysics. He calls into question precisely the metaphysics corresponding to this theme and horizon. In other contexts, he argues that the notions of transparency and the transcendental signifier are symptomatic of the *metaphysics of presence* (e.g., Derrida, 1974, pp. 44–65). Contrary to this metaphysical framework, Derrida proposes that the limits of signification (and thereby communication) indicate another necessity—namely that a pure transparency of signifier and signified or of text and translation is not possible ("We will never have, and in fact have never had, to do with some 'transport' of pure signifieds," etc.). In summary, in these passages Derrida explains why he subscribes to the view that all interpretation is translation and all translation is transformation. Accordingly, the transcendence that would enable pure transparency is, for Derrida, out of the question—or at least irreducibly problematic.

Wilber's reading is a bad misreading. In fact, this misreading twists what Derrida says into its opposite. The possibility for such a misreading serves only to reinforce Derrida's claim that language can never guarantee a particular understanding. And, consistent with this claim, the reader should remain alert to the possibility that the reading I propose as an alternative to Wilber's offers no guarantee of transparency with Derrida's text. Nevertheless, it is a reading that recommends itself because it does not require believing Derrida abdicated his entire project in one sentence, as Wilber too readily assumes. Wilber's misunderstanding confirms the constant potential in language for misunderstanding and verifies that a problematic difference between signifier and signified always operates to insure interpretation is little more than a species of translation. This interpretive translation always accomplishes transformations—and thereby potential misreadings—not only between languages but also within the same language.

Having established how he has misread Derrida, it remains to consider *why* Wilber has so easily misread him. Derrida and Wilber are both in agreement concerning the intimate connection—implicit in the metaphysical ground or core assumptions of philosophical and spiritual orientations—between transcendental signifiers and signifieds and notions of transcendence. However, according to Derrida—and in the wake of his broad deconstruction of metaphysics—any metaphysical position explicitly or implicitly providing a substantial role for forms of transcendence yielding transparency is a metaphysics necessarily resurrecting all the problems and dead ends of traditional metaphysics postmodern philosophers have labored to escape. Wilber's misreading of Derrida only adds further proof of strong attachment to belief in a particular tradition of transcendence. And this belief is odd, given Wilber's assertions in *Integral Spirituality* that he has arrived at a postmetaphysical spiritual and philosophical position. Wilber adheres to a species of transcendentalism and Derrida regards all such transcendentalism as classically metaphysical. The question, then, becomes: How can Wilber claim to be postmetaphysical in his thinking when Derrida has argued that the notion of transcendence to which Wilber subscribes is of a piece with the "entire history of metaphysics"?[2]

Wilber on Metaphysics and Postmetaphysics

In *Integral Spirituality*, Wilber argues lack of transparency of meaning—the problem of the sliding aspects of signifiers, the potential for different, yet valid, readings in communication and interpretation—opens the door to varieties of relativity of meaning. Radical relativity of meaning leads not only to problems in communication, which threaten the transmission of spiritual knowledge, but also problems of transcendence, which threaten the foundation, objectivity, and universal value of spiritual knowledge. In response, Wilber proposes the problem of relativity can be resolved by appeal to a system of *Kosmic addressing*.

Given terminologies achieve precise and repeatable meanings, according to Wilber, insofar as terms may be assigned coordinates in a matrix based on his four-quadrant division of being—the mapping device he refers to with the acronym AQAL (all quadrants, all levels). Briefly, the AQAL quadrant is a refinement of the subject/object relation, the classic relation of all modern philosophy. AQAL extends the subject/object relation from a duality to a quadrant. It does so by assigning singular and plural modes to the subject and singular and plural modes to the object.

In this quadrant partitioning, the upper left becomes the *I* quadrant (interior-individual or subjective) and *we* occupies the lower left (interior-collective or cultural), while *it* belongs to the upper right (exterior-individual or behavioral) and *its* the lower right (exterior-collective or social). The left/right dimensions of this division can also be understood as the difference between what can be experienced and what can be observed—where *experience* is understood to mean, among other things, *that which is not directly accessible to observation.* Each quadrant is further divided into developmental levels of complexity. The upper left, for example, manifests broader and deeper levels of consciousness; the lower left, increasingly complex orders of cultural beliefs and values; the upper right, growing complexity in organizations of atoms and molecules into limbic and neocortex systems; and the lower right, ever more sophisticated forms of social organization such as agrarian, industrial, and informational.

Wilber generates his Kosmic addressing coordinates against this AQAL background. With respect to how any object or any signified comes into existence and takes on meaning, Wilber asserts that "part of an object's Kosmic address is the fact that objects come into being, or are enacted, only at various developmental levels of complexity and consciousness" (Wilber, 2006, p. 252). Thus, the address of any particular object contains among its coordinates an indication of the quadrant and the level of development within the quadrant to be attained in order for that object to appear or make sense. For example, climate change and global warming will make sense only to a society having attained a level of consciousness and knowledge capable of observing and grasping the import of complex meteorological phenomena. Consistent with this level aspect of the quadrant system, an object's address must include designation of the quadrant coordinates for the developmental level of the perceiver (consciousness), as well as the coordinates of the perceived (external phenomenon).

Kosmic address referencing provides a system of grounded meaning and communication which, according to Wilber, supplants the need for positing ex nihilo an ultimate objective ground of reference or a pure *given.* Consequently, Wilber's ontological position shifts away from forms of classical realism and the positing of objects as existing entirely independent of perceivers. His view counts as a species of relativistic perspectivism, and he wants to clearly separate this view from any connection with traditional forms of philosophy or metaphysics. In fact, Wilber defines metaphysical thought in such a way as to make the departure from reliance on any manner of givenness count as postmetaphysical thinking:

> Whether they [objects] exist in some other way [apart from their "enactment" through various developmental levels as indicated in AQAL] CANNOT BE KNOWN in any event, and assuming that they do exist entirely independently of a knowing mind is nothing but the myth of the given and the representational paradigm—that is, is just another type of metaphysical thinking and thus not adequately grounded. At any event, post-metaphysical thinking does not rely on the existence of a pregiven world and the myth of that givenness. (Wilber, 2006, p. 252)[3]

Metaphysical thinking, in contrast to Kosmic addressing, posits a foundational ground as given, which means completely lacking in evidence and justification. The correction for this metaphysical magic trick of positing something out of nothing consists of willingness to give up on the myth of the given and simply refrain from imposing and positing any ultimate ground. With no such ultimate ground, however, everything becomes absolutely relative to everything else. In the absence of such a posited metaphysical ground, a reliable means of *location* can only be accomplished through something like Wilber's system of Kosmic addressing, whereby everything in existence can only be located within a network of relations of one thing to another.

Wilber believes his system of addressing can adequately take the place of what the metaphysical given was supposed to do but could not do—namely, provide a form of objective reference. The problems of location, assignment of meaning, and indeed existence itself are resolved insofar as Kosmic addressing serves as a collectively repeatable and communicable mode of identification for objects, events, and life-forms in the world. In other words, what is now required for existence is the specification of "the location of both the perceiver and the perceived, relative to each other" (Wilber, 2006, p. 255). This form of relativity, however, does not preclude the possibility for a science of meaning in the sense of calculable, repeatable, and communicable operations. And it does not, Wilber argues, preclude invariants and particular forms of absolute transcendence. The apparent contradiction of the continued role of a version of ultimate or absolute transcendence in Wilber's integral spirituality, despite his concessions to relativity, will be explained shortly.

Wilber's work supposedly ends the age of metaphysics, because it makes it possible to locate everything in mutually demonstrable ways. It now becomes possible to speak of interior or subjective phenomena and experiences with terminologies capable of corroboration by external procedures, such that these phenomena are demonstrable to others. This is so because the Kosmic addressing system avoids the pitfalls of mere abstraction and breezy postulating by referencing, through its AQAL coordinates, a set of observable operations for unobservable interior events, such as feelings, cognitions, concepts, ideas, revelations, or the like.

Meanings, when tied to some manner of observable performance tests, reliably produce the experience or existence corresponding to the signifier in question. More specifically, an injunction prompts a series of actions. These actions, in turn, produce an experience that calls forth the awareness or knowledge in question. The validity of this knowledge experience or meaning may, if desired, be further subjected to the tests of a community of those who have already performed the injunction and achieved the experience. With this methodological approach, it becomes possible to collectively verify the existence of everything by providing something like a map with directions for arriving at a direct experience with whatever is at issue.

This validation process includes especially inner experiences, such as the experience of God. In the case of modes of spiritual enlightenment, for example, if persons perform actions A, B, C, and so forth, they will have experience E (enlightenment). This process, according to Wilber, takes the form: "If you want to know this, do this" (Wilber, 2006, p. 267).

In summary, it may be said that Wilber has devised a postmetaphysical philosophical position, because it makes it possible to escape metaphysics (the postulating of givens) by introducing into the left interior side of the AQAL quadrant the kind of verifiability and objective reference possible in the right side of the quadrant. Previously unverifiable and loosely located meaning and value structures of the interior quadrants now acquire the same status of verifiability as the observable features of the exterior quadrants. The left side of the quadrant now escapes ungrounded metaphysical fuzziness. As Wilber expresses it, "The meaning of a statement is the injunction of its enactment. No injunction, no enactment, no meaning. That is, mere metaphysics" (Wilber, 2006, p. 268). Meaning must have a use and if it cannot be operationalized in or through a set of observable processes that can be noticed, repeated, and preserved by others, then it cannot count as meaningful. With respect to spirituality and the question of God, this means that in a very concrete sense the existence of God, the ultimate transcendental signified, is, in Wilber's view, verifiable and may be verified by any person who chooses to undertake the demonstration.

For Wilber, then, the genuine path to God consists of revelation through the practice or enactment of a set of prescribed behaviors or overt expressions rather than exclusively the incorporation of a set of particular, highly specific beliefs. God is authentically discovered through real *experience* rather than through faith or belief. This approach to spirituality shares some similarities with science in its operationalization of the path to proof or revelation. However, certain limits to the path to revelation through operationalization can be discerned even in behaviors as everyday as the use of language—the practice around which so much of Wilber's thinking turns.

Derrida and Wittgenstein: The Limits of Language and Science

The problem of inner experience and unobservable phenomena—mental processes especially—obsessed logical positivists such as Ludwig Wittgenstein and continued to preoccupy him in his later work. The view of the early positivists is sometimes represented by the dictum: If it exists, it can be measured—a dictum that also reads as: If it cannot be measured, it does not exist. Wilber's desire to locate meaning by operationalizing it through sequences of observable processes parallels Wittgenstein's later work, which highlights language as operationalization, as "operating with signs." Words are like currency in having material substance and social-exchange value or use value. For Wittgenstein, a person cannot have a private language any more than it would be possible to have a private currency. In this respect, meaning must be demonstrably viable within a marketplace in order to avoid becoming valueless word salad. Similarly, the claims to enlightenment and revelation from spiritual practitioners must be demonstrably viable within a larger community in order to be distinguished from hallucination and other forms of false consciousness.

Granting, for the moment, a similarity between Wilber and Wittgenstein with regard to a theory of meaning, and given the discussion thus far concerning differences between Wilber and Derrida, what might Derrida have to say about an operationalized theory of meaning? And, more specifically, since Derrida never read or commented on Wilber, what might Derrida have to say about Wittgenstein's view of meaning?

In the early 1990s, during a trip I took to the University of California at Irvine, where Derrida was a visiting professor, I asked him if he had read Wittgenstein. I focused on Wittgenstein because he was so prominent a theorist in the area of language theory, about which Derrida had written so much. To my surprise, Derrida said he had read only a few commentaries on him. He explained he did not want to begin reading such a formidable body of work unless he could devote a great deal of time to it, and, thus far, he had not found the time. Derrida died in 2004 before finding the time, so we will never have the benefit of his reading of Wittgenstein. But at our meeting, Derrida did respond briefly to a famous passage from Wittgenstein's *Philosophical Investigations*. Here is what I read to him:

> Suppose everyone had a box with something in it: we call it a "beetle." No one can look into anyone else's box, and everyone says he knows what a beetle is only by looking at *his* beetle. Here it would be quite possible for everyone to have something different in his box. One might even imagine such a thing constantly changing. But suppose the word "beetle" had a use in these people's language? If so it would not be used as the name of a thing. The thing in the box has no place in the language-game at all; not even as a *something*: for the box might even be empty. No,—one can "divide through" by the thing in the box; it cancels out, whatever it is. (Wittgenstein, 1953, 293)

With this imaginative illustration (called the beetle box analogy), Wittgenstein attacks the model of language that presupposes a crucial role for unobservable and inaccessible mental states in the communication transaction. However, his example is not intended to show unobservable mental states are not a possible part of what may transpire in thought and communication. It is only intended to show that whatever may transpire in the mind that may seem to remain inaccessible to public examination, need not be a *necessary* part of the processes called thinking and communication.

Though never comfortable commenting on excerpts taken out of context, on hearing the beetle box passage an immediate problem appeared to Derrida. He objected that the signifier itself, the word *beetle*, is as much a box into which no one can look as the "box with something in it." Cancelling out what is in each person's box, therefore, achieves nothing with respect to addressing problems of meaning and communication.

Derrida went on to explain that because the word *beetle* has a use in a given language does not mean this signifier becomes functionally transparent through verbal enactments.[4] The signifier is every bit as problematic, according to Derrida, as the signified. Cancelling out the thing in the box amounts to collapsing the distinction between signifier and signified, which, as noted earlier in the discussion of *Positions*, is no more possible in Derrida's view than drawing a clear distinction between signifier and signified. The material signifier (sign) does not and cannot escape issues of transparency besetting an immaterial signified (meaning). In other words, problems of meaning cannot be significantly alleviated, according to Derrida, by shifting the burden to whatever may appear to be the social-exchange value of material signifiers—words and sounds—in writing and speech.

By contrast, for Wittgenstein as well as for Wilber, all aspects of what may be collectively important about mental states are accessible in the sense that they *manifest themselves in corresponding observable operations*. If something were to remain fundamentally hidden from view, it would not be significant to the essence of these processes—"it cancels out, whatever it is." With respect to the role of mental processes in thought and communication, Wittgenstein remarks: "It is misleading then to talk of thinking as of a 'mental activity.' We may say that thinking is essentially the activity of operating with signs" (Wittgenstein, 1958, pp. 6–7).[5]

But thinking can safely be reduced to operating with signs only if it is possible to be certain it does not matter what is inside the beetle box. But to what extent is certainty warranted in such cases? Imagine, for example, that you know of no word in your language to fit what you have in your box. So you use several sentences to describe it. Others then take these sentences and, in a sense, reverse engineer them in order to construct for themselves what may be in your box. It seems most of the time, through social interaction, that others have adequately processed your description and have understood what is in your box. But, on some occasions, others make reference to this item in a way that seems to indicate they have not adequately understood. How might this be explained?

Consider, for example, the play of a chess grandmaster. The effects of the grandmaster's mental activity are observed as pieces on the board are moved and checkmate is achieved. When this happens often enough against other great players, the grandmaster's credibility rises. Others may ask how he does it. They may suggest he write a book. But could a book be written providing a set of instructions guaranteeing any other player who follows those instructions will become equally as good as the grandmaster? Even the grandmaster's close and attentive coaching may provide no guarantee of such success. In the world of chess, these measures have been taken many times among grandmasters and students and it may be safely said there are no set of operations ensuring the level to which any given player can rise. Coaching and practice may be important ingredients, but at a certain level of mastery it becomes difficult to instruct anyone on how exceptional greatness is achieved. The grandmaster's difference is operationalized in game performances, yet the secret of success remains hidden. The secret cannot itself be operationalized transparently in a set of words or routines and provides an ongoing stimulus to others to uncover it. The secret is unobservable (say, in the grandmaster's beetle box) but not therefore entirely inaccessible or untheorizable to the imagination, owing to its observed effects. This residual or partially hidden genius is anything but irrelevant to solving the puzzle of the game of chess, as those who have tried to program a computer to play like a grandmaster have discovered.

If it were decided in advance, as Wittgenstein seems inclined to decide, that what is inside the box does not matter, then the importance of communication (understood as successful social operations) has trumped the importance of aspiration and competition in the challenge of gaining insight through learning and inquiry. The importance of communication has perhaps even trumped the importance of that most controversial and besieged of values: truth.

In fairness to Wittgenstein, however, it should be noted that some commentators (e.g., Staten, 1984) have argued persuasively that his later views contain many important elements of a deconstructive view, such as appreciation for the role of context and the examination of particular cases. Other commentators (e.g., Hymers, 2005) show that it would also be a mistake to identify Wittgenstein too thoroughly with the varieties of verificationism associated with the Vienna Circle. Wittgenstein's radical operationism differs from verificationism in several respects, primarily with regard to differences between the former as a theory of meaning and the latter as a theory of truth. For Wittgenstein, the fact that a word has a use in a language and how language-users come to know the use of a word (the meaning of a word is its use) must be distinguished from verification theories of truth relying on immediate sense experience (the meaning of a statement is its method of verification). And other commentators (e.g., Lyotard, 1984) have noted Wittgenstein cannot be entirely summed up within the framework of a performative theory of meaning. So it is not obvious Wittgenstein's use of "operating with signs" needs be understood as offering a narrowly performative theory of meaning. Insofar as a convincing case can be made for this more complex reading of Wittgenstein, this reading would perhaps separate him to some degree from Wilber, as reflected in Wilber's dictum: "If you want to know this, do this."

However, in fairness to Wilber, it is important to be especially clear about this dictum. Wilber does not intend for it to imply a kind of behaviorism, verificationism, or scientism.[6] These interpretations would land his approach back in the two-dimensional "flatland" he rails against, which reduces all being to the right side of the AQAL quadrant. His operationism seeks to avoid reductionism by preserving immaterial quality alongside material phenomena. This entanglement of the immaterial and the material entails that qualitative phenomena remain accessible by way of the trace of the operational (or material) in their being just as material objects retain the trace of the immaterial in their being. In this way, Wilber seeks to overcome the traditional dualism of the material and the spiritual. For Wilber, spirit is one, includes matter, and manifests itself though all the expressions of creation. Derrida's departure from this position does not suggest a renewed dualism of spirit and matter. Instead, his departure consists primarily of the claim that the being of any such spirit must be divided in itself in an essential rupture, *a non-identity with itself*, in order for there to be anything at all. This self-division, touched on here, will be discussed more thoroughly in the remaining sections.

For purposes of broadening the scope and relevance of issues of observation and operationalization beyond language and into the wider arena of science, consider another analogy offered by Albert Einstein regarding attempts to decipher the operations of the natural world:

> In our endeavor to understand reality we are somewhat like a man trying to understand the mechanism of a closed watch. He sees the face and the moving hands, even hears it ticking, but he has no way of opening the case. If he is ingenious he may form some picture of the mechanism which could be responsible for all the things he observes, but he may never be quite sure his picture is *the only one* which could explain his observations. He will never be able to compare his picture with the real mechanism and he cannot even imagine the possibility of the meaning of such a comparison [emphasis added]. (Einstein and Infeld, as cited in Gregory, 1988, p. 189)

Einstein's watch analogy is similar to Wittgenstein's beetle box analogy. But there is also an important difference. Einstein does not suggest that what is inside the watch is irrelevant. There are several points to unpack in this analogy. First, there is the possibility of more than one explanation adequately accounting for all observations of the watch. Second—and this point grows from what is only implied in the example—there is the possibility that, over time, the initial explanation may prove inadequate to account for further observations and measurements. And third, there is the impossibility of ever opening the case and comparing the picture of the mechanism with the real mechanism.

This last point may seem strange, but it may help to see it in a slightly different way. Einstein intends to suggest that the problem of getting *inside* the watch is analogous to the problem of getting *outside* nature in order to objectively see it from the outside in. But this would, at bottom, require getting outside the entire universe in order to look inside. The inability to compare, the inability to "even imagine the possibility of the meaning of such a comparison," is precisely the problem of the inability to get outside *all context*, to reach a transcendent outside, which would provide an *absolute* position from which to compare. From within this way of conceptualizing nature, from within this model of being, knowing truth with certainty is *in principle* impossible.

In the domain of language theory, Derrida takes pains to point out no sign or set of signs can coerce or guarantee one particular interpretation. As a consequence, he argues further that choices *always* exist between competing alternatives that the evidence of material signs received from the senses is not sufficient in itself to decide. Instances where alternative interpretations do not appear or do not seem possible may be explained as a poverty of imagination. The presence of alternatives produces what Derrida calls an *undecidable* fork—*undecidable* not in the sense that a decision cannot be made on some basis, but rather undecidable in that a decision is not automatically made due to a preponderance of material evidence in favor of one alternative over another. As such, according to Derrida, whatever the relationship between signifier and signified may be, it is not a *causal* relationship—as language demonstrates every day through the misunderstandings to which it continually gives rise. Granted, such misunderstandings are open to repair, but the process of repair is itself conducted by way of processes the same as those already exposed to potential misunderstanding.

Returning to the domain of physical science, in a given instance of the reading of the "signs" of physical evidence, a clash of different explanations equally responsive to observation and evidence results in a dilemma referred to as the problem of *underdetermination*: Where a theory, meaning, or interpretation cannot be shown to be *uniquely* true or verified. The pervasiveness of underdetermination in relation to meaning in language explains why, in Derrida's view, there can be no determinate science or hermeneutics of meaning and no determinate science of the relationship between signifier and signified. This impasse accounts for statements of his to the effect that communication is (im)possible—possibly possible and possibly impossible, but certainly insolubly problematic (Derrida, 1982, pp. 309–330).

Derrida offers another way of expressing the consequences issuing from underdetermination in his use of notions such as *repetition-with-a-difference* and *iterability*. Both refer to the spatial/temporal embedment, whereby the limited number of signifiers in any given language necessarily involves their repeated use through constantly changing contexts. The meaning of signs must be flexible and interpretable enough to be used in changing contexts, otherwise the communicative function of language would be completely nullified. Yet this flexibility is precisely what also threatens and undermines fully transparent communication. Derrida finds this feature of language sufficiently ironclad to warrant calling it the *law of iterability* (for a full account of the law of iterability, see Derrida, 1977, p. 234). Iterability splits and divides the signifier through spatial/temporal difference and deferring, loosening and transforming the bond between signifier and signified, but not destroying the connection. This play in the system of signifiers insures that signifiers and signifieds always contaminate one another. Furthermore, this play insures not only the ever-present potential but also necessity for error or mistakenness in the reading and writing of signs through their radical incapacity to *locate in an absolute sense.*

In Derrida's view, there can be, in principle, no system of address escaping the law of iterability or repetition-with-a-difference. Yet Wilber sees this dependency of signs on changing context as a problem of relativism to be overcome in a manner analogous to the way in which the problem of measurement is overcome in special relativity. The following argument occurs in the context of Wilber's most recent and definitive defense of his Kosmic addressing account of language:

> As everybody knows, Einstein's theory [of special relativity] is badly misnamed; he thought about calling it things like absolute theory or invariance theory. The idea is that there is no fixed point anywhere in the universe that can be considered center;

> each thing can be located only relative to each other; this still creates absolutes and universals, but in a sliding system of reference to each other and to the system as a whole at any given time, with time itself being set by the invariant speed of light. (Wilber, 2006, p. 253)

But Wilber's use of special relativity in this sense is misleading at best, because it sidesteps the complicating role of context. Within any circumscribed context, certain invariants will become possible. The selected context for special relativity corresponds to four-dimensional Minkowski space. This Minkowski space *artificially* frames the cosmos and establishes a particular space within which specified events transpire. But this space has not proven sufficient for understanding all events occurring in the observed cosmos. This insufficiency, among others, led Einstein to formulate the theory of general relativity and a corresponding new context of *spacetimes* through interconnecting gravitational fields. This new context of space consistent with general relativity displaces Minkowski space. General relativity, in turn, has also proven inadequate in accounting for other observations of the physical world and has given way in the microcosmic realm to contextualizations imposed by quantum mechanics.

Within each of these selected spatial contexts, it becomes possible to work with particular types of invariants allowing for repeatable measurements. But this is perfectly consistent with Derrida's deconstruction, since the problems of underdetermination deconstruction underscores are a direct result of the problem of contextualization—which is the problem of the absence of an absolute context of contexts. Everywhere humans look, whether in language or in the cosmos, context is infinitely large, infinitely small, and infinitely divisible. This means the problem of context is a problem not only of *where* to draw the boundaries, but *how* to draw them in ways not so reductionistic as to become irrelevant to the complexity of the field of study. And this challenge is rendered more complex by the endless recontextualizations wrought by the passing of time or what Derrida refers to as the *yet-to-come*.

Wilber does acknowledge the important role of context and the constant shifting of context through time as presented in much of postmodern theory, yet he fails to theorize that role radically enough. Wilber's analogy between Kosmic addressing and Einstein's special relativity, therefore, remains inadequate to the challenge of deconstruction and the pervasive problem of contextualization. Wherever a context is drawn, there are always other ways of drawing it. These alternatives then signal other addresses for selected things and events. The crucial problem, then, is not so much one of relativity as it is one of multiple contexts, along with the underdetermination of signs—material, observable marks—within and through these shifting and overlapping contexts.

Furthermore, the limitation of addressing cannot be resolved by the notion that multiple contexts provide multiple addresses and thereby a complex convergence of object identity through an intersecting mapping of these multiple addresses. If each address is itself potentially incomplete and/or misdirecting, the accumulation of addresses may add stimulation and provoke thinking, but cannot fulfill identity and overcome the potential for a "misreading of signs." Problems of iterability and underdetermination necessitate that any given address, contrary to Wilber's claims and consistent with Derrida's theorizing of language, does not and *cannot ever* provide an instruction that will *guarantee* arriving at a particular location.

This is not to say Wilber's addressing system cannot be useful. Instead, it points out that his addressing system does not rest on the kind of foundation he claims for it in *Integral Spirituality*. For Wilber, language can be made to work and undecidability becomes, for him, a nonissue through his addressing system, whereas for Derrida, language and sign systems in general succeed as they also necessarily *fail*—not just occasionally, but always in some manner in every instance. And, as Derrida would insist, understanding and appreciating these limitations of sign systems are crucial for an adequate understanding of the nature of being. This is the case, because from the point of view of inquiry and understanding, everything material, the entire physical world, functions as a sign to the inquiring mind. This broadening of inquiry is reflected in the exasperatingly broad question: What does it all mean? An adequate understanding of the nature of being (to the extent that is possible) is necessary for achieving an adequate metaphysics—or at least an adequate understanding of the *limits* of metaphysics. Correspondingly, this understanding of the limits of metaphysics also provides an understanding of how the spiritual may be adequately approached.

Economies of Order and the Limits of Metaphysics

As mentioned in the previous section, play in the system of signifiers insures potential for mistakenness in the reading and writing of signs, combined with a necessary constraint against providing thoroughly objective location.

This necessarily incomplete, partial, or perspectival nature of human understanding may be viewed as the consequence of an essential flaw in the being of human being. This is the course of explanation often found in institutionalized spiritual traditions. Alternatively, this limitation may be viewed, as Derrida argues, as a consequence of being itself. The nature of being may be such that it can only reveal itself partially—in glimpses that enforce measures of omnipresent *blindness* precluding certainty and thereby necessitate some manner of *error*. The words *blindness* and *error* are italicized because these terms tend to lose their traditional meaning when applied to a system exceeding a traditional *economy* of order. The word "economy" is used to indicate a structured movement of exchange, interaction, and transaction. In the context of metaphysics, "economy" refers to the potential for transitions and transformations of being. An economy built around a principle of precise measurement, strict correspondence of cause and effect, and—speaking fiduciarily—a balance of payments, corresponds to a closed economy. Scientific theories of the natural world lean strongly in favor of theorizing whatever system is being observed as a *closed economy*, because closed economies are more amendable to basic mathematical strategies of measurement and calculation (think Newton's $F=ma$ and Einstein's $E=mc^2$).

But there are alternative economies of order, economies that see partiality (lack of fullness) and limitation (contamination) as a consequence of the nature of being itself, of the nature of all creation. Derrida (1978), following Georges Bataille, calls such an alternative economy of order a *general economy*. A general economy features the necessity of interrelation and dissemination of information or meaning as exceeding all measures of control and recuperation. It forms a law of irrecuperable loss. This general economy circulates around and through excesses irreducibly present in the nexus of causes and effects. Philosopher and literary theorist Arkady Plotnitsky (1994) explores Derrida's use of general economy in great detail, alongside parallel developments in theoretical physics. In Plotnitsky's analysis, derived from Bataille, a general economy "makes apparent that excesses of energy are produced, which, by definition, cannot be utilized. The excessive energy can only be lost without the slightest aim, consequently without any meaning" (Plotnitsky, 1994, pp. 1–2).

This possibility for irrecuperable loss is theorized by Derrida in his notion of the *trace*—a term he finds descriptive of the quality of being. The trace is an absenting presencing, disappearing as it appears. In the process of emergence there is also loss, a persistence/desistance similar to the flame of a candle. The flame moves through time, but it is not the "same" through every instant, because its previous existence has become its past. Its previous existence, its past being, is now apprehensible only as memory. Like words in language, the tracks of the trace are readable, but are also themselves traces. And what passes away in the tracings of being at any moment in time may be of incalculable value. Even if being is archived in a kind of library or museum or memory bank, there is no guarantee that "it" is preserved in its essence, because part of its essence consists of its temporal context. And since context is always on the move, there is no way to preserve without loss. This is the crucial consequence of a general economy. Because it is not possible to fully control this loss through any means of flawless preservation, this economy lacks closure and remains open to indeterminate change from the future. This feature of unpredictability (technically named *entropy*) is inherent in systems that lack strict causality.

Bataille calls the economy of order implicit in classical principles of cause and effect a *restricted economy*—restricted in the sense of a closure, whereby every action immediately or eventually provokes what can be understood and measured as a proportionate reaction. "Restricted economies consider their objects and the relationships between those objects as always meaningful and claim that the systems they deal with can avoid the unproductive expenditure of energy and control multiplicity and indeterminacy within themselves. General economy exposes such claims as untenable" (Plotnitsky, 1994, p. 2). The untenability of these claims became evident in the twentieth century, when lack of strict causality emerged as a notable limitation in the theorization of information systems, as well as the understanding of microcosmic particles in quantum physics.

A notable distinction between restricted and general economies arises from the different ways in which oppositional relation must be correspondingly structured. This difference will prove to be important in the upcoming discussion of transcendence. A restricted economy imposes a structuring principle establishing a strong polarity of opposites and clear lines of choice. In a restricted economy, the structural tension between opposites such as true and false or fact and interpretation operates with a clarity facilitating either/or alternatives and decision-making. In a general economy, however, every oppositional structure submits to a reversal and a displacement. This displacement involves an extraordinary reconfiguration of the structure or dynamic play between opposites.

Plotnitsky expresses this displacement of traditional oppositional tensions, using as key example the tension between description and reality, between interpretation and that which is interpreted. This tension points out an important distinction in his use of the terms *absolute* and *radical.* He says, for example, there cannot be "an absolute difference between an account and that which is being accounted for in a general economy. Once difference is absolute [between any set of classic opposites], *it is not radical enough* for a general economy. Absolute difference or exteriority of that type would always lead to a restricted economy, repressing the radical—but again never absolute—difference defined by and defining the field of general economy" [emphasis added] (Plotnitsky, 1994, p. 22).

A general economy displaces discrete and essential difference between opposites with a new structure, wherein the opposition presents a tension between elements both different yet connected; both penetrated to the core each by the other, yet irreducible one to the other. Plotnitsky calls this structure *complementary*—after Niels Bohr and the quantum theory of wave/particle duality. Thus, the quantum view of matter and energy is an example of a general economy, as is any economy in which a version of entropy operates—where entropy is understood as imposing an element of disorder, disjunction, or loss of information yielding unpredictability, incalculability, or irretrievability. In addition to quantum theory, deconstructive semiology falls into this category of entropic systems.

Applying the principle of *complementarity* to any oppositional pair yields a structure in which the two sides of the opposition penetrate each other in every instance, such that there is *no pure instance of either.* This circumstance then entails there can be no crossing over from an impure state to a pure state (complete transcendence) because there are no pure states or pure instances of anything. This circumstance of oppositional structure supports, according to Derrida, the notion of a universal law of contamination (analogous to the law of iterability). This universal contamination does not accord with degrees of mixture or gradations of difference. Instead, this law of contamination presents the circumstance of *superposition*—superposition of continuity (irreducible dependence) and discontinuity (irreducible separation). In the domain of language, complementarity is consistent with the emergence of meanings through contingent contexts precluding a calculus of discrete either/or discriminations. Discriminations or judgments are not so much coerced or caused, but rather *motivated*—motivated by a limited perception informed by the evaluation of what appear to be the most relevant factors of a here-and-now context. This universal law of contamination, consistent with a general economy and a complementary structure of oppositional relation, necessitates a deconstructive rethinking of the notion of transcendence. And, as might be guessed, this rethinking of the notion of transcendence bears importantly on the evaluation of Wilber's theorizing of transcendence, especially concerning his view of spiritual enlightenment.

Transcendence, Enlightenment, and Derrida's Radical Atheism

Among theological traditions, including a notion of God as creator and origin of the cosmos, one of the most commonly occurring distinctions may be found in the division between God and what God has made. Such distinctions follow the model of oppositional structure, in which there is a sharp division between the two sides of the opposition, whereby God exists completely separate from and independent of creation. Furthermore, God is perfect and God's creation is perfect—at least until corrupted by a contaminating element entirely separate from God (usually explained as brought into existence as a consequence of God's bestowal of free choice among the agents in creation). In these types of cosmologies, therefore, God remains wholly transcendent of creation. The possibility of transcendence for the beings of God's creation entails liberation from exposure to sources of contamination. This enables a crossing over into the realm of existence, which is, in essence, reunification with God and God's perfection. This transcendence is complete transcendence into perfected or fully realized being. In some spiritual traditions, this transcendence is called *salvation* and in others it is called *enlightenment.*

From the language Wilber uses in his current characterizations of spirit and enlightenment in *Integral Spirituality*, it becomes clear his spirituality remains within what Derrida calls a *restricted economy*. All restricted economies fall within classical metaphysical traditions and cannot be regarded as in any profound sense "postmetaphysical," as Wilber claims for his integral spirituality. There are two primary indicators for this assessment: 1) The deep structure of basic oppositions in Wilber's notion of Spirit; such as, for example, Emptiness and Form, timeless and temporal; and 2) The dominant role of notions such as union and oneness in his characterization of Spirit, as well as the transcendence of enlightenment.

Recall Wilber's definition of spirit in *Integral Spirituality*: "Spirit is defined as the union of Emptiness and Form (where Emptiness is timeless, unborn, unmanifest, and not evolving, and Form is manifest, temporal, and evolving)" (2006, p. 236). Spirit is the theological equivalent of God in Wilber's spirituality and oneness with spirit is Wilber's version of enlightenment.

Wilber acknowledges in *Integral Spirituality* that in ancient spiritual traditions, peak enlightenment was understood differently. It was thought to be achieved when novitiates attained, through difficult and focused practices, a state of enlightened oneness with *timeless* Spirit. But this practice reinforced, Wilber argues, a profound dualism between timeless Spirit and the temporal world of everyday experience. This profound dualism, with its unbalanced emphasis on the timeless, undermines the experience of oneness and renders it inauthentic against the realization in the current era that Spirit includes the temporal as well as the timeless. Spirit has always included the temporal and the timeless, but only in more recent times has human consciousness risen to the level of understanding the profound evolutionary or temporal aspect of Spirit's nature. Therefore, spiritual practices today, Wilber argues, attain only *partial enlightenment* if attending to and exclusively seeking union with the timeless quality of Spirit. Partial enlightenment consists of oneness with one side of the opposition—such as Emptiness, the unborn, the unmanifest—while failing to include the other side—Form, the temporal, and the manifest (e.g., Wilber, 2006, pp. 235–237).

However, Wilber's theorizing of the possibility of a partial enlightenment betrays an orientation toward the structure of oppositional relation consistent with a restricted economy. Such partial enlightenment would not be possible *even in principle* from within the dynamics of a general economy. It would not be possible, because in a general economy each side of the opposition does not exist in the manner of differentiated or pure being apart from its opposite. It would not be possible, now or in previous eras, to authentically realize the timeless aspect of Spirit because *no part of Spirit is timeless.* In a general economic structure of oppositional relation, each side of any given opposition is *already and everywhere contaminated by the other.* And this contamination necessarily entails a radical departure from the more traditional structure of oppositional relation.

The structure of opposition offered in a restricted economy undergoes a deconstruction such that, in the case of time and timelessness, both sides submit to a radical reconceptualization. If timelessness is already everywhere contaminated by time, *then there is no such thing as timelessness.* And, likewise, there can be no such thing as time as it is ordinarily understood. The notions of time and timelessness are exposed as having been markers for something else; as having something unexpected in their respective beetle boxes. The complex nature of this complementary relation of opposites is suggested in the yin-yang visual symbol, where the black swirl contains a dot of white and the white swirl contains a dot of black. The yin-yang symbol is often understood from within the frame of a restricted economy, but lends itself more credibly to the general economic way of understanding oppositional relation, whereby the dots represent inherent contamination of one side by the other.

To better understand the nature of the distinctions at stake and their relevance to Wilber's views, consider in greater detail his more recent formulations of his understanding of Spirit or Godhead, alongside a recent commentary on Derrida's views in relation to spiritual themes.

In his view of spirituality, Wilber retains the notion of timelessness, while also incorporating temporality as an inseparable part of Spirit. And he also retains for Spirit the quality of oneness and the potential for transcendence to full oneness with Godhead. Complete transcendence and oneness with Spirit—enlightenment—is the goal of his spirituality, which is also the overcoming of dualism in what Wilber calls *non-dual* spirituality. Non-dual spirituality is of the essence of an *integral* spirituality, because it exposes the illusory nature of essential divisions and thereby opens access to the subtle underlying reality through full realization of the oneness of everything in the Kosmos.

Oneness and ultimate transcendence go hand in hand in Wilber's thinking. This point cannot be emphasized enough. His insistence on ultimate transcendence *requires* his version of non-dual spirituality place *ultimate emphasis on oneness*. In describing his integral vision, he says, for example:

> Before Abraham was, I AM. I AM is none other than Spirit in 1st-person, the ultimate, the sublime, the radiant all-creating Self of the entire Kosmos, present in me and you and him and her and them—as the I AMness that each and every one of us feels. Because in all the known universe, the overall number of I AMs is but one. (Wilber, 2007, p. 224)[7]

Turning now to one of Derrida's commentators, Martin Hägglund, consider the steps in Hägglund's account of the structure of desire as Derrida sees it and how this structure is implicated in broader spiritual oppositions and the theme of transcendence. In this excerpt from his analysis, Hägglund approaches the question of desire from within a discussion of what he calls Derrida's *radical atheism*.[8]

Denial of the existence of God or Godhead defines, according to Hägglund, the general stance of traditional forms of atheism. But Hägglund believes Derrida goes further than denying the existence of God. For example, Hägglund asserts: "The atheism that Derrida expresses does not only deny the existence of God [substitute here also the I AM of Spirit in Wilber's sense] and immortality; it also answers to what I call radical atheism. Radical atheism proceeds from the argument that everything that can be desired is mortal in its essence" (Hägglund, 2008, p. 111).

Initially, Hägglund explains, it may seem the idea that "everything that can be desired is mortal in its essence" can be countered by the strategy of certain mystics such as Meister Eckhart. Desire and mortality, Eckhart might argue, are indeed linked and what we truly desire is to be rid of desire and to be rid of mortality. But this fails to imagine the situation from the direction of what is thereby necessarily implied about the nature of God. Without desire and without mortality, God could not possibly love any other creature, including humans. Love and desire are qualities arising only in *finitude.* Hägglund clarifies as follows:

> The experience of love *and the* beloved are necessarily finite. Such finitude is not something that comes to inhibit desire but precipitates desire in the first place. It is *because* the beloved can be lost that one seeks to keep it, and it is *because* the experience can be forgotten that one seeks to remember it. As Derrida strikingly puts it, *one cannot love* without the experience of finitude. This is the premise from which radical atheism necessarily follows. If one cannot love anything except the mortal, it follows that one cannot love God, since God does not exhibit the mortality that makes something desirable. The absolute being of God is not only unattainable but *undesirable,* since it would annul the mortality that is integral to whatever one desires [emphasis in original]. (Hägglund, 2008, p. 111)

Traditional atheism, according to Hagglund, remains within a traditional model of desire, because even though it denies the existence of God, it retains the notion that humans nevertheless desire absolute being. In other words, in traditional atheism the notion that humans *desire* absolute being, absolute transcendence, and immortality goes unquestioned. For the traditional atheist, this desire remains incapable of fulfillment, but nevertheless persists as a fundamental desire and therefore taints life with a peculiar nostalgia that Derrida finds unnecessary when the nature of being is adequately theorized.

The unity and fullness of ultimate transcendence is precisely what is precluded by temporality. The movement of time divides everything from itself and prevents any possible fullness of being or understanding. The spacing of time is what makes it possible for anything to happen. Without the constant interval between now and then, there would be no movement, no difference between being and seeing; and, hence, no desire, only stasis. By way of this analysis of the necessarily pervasive role of time, the highest state of conscious knowledge or attunement can only be, and must necessarily be, an incompleteness and a persistence of the sense of incompleteness. Being finite, being mortal, living within time, means being *always* in movement and incomplete.

Furthermore, movement brings not only the potential for, but the inevitability of the radical transformation intrinsic to mortality. As Hägglund interprets Derrida, the apparent desire for immortality is a false reading of desire—as is the reading of timelessness in the opposition of time and timelessness. In fact, the attainment of immortality would annihilate the possibility for any experience whatever. From within a general economy, immortality and timelessness are exposed as names for denoting phenomena other than what were thought to be the case. Hägglund argues (interpreting Derrida), immortality is a misleading name we give to desire. The notion of immortality actually reflects the desire to *extend* mortality, to extend our existence within time for a longer duration. We want to live in time without the ravages of time, while retaining all the advantages of time.

The ideal of timelessness masks a desire for survival—the desire for persistence through time into a future in which the last day is far away, unknown, and rarely confronted in the imagination. Timelessness is a way of thinking escape from the destructive effects of time, while not escaping from its constructive effects. Genuine timelessness entails a condition in which nothing can happen, a dimension of absolute stasis. Thus, the deconstructed opposition of time and timelessness emerges as the opposition of unremitting change through time, versus desired persistence through time. Similarly, the opposition of mortality and immortality, traditionally understood, is a confusion of the underlying opposition of deterioration and loss, versus endlessly extended survival within time.

A similar rethinking also happens in the opposition of good and evil. Evil in itself does not exist. It is inextricably bound up in all that is good. As Hägglund explains, "The possibility of evil is not a deplorable fact of our human constitution, which prevents us from achieving an ideal Good. Rather, the possibility of evil is intrinsic to the good that we desire, since even the most ideal fulfillment must remain open to the possibility of non-fulfillment" (Hägglund, 2008, p. 113).

This understanding of fulfillment requires, in turn, a rethinking of fulfillment as arising through, and only through, temporality. Nothing is untouched by temporality. Hägglund cites Derrida as saying, "The thought of 'radical evil' here is not concerned with it as an eventuality. It is simply that the *possibility* of something evil, or of some corruption, the *possibility* of the non-accomplishment, or of some failure, is *ineradicable*" (cited in Hägglund, 2008, p. 113). Hägglund then concludes: "For the same reason, everything that is good must be open to becoming evil. This threat of evil does not supervene on the good; it is part of the good that we desire" (Hägglund, 2008, p. 114). Evil is already everywhere part of the good. This means the potential for failure comes hand in hand with the potential for success. As soon as good becomes possible in any sense whatever, so too evil becomes possible. Evil, as the potential for failure, disaster, and annihilation, is therefore of the essence of the good. Like all oppositions in a general economy, good and evil contaminate each other to the core—even to the extent that in every good act, there is also evil and the need to weigh and choose between conflicting values.

For Derrida, structuring oppositional relations in accordance with a general economy and its notion of complementarity requires a displacement and rethinking of all the traditional oppositions. In fact, these oppositions are no longer oppositions in the old sense and preclude the old dualism. However, this complementarity also precludes the non-dual in Wilber's sense. Complementarity implies both one and two simultaneously, in the sense of retaining essential difference—one cannot be reduced to the other—while displaying essential relation—one cannot exist without the other. Here dualism is displaced but not subverted and oneness can be spoken of only as the system through that a displaced or deconstructed dualism inheres. Derrida would not use the word *non-dual* to describe the relation of opposites construed deconstructively, because it connotes too strongly in a direction obviating the irreducibility of twoness and division. However, it would also be misleading to suppose, on the other hand, that deconstruction may be aligned with any form of traditional philosophical dualism. The features of a general economy and complementarity of opposites belong to a different set of notions about division and opposition exceeding traditional dualistic and monistic notions.[9]

Summary and Conclusion

Despite showing attunement to postmodern philosophical developments, Wilber misses the point of deconstructive postmodernism as he continues to insist it does not imply what Derrida believes it implies. Ultimately,

Wilber adheres to his own version of a myth of the given in the belief that, for all practical purposes, clear, transparent communication and translation are as good as given when factored through his Kosmic addressing system. However, for Derrida, regardless of sophisticated sets of enactments or operations, transparency can never be taken as given. An absence of certainty in communication, a failure of objective location, persists—as is verifiable on a daily basis in attempts at communication, including this sentence. But this absence of certainty and failure of objective location are nothing to lament. The conditions of temporality and tensions of difference underlying this undecidability are precisely what make life, movement, change, experience—and any apprehension of the Kosmos whatever—possible.

In a deconstructive postmodern metaphysics/cosmology, traditional notions of time (as difference or change) and Being (as sameness or permanence) interpenetrate each other all the way through and at every point—which, as Derrida argues, does not prevent the existence of a functioning world. Indeed, a world functioning with movement and life requires this inextricable link between time and being. And this link produces dilemma as part of its essence, where modes of understanding, signification, and communication are always troubled by—but not destroyed by—undecidability.

If postmetaphysics is defined in the sense Wilber has indicated as deployment of a method of addressing or identification free of unwarrantable givens and allowing for transparent understanding and communication, then, for Derrida, there is no such thing as postmetaphysics, no escape from metaphysics. Not now, nor ever, in Derrida's view, can there be a postmetaphysical epistemology in the sense Wilber describes, because there can be no escape from the problem of undecidability created by the possibilities for multiple readings—whether of nature, text, or spirit. There remain only decisions about which metaphysical choices to make. The primary metaphysical decision involves a choice about how to view the structure of oppositional relation, as, for example, in the different choices for approaching oppositional relations inherent in restricted and general economies. For Derrida, restricted economies only *appear* to offer the promise of grasping the real and escaping troubling aspects of undecidability. They offer the illusion of such escape, while remaining metaphysics writ large.

Although offering no escape from metaphysics, Derrida's approach offers an escape from *traditional* metaphysics and its construction of notions of ultimate transcendence, which easily slide, however unintentionally, toward authorization of modes of certainty. Attitudes of certainty contribute to predispositions toward conceptual models and hierarchical arrangements immune to destabilizations, profound reversals, and unpredictable transformations. These kinds of models, consistent with restricted economies, ultimately imply forms of mastery and control that are without warrant.

The limitations of human communication and understanding disclosed by the conditions of a general economy, along with its temporal constraints on the nature of being, suggest three levels of implausibility for spiritual enlightenment as understood by Wilber. When reading these disclaimers, it must be kept in mind they are not offered as final pronouncements of truth, but must instead be understood as what is implied if—and only if—granting the nature of being as Derrida describes it:

1. Transcendent, totalized awareness of the Kosmos at any given point in time is not possible.
2. Even if such enlightenment were somehow possible, there could be no way of verifying with certainty it had been achieved.
3. And even assuming it had been achieved for oneself, there could be no reliable and unique set of instructions or operations for communicating to others how precisely to go about achieving it themselves.

Consequently, the notion of enlightenment as a state of full or peak awareness and oneness with the Kosmos has no practical role in a deconstructive postmodern spirituality. The nature of *what is* is such that oneness is not of the essence of *what is*. In this view, the fabric of the Kosmos is such that the possibility of enlightenment, as Wilber defines it, precludes the possibility of the Kosmos itself.

While Wilber's attempt to take the quackery and charlatanism out of spirituality by rendering it unto science and verifiability may be admirable, the problem is that spirituality, like language, cannot be made into the kind of science Wilber imagines. Its objects of investigation are not amenable to objective and transparent measurement. As Wilber understands, human experience in various fields of inquiry need not require subscribing to the Kantian notion that something remains always and essentially beyond observation in the thing-in-itself. But experience does suggest that observation will not yield singular and definitive answers to questions directed at the natural world. The answers to such questions always depend on context and context, theorized deconstructively, is an infinite finitude. This circumstance of infinite finitude creates what theorists such as Plotnitsky have referred to as an *anti-epistemology*. This orientation renders obsolete classical notions of objectivity, subject/object, and reality while retaining these notions under an alternative logic of oppositional relation. Nevertheless, anti-epistemology does not preclude forms of knowledge. Instead, it places an insurmountable limitation on achieving full transparency at any level of individual or collective consciousness and provides the rationale for understanding why this must be, in principle, the case.

At nearly every crossroad where Wilber could choose to depart from traditional metaphysics, he takes the traditional path. It is one thing to desire to be *integral* in spiritual approach and retain the best of all spiritual traditions, but another to do so while retaining the metaphysical foundation that has provided fertile ground for a long human history obviating the crucial role of time at the core of human being and all of creation. Adapting Wilber's myth metaphor to Derrida's metaphysics, the myth of the pure must be added to the myth of the given—as in the myth of pure transparency, the myth of pure communication, the myth of pure transcendence, the myth of pure consciousness, and the myth of pure oneness. To these must also be added the myth of repetition-without-difference (or loss) and the myth of the possibility of restricting being to a restricted economy.

Finally, the skeptical reader may continue to ask: Why be persuaded that the general economic metaphysics of deconstruction has found a better spiritual attitude in its seemingly radical embrace of temporality and finitude? Consistent with Einstein's watch analogy, this metaphysics may still be wrong, but it answers well to the current range of human experience and observation. Current theory in the fields of physics and semiology and related fields, such as biochemistry and information theory, reflects the dominance of the general economic metaphysical paradigm. If spirituality involves a measure of faith combined with reason, a measure of judgment combined with evidence—and it seems well that it should—then each person is left to make a metaphysical choice, the choice of which attitude more aptly describes the nature of being and more likely promotes the better life here and now. I hope to have persuaded the reader to at least consider the general economic metaphysics as the more philosophically justifiable position and, therefore, currently the better choice.

Notes

1. For the most thorough and concise explanation of Derrida's reasons for this assertion and for his view of language, see Derrida, 1988.

2. Derrida has been associated with transcendental philosophy, e.g., Rorty (1993); Doyon (2014), but care must be taken when aligning him with the transcendental tradition. It may be useful at this point to anticipate questions about how the term *transcendence* is being used in this context by distinguishing between notions of transcendence and transcendental philosophy.

Regarding transcendence, transcendental signifieds, and the grounding of language in something outside of language, one source of confusion comes from Derrida's famous dictum in *Of Grammatology* where he says what has been translated as "There is nothing outside the text"—a statement that has been widely misunderstood as implying the reduction of the entire external world of objects and referents to language and texts. This would be a shocking reduction, but it bears no resemblance to Derrida's position. Derrida has explained: "There is nothing outside the text" to mean "There is nothing outside context" (Derrida, 1988, pp. 136–137). According to Derrida, every text and its meaning emerges within an unbounded context, which includes other texts, as well as the physical world (and the entire cosmos, if you like). Any aspect of this unbounded context may prove relevant to understanding any given text. In this sense, it is not possible to get "outside"—absolutely transcend—the "text" any more than it is possible to get "outside" all context. Indeed, for human "readers" everything is semiotic (a "text") because everything may be understood to present information. Getting "outside the text" would be as impossible as getting outside the entire cosmos and looking in. Thus, Derrida's deconstructive position does not grant transcendence of context and is, in that sense, a version of contextualism.

On the other hand, transcendental philosophy considers conditions of possibility—for example, the conditions of possibility for knowledge, fulfillment, communication, etc. It is in this sense Derrida's work relates to the transcendental tradition and offers a reflection on the heterogeneous, yet indissociable, relation between immanence and transcendence, inside and outside—a relation precluding attaining the "outside" of absolute transcendence. Instead, this position aligns with what Derrida calls "quasi-transcendence," which is also consistent with what he calls transformation—a reaching or responding that opens up an expanded "inside." This developmental understanding of transcendence is consistent with developmental elements of Wilber's AQAL model, and so this kind of transcendence is not the point of difference between Wilber and Derrida explored herein. However, Wilber, as will be discussed below, posits an *ultimate* point of developmental process, which he refers to as "enlightenment." It is this notion of an ultimate transcendence—the merging of inside and outside in complete identification or *oneness* with Spirit—that is problematic in relation to Derrida's understanding of the nature of being as of the nature of the trace. This ultimate transcendence is also problematic with respect to what the nature of the trace entails—namely, that there can be no structural end, final reading, or ultimate experience of a "text" or the Kosmos. Terms such as "trace" and the deconstructive delimitation of transcendence are thoroughly explicated in the remainder of this essay.

3. This postmetaphysical way of understanding the non-givenness of the external world undermines the classic semiotic division of signifier/signified/referent corresponding to a version of metaphysical realism. There are no longer objects as referents, but instead operations or performances as referents. In this sense, the signified is materialized in actions (behaviors) and transactions (cooperation between people in tasks) and objects take on their significant being through semiotic operations. As will be seen in the next section, these features of Wilber's position resemble those of Wittgenstein's view of language.

4. W.V.O. Quine (1960) makes essentially the same point with his principle of indeterminacy of translation. This principle states: "Manuals for translating one language into another can be set up in divergent ways, all compatible with the totality of speech dispositions [utterances by native speakers], yet incompatible with each other" (1960, p. 27). Quine and Derrida share significant views about language, which makes it all the more surprising Quine was among the more prominent signatories of the group of intellectuals opposing the Cambridge award of an honorary degree to Derrida.

5. Here the phrase *operating with signs* is broad enough to include semiotic systems other than language, such as geometry and architectural drawings, picture stories, musical notation, mathematics, tarot cards, astrology, and similar systems. Furthermore, in Wittgenstein's approach, the traditional notion of semiotic reference falls away such that the meanings of signs are not hinged to objects to which they refer. Thus, the meanings of words and signs do not correspond to physical objects or to mental or ideal objects. But this does not reduce the world to a realm of circular sign exchanges. Instead, the role of reference is replaced by observable or measurable operations. The meaning of "Bring the slab to me" is understood when the person addressed brings the slab to me. For Wittgenstein, sign systems are public "life forms" or forms of communication and the success of communication is publicly tested and validated through overt operations. The "objectivity" of the external world is then, for the later Wittgenstein, rooted in operations, which notion bears some resemblance to the role of instrumentality (the ready-to-hand) in Heidegger's fundamental ontology of being. See, for example, Braver (2012).

6. As noted in the previous paragraph, verificationism may be distinguished from operationism in that the former is associated more with a theory of truth, whereas the latter is associated more with a theory of meaning. Verificationism is also closely associated with physicalism, which ties it to publicly observable objects and events. Operationism, however, as indicated by Wilber's addressing system, is used to tie words (such as enlightenment) to practices that can lead to unobservable experiences. So, in this respect, Wilber wants to avoid direct association with classic understandings of verificationism, which seek to tie words only to observable objects and events.

7. Wilber also emphasizes the unitary nature of Godhead when he speaks of the Ascending and Descending path to spiritual enlightenment. The words he uses to summarize this path apply to "any Nondual stance wherever it appears" when

he describes the practice as "flee the Many, find the One; having found the One, embrace the Many *as* the One. Or, in short: Return to One, embrace Many. The exuberant and loving and unconditional embrace of the Many is the fruition and consummation of the Perfection of the One, and without which the One remains dualistic, fractured, 'envious'" (Wilber, SES, p. 336). For Derrida, the Perfection of a pure and simple One would preclude the possibility of the Many. All being is "fractured" in nonidentity with itself and this is the perfection of imperfection required in order for there to be anything at all.

8. The primary text on which Hägglund bases his reading of Derrida's radical atheism is the essay "Faith and Knowledge: The Two Sources of 'Religion' and the Limits of Reason Alone" (found in Derrida and Vattimo, 1998). In reading the remainder of this section, it may prove useful to keep in mind that Martin Hägglund offers only one reading of Derrida. It is an important reading to consider and one that aligns with my own reading of Derrida, but there are other significant commentators on Derrida's later work who read him differently on the subject of theism and spiritual questions. The reader can only benefit from exposure to these alternative readings, e.g., Critchley, 1992; Caputo, 1997; Caputo and Scanlon, 1999; Kearney, 2001; Naas, 2012. Hägglund acknowledges these commentators have found Derrida to be an inspiration for deepening religious and ethical conviction and attunement to God. Nevertheless, he shows the ways in which he believes these commentators have failed to adequately interpret Derrida's relevant texts. The substance of Hägglund's disagreement with these views can be found primarily in two places: Hägglund, 2008, Chapter 3; and Hägglund, 2013. His argument hinges most significantly on noting a confusion between Derrida's terminology of unconditional openness or exposure implicit in phrases such as *messianism to come*, *justice to come*, or *democracy to come* and interpretations of this unconditional openness as a normative stance, rather than an irreducible and unavoidable feature of experience in time. As Hägglund explains: "The openness to the future is unconditional in the sense that every system or action necessarily is open to the future, but it is not unconditional in the sense of a normative ideal. The mistake is to assume that one can derive a normative affirmation of the future from the unconditional 'yes' to the future that Derrida analyzes as inherent in every system or action" (Hägglund, 2013, p. 106). This same criticism applies to those interpretations of Derrida's assertion that justice is undeconstructable that understand this statement to indicate a Neoplatonic ideal to which homage must be paid and from which guidance is received. Instead, according to Hägglund, Derrida intends this and similar statements about the future as indications of the radical openness of the future, the contours of which remain to play out in unpredictable ways owing to the fact that the otherness of the future and its influence cannot be controlled or reliably predicted.

9. The use of the word *traditional* here does not preclude the possibility that within ancient traditions such as Taoism and Buddhism there are lineages that may perhaps be interpreted as consistent with the deconstructive view of oppositional

relations (for a more direct discussion of these possibilities, see Desilet, 2007b). The yin-yang symbol has already been mentioned as an image suggesting this type of understanding. Nevertheless, tasks of translation and interpretation, as Derrida has argued, are never simple and this is especially so in the case of ancient texts and symbols.

References

Braver, Lee. 2012. *Groundless Grounds: A Study of Wittgenstein and Heidegger*. Cambridge, MA: MIT Press.

Caputo, John D. 1997. *The Prayers and Tears of Jacques Derrida: Religion Without Religion*. Bloomington, IN: Indiana University Press.

Caputo, John D., and Michael J. Scanlon (eds.). 1999. *God, the Gift, and Postmodernism*. Bloomington, IN: Indiana University Press.

Critchley, Simon. 1992. *The Ethics of Deconstruction: Derrida and Levinas*. Cambridge, MA: Blackwell Publishers.

Derrida, Jacques. 1974. *Of Grammatology*, trans. Gayatri Chakravorty Spivak. Baltimore: Johns Hopkins University Press.

Derrida, Jacques. 1977. "Limited Inc abc." *Glyph 2: Johns Hopkins Textual Studies*, trans. Samuel Weber. Baltimore: Johns Hopkins University Press.

Derrida, Jacques. 1978. *Writing and Difference*, trans. Alan Bass. Chicago: University of Chicago Press.

Derrida, Jacques. 1981. *Positions*, trans. Alan Bass. Chicago: University of Chicago Press.

Derrida, Jacques. 1988. *Limited Inc*, trans. Samuel Weber; ed. Gerald Graff. Evanston, IL: Northwestern University Press.

Derrida, Jacques, and Elisabeth Roudinesco. 2004. *For What Tomorrow . . . A Dialogue*, trans. Jeff Fort. Stanford, CA: Stanford University Press.

Derrida, Jacques, and Gianni Vattimo (eds.). 1998. *Religion*. Stanford, CA: Stanford University Press.

Desilet, Gregory. 2002. *Cult of the Kill: Traditional Metaphysics of Rhetoric, Truth, and Violence in a Postmodern World*. Philadelphia: Random House Ventures/Xlibris.

Desilet, Gregory. 2007a. "Misunderstanding Derrida and Postmodernism: Ken Wilber and 'Post-metaphysics' Integral Spirituality." *Integral World*. Posted March 2007.

Desilet, Gregory. 2007b. "Derrida and Nonduality: On the Possible Shortcomings of Nondual Spirituality." *Integral World*. http://www.integralworld.net/desilet2.html. Posted April 2007.

Doyon, Maxime. 2014. "The Transcendental Claim of Deconstruction." In *A Companion to Derrida*, ed. Zeynep Direk and Leonard Lawler. Malden, MA: John Wiley.

Gregory, Bruce. 1988. *Inventing Reality: Physics as Language*. New York: John Wiley.

Hägglund, Martin. 2008. *Radical Atheism: Derrida and the Time of Life*. Stanford, CA: Stanford University Press.

Hägglund, Martin. 2013. "Beyond the Performative and the Constative." *Research in Phenomenology* 43: 100–107.

Hampson, Gary P. 2007. "Integral Re-views Postmodernism: The Way Out is Through." *Integral Review* 4.

Hymers, Michael. 2005. "Going Around the Vienna Circle: Wittgenstein and Verification." *Philosophical Investigations* 28:3: 205–234.

Kearney, Richard. 2001. *The God Who May Be: A Hermeneutics of Religion*. Bloomington, IN: Indiana University Press.

Lyotard, Jean-Francois. 1984. *The Postmodern Condition: A Report on Knowledge*, trans. Geoffrey Bennington and Brian Massumi. Minneapolis, MN: University of Minnesota Press.

Meyerhoff, Jeff. 2006. "*Bald Ambition*, Chapter 7: Poststructuralism and Postmodernism." *Integral World*. http://www.integralworld.net/meyerhoff-ba-7.html. Posted July 2006.

Meyerhoff, Jeff. 2010. *Bald Ambition: A Critique of Ken Wilber's Theory of Everything*. Inside the Curtain Press.

Naas, Michael. 2012. *Miracle and Machine: Jacques Derrida and the Two Sources of Religion, Science, and the Media*. New York: Fordham University Press.

Plotnitsky, Arkady. 1994. *Complementarity: Anti-Epistemology After Bohr and Derrida*. Durham, NC: Duke University Press.

Quine, W.V.O. 1960. *Word and Object*. Cambridge, MA: MIT Press.

Rorty, Richard. 1993. "Is Derrida a Transcendental Philosopher?" In *Working Through Derrida*, ed. Gary B. Madison. Evanston, IL: Northwestern University Press.

Staten, Henry. 1984. *Wittgenstein and Derrida*. Lincoln, NE: University of Nebraska Press.

Wilber, Ken. 1996. *A Brief History of Everything*. Boston: Shambhala.

Wilber, Ken. 2000. *Sex, Ecology, Spirituality: The Spirit of Evolution* (2d. ed. rev.) Boston: Shambhala.

Wilber, Ken. 2006. *Integral Spirituality*. Boston: Integral Books.

Wilber, Ken. 2007. *The Integral Vision: A Very Short Introduction to the Revolutionary Integral Approach to Life, God, the Universe, and Everything*. Boston: Shambhala.

Wilber, Ken, and Andrew Cohen. 2004. "Transcend and Include: The Guru and the Pandit, Ken Wilber and Andrew Cohen in Dialogue." *EnlightenNext Magazine* Oct.–Dec. 2004. Available at http://www.enlightennext.org/magazine/j27/gurupandit.asp.

Wittgenstein, Ludwig. 1953. *Philosophical Investigations*, trans. G.E.M. Anscombe. New York: Macmillan.

Wittgenstein, Ludwig. 1958. *The Blue and the Brown Books*. New York: Harper & Row.

Chapter 10

Ontological and Epistemic Considerations for Integral Philosophy

Toward a Critical Realist Integral Theory

Nicholas Hedlund

Author's Note

This chapter was the basis of an essay I published in *Metatheory for the Twenty-First Century: Critical Realism and Integral Theory in Dialogue* (Bhaskar et al., 2016), entitled "Rethinking the Intellectual Resources for Addressing Complex Twenty-First Century Problems" (Hedlund, 2016). While the overall structure remains largely the same, a fairly substantial portion of the content is different. For example, the other version was dialectized in terms of my approach and my position was, therefore, more pronounced in some ways with respect to the nature of the synthesis I sought to forge between critical realism and integral theory. Specifically, I argued for an explicitly non-preservative synthesis in which some elements of each theory are negated on the way to synthesis. More technically, I argue for a synthesis or sublation of an explicitly transformative-negational variety. As I state: "To be sure, my method here is dialectical in a *transformative-sublatory* sense (à la Bhaskar), as opposed to preservative-synthetic (à la Hegel) . . . by that I mean that I aim to engage each metatheory with an eye for identifying generative contradictions and absences (or other inconsistencies, anomalies, and aporias), while (hopefully) shedding some preliminary light on their potential causes. Such a method initiates a movement toward the rethinking of (aspects of) each metatheory's architechtonics—beginning to chart a trajectory toward an expanded conceptual field (namely, a critical realist integral theory or CRIT) that eschews and remedies absences and contradictions in each theory's preexisting form. Importantly, this involves a negative transfiguration of elements within both theories (p. 186). This transformative negativity is clearly thematized in the other version of this essay. Additionally, in the present chapter, there is a sub-section toward the end of the section on "Critical Realism's Ontology and Epistemology" on critical naturalism and the philosophy of social science. This section adds nuance and depth to the overall discussion of critical realism's approach.

Introduction

As postmodernism's anti-realism continues to wane, and its inadequacies as a philosophical response to the complex global challenges of the twenty-first century become evermore glaring, there is an urgent need for more sophisticated and efficacious alternatives.[1] But what will rise from the rubble that postmodernism has bequeathed us? What intimations of an alternative intellectual formation can be discerned? And what are (or will be) its key motifs and thematics?

To begin to address these questions, one can start by noting some of the leading philosophies in the academy that are gaining credence as alternatives to postmodernism—namely, critical realism,[2] integral theory, and speculative realism.[3] These approaches are broadly aligned in an interest in the re-vindication of ontology[4] or some variant of *realism* in the face of the neo- and post-Kantian epistemological critiques undergirding postmodernism's myriad inflections of anti-realism.[5] Concomitantly, they diverge in important ways in terms of their particular approaches and histories related to surmounting these challenges to the status of ontology and their impact. In contrast to critical realism, for whom the re-vindication of ontology in philosophy has been a central goal explicitly developed since the 1970s, integral theory approaches the issue from a more interdisciplinary,[6] metatheoretical perspective and has only recently begun to address the issue, which remains somewhat peripheral, more explicitly (see Esbjörn-Hargens, 2010; Wilber, 2012a, 2012b). Finally, speculative realism is itself a very new movement, emerging in 2007, which employs a number of divergent approaches to the re-vindication of ontology[7] (and has, to some extent, been influenced by critical realism [see e.g., Levi Bryant, 2011]).[8]

Of the aforementioned approaches, I will focus on only two here: The respective positions articulated by the contemporary European-based philosophy of critical realism, founded by Roy Bhaskar, and the American-based metatheoretical approach of integral theory,[9] founded by Ken Wilber. While certain currents within the much more heterogeneous and loosely connected philosophical movement known as speculative realism are also worthy of consideration (see, e.g., Graham Harman's object-oriented philosophy and Levi Bryant's onticology), for purposes of this short essay, I must necessarily limit myself to addressing only IT and CR.

Thus, in this chapter, I want to suggest that each of these movements have substantial relevance for the iterative and reflexive process of envisaging and bringing forth an integral (or post-postmodern) philosophy. Rather than a singular approach or particular philosophical theory (e.g., Ken Wilber's articulation of the AQAL model), I argue that integral philosophy might be better understood as a broad and pluralistic movement (i.e., inclusive of multiple schools or streams) defined largely as an emergent structural formation arising in the wake of the philosophical discourse of both modernity and postmodernity[10] and characterized by the key motif of a resurgence of ontology, or *the new realism.*[11] In this way, I am suggesting that we may indeed be in the early phases of integral philosophy's rise as a definitive alternative to postmodernism and its marked limitations—but of course, only time will tell. Yet if integral philosophy is to constitute an authentically novel movement within the geohistorical trajectory of Western philosophy, rather than a mere recapitulation or variant of postmodernism (or regressive championing of [pre]modern approaches under the guise of the new), then it must be more than an alternative—it must actually go *beyond* or transcend both modernism and postmodernism, while simultaneously including their most important enduring contributions. That is, integral philosophy, I want to suggest, should forge a higher-order *sublation* (synthesis and transcendence) of the philosophical discourse of both modernity and postmodernity. Thus, rather than a mere recapitulation or re-iteration of the core tenets of modern or postmodern philosophy, I argue that a definitive signature of integral philosophy is its fundamental *break* or asymmetry in relation to the ontological and epistemic foundations of its antecedent philosophical formations concomitant with their enfoldment. It thereby must be an emergent dialectical synthesis that modifies and repatterns aspects of them, catalyzing their integration in the process of birthing an emergent holistic pattern or structure. In short, integral philosophy, defined as such, should strive to enact a kind of *post*-postmodernism worthy of such a designation in a definitive structural sense, as opposed to the all-too-common rhetorical 'post-'holing that often seems to reflect trivial academic fence-building more than a substantive differentiation or break from antecedent approaches.[12]

Based on these criteria for an integral philosophy (i.e., a post-post-modern philosophical formation sublative of the philosophical discourse of modernity and postmodernity; an epistemologically mature or post-critical championing of ontology), I argue that CR and IT appear to be among the most comprehensive and sophisticated expressions of a still yet-to-be fully consolidated integral, post-postmodern philosophy. Both CR and IT explicitly situate themselves not only as alternatives to postmodernism, but claim to go beyond both positivism and social constructivism while integrating key aspects of their respective philosophical discourses.[13] In the face of radicalized forms of post-Kantian skepticism and anti-realism characteristic of postmodernism, both approaches champion a return to ontology at a higher turn of the spiral—a return to some form of realism that substantially integrates the epistemic advances of both (post)positivism and social constructivism, and thus is not a regression to a form of precritical, first philosophy (*prima philosophia*) or dogmatic metaphysics. Both IT and CR articulate unique justifications for such a return to an ontology inclusive of the post-Kantian, postmodern principle of *epistemic relativity/fallibility* in some form, to some degree. They both seem to acknowledge that philosophy can no longer be formulated from what Thomas Nagel (1986) calls the "view from nowhere," which characterizes most pre-critical metaphysical projects. Rather, they both self-reflexively argue that philosophy should necessarily be *situated* in various important ways, be it in a geohistorical trajectory, cultural milieu, psychological structure, or otherwise. As such, they are both helping to fashion the emergent features of an integral philosophical discourse through an epistemologically sophisticated return to ontology or (neo-)realism, but do so in different, yet complementary, ways.

As I will contend, IT, as it has been expressed to date, maintains a post-Kantian position and develops a sophisticated, postmetaphysical theory of enactment, the strengths of which lie primarily in the epistemic domain.[14] In contrast, CR expounds a powerful critique of neo- and post-Kantianism, yet uses a Kantian method of transcendental argumentation to derive a depth ontology, which is arguably its signature advance and principal strength. Thus, in this short essay, I aim to explore the most salient strengths and weaknesses (absences and contradictions) of both CR and IT[15] within the domains of ontology and epistemology, highlighting their striking complementarities, on the way to forging the outlines of a provisional synthesis of these two approaches to being and knowing—that is, an integral realism or critical realist integral theory (CRIT).[16] As such, I am broadly attempting to begin to do with CR and IT what they each claim to do with the philosophical discourse of modernity and postmodernity: Namely, to transcend and integrate them into an emergent structural formation.

First, I begin by providing a high-level synoptic overview of IT in the domains of ontology and epistemology, followed by a comparable exposition of CR. I then critically analyze IT in light of CR, before exploring CR from the perspective of IT. Finally, I sketch some initial propositions with respect to how the two schools might begin to be synthesized into a more comprehensive and robust integrative metatheory and expression of integral philosophy—a CRIT—that could potentially unite the strengths of both, while addressing and mitigating their respective weaknesses. I conclude by reflecting on the social and ecological relevance of the ontological and epistemological questions underpinning this inquiry, suggesting that something like a CRIT may offer crucial intellectual resources for addressing the complex global challenges of the twenty-first century, such as climate change.

Integral Theory's Ontology and Epistemology

Since a comprehensive overview of IT's ontology and epistemology is beyond the scope of this essay, I will, rather, summarize certain key features relevant to my argument. IT, at least in a formal philosophical sense, lacks an explicit, fully articulated and justified (a priori) philosophical ontology; it thus remains largely implicit and therefore will be assessed in a reconstructive manner.[17] Having clarified this caveat, IT, as it has been expressed to date, builds on the German philosopher and social theorist Jürgen Habermas's (1992, 2003) postmetaphysical thinking in articulating a post-Kantian theory of enactment, or integral postmetaphysics (also called *phase 5* in the development of Wilber's philosophy). Integral postmetaphysics, as expounded by Wilber[18] (2001, 2003, 2006) and Esbjörn-Hargens[19] (2010) links ontology to epistemology and methodology such that (at least in some sense) it appears to assert the primacy of epistemology and methodology over ontology. That is, I argue that in practice it underscores the ways in which ontology is essentially derivative of, or contingent on, epistemology (and methodology), despite countervailing claims that they are synchronically emergent ("arise concurrently") and mutually interdependent ("co-enact concurrently").[20] Moreover, maintaining the primacy of epistemology (and methodology) over ontology is closely connected to IT's postmetaphysical attempt to jettison ontology or metaphysics in its precritical or dogmatic form. As Wilber (2006) articulates it:

> If metaphysics began with Aristotle, it ended with Kant. Or at any rate, took a turn that has defined the way sophisticated philosophers think about reality ever since. Kant's *critical philosophy* replaced ontological objects with structures of the subject. In essence, this means that we do not perceive empirical objects in a completely realistic, pregiven fashion; but rather, structures of the knowing subject impart various characteristics to the known object that then appear to belong to the object—but really don't; they are, rather, co-creations of the knowing subject. Various *a priori* categories of the knowing subject help to fashion or construct reality as we know it. Reality is not a perception, but a conception; at least in part. Ontology per se just does not exist (p. 231).

Thus, Wilber's articulation of his postmetaphysical position appears to involve a relatively strong post-Kantian irrealist and constructivist stance,[21] including an alignment with Kant's basic notion that the a priori categories and structures do not have independent, real referents in the world (that is, *categorial irrealism*), but, in Wilber's terms, "enact" the referent.[22] Wilber (2006) goes on to note that

> [ontological] objects come into being, or are enacted, only at various developmental levels of complexity and consciousness. Whether they exist in some other way CANNOT BE KNOWN in any event, and assuming that they do exist entirely independently of a knowing mind is nothing but the myth of the given and the representational paradigm—that is, is just another type of metaphysical thinking and thus not adequately grounded. At any event, post-metaphysical thinking does not rely on the existence of a pregiven world and the myth of that givenness. (p. 252, capitalization in original)

This passage seems to reveal Wilber's correlation of ontology and epistemology: The ontological, mind-independent existence of objects "CANNOT BE KNOWN," and therefore, in a (characteristically postmodern) radicalization of Kant, if they cannot be known, then sophisticated philosophy, for Wilber, would make no claim to their existence; the ontological status of an object is contingent on its epistemological enactment vis-à-vis developmental structures and methods. Accordingly, Wilber seems to suggest that we cannot have knowledge of being (the ontic) *as such*, but only being as it is known by subjects (human and nonhuman), and therefore we can collapse Kant's transcendental dialectic and functionally equate being with *access* to being, being itself with the (inter)subjective interpretation or enactment of being: "there is no 'apart from' how a thing appears; there is simply how it appears." (Wilber, 2006, p. 252); thus, " 'enter consciousness' and 'exist' are essentially identical in the post/modern world" (Wilber, 2006, p. 250). Thus, in the face of this Kantian *problem of access,* Wilber argues for what seems to be a subject-oriented position, albeit a non-anthropocentric or panpsychic one,[23] which apparently sees no way for there to be realities that are fundamentally mind independent—he sees no way to grant ontology an autonomy from epistemology[24] (and methodology) without regressing to dogmatic metaphysics, or some kind of precritical ontotheology that sidesteps the demands of modern *procedural rationality*[25] (Taylor, 1989; Habermas, 1992). As such, from the perspective of integral postmetaphysics, any claim to a truly mind-independent object-world is apparently a form of the "myth of the given," or precritical metaphysics.[26]

To be sure, Wilber's (2006, 2012a, 2012b) notion of "intrinsic features" and related distinction between "subsist" and "exist" adds complexity and nuance to his scheme, and prima facie, appears to undercut the assessment that "any claim to a truly mind-independent object-world is apparently a form of the 'myth of the given.' " However, Wilber (2006) goes on to point out that his "intrinsic features . . . are not intrinsically intrinsic features," but rather that "whatever is actually 'intrinsic' to the Kosmos changes with each new worldspace; and thus both what ex-ists and what sub-sists are con-structions of consciousness" (pp. 250–251). Moreover, he goes on to reiterate this position by claiming that "signifiers have real referents in the only place that referents of any sort exist anyway: in a state or structure of consciousness. All referents exist, if they exist at all, in a worldspace." (p. 266). Therefore, while Wilber argues for the existence of "real" objects, referents, and "intrinsic features" that subsist, upon scrutiny, it seems that such notions are, for Wilber (2012a), a contingent function of mind/consciousness/interiority and its structures: "[W]hen we actually get down to explaining what this subsistence reality is—the 'real'—it changes with each new structure (red, amber, orange, green, etc.)" (p. 44). So for Wilber, it appears that there are realities that are not totally mind-dependent in the sense of what is brought forth synchronically in the epistemic, subject-centered process of enactment (that is, "intrinsic features" that "subsist" relatively independent of a given subject's perception of it), but those realities are themselves inexorably mind-dependent (at least in the Whiteheadian sense of prehension[27]). So we might thereby conclude that, according to integral postmetaphysics, realities are not only constituted individually and synchronically, but also diachronically and relationally, and they are contingent on specific developmental structures. While this can certainly help to distinquish Wilber's position from solipsism and classical (e.g., Berkeleyian) forms of subjective idealism, for example, to my mind it does little to establish a foothold in the domain of an authentic realism that honors the epistemic anteriority and independence of the world. While Wilber has recently shifted his rhetorical emphasis with respect to ontology, moving from statements such as "ontology per se just does not exist" (2006, p. 231) to making explicit that "ontology is real" (quoted in Marshall, 2012c, p. 37), it seems relatively clear that for Wilber and IT at large, ontology is enactively or *empirically contingent* (i.e., a product or "co-creation" of the knowing-consciousness of sentient beings/holons), *developmentally stratified* (i.e., according to species and psychological levels of consciousness), and therefore *pluralistic* (i.e., there are multiple ontologies and many worlds that may or may not overlap). In short, IT champions an ontology of the phenomenal, which, as we will see, is in marked contrast to that of CR.

Despite positing this inexorable post-Kantian coupling of epistemology (and methodology) and ontology and interrelated rejection of the possibility of generating a critical/post-Kantian, realist ontology (i.e., an ontology that is disambiguated from epistemology and thereby makes claims about being as such or objects that exist independent of mind and method) it is important to emphasize that Wilber attempts to differentiate his position from that of most strong forms of postmodern social constructivism[28] and untempered epistemic relativism in, for example, the following ways: 1) he argues for a weaker form of social constructivism by virtue of the fact that he claims to not deny *entirely* the existence of a real world "out there" by reference to his "intrinsic features" and "ex-ist"/"subsist" distinction; 2) by emphasizing the highly structured (e.g., through developmental structures), interactively performative, and therefore nonarbitrary process of enactment on both epistemic and methodological levels (which could be said to resonate with aspects of structuralist anti-humanism[29]); and 3) through his underscoring of the principles of *epistemic reflexivity* and *positionality* implied in his articulation of the notion of "kosmic address."

Moreover, in the domain of epistemology, it should be noted that IT possesses a sophisticated epistemic taxonomy, including its matrix of (inter)subjective structures (e.g., levels, lines, states, types [see Figure 1]), as well as its methodological taxonomy known as integral methodological pluralism (IMP; see 2). IT's taxonomy of such myriad (inter)subjective epistemic structures builds forth on the pioneering work of the Swiss psychologist and philosopher Jean Piaget (1896–1980). Piaget employed empirical methods to observe and code the patterning of diverse capacities for thought and action, disclosed as human beings develop from infancy to adulthood. In this way, he rationally reconstructed the conditions for the possibility of various cognitive skills/events, and designated numerous (epistemic) structures that he saw as the fundamental mechanisms necessarily undergirding them. Over the course of his career, Piaget amassed a copious body of evidence for his developmental theory—known as *genetic epistemology* (referring to the genesis or origins of knowledge, *not* genes or biological genetics)—essentially birthing the field of developmental-structuralism and inspiring many researchers to further probe, test, and expand his model to delineate the higher reaches of adult development (i.e., beyond his "formal operational" stage of linear rationality). As such, this neo-Piagetian stream of developmental-structuralism has subjected Piaget's model to careful scrutiny within multiple research paradigms, and the model has generally stood the tests of time and demonstrated both its scientific validity and cross-cultural universality across the globe (Gardiner and Kosmitzki, 2004).[30] At the same time, the neo-Piagetians have introduced a number of important nuances and distinctions that do much to address a number of common objections and criticisms to developmental models, including their potential abuses when coupled with simple "growth to goodness" normative assumptions, their purported uni-linear and uni-directional trajectory of "progress," and their alleged Eurocentricity, to name a few. Additionally, various researchers have used a broadly neo-Piagetian developmental-structural approach to delineate their own similarly forged (and generally more advanced) stage models in a number of domains or lines such as cognition (Commons, et al., 1984; Rose and Fischer, 2009), consciousness (Kegan, 1982a, 1994, 2001), ego-identity (Cook-Greuter, 1999, 2000, 2002; Loevinger, 1977, 1987), and morality

(Kohlberg, 1984). IT, based on neo-Piagetian developmental-structural psychology, thereby posits that empirical human knowing is situated within an invariant, though dialectical and non-unilinear, trajectory through hierarchically-structured stages—stages that function as key generative mechanisms in the enactment of what "ex-ists" out of the "subsist" level. Based on a meta-analysis of many of the best neo-Piagetian theories, IT articulates a synthetic metatheory that is arguably among the comprehensive taxonomy of these epistemic structures brought forth to date.

In addition to its matrix of (inter)subjective structures, IT also articulates a robust methodological taxonomy, IMP, which can be seen as an important aspect of its overall epistemic taxonomy (see Wilber, 2003, 2006; Wilber and Esbjörn-Hargens, 2006). IMP is a meta-methodological map of eight *event horizons* that situate eight corresponding methodological families to explore and disclose the dynamic interrelationships between (inter)subjective and (inter)objective aspects of reality. IMP also articulates the systematic interrelationships between each of the major methodological families, allowing one to combine, coordinate, and *systematically integrate* the multiplicity of methodologies (both qualitative and quantitative) available for scientific inquiry. IMP has been operationalized as a practical framework, known as integral research (IR), which supports researchers to reflect on

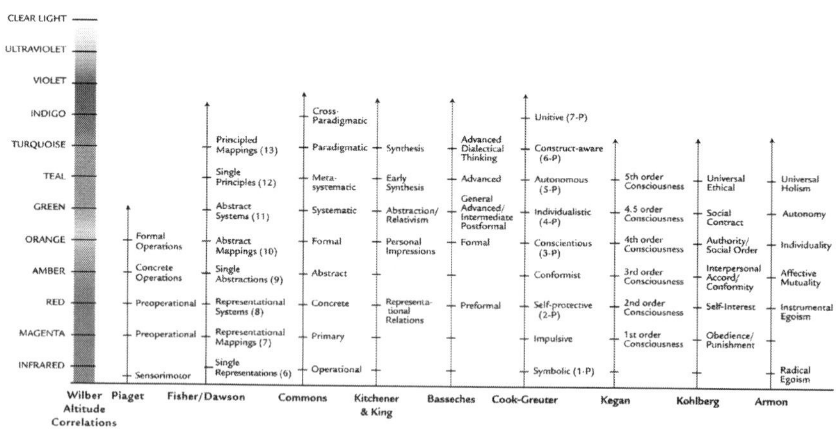

Figure 10.1. Lines of development. *Source:* author.

and self-reflexively situate the unique interpretive lens (and its strengths and weaknesses) that each researcher brings to their inquiry (see e.g., Esbjörn-Hargens, 2006; Hedlund, 2008, 2010). In these ways, it offers a (broadly) scientific framework that goes beyond the unprincipled eclecticism that plagues many other integrative and multi-methodological approaches.

IT's epistemic taxonomy can be understood to represent an important scientific ontology that must be grappled with by any panoptic or comprehensive metatheory. In short, while IT lacks an explicit philosophical

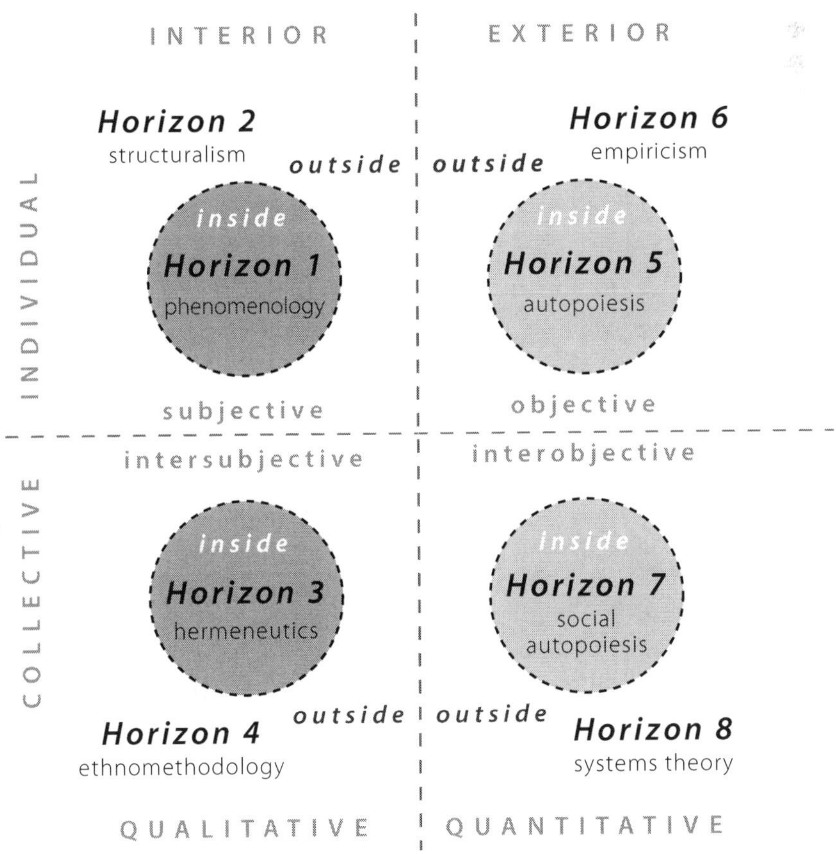

Figure 10.2. Integral methodological pluralism. *Source:* author.

ontology, it nonetheless has a highly comprehensive and sophisticated, systematically structured scientific ontology of the psychological, cultural, and methodological mechanisms that help to construct knowledge. Taken together, IT's epistemic taxonomy constitutes a kind of robust scientific model or metatheory of the varied and often divergent ways that human beings experience and relate to aspects of the world—and is among its primary contributions.

Critical Realism's Ontology and Epistemology

In this section, I will provide a synoptic overview of CR's basic (transcendental realist and critical naturalist) ontology and epistemology (also see Marshall, 2012b, for a more detailed overview), while omitting CR's more complex dialectical and spiritual turns, since they do not fundamentally shift or depart from CR's basic ontology and epistemology. The later two phases in the development of critical realism, dialectical critical realism and the philosophy of meta-Reality, respectively, both bring greater depth, complexity, and internal cohernece to the ontology articulated in basic critical realism, but fundamentally do not alter the fundamental propositions of basic critical realism. Basic critical realism articulates an ontology in which being is *structured and differentiated* (in terms of the domains of real, the actual and the empirical; the intransative and the transative dimensions). Dialectical critical realism deepens the basic critical realist ontology by explicitly thematizing the primacy of *negativity* or ontological absence (and highlighting its essential role for an adequate theorization of process and change). It also highlights that objects are complex *totalities* with internal relatedness and holistic causality; and by thematizing *transformative agency and reflexivity* as inherent in being. Meta-Reality thematizes the *inwardness* or interiority and secular spirituality of being; being as *reenchanted* and accordingly posessing intrinsic value and meaning; and being as incorporating identity over nonidentity, or *non-duality.*

In contrast to IT, CR has an explicit philosophical ontology, grounded first and foremost in its philosophy of natural science: transcendental realism. Transcendental realism deploys a variation on a Kantian transcendental mode of argument[31] vis-à-vis experimental science to arrive at a definitively non-Kantian (object-oriented), realist position. This position argues for a world composed of objects (that is, generative mechanisms) existing anterior to and *independently* of human interpretation, knowledge, enactment, or discourse.[32]As such, CR thoroughly decouples and disambiguates ontology from epistemology, while making epistemology secondary to ontology (the former is 'constellationally contained by the later), since knowledge of the world (in some domain) depends evidently on the nature of the world (i.e., what the world is like in that domain).[33] This stands in stark contrast to IT's neo-Kantian position that leads with epistemology and developmental levels in expounding its notion of relationally constituted, "enacted objects." Bhaskar (1975/2008) arrives at CR's basic ontology by asking an (inverted) Kantian-transcendental question: Not "What must the mind be like for science to be possible?" as Kant asked, but rather "What must the *world* be like for science to be possible?" As Bhaskar (1975/2008) highlights through rigorous Oxford-style deductive logic, and as will be delineated below, it is the ontological reality and existence of a mind-independent object-world that must be presupposed, on an a priori philosophical level, if a posteriori science is to be intelligible at all—it is a necessary condition for the possibility and intelligibility of experimental science. (This premise of human experimental practice is later generalized to include all forms of human practice.) More precisely, Bhaskar (1975/2008) claims that a necessary condition for the possibility and intelligibility of science is the existence of "intransitive objects," by which he does not mean simple gross-material entities (as in IT's right quadrants), but rather real generative mechanisms, structures, and powers that exist relatively autonomously of human minds and can be uncorrelated or "out of phase" with actual patterns of events or empirical observations (p. 13). Consequently, according to CR, all socially produced scientific theories or interpretive knowledge-claims (the *transitive* dimension) are concerned with an absolutely (most natural mechanisms) or relatively (most social mechanisms) theory-independent object-world (the *intransitive* dimension), whether they explicitly acknowledge it or not. To be sure, "intransitive," for Bhaskar, does not mean that objects/generative mechanisms are somehow static (they are more like dynamical morphic attractors), but rather that they are either absolutely or relatively independent of human knowledge and practices in relation to them (in the natural and social worlds, respectively). In the social world, objects are cultural and historical. Therefore, in the social sciences, the objects of inquiry are existentially independent in the sense that once constituted, nothing can then alter the reasons for this, while the generative structures of the natural world are also causally independent. Referring to this notion that "knowledge" has both a constructivist (transitive) as well as realist (intransitive) element, Bhaskar writes:

> Any adequate philosophy of science must find a way of grappling with this central paradox of science: that men in their social activity produce knowledge which is a social product much like any other, which is no more independent of its production and the men who produce it than motor cars, armchairs or books, which has is own craftsmen, technicians, publicists, standards and skills and which is no less subject to change than any other commodity. This is one side of "knowledge." The other is that knowledge is "*of*" things which are not produced by men at all: the specific gravity of mercury, the process of electrolysis, the mechanism of light propagation. None of these "objects of knowledge" depend on human activity. If men ceased to exist sound would continue to travel and heavy bodies fall to the earth in exactly the same way, though ex hypothesi there would be no-one to know it.[34]

As Bhaskar suggests in this passage, CR holds that the world is characterized by a kind of duality in which (intransitive) objects (in a general categorical and dispositional/tendential sense) have their own existence (and agency) outside of human knowledge and interpretation, but can only be known in their specific contents, rich textures, and nuances in and through (transitive) scientific inquiry and human interpretation/construal.

The proposition that intransitive objects can be (and often are) "out of phase" with actual patterns of events means that certain aspects of an object's generative powers may either act or lie dormant depending on various conditions. Accordingly, an intransitive object (generative mechanism) will not produce the same actual events in all contexts. Bhaskar (1975/2008) justifies his proposition that intransitive objects are the necessarily presupposed condition for science by transcendental analysis of the social practice of scientific experiment by stating that:

> an experiment is necessary precisely to the extent that the pattern of events forthcoming under experimental conditions would not be forthcoming without it. Thus in an experiment we are a causal agent of the sequence of events, but not of the causal law which the sequence of events, because it has been produced under experimental conditions, enables us to identify (p. 33).

In this way, as Bhaskar elucidates, the (closed systemic) experimental conditions draw out or disclose a particular pattern of events that would not otherwise have manifested (in an open systemic context). The experiement therby illuminates the real mechanisms producing the empirically observable pattern of events—it brings the real and the actual into phase. In the extraordinary circumstance of an experimentally closed systemic context, objects tend to "obtain" or disclose unique (linear, causal) patterns of events, or aspects of their potential event horizon. But in the nearly ubiquitous (ordinary) context of open systems, objects/generative mechanisms can be either dormant or occluded by the complexity ("multi-mechanicity") of other causes within a network of mechanisms. Furthermore, the experience of particular patterns of events can also be "out of phase" with the events themselves. It is on this basis that CR posits that the world is structured or stratified in terms of three overlapping, but distinct domains: the *real* (generative mechanisms; tendencies; powers): the *actual* (events): and the *empirical* (experiences) (see Figure 10.3). Moreover, as the intelligibility of scientific change and development shows, the domain of the real is itself

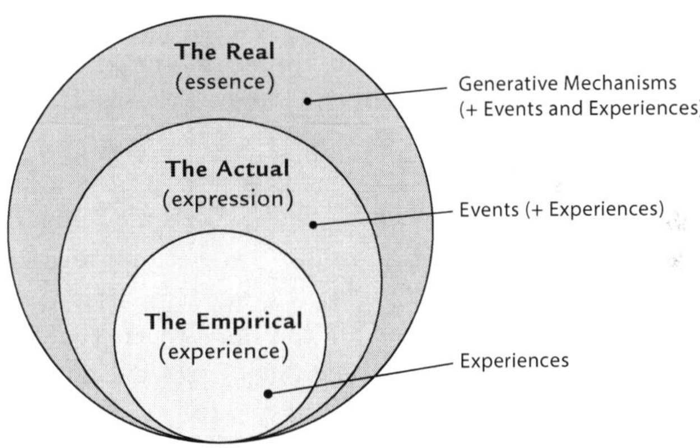

Stratum in CR's Depth Ontology	Refers to:
The Real = Generative Mechanisms (+ Events and Experiences)	Underlying generative (causal) mechanisms or structures or fields that co-produce the flux of phenomena (events). These are themselves depth-stratified or layered (e.g., mechanisms of the inorganic world, the biosphere, and the sociosphere).
The Actual = Events (+ Experiences)	Events (whether observed or not) (e.g., Big Bang, the French Revolution, a human action)
The Empirical = Experiences	Experiences, empirical observations of events (e.g., what you see through microscopes or in historical documents)

Figure 10.3. Three levels of depth in critical realism's ontology. *Source:* author.

depth-stratified or ontologically deep such that the levels overlap in a hierarchically nested manner: the real>the actual>the empirical, where '>' means co-includes or constellationally overreaches.

In noting the differential expression of objects in open and closed systemic contexts (i.e., what Bhaskar refers to as their "transfactuality") and distinguishing between objects/generative mechanisms (level of the real), events/actualities (level of the actual), and the experiential and semiotic (level of the empirical), CR is, in effect, espousing a notion resonant with aspects of the profoundly anti-reductionistic notion of *withdrawal*. That is, for CR, the being of an object in its essence and potentialities infinitely exceeds or is "withdrawn" from its manifestation on the level of the actual and empirical (or even the sum of those actual and empirical qualities). For example, taking a human social actor as an "object," the being of that human always exceeds the particular ways it is expressing in form and being experienced/enacted by other actors—it cannot be reduced to the pattern of its manifestation and/or interpretation in any context.[35] It is important to note, however, that withdrawal cuts both ways, and is not a one-sided, anthropocentic phenomenon, meaning that human experience is withdrawn from the object (whether human or nonhuman) we are encountering too—from the perspective of objects in the world (who are themselves subjects), knowing subjects and their experience are likewise withdrawn from objects in the world. As such, CR lends a powerful blow to all forms of (post)positivism, empirical verificationism, and the like—even in their most expanded forms that are inclusive of interiority (e.g., James's "radical empiricism" and Wilber's "deep/broad empiricism"). In short, CR's ontology posits the existence of a real, differentiated, and depth-stratified world, independent of human epistemology and methodology, in which the domains of the real, actual, and empirical are categorically distinct. At the level of the real, objects have an undeniable, but often somewhat opaque and elusively withdrawn, existence. At the level of the actual and the empirical, aspects of the real can be disclosed through human inquiry, and rich knowledge of the nuances, contours, and textures of objects' contextual manifestations can be obtained, despite the fallibility and inevitable partiality of human knowledge production.

Having established a robust philosophy of experimental natural science (transcendental realism), CR progressed to articulate a philosophy of social science, known as *critical naturalism*. Critical naturalism distinguishes some important differences between the natural sciences and the social sciences and their respective object domains of inquiry. These distinctions, as we will see, have some important implications.

In Bhaskar's (1979/1998) primary text on critical naturalism, *The Possibility of Naturalism: A Philosophical Critique of the Contemporary Human Sciences,* he explores the extent to which his transcendental realist account of the natural sciences is applicable to the social sciences. In doing so, he formulates the basis for the (modified) application of his transcendental realist philosophy of natural science within the social sciences ("critical naturalism"). This exploration depends on formulating some conception of the differing subject matter of the social and natural sciences, since for transcendental realism it is the nature of the objects that determines their cognitive possibilities for human inquiry. Hence, Bhaskar formulates a systematic response to the following question: What properties do human societies possess that make them possible objects of knowledge for human beings and differentiates them from the objects of inquiry in the natural sciences?

Analysis of the subject matter of the social sciences lead Bhaskar to the employment of the method of imminent critique within extant philosophy of social science to reveal its own internal contradictions, aporias, or inadequacies, and establish the basic validity of critical realism's application within the social sciences. Just as experimentation or recourse to experience was a very prominent feature of the philosophy of natural science, a prominent feature of the philosophy of social science, according to Bhaskar, was the existence of sharp theoretical dualisms, both macro and micro. The macro-dualisms Bhaskar identified include the following:

- structure and agency
- individualism and collectivism (holism)
- conceptuality (language) and materiality (behavior)

These macro-dualisms, Bhaskar argues, are sustained by four micro-dualisms:

- mind and body
- reason and cause
- fact and value
- theory and practice

Bhaskar critiques these dualisms on the way to drawing out characteristic features of society and ultimately sublating them in a critical realist resolution. Additionally, Bhaskar identifies an epistemological meta-dualism, supervening these macro- and micro-dualisms, vis-à-vis the question of the extent to which the social sciences can be studied in the same way as the natural sciences. On the one hand, positivism (or naturalism) holds that the social world can be studied in essentially the same way as the natural world—and that this is the only "scientific" way. On the other hand, social constructivist hermeneutics, according to Bhaskar, argues that there is a rupture between the social and natural sciences, and we cannot study the social world naturalistically due to the inexorably linguistic/conceptual nature of social life. For CR, however, hermeneutics is a first step in the social sciences—it is a necessary, but not sufficient component of the social landscape and social science. What it argues to be the central feature of social life—complex conceptuality and language—marks a crucial difference from the natural world. In this way, CR argues that while social life is indeed conceptual and concept-dependent, it is not exhaustible by conceptuality (and language). The critical realist view of social life is that we are not just conceptual, but also material and embodied. Hence, for CR the partiality of the hermeneuticist claims must be situated and its enduring insights integrated into a wider critical naturalist position.

CR's understanding of the relationship between the natural and social sciences also contrasts with the Habermasian perspective (Habermas, 1970/1996), which IT largely adopts, that argues for a domain-specific differentiation of the positivistic natural and hermeneutic/human sciences. In this conception, there is no imminant critique of the architechnonics of positivism, but rather a plea for its non-encroachment on the human sciences, which, Habermas argues, should be the domain of the hermeneutic sciences. In contrast, CR wages a root-level, devastating critique of positivist science that calls into question its fundamental validity in the natural sciences, as well as the social/human sciences. CR likewise expounds a qualified anti-positivist (or critical) naturalism that: articulates the essential differences between the subject-matters of the natural and social sciences; provides a basis for their irreducibility; and calls for a differentiation in methods. For CR, social science is recursively and internally related to its own subject matter, but this is not true in the same way for natural science. As such, social scientific descriptions of the social world are necessarily reflexive reproductions and/or transformations that, in part, constitute the social world itself. For CR, however, this does not result in an infinite regress and strong social constructivism, but rather, CR argues that once an object or structure has come into being in the social world, just as in the natural world, it is both determined and determinate, and inalterable—that is, it is *existentially intransitive*. As critical realist Mervyn Hartwig (2007) states, "once an entity has come into existence at t_1 there is nothing that can happen at t_2 which can alter the fact and causes of its existence at $t_{1.}$" (p. 264). Such an entity or structure may be partly causally constituted in a recursive manner (as in social science), and therefore only relatively intransitive in a causal sense, but not an existential one.[36] This existential intransitivity is a key basis for CR's argument that the transitive/intransitive distinction can be maintained in the social domain. In short, social scientific knowledge (in the transitive dimension) of a social reality (in the intransitive dimension) is partially constitutive of the social reality it describes, such that the transitive and intransitive dimension remain categorically distinct but not descrete—that is, the are recursively interconnected on a causal level in the sociosphere. The acknowledgment of this causally recursive interdependence, however, by no means is a conflation or reduction of ontology and epistemology as in the epistemic fallacy. Rather, it is an important part of the basis for a realism that is critical in the sense that it both acknowledges epistemic relativity and fallability, as well as the complex causal recursivity of epistemology and ontology in the social domain.

In short, CR offers a compelling ontology that shares positivism's interest in the objective world and identifying causes, yet it diverges radically from it in claiming that the study of the empirical, in-and-of-itself, is too superficial, since it disregards the unobservable generative mechanisms that produce the actual events and empirical phenomena that positivists seek to measure and explain.[37] CR argues simultaneously for a weak constructivism and (critical) ontological realism—that is, an epistemological relativism that simultaneously acknowledges a universal, intransitive ontological dimension to reality, albeit a causally relative one in the social domain. And just in virtue of ontological realism and epistemic relativity, CR espouses a third element in its "holy trinity:" *judgmental rationality*—the possibility of arriving at nonarbitrary views about the world. CR is, therefore, a higher-order sublation (transcendence and inclusion) of naturalistic positivism and constructivist hermeneutics that articulates an ontology and epistemology, honoring not only the creative agency of the human subject, but also the reality (and agency) of objects and structures in the world (Alvesson and Sköldberg, 2000/2009). Accordingly, CR argues persuasively against the reduction of ontology to epistemology (referred to as the "epistemic fallacy"), and against the reduction or conflation of the domain of the real to the domain of the actual (and empirical). That is, it argues for the irreducibility of the reality of causal structures and generative mechanisms to the manifest patterns of events that they produce (Alvesson and Sköldberg, 2000/2009).

Having now provided a synoptic overview of IT and CR's respective basic ontologies and epistemologies, I will now evaluate IT from the vantage point of CR.

Integral Theory through the Lens of Critical Realism

From a critical realist standpoint, it could be argued that IT's postmetaphysical coupling of ontology and epistemology (and methodology), constitutes a form of neo-Kantian reductionism that CR refers to as the *epistemic fallacy*, a philosophical stance that harkens back to ancient Greek philosophy (i.e., Parmenides, Protagoras, and Plato),[38] and has arguably been dominant in Western thought since the seventeenth century, which can be largely attributed to the work of Descartes, Hume, and Kant.[39]According to Bhaskar (1975/2008), the epistemic fallacy,

> consists in the view that statements about being can be reduced to or analysed in terms of statements about knowledge; i.e., that ontological questions can always be transposed into epistemological terms. The idea that being can always be analysed in terms of our knowledge of being, that it is sufficient for philosophy to "treat only of the network, and not what the network describes," results in the systematic dissolution of the idea of a world (which I shall here metaphorically characterize as an ontological realm) independent of but investigated by science. (pp. 36–37)

In short, the epistemic fallacy refers to the conflation of ontology and epistemology—the reduction of being as such to our knowledge of being. To be sure, IT's postmetaphysical approach commits the epistemic fallacy in claiming that the being of ontological objects is entirely constituted through a subject's epistemic structures (e.g., developmental levels of consciousness) and methodological injunctions in the process of enactment.[40] It appears that IT therefore transposes or reduces questions of the ontological status of being as such to epistemological questions of being as it is brought forth and known in actual events and (broad) empirical experience. In Wilber's (2006) words, the ontological status of objects in themselves "CANNOT

BE KNOWN," and thus IT posits that the object has no existence, ontic status, or reality outside of the epistemic-hermeneutic process of enactment. While CR would concede that *actual events* cannot be known outside of the epistemic translations inevitably associated with substantive empirical inquiry, it would, of course, claim that the ontological status of objects in their most abstract and categorical features, *can* be known through transcendental analysis and indeed must be presupposed. This is a key difference between CR and IT: For CR, ontological questions can in principle be clearly differentiated and answered without being transposed into epistemological ones; whereas for IT, the former is always fused to the latter.

In short, it appears that IT is essentially saying the following: The traditional concept of knowing has now lost its cachet, since there is actually no given thing or object to be known. Hence, knowing and being *implode* in the notion of enactment—knowing is comprehensively constitutive of being, ontology is comprised by epistemology (and methodology). The claim here is that the ontological status or being of an object is brought forth through the consciousness (epistemic structures) and behavior (methodological injunctions) of the knowing subject—the being or agent engaged in the enactment. But what then, a critical realist might ask, is the ontological status of the one who enacts? This appears to be overlooked by IT as it has been explicitly articulated to date, yet there seems to be an implicit presupposition and thus implicit concession of the ontological existence or reality of at least one object—that is, the being engaged in the process of enactment—since in order for that being to enact anything at all, it must first exist as a real entity or object.[41] In this way, IT and its postmetaphysical theory of enactment seems to necessarily presuppose the ontological existence or "givenness" of at least one *intransitive object*. How can the being of an object be constituted through the process of enactment, if the process of enactment is inexorably driven by—and contingent on—a being that is *itself* an object?[42] Whether the "being" here is a human or an atom, the argument holds: IT's panpsychism appears to be unable to help it escape the necessity of a realist position, or (transcendental) *TINA formation (there is no alternative)*, as CR calls it.[43] In this way, from the vantage point of CR, in order to begin the process of enacting or knowing anything, one must presuppose some kind of philosophical ontology—some kind of "metaphysics," if you will. Furthermore, following Bhaskar's powerful transcendental argument, such an ontology or metaphysical proposition must presuppose the existence of an enactment-independent or pre-given world. Therefore, when Wilber claims that "post-metaphysical thinking does not rely on the existence of a pregiven world," he appears to be unaware of the *performative contraction* undergirding this so-called postmetaphysical position, as an implicitly pre-given or mind-independent world is *precisely* what it relies on.[44] And this problem is not unique to IT, but is the inevitable outcome of any philosophy or theory that commits the epistemic fallacy, which as we can see now is indeed a *fallacy* in the proper sense. Put differently, CR might say that IT's commitment of the epistemic fallacy condemns it to rely on an implicit philosophical ontology. As Bhaskar (1975/2008) elucidates,

> The metaphysical mistake the analysis of experimental episodes pinpoint, viz. the epistemic fallacy, involves the denial of the possibility of a philosophical ontology. But if transcendental realism is correct, and ontology cannot in fact be reduced to epistemology, then denying the possibility of an ontology merely results in the generation of an *implicit ontology* and an *implicit realism*. In the empirical realist tradition the epistemic fallacy thus covers or disguises an ontology based on the category of experience, and a realism based on the presumed characteristics of the objects of experience, viz. atomistic events, and their relations, viz. constant conjunctions" (pp. 39–40).

In light of the above passage, it is precisely IT's implicit philosophical ontology and implicit realism, because it has not been sufficiently justified and thereby sidesteps it own demands for methodological and epistemic transparency, that it cannot self-reflexively situate and coherently sustain itself—that is, its postmetaphysical commitments are necessarily metaphysical commitments. Without an explicit and procedurally transparent (and hence, postmetaphysical) philosophical ontology, the internal logic of IT's own postmetaphysics inexorably eclipses itself, thereby unconsciously "scrambling back behind Kant's transcendental dialectic," to borrow a phrase from Habermas (1992, p. 28), and to some extent succumbs to the very precritical position that it sought to depart from.[45] Put differently, IT's own internal commitments logically lead it toward the incorporation of a procedurally rational ontological foundation, like that of CR's transcendental realism.

Furthermore, as Bhaskar explicates in the above passage, the epistemic fallacy has its roots in the tradition of empirical realism, which is closely connected to logical positivism and its *verificationism*. Bhaskar (1975/2008) goes on to explain that

> The logical positivists committed it [the epistemic fallacy] when arguing, in the spirit of Hume, that if a proposition was not empirically verifiable (or falsifiable) or a tautology, it was meaningless. Verificationism indeed may be regarded as a particular form of the epistemic fallacy, in which the meaning of a proposition about reality (which cannot be designated "empirical") is confused with our grounds, which may or may not be empirical, for holding it. (p. 37)

This logical positivist verificationism bears a striking resemblance to IT's postmetaphysical dictum: "*the meaning of a statement is the injunction of its enactment* [. . .] No injunction, no enactment, no meaning,"[46] which implies that without specification and disclosure of the methodological conditions of a statement about reality, it is considered to be meaningless (Wilber, 2006, p. 268). Therefore, in the light of CR, IT's postmetaphysical approach can be seen, at least with respect to ontology, as a kind of empirical verificationism marred by the epistemic fallacy and unable to intelligibly sustain its own ontological and epistemological commitments. Furthermore, the epistemic fallacy is rooted in the metaphysical (in its precritical, pejorative sense) presupposition of actualism[47]—the proposition that actually manifest events, and not the underlying mechanisms that CR posits they are generated by, are comprehensively constitutive of an object. Accordingly, without adopting a critical realist stratified depth-ontology to avoid such a reduction of the real to the actual (i.e., actualism), postmetaphysical enactivism might therefore better be understood a kind of metaphysical *(en)actualism.*

From a CR perspective, however, IT's interest in formulating a post-critical, post-postmodern philosophy does not inevitably lead to a neo-Kantian, subject-centered (strong) constructivism (and an entanglement in the epistemic fallacy and [en]actualism).[48] As Bhaskar's work highlights, the use of transcendental argumentation is a transparent *methodology* that arguably meets the demands of procedural rationality (a key criterion of a postmetaphysical approach) and thereby constitutes a crucial pathway to a post-critical revindication of an ontological realism that is not committed (implicitly or explicitly) to the epistemic fallacy and the philosophy of actualism. It is a methodologically sophisticated approach to forging an intelligible realist ontology that, in effect, sublates the essential epistemic advances of neo- and post-Kantian philosophy, without succumbing to performative contradiction or tautology. It may therefore, in practice, be more postmetaphysical relative to integral theory's implicit realist ontology on the one hand, and "minimalist metaphysics" on the other, which remain procedurally opaque and lacking adequate justification vis-à-vis the mandates of its own postmetaphysical position. Moreover, as CR implicitly highlights, transcendental argumentation is a method of knowing that is *not* included in IT's meta-methodological map (IMP), which claims to account for all the general categories of human knowing. While one might speculate with respect to if and where transcendental argumentation might fit in the context of IMP's categories, as we can see by way of Bhaskar's theory, transcendental argumentation can be considered a foundational (a priori) method for garnering knowledge of the basic status and categorical structure of reality—and at present, it has no place in IT's meta-methodological map.[49] In short, from a CR vantage point, IT's attempt to jettison precritical metaphysics and arrive at an integral postmetaphysical position has not been entirely successful and appears to be entangled in a number of intractable philosophical problems, including its reliance on an implicit realist ontology it cannot self-reflexively account for. As such, IT's metatheoretical edifice could be importantly strengthened by adopting CR's transcendental realist and critical naturalist ontology and epistemology.

Critical Realism through the Lens of Integral Theory

When examined through the lens of IT, it could be argued that CR, given its lack of an adequate epistemic taxonomy, is not sufficiently nuanced and careful in its consideration of the epistemic categories that it uses to describe the world—and at a meta-level, of *reflexivity*, its own epistemic theorizing about it. While CR appears to have a solid ontological foundation and epistemology (in the sense of a formal philosophical theory with which to generally and categorically justify how humans acquire/produce knowledge), from the perspective of IT, CR has not paid sufficient attention to the variety of *epistemic* structures through which the world is known substantively and concretely, as well as the problem of epistemological self-consciousness in the sciences.[50] As a result, CR appears to be somewhat deficient in terms of providing a detailed account of the various discrete epistemic structures or categories that explain and shape (the transitive dimension of) knowledge production in our contemporary world—that is, it does not have an adequate explanatory account of the widespread phenomenon of inter-individual epistemic-hermeneutic variability (e.g., the ontological, epistemological, methodological, axiological, anthropological, and societal visionary orientations, or worldviews that individuals inhabit [see, e.g., Hedlund-de Witt, 2012; De Witt and Hedlund, 2017]).

In contrast, IT has a rich and nuanced taxonomy of such myriad epistemic structures, which can be understood to represent an important *scientific ontology* of the categories of human knowing, which could strengthen CR's theory of the substantive psychological and cultural mechanisms that help to condition knowledge (the transitive dimension), and successfully be integrated with its compelling *philosophical ontology* (the intransitive dimension).[51] Moreover, given CR's commitment to *epistemic relativism* (that is, the principle that all knowledge is socially produced, and concomitantly transient and fallible, and is conditioned by a geohistorically determined epistemic framework) and the concept of *developing integrative pluralism* (that is, incorporating the findings of valid empirical inquiry in the form of an evolving scientific ontology), CR's own internal commitments logically lead it toward the incorporation of a broader taxonomy of epistemic categories like that of IT (Bhaskar, 1986).[52]

Following Kant's (1781/1998) basic intuition regarding the a priori categories and structures of the mind, which contemporary scientific research (e.g., neo-Piagetian developmental structuralism) has established and arguably honed and advanced, IT underscores the extent to which our psychological/subjective structures mediate and profoundly shape our knowledge of the world, not to mention the various neurobiological, cultural, and social structures. As mentioned above, IT's epistemology is deeply informed by the work of Piaget and the neo-Piagetians, who have empirically illumined (or retroduced) the conditions for the possibility of various events disclosed in consciousness, designating numerous epistemic structures that they saw as the fundamental generative mechanisms necessarily undergirding them. Thus, as Piaget suggested in his discussions of epistemology, the developmental structures of cognition he (and many others in his wake) identified, are essentially a more nuanced and empirically grounded articulation of Kant's structures of the understanding or mind. Hence, they can be conceptualized as neo-Kantian structures identified a posteriori.[53]

While CR concedes that knowledge is indeed transitive and fallible, as it is situated within a geohistorical trajectory and social context, when compared to IT it seems to largely overlook such neo-Kantian/neo-Piagetian epistemic structures of consciousness that are so deeply implicated in the production of substantive knowledge. These structures, I argue, cannot be written off simply on the basis of a critique of (neo-)Kantian irrealism. The evidence presented in the neo-Piagetian literature makes abundantly clear that these structures are causally efficacious with respect to how humans construe the world, and therefore cannot be curtly cast aside as relics of a neo-Kantian epistemic fallacy. Moreover, it is indeed possible, I propose, that such neo-Kantian/neo-Piagetian structures can be coherently construed in a transcendental realist manner. CR already acknowledges the existence of Kantian categories (e.g., space, time, and causality) and structures, situating them not as (transitive) epistemic impositions on the world by the subjective human mind (as Kant would have it), but as having real reference in the (intransitive) world.[54] However, these categories and structures, part and parcel of an intransitive ontological world, and when inhabited and employed in the context of inquiry, are also transitive epistemic structures that fashion our construal and re/production of that intransitive world, as ontology necessarily precedes and constellationally contains or enfolds epistemology—and this means that knowing subjects and their epistemic structures are part of the world, part of ontology. Thus, CR rejects (neo-)Kantian *categorial irrealism* while embracing a categorial realism, allowing it, in principle, to include the Kantian categories and structures while only jettisoning their status as unreal subjective impositions of the mind. However, the neo-Kantian structures (à la Piaget) do exist as (inter)subjective structures necessary for disclosing aspects of the world; they are structures in the transitive dimension that refer to real entities in the intransitive dimension. Concomitantly, since these neo-Kantian structures are clearly causally efficacious generative mechanisms in the real domain of consciousness, they are themselves, by definition, constitutive objects of the (intransitive) world. For example, formal operations, in the (neo-)Piagetian scheme, refer to the structural capacity of a human subject to see or disclose linear causality, a reality that actually exists in the world. Similarly, meta-systematic operations (Commons et al., 1984) refer to the capacity to disclose the *holistic causality* emerging from the interaction of multiple causal mechanisms across multiple nested systems, which again has an independent and anterior existence as a reality in the world. This meta-systematic structure discloses, meta-reflexively, the pluralism of interwoven epistemic structures that are themselves also part of the intransitive world—the world itself generates the structures through which facets of its own depth and complexity can be disclosed in consciousness. More of the complexity of reality is revealed in the later-stage epistemic structures, and therefore each higher-order structure confers the possibility of a progressive de-centration or diminishing of elements of what Bhaskar (2002b, 2002/2012) refers to as the "demi-real," or that which is falsely premised but real, owing to its causal efficacy. CR, therefore, could adopt aspects of IT's robust taxonomy of the neo-Kantian epistemic structures rooted in neo-Piagetian developmental structural research, integrating them into its scientific ontology and epistemology in a coherent transcendental realist and critical naturalist manner. Such a move would offer a more substantive and detailed account of the structured nature of the transitive/epistemic dimension and its causal interconnection and internal relationality with the intransitive/ontological dimension in the social world, lending due credence to the causal power of the transitive dimension in a structuralist, non-voluntaristic manner. Moreover, this move seems particularly apt, given CR's emphasis on structure and the dialectical (and implicitly developmental) logic already present within CR.

Beyond its theoretical value, the integration of IT's epistemic taxonomy into CR's ontology and epistemology also would strengthen CR in the context of applied scientific research, potentially advancing it particularly in the context of social scientific research. While CR's critical naturalist approach to social science (see, e.g., Bhaskar, 1998) and "critical methodological pluralism" (Danermark et al., 2002) has been lauded in the academy as a leading alternative to both (post)positivism and social constructivism alike, it has also been criticized for its insufficient engagement, in practice, on the level of the transitive, epistemological dimension, which appears to be due in part to its lack of a robust scientific ontology of epistemic structures (such as that of IT). From the vantage point of IT's intricate taxonomy of epistemic structures and its appreciation of the profound importance of the transitive-constructivist dimension of knowledge production, CR may run the risk of unknowingly hypostatizing various subjective and intersubjective phenomena, thereby potentially transposing various epistemic elements into "ontological" elements in an insufficiently critical manner. For example, Alvesson and Sköldberg (2009) state, in their discussion of critical realism as a leading alternative to (post)positivism and social constructionism, that while critical realist researchers

> are aware of the precarious nature of research (as inevitably problematic and arguable) . . . little space is granted to such discussions, apart from occasional confessions that come across as highly peripheral to what they otherwise consider themselves to be doing . . . . the approach runs the risk of becoming rigid and lacking in terms of reflexivity, presenting subjective and arbitrary representations as self-evident and robust findings (p. 49).

In this way, while CR acknowledges the constructivist element (or transitive dimension) in social scientific inquiry, devoid of a robust epistemic taxonomy, it may tend to pay too little attention to these transitive elements and their crucial role in the social process of knowledge production. CR social science might therefore be at risk of insufficiently accounting for the transitive-constructivist dimension of inquiry and therefore insufficiently safeguarding against the potential import of hidden ideologies (see, e.g., Foucault, 1966/2002, 1972, who discusses such hidden ideologies in the context of the human sciences). It may consequently run the risk of being written off or marginalized by those concerned with the hermeneutical and social constructivist complexities of inquiry. Concomitantly, CR social science may likewise run the risk of being co-opted by those with a positivist affinity who do not acknowledge the intricacies of knowledge production in any substantive way. Those individuals who consider themselves to be under the broad umbrella of critical realism, yet (tellingly) propose to drop the *critical* from *critical realism* might indeed be suspected of such an implicitly positivistic disposition.

CR's insufficient account of the complexities of the transitive dimension, rooted in its lack of a model of inter-individual epistemic-hermeneutic variability, leads to a number of other problems in practice as researchers apply CR's DREIC schema (Bhaskar, 1998; Danermark et al., 2002) to social scientific research. In the DREIC schema, researchers attempt to *describe* a particular pattern of events, *retroduce* an explanatory model, *eliminate* competing explanations, *identify* principal generative mechanisms, and *correct* the model in an iterative manner. Without an adequate epistemic taxonomy, such an approach may be somewhat problematic in practice. As Alvesson and Sköldberg (2009) argue,

> different researchers have different views regarding the "necessary constitutive properties" and even if one had the good fortune to find researchers sharing the assumption about such properties, they would most likely come up with different ideas on the nature of such properties, and they would probably disagree over the events that the objects can be seen as capable of producing. Use of different perspectives would probably lead to different properties and different produced objects. (p. 45)

Given this perspectival variability among researchers, in order to effectively engage in explanatory social science, particularly with respect to the elimination of competing explanations, data and explanatory theories need to be situated within comprehensive methodological and epistemic taxonomies. Integral theory's emphasis on situating the positionality of the researcher in relation to its epistemic taxonomy (Hedlund, 2008, 2010) could help to mitigate problems of inter-individual hermeneutic-epistemic variability—critical realists need only recontextualize this in terms of making transparent salient socially produced, fallible elements of our knowledge of objects. The epistemic and methodological positionality of the researcher is not constitutive of the ontological reality of an object, but it does profoundly shape not only the ways in which the researcher cognizes and interprets the object of inquiry, but also interfaces with—and impacts—the object of inquiry internally as it comes in to a relational assemblage as a part of a complex totality or open system. As follows, this internal relationality potentially generates specifically structured forms of what social scientists call *reactivity* (e.g., "the Hawthorne/observer effect") wherein individuals modify aspects of their behavior or attitudes owing to the effects of being studied, including a simple awareness of being observed (Heppner et al., 2008, p. 331).

The heightened self-reflexivity that IT's epistemic taxonomy supports can help to both mitigate and situate specific reactivity effects, which, in turn, may help CR social scientists articulate more reliable and valid explanatory models. In this way, IT's methods for fostering such methodological and epistemic reflexivity by "researching the researcher" (Hedlund, 2008, 2010) and locating one's scientific positionality vis-à-vis IT's taxonomy of structures (integral epistemological pluralism) and meta-methodological map (IMP), may have much to offer CR in general, and its social scientific approach in particular.

While CR claims to go beyond the myth of a God's-eye-view or Nagel's "view from nowhere" by self-reflexively locating its own theorizing within a geohistorical trajectory, it could substantially enhance its epistemological self-reflexivity by adopting IT's epistemic taxonomy as a tool for generating much more specificity in terms of its own positionality within a matrix of structures. Bhaskar (2012) refers to "reflexivity, or the capacity of a theory or discourse to coherently situate and sustain itself, is very important, indeed the supreme, criterion of philosophy" (p. 176). In short, IT holds the potential to complexify CR's scientific ontology and theory of the transitive dimension with its taxonomy of epistemic structures to complement its depth ontology.

Lacking such a robust *scientific* ontology of human knowing, CR generally seems to deal with divergence by leaning toward the philosophical ideal of *rational adjudication,* which IT would acknowledge is important under certain conditions, but is inadequate as an overall approach from IT's developmental-structural vantage. From an IT perspective, it is not always practical or ethical to try to rationally adjudicate disagreements that reflect deep structural differences in worldview. This is not always a simple matter of rational adjudication, but requires an understanding of developmental differences, as well as an appropriate strategy for compassionately and effectively relating across worldview structures (De Witt and Hedlund, in press). While it is more obvious when one considers a case of child development, the same principle holds for adults and their disputes, as they continue to develop through the many structure-stages articulated by IT. IT might, therefore, lean toward an integrative-pluralistic concept of what could be called *rational-structural adjudication*, rather than the more monistic rational adjudication that a CR approach would lend itself toward. Such rational-structural adjudication would attempt to mediate divergence in perspective, not only on the basis of a singular rationally founded reality, but would attempt to do so also by acknowledging a multiplicity of (inter) subjective structures and their corresponding "demi-realities" imbued with varying degrees of falsehood and truth. Having now critically assessed CR in light of IT, I will now turn to my concluding remarks.

Conclusion: Toward a Critical Realist Integral Theory

In this essay, I set out to explore the most salient strengths and weakness of both CR and IT within the domains of ontology and epistemology, attempting to highlight their key points of complementarity, and in doing so, moving toward the forging of a provisional synthesis by highlighting key considerations. I began by providing a synoptic overview of IT in the domains of ontology and epistemology, noting that IT's postmetaphysical approach asserts the primacy of epistemology (and methodology) over ontology, thus emphasizing the phenomenal pole of Kant's transcendental dialectic, and championing a kind of subject-oriented, enactivist ontology, rich with epistemic distinctions and categories. I then offered an analogous overview of CR, noting that its transcendental realism and critical naturalism uses the method of transcendental argument to assert the primacy of ontology over epistemology (and methodology), thereby emphasizing the noumenal pole of Kant's transcendental dialectic and articulating an object-oriented, realist depth-ontology equipped with multiple distinct and stratified categories. I then critically analyzed IT in the light of CR, demonstrating the ways in which IT's postmetaphysics is marred by performative contradiction rooted in its commitment to what CR calls the "epistemic fallacy," which reduces ontology to epistemology and necessarily presupposes an implicit philosophical ontology or precritical metaphysics. I then highlighted the consequent problematic of IT's inability to coherently account for and sustain itself on a meta-level (i.e., its lack of adequate *philosophical self-reflexivity*) and contrasted it with CR's transcendental realism, which offers a sophisticated, procedurally rational pathway to arriving at a philosophical ontology that IT would do well to consider. Finally, I evaluated CR in light of IT, illustrating the ways in which it lacks nuance vis-à-vis the epistemic categories it uses to describe the world and its own substantive theorizing (i.e., its lack of adequate *scientific self-reflexivity*) and suggested that this deficiency also amounts to a blind spot in terms of CR's account of inter-individual epistemic-hermeneutic variability. I then contrasted CR's model with IT's epistemic taxonomy, which offers a robust scientific ontology or meta-model of the varied categories of human knowing, and which might support both CR's scientific and emancipatory projects.

While this account of CR and IT's respective ontological and epistemological foundations is notably limited by the synoptic method I have employed in this essay (as opposed, for example, to a more detailed comparative philosophical method), as well as by virtue of my own epistemic-hermeneutic positionality as a researcher and embodied personality,[55] I nonetheless have attempted to be as precise and evenhanded as possible, striving to highlight salient absences and internal contradictions in each approach in an effort to incite reflection and foster the theoretical development of both. Moreover, aspects of my interpretations have been informed by the 2011 Critical Realism and Integral Theory Symposium, which could be seen here to constitute a kind of informal peer-validation of a number of these perspectives, thereby arguably enhancing their validity. Whether one agrees with my substantive interpretations in full, I hope to at least have drawn attention to some problem fields that need to be considered and addressed in both communities of discourse in the coming years or decades.

With respect to the project of synthesis of the two schools, which is where my principal interest lies, my analysis has arguably begun to demonstrate how the respective internal logoi of both CR and IT naturally flows in the direction of their integration into a more comprehensive and sophisticated metatheory that can unite the strengths of both, while jettisoning their respective shortcomings. In my view, CR and IT are, in essence, clearly born from the same dynamic patterning—cut from the same cloth—as evidenced in their stunning conceptual resonance and similarity across many domains (e.g., CR's four-planar social being and IT's four quadrants; CR's emergent levels and IT's developmental levels) (Marshall, 2012a). Yet, as I hope to have highlighted in this article, CR and IT are not mere recapitulations of one another, but rather each bring forth unique and complementary gifts that cannot be found in the other—the strengths of each remarkably seeming to coincide with the deficiencies, or areas in need of further theoretical reflection and development, in the other. This feature thereby suggests a propitious, mutually enriching encounter between these approaches—and highlights the potential for forging a fruitful synthesis. Such a synthesis would unite the complementary panoptic visions of both CR and IT into a more encompassing integrative approach—a critical realist integral theory (CRIT). While the specific contours of such a CRIT will have to be the subject of future writings and indeed will be developed at length in my PhD research (Hedlund, forthcoming), I have begun, in this essay, to articulate a basis for such a synthesis.

In the domains of ontology and epistemology, we can readily envision CR's philosophical depth ontology emboldened by IT's scientific ontology of epistemic categories. Such a basic synthesis would potentially help move toward an integration of approaches along the two poles of the axis of Kant's transcendental dialectic, IT's enactivism representing a sophisticated subjected-oriented approach to returning to ontology (emphasizing the primacy of the *phenomenal* pole), while CR's transcendental realism representing a compelling object-oriented approach to re-vindicating ontology (emphasizing the primacy of the *noumenal* pole). A CRIT might better honor and integrate these two key dialectically constellated attempts to re-vindicate ontology in a way that can sublate the philosophical discourse of modernity and postmodernity. CR's transcendental realist arguments offer a fundamental break from, and transcendence of, the irrealist philosophical discourse of (post)modernity, while IT's deep appreciation of the complexities of knowledge production ensure that a CRIT has sufficiently included its enduring epistemological insights. Furthermore, a CRIT could bring together the superior moments of self-reflexivity with respect to the philosophical and scientific aspects of metatheorizing within CR and IT, respectively. Together, given their particular philosophical and scientific strong suits, along with their shared interdisciplinary, integrative, metatheoretical natures, a CRIT will be notably powerful as an approach studying and addressing complex phenomena and "wicked problems," such as climate change.

Amid all this somewhat arid talk of ontology and epistemology, it is crucial to note that these debates have profound, far-reaching implications for real-world practice and social and ecological well-being. Debates about what is real and how we know, ultimately invoke the normative and political aspects of social life. In some sense, ontological and epistemological questions are key determinates of a formative process that determines a view of who we are as human beings, our conception of nature, the divine, our ethical and aesthetic values, and our vision of the social order. And the totality of those views—our worldview at large—is deeply implicated in our contemporary practice. Pulling back from our given method and practice to a deeper level of ontological and epistemological theory is very important, as we start to see the ways in which our manner of approaching our practice is profoundly shaped by our basic ontological and epistemic disposition. Take, for example, the ontological and epistemological position of the epistemic fallacy and its impact on how we see ourselves in relation to nature, building our practices and institutions on that vision. As the critical realist Andrew Collier (1994) put it,

> If there is a single philosophical idea which reflects more closely than any other this commercial (rather than technological) spirit, it is the epistemic fallacy, which reduces nature to our cognitive appropriation of it, just as this spirit reduces it to our economic appropriation of it. This epistemic fallacy has dominated philosophy for just the same period. In offering us the chance to break decisively with this fallacy, and the consequent anthropocentric world-view (Russell's "three centuries of subjectivistic madness"), Bhaskar's realism makes possible . . . a much greater respect for the integrity of things independent of us (p. 149).

As this passage suggests, our ontological and epistemic suppositions are fundamentally intertwined with our collective social forms and ecological well-being—and we can deduce from this that our dominant philosophy in these domains needs to transform. As the profound social and ecological crises of the twenty-first century indicate, we are being forced at a species level to move beyond anthropocentrism and the philosophy of the (inter) subject—to honor the integrity of things and beings independent of us. In light of intractable global crises such as climate change, it does not seem all that far-fetched to suppose that the world itself may be reasserting the reality principle, and therefore we need an epistemically sophisticated (neo-) realism—an integral realism or CRIT—that can help us to honor reality and address such complex problems. Perhaps, I will be so audacious as to suggest, something like a CRIT could offer precisely the kind of intellectual resources that are urgently needed on the planet right now. In their own right, I see both CR and IT as harbingers of an emergent, intellectual formation or integrative worldview that we might call a post-postmodern, integral philosophy, perhaps somehow responding to whisperings of a higher order reality or morphic attractor.[56] Yet perhaps it is possible that in joining forces they can become something greater than their sum: A force that might thereby more powerfully address the urgent global challenges of the twenty-first century and forge the foundations for a sustainable, eudaimonistic global society in which all are free to flourish.

Acknowledgments

I would like to thank Roy Bhaskar, Sean Esbjörn-Hargens, Paul Marshall, Annick de Witt, Petter Naess, and Michael Schwartz, and for their valuable feedback and encouragement in writing this chapter.

Notes

1. When refering to *postmodernism* in the chapter, I am using it in a broad sense of the term, not beholden to any single theoretical perpective on it. I will assume it to be relatively unproblematic at this point to postulate that, while there is heterogeneity in perpective among scholars such as Jürgen Habermas, Charles Taylor, Roy Bhaskar, and Ken Wilber, there also appears to be substantial referential overlap and broad agreement among them with respect to postmodernism. While I hightlight its limitations, it should be noted that postmodernism has pioneered many important theoretical advances of enduring value and which any aspiring integral, post-postmodern approach ought to deeply engage (see e.g., Gary P. Hampson's [2007] important essay "Integral Re-views Postmodernism: The Way Out Is Through" for a rich disscussion of such enduring advances and the need for integral studies to engage and include them more substantively). For a discussion of the problematics associated with postmodernism, including the myriad instantiations of its "performative contradiction," see e.g., Karl-Otto Apel (1994), *Selected Essays*; Jürgen Habermas (1987, 1990), *The Philosophical Discourse of Modernity, Moral Consciousness and Communicative Action*; John Searle (1995), *The Construction of Social*

Reality; Thomas Nagel (1997), *The Last Word*; Charles Taylor (1989), *Sources of the Self*; Ken Wilber (1995), *Sex, Ecology, Spirituality*, and Roy Bhaskar (2002/2012), *Reflections on MetaReality: Transcendence, Emancipation, and Everyday Life*.

2. See Chapter 1: "Critical Realism: Beyond Modernism and Postmodernism," in Bhaskar (2002/2012) *Reflections on MetaReality*. Also see Lopez and Potter (2001), *After Postmodernism: An Introduction to Critical Realism*. It is important to note here that for Bhaskar, modernism and postmodernism are a kind of dialectically constellated assemblage, and thus postmodernism is *not* to be understood as a fundamentally novel or discrete intellectual formation vis-à-vis modernity. Rather, postmodernism is seen as merely one of five phases in the development of the philosophical discourse of modernity. These stages are as follows: 1) classical modernism; 2) high modernism; 3) modernization; 4) postmodernism; and 5) bourgeois triumphalism and endism/ renascent fundamentalism. For an exposition of this conception of postmodernism as a sub-movement within the philosophical discourse of modernity, see Bhaskar (2002/2012), *Reflections on MetaReality*. For a more concise overview, see Hartwig (2011) "Bhaskar's Critique of the Philosophical Discourse of Modernity."

3. Other philosophies could be noted here, such as that of the contemporary French philosopher Alain Badiou, who also professes to be neither modern nor postmodern, but my intention here is to focus on integrative metatheories arising in the wake of postmodernism, not to be exhaustive.

4. While much more could be said with respect to the similarities shared by these three approaches, my interest here is focused on the domains of ontology and epistemology.

5. Beyond the neo- and post-Kantian critiques of realism, which were radicalized by the postmodernists (according to Bhaskar [2002/2012], "the post-modernists are non-dialectical post-Kantians" [p. 30]), it is important to note, following numerous theorists, including Roy Bhaskar and Quentin Meillassoux, that most of Western philosophy, running all the way back to the ancient Greeks (e.g., Paramenades and Protagoras) has somewhat of an "irrealist" or "correllationist" tendency, which privileges epistemology over ontology in some form.

6. Technically, integral theory situates itself as *postdisciplinary* or *metadisciplinary*, which it contrasts with transdisclinary, cross-disciplinary, multi-disciplinary, and interdisciplinary (see, e.g., Esbjörn-Hargens and Zimmerman, 2009). However, here I am using interdisciplinary as a general catchall phrase to signify scholarship that pursues some form of integration across disciplinary boundaries.

7. Speculative realism is a broad and heterogeneous family of emerging philosophical positions that are generally understood to be responses to the French philosopher Quentin Meillassoux's (2008) "correlationism" thesis. As Bryant (2011) states, speculative realism is "a loosely affiliated philosophical movement that arose out of a University of London, Goldsmiths College conference organized by Alberto Toscano in 2007. While the participants at this event—Ray Brassier, Iain Hamilton Grant, Graham Harman, and Quentin Meillassoux—share vastly different philosophical positions, they are all united in defending a variant of realism and in rejecting

anti-realism or what they call 'correlationism' " (Bryant, 2011, p. 26). In this way, many speculative realists argue for various inflections of realist ontology that avoid the treatment of objects as mere constructions or correlates of the human subject/mind or culture/language, and in that sense seems to diverge from postmodernism (Bryant, 2011, p. 26). Finally, it is worth noting that Robert Jackson (2013) has provisionally outlined four main schools or strains within speculative realism, mapped along two axes: 1) "the primacy of epistemological fact/knowledge" vs. "the primacy of ontological existant;" and 2) "intensional" vs. "extentional." His blog article provides a clarifying overview of the relationships among the various positions within the speculative realism movement.

8. With respect to critical realism's influence on speculative realism, the foundation of Bryant's "Onticology" is grounded in Bhaskar's transcendental realism, and therefore appears to be largely critical realist in terms of its fundamental ontological and epistemological positions, although he builds on it in novel ways. Bryant also seems to share a resonance with critical realism's sublative disposition in relation to the philosophical discourse of modernity and postmodernity. As Bryant (2011) states, the aim of his book is to develop a "a post-humanist, realist theory of being capable of breaking with correlationism, that is nonetheless capable of integrating the most important and significant findings of the correlationists." (p. 42).

9. This article assumes readers to be basically familiar with both integral theory and critical realism. For an introductory overview of IT, see Esbjörn-Hargens (2009) and Wilber (2006). For an introductory overview of CR, see Bhaskar and Hartwig (2010), *The Formation of Critical Realism: A Personal Perspective*, an accessible book in the form of Mervyn Hartwig's interviews of Roy Bhaskar. As well as Bhaskar's "General Introduction" to the anthology *Critical Realism: Essential Readings*, edited by M.S. Archer et al., I have also published an overview (Hedlund, 2013) entitled "Critical Realism: A Synoptic Overview and Resource Guide for Integral Scholars" available on the MetaIntegral Foundation website: https://metaintegral.org/sites/default/files/Critical%20Realism_4-12-2013.pdf.

10. In this chapter, I am employing a generally dialectical, developmental view of consciousness, culture, and society. It is important to note that this position contrasts in important ways with the notion of development in its modernist connotations—that is, of a uni-linear, triumphalist developmental progression from "primitive" levels of social evolution toward the "civilized" status represented by the modern West. Such an approach has, in my eyes rightfully, been deconstructed by (notably postmodern) philosophers, anthropologists, and sociologists alike, mainly because of its Eurocentric, neocolonial, and derogatory implications, and its commitment to an oversimplified ontological parsimony that is out of step with the complexities and messiness of the empirical evidence (see e.g., Ferguson, 2002; Marshall, 1998). Rather, I argue for a much more complex, dialectical, open-ended, and unpredictable process of change. In this understanding, development is de-coupled from the notion of "progress" (i.e., one can also speak of negative developments),

while some form of qualitative or structural change can nonetheless be observed. This means that not only do certain qualities increase or decrease according to specific criteria, but also that different criteria are appropriate for an adequate description of a new developmental stage. Thus, in a developmental movement two or more qualitatively different stages can always be systematically distinguished (Van Haaften, 1997). Moreover, new stages do not randomly arise, but they evolve out of, and are in some sense "produced" by, the antecedent stage. In the words of Van Haaften, the later stages "depend on the earlier ones in the sense that the prior stages are necessary (but not sufficient) conditions for the coming about of the later ones. It is in this sense that several stages can be identified as causally and conceptually connected parts of a single developmental sequence" (1997, p. 18). Accordingly, I invoke a notion of development as a structural change toward increasing complexity, differentiation, and integration, in line with the insights of the developmental-structuralists (or constructive developmentalists) in the field of psychology (see e.g., Cook-Greuter, 1999; Kegan, 1982; Kohlberg, 1984; Piaget and Inhelder, 1969/2000) as well as with, for example, Inglehart and Welzel's (2005) notions of nonlinear societal development, based on the empirical finding that over time the *direction* of change changes. This notion of development is thus complex and dialectical (rather than uni-linear and triumphalist), and describes a process without an a priori positable telos, endpoint, or formal trajectory. As Hartwig (2011, p. 501), writes, "while rejecting any view of geo-history that sees it as an inexorable process of development towards a pre-ordained goal, viewing it rather as a radically contingent, uneven and multiform process punctuated by regression and foldback, critical realism does hold that there is a certain 'tendential rational directionality' in history" (p. 501). The view I am espousing here also implies that the later stages of development are not univocally "better"—morally or otherwise. Similarly, Habermas (1976, p. 164) speaks of the *dialectics of progress*, observing that "evolutionarily important innovations mean not only a new level of learning but a new problem situation as well, that is, a new category of burdens that accompany the new social formation" (p. 164). Moreover, as Kegan (1982) argues: "A developmental perspective naturally equips one to see the present in the context both of its antecedents and potential future, so that every phenomenon gets looked at not only in terms of its limits but its strengths" (p. 30). So despite what are in my eyes warranted (largely postmodern) critiques, part and parcel of our understanding of dialectical development is a critical distancing from the "growth to goodness" assumptions that have often plagued the discourse, and a concurrent differentiation between *descriptive* and *normative* dimensions of development (see e.g., Stein, 2012).

11. This a very provisional suggestion, and there are several other elements of integral philosophy that we might want to delineate, including a focus on the scholarship of integration (Boyer, 1990), a metatheoretical orientation, a post-formal or dialectical mode of thought, and a break with the characeristically post/modern bias toward anthropism or anthroporealism, to name but a few.

12. That said, I do not generally prefer the term *post-postmodern*, which necessarily must sustain itself in dialectical constellation with the post/modern. *Integral* (or *integrative*) are better general terms in my view, but *post-postmodern* can nevertheless be a useful term for certain rhetorical purposes, especially invoking a sense of geohistorical directionality.

13. It is also worth noting that both CR and IT not only claim this themselves, but also various commentators have recognized them as such. Also, keep in mind that positivism and social constructivism are invoked here as key (ontological and epistemological) moments within a constellation of modern and postmodern philosophies, respectively. They thereby are not to be conflated with the larger totalities of modernism and postmodernism.

14. Here I am generally using *epistemic* in the sense of relating to informal knowledge or cognition, in contrast to *epistemology*, which refers to formal *theories* of knowledge and how it is produced or aquired. However, these terms often overlap and can be used interchangably in some contexts.

15. Also, see Marshall (2012a) for an excellent overview of the points of connection and complementarity between CR and IT as integrative metatheories.

16. In many ways, this essay was inspired by and born out of my participation in the Critical Realism and Integral Theory symposium, held on September 15–18, 2011 at John F. Kennedy University in the San Francisco Bay Area, and hosted by Integral Institute and the Integral Research Center. The event, founded by Roy Bhaskar, Sean Esbjörn-Hargens, and myself was envisaged with the intention of bringing together scholars associated with each approach to explore the points of contact and divergence between CR, on the one hand, and IT on the other. For a detailed overview of the CR-IT dialogues and symposia series, see the introduction (Hedlund et. al, 2016) to *Metatheory for the Twenty-First century: Critical Realism and Integral Theory in Dialogue* (Bhaskar et. al, 2016).

17. Wilber (2012a), in response to recent publications on the relationship between CR and IT, states that "virtually all of them say the same thing" in pointing out that integral theory can benefit from critical realism through "essentially, 'a grounding in ontology.' " He goes on to state that ". . . in some ways this is unfair to Integral Theory. As several responding critics have pointed out, Integral Theory has an extensive ontology—from 'involutionary givens' to the 20 tenets, whose first tenet is: 'Reality is composed neither of things nor of processes, but of holons.' Holons, of course, are wholes that are parts of other wholes (as a whole atom is part of a whole molecule, a whole molecule is part of a whole cell, a whole cell is part of a whole organism, etc.). This is sometimes worded, 'Reality is composed of perspectives that are holons' (for reasons explained below). Since all of the items in the quadrants are holons, the Integral map is drenched in ontology . . ." (p. 1). In some sense, I agree with Wilber's assessment here: Integral theory does have an ontology. However, he goes on to indicate that, unlike in critical realism "this is an ontology inseparable from epistemology and methodology, all interwoven aspects of

the Whole." But what seems to cause some confusion here is the failure to differentiate *philosophical* from *scientific* ontologies, which I see as a crucial distinction. To be sure, integral theory does indeed have a philosophical ontology (since, as we will see below, there is no alternative), but to my mind, it is essentially *implicit.* An exception to this is Wilber's (2006) admission that integral theory's postmetaphysical position actually relies on a "minimalist metaphysics," which includes his aforementioned "involutionary givens," such as *Eros, Agape,* and a *morphogenetic field of potentials* (see endnote 26 in Wilber's (2003a) "Excerpt A: An Integral Age at the Leading Edge"). This so-called minimalist metaphysics indeed seems to be the closest proxy to an explicit philosophical ontology in integral theory, although in my view, if it is to cohere with its postmetaphysical position, it is in need of elaboration and justification vis-à-vis its methodological status. Until then, it is in contradiction with its postmetaphysical commitments. In many of Wilber's writings, despite claims that IT is post- or minimally metaphysical, it often appears to be the case that his metaphysics are explicit and not at all transcended or minimalist, but that IT relies to some extent on a neo-Hegelian metaphysics of Spirit-in-action. Wilber attempts to resolve the contradiction (between postmetaphysics and metaphysics) by dropping the "metaphysics" of his early work based on the perennial philosophy and adopting a "deep empiricism" in which various elements of his metaphysics of Spirit-in-action can be postmetaphysically justified. This is a potentially promising direction, in my view, but it is underdeveloped in his overall system and his position, as he acknowledges in the above quote, remains metaphysical. Wilber larglely claims that his metatheoretical narrative isn't metaphysical, while occasionally admitting that it is minimally so, but in reality it appears to be (non-minimally) metaphysical (methodologically opaque and unjustified) and in contradiction with his postmetaphysical stance.

When it comes to the twenty tenets (see Wilber, 1995), my view is that they constitute an important aspect of integral theory's *scientific* ontology, although they are far from exhaustive of it. The twenty tenets, as I understand them, are essentially the result of Wilber's impressive coding of the meta-patterns or tendencies governing evolution in the purely physical domain of the universe or "physiosphere." They are derived from a deep study of the systems/complexity sciences, which have their basis largely in the physical sciences. As such, unless otherwise argued for and justified, the twenty tenets should be regarded, in my view, as aspects of integral theory's scientific ontology. The situation gets more convoluted when Wilber moves from his (Wilber-4) statement that "reality is composed neither of things nor processes, but of holons" to his (Wilber-5) stronger constructivist statement that "reality is composed of perspectives." In doing so, it seems that Wilber has extrapolated from (the first tenet in) his scientific ontology a quasi-philosophical ontological proposition in which to attempt to ground his postmetaphysical position. However, the procedure or method by which he arrived at this claim has not been made transparent, and therefore appears to be, by default, an essential "metaphysical" claim based on speculation. Interestingly, Wilber (2012b) augments his position by claiming in note 1 that " 'Reality is composed of holons' is often stated 'Reality is composed of perspectives that are holons,' " thus explicitly linking a key ontological proposition in Wilber-4 with that of Wilber-5 for the first time in a published work (p. 2). In my view, this appears to be an important (retrofit) move toward redressing problematic aspects of his (phase 5) postmetaphysical stance and grounding it clearly in his earlier (phase 4) work.

On the other hand, Wilber's recent writings on CR tend to skirt the key issues, in my opinion, continuing to avoid a substantive engagement with Bhaskar's transcendental argument for the disambiguation or differentiation of ontology and epistemology. Such differentiation is clearly not the same as them "being violently torn from each other." Rather, differentiation, according to Wilber's own developmental logic, is the necessary condition for the possibility of authentic integration, in contradistinction to pre- or de-differentiated fusion. Bhaskar's argument implies that integral theory is *necessarily* beholden to ontological realism in the manner of TINA formation—*there is no alternative.* That is, IT is dependent on an implicit ontology that precedes, and therefore can be disambiguated or de-coupled from epistemology/methodology, and cannot intelligibly claim otherwise (i.e., at least not without simultaneously succumbing to a fundamental performative self-contradiction or self-referential paradox). This point will be returned to below. Furthermore, Wilber's position here depends in large part on his "genuine panpsychism," which methodologically speaking, is in need of a justification to show its alignment and coherence with his phase-5 postmetaphysical emphasis on methodological reflexivity and transparency and demonstrate that it is not "just another type of metaphysical thinking and thus not adequately grounded" (Wilber, 2006, p. 252). Based on published articulations to date, Wilber's panpsychic position appears to be largely unjustified from a methodological perspective. I intuitively resonate with panpsychism/paninteriorism, but I do not think it can be coherently proclaimed (in an apparently metaphysical manner) as a crucial component of his "postmetaphysical" philosophy without a more elaborated justification

18. However, it is important to note that integral postmetaphysics, which stereotypically "overcomes and rejects a metaphysical viewpoint and replaces it with an empirical, phenomenological, experiential, and evidential approach" (Wilber, 2001, p. 2) does not appear to be able to justify itself in accord with its own criteria. As Wilber (2006) admits, integral postmetaphysics cannot actually transcend metaphysics in practice, but rather relies on a "minimalist metaphysics," as mentioned above. Specifically, in order to cohere his philosophy, Wilber posits a number of "involutionary givens" such as *Eros*, *Agape*, and a *morphogenetic field of potentials.* These involutionary givens are apparently grounded only in substantive speculation and presuppossed as ontological givens.

19. While Esbjörn-Hargens (2010) refers to his extension of Wilber's (2003, 2006) approach as "integral enactment theory," I will, for purposes of this chapter,

include it under the umbrella of "integral postmetaphysics" or simply "postmetaphysics," since its fundamental innovation is to thematize ontology and make explicit integral theory's previously implicit ontological pluralism.

20. In my view, this assessment holds, despite some obfuscating statements arguing for the synchronically emergent and mutually interdependent nature of ontology and epistemology—e.g., Wilber's (2012b) claim that "epistemology (and methodology) and ontology are all integrally interwoven and mutually enactive, each contributing an irreducible aspect of the whole of reality, and none can be privileged (without resorting to first tier thinking). . . . This approach neither commits the epistemic fallacy (epistemology is privileged and ontology derived from it) nor the ontic fallacy (ontology is privileged and epistemology derived from it). Nor does it see ontology separated and consigned to its own realm, and epistemology separated and consigned to its own realm—but rather both arise concurrently (as part of a four-quadrant tetra-arising), co-evolve concurrently, and co-enact concurrently" (p. 1). As will be expounded, these claims seem to becloud the otherwise clear logic of integral postmetaphysics, which precisely depends on the transposing of ontology into epistemology, such that the former is derived from the latter. Merely claiming (and not providing an argument) that they both co-arise and co-enact each other concurrently does nothing, in my view, to resolve the contradictions between such claims and other statements such as the following: "[ontological] objects come into being, or are enacted, only at various developmental levels of complexity and consciousness" (Wilber, 2006, p. 252), or "critical (Kantian) philosophy replaced metaphysics (or ontological objects) with epistemology (or structures in the subject), and this general move is unavoidable in the post/modern world." (Wilber, 2006, p. 271).

21. I argue that Wilber's position is indeed a strong (but not extreme) constructivism, despite his inclusion of various qualifiers and apparent caveats such as "we do not perceive empirical objects in a *completely* realistic, pregiven fashion" and "reality is not a perception, but a conception; *at least in part*" (italics added). This should clarify as my argument unfolds and I address Wilber's "ex-ist"/"subsist" distinction in more depth.

22. As Kant stated, "[H]itherto it has been assumed that all our knowledge must conform to objects," but he then offers a new proposition: "that objects . . . conform to our knowledge" (quoted in Braver, 2007, p. 35).

23. Wilber (2012a) also refers to his neo-Whiteheadian position as "pan-interiorist," wherein the Kosmos is composed of sentient holons with perspectives from humans all the way down to subatomic particles (who have "prehension"). For Wilber, his paninteriorism constitutes a key point of demarcation between his position and that of Bhaskar: "CR maintains that there are ontological realities that are not dependent upon humans or human theories—including much of the level of the 'real'—including items such as atoms, molecules, cells, etc.—and IT agrees, with one important difference: IT is panpsychic (a term I'm not fond of, preferring 'pan-interiorist,' meaning all beings have interiors or proto-consciousness, à la

Whitehead, Peirce, Leibnitz, etc.)—to wit, atoms do not depend upon being known by humans, but they do depend upon being known by each other. The 'prehension' aspect of atoms (proto-knowing, proto-feeling, proto-consciousness) helps to co-enact the being or ontology aspect of the atoms for each other—their own epistemology and ontology are thus inseparable and co-creative. The atom's prehension is part of its very ontology (and vice versa), and as each atom prehends its predecessor, it is instrumental in bringing it forth or enacting it, just as its own being will depend in part on being prehended/known/included by its own successor" (p. 43). While the panpsychic qualification of Wilber's postmetaphysical/enactivist position does indeed distinguish it from the standard anthropocentric expressions of actualism and the epistemic fallacy, it does little, to my mind, to refute the core critiques that CR's transcendental realism levels against it. Wilber's panpsychic enactivism still necessarily must presupposes a mind- or prehension-independent world—an implicit ontology anterior to enactment. This is what CR refers to, as mentioned above, as a TINA formation. So while Habermas (1992) argues that "there is no alternative to post-metaphysical thinking," we can be fairly certain that there is indeed a viable, post-critical alternative to postmetaphysical thinking in critical realism, and its transcendental realism in particular (to which there appears to be no alternative). (Alternatively, transcendental realism could be considered to be highly postmetaphysical in certain respects, as will be explained.) I will discuss this critique of enactivism/postmetaphysics in the forthcoming section "Integral Theory in the Light of Critical Realism."

24. For CR, however, ontology is granted autonomy from epistemology, but is not seen as separate or descrete.

25. According to Habermas (1992), procedural rationality is a mode of knowledge production that came to prominence in the seventeeth century through the rise of the empirical methods of the natural sciences, while expanding its influence and reach in the eighteenth century via formalism in moral and legal theory, as well as the institutions of the constitutional state (p. 33). It emergence was importantly linked with a project of undermining a totalizing and dogmatic tendency toward the speculative assertion of a priori concepts such as "the One" in premodern philosophy. Such a tendency was strongly associated with a kind of *substantive* (or theoretical) rationality whose claims were implicitly to be assessed in terms of a "rationality of contents" rather than a rationality of procedure or method concerned with "the validity of results." (p. 35). The former mode, which generates *anamnestic* knowledge, is associated with first philosophy or what Habermas calls "metaphysical thinking," while the latter concerns itself with *discursive* knowledge and is associated with the epistemological and methodological transparency and rigor associated with modern science (p. 31). Procedural rationality, for Habermas, is closely connected, as a key criterion, to "postmetaphysical thinking."

26. For Wilber (2006), ". . . there is no pregiven world, existing independently and apart from all perception of it. Nor are all things merely perceptions. Rather, there is a sum total of the mutually disclosing things and events that disclose themselves

relative to each other (i.e., relative to each other's perspective)." (p. 255) Moreover, he states, "assuming there is something pre-existing in an ahistorical world and waiting to be seen is just metaphysics (and the myth of the given) . . . there is no 'apart from' how a thing appears; there is simply how it appears, and it ALWAYS ALREADY appears as a perspective" (p. 252).

27. See Whitehead, A.N. 1978. *Process and Reality*.

28. The critical realist Andrew Collier (1994) makes the distinction between "strong" and "weak" forms of social constructivism, claiming that CR is a weak social constructivism, in contrast to strong, voluntaristic forms of social constructivism (e.g., post-structuralism). While I occasionally deploy these terms in this essay, it should be noted that Bhaskar (personal communication, June 16, 2013) prefers to refer to "the social construal of reality," or *social construalism* to describe CR's position, rather than a weak social constructivism. For Bhaskar, there is always a pregiven structural starting point for agential action and thus construction is not voluntaristic—hence, his preference of the term *construal* over *construction.*

29. While I would not go so far as to claim that Wilber's enactivism should be called a form of "structuralist anti-humanism," I do see some notable resonance in aspects of it in the sense that it emphasizes that reality is not merely a construction of an individual human mind flowing from the personal agency of transcendental subjectivity, but rather is more of a product of impersonal or anonymous structures that are partly autonomous from any such agency (see, e.g., Bryant, 2011). To be sure, Wilber's staunch defense of the subject/agent and anti-reductionism (of individual subjectivity and agency to collective and impersonal intersubjective structures, as often championed by postmodern theorists) disavows him of such a designation (P. Marshall, personal communication, June 16, 2013).

30. As Gardiner and Kosmitzki (2004, p. 123) state, "These stages have been studied from a cross-cultural perspective, and research evidence suggests that some aspects may be universal (the sequence of stages) while others (the stage of formal operations) may not." More specifically, most researchers in the field appear to agree that Piaget's stage-sequence and fundamental model is cross-culturally valid, yet this does not mean that all people in all cultures will reach the formal operational stage. Moreover, researchers in the neo-Piagetian tradition have found evidence for cognitive development beyond the level of formal (abstract, rational) operations—that is, various levels of *post-formal* (systemic, dialectical) thinking (Commons, Richards, and Armon, 1984; Kegan, 1994; Rose and Fischer, 2009).

31. A transcendental mode of argument, or transcendental argument, is generally understood to be a philosophical argument that takes some manifest phenomenon or aspect of experience as given, and then deduces the necessary conditions for the possibility of that phenomenon—that which must be the case for it to be possible or intelligible.

32. One of Bhaskar's innovations is to propose a decoupling of transcendental modes of argumentation from their characteristically Kantian orientation

toward subjective and intersubjective structures. As Bhaskar writes in *The Possibility of Naturalism: A Philosophical Critique of the Contemporary Human Sciences* (1998, Routledge): "If philosophy is to be possible (and I want to contend that it is in practice indispensable) then it must follow the Kantian road. But in doing so it must both avoid any commitment to the content of specific theories and recognize the conditional nature of all its results. Moreover, it must reject two presuppositions which were central to Kant's own philosophical project, viz. that in any inquiry of the form 'what must be the case for Φ to be possible?' the conclusion, X, would be a fact about us and that Φ must invariably stand for some universal operation of the mind. That is to say, it must reject the idealist and individualist cast into which Kant pressed his own inquiries" (p. 5).

33. However, it is important to note that such a disambiguation is understood by CR not in the sense that ontology and epistemology are fundamentally split off from each other, but rather that ontology contellationally contains (or hollarchically embraces) epistemology, meaning that they are two differentiated (not dissociated) and asymettrically related facets of a unity. Hartwig (2007) underscores this point, stating that "the two dimensions, whilst distinct, are not discrete; dialectically speaking, they . . . constitut[e] a constellational identity . . . wherein epistemology/the TD is seen as constellationally contained within ontology/the ID. . . . There is not a transative dimension 'in here,' and an intransative one 'out there,' though of course the causal laws of nature endure and operate independently of us. Everything—including the knowledge-seeker—is within being, of which epistemology/the TD is an emergent stratum" (p. 256).

34. See Bhaskar (1975/2008, p. 21).

35. It is worth noting here that integral theory has it own implicit notion of withdrawal, as seen, for example, in Esbjörn-Hargens and Zimmerman's (2009) "there is no single tree" section of their impressive book, *Integral Ecology: Uniting Multiple Perspectives on the Natural World*. They claim that all the enactments of the tree (be they human or nonhuman) do not exhaust the tree.

36. In contrast to a more voluntarist reading of CR's acknowledgment of the causal relativity and internal relationality of the social sciences and the social world, CR highlights that many social realities, such the core social structures that define and reproduce the capitalist sociosphere or the structure of the German language, although they are partially causally constituted by the agency of social actors, have reproductive momentum and potential insularity to transformative social action.

37. Alvesson, M., and K. Sköldberg. 2000/2009. *Reflexive Methodology: New Vistas for Qualitative Research:* London: Sage Publications.

38. Bhaskar (1993/2008) and Norrie (2010) insist that the roots of the epistemic fallacy were laid down by the Greeks—especially Parmenides (in his two ways of knowledge) and then more explicitly by Plato (in his theory of Forms). Bryant (2011) also ascribes Protagoras that status of a root-source philosopher asserting epistemology over ontology (i.e., correllationism).

39. The Greek move toward crowning the primacy of epistemology was consumated by Descartes, who "subjectivized and inwardized" the rational criteria for knowledge. Descartes also initiated what would later become known as the "Cartesian-Lockean-Humean-Kantian paradigm," which holds that we can only know reality from the immediate data of consciousness (P. Marshall, personal communication, June 16, 2013). See Descartes (1637/2006), Hume (1739/2000, 1748/1999), and Kant (1781/1998).

40. While Wilber (2012a, 2012b) claims that integral theory does not commit the epistemic fallacy, I hope to make a convincing case in this essay to the contrary. Without a stratified ontology that distinguishes the real, the actual, and the empirical, as well as the intransitive and transitive dimesions, it is likely that it will continue to succumb to the epistemic fallacy—to be stuck in the "correllationist circle." Wilber also argues that his distinction between "ex-ist" and "subsist" is "similar to CR's transitive (ex-ist) and intransitive (subsist) with one major exception: as noted, IT is panpsychic—epistemology and ontology/consciousness and being cannot be torn asunder. What we call 'pre-human ontology' is actually a *pre-human sentient holon's epistemic-ontic Wholeness,* and not merely a disembodied, floating, 'view-from-no-where' ontology. As molecule's prehension-knowing-proto-feeling is an inseparable part of its being-ontological makeup at the molecular level, and both are necessary to co-create each other. Ignoring prehension (and consciousness) just leaves ontology-being for the molecule, and epistemology-consciousness is just given to humans (or higher mammals), not to all sentient being—they only get being, not knowing. But if a human consciousness-knowing is not involved in co-creating the ontology of atoms, molecules, or cells, *their own* consciousness-prehension is involved, all the way down (à la Peirce and Whitehead)" (Wilber, 2012a, p. 44). While Wilber argues that his distinction between "ex-ist" and "subsist" is "very similar" to critical realism's distinction between the transitive and intransitive dimensions, respectively, I argue that they differ in a number of important ways, including that both Wilber's ex-ist and subsist refer to realities that are both fundamentally constructions of consciousness. Subsistent realites can apparently be distinquished from ex-istent realities on a perspectival and temporal basis—they are constructions of consciousness that are perpectivally anterior to a given subject's process of enactment in the present moment, and may or may not exist for other subjects depending primarily on their developmental complexity of that subject's consciousness. Furthermore, on the issue of panpsychism, CR clearly does not reserve consciousness in the sense of prehension only for humans, but rather ascribes it to all entities in the form of various gradations of what Bhaskar calls "enfolded consciousness."

41. Bhaskar (1993/2008) makes essentially the same argument in chapter 4.3. Also, see Bryant (2011) for a similar argument drawing on CR's transcendental realism.

42. For example, when Wilber (2006) states that "[ontological] objects come into being, or are enacted, only at various developmental levels of complexity and consciousness," he is, at minimum, logically presupposing at least one epistemic

subject, embedded in developmental structures of consciousness, capable of employing methods to enact ontological objects (p. 252). But for that claim to be intelligeble, that subject must itself have some ontological status. That is, the epistemic subject (or enactive agency) must itself be an ontologically real object.

43. To illustrate this point, I will offer an example: To recap, having made the ontological status of the being of objects contingent on *access* to them, IT then points out that different entities (e.g., quarks, atoms, molecules; cells, reptiles, mammals; humans at different stages in their psychological development) access or enact the world and its objects differently. For example, drawing on Maturana and Varela's biological phenomenology (zone-5 in the IMP map), IT claims that a frog's "view from within" discloses a tree in a very different way than a human. As Wilber (2012a) states, "the frog enacts its own reality—its own epistemology and consciousness brings forth and co-creates its own ontology or world" (p. 45). Thus, within the frog's *umwelt*, the "tree" is brought forth very differently, and may not even exist at all as a discrete qualitative pattern. And the same would be true for an atom's prehension of the "tree." This is a key basis of IT's rejection of the CR's realism. As Wilber states, "according to IT, the level of the 'real' described by CR doesn't exist as CR describes it. Rather in IT's view, in actuality is either the product of both the prehensive-feeling-knowing plus holonic-being-isness of each of the holons at the particular level of the real (e.g., quarks, atoms, molecules, genetics) and their relations—all of which are tetra-enacted and tetra-evolved; and/or it is the result of the way the world emerges and is tetra-enacted at and from a particular level of consciousness-being" (p. 45). Finally, Wilber adds, "these levels of being-consciousness (red, amber, orange, green, turquoise, etc.) are not different interpretations of a one, single, pregiven reality or world, but are themselves actually *different worlds* in deep structure (an infrared world, a red world, an amber world, an orange world, a green world, a turquoise world, etc., *each of which is composed of Nature's or Kosmic habits tetra-created by the sentient holons at those levels,* as are atomic, molecular, cellular, etc. worlds)" (p. 45). So in short, the being of objects has no existence or ontological status apart from the sentient holons enacting them at their own level of complexity and consciousness—and these different worldviews or *umwelts* actually enact different worlds. But in all of these cases, the being of each of these holons, whether a frog, an atom, or a human, is presupposed to exist as an ontologically *real* entity or object. For the frog to enact the tree, the frog must first exist as a real ontological entity—and the same holds for the tree and the human in their enactment of objects in their worlds. In short, IT's panpsychic position still must presuppose an ontic reality independent of and anterior to the epistemological process of enactment. It thus does not escape the epistemic fallacy—it merely attempts to render it non-anthropocentric.

44. IT's postmetaphysics can be said to commit a performative (self-)contradiction (*performativer widerspruch*) in the sense that in the act of stating its central argument, the propositional content of the statement contradicts the implicit claims or

presuppositions of its assertion (see, e.g., Habermas, 1990). Bhaskar makes a similar argument with respect to the central problematic of irrealist philosophies in *Dialectic: The Pulse of Freedom*, chapter 4.3, which he refers to as a "self-referential paradox."

45. While one could argue that much of Wilber's speculation and argumentation is in the form of a Habermasian "reconstructive science," which in principle bears some strong methodological resemblances to that of transcendental argument and could therefore be considered to possess a procedural rationality, in practice the necessary epistemic self-reflexivity and transparency necessary to substantiate such claim appears to be lacking, as theorists such as Edwards (2010) have pointed out.

46. In many ways, Wilber's (2006) articulation of integral postmetaphysics seems to amount to a kind of expanded or "broad" empirical verificationism in which the self-reflexive and transparent disclosure of the postionality of the researcher (i.e., the "means" of enactment) is theoretically paramount. Wilber calls this positionality "Kosmic address," and states that at a minimum, it should include the specification of key epistemic structures and methodological injunctions employed by an author in making an ontic claim. According to Wilber (2006), "metaphysics from an AQAL perspective means anything that does not (or cannot) generally specify the quadrant, level, line, state, and type of an occasion. If a writer does not specify those components—that is, if some version of a Kosmic address is not specified—it is virtually always because that writer is unconsciously assuming that those components are pregiven and thus don't need to be specified . . . So they present their maps of reality as if there is a pregiven reality and they have the correct representation of it. That is horrid metaphysics even according to the postmodern definition of metaphysics!" (p. 257). Wilber continues: "But I am going a step further and claiming that even the postmodernists who claim to overcome metaphysics are actually caught in subtler versions of it, because metaphysics is anything that does not self-consciously disclose all of the AQAL components of any occasion. When a writer does not disclose those components it is almost always because he or she doesn't know they are there; and not knowing they are there, cannot stop those realities from unconsciously slipping into extensive versions of the myth of the given" (p. 257). However, Wilber's only reflexive disclosure of his positionality in *Integral Spirituality* was (jokingly?) as follows: ". . . say, in a cognitive 3rd-person stance by a male (let's be generous and say that I am) at an ultraviolet altitude in line/cognitive . . ." (Wilber, 2006, p. 266). So it seems that some integralists (in this case, Wilber) "who claim to overcome metaphysics" by evoking the *rhetoric* of postmetaphysics, yet "do not self-consciously disclose all of the AQAL components of any occasion . . . are actually caught in subtler versions of it." But as I am attempting to show in this essay, failure to disclose one's epistemic positionality is not the only a subtler version of metaphysics that postmetaphysics can find itself caught in; far more consequential, in my view, is when postmetaphysics attempts to deny its dependence on a philosophical ontology, thereby implicitly committing itself to a form of precritical metaphysics.

47. Actualism can consisely be defined as the proposition that the domain of the real can be reduced to the domain of the actual (actually manifest events and patterns of events).

48. Wilber (2006), however, sees the neo-Kantian approach as the only viable philosophical pathway in our contemporary context: "critical (Kantian) philosophy replaced metaphysics (or ontological objects) with epistemology (or structures in the subject), and this general move is *unavoidable* in the post/modern world" [emphasis added] (p. 271).

49. Sean Esbjörn-Hargens has suggested (personal communication, March 16, 2013) that trascendental argument may be a Zone-1 method in combination with a Zone-6 focus, following Wilber's claim that mathematics and logic are associated with the "eye of mind" in his "three eyes" scheme (the other two being the "the eye of flesh" and "the eye of spirit") and thus are fundamentally a facet of subjective mental experience, or introspection. However, I argue that since transcendental argumentation is an a priori philosophical method (that is, it refers to that which is *prior to* the subjective experience associated with Zone-1), such a valid placement in the IMP map seems questionable. In my view, IMP is a map of the a posteriori scientific methodologies of human knowing. This suggests that IMP might be better understood as a map of a posteriori, scientific methodologies and points to the possibility of developing *philosophical methodological pluralism* to complement its scientifically oriented methodological pluralism. Such a development might lead to a more comprehensive articulation of IMP. In this way, I am not trying to criticize IMP for omitting transcendental argument, but rather highlighting the potential for developing a more comprehensive taxonomy of methods that includes a priori or ex ante philosophical methods, such as transcendental argument.

50. While is has been suggested by some integral theorists that CR tends toward an *ontic fallacy* (e.g., Esbjörn-Hargens, personal communication, 9/17/11) in the loose sense of an insufficient consideration of its epistemic categories, in a proper sense, the ontic fallacy can be said to refer to a reduction of epistemology to ontology, wherein knowledge is conceptualized as a direct or unmediated representation of being by a disengaged subject in which the psychological, cultural, and social mechanisms through which knowledge is constructed vis-à-vis antecedent knowledge are either denied or ignored. It is important to note that, from a CR perspective, the ontic fallacy follows closely from the epistemic fallacy. As Hartwig (2007) puts it: "[T]he epistemic (together with its logicising variant) and ontic fallacies are dialectical counterparts or duals which, while apparent antagonists, in reality mutually presuppose and support each other" (p. 174). As a logical consequence, for CR to commit the ontic fallacy, according to its own definitions, it would also have to commit the epistemic fallacy, which it does not. Clearly, given CR's concept of the transitive dimension and fallibilist epistemology, which acknowledges that knowledge is always already situated within a geohistorical trajectory, CR does *not* commit an ontic fallacy in any proper sense. However, viewed from the

vantage point of IT's robust taxonomy of epistemic structures and its appreciation of the profound importance of the transitive-constructivist dimension of knowledge production, CR, I argue, may run the risk of unknowingly hypostatizing various subjective and intersubjective phenomena, thereby potentially transposing various epistemic elements into ontological elements in an insufficiently critical manner.

51. A philosophical ontology delineates the most abstract, general categorical features and form of the world, which science and other social activities presuppose. A scientific ontology discloses the *specific contents* of the world established a substantive scientific theory (Hartwig, 2007, 178). It is one thing to have a theory generally positing that psychological, cultural, and social elements help to condition human knowing—it is quite another to have a detailed theory that actually specifies them as discrete, substantive mechanisms, grounded in far-reaching synthesis of scientific evidence.

52. As Bhaskar (2012) articulates it, critical realism "remedies incompleteness in its own discourse itself, that is in its previous phases: thus critical realism is a process of development in thought which builds ever more complete and rounded totalities, continually self-critical in a process of self-transcendence without any conceivable a priori positable end. This duplex dialectical process means that critical realism always consists in a double immanent critique—of the external manifold of received theory, and of its own dialectical past" (pp. 178–179).

53. Paul Marshall (2012) also makes a similar point in his excellent article, "Toward an Integral Realism: Part 1: An Overview of Transcendental Realist Ontology" published in the *Journal of Integral Theory and Practice* 7(4): 1–34.

54. In Bhaskar's writings, he stesses that the Kantian categories (and structures) are in the world (categorial realism). What I am suggesting in the context of a CRIT, however, is that the neo-Kantian/neo-Piagetian structures are both in the world and in the human mind. This proposition appears to be comensurable with CR's categorial realism, as it in no way is implying that the neo-Kantian structures are mere subjective impositions, but rather that they are intransative objects that can be employed in transative knowledge production to construe aspects of the intransative world.

55. See Hedlund (2008, 2010) for detailed accounts of my own positionality as a researcher, situated in relation to IT's epistemic taxonomy.

56. The German philosopher Karl Jaspers was the first to propose the notion of the Axial Age, ranging from approximately 800 to 200 B.C.E. This period witnessed the essentially synchronic manifestation of many of the world's great wisdom traditions, including the first Greek philosophers (e.g., Thales, Pythagoras, Plato, and Aristotle), Siddhārtha Gautama Buddha, the Bhagavad Gita, Zoroastrianism, Confucianism, Taoism, and the Jewish prophets (from Isaiah to Ezekiel). Also, see Karen Armstrong's *The Great Transformation: The Beginning of Our Religious Traditions* for a more contemporary view on the Axial period. Much like the way in which many of the world's great wisdom traditions of the Axial Age—from Platonism

to Buddhism to Taoism—synchronically emerged across the globe (Jaspers, 1968), devoid of direct communication or physical mediation, one might speculate that the traditions of the post-postmodern, integral age (e.g., CR and IT) seem to be being birthed together, each revealing and bringing forth unique facets of a larger emergent totality. Experimental evidence generated by scientists such as Rupert Sheldrake suggests that patterns of actual events and behaviors tend to resonate with and formatively influence other similar patterns of actual events, which apparently cannot be explained via material cause or direct physical mediation, but rather must be explained in terms of deeper generative mechanisms, or morphic attractors, that probabilistically influence the formation, patterning, and evolutionary trajectory of a given phenomena on the level of the actual. This is one speculative hypothesis that might explain such non-locally co-emergent phenomena.

References

Apel, Karl-Otto. 1994. *Selected Essays, Volume 1: Towards a Transcendental Semiotics*, ed. Edward Mendieta. Atlantic Highlands, NJ: Humanities Press.

Armstrong, Karen. 2006. *The great Transformation: The Beginning of Our Religious Traditions.* New York: Knopf.

Bhaskar, Roy. 1975/2008. *A Realist Theory of Science.* New York: Routledge.

Bhaskar, Roy. 1979/1998. *The Possibility of Naturalism: A Philosophical Critique of the Contemporary Human Sciences.* New York: Routledge.

Bhaskar, Roy. 1993/2008. *Dialectic: The Pulse of Freedom.* New York: Routledge.

Bhaskar, Roy. 1986. *Scientific Realism and Human Emancipation.* Sussex, UK: Harvester Press.

Bhaskar, Roy. 2002a. *From Science to Emancipation: Alienation and the Actuality of Enlightenment.* New Delhi, IN: Sage Publications.

Bhaskar, Roy. 2002b. *meta-Reality: Creativity, Love and Freedom.* New Delhi, IN: Sage Publications.

Bhaskar, Roy. 2002/2012. *Reflections on Meta-Reality: Transcendence, Emancipation and Everyday Life* (2d. edition). New York: Routledge.

Bhaskar, Roy, Sean Esbjörn-Hargens, Nicholas Hedlund, and Mervyn Hartwig. 2016. *Metatheory for the Twenty-First century: Critical Realism and Integral Theory in Dialogue.* London: Routledge.

Boyer, Ernest. 1990. *Scholarship Reconsidered: Priorities of the Professoriate.* New York: The Carnegie Foundation For the Advancement of Teaching.

Braver, Lee. 2007. *A Thing of this World: A History of Continental Anti-Realism.* Evanston, IL: Northwestern University Press.

Bryant, Levi. 2011. *The Democracy of Objects.* Ann Arbor, MI: Open Humanities Press.

Collier, Andrew. 1994. *Critical Realism: An Introduction to Roy Bhaskar's Philosophy.* London: Verso.

Commons, Michael L., Francis A. Richards, and Cheryl Armon (eds.). 1984. *Beyond Formal Operations: Late Adolescent and Adult Cognitive Development.* New York: Praeger.

Cook-Greuter, Susanne. 1999. *Postautonomous Ego Development: A Study of Its Nature and Measurement.* PhD dissertation, Harvard University.

Danermark, Berth, et al. 2002. *Explaining Society: Critical Realism in the Social Sciences.* New York: Routledge.

Descartes, René. 1637/2006. *Discourse on Method,* trans. Ian Maclean. Oxford, UK: Oxford University Press.

De Witt, A., and N. Hedlund. (2017). "Toward An Integral Ecology of Worldviews: Reflexive Communicative Action for Climate Solutions." In *The Variety of Integral Ecologies: Nature, Culture, and Knowledge in the Planetary Era,* eds. S. Mickey, A. Robert, and S. Kelly. Albany, NY: SUNY Press.

Edwards, Mark. 2010. *Organizational Transformation for Sustainability: An Integral Metatheory.* New York: Routledge.

Esbjörn-Hargens, Sean. 2006. "Integral Research: A Multimethod Approach to Investigating Phenomena." *Constructivism and the Human Sciences* 11(1): 79–107.

Esbjörn-Hargens, Sean. 2009. "An Overview of Integral Theory: An All-Inclusive Framework for the 21st-Century." Integral Institute, *Resource Paper No. 1* (March 2009): 1–24.

Esbjörn-Hargens, Sean. 2010. "An Ontology of Climate Change: Integral Pluralism and the Enactment of Multiple Objects." *Journal of Integral Theory and Practice* 5(1): 143–174.

Esbjörn-Hargens, Sean. 2011. Editorial Introduction. *Journal of Integral Theory and Practice* 6(3): v–xi.

Esbjörn-Hargens, Sean, and Ken Wilber. 2006. "Towards a Comprehensive Integration of Science and Religion: A Post-Metaphysical Approach." In *The Oxford Handbook of Science and Religion,* eds. P. Clayton and Z. Simpson, 523–546. Oxford, UK: Oxford University Press.

Esbjörn-Hargens, Sean, and Michael Zimmerman. 2009. *Integral Ecology: Uniting Multiple Perspectives on the Natural World.* Boston: Integral Books.

Ferguson, James. 2002. "Development." In *Encyclopedia of Social and Cultural Anthropology,* eds. Alan Barnard and Jonathan Spencer. London: Routledge.

Foucault, Michel. 1966/2002. *The Order of Things: An Archaeology of the Human Sciences.* London: Routledge.

Foucault, Michel. 1972. *The Archaeology of Knowledge and the Discourse on Language,* trans. A. Sheridan Smith. New York: Pantheon Books.

Habermas, Jürgen. 1987. *The Philosophical Discourse of Modernity: Twelve Lectures,* trans. Frederick Lawrence. Cambridge, MA: MIT Press.

Habermas, Jürgen 1976. *Communication and the Evolution of Society,* trans. Thomas McCarthy. Boston: Beacon Press.

Habermas, Jürgen. 1990. *Moral Consciousness and Communicative Action*, trans. C. Lenhardt and S. Nicholsen. Cambridge, MA: MIT Press.

Habermas, Jürgen. 1992. *Postmetaphysical Thinking: Philosophical Essays.* Cambridge, MA: MIT Press.

Habermas, Jürgen. 1970/1996. *On the Logic of the Social Sciences.* Cambridge, MA: MIT Press.

Habermas, Jürgen. 2003. *The Future of Human Nature.* Cambridge, UK: Polity Press.

Hampson, G. 2007. "Integral Re-views Postmodernism: The Way Out Is Through." *Integral Review* (4): 108–173.

Hartwig, Mervyn. 2007. *Dictionary of Critical Realism.* London: Routledge.

Hartwig, Mervyn. 2011. "Roy Bhaskar's Critique of the Philosophical Discourse of Modernity." *Journal of Critical Realism* 10(4): 485–510.

Hedlund, Nicholas. 2008. "Integrally Researching the Integral Researcher: A First-Person Exploration of Psychosophy's Holding Loving Space Practice." *Journal of Integral Theory and Practice* 3(2): 1–57.

Hedlund, Nicholas. 2010. "Integrally Researching Integral Research: Enactive Perspectives on the Field." *Journal of Integral Theory and Practice* 5(2): 1–30.

Hedlund, Nicholas. 2013. "Critical Realism: A Synoptic Overview and Resource Guide for Integral Scholars." MetaIntegral Foundation, *Resource Paper* (April 2013): 1–19.

Hedlund, Nicholas. "Towards a Visionary Realism: And the Emergence of a Eudaimonistic Society: Metatheory in a Time of Meta-Crisis." PhD dissertation. University College London, forthcoming.

Hedlund, Nicholas. 2016. "Rethinking the Intellectual Resources for Addressing Complex Twenty-First Century Problems: Towards a Critical Realist Integral Theory." In *Metatheory for the Twenty-First Century: Critical Realism and Integral Theory in Dialogue*, eds. R.S. Bhaskar, N. Esbjörn-Hargens, M. Hedlund, M. Hartwig. London: Routledge.

Hedlund, N., S. Esbjörn-Hargens, M. Hartwig, R. Bhaskar. 2016. "Introduction: On the Deep Need for Integrative Metatheory in the Twenty-First Century." In *Metatheory for the Twenty-First Century: Critical Realism and Integral Theory in Dialogue*, eds. R.S. Bhaskar, N. Esbjörn-Hargens, M. Hedlund, M. Hartwig. London: Routledge.

Hedlund-de Witt, A. 2012. "Exploring Worldviews and their Relationships to Sustainable Lifestyles: Towards a New Conceptual and Methodological Approach." *Ecological Economics* 84: 74–83.

Heppner, Paul, Bruce Wampold, and D. Kivlighan. 2008. *Research Design in Counseling* (3rd ed.). Belmont, CA: Thomson.

Hume, David. 1739/2000. *A Treatise on Human Nature.* Oxford, UK: Oxford University Press.

Hume, David. 1748/1999. *An Enquiry Concerning Human Understanding.* Oxford, UK: Oxford University Press.

Inglehart, Ronald, and Christian Welzel. 2005. *Modernization, Cultural Change, and Democracy: The Human Development Sequence.* New York: Cambridge University Press.

Jackson, Robert. 2013. "The Fourfold of Speculative Realism: A Work in Progress." Retrieved April 5, 2013, from http://robertjackson.info/index/2013/04/the-fourfold-of-speculative-realism-a-work-in-progress/.

Jaspers, Karl. 1968. *The Origin and Goal of History*, trans. Michael Bullock. New Haven, CT: Yale University Press.

Kant, Immanuel. 1781/1998. *Critique of Pure Reason*, trans. Paul Guyer and Allen W. Wood. Cambridge, UK: Cambridge University Press.

Kegan, Robert. 1982. *The Evolving Self: Problem and Process in Human Development.* Cambridge, MA: Harvard University Press.

Kohlberg, Lawrence. 1984. *The Psychology of Moral Development: The Nature and Validity of Moral Stages.* San Francisco: Harper & Row.

Kuhn, Thomas. 1970. *The Structure of Scientific Revolutions.* Chicago: University of Chicago Press.

López, José, and Garry Potter. 2001. *After Postmodernism: An Introduction to Critical Realism.* London: Athlone Press.

Marshall, Gordon. 1998. *Oxford Dictionary of Sociology.* Oxford, UK: Oxford University Press.

Marshall, P. 2012a. "The Meeting of Two Integrative Metatheories." *Journal of Critical Realism* 11(2): 188–214.

Marshall, P. 2012b. "Toward an Integral Realism: Part 1: An Overview of Transcendental Realist Ontology." *Journal of Integral Theory and Practice* 7(4): 1–34.

Marshall, P. 2012c. "Ken Wilber on Critical Realism." *Journal of Integral Theory and Practice* 7(4): 35–38.

Meillassoux, Quentin. 2008. *After Finitude: An Essay on the Necessity of Contingency.* New York: Continuum.

Nagel, Thomas. 1986. *The View from Nowhere.* New York: Oxford University Press.

Nagel, Thomas. 1997. *The Last Word.* New York: Oxford University Press.

Norrie, Alan. 2010. *Dialectic and Difference: Dialectical Critical Realism and the Grounds of Justice.* London: Routledge.

Piaget, Jean, and Bärbel Inhelder. 1969/2000. *The Psychology of the Child.* New York: Basic Books.

Searle, John. 1995. *The Construction of Social Reality.* New York: Free Press.

Stein, Zachary. 2012. "On the Use of the Term *Integral*: Vision-Logic, Meta-Theory, and the Growth-to-Goodness Assumptions." Paper presented at the 2nd Biennial Integral Theory Conference, Pleasant Hill, California.

Taylor, Charles. 1989. *Sources of the Self: The Making of Modern Identity.* Cambridge, MA: Harvard University Press.

Van Haaften, A.W. 1997. "The Concept of Development." In *Philosophy of Development. Reconstructing the Foundations of Human Development and Education,* eds. A.W. Van Haaften, M. Korthals, and T. Wren, 13–29. Dordrecht, NL: Kluwer Academic Publishers.

Whitehead, Alfred North. 1978. *Process and Reality*. New York: Free Press.

Wilber, Ken. 1995. *Sex, Ecology, Spirituality: The Spirit of Evolution*. Boston: Shambhala.

Wilber, Ken. 2001. "On the Nature of a Post-Metaphysical Spirituality: Response to Habermas and Weis." Retrieved November 18, 2009, from http://wilber.shambhala.com/html/misc/habermas/index.cfm/.

Wilber, Ken. 2003. *Excerpts A, B, C, D, G from the Kosmos Trilogy, Vol. 2: An Integral Age at the Leading Edge*, http://www.kenwilber.com/professional/writings/index.html.

Wilber, Ken. 2006. *Integral Spirituality: A Startling New Role for Religion in the Modern and Postmodern world.* Boston: Integral Books.

Wilber, Ken. 2012a. "In Defense of Integral Theory: A Response to Critical Realism." *Journal of Integral Theory and Practice* 7(4): 43–52.

Wilber, Ken. 2012b. "Critical Realism Revisited." MetaIntegral Foundation, *Resource Paper* (May 2013): 1–3.

Chapter 11

Embodied Realisms and Integral Ontologies

Toward Self-Critical Theories

Tom Murray

Introduction: Ontological Pink Elephants and Self-Critical Theories

Ontological claims in philosophy attempt to describe the nature of ultimate or foundational components of reality. At stake is what can be considered *real*—vs. epiphenomenal or derivative; imaginary or fictitious; merely subjective or illusory, or fallacious and groundless. And differences about what is considered real or to exist is often at the core of disagreements about the *truth* of claims—giving ontological considerations significant importance in dialogue that are not explicitly ontological. In other papers, I have discussed integral theory from the perspective of postmetaphysics and epistemology, metaphysics and mysticism, knowledge-building processes, and ethics, and here I wish to focus on the relationships between ontology and integral theory.[1]

Integral theory (IT) has been criticized (primarily from the perspective of Critical Realism, CR) for committing the "epistemic fallacy" in conflating statements about being with statement about knowledge of being, and thus in prioritizing epistemology over ontology. IT is a metatheoretical framework grounded in perspectives (as "primordial") and is motivated by goals to explain and advance the human condition (in terms of human potential, spirituality, and ego development). It is thus naturally sensitive to how knowledge or beliefs about reality depend on characteristics of the believer.

That is, though its transdisciplinary scope includes science and the scientific method, IT is not primarily designed to answer basic explanatory questions about the natural world, but is more oriented to the meaning-generative goal of helping people make sense of (and better) the world. On the other hand, integral theory makes strong ontological commitments about being (including constructs such as Eros, the non-dual ground of being, and perspectives as primordial) and becoming (e.g., in the concepts of involution and tetra-emerging holons) that border on metaphysics, without much hedging around the epistemologically imposed limitations of these claims.

Maintaining the tidiness of foundational categories and the meaning-generative power of grand teleological evolutionary narratives is important to the populist slant of Wilber's writings and the activist streak within the community, but this tidiness is difficult to maintain within the postmetaphysical framework that recent versions of integral theory embrace. In philosophical discourse, definitive statements can easily lead to the pink elephants dodged in an extended argument, or the endless mazes of clarification and hedging that seem necessary to keep from contradicting oneself. For some, the solution is the anti-foundationalists (or anti-essentialist) perspective that all claims about the essential or foundational elements or structures of reality are wrongheaded or meaningless, and should be avoided. Yet foundational claims, even if fallible, do have significant meaning-generative potential. In fact, those probing into the deepest philosophical questions can hardly avoid taking on foundational models, if only hypothetically.

In a post-postmodern (and postmetaphysical) milieu, the philosophical projects of ontology (making claims about being and/or nature) and epistemology (understanding the nature and limits of knowing) are inextricably interwoven. Yet, even given contemporary sophisticated metatheoretical approaches such at IT and CR, fundamental ontological questions about the nature of reality and fundamental epistemological questions about the relationship between reality and *ideas about* reality remain controversial and problematic. In this chapter, I will explore recent philosophical themes related to the *embodiment* of reason, including Lakoff and Johnson's embodied realism and extensions to this theory that describe "epistemic drives." Embodied approaches can deepen metatheoretical endeavors by adding nuance to their primary categories and methods of inquiry toward a more deeply "construct aware" approach to philosophy than is seen even within communities working on metatheories. And importantly, embodied approaches allow for a layer of "immanent critique" that is self-reflective, appreciative, and self-emancipatory, allowing strong (meta) theoretical systems to account for more indeterminacy and unknowing (within the theories themselves, in addition to within phenomena they are applied to explain), and to be more portable, porous, and forgiving as they interface with other theories that present opposing assumptions.

Negotiations in the Real vs. Ideas

Contemporary metatheoretical approaches, including integral theory, critical realism, the works of Habermas, Latour, and many others, share the goal of skillfully combining the gifts of classical and positivistic philosophies with the caveats and unsettling disclosures that emerged in postmodern and deconstructivist philosophies.[2] Postmodernism swung the epistemology-ontology pendulum far in the direction of discounting any validity in truth claims, and left a wake of solipsism and cynicism that undermined the natural human drives to know and to do good through valid knowledge. A conundrum being worked out by meta-theoretical approaches is how to make strong claims, while remaining appropriately humble and acknowledging of a fallibilism that is compatible with the postmodern and constructivist critiques of knowing.

One can see three overarching steps or gestures in most contemporary approaches to the ontology-vs.-epistemology conundrum. *First* is the weak realist claim that a reality exists outside of our knowing or perceiving of it (even if any particular claim about that reality is fallible).[3] This what Wilber is referring to by subsistence and is called "ontological intransitivity" by Bhaskar, who supports it with transcendental arguments.[4] That is, to deny that there is a reality is to engage in performative contradiction or absurdity. Antecedent to this first step, and supported by similar arguments, is the assumption (epistemologically speaking) or claim (ontologically speaking) that reality has stable forms of structure, regularity, and pattern—which, for example, allows for experiences of external reality that are more stable than dreams or imaginations.

The common *second* step is a constructivist move to fully acknowledge that there are epistemic limitations and fallibilities to all human knowledge (implied in Wilber's adages "the map is not the territory," "everyone is at least partially right," and in his Three Strands description of scientific inquiry, and corresponding to CR's "epistemic relativity"). The *third* step is meant to transcend and include the first two, and offers a middle path between ontology and epistemology: To claim that validity is graded such that some claims are stronger than others, which implies that some claims more closely correspond with reality (related to what Habermas calls "the force of the better argument"). This corresponds with Wilber's "we can accept the valid truth claims . . . insofar as they make statements about the existence of their own enacted and disclosed phenomena" (excerpt B) (and is called "judgmental rationality" in CR).

These three steps are much more accepted in current scholarly circles than they were in the mid-twentieth century when Wilber, Bhaskar, and Habermas were working out their original contributions—in full battle gear—vs. the excesses of postmodernism prominent in academia (and progressive culture) at the time (though by no means disappeared). As a more recent example, in *Philosophy in the Flesh* (PITF) Lakoff and Johnson describe traditional "disembodied objective scientific realism" as containing three claims or assumptions (PITF, p. 90): 1) There is a world independent of our understanding of it; 2) We can have stable [practical, trustable] knowledge of it; and 3) Our concepts and forms of reason are *not* constrained by physicality, allowing science to discover absolute truths. They take the first two as true, paralleling the above discussion, and see the last as problematic. The second claim is the epistemological antecedent to the ontological claim of stable structures in reality. For example, as Lakoff and Johnson put it, though all knowledge is fallible, "we are not likely to discover that there are no such things as cells or that DNA does not have a double-helix structure" (p. 89).

After these initial three moves, the problem of exactly how to argue for strong validity or confidence in specific truth claims is more problematic.[5] Following the three steps, integral theory often moves quickly on to "so let us find and use the best model we possibly can" (i.e., AQAL), and proceeds with a relatively positivist style.[6] But the challenge of working out exactly how to argue that one truth claim is more valid than another, or that one entity is more real than another, is only weakly met. The embodied philosophical approaches described in this chapter help address those challenges.

Integral theory faces several challenges from an ontological perspective. First, as claimed by critical realists, it does not contain a rigorous analysis of its ontological assumptions (see Murray, 2015 for more on this). Second, IT relies heavily on definitive categories such as subject vs. object, singular vs. plural, and state vs. stage, which are problematized in the light of embodied philosophical approaches. Third, it makes quasi-metaphysical claims about cosmic essences and processes including Eros (as driving evolution), ground of being, and involution. Again, embodied approaches imply a more fallible treatment of the reality of these constructs than IT offers.

Though contemporary philosophical systems acknowledge that there *are* inherent limitations to reason, most do little to specify specific structural limitations and inherent biases. Embodied approaches do just that, and in so doing they can increase the *negative capability* to cope with indeterminacy and increase the *positive capability* for self-critique, articulating limitations, and (partially) compensating for biases.[7]

Embodied Approaches and Sources of Fallibility

One of the primary principles of postmodern philosophies is that there is no privileged perspective, no philosophically pure "view from nowhere," and that no truth claim should be taken as absolute. This generally leads postmodernists to avoid and critique claims even vaguely smacking of foundationalism or universality (which can lead to the performative contradictions inherent in extreme postmodernism). In contrast, while *post*-postmodern theories are constrained by this insight, they are not hamstrung by it. They allow themselves to propose theories containing essences, foundations, and universals, knowing they are fallible. I propose that most of the sources of this fallibility are results of embodiment.[8] Below, I will summarize a number of these sources.

First, there are inherent limitations in perception (human vision, hearing, etc.; e.g., the neurological structures that lead to optical illusions) and measurement (calibration, accuracy, etc. in of tools used to measure or observe). Secondly, as the earliest philosophers were aware and modern cognitive science has proven, emotion (desire, fear, preference, mood, etc.) highly influences reason and belief.[9] Third, since Freud, it is understood that human thought and action are deeply influenced by un- or pre-conscious processes; that conscious thought is only the tip of the iceberg, and that one's personal history, including childhood traumas, have insidious effects on reason. Fourth, following from Darwin, we increasingly see that the human brain is a lump of advanced mammalian wetware with idiosyncratic capacities, created through random evolutionary processes. Reason is seen as a collection of evolved tools, more than a unified pure capacity. Fifth, as articulated by Foucault and other postmodern and social constructivist thinkers, culture situates individuals within a host of invisible biases that are in large part determined by structural power dynamics. Sixth, modern cognitive scientists, including Kahneman and Tversky, have researched a host of "cognitive biases" such as loss aversion and confirmation bias that underlie much of everyday thought.[10] Seventh, even in the rarified strata of mathematics, logic, and theoretical physics, theories such as Gödel's Incompleteness Theorem, Tarski's Undefinability Theorem, and Heisenberg's Uncertainty Principle demonstrate the limits to rational thinking and theorizing, while quantum science and cosmology in various ways question whether reality can be known at all.

It seems that each generation reveals new sources of fallibility that further unseat knowledge from any privileged position. I mention these seven sources of the fallibility of reason only briefly and for completeness, as I move on to those more central to this chapter, which are most closely related to the cognitive biases category (number 6 above). We will focus on sources of fallibility that I call "epistemic drives," including the indeterminacy of conceptual structures, which are most directly related to ontological claims about the nature of reality. While the scientific method and its extensions are meant to ameliorate some of the sources of fallibility above (as illustrated by Wilber's "strands" framework), epistemic drives have not been adequately explored or acknowledged, and thus even post-postmodern philosophical frameworks are susceptible to these sources of bias and overconfidence. The specific biases implied by epistemic drives are universal to human reason and might be said to strike more deeply and even more invisibly than those based on personal history, psychology, and sociocultural conditioning. These sources of fallibility uncovered through cognitive science are thus less well expunged by the methods of "objective" and careful reasoning developed historically by scholars (scientists, philosophers, etc).

Lakoff and Johnson describe the *three major findings of cognitive science* this way (PITF, p. 3–4): 1) the mind is inherently embodied; 2) thought is mostly unconscious; and 3) abstract concepts are largely metaphorical. The first two points are elaborated upon by many others, while Lakoff and Johnson's main contribution is on the third point, which I will discuss in depth in the next section. Also, the first two items might be readily acknowledged by Wilber, while the third is more problematic for IT. Lakoff and Johnson go on to say that "More than two millennia of a priori philosophical speculation about these aspects of reason are over," and that because these "findings from the science of the mind are inconsistent with central parts of Western philosophy . . . philosophy can never be the same again" (p. 4). Lakoff and Johnson are telling us that the understanding of human reason that underpinned traditional philosophy was deeply flawed, and so are many of its methods and conclusions. Here are more of their claims (pp. 4–8):

- "Reason is not disembodied [but] arises form the nature of our brains, bodies, and bodily experience [such that] every structure of reason . . . comes from the details of our embodiment, [from] the same neural and cognitive mechanisms that allow us to perceive and move around."

- "Reason is evolutionary . . . [it builds upon forms present in] 'lower animals' . . . reason makes use of, rather than transcends, our animal nature."
- "Reason is not 'universal' in the transcendent sense; that is, it is not part of the structure of the universe. It is [however] a structure shared universally by all human beings."
- "Reason is not dispassionate, but emotionally engaged."[11]

Though these critiques of classical, modern, and postmodern philosophy will appeal to integralists, embodied realism contains a radical critique of reason based on the nature of concepts that has challenging implications for IT. An important source of fallibility in truth claims is indeterminacy in the concepts (constructs) of which they are composed. The claim that "all dogs bite" is indeterminate to the extent that the constructs "dog," "bite," and even "all" are poorly defined or not well definable (in general or within a particular dialogue). Embodied realism illustrates how the central concepts of philosophy are radically indeterminate and cannot be confidently said to point to anything in reality. Integral theory relies on strong categorical distinctions such as subject vs. object, individual vs. collective; lines, levels, and types; and concepts such as Eros, Spirit, and the non-dual ground of being. Although ITs key constructs have strong meaning-generative potential, any particular claim made using these constructs has sources of fallibility that are unexplored within IT. And, in particular, the way in which these constructs can be confidently said to point to aspects of reality is further problematized, as we will see.

Embodied Realism: Prototype Theory and Metaphorical Pluralism

Graded Concepts and Prototype Theory

Conceptual categories split the world into parts while joining parts into categories.[12] When we employ the knife of the concept, important truths or nuance can get left on the cutting room floor, so to speak, and troublesome gray areas can be ignored. The mind (or, we could say, the symbolic nature of language) has a tendency to treat conceptual boundaries as black-and-white.[13] As Bateson says: "[the] world begins by making splits, then drawing boundaries, then solidifying these boundaries. Then we fool ourselves into believing what we have made ourselves see. Solidifying boundaries is very comfortable, because it allows us to deny our experience . . . We miss the whole system" (1979). This "symbolic impulse" (my term) compels us to, for example in integral studies, to classify some phenomena as a state phenomena vs. a stage phenomena (or neither, but not both); or to classify a performance as being on the cognitive line or the ego line or some other specific line, when the phenomena in question may more accurately be said to exist between categories, outside of them, or in more than one category.

Lakoff and Johnson illustrate how real phenomena don't tend to exist in the neat categorical boxes that correspond to the constructs we create. Sophisticated modern thinkers *intellectually* know this about concepts—we know that things do not exist according to black-and-white categories—and our language often tries to compensate for the distortions introduced by this symbolic impulse (e.g., with qualifiers and hedges). However, the impulse and its consequences go deeper than most imagine.

Prototype theory in cognitive science has revealed how the nature of concepts differs from what we normally assume about them (Mervis and Rosch, 1981; Lakoff, 1987). *All* concepts, not just poorly defined, culturally relevant, or complex ones, have "graded" or indeterminate boundaries (though some are more indeterminate than others). Some conceptual exemplars are more central than others (the most central are called "prototypes" of the concept). Conceptual categories universally admit to fuzzy boundaries as an outcome of how cognition works. The traditional logic-based notion of concepts from Aristotelian Logics, based on necessary and sufficient conditions, does not match well to actual human cognition. One can usually imagine things that exist in the gray area between being X and not-X, things that are sort-of X or more-or-less X (or not X).[14] Exactly what exists at these boundaries will vary according to individual or group, but the indeterminacy itself is a universal cognitive phenomena.

Graded concept boundaries make universalizing claims of the form "all X's are Y" particularly fallible, because there will always be examples of things that are not exactly X but not exactly not-X either. It would be more correct to say "all X's are Y *to the extent that* instances of X and Y are prototypical of the categories as the speaker intends them."[15] Disagreements about whether "all X's are Y" will often hinge on the fact that the objects offered up as exemplars may not be included in both party's meaning of X or Y. I will call the mutually exclusive, black-and-white, definitive, clear-boundaried model of concepts the "simple" model, and graded, fuzzy-boundaried, prototype-centered, or otherwise complex models of concepts "indeterminate."

Abstract Concepts

Lakoff and colleagues' research on conceptual structures indicates that the indeterminacy of concepts becomes progressively worse the more *abstract* they are; i.e., the further removed from concrete sensory experience and exemplars.[16] The concepts at the heart of integral studies—e.g., holon, perspective, subjectivity, spirit, omega point, collective consciousness, and non-duality—are abstract and wildly indeterminate. This, of course, is not a problem for integral theory alone, as a substantial segment of philosophical text labors to work out the hermeneutic issues of what others mean by their terms.

For example, Steven Wagner notes: "Everyone knows Poincare insisted, against Russell, that logic depends on psychology, which makes him a 'psychologist about logic.' What Poincare actually meant by 'logic' or 'psychology' and what drove his insistence are far less clear" (Wagner 2001, p. 35). Among philosophers who disagree on whether "knowledge is justified true belief"—do they agree on the definitions of these five terms? What did Heidegger mean by being? Plato by form? Freud by ego? Kant by things-in-themselves? These questions are highly contentious within philosophical discourse.[17] In all disciplines scholars bemoan, in their introductory paragraphs, that one of the problems needing to be addressed in their field is insufficient agreement or excessive ambiguity about the meaning of the key terms of the field.[18] Particularly in the "soft" sciences and humanities, though understanding surely evolves, this problem never seems to go away. Many authors do not seem to acknowledge what embodied realism shows: that indeterminacy is, to some degree, natural and unavoidable, and a great deal of the indeterminacy must be "coped with," rather than solved or debated.

The graded nature of abstract concepts sheds light on many philosophical conundrums. Scholarly inquiries into cognition vs. affect; or mind vs. body, are often hindered by the under-acknowledged fact that phenomena fall within the gray (graded) area between core constructs. The same issues arise for facts vs. values; a prior vs. a posteriori, and many other constructs debated in philosophy. In psychology one will see debates about long-term memory, short-term memory, and working memory that ignore the fact that these are somewhat arbitrary categorical delineations for what is really a graded spectrum of memory functionality.[19] Is the universe made of matter/energy or more mind-like stuff such as consciousness, spirit, or information? What embodied realism implies is that we don't have to choose—and that we can never fully know. Embodied human comprehension is a feeble tool for understanding things that have a nature and structure far from what our underlying sensorimotor metaphors can describe. Just as physicists have had to live with the particle-and-wave nature of matter/energy without having to choose, philosophers can acknowledge that, for example, the underpinnings of reality are matter-like in some ways and mind-like in other ways, and move forward working out the details of each perspective, in the humility that reason's deep fallibility requires. New models might integrate such differences and polarities, but this does not diminish the limits imposed by the embodiment of thought.

Metaphorical Pluralism

The reader is likely to be familiar with the notion that much of language and thought is metaphorical. Lakoff and Johnson argue that thought and reason are *primarily* and *fundamentally* metaphorical, and that the metaphors we employ are grounded in our embodiment—that abstract thought is composed of conceptual building blocks at the sensory-motor level.

Of course, there are an infinite number of variations built up from any set of primitive building blocks—so thought is limited in one sense and unlimited in another. The key point for us is the (perhaps exaggerated) conclusion that if it can't be built up from basic sensory-motor primitives, *we can't think it*. Our embodied experience determines the limited conceptual pallet that we have at our disposal with which to paint all of our ideas (a pallet determined both by the genetically established structure of the brain and the embodied experiences of early childhood mental development).

Developmental theory (Piaget, 1972; Fischer, 1980; Commons, 1984; Kegan, 1994) shows us how mental constructs are built up from lower-level constructs, in response to (in interaction with) events and pressures from our environment. As far as we know, people cannot directly transmit ideas or concepts mind-to-mind. Concepts and ideas come from (one's own) prior concepts and ideas, and from sensory-motor experiences (including verbal and textual communication)—they have nowhere else to come from (as far as we can tell). Even if one assumes that we have direct access to intuitive or creative knowledge outside the self, to be expressed, the preverbal knowing must be translated into symbolic language and metaphorically-bound concepts.

Lakoff and Johnson show how all abstract ideas "such as importance, similarity, difficulty, and morality" and our abstract understanding of subjective experiences such as "desire, affection, intimacy, and achievement" are based on concrete metaphors (p. 45). "As rich as these experiences are, much of the way we conceptualize them, reason about them, and visualize them come from [concrete, mostly sensory-motor] domains of experience" (ibid). For example, our understanding of friendship or intimacy is not simply *related* to experiences and concepts of closeness, warmth, smiling, touch, and satisfying conversation; in a sense it *is* the combination of such things and nothing more. One can think of the abstract concept as the node in a semantic network that has no content in itself, but serves as the connection point pulling together other nodes (which, according to Lakoff and Johnson, bottom out in concrete experiential categories).

This connection between abstract thought and concrete experience is at the center of Lakoff and Johnson's primary theory of metaphor. In their theory, "metaphor is *not* the result of . . . interpretation [it is] a matter of immediate conceptual mapping via neural connections" (emphasis in original; p. 57). (Nonabstract or literal ideas need not be metaphorical; grasping a hammer is literal, while grasping an idea is metaphorical.)

Lakoff and Johnson map out the sensory-motor roots of abstract concepts. I list some below. The first concept in each list is abstract and the second is concrete. I have highlighted those abstract concepts that are particularly important in philosophy and theory-making:

> Importance as bigness; happy as up; bad as stinky; *knowing* or *understanding* as seeing or grasping; difficulties as heavy burdens; more as up; *similarity* as closeness; *organization* as physical structure; time as motion; *change or transformation* as motion; *states* as locations; *purpose* as destinations or desired objects; *causes* as physical forces; *relationships* as enclosures (PITF, pp. 50–54).

The metaphorical connections between abstract ideas and concrete metaphors are not always simple or obvious. Primary metaphors are combined in complex ways. For example, Lakoff and Johnson examine the "life as a journey" metaphor and uncover a wealth of depth and breadth.[20] Another example is importance, which is metaphorically associated with bigness, but also with other sensory-motor metaphors.

Lakoff and Johnson's *Philosophy in the Flesh* is not only about the pervasive role of metaphor in reason and language (their prior books,

Women, Fire, and Dangerous Things [Lakoff, 1987]; and *Metaphors We Live By* [Lakoff and Johnson, 1980], covered that territory). They have bigger fish to fry. They are out to show how the most prestigious of all ideas and theories, philosophical and scientific ones, which are also among the most abstract ideas and theories, are on dubious ground—they point not so much to eternal truths, but back to concrete embodied experience. "Our most fundamental concepts—time, events, causation, the mind, the self, and morality—are multiply metaphorical" (or metaphorically pluralistic, p. 128). Metaphysical philosophical arguments seem to be telling us more about how the mind works than about how the universe works.[21]

Metaphorical Pluralism: The Ontology of Time and Causality

We can now relate these ideas to ontological questions in philosophy. Lakoff and Johnson show that many abstract concepts are understood in terms of a "metaphorical patchwork, sometimes conceptualized by one metaphor, and at other times by another." For example, consider our concept of time, which is based on a patchwork conglomerate of more fundamental experiences and schema, mostly involving space and motion (from PITF, Chapter 10). The future is in *front* of us and the past *behind* us. We *face* the future. Time *passes* by or the time has *arrived.* Time durations can be *large* or *small.* One date is *close* to another. Events occur *at* times or *in* time. Also mentioned is the "time as a resource" metaphor: we can waste time, steal time, budget our time, etc.[22]

These metaphors "structure not only the way we conceptualize the relationship between events and time but the very way we experience time" (p. 153). "We have found that we cannot think (much less talk) about time without those metaphors" (p 166). Thus "the metaphorical conceptualization of time is constitutive, at least in significant part, of our concept of time" (p. 166). That is, the metaphors are not just *an aspect* of our understanding of time; together they *are* our understanding of time.[23]

Lakoff and Johnson go on to "consider the classical ontological question: *Does time exist independent of minds*, and if so, what are its properties? [We] reject the question. It is a loaded question" (p. 167). Answers to the question are meaningless or not useful. "Yet the biological and cognitive construction of time does not make it subjective or arbitrary or merely cultural . . . the metaphors are not arbitrary; they are deeply motivated. They permit the measurement of time, our very notion of history, the science of physics, and much more" (p. 168). The metaphors are "apt" and extremely useful, but "being metaphors, can get us into silliness if we take them literally" (ibid). And, reading Lakoff and Johnson, there seems to be much of such silliness in traditional philosophy.

Importantly, the metaphors that underlie a particular concept can be incompatible or contradictory, and yet we unreflectively jump from one metaphorical basis to another. For example, on the nature of *causality*, Lakoff and Johnson's analysis shows that "over the course of history, philosophers have formulated a wide variety of theories of causation, each substantively different from the others and therefore each with its own distinct logic" (p. 173). Are they talking about the same thing? "Philosophers may disagree as to what is the *right* theory of causation, but the philosophical community recognizes all of them as theories of the same thing. Why should philosophers have come up with this particular range of theories of causation?" (ibid). We will never answer this question if we only keep looking "out there" to the external world of physics for the real answer. The answer comes only when we investigate the cognitive aspects of the concept itself.

Lakoff and Johnson show how our conceptualization of the abstract concept of causation is based upon a plurality of metaphors, not all of them compatible with each other, which are brought in and used unawares as philosophers base their theories on different metaphorical bases of the concept, and so they come to different conclusions.[24] Like the concepts of chair and game (try to define them!), the concept of *causation* is understood in terms of a loose collection of features and exemplars having a fuzzy "family resemblance" or "multivalent radial structure," but having no precise definition, specific nature or essence beyond human thought. Though having diverse facets, these concepts have an undeniable unity. The various senses of the word have enough overlap of use and understanding that the mishmash holds together as a single conceptual gestalt for us.

At this point, it is worth reminding the reader who may feel as though embodied realism is veering into idealism in terms of denial of reality, or solipsism/nihilism in terms of denial of valid knowledge. Embodied realism is a weak realism. Our efforts to understand causality (or time) *are* pointing to some actual phenomena, and may (in Bhaskar's terms) be pointing toward actual underlying mechanisms. But embodied realism says that we cannot presume that our attempts to understand reality produce simple or fully accurate mappings between ideas and reality.

"Does Free Will Exist?" and Other Victims of Metaphorical Pluralism

Lakoff and Johnson continue with an in-depth analysis of *mind* and *self* (constructs more central to integral theories than time and causality), and find a similar type of metaphorical pluralism. Along the way, they illustrate metaphorical pluralisms in the concepts of thing, object, truth, law, and reality. We noted above that because all such abstract concepts are graded, metaphorical pluralisms, and/or otherwise indeterminate, that any claims containing them are likewise fallible.

Many classic philosophical and academic debates lose much of their steam in the light of embodied realism. Do slugs have *emotions*? Are dolphins *intelligent*? Are computers intelligent (could they become so)? Do apes use *language*? Are rocks or trees or atoms *conscious*? Do humans have *free will*? Do we have a *soul*? Heated arguments ensue without a thorough investigation into how each party's interpretation of abstract concepts may differ. Slugs, dolphins, apes, computers, rocks, atoms, and people do what they are *observed* to do, and scientists can propose deeper *mechanisms* that predict or explain phenomena. But the *categorical* types of questions are uninteresting in the light of embodied realism. Humans have free will in a sense and they don't in another sense (arguments on both sides are no doubt familiar to the reader). Dolphins are intelligent depending on the central exemplars and metaphors that are built into one's meaning of *intelligent* (this does not mean that it is useless to study dolphin intelligence). Is moral development justice-based, as Kohlberg found, or care-base, as Gilliam found? Both types of phenomena are observed and there are important questions of how/when/why/who to be investigated, but whether moral development "*is*" *[something]* is not among them.[25]

Ontological Questions about Existence

We can focus this exploration of the fallibility of statements specifically on ontological claims about existence, foundations, universals, and essence. Disconcertingly, based on embodied realism, causation, free will, life, intelligence, evolution, mind, the self, and morality cannot be said to exist independent of human ideation. They are names that we give to patterns (arguably real patterns involving real phenomena, and certainly important to study). "Does [X] exist (or subsist, or have being)? If so, what are its essential properties?" With Lakoff and Johnson, we can "reject the question."

Even the constructs of real/reality/exist and truth are shown to be problematic metaphorical pluralisms in PITF. In the last century, philosophers have worked out that each of these things are "real" in different ways: concrete individual objects (the dog); classes and abstractions over concrete objects (e.g., dogs, mammals); properties such as red or bigness;[26]

processes and gerunds (e.g., reproduction, running); so-called social constructs, such as money and gender (see Searle, 1995); and natural laws and causal mechanisms, such as gravitation and evolution (see Elster, 1999, Bhaskar, 1975). Yet many still hold onto the notion that "reality" can point to a single totalizing referent. To ask *whether* of each of these things is real is uninteresting, but articulating *in what sense* each is real is useful.

Lakoff and Johnson make the radical claim that "the question of what we take truth to be is therefore a matter for cognitive science because it depends on the nature of human understanding . . . Truth is, for this reason, not something subject to definition by an a-priori philosophy" (PITF, 1999, p. 108).[27]

Epistemic Drives

Ontology and epistemology must interweave in a dance. At some point, any claim about reality must be open to epistemological critiques about its validity, and, as noted in embodied realism, all such claims are inherently fallible. Yet, pragmatically and performativity, one must get on with the job of making meaning of reality as best one can, and bracket or put aside investigations or admissions of fallibility and speak with confidence without constantly hedging in the bulk of discourse. As Bhaskar and others point out, ontological (and perhaps even metaphysical) assumptions exist within all discourses, and usually go unexamined. We often speak as if we refer to objects in the real world, and this is not only pragmatically necessary, but inherently necessary. What embodied realism does is not so much critique or expose any particular ontological claim, as it critiques the levels of *certainty* and confidence, and the methods of *argument*, employed in philosophical discourse. Critical realism and Pragmatism give us the permission to make ontological claims, but they do not alleviate the underlying fallibilities. The embodied approach allows one to move from simply exposing fallibilities to deeper questions about whether a given source of fallibility significantly impairs a given claim.

In what follows, I broaden the discussion of fallibilities from those based specifically on Lakoff and Johnson's embodied realism to include other "epistemic drives." The discussion will be more speculative and superficial, but no less important. While Lakoff and Johnson's claims from embodied realism are based in empirical studies in cognitive science, my description of epistemic drives is meant as a rough sketch of a useful concept, awaiting more thorough treatment.[28] *Epistemic drive* is an umbrella term I use for any tendencies of thought that influence what is perceived as real or true. Epistemic drives are analogous to biologically innate "emotional" drives, such as the drive to reproduce, the fight/flight/freeze responses, territoriality, maternal/paternal care, and social dominance/submissiveness drives, but would seem to involve higher brain centers. The term *epistemic drive* substantially overlaps with other classifications of cognitive phenomena, such as cognitive biases and heuristics (see references to Kahneman and others above), but frames such cognitive phenomena in terms of phenomenological and motivational considerations. The usual treatment of cognitive biases emphasizes the *results* of fallible cognition and the shape of systematic distortions. My discussion of epistemic drives will emphasizes the *impulse* or motivation that draws us into enacting these distortions.

A plethora of drives or hardwired urges exist within humans, mostly dormant until conditions trigger them, and often operating in competition (Will I fight or run? Eat, work, or play?). Like other drives, epistemic drives are unconscious processes that, on the one hand, can have unseen control over us and on the other hand, can be managed or controlled to some degree through learned metacognitive (or meta-emotional) skills.

I found it striking that Lakoff and Johnson's 624-page tome on embodied philosophy barely mentions the influence of *emotions* and basic human drives on cognition.[29] Lakoff and Johnson seem to focus on sensorimotor experience as the basis of their theory of metaphoric thought, but leave out a critical aspect of early prelinguistic experience—emotional experience and other non-sensorimotor experiences—that are just as available for the foundation of metaphorical building blocks of later abstract thought. The feelings of anger, disappointment, longing, or even more physiological states like nausea and itching can also be the origins of primary metaphors.

I use the term *symbolic impulse* to implicate the tendency, which is akin to a drive or compulsion. The symbolic impulse is a tendency of thought that biases one to perceive or interpret concepts as having mutually exclusive, black-and-white, definitive, clear boundaried (i.e., as "simple" as opposed to indeterminate). In calling it a drive, diverging from Lakoff, I imply that it is a tendency that can be observed (reflectively experienced), examined, and at least partially compensated for. I also imply that its impact varies and that certain conditions exacerbate it (as with more commonly noted human drives). Also, as with other impulses and drives, one can observe that conditions of stress or complexity can compromise one's efforts to manage or gain perspective on the symbolic impulse.

A related epistemic drive is the desire, need, or compulsion for certainty (and the avoidance of dissonance-incurring uncertainty, doubt, or unknowing).[30] In Murray [2011, Table 2] I list about a dozen epistemic drives, including drives toward oneness, completeness, purity, simplicity, wholeness, generality, and abstraction. They serve positive functions, but can also over-function to create the "violence and folly" of biases, errors; and can cause ethical problems, leading, at the extreme, to phenomena such as grandiosity, hegemony, elitism, delusions of reference, and protofascism.[31] We can imagine that such drives contribute to the degree of certainty, foundationalism, essentialism, and universalism witnessed in the theories of various philosophers. However, the main goal here is the self-emancipatory power of considering the impact of epistemic drives on the theories that one creates or uses.

Like the more basic biological drives, epistemic drives exist within an ecology of psychological and cognitive forces—interacting and often competing. For any drive to not over-function it needs one or more balancing drives. In my article (2011, Table 2), I suggest that each epistemic drive has a polar opposite. For example, there is a drive to notice differences, as well as one to perceive wholes; a drive toward diving into the concrete, as well as one for leaping into the abstract.

An important epistemic drive, related to both conceptual gradedness and the metaphorical nature, is "misplaced concreteness" (coined by Whitehead, 1929). Misplaced concreteness is the tendency to imbue abstract concepts with the properties of concrete objects (e.g., to give them definitive boundaries). It is at the core of fallacies of the "myth of the given" and "confusing the map for the territory"—which are often mentioned by Wilber. In Murray (2011), I discuss how misplaced concreteness manifests differently at different levels of abstract thought (or different developmental levels of reflective abstraction). Though philosophers and intellectuals may not be prone to its more primitive manifestations, as we can see from Lakoff and Johnson's arguments, intellectuals are not immune from the influence of certain forms of misplaced concreteness.

One property of drives is that one can experience their pull if one observes closely. In this section, I focus on the drives that seem to most afflict intellectual, philosophical, or ontological threads of human activity. One can become aware of that in the human mind that wants to pull the disparate, the many, the diverse into a unifying whole; achieve the simplicity and power of a general concept or rule; to determine and rest in what is at the center of, or underneath things. One can identify these drives or urges working within us at the level of felt experience. There is a sense of ease, certainty, and mastery when one ignores details and differences and trusts a sturdy generality. There is a sense of elegance and wholeness when one embraces many things into a circle of unity. One gets a certain satisfaction from ordering things or collecting them into tidy groups. The inquisitive and meaning-hungry mind wants to know the causal root, foundation, source, or origin of things. With many philosophical frameworks available to the modern thinker, one must ask how such factors influence how particular ideas are spread, which ideas one finds convincing, and which ideas one espouses and builds upon. Though the existence of epistemic drives cannot disprove ideas, they offer a critique of many forms of performative confidence and persuasion.

Implications of ER for Integral Theories and Practices

Ontology addresses the essential nature, structure, or properties of reality and also addresses the simple reality, existence, or being of things, i.e., the "ontological status" of fundamental concepts. Ontological status determines what can be considered *real* vs. epiphenomenal, merely subjective, illusory, or fallacious.[32] Embodied realism shows that the concepts of real/existence/being are both fuzzy and metaphorically pluralistic. This supports approaches that nuance the issue by describing *ways* that things can be real, rather than defining *whether* something is real. Embodied realism reveals and explains sources of fallibility in claims and indeterminacy in concepts, but provides only a few tools for dealing or coping with these phenomena. IT contributes to these themes by introducing models and distinctions that nuance the questions of what it means to "exist" and what it means to "know." I describe these contributions next. (CR makes additional, compatible distinctions; see Murray, 2015.)

Integral Pluralism and Kosmic Address

The integral postmetaphysics of Wilber and Esbjörn-Hargens involves reframing the overly simplistic question of *whether* something exists (i.e., is real) to ask *how* it exists *for whom?* Integral pluralism (one aspect of integral postmetaphysics) says that what is perceived to exist depends on the methodology used to inquire and the developmentally determined capacity of the observer/inquirer to perceive (Wilber 2006; Esbjörn-Hargens, 2010; Esbjörn-Hargens and Zimmerman, 2009; Wilber, in preparation). It proposes a specific framework for classifying methodologies (using eight "primordial perspectives" or "methodological zones") and developmental capacity (Wilber's Levels of Consciousness stage model). The move from "whether" something exists to "how and for whom" something exists enables one to loosen a number the ontological knots mentioned above.

For example, Santa Claus can be said to "exist;" to be real, for those within a circle of five-year-old believers having a conversation about him. "What kind of cookies does Santa Claus like best?" is a valid question in such a circle.[33] Esbjörn-Hargens and Zimmerman give the example of "eco-system," which can exist, and claims about one can be made, only for those who have an adequate understanding of the concept, which in itself requires the capacity to think at a certain level of complexity. Integral pluralism also stresses the importance of methodology. What one perceives, and thus considers real, depends in part on the methods and equipment one uses to observe (objects are thus said to be "enacted").

Wilber and Esbjörn-Hargens's integral postmetaphysics is one among a number of recent theories that see objects and phenomena in reality as *enacted*. Esbjörn-Hargens says "the ontological status of [a soda] bottle is enacted in part by the method of interacting with it . . . The reality of the bottle as instrument, vase, or cash refund is not dependent on your viewpoint but rather on the social practice of interacting with the bottle" (2010, p. 13). Integral pluralism proposes that many objects of deliberation are "decentered multiple objects" that exhibit an "ontological pluralism" (Esbjörn-Hargens, 2010). That is, when interlocutors (experts or citizens) talk about a complex object such as "climate change," they are often referring to different aspects of the totality of what is related to climate change. So far, this is similar to embodied realism's idea of metaphorical pluralism, but from here integral pluralism takes a different tack. It proposes that the perspectives that give rise to different perceived "objects" can be located with a "Kosmic Address" that includes the methodological zones of integral methodological pluralism and the developmental levels of consciousness of integral epistemological pluralism. Ontological pluralism says that observers will enact different objects if they are using, for example, phenomenological vs. empirical modes of inquiry; or are perceiving reality from a conventional vs. post-conventional developmental level.

AQAL Categories

The core orienting model in integral theory is the AQAL model (or meta-theory). It proposes "five irreducible categories of . . . manifest existence":

quadrants, levels, lines, states, and types. There are said to be "the five most basic elements that need to be included in any truly integral or comprehensive approach . . ." to understand the cosmos as a whole or any aspect of it (Wilber, 2006, p. 31). AQAL includes not only these five dimensions as distinct categories, but within each category Wilber defines a classification of elements: the four quadrants (8 zones), 4–6 states, 3–17 stages, 3–12 lines, etc.

In the Murray (2011) section "An Indeterminacy Analysis of Some Integral Theory Constructs," I explore the implications of the fact that the foundational categories of Wilber's four quadrant model, "subjective vs. objective" and "singular vs. plural" are graded concepts exhibiting metaphorical pluralism. To quote: "For example, unconscious mental processes are not exactly subjective, but are they objective? It seems to me that the category fails to be useful here . . . As to the category singular vs. plural, we can find or imagine things that are sort of singular but also sort of plural . . . We can also apply indeterminacy analysis to the . . . concept of holon . . . some objects of interest may fall into a gray area between heaps and holons, or between holons and artifacts . . ." (p. 106). (The same arguments can be made of the eight zones of integral methodological pluralism.)

In "Integralist Mental Models of Adult Development: Provisos from a Users Guide" (Murray, to be published), I explore the indeterminacies in the constructs central to AQAL's theory of development: the lines and levels of the AQAL psychograph, and the concept of developmental tiers. I show how certain commonly held beliefs about development within the integral community are more fallible than is assumed because of the graded nature of and metaphorical pluralism of the core constructs.

The question of whether boundary objects are common or rare, important or irrelevant, is a *pragmatic* question—the ontological issue remains: That proponents of IT often treat such categories as 1) mutually exclusive; 2) having no fuzzy boundaries; and 3) properties of reality that valid inferences must abide by. And of course, if one habitually looks at the world through the lens of such a model, then boundary objects will automatically appear rare and irrelevant. Wilber does employ various epistemic forms (as implied in "tetra-enact") to indicate that the concepts and models he uses do not have a simple categorical form. Wilber uses multiple metaphors for key concepts: developmental levels are also referred to as stages, ladders, spirals, concentric circles, waves, etc. Developmental lines are sometimes referred to as streams.[34]

These uses of metaphor notwithstanding, it can be noted that 1) in the majority of Wilber's writing and dialogue, he uses the categories without such qualification; and 2) when he notes the non-simplicity of the constructs, he is claiming that this non-simplicity (intermeshing, etc.) represents nature, which, though it may be true, is not the same as noting the indeterminacies and fallibilities of the concepts themselves.[35]

Though Wilber clearly notes that his system is an evolving one, open to improvement, the confidence and directness of his rhetoric and the steadfast adherence of many of his colleagues to the model *implies* that AQAL contains deep and stable truths about external reality. Though much of Wilber's writings, and especially recent "Wilber-5" texts (most associated with postmetaphysics) and the work of his most prominent academic colleagues, are more based on principles and methodologies, and are thus less susceptible to the problems of indeterminacy, the AQAL model is still the foundation of integral theory as it is presented to the masses. The model seems designed to be understandable in terms of simple categories, taxonomies, and charts that appeal to more linear and less complex "epistemic forms," though a deeper reading of integral theory invokes higher-stage forms such as ecologies, fractals, and co-referential dialecticals. The rub is, that if the model did not contain these easily digestible categories, then it surely would not be so popular, and fewer would benefit from what IT has to offer.

The related concepts of "The True, the Good, and the Beautiful," often referenced in the integral theory, are similarly problematic. Associated with the I, We, and It primordial perspectives, they are given a foundational ontological status. But the True, the Good, and the Beautiful are metaphorical pluralisms that turn out to be difficult to pin down, and their meanings are contentious among philosophers.[36]

Primordial Perspectives

The quadrant model and related and eight "primordial perspectives" or zones ground integral theory's treatment of *perspectives*. In *Integral Spirituality*, Wilber says: "all objects are first and foremost perspectives. NOT 'are seen from perspectives,' but ARE perspectives . . . there is no 'apart from' how a thing appears . . . 'things' do not exist in a pregiven world . . ." (p. 252). There are several assumptions or implications here. The idea that our mental apparatus constructs our perception of objects and even their appearance *as* objects, is generally accepted. But this quote leaves open the question of whether *perspectives* exist in a pregiven world (and whether they might reasonably be considered "things"—which would lead to a contradiction in the quote). One of Wilber's primary students and colleagues, Clint Fuhs, says that "Put as simply as possible: perspectives are primordial, which is to say they are the most fundamental or primeval elements of reality, existing at or from the beginning of time" (2010, p. 1). On the other hand, in the same paragraph, he says, "It is through perspectives and perspectives alone that we come to understand anything about our world."

Are perspectives, then, things that humans have/use, or are they fundamental components of the world?[37] Wilber's claim that "there is no 'apart from' how a thing appears" as well as the "enactive" interpretation of reality from integral pluralism, verges on a non-realist (constructivist) position that a world "out there" does not exist. These types of statements lead critical realists to claim that IT falls prey to the epistemic fallacy: '"the view that statements about being can be reduced to or analyzed in terms of statements about knowledge" (Bhaskar 1975, p. 36; and see Collier, pp. 76–84). However, in general IT has a more nuanced stance.

From the perspective of embodied realism, these sorts of conundrums are natural and even unavoidable. Perspective, reality, object, thing, and even "are" are metaphorical pluralisms that must be coped with, rather than hammered down. Claims about these constructs are not so much true (or false) as true *to the extent that* the exemplars considered in any actual situation are prototypical to the commonly accepted prototypes of the core categories. However, Wilber's positivistic style does not include caveats of the type offered by embodied realism, and thus he is forced to interleave explanations that may seem contradictory.

Kosmic Address

Integral pluralism highlights how different objects arise from the different defined perspectives of the Kosmic Address model. It thus offers developmental and ontological categories that are very useful in nunacing the question of how something does or can exist. However, it does not directly address the question of how individuals operating from the same Kosmic Address might differ in their conceptualizations. Also, it is not yet apparent whether the concept of Kosmic Address itself is sufficiently determinate. In contentious dialogues about the validity of specific claims, will participants be able to agree on the parameters of the Kosmic Address itself? How contentious will the specification of the developmental levels or formal perspective of interlocutors become?

The strategy of concluding that another person is developmentally not up to snuff and accepting that they don't have the capacity to engage with our beliefs or engage at the level of discourse we hope for is, though sometimes perfectly valid, also problematic. In doing so we 1) risk misdiagnosing the other using a simplistic categorization system; 2) miss an opportunity to connect more deeply with both the person and the ideas in front of us; and 3) miss an opportunity to more seriously reflect on our beliefs and selves in the face of an authentic encounter with another (and see Kögler, 1992, on critical hermeneutics and self-distanciation). Admitting that I, and all of us, unavoidably constantly make these sorts of calls to judge the "adequatio" of the listener and gauge how deeply we will engage, we want to take seriously the question of how integral beliefs are explained and argued for in rational public discourse. Embodied realism provides an additional resource for explanations of why interlocutors may disagree.

Spiritual Ontologies

In *Integral Spirituality*, Wilber defines the spiritual line of development as addressing "what is it that is of ultimate concern." This includes the "perennial" ontological/metaphysical questions central to all religions: Who am I (are we)? Where do we come from and where are we going (life, death, and soul)? Where did the universe (or everything) come from and where is it going (cosmology)? What is it made of (what are its essences)? Does God exist (and what does he/she do and want)?[38] Wilber's spiritual and esoteric themes are a primary draw for many of his readers. His *Integral Spirituality* is in part an attempt to provide a postmetaphysical treatment of spiritual realities, transpersonal phenomena, and perennial principles from religions and wisdom traditions. Spiritual themes in integral discourse include the three faces of God; the primordial, the non-dual Ground of Being (the Absolute); Higher/Authentic self; Eros and Agape; and Omega Point.[39] Though Integral Theory is explicitly post-metaphysical (especially in the "Wilber-5" phase), some of Wilber's concepts veer uncomfortably close to the metaphysical—e.g., Primordial Perspectives, Eros and Agape, involution, Kosmos, Omega Point, and nonduality.

In Murray (2013) I explore some of the challenges that arise in discussing mystical, metaphysical, and spiritual concepts in a post-postmodern and postmetaphysical age. Below, I will briefly summarize some of the key points that relate to embodied realism and epistemic drives"

1. We can note that metaphysical questions call out for answers from deep within the human psyche—they are often, as Wilber notes, themes of ultimate concern. From the perspective

of epistemic drives, this might imply that the human drive to find answers to these questions is quite strong—and the more certain the answer, the better. Many of the concepts involved, such as Truth, Morality (goodness), and Beauty, are quite abstract and thus particularly susceptible to indeterminacy (fuzzy boundaries and metaphorical pluralism). The marriage of high levels of importance with high levels of indeterminacy explains some of the chaos and vigorous disputation around religious and metaphysical themes.

2. Wilber's approach to these themes combines the idea of Kosmic Address (from integral pluralism) and his three strands summary of the scientific method, and is best summarized in his excerpt *Integral Semiotics*.[40] He basically says that what he is referring to when he speaks of God, Agape, non-duality, etc. is only observable or comprehendible from advanced states of development and state-practice realization. Those who do not agree with the whole premise of the Kosmic Address will find this to be a cop-out—and it begs the question of "privileged access" decried by constructivists. Part of the postmetaphysical attitude is that, call it what you will, there is no avoiding differences in expertise and developmental capacity in questions of truth. Yet, while Wilber's spiritual themes are important and his analysis is insightful, he faces a conundrum in justifying them. To meet the modern criteria, they must anchor in experiences that his audience has access to (given certain injunctions). But, based on his own description of developmental levels, the vast majority of his audience will have, at most, fleeting glimpses or frequent but vague tastes of the deeper realities the concepts point to. This would seem to call for massive misunderstanding and misplaced concreteness around IT's spiritual ontology (though it may be a risk worth taking if the exposition helps a sufficient number understand and integrate something they have a taste of).

The theory of Kosmic Address says that to understand a thing one must first have access to it experientially in the world-space that reveals it (which might require contemplative training) and secondly, must have the developmental capacity to see it as intended (which might mean at a given level of *complexity*; and might mean at a given level of *purity* in which certain biases and filters have been transcended). However, even if these conditions are met, all of the concerns brought up in embodied realism hold. To those developed enough to have these experiences, they are still raw experiences for which one must use language to bring them into intersubjective space. In this sense, describing non-duality is similar to describing the taste of chocolate. To one who has not experienced it (or something like it), no amount of language will reveal the referent. And for those who have experienced it, all the same sources of indeterminacies are present. More developed individuals will have more skill in observing and ameliorating the sources of indeterminacy. Yet, as is proven out by differences of opinion expressed by accomplished adepts and brilliant philosophers throughout history, there is no avoiding the indeterminacies in abstract philosophical discussion about essential aspects of reality, self, or spirit.

Conclusions: Enacting Ethical Ontological Reasoning

The arc of progress in Western philosophy and science can arguably be described through a developmental lens as having two chapters. In this simplistic narrative, the first chapter is of increasing mastery of the faculties of reason and rational control (formal operations) and "mastery" of much of the natural world. During this period (i.e., up though modernity) many of the physical needs of man have been satisfied (food, shelter, medicine, education, transportation, etc.—for a large percentage of Westerners). We are currently beginning the second chapter, in which man, through his ideations and "solutions," has created our direst contemporary problems (climate change, species extinctions, economic inequality and instability, obesity, terrorism, existential despair and isolation, etc.). In our struggles, we increasingly see that in modernity it is *human* nature that must be understood and mastered in order to create sustained happiness.[41] Embodied philosophies say that a root cause is the *disembodied* character of Western-style reason, and that deeply understanding the implications of embodiment is one path home. In developmental terms, this means building post-rational or post-formal faculties—e.g., understanding of the limitations of formal/logical reason and learning the "wisdom skills" of incorporating intuition, unknowing, ethics, critical self-reflection, and body-based self-knowing into reason.

Embodiment has many branches. In addition to the epistemological and cognitive science–oriented themes central to this paper, and the situated and social-constructivist themes also mentioned, are pragmatic and ethical themes. Increasingly, thinkers and leaders are called upon to be more integrated. That is to: enact a life consistent with their ideas and ideals; consider the real moral/ethical/spiritual implications of ideas (including theories, models, etc.); and consider the wider systemic implications of ideas (in AQAL terms: to integrate first, third, and fourth quadrants).

Habermas speaks about "emancipatory" knowledge and interests in dealing with self-knowledge and self-refection (1971).[42] Embodied philosophies that expose universal sources of fallibility provide tools for emancipatory self-critique. They also help good ideas spread in more ethical ways. As long as one is developing and using integral theories and models within the community of the enculturated (preaching to the choir), sources of fallibility may seem inert or unimportant. But this (meta-) knowledge is important when we try to 1) cross disciplinary boundaries to interact with other communities; 2) apply these ideas and explain one's purposes to stakeholders; or 3) have a constructive dialogue with others who don't agree with some aspect of the theory or model—that is, when the integral worldview needs to reach across and communicate with other worldviews or conceptual frames.[43] And of course, such reaching out to—positively affecting *and being affected by* individuals with other conceptual frames—is the real end goal of integral theory and practice.

Integral theories straddle and connect multiple (one could say all) disciplines and modes of inquiry. To build credible arguments for and relationships with multiple disciplines, it behooves integralists to develop styles of argumentation, meta-dialogue, and self-reflection that speak directly to the sources of indeterminacy of particularly abstract, metaphysical, or esoteric claims. The implications are important because, as Lakoff and Johnson put it: "[R]adical change in our understanding of reason [leads to] a radical change in our understanding of ourselves" (p. 3).

Notes

1. Two papers in particular are companion or complementary to this one, one dealing with embodied realism and critical realism, and another with mystical and metaphysical claims in integral theory.

2. The approaches also respond to the problems of scientific materialism, logical empiricism, and positivism, which tend to marginalize non-concrete objects and nonrational modes of thought.

3. Collier notes that "Heidegger . . . argues forcefully that non-realism is a non-starter, as it presupposes a worldless subject, and we are essential Being-in-the-world" (Collier, 1994, p. 30).

4. The transcendental argument is that we always already make this assumption, or that this assumption is a necessary condition for the possibility of for either further (serious) philosophical deliberation, and/or a necessary condition for any reasoned action or communication. The latter is more along the lines of Habermas, and see Murray (2015) for how transcendental arguments relate to Habermas's rational reconstructive arguments.

5. A primary problem in the systematic comparison of truth claims (or models) is that the space of evaluation is not monotonic or linear. There are multiple characteristics that bear on quality (coverage, explanatory depth, parsimony, intuitive appeal, etc.), with no simple or generally agreed-upon method for prioritizing or weighing them.

6. Positivistic in the sense of "positive capability" vs. "negative capability," as described later.

7. Positivistic approaches provide models, insights, and distinctions enabling more reasoning power, more meaning generation, and increased clarity and confidence; while approaches with more negative capability have a higher tolerance of and skill with the cognitive dissonance, fallibility, ignorance, mystery, and paradox, when inquiry exposes indeterminacies revealing ever-deeper unsettling territories of unknowing and fallibility (see PME).

8. Fallibility and bias cannot be erased in general but, to speak metaphorically, the better one characterizes the coloring and distortion contributed by a lens (or any tool, especially the mind) the better one can compensate for the limitations that accompany its use. A popular quote attributed to Voltaire says: "Doubt is uncomfortable, certainty is ridiculous."

9. Contemporary thinkers have put to rest the rationalist vs. empiricist debate over whether the senses or reason can yield valid knowledge—both are eminently fallible and, moreover, perception and reason are too entwined to differentiate their reliability so strongly.

10. On bounded rationality see: Kahneman et al., 1982; Gigerenzer and Selten, 1999; Gladwell, 2002; Meyers, 2002; Sunstein, 2002; Shermer, 2011b. For work specifically addressing the role of emotions in reason see: Goleman, 1995; Damasio, 1999; Matthews et al., 2002; Fischer et al., 1990. And on systematic errors of memory and perception, see Travis and Aronson, 2007; Wilson, 2002.

11. Lakoff and Johnson go on to describe how the embodied perspective contradicts common philosophical positions: "there is no Cartesian dualistic person with

a mind separate and independent from a body;" "since reason is shaped by the body, it is not radically free [and] we have no absolute freedom in Kant's sense . . . no full autonomy;" "the utilitarian [economically rational] person does not exist;" "phenomenological introspection alone [can not] discover everything there is to know about the mind;" and "there is no . . . decentered subjective . . . poststructuralist person . . . for whom all meaning is arbitrary, totally relative, and purely historically contingent, unconstrained by body and brain."

12. With each split-and-join operation we risk making two types of errors: overgeneralization and overspecialization, i.e., treating things as similar that are in some important way different, and treating things as different that are in some important way similar (analogous to type I and type II errors from statistical analysis).

13. In part, such categorization is the mind's attempt to establish a comfortable condition of certainty, and avoid dissonance-producing states of uncertainty and ambiguity. Definitive categorizing enables definitive decision and action. In evolutionary terms, quick and certain categorization means catching the prey or avoiding the predator. Bio-evolutionary approaches to cognition, as in Daniel Kahneman's *Thinking, Fast and Slow*, are rarely applied to scholarly or philosophical thought, but can be.

14. This is true for concepts indicated by words that have evolved naturally in language. We can, of course, define a new concept in a very specific way and, until it undergoes the hermeneutic transformations in the "telephone game" of real use over time, it can maintain a strict definition.

15. Lakoff and Johnson describe *graded propositions* that ". . . contain linear scales [that] define the degree to which a given property holds of an individual [as] defined by a graded category . . ." (p. 288).

16. Similarly, Chris Argyris says "the likelihood of differences in the interpretations of different observers increases the higher one goes on the ladder of inference" (1995, p. 58). Rungs along this "ladder" are inferential steps that can represent increases in abstraction, complexity, or just a sequence of inferences—any of which lead one ever further from concrete facts. Esbjörn-Hargens (2010) uses the term *epistemological distance* (from Carolan, 2004) to describe differences along this ladder of inference that, to my reading, map to hierarchical complexity, which is essentially a combination of complexity and abstraction (Commons and Richards, 1984).

17. It is still true that, as Descartes said four centuries ago, that "[philosophy] had been cultivated for many centuries by the best minds that have ever lived and that nevertheless no single thing is to be found in it which is not a subject of dispute and in consequence is not dubious" (Descartes, 1637, p. 10). Descartes actually thought he had discovered a solution, and did not count himself among the plagued philosophers. Postmetaphysical philosophy, which foregrounds knowledge fallibility, better avoids such blind spots.

18. Many areas of scholarly work are, as Michael Shermer puts it, "notoriously fraught with definitional disagreement" (Shermer, 2011a).

19. We should differentiate between two types of problems: First, that definitive concepts mismatch graded phenomena in *nature*; and second, that we treat concepts as definitive, when in fact they operate within *cognition* as graded.

20. For claims about instances whose categories follow a *graded or prototype* structure, the claim is true to the extent that the instance fits the prototype or central meaning. But for concepts with more *metaphorical pluralism*, the situation is even more fraught with indeterminacy because the structure of the category may be more like distant islands of prototypes with no central meaning.

21. Lakoff and Johnson may make metaphorical pluralism sound like a more revolutionary idea than it is, especially to philosophers. It is the multi-perspectival nature of the metaphorical pluralism of core concepts that enables scholars over the ages to write entire books exploring single constructs such as cosmopolitanism, hope, patriotism, being, selfishness, pluralism, bullshit, or insecurity (this random list from looking at the books on my shelf). That cognitive science supports the inescapability of metaphorical pluralism is, however, new in our era.

22. These metaphorical explorations are for English-language speakers, but the authors give interesting examples of alternative conceptualizations from other languages and cultures.

23. Or most of it, as Lakoff and Johnson mention, there are some nonmetaphorical; i.e., *literal,* aspects of time such as its directionality and irreversibility.

24. They also make the argument (p. 198) that for incompatible metaphorical senses of a concept, we have to (usually unconsciously) choose between them and can't conceive of the concept in a way that includes both. They make an analogy to perceiving vs. ground.

25. Even the verb *to be* is a metaphorical pluralism. It can imply identity, class membership, existence, or predication. (President Clinton famously and disastrously said, as he was trying to deceive his interrogators: "It depends on what the meaning of the word 'is' is.") Alfred Korzybski describes E-Prime, "a version of the English language that excludes all forms of the verb to be" as a ". . . a device to clarify thinking and strengthen writing [that] leads to a less dogmatic style of language that reduces the possibility of misunderstanding and conflict . . . For example, the sentence 'the film was good' could translate into E-Prime as 'I liked the film' or as 'the film made me laugh.' The E-Prime versions communicate the speaker's experience rather than judgment, making it harder for the writer or reader to confuse opinion with fact" (Wikipedia, August 20, 2011).

26. Lakoff and Johnson, in Chapter 3, explain that "color does not exist in the external world . . . light is not colored . . . it is electromagnetic radiation" and the relationship between perceived color and the combination of color frequencies hitting the eye is not a simple mapping of the rainbow spectrum of frequencies.

27. This notion is backed up in a strictly philosophical sense, rather than from cognitive psychology, in Kirkham's (1992) *Theories of Truth: A Critical Introduction.* Kirkham shows that there are a multitude of definitions of truth implied

in philosophy and logic. He claims that philosophical disagreements and confusions about the nature of truth are often the result of scholars being unaware that each is talking about different things (both called truth), or that a single author implies different definitions of truth in different places. He classifies the implicit definitions of truth into categories, including extensional, possible worlds, metaphysical, naturalistic, essential, justificatory, assertional, and ascriptional.

28. There seem to be threads in the literature from psychology and brain science that would or could support and expound upon epistemic drives, but such research is still emerging.

29. It was also surprising that no mention was made of developmental theories. This is one indication among many of the surprising marginalization or ignorance of developmental theories in academia. Though developmental theory has deep implications for all of the social sciences, even in closely related branches such as cognitive science, developmental theory is unused except for passing references to Piaget's work with young children, missing the critical contributions of neo-Piagetian theories relevant to adults.

30. The very general urge to find understanding or meaning in our experience is an epistemic drive that includes many others. Many of the drives I will mention are overlapping—I am not proposing any clear taxonomy of them here.

31. Maeve Cooke notes the potential of "repressive metaphysical projections" in language and (hyper-) rationality (1994, p. ix; in framing Habermas's postmetaphysics).

32. Simply *naming* something can confer an ontological status. The "ontological legislation" of giving things names, and thus tendering more reality to the objects they denote, whether it happens culturally (organically, bottom up), or through the power structures of institutions (top-down sanctioning), partitions the buzzing, booming chaos of reality into things of importance, those of lesser importance, and that which can barely be considered or known to exist because they have not been named. Cultures that have no name for the "ecosystem" may have difficulty considering its health. The differentiations (and integrations) provided by ontologies-in-use constrain the set of choices one has in dialogue, action, and thought.

33. Santa Claus can also exist for *us* if we take the magical-thought perspective of that developmental level, which remains ever-available within our consciousness (some would call it suspension of disbelief).

34. Metaphorical pluralism and ontological pluralism imply that when Wilber uses ladders vs. spirals to refer to developmental levels, he may actually be referring to a slightly different (multiple) object.

35. Critiques of integral theory suggest that in countering postmodern theories, integral theory has overshot and has not fully incorporated the lessons of postmodernism, as suggested by the subtitle of Gary Hampson's paper: "The [only] way out [of postmodernism] is through [it]" (Hampson, 2007). See also Mark Edwards (2010, p. 409): "an integral metastudies needs a decentering postmodernism that it cannot

integrate, that lies outside of its scientific purview, which continually challenges it and is critical of its generalisations, abstractions and universalisings."

36. Habermas uses a parallel conceptualization of subjective, objective, and intersubjective (which Wilber cites as an influence). But Habermas is not interested in whether these are primordial aspects of nature—he describes them in terms of enacted *human* interests, perspectives, and innate orientations.

37. In Wilber (Excerpt A, online) he again seems contradictory regarding whether perspectives are inherent in the universe or aspects of human cognition: "These four perspectives are not merely arbitrary conventions. Rather, they are dimensions that are so fundamental that they have become embedded in language as pronouns during the natural course of evolution. These embedded perspectives show up as first, second, and third person pronouns." That something seems to be universally embedded in human languages tells us something about how the mind works, but not, I would argue, anything about the deep nature of reality.

38. We eschew the less ontological perennial questions such as: How can I know the right/moral thing to do? Is there an ultimate purpose for the universe or for me? How do I cope with suffering and respond to evil? How do I improve myself (spiritually)?

39. Bhaskar's most recent work on meta-reality touches on overlapping themes. However Bhaskar's audience is primarily philosophers, while Wilber's addresses a more general audience, so their styles of argument are quite different.

40. In preparation, with a draft available online at http://www.kenwilber.com/blog/show/758.

41. Again, this is clearly a Western story. The East figured this out without needing to develop modern forms of life or technology. However, the answers lie not only in mastery and liberation of the *individual* mind/body, but in the understanding and liberation of *collective* forms of fallibility—an area in which the East does not have a strong advantage.

42. Habermas (1971) defines three types of human knowledge and interests: instrumental (objective), dealing with understanding and control over our environment; practical (intersubjective), dealing with social norms—expectations about social behavior; and emancipatory (subjective), dealing with self-knowledge and self-refection.

43. In Murray (2011), I call this "The Idea Portability Principle:" that *understanding and dealing with the indeterminacy of ideas is more important the greater the distance between the worldviews or beliefs of interlocutors.*

References

Argyris, Chris, Robert Putnam, and Diana Smith. 1985. *Action Science*. San Francisco: Jossey-Bass.

Bateson, Gregory. 1972. *Steps to an Ecology of Mind: Collected Essays in Anthropology, Psychiatry, Evolution, and Epistemology*. Chicago: University of Chicago Press.

Bateson, Gregory. 1979. *Mind and Nature: A Necessary Unity*. New York: Hampton Press.

Bhaskar, Roy. 1975. *A Realist Theory of Science*. Brighton, UK: Harvester Press.

Bhaskar, Roy. 1997. "On the Ontological Status of Ideas." *Journal for the Theory of Social Behaviour* 27(2/3): 139–147.

Bhaskar, Roy. 2002. *From Science to Emancipation: Alienation and the Actuality of Enlightenment*. New Delhi, IN; Thousand Oaks, CA; London: Sage.

Carolan, M.S. 2005. "Society, Biology, and Ecology: Bringing Nature Back into Sociology's Disciplinary Narrative Through Critical Realism." *Organization & Environment* 18: 393–421.

Collier, Andrew. 1994. *Critical Realism: An Introduction to Roy Bhaskar's Philosophy*. New York: Verso.

Commons, Michael L., and Francis Richards. 1984. "A General Model of Stage Theory." In *Beyond Formal Operations: Late Adolescent and Adult Cognitive Development*, eds. Michael L. Commons, Francis Richards, and Cheryl Armo, 120–141. New York: Praeger.

Cooke, Maeve. 1994. *Language and Reason: A Study of Habermas's Pragmatics*. Cambridge, MA: MIT Press.

Cook-Greuter, S.R. 2000. "Mature Ego Development: A Gateway to Ego Transcendence." *Journal of Adult Development* 7(4): 227–240.

Corning, Peter A. 2002. "The Re-emergence of "Emergence": A Venerable Concept in Search of a Theory." *Complexity* 7(6): 18–30.

Damasio, Antonio. 1999. *The Feeling of What Happens: Body and Emotion in the Making of Consciousness*. New York: Harcourt Brace.

Darwin, Charles. 1871. *The Descent of Man, and Selection in Relation to Sex* (1st ed.). London: John Murray.

Descartes, René. 1637/2005. *Discourse on Method and Meditations on First Philosophy*, Trans. E.S. Haldane. Stillwell, KS: Digireads Publ.

Edwards, M. 2010. "Of Elephants and Butterflies: An Integral Metatheory for Organizational Transformation." In *Integral Theory in Action*, ed. Sean Esbjörn-Hargens. Albany, NY: SUNY Press.

Esbjörn-Hargens, Sean. 2005. "Integral Ecology: The What, Who, and How of Environmental Phenomena." *World Futures* 61(1–2): 5–49.

Esbjörn-Hargens, Sean. 2010. "An Ontology of Climate Change: Integral Pluralism and the Enactment of Multiple Objects." *Journal of Integral Theory and Practice* 5(1): 143–174.

Esbjörn-Hargens, Sean, and Michael E. Zimmerman. 2009. *Integral Ecology: Uniting Multiple Perspectives on the Natural World*. Boston: Integral Books.

Fischer, Kurt. 1980. "A Theory of Cognitive Development: The Control and Construction of Hierarchies of Skills." *Psychological Review* 87(6): 477–531.

Fischer, Kurt W., P.R. Shaver, and P. Carnochan. 1990. "How Emotions Develop and How They Organize Development." *Cognition and Emotion* 4(2): 81–127.

Gigerenzer, Gerd, and Reinhard Selten (eds.). 1999. *Bounded Rationality: The Adaptive Toolbox*. Cambridge, MA: MIT Press.

Gladwell, Malcolm. 2002. *Blink*. New York: Little, Brown.

Goleman, Daniel. 1995. *Emotional Intelligence*. New York: Bantam Books.

Habermas, Jürgen. 1971. *Knowledge and Human Interests*. Boston: Beacon Press.

Habermas, Jürgen. 1992. *Postmetaphysical Thinking*. Cambridge, MA: MIT Press.

Hampson, Gary P. 2007. "Integral Re-views Postmodernism: The Way Out is Through." *Integral Review* V.4: 108–173.

Kahneman, Daniel. 2011. *Thinking, Fast and Slow*. New York: Macmillan.

Kahneman, Daniel, Paul Slovic, and Amos Tversky (eds.). 1982. *Judgment Under Uncertainty: Heuristics and Biases*. New York: Cambridge University Press.

Kegan, Robert. 1994. *In Over Our Heads: The Mental Demands of Modern Life*. Cambridge, MA: Harvard University Press.

Kegan, Robert, and Lisa Laskow Lahey. 2009. *Immunity to Change: How to Overcome It and Unlock the Potential in Yourself and Your Organization*. Boston: Harvard Business Press.

Kirkham, Richard L. 1992. *Theories of Truth: A Critical Introduction*. Cambridge, MA: MIT Press.

Kögler, Hans Herbert. 1999. *The Power of Dialogue: Critical Hermeneutics after Gadamer and Foucault*. Cambridge, MA: MIT Press.

Lakoff, George. 1987. *Women, Fire, and Dangerous Things: What Categories Reveal About the Mind*. Chicago: University of Chicago Press.

Lakoff, George and Mark Johnson. 1999. *Philosophy in the Flesh: The Embodied Mind and its Challenge to Western Thought*. New York: Basic Books/Perseus Books Group.

Matthews, Gerald, Moshe Zeidner, and Richard Roberts. 2002. *Emotional Intelligence: Science and Myth*. Cambridge, MA: Bradford Book/MIT Press.

Mervis, B., and E. Rosch. 1981. "Categories of Natural Objects." *Annual Review of Psychology* 32: 89–115.

Meyers, David G. 2002. *Intuition: Its Powers and Perils*. New Haven, CT: Yale University Press.

Murray, Tom. 2008. "Exploring Epistemic Wisdom: Ethical and Practical Implications of Integral Theory and Methodological Pluralism for Collaboration and Knowledge-Building." Presented at the 1st Biannual Integral Theory Conference, John F. Kennedy University, Pleasant Hill, CA, August 2008.

Murray, Tom. 2011. "Toward Post-metaphysical Enactments: On Epistemic Rrives, Negative Capability, and Indeterminacy Analysis." *Integral Review* 7(2): 92–124.

Murray, Tom. 2013. "Mystical Claims and Embodied Knowledge in a Post-metaphysical Age." Presented at the 2013 Integral Theory Conference, San Francisco, July 18, 2013.

Murray, Tom. (in press). "Integralist Mental Models of Adult Development: Provisos from a Users Guide. In *True But Partial: Essential Critiques of Integral Theory*, ed. Sean Esbjörn-Hargens. Albany, NY: SUNY Press.

Murray, Tom. (in press). "Contributions of Embodied Realism to Ontological Questions in Critical Realism and Integral Theory." In *Metatheory for the 21st-Century: Critical Realism and Integral Theory in Dialogue.*

Piaget, Jean. 1972. *The Principles of Genetic Epistemology*. New York: Basic Books.

Searle, John. 1995. *The Construction of Social Reality*. New York: Free Press.

Shermer, Michael. 2011a. "What is Pseudoscience?" *Scientific American* September 2011.

Shermer, Michael. 2011b. *The Believing Brain: From Ghosts and Gods to Politics and Conspiracies—How We Construct Beliefs and Reinforce Them as Truths*. New York: Henry Holt.

Sunstein, Cass R. 2002. *Risk and Reason*. New York: Cambridge University Press.

Travis, Carol, and Elliot Aronson. 2007. *Mistakes Were Made (but not by* me*): Why We Justify Foolish Beliefs, Bad Decisions, and Hurtful Acts*. New York: Harcourt.

Wagner, Steven 2001. "Searching for Pragmatism in the Philosophy of Mathematics." *Philosophia Mathematica* 9(3): 355–376.

Whitehead, Alfred North. 1979. *Process and Reality: An Essay in Cosmology*. New York: Free Press.

Wilber, Ken. 2000. *Sex, Ecology, Spirituality* (In *Collected Works of Ken Wilber, Vol. 6*). Boston: Shambhala.

Wilber, Ken. 2002. "Excerpt A: An Integral Age at the Leading Edge, Part I." Ken Wilber Online. http://wilber.shambhala.com/html/books/kosmos/excerptA/part1.cfm. Retrieved October 10, 2011.

Wilber, Ken. 2006. *Integral Spirituality*. Boston: Shambhala.

Wilson, Timothy D. 2002. *Strangers to Ourselves: Discovering the Adaptive Unconscious*. Cambridge, MA: Harvard University Press.

Chapter 12

Making Sense of Everything?

Integral Postmetaphysics and the Theological Turn in Continental Philosophy

Cameron Stewart Rees Freeman

> For wherever the name of God would allow us to think something else, for example a vulnerable non-sovereignty, one that suffers and is divisible, one that is mortal even, capable of contradicting itself or repenting (a thought that is neither impossible or without example), it would be a completely different story, perhaps even the story of a God who deconstructs himself in his ipseity.[1]
>
> —Jacques Derrida

One of the more unexpected features of Continental philosophy at the beginning of the twenty-first century has been the reemergence of religious and theological questions, particularly in relation to the discourse about the "end of metaphysics" and the possibility of a postmetaphysical approach to philosophy (and spirituality). This turn toward the sphere of religion in contemporary postmodern philosophy (in figures such as Derrida, Levinas, Žižek, and Caputo) has taken many by surprise, for it has occurred just as the modern Enlightenment—with its rational critique of religion (Freud, Marx, Nietzsche)—was believed to have done away with the theistic God of the premodern religion and cosmology once and for all.

However, if the Age of Reason in the modern world means the death of the mythic God of the premodern cosmology, then postmodernity means the critique of modernity, and the delimitation of its rational (secular-humanist) critique of religion. That is, in becoming enlightened about the autonomous-rational ego of the modern Enlightenment,[2] postmodern philosophy involves a renewed openness to the question of God and the nonrational dimensions of human experience in its unyielding attempt to break free of the grip of the modern Enlightenment paradigm, with its all too rational-objectifying, logocentric discourse.

This postmodern return to the sphere of religion is evidenced in many of the postmodern "prophets of unreason," with their critical unmasking of the hubris of modern Enlightenment rationality. Back in the nineteenth century the Danish father of existentialism, Søren Kierkegaard, howled with laughter at Hegel's claim that the paradoxical madness of the Christian faith is to be subsumed (transcended and included) by the Absolute Idea—the clarity of conceptual thinking provided by German Idealist metaphysics. In a similar, but decidedly anti-Christian vein, Nietzsche's radical perspectivism undermined the traditional foundations of not just morality and religion, but also science and philosophy in his prophetic-intuitive vision of the Overman (Zarathustra) beyond good and evil that affirms this body and this life and refuses the metaphysical consolations of another world behind the scenes.

In the same way, in the twentieth century we have Heidegger's critique of metaphysics as onto-theology (conceptual idolatry) and his call for "the gods before who I can sing and dance," as well as the mystical-poetic turn of his later writings, which were deeply inspired by Christian medieval mystic Meister Eckhart and Zen scholar D.T. Suzuki. Following this, there is the prophetic appeal of Emmanuel Levinas to God as the "wholly Other," which absolves itself from human knowledge, and where the ethical response to each and every other (the poor, widow, the orphan, etc.) and comes before any rational accounting of the "the totality of Being." In the same postmodern trajectory we also have Catholic philosopher Jean Luc-Marion, who also affirms both the vanity of metaphysics and the mystery of God as a "saturated phenomenon," given in a way that far exceeds our grasp, where the shortcoming has to do with the failure of our metaphysical concepts, not with overflowing excess of the divine.

In a more secular and post-structural vein, Foucault spent most of his life seeking out limit-experiences and transcendent release in everything from madness to psychedelics, to Zen meditation, to eroticism and sadomasochism.[3] And even Derrida said that the least bad definition of deconstruction is an "experience of the impossible" and spent his last years writing on the "un-deconstructable," i.e., on how the aporetic structure of religious concepts (e.g., gift, hospitality, justice, forgiveness, and death) twists free from conceptual presence and the realm of identificatory knowledge, in a paradoxical passion for the impossible. Finally, French psychoanalytical theorist Jacques Lacan was also deeply interested in mysticism as a specific kind of feminine (non-phallic) enjoyment (*jouissance)* and pushed into the "fear and trembling" of Kierkegaard's religious sphere with his concept of the Real as an impossible traumatic/excess that resists any symbolic articulation.

So while there is indeed a strong mystical/religious current running through many of the pioneers of postmodern philosophy, if there is a single lesson of Continental thought in the twentieth century, it is that there is no Deep Order (i.e., no transcendent structure or necessary reason) to reality to which philosophers or anyone else has access. In other words, what all of the most influential Continental thinkers in postmodernity have in common is a desire to break free from the grip of metaphysics as the search for an unshakable foundation for truth and meaning, and to finally relinquish the age-old quest for a single encompassing philosophical narrative that can claim to "make sense of everything."

In the face of what Lyotard called this "incredulity towards meta-narratives,"[4] with the end of metaphysics (Heidegger/Derrida) the secret is there is no Secret.[5] There is no "deep structure" waiting for us just beneath the surface, and there is no Big Story (e.g., historical progress through advance of science, the inexorable march of democracy and freedom, the self-development of Spirit working itself out through history, etc.) that explains to all people everywhere the meaning of the universe. What we have then, after the end of metaphysics, are provisional, contingent, historically constituted "unities of meaning" (e.g., AQAL) as effects of a play of non-totalizable differences, leaving us with the instability of traditional foundations, the ambiguities of the old absolutes, the destabilization of rigid modernist binaries (subject/object, religious/secular, faith/reason) and complex, decentered systems that link endlessly without closure (e.g., the Internet).[6]

This postmodern predicament presents a significant challenge to integral philosophy, particularly in regards to this influential discourse surrounding the end of metaphysics. Insofar as the AQAL (Wilber V) framework that constitutes integral philosophy takes itself to be the most comprehensive and inclusive account of reality currently available, it is clearly open to the charge of metaphysics.[7] That is, integral philosophy, with its systematic aspirations to "make sense of everything" (at least in its more popular instantiations) repeats the classical metaphysical gesture from Plato to Heidegger of wanting to take its adherents out of the shadows and into the light beyond (i.e., out of the flat-land world of partial and fragmented perspectives into the all-encompassing vision-logic of integral awareness) via an externally imposed formal framework within which positive elements fill their preordained place.

In other words, given that the end of metaphysics consists in a vigilant skepticism toward any grand narrative that purports to provide direct access to Truth or comprehend the meaning of Being as a whole, the obvious question here is: Is the overarching Kosmic vision of integral philosophy simply the foremost contemporary example of just another historically contingent Big Story that claims to make everything make sense—or is integral philosophy able to escape the charge of metaphysics with its fundamental constitution still intact? In other words, to what extent is integral philosophy (even with its dialectical vision-logic and critically reflexive self-understanding) simply another grand meta-narrative that a particular tribe tells itself about itself, where ever-higher Levels of consciousness are fleshed out through four irreducible Quadrants that tetra-evolve through different Lines, States, and Types (AQAL)?[8]

In the most recent phase of his thought—integral postmetaphysics (IPM)[9]—Ken Wilber attempts to respond to just this postmodern critique of metaphysics. Wilber deploys the notion of "Kosmic Habits" to replace the traditional Great Chain of Being ontology, as well as a calculus of perspectives within a Kosmic address system to replace the postulation of independently existing realities.[10] With this postmetaphysical gesture in mind, then, the pressing question for integral philosophy is: How well does IPM stand up to and survive the postmodern critique of grand meta-narratives? Given that the metaphysical impulse to "make sense of everything" is the primary object of critique of recent Continental thought, to what extent does integral philosophy (i.e., Wilber V) provide a genuinely postmetaphysical opening for philosophy and spirituality? That is, is the multidimensional Kosmos disclosed by an IPM just another totalizing (if structurally open-ended) map of reality that pretends to universality, or is it a genuinely new point of departure for the future of metaphysics? This key question will be examined here primarily in relation to theological turn in contemporary Continental philosophy in figures such as Žižek, Derrida, and Caputo. In drawing out some of the key tensions and differences between integral philosophy and recent trends in Continental thought, we will attempt to bring IPM (Wilber V) into a dialogue with an alternative postmetaphysical opening, one that is based not upon the quest for an all-embracing and comprehensive Kosmic totality, but the ontological incompleteness of reality itself as the very conditions of possibility for the further evolution of human consciousness.

The *Aufhebung* in Hegel and Schelling

Georg F.W. Hegel, the nineteenth century German Idealist philosopher, is probably the foremost precursor to integral philosophy from within the tradition of Continental philosophy. Hegel's dialectical philosophy conceived of the world-historical process as the self-development of the Absolute Spirit through successive stages in the evolution of consciousness, a theme that is virtually definitive for every major integral thinker ever since.[11] As is well known, such all-encompassing or totalizing aspirations have been widely lampooned by postmodern philosophy since the time of Nietzsche and Kierkegaard in the nineteenth century, which has criticized Hegel as an absurd "absolute idealist" who "pretended to know everything," to possess absolute knowledge, to know the mind of God and make sense of all of reality out of the self-development of the Absolute Spirit.[12]

The integral notion that each new structure-stage of consciousness in human evolution "transcends and includes" its preceding stage originally stems from Hegel, who coined the term *Aufhebung* to stipulate the moment of dialectical reconciliation between opposites into a higher unity at each new stage of development. It is precisely this Hegelian notion of "transcend and include" as a higher stage that aims to go beyond and embrace its previous stages (Wilber) that has been put into question in twentieth century Continental philosophy, most recently by Slavoj Žižek, who wants to rescue Hegel from his postmodern caricature as a totalizing thinker of the self-development of Absolute with a radical rereading of the original meaning of the *Aufhebung*.[13]

Žižek begins his reading of Hegel by drawing on Friedrich Schelling, another central figure in the brief history of integral philosophy. While Wilber employs Schelling to drive home a peaceful evolutionary reconciliation of Ascending (Ego) and Descending (Eco) currents into a non-dual union in volume 1 of the (still forthcoming) Kosmos Trilogy *Sex, Ecology, Spirituality*,[14] Žižek draws on Schelling's later works and argues for a very different, and even heretical reading. In contrast to Wilber's appropriation of German Idealism, in his later works Schelling undermines the very foundations of traditional metaphysics by invoking a pre-ontological darkness or insurmountable trauma in the heart of the Absolute, and as such Schelling opens the way for a reconfiguration of the Wilberian developmental-dialectic that informs much of integral philosophy with a more radical understanding of this key integral-Hegelian motif of the *Aufhebung*.

While one of the central points of departure for integral philosophy is that the Kosmos "hangs together" as an integrated, ordered, and meaningful Whole (to be apprehended via vision-logic), for Schelling the rational order of the Kosmos (i.e., the "patterns that connect" across all domains in evolution) is not self-evident. As Schelling asks, writing at the height of the Western Enlightenment, "the whole world is thoroughly caught in Reason, but the question is, 'how did it get caught in the network of reason in the first place'?"[15] In his unfinished *Weltalter* drafts (*The Ages of the World*), Schelling attempts to account for the Logos of the universe, the patterned order of the Kosmos, by answering the age-old question of what God was doing before the creation of the world.[16]

Prior to the beginning of the world, there is precisely nothing for Schelling, by which he means an abyss of pure undifferentiated freedom (*UnGrund*). This primordial abyss of freedom is, to be precise, not-yet God, but simply a pure impersonal Will that wills nothing in particular, a pure Nothingness that "enjoys its own non-being."[17] So the urgent question is: How does this "not-yet" God become God, the Creator of everything that exists who brings forth a space-time universe?

For Schelling, this state of primordial freedom prior to the beginning is interrupted when this "not-yet" God switches from willing *nothing* in particular to willing *nothingness itself*.[18] This shift produces a radical self-contraction within the primordial Will itself, which then opposes itself to itself in the guise of its own inherent opposite, the Will that *wants something*, i.e., the positive will to expansion.[19] With the primordial freedom of the *UnGrund* caught up in this tension between contradictory drives, it is converted into a vortex of "divine madness" with nothing outside itself, a wild fury tearing itself apart.[20] This rotary motion of expanding and contracting drives is for Schelling an unbearable antagonism within the *UnGrund* itself which, *stricto sensu*, does not yet exist. In order to resolve this internal deadlock, this "not-yet" God of blind, pre-rational drives pronounces his Word/Logos,[21] creates Order out of the primordial madness, and time begins:

> The Absolute "opens up time," it "represses" the rotary motion into the past, in order to get rid of the antagonism in its heart which threatens to drag it into the abyss of madness . . . *eter-*

nity itself begets time in order to resolve the deadlock it became entangled in.[22]

For Schelling then, before God becomes God, there is only a primordial, irrational Will that then "contracts."[23] Being in order to overcome this unbearable conflict within itself. Schelling's Absolute, then, is not "at one" with itself in a state of primordial presence (Wilber's non-dual reading), but at the mercy of a fundamental and irreconcilable antagonism. Before the beginning, the Absolute is "escaping from hell,"[24] locked into a dark, irreconcilable conflict between God as *Ground* and God as *UnGrund* and without any guarantee that the spiritual principle of Light would eventually prevail over the obscure principle of Ground.[25] The turning point in the history of the Absolute is the divine act of resolution, the pronouncement of the Word (*Ent-Scheidung*)[26] which—by rejecting the chaotic-psychotic vortex of blind drives into the darkness of the "eternal past"—establishes the Kosmos, the universe of temporal "progression" dominated by Logos.[27]

This darker, more risky tradition is on the verge of both integral philosophy and the theological turn in recent Continental philosophy. It takes its point of departure from a more radical strand in the writings of Meister Eckhart, which then runs through Jacob Boehme through to Schelling and on to recent Continental and radical theological thought.[28] These German Christian mystics invoke a principle of genuine negativity in the heart of the Absolute (Schelling's *UnGrund*)—a primordial, insurmountable trauma in the abyssal ground of Godhead itself. As Schelling emphasizes over and again, this fundamental antagonism in the heart of the Absolute remains the innermost base of all reality[29] wherein all new creation is "a birth out of the chaos into the light."[30] That is, the order and structure that we discern in the Kosmos comes out of this tumultuous unruly abyss in which God wrestles with God's self, driven by this dark nature, until God pronounced his Word and the principle of Light (Logos/Reason) can emerge.[31]

This key insight in Schelling's philosophy also shows up in Žižek's unorthodox (Lacanian) reading of Hegel, and particularly the central integral/Hegelian notion of the *Aufhebung*. The Hegel that Žižek disavows is precisely the Hegel of the "transcend and include," the moment of dialectical reconciliation between opposites (*Aufhebung*) at the core of Wilber's developmental-holarchical approach—where each new stage in the Spirit's self-realization negates and preserves its preceding stage, in accordance with the deeper "self-organizing, self-transcending"[32] currents at work within the Kosmos.

In Žižek's more eccentric reading of Hegel's dialectical logic, the definitive gesture of integral philosophy to "transcend and include" partial perspectives in a higher stage of development always fails, for the Absolute in Hegel is "always-already . . . the subversion of what it purports to achieve."[33] In other words, with the sweeping evolutionary visions of the German Idealists (Schelling and Hegel), even the Absolute is not at one with itself, but something that is structured by a fundamental rupture or antagonism and is therefore, in a sense, structurally incomplete and at odds with itself. The overarching reconciliation that an integral vision provides (i.e., the tetra-meshing of indigenous perspectives into Quadrants, the organizing of different worldviews into ever higher Levels, supplemented by Lines, States, and Types) is for Žižek/Schelling merely a *Deck-Erinnerung* (screen-memory), a fantasy-formation designed to cover up the traumatic truth: The irreconcilable gap or paradoxical tension at the heart of the Absolute, the dark kernel of the Real that resists any proper resolution or higher synthesis.[34]

By refusing the standard charge of totalizing clarity directed at Hegel by his postmodern critics, Žižek's more radical reading of Hegel is itself, he argues, the true movement from outdated metaphysics into a post-metaphysical horizon, i.e., "the moment of passage between philosophy as Master's discourse, the philosophy of the One that totalizes the multiplicity, and anti-philosophy which asserts the Real that escapes the grasp of the One."[35] The problem of integral philosophy from a Žižekian perspective in particular (and the theological turn in Continental philosophy in general) is that to the extent that the all-encompassing vision provided by an integral framework (e.g., AQAL) glosses over this irreducible gap in the heart of the Absolute itself (Schelling), it becomes a fiction of all-encompassing primordial harmony, or a fantasy of Kosmic balance that obfuscates the antagonistic darkness within the Godhead itself. That is, the systematic aspirations of integral philosophy can tend toward a domestication or covering over of the fundamental antagonism of the Real by establishing a global harmony of perspectives that incorporates everything in its comprehensive embrace, whereas for Žižek "there's a crack in everything/that's how the light gets in" (Leonard Cohen).

In other words, the key integral motif of the *Aufhebung* (transcend and include) that accounts for the emergence of higher stages of development in integral philosophy masks the more original Hegelian/Schellingian notion of an irresolvable conflict or strife at the founding gesture of the self-becoming of the Absolute, i.e., the passage through a pre-ontological madness in emergence of a rationally ordered universe of Logos. In the same way, the standard Wilberian dialectical vision-logic that tries to contain everything within its borders lacks the genuine negativity or the insurmountable trauma at the heart the self-development of Spirit from Eckhart to Boehme to Schelling. It is this insight into the fundamental rupture in the Real, and how a crucible of divine disruptive darkness constitutes the emergence of freedom and human consciousness (Schelling) that has been developed recently in post-Hegelian radical theology,[36] while also showing up in what is today called the "Non-All," a wide-ranging contemporary attempt of recent Continental philosophers to twist free from the grip of metaphysics (see below).

In Žižek's alternative reading of the German Idealist tradition (which is itself one of the formative influences of integral philosophy), the driving force of the Kosmos is this agonistic tension internal to the Absolute itself, a principle of ir-reconciliation where the Real always returns as the imminent gap or obstacle on account of which our cognitive maps and representations cannot ever totalize themselves.[37] As Žižek states: "dialectics is for Hegel a systematic notation of the failure of all such attempts—'absolute knowledge' denotes a subjective position which finally accepts 'contradiction' as an internal condition of every identity."[38] Hegelian reconciliation (*Aufhebung*) is not, then, the story of Spirit guiding things by its deep providential Logos that contains all reality within an overarching conceptual framework, but an affirmation of a kind of irreducible gap or incompleteness in the fabric of Being itself that cannot be totalized; where the more we look for deeper order and meaningful patterns in the universe the more the arbitrariness of phenomena and the sheer meaninglessness of our sufferings comes into merciless focus.[39]

In Žižek's contemporary "de-mythologization" of Hegel's dialectical logic, Absolute knowledge is not (the postmodern caricature of Hegel's system as . . .) a monster of conceptual clarity drawing every contingency into its grasp in the teleological advance of Sprit working itself out in human history. There is, rather, a radically contingent, fissured ontology at the very core of Hegel's System, where the Real is itself fundamentally antagonistic, out of balance and "not" at one with itself. Where for Kant the dualities, antinomies and contradictions of conceptual reasoning has to do with epistemology (e.g., the limits of reason and human understanding when faced with the Absolute, the thing-in-itself), while the standard reading of Hegel claims to have overcome this obstacle through the dialectical development of the Absolute Spirit coming to know itself in human consciousness ("substance becomes subject"), Žižek makes a far more radical/postmetaphysical gesture.

Drawing on Jacob Boehme's reading of Meister Eckhart, as well as his own eccentric reading of German idealism, in Žižek's heterodox reading of Hegel, this purely epistemological point in Kant about the limits of human reason is now an ontological point about the structure of the reality itself. It is not simply that there is some kind of limit or obstacle in human consciousness (or in external reality) to be overcome and reconciled in a higher unity of opposites via Hegel's developmental-dialectic (which is the standard reading of how Hegel resolves the Kantian dualism between the noumenal and the phenomenal). No, this irreducible tension is inscribed in the Real itself, as a tear or cut in the very fabric of things, and as a parallax gap that also informs all aspects of our imperfect knowledge. The only genuine reconciliation (*Aufhebung*) for Žižek is in the recognition that there is no proper reconciliation, the Real itself is fundamentally conflictual (Schelling), an impossible trauma (Lacan), an aporia (Derrida/Caputo), and Žižek insists that this parallax gap is not a contingent obstacle to be overcome, but goes all the way to the ontological edifice of reality itself.

On Žižek's reading, then, the Kosmic vision of integral philosophy is, in mythological terms, like the Logos (Light/Reason) that emerges from the prerational vortex of blind drives in Schelling. That is, the vision-logic of integral philosophy (i.e., AQAL as it has hitherto been modeled by Wilber) is an ideological screen trying to hide from or escape the insurmountable conflict in the heart of Being; i.e., just another version of the Big Other (Lacan) that installs itself in the socio-symbolic order and attempts to regulate meaning and action while covering over the Real of irreducible antagonism.[40] The cure, for Žižek, is to realize that "There is No Big Other" (i.e., the Death of God), to get rid of the (metaphysical) illusion that there is or ever was any overarching meta-narrative about the Kosmos that makes things make sense or guarantees the ultimate meaning of our enactments—and deal with the Real (insurmountable trauma). In other words, for Žižek there is a structure of imbalance at the heart of things that cannot be resolved, and the comprehensive grasp of integral philosophy (particularly in its more popular formulations) is just another totalizing gesture set on effacing the trace of its own impossibility; just another in a series of failed attempts in the history of philosophy to both contain and evade the traumatic gap of the Real.

Žižek's Schellingian/Lacanian reading of Hegel is, then, as far as possible from establishing a comprehensive integral framework that can "make everything make sense" (which is the explicit aim of integral philosophy)—the parallax tension or gap between perspectives is irreducible and irresolvable. In other words, the contradictions and conflicts that constitute our embodied finitude and temporality are not epistemological obstacles to be resolved by a developmental synthesis into a higher level of consciousness (e.g., by implementing an integral operating system, perhaps), but an ontological fault or incompleteness in reality itself to be embraced and affirmed. To put it simply, for Žižek, the Real is irreconcilable, and the irreconcilable is the Real.[41]

Postmetaphysics and Žižek's Christology

In order to further draw out this key point of difference between integral philosophy and the central postmetaphysical turn in recent Continental philosophy, we will now turn to the theological dimension of Žižek's writings, and particularly his radical or "Death of God" theology as outlined in *The Monstrosity of Christ: Paradox or Dialectic?* (2009) For Žižek, integral philosophy can still be charged with being metaphysical insofar as its Kosmic meta-narrative is "a frame containing all worldly antagonisms, guaranteeing their final reconciliation, so that, from the standpoint of divine eternity, all struggles are moments of a higher Whole, their apparent cacophony a subordinate aspect of the all-encompassing harmony?"[42] In other words, if the totalizing clarity of the integral vision is just another version of the Big Other, a master discourse that contains everything within its grasp, for Žižek we are to assume all the consequences of the death of God (Nietzsche/Heidegger/Derrida) and the nonexistence of the Big Other (Lacan) and resist precisely this integral temptation to construct a meta-narrative or meta-paradigm that aspires to makes sense of everything in an overarching Kosmic embrace.

In this respect, it is Christianity that provides the properly postmetaphysical gesture.[43] For Christianity is the religion of a godforsaken God, where the Incarnation and the shattering impact of the death of Christ is what Hegel called a "monstrosity"—a scandalous obstacle that resists all our attempts to make reality make sense. For Hegel (and Žižek) God incarnate (Christ) showed up on the world scene in the spectacular otherness of a diabolical monstrosity, in a way that disrupts the security of our predictable commonsense world. Not only do the teachings of Christ embody deeper internal discord than the teachings of any other religious founder or tradition,[44] the monstrosity of Christ is the sheer "inappropriateness" of a powerless, crucified and god-forsaken God—an unfathomable X so outlandish, so beyond the social consensual reality as to constitute a shattering rupture in all existing forms of meaning-making and social belonging.

As an unpredictable irruption of the impossible/Real, at the perverse core of Christianity is the paradoxical scandal of Christ crucified. For Žižek, this is an explicit expression of the death of God and the "good news" that there is no transcendent God (Big Other) behind the scenes, keeping things safe or guaranteeing the outcome of events in advance. In contrast to the tetra-evolving rainbow of awareness that constitutes Wilber's integral philosophy (where successively higher Levels of consciousness are laid down as Kosmic habits in four irreducible Quadrants while moving through Lines, States and Types toward a higher evolutionary synthesis), for these emerging radical theologies (Žižek/Caputo/Rollins) the properly Christian experience is an encounter with the genuine negativity of the Absolute itself (Schelling's *UnGrund*), as an irresolvable tension or agonistic gap in the heart of God's own self (Christ crucified), an ontological incompleteness that reveals the deep ambiguity in things and the nonexistence of the firm, impenetrable ground of the Big Other (i.e., the death of God).

In Žižek's radical post-Hegelian theology, with the experience of God (the Absolute) in the crucified Christ, we are at one with God precisely when God is *not* at one with God's self. That is, with Jesus' final words from the Cross, his cry of dereliction: "My God, my God, why hast thou forsaken me?" God incarnate loses faith and "laments that he too is forsaken by God, which means that God too is for an instant an atheist, that God doubts, that God rebels against himself."[45]

There is, then, an irreducibly atheistic moment in the genuinely Christian experience, for when we are identified with the Christ, we come to see that there is no transcendent order that can guarantee the objective meaning of our lives, but only the stark reality of God made vulnerable in the suffering and death of the god-forsaken Christ.[46] In this more radical view of "God made flesh" in Christ, Žižek fundamentally rejects the Hegelian *Aufhebung* that drives the integral impulse to "transcend and include" in a higher level of consciousness, and disavows the moment of the reconciliation of opposites in a higher unity. Instead, in following the pioneering work of Schelling, for Zizek "antagonism [is] inscribed into the very heart of God," where the Absolute is now the name for a contradiction that tears apart the very unity of the All.[47]

In Žižek's view, then, Christ is not shining metaphysical Logos that clears up all partial and fragmented perspectives in an all-embracing unity or wholeness; but a parallax gap, a dynamic point of irreconcilable tension between opposing perspectives from which new possibilities for human freedom and consciousness may spring forth. As a more radical "negation of the negation" (Hegel)—an *Aufhebung* without dialectical reconciliation, on Žižek's reading the Hegelian dialectic works not by reconciling opposites (e.g., according to the standard developmental dialectical of thesis/antithesis/ synthesis). Instead, the two opposed moments are reconciled when the gap that separates them is posited as inherent to one of the terms (e.g., the gap between God and humanity is transposed into God's own self).[48]

In drawing out the implication of this heterodox reading of Hegel, the Christ-event (the decisive self-revelation of the Absolute) is a "weird intrusion from the Real" (Žižek) that discloses an irreducible gap in the very fabric of Being itself, a shattering disturbance in the universe that de-centers all our socio-symbolic fictions, or a radical singularity that interrupts and reorganizes the landscape in ways that are not foreseeable, predictable or rule-governed. In these emerging radical theologies (Žižek, Caputo, Rollins) the crucified body of Christ is the incarnation of the death of God, the revelation that there is no theistic God "out there" guaranteeing in advance that we live in a meaningful and rationally ordered universe. Moreover, this scandalous irruption is, at the same time, the resurrection, where the site of a truth-event (Badiou)[49]is the condition of possibility for the emergence a universal collective engaged in a revolutionary struggle for justice and social transformation. In other words, with the Incarnation, the death of God (in Christ) is also the birth of the Holy Spirit: A community of believers unplugged from the Big Other and fully engaged in a public struggle for freedom and justice against the "powers and principalities" that can only pretend to universality.

This fragile absolute of the Christian legacy is also what Žižek calls a "fighting universal" where the true universality of humankind is made visible precisely in Christ's abjection, in his exclusion from the Big Other. As the site of a truth event, Christ as the charismatic individual (concrete universal) comes to us in the sheer otherness or paradoxical strangeness of a crucified God, as the abject "no-part" of the universal, as the category that humanity excludes. It is this element that has no place in the socio-symbolic structure that is the true universal for Žižek, a scandal/obstacle that disturbs the complacency of the moral order of things in a radical refusal to fit into or compromise with any preexisting power structure. With the "fighting universal," then, that which claims to be universal (the totality or whole) contains something that it cannot contain; i.e., there is always a particular (e.g., Christ) whose particularity is to be "no part" of the universal. That is, since the whole is what it is by way of exclusion (as Badiou maintains: Every time you form a totality it's because you have left something out), the true universal is the "part of no-part;" i.e., it is in the outrageous intrusion into the safe and settled ways that pretend to universality that the true universality of humankind is made visible. In other words, the universal appears as such in its singular exception, as a fragile appearance (i.e., a crucified body), and thereby forces the universal—because it has constituted itself by its acts of exclusion, to reconfigure itself.[50]

Dancing with Sophia: The Real as Non-All

We can further clarify this contrast between Žižek's neo-Hegelian death of God theology and the comprehensive, all-inclusive grasp of an integral post-metaphysics by turning to an emerging motif within the theological turn in Continental philosophy in recent decades.[51] As we have seen, in contrast to one of the basic presuppositions of integral philosophy, there is no Big Story for these thinkers; there is no overarching vision or meta-paradigm that can make sense of all dimensions of reality, or clear up all the ambiguities of human existence without remainder. Instead, reality is what's called a "Non-All" (not-whole), where an abyssal structure of ontological incompleteness goes all the way down into the very heart of what is there. The Non-All (ontological incompleteness of reality) not only exposes the undecidability and inconsistency of all our scientific and philosophical meta-narratives, but also—and more significantly—it is precisely the non-totalizability or open-ended contingency of all our integral meta-paradigms that makes things revisable and transformable.

The Non-All stems from the psychoanalytic theories of the French post-structuralist Jacques Lacan, who offers, perhaps, an alternative point of departure for integral philosophy by making a distinction between what he calls masculine sexuation and feminine sexuation. For Lacan, these two logics differentiate two ways to treat any formal system (e.g., the AQAL framework), i.e., they constitute two different approaches to the systematic impulse within integral philosophy to contain all finite, temporal perspectives in an all-embracing reach and thereby "make sense of everything."

In the first approach (masculine sexuation), every contingent, sentient being (or perspective) belongs to a given order of being (e.g., it has a Kosmic Address) except the necessary Being or principle that constitutes or orders it (e.g., the AQAL framework itself). In other words, not everything can be a finite, relative or partial perspective: There must be something outside the totality of things, an exception to the order that is also beyond all the elements within it, which is able to ground the totality. The God of classical theology is a well-known example of this masculine logic, where a given a totality of contingent beings (creation) is sustained by a constitutive exception (Creator) that is beyond the totality—i.e., there is a supreme being exempt from the totality that sustains the totality.

This logic of masculine sexuation is also evidenced in the systematic aspirations of integral philosophy. Even with the nuances of its postmetaphysical coordinates and its methodological pluralism (Wilber V), the AQAL framework is often explicitly deployed as a kind of overarching or constitutive exception that stands over and above everything that it contains, as a meta-paradigm that grounds and orders all other paradigms and perspectives within the borders of its Kosmic address system.

According to this view, the fundamental problem with integral philosophy is that by presupposing and working within this logic of masculine sexuation, an integral approach "always already" imposes its framework on absolutely everything that it encounters in this multidimensional Kosmos. So rather than approaching each and every other (sentient being, perspective, etc.) in its "this-ness"—i.e., as a finite, irreplaceable singularity (Levinas, Derrida, Caputo), integral philosophy welcomes what is (wholly) Other only as an auxiliary, as a secondary derivative to be assimilated and consumed by its pre-given frame of reference, in a self-serving move that functions by reaffirming its own higher authority.

That is, the temptation of integral philosophy is to respond to the critical insights of Continental philosophy outlined here (ontological incompleteness, parallax gaps, the Real as irreducible antagonism) simply by apprehending these themes on the basis of its own governing framework (e.g., by situating post-structural hermeneutics within a Kosmic address system that allocates it to a lower level of consciousness: postmodern pluralism). However, this move only diminishes and flattens the opening of integral philosophy to the irreplaceable singularity of what it encounters in the world. Each and every other (or sentient being) contains a uniqueness that transcends conceptual capture and therefore represents a gap in the horizon of conceptual understanding. In other words, the identity of each and every other cannot be constituted entirely by reference to integral philosophy and its Kosmic Address system (Wilber V), but contains uniquely irreplaceable elements that resist all such systems of collective designation. Or as Levinas said, "Generalization is death."[52]

For our purposes here, however, the simple point is that the Kosmic architecture established by the integral (AQAL) framework corresponds well with Lacan's logic of masculine sexuation, in that integral philosophy constitutes a meta-framework that contains and orders all other frameworks, while functioning as an implicit background against which all other perspectives are to be appropriated and evaluated.[53]

In feminine sexuation of the Non-All, on the other hand, the structuring principle of a totality (or formal system) is not powerful enough to order it.[54] What there is, in other words, is the totality of finite, contingent beings (i.e., the Kosmos), but the totality is itself "non-totalizable;" it cannot reach closure without remainder. Instead of a first being outside a totality (a constitutive exception that orders it), in feminine sexuation there is nothing outside or beyond the totality that grounds the totality. Rather, in the feminine logic of the Non-All, there is something elusive, undecidable and endlessly reconfigurable within the totality itself that means the totality itself cannot ever be totalized. That is, there is always something left outside any given totality in each and every attempt to totalize it, what is called the Non-All, where the non-totalizability of the Real denotes an aporia, an irreducible paradox within any formal system that prevents its closure while rendering the totality of things inherently incomplete.[55]

The Non-All, then, rejects the masculine logic of an integral embrace wherein multiple perspectives "hang together" in an overall self-consistent harmony (AQAL) by affirming an irresolvable incompleteness within the very structure of things that cannot be either fully mastered or extinguished. According to the logic of feminine sexuation, then, the Real is a kind of "not being at one" with oneself, whereby the engine room of the Kosmos is "always already" inconsistent or out-of-joint. From this contemporary philosophical perspective, where nothing is (or can ever be) identical with itself, the integral model (AQAL) is a provisional, historically constituted "unity of meaning" that provides the illusion of the Big Other—a fantasmic order of Being that stabilizes the flux and protects us from the promise/threat of the fundamental incompleteness of the Non-All. And so, in coming to grips with the all-important question of what integral philosophy does not encompass or include in its universal embrace, in the second half of this chapter it will be argued that integral philosophy (in its present configuration) has a tendency to foreclose or prevent the event that most or ultimately concerns it (see note 11). That is, while integral philosophy is lucid and even breathtaking when it comes to framing "what" happens both individually and collectively in human consciousness development, it is virtually silent when it comes to the critically important question of precisely "how" consciousness develops, or how it is that new forms and structures emerge in the overall trajectory of cosmic, biological and human evolution, a theme will be explored in more depth toward the end of this chapter.

Nevertheless, in *Sex, Ecology, Spirituality* (1995) Wilber attempts to come to grips with the Non-All in his IOU (Incomplete or Uncertain) principle. As a simultaneous whole/part, for Wilber every holon (or actual occasion) has a dual or contradictory tension built into its very constitution. As an autonomous whole, each holon has a drive to consistency and coherency, while as a communal part of a greater whole, each holon has a simultaneous drive for completeness. Drawing on Gödel's incompleteness theorem, the IOU principle states that the more complete (all-encompassing) any formal system is, the less consistent/coherent it will be, and vice versa: The more consistent/coherent it is, the less complete it will be.[56] This means that any formal system can be either complete but incoherent (masculine, in this context) or it can be coherent/consistent but incomplete (feminine), the more of one, the less of the other, and with no side of this contradictory tension ever finally winning the battle. In view of this intrinsic tension or contradiction within all actually existing phenomena, for Wilber the upshot of the IOU principle is that each and every holon issues a promissory note to the universe, but it is a promise that it can never deliver on: an IOU.[57]

As far as it goes, the IOU principle is structurally isomorphic with the logic of feminine sexuation and the Non-All, but only up to this point. For following this, Wilber maintains that all IOUs (holons) are redeemed in non-dual Emptiness, when consciousness awakens to the primordial Source and Summit of manifest reality.[58] This move, however, simply installs the masculine logic of the constitutive exception, where the structural incompleteness/incoherence of all finite, manifest holons is undone and subsumed in a direct apprehension of the infinite, ever-present, non-dual ground of the one and the many.[59] Non-dual Emptiness as the "constitutive exception" within which everything arises can also be witnessed in Nagarjuna's dialectical philosophy, which is founded upon the Two Truths doctrine: One of the founding gestures of Wilber's integral philosophy, from its inception in *The Spectrum of Consciousness* (1973). For Nagarjuna established his philosophical system by way of a relentless critical destabilization of every single dualistic category of thought imaginable, with the constitutive exception of the distinction between Absolute knowledge (the direct experience of non-dual Emptiness) and relative knowledge (conventional spacio-temporal reality), and it is this distinction that grounds his entire Buddhist philosophy.

That is, for Nagarjuna and other mystically oriented philosopher-sages, once one has glimpsed the non-dual ground of the one and the many, all finite things are *by comparison*, pale, incomplete, uncertain, shifting and shadowy.[60] In other words, the Two Truths doctrine is an instance of the classic metaphysical distinction between appearance and reality, a two-worlds theory where non-dual Emptiness is the primordial "always already" truth of Absolute knowledge, the constitutive exception that grounds and sustains all finite occasions in space-time; whereas all other finite, temporal phenomena, insofar as they move, have impulse, or activity, are self-contradictory.[61]

So where Wilber argues, along with Nagarjuna, that "if you don't want to be a complete self-contradiction, then you must rest in infinity"[62] (non-dual Emptiness) in view of the logic of feminine sexuation, things here are turned upside down: If you don't want to be the self-contradiction of a timeless Absolute untouched by the push and pull of contradictory forces, then you must be exposed to the trembling of the Non-All, the structural incompleteness of the Real, or the noncoincidence of the One with itself. In this reworking of the non-dual Absolute that grounds and sustains integral philosophy, this inherent tension (incompleteness or inconsistency) is not merely built into all manifest holons in the relative domain, but it goes all the way into the heart of the Absolute itself in the German Idealist tradition (Schelling's *UnGrund*, Hegel's death of God), where the Absolute is nothing but the Absolute's self-revelation in time and space, i.e., where God can only fully realizes God's self in the heart of flesh, in the midst of this built-in incompleteness/inconsistency in the heart of things.

One of the important consequences of this is that Wilber's appropriation of the German Idealist tradition in SES (volume 1 of the Kosmos Trilogy, 1995) falls well short of the pioneering insights that are to be found within this radical tradition. The very point of departure of Hegel's dialectical philosophy is to reject the Kantian distinction between Absolute truth (noumenon) and the relative domain (phenomenon), a distinction that remains at the core of Wilber's integral model in the form of the Two Truths Doctrine (Nagarjuna). Moreover, it also seems important to point out that Wilber's reading of Schelling is at best a partial appropriation of an earlier phase of Schelling's work conveniently deployed by Wilber in the service of his own developmental-hierarchical conclusions—or at worst, a serious misrepresentation of Schelling that obfuscates the antagonistic darkness within the depths of the Absolute, an insight that informs so much of contemporary Continental philosophy and the philosophy of religion.

In view of this critique of Wilber's integral framework, which is based on a contemporary (Žižekian) reading of the Hegelian *Aufhebung* and Schelling's primordial *UnGrund* (both of which inform recent trends in radical theology), there is potential here for a postmetaphysical short-circuit here between the masculine logic that informs integral philosophy and the feminine logic of the Non-All (the death of God and the nonexistence of the Big Other). For as Gödel reminds us, if any formal system (e.g., a Kosmic totality) is made to be a self-consistent whole (e.g., AQAL), then there remain fundamental truths that cannot be derived from the system itself—for instance, the insurmountable cut/gap in the heart of the Absolute. And while this comprehensive self-consistency makes the system incomplete, when the same system is made to include these other truths (the Non-All and the rupture of the Real) and thus attempts to become complete, then it inevitably contradicts itself at certain crucial points, and thus becomes open to the emergence of new configurations and creative reinventions.

Perhaps, then, this is the verge of integral philosophy, where the ontological inconsistency/incompleteness of things is not a debt that needs to be redeemed in non-dual awareness, or a problem to be solved by a comprehensive embrace of an integral philosophy, but an ontological cut in the Real itself that depicts the contingency, revise-ability, and transformability of all formal systems, including our overarching integral meta-narratives? From this perspective, it can also be seen that the incomplete/unfulfilled integral vision (i.e., the still unpublished third volume of the Kosmos Trilogy) is not so much the loss of a transcendent ideal that sustains us, but a never-finished production of what is always, already "to come" . . .

The feminine logic of the Non-All is also crucial to a wide range of other thinkers on the verge of philosophy and theology in contemporary continental philosophy, and provides an unpredictable opening for the future of integral philosophy, a still-unexplored trajectory only hinted at in Wilber's (still forthcoming) Kosmos Trilogy.[63] We have already seen that it is central to Žižek's neo-Hegelian/Lacanian account of the Real as a parallax gap, which itself stems from Schelling's *UnGrund* and the inner antagonism in the primordial depths of the divine.[64] The Non-All is also pervasive in Catherine Malabou's deconstructive reading of Hegel, which pushes contingency and temporality into the heart of the dialectical self-development of the Absolute. With her signature notion of "plasticity" as the self-transforming, self-shaping, self-reforming structure and function of the human brain, Malabou re-reconfigures the Absolute (Hegel) in terms of a Non-All, which makes porous the distinction between consciousness (interior) and the brain (exterior). For Malabou, the brain is an open system that cannot be formalized or totalized (i.e., Non-All), where things become what they are by refusing to submit to a model, i.e., by being un-programmable and by being exposed to the future as an unforeseeable, unpredictable "to come" (*l'avenir*).[65]

In *The Future Christ: A Lesson in Heresy* (2001),[66] Francois Laruelle makes use of the Non-All by making a distinction between the outdated tradition of Western philosophy, which totalizes and only pretends to universality (metaphysics), and what he calls "non-philosophy," which is caught up in the non-totalizable or uncontainable multiplicity of life within the sphere of radical immanence. For Laruelle, the central figure of non-philosophy is the heretic, which represents the pure inconsistency of the human that is "always, already" enfleshed in the place of radical resistance to those regional hegemonic powers that pretend to be universals. The heretic is engaged in a profound ontological struggle of the human against everything that tries to capture, dominate, control, regulate, subjugate, normalize, subordinate or rule the human, and in breaking the grip of the totalizing gesture of metaphysics that can only foreclose the sphere of radical immanence (e.g., with two-worlds theories of transcendence, etc.), the heretic reveals the human *as such* in its non-consistency, irregularity and irreducibility; what Caputo calls "the Real with a human face."[67]

Integral Postmetaphysics and Derrida's Deconstruction

Another name for the Non-All is what Jacques Derrida called *différance*, the ever-shifting play of differential spacing within which we derive all our relatively stable "constituted unities of meaning" (e.g., AQAL).[68] For Derrida, we are always already situated within the effects of différance, which is a non-concept (quasi-transcendental)[69] that precedes and sets up the very "conditions of possibility" for establishing meaning and signification, including the categorical distinctions that structure integral philosophy (interior/exterior, singular/plural, levels/lines, states/stages, etc.). Derrida's deconstruction deploys the destabilizing effects of différance (which in French means to both differ and to defer) to expose the internal inconsistency (Non-All) in the very constitution of all our fundamental concepts and the instability that inscribes all our institutional beliefs and practices, in order to delimit the dominance of the traditional logocentric, theological, hierarchical, and metaphysical way of thinking about reality.

With a relentless questioning of the persistent desire in the Western metaphysical tradition to arrest this endless play différance with some deep ontological structure as certain grounds for timeless truth and unchanging meaning (e.g., the "myth of the given," or the "metaphysics of presence"), Derrida's deconstruction is a way of twisting free from metaphysical determinations by showing that all our conceptual formations are forged in the economy of culture and the contingencies of history and rest on "a delusion and non-respect for their own condition of origin."[70]

Integral postmetaphysics (Wilber V) responds to the fundamental critique of Derrida's deconstruction, firstly by celebrating the deep resonance between deconstruction and negative theology (mysticism), and then—more importantly—by jettisoning any deep ontological structures from its representations. Specifically, integral postmetaphysics replaces the levels of on the Great Chain of Being with the notion of Kosmic habits.[71] In an IPM, the stratification of the different levels of Reality in the premodern Great Chain cosmology (matter, life, mind, soul, spirit) is not based on a "myth of the given" (i.e., independently existing realities) but rather these levels of consciousness are now considered habits, or tendencies laid down by evolution through creative repetition, as relatively stable grooves that have emerged through time. The notion of Kosmic habits is a significant contribution to any form of postmetaphysics that seeks to take the cosmic, biological and human context of modern evolutionary science as its point of departure. Rather than postulating any preexisting ontological structures (Logos), the levels of consciousness in integral philosophy have emerged within the Kosmos and evolve in time, so much so that the evolution of higher stages of consciousness is itself wildly unpredictable and open-ended: We produce what we are repeating, and we invent what we are discovering.

Nevertheless, there are still a few things that integral postmetaphysics must postulate in advance (as involutionary givens) in order to explain anything that happens in evolution, and as such, integral philosophy still ascribes, at least minimally, to the ontological structures of metaphysics, i.e., the primary object of the deconstructive critiques of postmodernity (Heidegger, Foucault, Derrida, Deleuze). For Wilber, the Kosmos requires at least three involutionary givens in order to get itself going, i.e., three ontological structures that must be given in advance prior to the beginning of time (e.g., before the Big Bang): 1) Eros (Whitehead's gentle persuasion toward love, self-organizing principles, etc.); 2) Logos (e.g., the Twenty Tenets, the patterns that connect across all domains of evolution); and 3) Cosmos (AQAL as a game board or space-time matrix).[72] So while structure-stages of consciousness (archaic, magic, mythic, rational, etc.) are no longer pre-given realities, but Kosmic habits or time-honored evolutionary patterns/grooves laid down over past epochs, the evolution of these structures of consciousness themselves depends of still other ontological givens: Eros, Logos, and Cosmos.[73]

From here, however, Wilber employs the dialectical vision-logic of integral philosophy to affirm an irreducible multiplicity of indigenous perspectives, i.e., the equi-primordiality of the four zones (interior/exterior, singular/plural) and thereby argues that this goes a long way toward overcoming the Derridean challenge. Since integral theory deliberately refuses the "either/or" dualities (value-hierarchies) that constitutes the founding oppositions of Western metaphysics, and instead affirms the "both/and" dialectics of vision-logic, where one quadrant is neither reduced to, nor elevated over any other, it can be argued that this irreducible multiplicity of primordial perspectives at the heart of integral philosophy is dynamic and fluid enough to evade Derrida's deconstructive critique of any centered structure that stabilizes the differential flux.

However, the founding categorical distinctions of integral philosophy still fall prey to deconstruction, for Derrida's différance is not to be equated with such dialectical difference (irreducibly multiple, equi-primordial or otherwise). That is, the pure form of the play of differences first deployed in Heidegger (Being/beings) was deformed by Derrida in the direction of a more radical (post-structural) hermeneutics by divesting it of either a dialectical opposition (where the differences derived are still subsumed in a higher unity or synthesis), or any deep grammar (e.g., first-person, second-person, third-person perspectives, etc.), which is precisely what underpins the four quadrants and their associated eight zones.[74]

In other words, while this kind of dialectical difference (e.g., the equi-primordiality of the zones, the holonic whole/part nature of the Kosmos, both/and vision logic, etc.) is fundamental to the very constitution of integral philosophy, for Derrida any form of difference that is based on dialectical opposition is still just one species of difference. That is, this specific kind of dialectical difference is itself an effect of the more unsettling differential spacing of Derrida's différance, which precedes and sets up the very conditions of possibility for distinguishing between binary oppositions such as interior/exterior, singular/plural, and so on. In other words, différance is not something we (or Derrida) invented (e.g., the conceptual clarity of AQAL), but a fundamental situation in which we find ourselves. As the enabling condition of all our philosophical concepts, différance is always already at work destabilizing the metaphysical decisions that constitute our fundamental categories and rupturing the way in which oppositional tensions are structured.

In deconstruction, then, the Alpha and Omega of any Kosmic totality (Spirit, Being, Consciousness) is split by difference all the way to the core.

This means that our metaphysical categories are divided in their very constitution and cannot be so easily stabilized or fixed in place, i.e., they are structured by an aporetic tension (impossibility/paradox), and thereby remain un-totalizable and undecidable. As such, Derrida exposes the totalizing clarity of the great metaphysical systems of the past as futile attempts to master the un-masterable, to fix the endlessly sliding meaning of conceptual oppositions and freeze the play of linguistic differences. As Rowan Williams also attests, "[O]ur pigeonholes for things, people, emotions, and perceptions are often lagging well behind the fluidity of the real world, with its subtle rapid interactions and puzzling quality."[75]

Moreover, while it is precisely these dialectical opposites and value-hierarchies that constitute the most powerful conceptual distinctions in integral philosophy (e.g., interior/exterior, states/stages, levels/lines, pre/trans) and thereby become potential targets of a deconstructive critique, Derrida's deconstruction opens up another, more risky way to probe and examine limits of thought after the end of metaphysics. Instead of the standard metaphysical way of thinking about things in terms of wholes and parts, where the particular instance (perspective) is circumscribed or captured by its universal (quadrant, level, etc.), in deconstruction we are always already haunted by a radical singularity, solicited by an irreducible otherness and brought up short by an undecidable paradox (aporia) that cannot be assimilated, encompassed or appropriated within a single overarching narrative.

As Caputo maintains, in deconstruction the truth is there is no Truth, which means there is no deep structure at the heart of things that is able to stabilize the endless differential play of forces.[76] We are not hardwired to underlying architecture of the Kosmos, since we have no direct access to reality except through différance, Derrida's anonymous quasi-transcendental structure of radical difference and radical temporality. Therefore, while it can be argued that the conceptual formations of the integral AQAL framework do indeed avoid the pitfalls of "either/or" logic of many strands of traditional metaphysics and its time-honored propensity to divide things into mutually exclusive opposites (a legitimate target of Derrida's deconstructive strategy)—even when it deploys a dialectical form of "both/and" vision-logic to carve out its fundamental vocabulary, the AQAL framework is itself just another constituted unity of meaning that is beset by the differential spacing of différance (the Non-All). In other words, even with its second-tier version of dialectical vision-logic, integral philosophy still betrays the structural inconsistency and undecidability of its fundamental concepts. For the AQAL vocabulary is forged by way of a series of clear and powerful distinctions that constitute the fundamental categories of the integral framework (e.g., interior/exterior, autonomy/communion, states/stages, etc.), where the meaning of these fundamental categories is then taken for granted and presupposed. However, a deconstructive reading is able to show, in spite of the powerful explanatory distinctions that constitute integral philosophy, that each side of these fundamental binary oppositions is "always, already" contaminated by the other—thereby rendering any fixed or stable meaning that is attributed to these concepts as nothing more than a contingent effect of a non-totalizable play of differences, rather than something that is simply present or given in any self-evident way.

For Derrida, then, the founding distinctions established by integral philosophy (inside/outside, singular/plural, states/stages, etc.) once exposed, are permeable, mobile and reconfigurable. By showing that those fundamental distinctions that constitute the vocabulary of integral philosophy (AQAL) simply cannot be maintained with rigor and transparency, a deconstructive reading can make us aware of the inherent fissures, gaps, and incompleteness in the way we forge these categories. For everything that is constituted within an endless play of differential traces can be de-constituted, and in the same way, just as any formal rule-governed totality (the AQAL framework) is a finite system, différance is itself non-totalizable. However, such deconstructive interventions are not meant to create relativistic chaos but, as Caputo argues, deconstruction keep things from getting too safe; it keeps hope alive and keeps the cut of difference and temporality open and vulnerable to what Derrida calls the absolute future (*l'avenir*): The unforeseeable, unpredictable, and unknowable future as an event that shatters "the comfortable horizons of expectation that surround the present."[77]

So in spite of many nihilistic and relativistic assumptions to the contrary, the fundamental impulse of integral theory to reinvent things for the future is precisely what Derrida's deconstruction is all about. As Derrida says, the least bad definition of deconstruction is "an experience of the impossible,"[78] where the impossible is an experience of something unforeseeable that traumatizes and shocks us—the in-coming of the wholly Other that interrupts the circle of the same. For this reason, the experience of the impossible has the structure of the "to come" for Derrida, where the impossible comes to us as an irruptive event that we cannot see coming from within the given order of things. The "to come" in Derrida is not, to be sure, the future present as a horizon that you can plan for or anticipate (e.g., a higher stage or state of consciousness to be enacted by a rule-governed program of practical injunctions), but an unconditional affirmation of the absolute future as something that we cannot see coming, and which has the structure of a radically unexpected event that shatters the established horizons of what's possible.

With Derrida's heretical phenomenology, the experience of the impossible is also an experience of the absolute paradox (*aporia*) of the un-deconstructable.[79] As an event that interrupts our horizons of identificatory knowledge, the un-deconstructable is a solicitation, a laying claim to us of a call, an unconditional address or call from the irreducible singularity of the Other that slips away from the comprehensive grasp of any Kosmic address system. As an experience of the "possibility of the impossible," the un-deconstructable is therefore a "qualitative intensification of an immediate and pressing demand,"[80] what Derrida also calls the undecidability (aporia/paradox) of our fundamental religious concepts (gift, justice, forgiveness), in a pure experience of faith; a faith without belief and beyond the horizon of the normalizable, the programmable, or the calculable.

In Caputo's quasi-religious appropriation of Derrida, as soon as you know for sure who it is that calls you out of yourself, and as soon as you are sure where you're going by seeking to make everything turn on clear-cut distinctions (e.g., the distinction between prerational and transrational, the way up and the way down, the post-conventional saint and the pre-conventional heretic, a democratic nation and the rogue state), i.e., as soon as you think you have a handle on these value-hierarchies, then things soon become too safe and settled. In other words, when the powerful distinctions that constitute the unity of integral philosophy become hardened and self-certain, they arrest the play of differences and thereby foreclose on the event that is harbored in its name, the singular risk of the "to come," the incoming of the unforeseeable future. For Derrida, then, the un-deconstructable is never a matter of just the application of a rule or program (i.e., the practical injunctions of a Kosmic Address system) for the event that is harbored in the name integral (i.e., evolution becoming conscious of itself: see note 11) does not exist, but rather it insists—as a passion for the impossible, an unexpected irruption that is structurally unforeseeable, or the open-ended venture of what Caputo calls the promise/risk.[81]

This unconditional affirmation of the future breaks absolutely with the constituted normalacy of the rule-governed and the programmable, for the future can only be anticipated in the form of an undecidable risk, where the promise of the "to come" is made in the midst of a threat, where the horizon of what is possible is unhinged by the impossible, and where there are no guarantees that all will work out for the best.[82] As the ambiguity of an event at the very limits of human experience, then, the un-deconstructable is the very structure of hope and expectation, not a hope or expectation in this or that determinate belief-system (to be verified by the three strands of good knowledge), but a passion for the impossible, or a hope against hope that keeps the future open—and a hope that is not immune from secretly hoping that the Truth never shows up.[83]

Integral Philosophy on the Verge: A Fragile Absolute

The unprecedented event that is harbored in the name of integral is "evolution becoming conscious of its self" (see note 11). The discovery that we are part and parcel of a 13.7 billion–year process of cosmological, biological, and sociocultural evolution has wide-ranging implications for the formation of a postmetaphysical philosophy (and spirituality). This evolutionary epic, which has only recently become conscious of itself in our species through the discoveries of modern science—is marked by radical contingency, chaotic instabilities, disruptive symmetry breaks, catastrophic decimations, and wildly unexpected bursts of creative novelty (punctuating long period of relative stasis)—in an unfinished process that has most likely only just begun, and is also, perhaps, moving toward an unimaginable and unforeseeable future. And while the deeper implications of this discovery are still to be fully unpacked[84] a dialogue between integral philosophy (Wilber V) and the post-Hegelian radical theologies (Žižek, Derrida, Caputo, Laruelle) that are emerging in contemporary Continental philosophy leads to some intriguing new possibilities for an integral philosophy on the verge, as well as some specific suggestions for further inquiry.

Given the new evolutionary context for our understanding of spirituality in the postmodern world, as well as the radical theological turn in recent Continental thought (the death of the transcendent God), integral philosophy is on the verge when it is "always already" at risk and exposed to the unpredictable earthquake that is harbored in its name, i.e., the undecidability and "the dread of the new," which is evoked in us by the singular event of evolution becoming conscious of itself. In coming to grips with this relatively recent and unprecedented event of evolution becoming conscious of itself, from the perspective of deconstructive postmodernity and radical theology, the heretical impulse of integral philosophy is therefore likely to lay in a destructive longing for final clarity, in which all tensions and ambiguities are eliminated; a totalizing vision that brings forth the monsters of religious and political idolatry.

The critical question to be asked here, then, is: What does integral philosophy (in its currently existing form) exclude or leave out of its picture of the Kosmos? Wilber and virtually all integral theorists openly acknowledge that even the most fully developed integral philosophy is itself incomplete, provisional and "true but partial," i.e., awaiting newer and higher dawns in the future, etc. So in response to the basic drift of the logic of the Non-All set out here and the subsequent critiques that have been levelled against it here, integral theorists are (for the most part) acutely aware that they are working with a revisable and open-ended system, and would therefore readily accept that there is a coefficient of contingency and uncertainty woven into its totalizing and aspirations.

So again, what does integral philosophy fail to deliver upon? What does it tend to foreclose or disavow? The provocative (yet tentative) suggestion to be made here is that while integral theory does well in explaining the "what" of evolution becoming conscious of itself (i.e., what happens in the evolution of matter to life to mind, etc.), the one thing integral cannot explain is the "how" of evolutionary transformation, particularity in our own species. That is, integral philosophy, virtually since its inception, has failed to come to grips with what is the critically urgent and profoundly significant question of how consciousness evolves, i.e., how do we set up the conditions of possibility for bringing about, enacting and embodying a deep shift or qualitative transformation in human consciousness (both personally and culturally)?

The suggestion here, then, is that by failing to come to grips with the question of "how" human consciousness undergoes evolutionary transformation, the real danger for integral philosophy is that it has become too safe. That is, without the logic of the Non-All, the effects of which are always unpredictable and un-programmable, an integral approach becomes immunized against the promise/risk of the unforeseeable future (Caputo) and prevents the transformative event that it explicitly seeks to embody. The central post-structural argument in contemporary Continental philosophy concerning the Non-All (the non-totalizability of all formal systems in Derrida, Lacan, Deleuze, Foucault, Badiou, Žižek, and Caputo) not only challenges the prevailing tendency of integral philosophy to keep everything contained within its holarchically organized developmental boundaries (as dynamic as the boundaries of vision-logic purport to be), it also puts into question the built-in propensity of integral philosophy to cover over or prevent any deep rift in the structure of things. On the other hand, the feminine logic of the Non-All keeps these simmering tensions, fractures, and ambiguities alive. It does not resolve these tensions into the firm and fast categories of an IPM with its all-encompassing Kosmic Address system, thereby making everything predictable, decidable and calculable. Instead, the Non-All opens up a gap and lives with these undecidable tensions in a way that keeps the future open to the incoming of the event.

And in this sense, the fundamental categories and distinctions of integral philosophy (AQAL), particularly when they're implemented and enacted in systematic and rule-governed ways, are not simply false; rather, they are too strong, too determinate and too powerful in their attempt to stabilize an endless differential flux that can itself never be totalized. By functioning as a kind of Kosmic filing and ranking system, Integral philosophy is, in the end, ultimately at risk of constituting a model of consciousness development that accounts for too *little* of the complex dynamics of history and irreducible ambiguities of our lived experience. In this respect, the strategy of post-structural hermeneutics and deconstruction is to consistently show integral (and other) philosophies that its fundamental categories, its esteemed developmental value-hierarchies and its privileged conceptual formations, cannot be maintained without foreclosing on the possibility of the impossible, the radical singularity of evolution becoming conscious of itself, i.e., the very event that gave rise to the name of integral philosophy in the first place.

So in order to keep the future open to the singular event that integral philosophy aspires to contain: Evolution becoming conscious of itself (which is itself a critical threshold in the process of Spirit's self-actualization), we can here begin by briefly outlining an alternative conception of Spirit or the Absolute, in the light of the insights already set out above. For when it comes to the question of the Absolute—as either primordial Emptiness within the Eastern Enlightenment traditions or the transcendent God of the Judeo-Christian tradition ordering all things for the best with his all-seeing, providential eye—it now seems that both of these notions have run their course and need to be revised.

From its earliest inception in Wilber's published works, the Absolute has been construed in terms of non-dual awareness or the direct apprehension of unqualifiable Emptiness that is itself untouched by time and space. On the other hand, in the standard Hegelian frame, the Absolute Spirit loses itself in temporal manifestation, works itself out via a dialectical process of reconciling opposites and overcoming dualities through various world-historical epochs, and then returns to itself in the Absolute's knowledge of itself as the Absolute Spirit.

The important point here, however, is that there can be no event, no explosive singularity or unexpected shock in either of the two major options that inform integral philosophy as it currently stands. Firstly, literally nothing ever happens in non-dual Emptiness (as the Great Unborn it is untouched by time and space). So as an initial first step, then, and in beginning to shift integral theory toward the feminine logic of the Non-All, we can begin by jettisoning Wilber's enduring reliance on primordial awareness and follow the lead of Hegel by reconfiguring the Absolute as constitutionally, inherently and intrinsically *temporal* (which is precisely why Hegel was considered as atheist by Lutheran theologians). That is, the Absolute does not fall into time from a timeless Eternity, the Absolute is time temporalizing itself, the world worlding itself, where Spirit is nothing but its own incarnation and en-fleshment within the vicissitudes of finitude and temporality. For Hegel, then, there is no timeless or preexisting Absolute Spirit "behind the scenes," making sure everything turns out for the best, but rather "the finite existence of mortal humans is the only site of the Spirit, the site where Spirit achieves its actuality."[85]

However, even in Hegel's dialectical logic, where the self-development of the Absolute is fully inscribed within time and space, it is still the case that there can be no event, for nothing can absolutely surprise or shock the Absolute. The Absolute Spirit goes out of itself and returns to itself in time, making explicit what's implicit, and actualizing its potential in accordance with the dialectical logic of the developmental process (AQAL framework, the Twenty Tenets, self-transcending Eros, etc.). That is, no matter what happens in the contingent, temporal process of world-historical becoming, one way of another, the Absolute is guaranteed in advance to return to itself as the Absolute. So again, there can be no event or unforeseeable rupture in the self-actualization of Hegel's Absolute Spirit. For so as long as the Absolute follows this developmental unfolding wherein Spirit gradually realizing itself through the standard Hegelian dialectic of the "transcend and include" (*Aufhebung*), things are too safe and predictable, too rule-governed, and always already bound by a fundamental framework in which the Absolute guarantees that everything is working out for the best.

However, by drawing on the more marginal tradition being explored here that stems from Meister Eckhart, and then moves through German Idealism and onto the radical theologies emerging out of contemporary Continental philosophy, we can now begin to see what a reconfiguration of the Absolute might look like. Firstly, there is a shift away from the primordial peace of Wilber's non-dual awareness towards Hegel's Absolute as fully inscribed within the spacio-temporal universe. But then we need to make a further shift away from the standard reading of Hegel, where everything is guaranteed in advance and into the feminine logic of the Non-All, where it is the ontological incompleteness in things that exposes us to the incoming of the event, and opens up the "possibility of the impossible" (Caputo) as a shattering rupture of the Real that resists the totalizing aspirations of integral theory.

As an alternative order or rule for the unpredictable emergence of new forms and structures, the proposal here is that by way of this decidedly more feminine logic of the Non-All, integral philosophy may truly begin to dance with Sophia. And as such, the event that is promised in the name of integral philosophy is ruled not so much by differential relations within the stable conceptual determinations of an integral framework, but more by an elliptical openness to the fragility and incompleteness in things, or a poetics of paradox that can speak the unspeakable while unsaying what it says—while simultaneously putting its own assumptions into question in a full-blooded embrace of the ambiguity and undecidability of those unpredictable events at the very limits of human experience . . .

The cutting edge of evolution becoming conscious of itself, according to the feminine logic of the Non-All, is therefore the promise/risk of an event that comes to us as something we can't see coming. And as such, it resists inscription in any formal system; for as soon as we get our conceptual teeth around it, or appropriate it and make it our own, we cover it over and immunize ourselves from the riskiness and unpredictability of the "to come." That is, the radical singularity that stirs within the name integral is structurally unforeseeable, which means that the event does not constitute the conditions of possibility for the further evolution of human consciousness: It interrupts or deconstitutes its conditions of possibility with the incoming of the impossible. The transformative event that integral names, then, is the shattering of the horizon of what is foreseeable by the unforeseeable, the breaking open of the horizons of what's possible by the impossible, where the "to come" is not what we can see coming up ahead, but precisely what takes us by surprise as something unimaginable, un-programmable and non-totalizable.

The important question to be asked here, then, is: Is Integral on the edge-of-chaos, exposed to the irruptive singularity of "evolution becoming conscious of itself" and capable of interrupting and reconfiguring the existing horizons of meaning and action that currently constitutes the further reaches of human consciousness development? Does integral keep us on the verge, on the edge of experience, exposed to the irreducible gap or paradoxical tension (aporia) at the heart of things, or is it too rule-governed and predictable, while protecting itself against the ambiguity, undecidability and the non-programmability of the Non-All with the all-consuming reach of its masculine logic? That is, Does integral philosophy keep us off-center, in disequilibrium and sensitized to the precariousness of life—as well as self-critical enough to be worried about how the totalizing aspirations of an integral embrace always leave something out, while simultaneously understanding our responsibility to the event that solicits us? In other words, is integral philosophy, if it is to remain on the verge, a philosophy "to come"?

In this sense, one version of the radical singularity that potentially reconfigures integral philosophy may be the Absolute paradox of the Incarnation, where the Absolute is nothing but the risky venture of God's self-embodiment in Christ. As radical theologians from Hegel in the nineteenth century to Caputo and Rollins in the twenty-first century attest, the decisive self-embodiment of Spirit is a monstrosity of prodigious proportions, where Christ is the abject one, ripped out of the political, the cultural and the religious spheres of human existence, and where God actually becomes more fully God only by being made vulnerable to the senseless nightmare of meaningless suffering and death.

Moreover, as we saw previously with Schelling's *UnGrund*, there is ontological turmoil and pain in the very coming-into-being of God. It's the same with the Incarnation—and the radical theological turn in Continental philosophy, for here also the Absolute must undergo its own Golgotha in order to become actualized. In this respect, Caputo emphasizes how radical the death of God is in Hegel's philosophy—once we suspend its overarching metaphysical framework in which the end of the process is guaranteed in advance, when he writes: "[C]ould God, unawares, step on an explosive? Could God be blown to bits without so much as knowing what hit him?"[86]

In other words, in order for there to be a future for God, for Caputo "God would have to be exposed to the final and uttermost risk of death,"[87] where this death would be something more than a transitional moment in a developmental dialectic (i.e., the masculine logic of integral philosophy). And is this not precisely what we see in the Christ-event, where God incarnate is exposed to the possibility of irreversible extinction in the process of Spirit's own self-actualization? The radical singularity of evolution becoming fully conscious of itself that integral aspires to is also, then, the embodied story of God on a cross and the divine madness of an event that is marked by the irreducible ambiguity of a promise/risk and the non-programmability of our fundamental decisions, i.e., where one's passion for life is structured by its exposure to mortality and death, where there is no guarantee that an unconditional gift might not be an unmitigated disaster—and where the horizons of what's possible is unhinged by the impossible . . .

In this sense, then, perhaps the synthesis (or higher level of consciousness) that integral philosophy sets out to accomplish is not so much a comprehensive Kosmic embrace that aspires to contain all worldly conflicts within its overarching meta-framework, but an antagonistic gap or paradoxical tension in the Real that refuses any proper resolution from within the existing order of things, i.e., something altogether otherwise than the seamless clarity of a higher level of consciousness that makes sense of everything in a vision of totalizing clarity? For just as we see in radical theology and the central Christian experience of the death of God, perhaps there will be no deep or abiding reconciliation, integration or peace so long as we persist in looking for a unified or seamless picture of our lives, which our consciousness can take in without the difficulty of painful and irreconcilable contradiction. In confronting this irreducible antagonism of the Real, then, perhaps for there to be an event, or a rupture of the Real in integral philosophy, things also need to be exposed to the possibility of an unmitigated failure and death—where the only integration we can achieve in this life is found in acknowledging of our own failure to achieve integration? And isn't this precisely how contemporary Continental philosophy now understands the most influential precursors to integral philosophy in the German Idealist systems of Schelling and Hegel?[88]

For as these German mystic-philosophers, as well as the more recent contemporary thinkers consistently show us, the event that integral philosophy actually gives voice to is not the "blinding sun" of Christian Neoplatonism, with its high-altitude vision, but the "face of the deep" of Catherine Keller's postmodern process theology. And moreover, this dark precursor at the verge of integral theory is not the ideal of being "at one with everything," but the ordeal of an event astir within being[89]—an event that slips through the grasp of our conceptual schemas as a shattering disturbance in the very fabric of reality that refuses to make things make sense. And given this shift toward the darker, more feminine texture of the Non-All, what if the brilliant clarity of the integral AQAL framework is simply a form of systematic regulation, moderation and balance, i.e., the very form of homeostasis and moderation that forecloses on the irruptive event that integral philosophy harbors in its name?

This raises and underlines once again the all-important question here: Does integral philosophy prevent the event that simmers at its heart—evolution becoming conscious of itself? And if this is indeed the case, then does its exposure here to the feminine logic of the Non-All (Lacan), the non-totalizability of all formal systems (Derrida), the ontological incompleteness of reality (Žižek), the fundamental antagonism in the depths of the divine (Schelling/Hegel) and the call of contemporary radical theology to be exposed to the trembling in things (Caputo/Rollins/Keller)—does all of this amount to a radical break in the very constitution of integral philosophy as it stands today? And if so, then does the "disruptive novelty" of consciousness transformation—as the event that integral aspires to contain, now comes to us as the shattering rupture of the Real that resists any full articulation or enactment from within the coordinates of existing order of things in integral philosophy?

Notes

1. Derrida (2005), 157.
2. Wilber (1995), 72–73.
3. Wilber (1995), 419–420.
4. As Wilber and others have argued, it is important to keep in mind here that the discourse about the "end of metaphysics" can itself be framed as a grand meta-narrative, i.e., another overarching (metaphysical) story about the history of Western philosophy from Plato to Nietzsche. Significant here is Derrida's critique of Heidegger in his essay *The Ends of Man*, where Heidegger's quest to overcome metaphysics by invoking the primordial opening or clearing of Being among the pre-Socratic philosophers is still dominated by the lexicon of traditional metaphysics: "an entire metaphorics of proximity, of simple and immediate presence, a metaphorics associating the proximity of Being with the values of neighbouring, shelter, house, service, guard, voice, and listening" (Derrida [1982], 130).
5. Caputo (2000), 1. As Heidegger argues, the whole history of Western metaphysics is one or another of a long series of failed attempts to "master the Real," to grasp the meaning of Being under the forms of one or another set of ontological structures (e.g., Platonic *Ideas*, Aristotelian *Substance*, Cartesian *Cogito Sum*, Spinoza's *Causa Sui*, Trinitarian *Logos*). Heidegger calls this history of metaphysics in the West a series of various constellations of "onto-theology," which he

unmasked as a philosophical project that itself was constituted by the forgetfulness or the oblivion of the more primordial question of Being. And where Heidegger attempted to uncover the lost origin of Being in the pre-Socratic philosophies of ancient Greece, soon after Derrida's deconstruction hammered in the last nail into the coffin of metaphysics by doing away with the search for any "deep structure" or "transparent essence" altogether.

6. Caputo (2010).

7. The primary focus of this paper is the integral philosophy pioneered by Ken Wilber and culminating in what is commonly called integral postmetaphysics (Wilber V). However, in recent and more sophisticated developments of integral theory by Sean Esbjörn-Hargens, integral philosophy has shifted focus from this more popular model of representing a Theory of Everything (integral monism) to a post-formal, more nuanced and more contextualized version of a Theory of Anything (integrative pluralism) involving the development of an integral ontological pluralism, and the intricate relations between "who" (epistemological distance), "how" (methodology variety) and "what" (ontological complexity)—particularly in relation to climate change. The implications of this shift may be more than just semantic; however, they will not be explored in great detail in this paper. (For more, see Fuhs [2010].)

8. As Wilber states in regards to the comprehensive and all-inclusive reach of his integral philosophy: "I'd like to think of it as one of the first believable world philosophies, a genuine embrace of East and West, North and South" Wilber (2000), 17.

9. Integral postmetaphysics (Wilber V) is outlined in Wilber (2006a) and Wilber (2006b).

10. The notion of "Kosmic habits" also displaces the binary structure of the quadrants (interior/exterior, individual/collective) as primordial. In a more recent extension of integral philosophy by Clint Fuhs, perspectives are said to be more primordial than the quadrants, and even within quadrants there are sundry different perspectives that come into play with higher development. At the same time, it can be argued that any given perspective (first-person, second-person, third-person, etc.) presupposes an interior and an exterior, for a perspective is always a perspective on something, just as consciousness (in phenomenology) is always consciousness of something. So while the distinction between quadrants and perspectives can become fluid and somewhat arbitrary at this point, this displacement of the quadrants into perspectives does begin to dissolve the rigidity and solidity of the quadrants as primordial givens. For more, see Fuhs (2010).

11. In the context of this essay, integral philosophy is the name given to an event, where the event that is harbored within the name of integral philosophy is "evolution becoming conscious of itself," i.e., the 13.7 billion year–process of cosmic, biological and human evolution becomes aware of itself for the first time in our species (as far as we know) about two hundred years ago. This understanding of evolution as Spirit-in-action in the emergence of human freedom and consciousness

was first recognized by Schelling, Hegel, and the German Idealists and then taken up by all of the key pioneers of Integral philosophy: Whitehead and Teilhard de Chardin, as well as Sri Aurobindo, Jean Gebser, and most recently Ken Wilber.

12. Žižek (2009), 27.

13. Žižek, et al. (2011). According to Žižek, Hegel's thinking was marginalized by much of French and American analytic philosophy in the twentieth century to such a degree that he eventually becomes a scarecrow who represents the dark shadow side of Western colonialism and imperialism. This fake Hegel can be seen in Levinas's critique in *Totality and Infinity*, in Jacques Derrida from the mid-1960s to the late 1980s, and in Gilles Deleuze.

14. Wilber (1995), 486.

15. Schelling quoted in Zizek (1996), 16. The central problem for Schelling is not how, in a universe of inexorable natural laws, freedom is possible, but how this abyss of primordial freedom becomes entangled in the casual chains of reason.

16. Žižek (1996).

17. Schelling, cited in Žižek (1996), 22, note 11.

18. Koysko (2008), 53.

19. Žižek (1996), 2.

20. Žižek (1996), 1.

21. The reference here is to the Gospel of John: "In the beginning was the Word/Logos."

22. Schelling, cited in Žižek (1996), 31.

23. In Schelling's original German, the word *contracts* here is meant in the dual sense of both "harden/condense/concentrate" as well as "contracting" a disease (Kotsko [2008], 53).

24. Kotsko (2008), 53.

25. Žižek (1996), 23, 32.

26. Žižek (2006), 17. The blind rotary motion of God prior to the pronouncement of the Word is not yet temporal, for time would already presuppose that God has broken free from the *UnGrund* of antagonistic drives. The common expression *from the beginning of time* is to be taken literally here for Žižek: it is the Beginning, the primordial act of decision/resolution, which allows for the linear succession of time to begin.

27. Žižek (1996), 42.

28. This lineage stems from Eckhart's more heretical and incarnational Christology, not his Neoplatonism.

Žižek (2009) argues that what made Eckhart's work so shocking to the medieval Church was his claim that since it is of the very essence of the Son (Logos) to enable God to manifest himself, it is humanity itself that gives birth to God; what he called the "birth of the Son" (32–33). It is precisely this ex-centricity of God's own self, on account of which God needs man in order to actualize God's self that raised the attention of the pope, as Schurman writes of Eckhart's heretical teachings: "while one's [human] being has a center outside of it, i.e., in God, God's (being) too has a corresponding eccentricity;" i.e., a center outside himself (cited by Davis in Žižek [2009], 3).

29. For instance, "[I]f we were able to penetrate the exterior of all things, we would find that the true stuff of all life and existence is the horrible" (Schelling, cited in Žižek [1996], 24, n.15.) Increasingly, in his later years, Schelling emphasized the irrational (real) out of which reason (the ideal) emerges: *Order and form nowhere appear to have been original, but it seems as though what had initially been unruly had been brought to order. This is the incomprehensible basis of reality in things, the irreducible remainder which cannot be resolved into reason by the greatest exertion but always remains in the depths. Out of this which is unreasonable, reason in the true sense is born. Without this preceding gloom, creation would have no reality; darkness is its necessary heritage.* Schelling (1936), 34.

30. Schelling (1936), 35.

31. And in the same way, human beings are constituted by this abyssal turmoil; it is in the passage through this pure untrammeled freedom that one chooses their phenomenal character and thus enters the temporal world with a certain kind of identity. With this inquiry Schelling launches his own highly original inquiry into the problem of evil and human freedom. Schelling (1936).

32. Wilber (1995), 32–43.

33. S. Žižek, "Preface: Hegel's Century," in Žižek, Crockett, and Davis (eds.) (2011, ix–xi).

34. While the Lacanian Real may initially appear to be synonymous with non-dual awakening (i.e., there is no Big Other), for Žižek the Lacanian Real as trauma also implies the impossibility of direct or unmediated access to any kind of pure presence or primordial peace (e.g., non-dual awakening), i.e., the structural incompleteness or irreducible antagonism at heart of reality itself. And while Wilber continually insists (especially in his early works) that the synthesis provided by an integral philosophy is indeed a kind of substitute gratification to be relinquished and dissolved in unqualifiable emptiness, the precise relation between the Lacanian Real and non-dual realization remains an intriguing topic of comparative research and inquiry.

35. Ibid.

36. See the works of John D. Caputo, Catherine Keller, Slavoj Žižek, and Peter Rollins.

37. Žižek, et al. (2011).

38. Žižek's thesis was originally submitted to *Le plus sublime hysteriques: Hegel passé* (C. Davis, "Introduction," in Žižek, Crockett, and Davis (eds.) (2011, 6). The notion that contradiction is an internal condition of every identity is congruent in some ways with Wilber's claim that all holons contain four contradictory tensions or drives: agency vs. communion, and eros vs. agape. Integral philosophy here acknowledges the post-structural insight that an internal tension or contradiction

constitutes every identity in its depiction of the holonic nature of reality, although the subsequent interpretations of this interior tension take different directions. For example, these contradictory forces are still very much self-identical and mutually exclusive in the conceptual formations of the AQAL framework, whereas these oppositions tend to be more ambiguous or inextricably intertwined in contemporary forms of postmetaphysics, where the hard-and-fast distinctions of integral philosophy (such as interior/exterior, individual/collective, states/stages or levels/lines) are more fluid, more porous and tend to bleed into each other.

39. In Ken Wilber's collected body of writings, there is a notable example of this primordial cut/wound or rupture in the very fabric of the Real in *Grace and Grit: Spirituality and Healing in the Life and Death of Treya Killam Wilber* (Wilber, 1992), a profoundly moving love story that follows the journey of Wilber and his second wife, Treya, as she battled and eventually succumbed to cancer, a cancer that was first diagnosed within weeks of their first meeting and just days after they got married. *Grace and Grit* is a singular text in Wilber's voluminous writings, for it is his only published work that simply "suspends" the ever-evolving and systematic impulse of integral philosophy (from his first book, *Spectrum of Consciousness*, published in 1973, to Wilber [2006a]) in its all-encompassing quest to provide the most comprehensive map of reality currently available. In departing from the integral impulse that drives Wilber's other theoretical writings, and in what many claim to be Wilber's best published work, the agonistic darkness that we see in Schelling's *UnGrund*, and the principle or ir-reconciliation (or the parallax gap) we see in Žižek's (Lacanian) reading of Hegel, is depicted here in one of the most anguished and heart-wrenching passages in the book:

> From the top of this tower I could see for perhaps a hundred miles in all directions . . . I looked up: Heaven; I looked down: Earth. Heaven, Earth; Heaven, Earth. And that's what started me thinking of Treya. In the past few years she had returned to her roots in the Earth, to her love of nature, to the body, to making, to her femininity, to her grounded openness and trust and caring. While I had remained where I wanted to be, where I myself am at home—in Heaven . . . the Apollonian world of ideas, of logic, of concepts and symbols. Heaven is of the mind, Earth is of the body. I took feelings and related them to ideas; Treya took ideas and related them to feelings . . .

Wilber goes on to describe the more "formal" non-dual union of opposites that underpins integral philosophy:

> In the traditions, Spirit is found neither in Heaven nor in Earth, but in the Heart. The Heart has always been seen as the integration or the union point of Heaven and Earth, the point that Earth grounded

> Heaven and Heaven exalted the Earth. Neither Heaven nor Earth alone could capture Spirit; only the balance of the two found in the Heart could lead to the secret door beyond death and mortality and pain.

With this non-dual union of Heaven and Earth—and this precious embodiment and realization of what conscious love means in an integral approach, Wilber then undoes this non-dual union and exposes us to the shattering impact of the Real as a traumatic intrusion that resists all our existing forms of language and signification: "I kept thinking, as my eyes looked up, looked down. With Treya, I thought, I am beginning, just beginning to find my Heart. *And Treya is going to die . . .*" (Wilber [1992], 304, italics added).

40. The Big Other is any sociohistorical linguistic structure or communal network of social institutions, customs and laws that secure the objective meaning of our lives, assuring us in advance that things are working out for the best (e.g., the Church, Communism, Capitalism, the Nation, Historical Necessity, Spirit, Gaia, Integral philosophy, etc.

41. Caputo (2009), 9.

42. Žižek (2009), 49. While Wilber counters this charge by replacing the ontological structures of the Great Chain of Being with the notion of Kosmic Habits laid down by evolution, his integral philosophy is still within the most dominant metaphysical tradition of Western philosophy: e.g., Plato's Cave and the movement from fleeting, shadowy appearances to the timeless light beyond, or from chaos to order, from the simple to the complex, or from the sensible world to the supersensible world (Neoplatonism), i.e., from the fragmented world of postmodernity to the integral vision.

43. See Žižek's theological works: Žižek (2001), Žižek (2003), and Žižek and Milbank (2009).

44. Freeman (2010).

45. Caputo and Alcoff (2009), 14.

46. As Catholic author G. K. Chesterton maintains:

> "In this indeed I approach a matter more dark and awful than it is easy to discuss . . . a matter which the greatest saints and thinkers have justly feared to approach. But in that terrific tale of the Passion there is a distinct emotional suggestion that the author of all things (in some unthinkable way) went not only through agony, but through doubt . . . When the world shook and the sun was wiped out of heaven, it was not at the crucifixion, but at the cry from the cross: the cry which confessed that God was forsaken of God (Matthew 7:46 quoting Psalms 22:1). And now let the revolutionists choose a creed from all the creeds and a god from all the gods of the world, carefully weighing all the gods of inevitable recurrence and of unalterable power.

> They will not find another god who has himself been in revolt . . . Nay (the matter grows too difficult for human speech), but let the atheists themselves choose a god. They will find only one divinity who ever uttered their isolation; only one religion in which God seemed for an instant to be an atheist." (2014), 344

47. 49.

48. Žižek (2006), 106. To further explain this new reading of Hegel in relation to one of the basic presuppositions of integral philosophy, it is not that Spirit is first whole, then lost itself in manifestation in time and space (i.e., the involution of the One into the Many), and then made whole again in a return to Spirit (i.e., the evolution/return of the Many to the One) as either an integral "growth towards goodness" or a retro-Romantic "recaptured goodness" model. Rather, for Žižek, the healing and wholeness that is available to us comes by erasing the "transcend and include" involution/evolution scheme at the core of integral philosophy altogether and by getting rid of the idea of being whole to begin with. We get ourselves into trouble by imagining we were once whole, but then lost this original innocence, and that we need to return/recapture this lost wholeness. Rather, the dialectical move here is to see that the antithesis (loss) is "always already" the synthesis (innocence): There is no wholeness to get back or return to. The Hegelian "negation of the negation" here leaves us not with an affirmation (higher synthesis), but with an even deeper negation: We negate the notion that something was lost, and face up to the disorientating rupture in the very fabric of what is. In other words, we don't become whole (integral), we lose the loss, i.e., we relinquish the search for an original innocence that was once lost (in involution) and that needs to be regained (evolution); i.e., we accept that there is an irreducible gap or traumatic cut at the very heart of things that cannot be overcome or resolved.

49. For more on the emergence of Christianity as a "truth-event" in postmodern philosophy, see Badiou (2003).

50. Caputo (2010b), lecture 11: on Žižek's *Parallax View.*

51. Caputo (2010b), lecture 10: on Brassier's *Nihil Unbound.*

52. Levinas (1991), 27.

In seeking to break the grip of the all-consuming logic of masculine sexuation, one proposal for bringing integral philosophy into a deeper accord with the feminine logic of the Non-All would be to make integral philosophy visible to itself from the outside. The task here would be to reverse the primary relationship between integral (which sees itself as representing a comprehensive and inclusive synthesis of all existing knowledge) and its Other (the partial, fragmented, unbalanced and unreconciled). That is, instead of looking at everything in the world through its own all-encompassing frame of reference, what if integral philosophy was able to de-center itself by looking at itself from the perspective of that which it considers strange, different and even the incongruent? And here, once we suspend the self-justifications about higher levels of consciousness stemming from second-tier elitism, for those outside the sphere of integral philosophy, its various conceptual formations, such as AQAL framework (as well as its more recent mutations), are likely to show up as incomprehensible, alienating, convoluted and insular, i.e., anything but integrated.

53. In a similar vein, as a meta-perspective on the class of all perspectives, the AQAL model is also implicit again in the Lacanian notion of a symbolic Big Other that orders any sociolinguistic system by erasing the trace of its own structural incompleteness or inherent impossibility, where in so doing the Big Other pretends to grasp an unshakable foundation or deep structure at the heart of things (AQAL) and thereby achieve (the illusion of) a kind of mastery over the Real.

54. Caputo (2010b).

55. Ibid.

56. Wilber (1995), 502.

57. Ibid., 503.

58. Ibid., 505.

59. Wilber (1995): "Emptiness is the reality of which all wholes and all parts are simply manifestations . . . the groundless Ground, the empty abyss, that never enters the stream of endless IOU's, that never lives the transfinite nightmare of ceaseless contradiction" (505–506). Now, this is not to deny the authenticity of the stateless state of non-dual consciousness, but simply to question its ontological and epistemological status as Absolute truth (the union of Form and Emptiness), based upon Nagarjuna's two truths doctrine.

60. Wilber (Ibid.), 501.

61. While it must always be kept in mind that un-qualifiable Emptiness (non-dual awareness) is not a concept, but a direct apprehension of an ever-present reality in the immediacy of primordial awareness, the status of the Absolute in integral philosophy (non-dual awareness) is founded upon precisely the kind a "two-worlds" metaphysics that has been deconstructed by virtually all major thinkers in the Continental philosophical tradition since the beginning of the twentieth century. For more on this central problematic of the non-dual as the union of the Absolute (timeless) and the relative (time), see *Integral Spirituality*, especially Appendix II, as Wilber writes: "Even if Spirit is defined as the union of Emptiness and Form (where Emptiness is timeless, unborn, un-manifest, and not evolving, and Form is manifest, temporal, and evolving), the 'temporal' or 'world-of-Form' part puts stress on the meaning of Enlightenment that is not easily remedied" (Wilber [2006a], 236).

62. Wilber (1995), 502.

63. As Wilber suggests toward the end of *Sex, Ecology, Spirituality* (1995):

> In volume 3, I attempt to explain this IOU principle in much greater detail, and this is meant only as a brief introduction. I attempt to show that agency across time and communion across space, as the two fundamental "drives" of all holons (on a given level) show up in various fields as, respectively: time and space, coherence and correspondence,

> rights and responsibilities, etc. . . . the central point is that these typical dualisms (such as coherence vs. correspondence in epistemology) are dual partners forever fated to battle it out with each other . . . and never, never win. (Wilber [1995], 506)

64. The feminine logic of the Non-All is also evidence in the quantum revolution in twentieth century physics, where matter is not a totality: It is a Non-All. Clearly quantum physics works in a way that is strange, odd or perplexing in the light of our normal experience of reality. In accordance with the standard materialist ontology of contemporary science, matter is indeed all there is, but "matter" is a Non-All—i.e., something fragile, questionable, undecidable, a provisional unity full of spaces, gaps, voids and openings. Where Einstein resisted the implications of the Non-All (e.g., "God doesn't play dice"), the drift of contemporary physics is toward unpredictable and random indeterminacy, i.e., the direction of feminine sexuation. Moreover, mathematical theory also affirms the Non-All (Gödel: formal systems are non-totalizable; also see Cantor on set theory), and the later Wittgenstein also moved in this direction: Discourses follow rules, but there is no meta-language, just a multiplicity of games that cannot themselves ever be formalized or totalized.

65. Malabou (2004).

66. Laruelle (2001).

67. Caputo (2010b), lecture 1: Intro to Derrida and on Derrida's *Of Grammatology*.

68. Derrida asks, "[H]ow is it that philosophy finds itself inscribed . . . within a space which it seeks but is unable to control . . . How is one to name the structure of this space?" (Derrida [1983], 45).

69. As a quasi-transcendental, différance is not a transcendental in the strong Kantian sense where a transcendental specifies the conditions of possibility under which something happens. Rather, Derrida is interested in interrupting the conditions of possibility under which something happens, where the real conditions under which something happens are the conditions of not possibility, but of impossibility.

70. Derrida (1996), 139.

71. Wilber (2006b).

72. Wilber (2006a), Appendix ii on integral postmetaphysics.

73. Moreover, while more recent versions of integral philosophy may differ (see notes 7 and 10), the fundamental distinctions of AQAL theory (interior/exterior, singular/plural) that structure the evolution of form also constitute a "myth of the given" in IPM in the sense that the Kosmos comes into being with these indigenous perspectives (the four Quadrants) already at work, they go all the way down, and already exist at the beginning of time.

74. Caputo (2010b), Lecture 1: Introduction to Derrida's *Of Grammatology*.

75. Williams (1995), 100. In this collection of sermons, Williams deals head-on with the centrality of paradox in the journey toward God. The title phrase, borrowed from the fifth-century Syrian Dionysius, captures both the luminosity

that occurs when God "interrupts our blindness and ignorance" (100) and the disorientation that comes when this very illumination cuts through our familiar sense of ourselves. Far from making everything clear, the encounter with God makes everything unfamiliar, and Williams affirms that this sense of bewilderment is essential to Christian discipleship. He desires "a discipline that stops me taking myself for granted as the fixed center of a little universe, and allows me to find and lose and re-find myself constantly in the interweaving patterns of a world I did not make and do not control" (101).

76. Caputo (2000).

77. Caputo (2001), 8.

78. Derrida (2007), 15. To be precise, as Caputo maintains, "*the* impossible" refers not to a logical but to a phenomenological impossibility—a horizon-shattering structure of human experience.

79. Caputo (2007).

80. Ibid., 191.

81. Caputo (2013).

82. Caputo (2010b).

83. Caputo (2010b).

84. The second and third volumes of Wilber's projected three volume Kosmos Trilogy are currently unpublished, although large sections of Volume II are available at Wilber (2006b).

85. Žižek (2009), 287.

86. Caputo (2013), 131.

87. Ibid., 133.

88. Žižek (2012). Significantly, this proposal for integral philosophy to embrace the feminine logic of the Non-All does not constitute another binary opposition or value hierarchy. Žižek's ontological incompleteness is instead the parallax gap from which both masculine and feminine logics of sexuation emerge as explanatory constructs and is nothing less than an attempt to understand the Real as the failed attempt. As Zizek states: "However, it would be too easy to simply privilege the 'feminine' non-All and to reduce the 'masculine' totalisation through-exception to a secondary illusion—here, more than ever, we should insist on (sexual) difference itself as the primary fact, as the impossible Real with regard to which both positions, "masculine" and "feminine" appear as seconder, as two attempts to resolve its deadlock (ibid., 934–935).

89. Caputo (2011), 39.

References

Badiou, Alain. 2003. *Saint Paul: The Foundations of Universalism*. Stanford, CA: Stanford University Press.

Caputo, John D. 2000. *More Radical Hermeneutics: On Not Knowing Who We Are.* Bloomington, IN: Indiana University Press.

Caputo, John D. 2001. *On Religion.* New York: Routledge.

Caputo, John D. 2007. *What Would Jesus Deconstruct?: The Good News of Postmodernity for the Church.* Grand Rapids, MI: Baker Academic.

Caputo, John D. 2009. Review of Slavoj Žižek and John Milbank, *The Monstrosity of Christ: Paradox or Dialectic? Notre Dame Philosophical Reviews.* http://ndpr.nd.edu/news/24179-the-monstrosity-of-christ-paradox-or-dialectic/.

Caputo, John D., Linda Alcoff (eds.). 2009. *Saint Paul Among the Philosophers.* Bloomington, IN: Indiana University Press.

Caputo, John D. 2010. "The Gap God Opens." http://www.booktalk.org/the-gap-god-opens-by-john-caputo-t10017.html.

Caputo, John D. 2010b. Online Lecture, Fall 2010 (audio), at http://trippfuller.com/Caputo/Fall2010%20Caputo/.

Caputo, John D. 2011. "The Return of Anti-religion: From Radical Atheism to Radical Theology." *Journal of Cultural and Religious Theory* 11: 32–124.

Caputo, John D. 2013. *The Insistence of God: A Theology of Perhaps.* Bloomington, IN: Indiana University Press.

Chesterton, G.K. 2014. *The Everlasting Man.* Nashville, TN: Sam Torode Book Arts.

Derrida, Jacques. 1982. *Margins of Philosophy*, trans. Alan Bass. Chicago: University of Chicago Press.

Derrida, Jacques. 1983. "The Time of a Thesis: Punctuations From." In *Philosophy in France Today*, ed. Alan Montefiore. New York: Cambridge University Press.

Derrida, Jacques. 1996. *Of Grammatology*, trans. G. Spivak. Baltimore, MD: Johns Hopkins University Press.

Derrida, Jacques. 2005. *Rogues: Two essays on Reason*, trans. Pascale Anne-Brault and Michael Nass. Stanford, CA: Stanford University Press.

Derrida, Jacques. 2007. *Psyche: Invention of the Other, Volume 1*, trans. Peggy Kamuf and Elizabeth Rottenberg. Stanford, CA: Stanford University Press.

Freeman, Cameron. 2010. *Post-Metaphysics and the Paradoxical Teachings of Jesus.* New York: Peter Lang.

Fuhs, Clint. 2010. "An Integral Map of Perspective-taking." In *Integral Theory in Action,* ed. Sean Esbjörn-Hargens, 273–302. Albany, NY: SUNY Press.

Kotsko, Adam. 2008. *Žižek and Theology.* London and New York: T&T Clark.

Laruelle, François. 2001. *The Future Christ: A Lesson in Heresy*, trans. Anthony Paul Smith. London and New York: Continuum.

Levinas, Emmanuel. 1991. *Otherwise Than Being or Beyond Essence*, trans. Alphonso Lingis. Dordrecht, NL: Kluwer Academic Publishers.

Malabou, Catherine. 2004. *The Future of Hegel: Plasticity, Temporality and Dialectic.* New York: Routledge.

Schelling, F.W.J. 1936. *Philosophical Inquiries Into the Nature of Human Freedom*, trans. James Gutmann. LaSalle, IL: Open Court.

Wilber, Ken. 1992. *Grace and Grit: Spirituality and Healing in the Life and Death of Treya Killam Wilber.* Boston: Shambhala.

Wilber, Ken. 1995. *Sex, Ecology, Spirituality.* Boston: Shambala.

Wilber, Ken. 2000. *One Taste: Daily Reflections on Integral Spirituality.* Boston: Shambhala.

Wilber, Ken. 2006a. *Integral Spirituality: A Startling New Role for Religion in the Modern and Postmodern world.* Boston: Shambhala.

Wilber, Ken. 2006b. *The Kosmos Trilogy*, Volume II, at http://www.kenwilber.com/professional/writings/index.html.

Williams, Rowan. 1995. *A Ray of Darkness.* Plymouth, UK: Cowley Publications.

Žižek, Slavoj. 1996. *The Indivisible Remainder: An Essay on Schelling and Related Matters.* London and New York: Verso.

Žižek, Slavoj. 2001. *The Fragile Absolute.* London and New York: Verso.

Žižek, Slavoj. 2003. *The Puppet and the Dwarf: The Perverse Core of Christianity.* London and New York: Verso.

Žižek, Slavoj. 2006. *The Parallax View.* Cambridge, MA: MIT Press.

Žižek, Slavoj, and John Milbank. 2009. *The Monstrosity of Christ: Paradox or Dialectic?* ed. Creston Davis. Cambridge, MA: MIT Press.

Žižek, Slavoj, Clayton Crockett, and Creston Davis, C. (eds.). 2011. *Hegel and the Infinite: Religion, Politics and Dialectic.* New York: Columbia University Press.

Žižek, Slavoj. 2012. *Less Than Nothing: Hegel and the Shadow of Dialectical Materialism.* London and New York: Verso.

PART IV

Philosophy and Meta-Philosophy

Chapter 13

Sophia Speaks

An Integral Grammar of Philosophy

Bruce Alderman

Since Ken Wilber first introduced the four-quadrant model in *Sex, Ecology, Spirituality*, it has become practically synonymous with integral theory itself, and for good reason. The four fundamental perspectives around which the model is organized have yielded impressive explanatory and integrative potential. Arguably, the broad applicability and appeal of these basic distinctions is attributable to their near universality: The personal pronouns, *I*, *We*, *It*, and *Its*, representing the first-, second-, and third-person singular and plural perspectives of the quadrant map, are grammatical distinctions common to most major languages. As Wilber notes, these pronouns encode within our natural languages "four major dimensions of being-in-the-world;" four ubiquitous ways of perceiving and relating to reality.

Wilber is not the first to build a philosophy around the personal pronouns, as I will explore later in this chapter. While it would be limiting and simply incorrect to describe integral theory as a "pronoun philosophy" in any *exclusive* sense, I would nevertheless like to hold up integral theory as an exemplar of this form of philosophy for the purposes of this discussion. I would like to highlight Wilber's place in the lineage of thinkers who have reflected on and mined the pronouns for their metaphysical and epistemological implications. If anything, integral theory demonstrates the rich philosophical, pragmatic, and meta-paradigmatic yield of taking a common grammatical category, which is found across most human languages, as a central organizing lens or metaphor.

But in noting and celebrating the fruitfulness of such an approach, we must confront at once also its limitation: It focuses on only one of several possible grammatical categories, each of which is arguably just as common to our human languages, and each of which may have similarly rich metaphysical yields. If employing pronouns as a central organizing principle enables us to generate a metaphysics of sentient beings or a postmetaphysical philosophy of perspectives, for instance, what might we expect to find if we were to place nouns or verbs at the center, or adjectives, adverbs, or prepositions? A broad survey of philosophy from the perspective of multiple grammatical lenses, in fact, makes it clear that many philosophical systems have been implicitly or explicitly organized around one or another of the major parts of speech. Importantly, especially for those interested in integral theory as a "theory for anything" or as a form of "integral methodological pluralism" (IMP), the deep grammatical commitments or foci of these traditions, and their relationships to each other, are not things readily disclosed when we rely upon the pronouns alone—or even their extension to the eight zones of IMP.

In an article advocating for a more verbal, process-oriented reading of integral theory, for instance, Bonnitta Roy (2006) has noted that the first-, second-, and third-person lenses at the center of the integral model are insufficient, in themselves, to disclose the deeper metaphysical view in and through which first-, second-, or third-person research is pursued and articulated. In particular, these lenses alone cannot account for the different territories enacted by structural or process-oriented metaphysics. In contrasting her preferred "pure process" view with the commonly nounal character of substance metaphysics and structuralist orientations, she emphasizes the need to shift to a more verb-centered language. We will return to her specific arguments about this later in the chapter, when we are reviewing various verb-oriented metaphysics; for now, I would like only to note that we already have, here, the suggestion of *at least three* possible grammatical-philosophical approaches: a pronoun-centered perspectival epistemology; a noun-centered metaphysics of things or structures; and a verb-centered metaphysics of processes or events. But, while Roy (2006) emphasizes that the structural and process views are deeper than the perspectival lenses that comprise the quadrants, and thus are not explicitly disclosed by them, I will argue that all are also related, in that each employs and organizes itself around a particular grammatical category or metaphor.

In this chapter, then, I would like to review a number of the major philosophical approaches or metaphysical systems that have developed around each of six basic grammatical categories: pronouns, nouns, adjectives, verbs, adverbs, and prepositions.[1] As I have already suggested above, these approaches range from various perspectival epistemologies, to substance, process, or relational metaphysics, among others. When considering these systems alongside one another, we may be led, in integral fashion, to perceive each as true but partial: As necessarily limited in scope, but still delivering important and irreducible truths. In this way, I hope to demonstrate the merit of expanding the integral model beyond its pronoun focus, to enact a broader integrative approach employing multiple grammatical lenses. But as I will discuss below, each grammatical-philosophical system in itself can also be a site for integral theorizing: Just as the pronouns can be used as a base to construct a broadly integrative model, so can nouns, verbs, or other grammatical elements. As we will see, both object-oriented (nounal) and process-oriented (verbal) philosophical systems, for instance, have already realized their own integral formulations. Thus, the six grammatical lenses or philosophemes I will introduce here can be understood from two perspectives at once: *Collectively*, as true-but-partial elements of any comprehensive philosophical system; and *individually*, as unique, generative centers around which a number of philosophical models and emergent integrative metatheories have been organized.

With these distinctions in mind, I will introduce two new terms to frame and guide our explorations: *onto-choreography* and *heno-ontology*. I will save fuller discussion of the former term until the end of this chapter, when I will review the ground we have covered and will reflect on various integrative metatheories that have been proposed. But in brief, by onto-choreography, I mean the integrative task of weighting and coordinating the grammatical elements or philosophemes into various metaphysical systems. How do these ontological elements dance together in the different philosophical models we will consider here? This question is related also to the second term I have coined, heno-ontology, by which I mean a meta-philosophical approach that allows for metaphysical pluralism, both across stages of development and even at the same level of development. As in henotheism—where multiple gods are recognized, but only one might be worshipped at a given time as supreme, depending on the circumstance or the proclivities of the devotee—I intend here to evoke an ambiguous field of multiple possible ontologies and integrative lenses, a chthonic matrix with a shifting absolute (which, in each "form" that it manifests, may be seen to enfold in its own way certain of the qualities of the other "deities"). This is not an argument for the full equality of each choice of metaphysical or ontological center, however, or of the integrative models they may support. Each has its weaknesses as well as strengths, and I will review a number of them in the discussion to come. But rather than arguing for the ultimate superiority of one metaphysical or integrative model over all others, I prefer to adopt a meta-metaphysical, heno-ontological approach: A robust, speculative, experimental form of philosophical engagement that does not shy away from, but rather embraces and enacts, metaphysical pluralism.

Before beginning a selective review of philosophers and metaphysical systems associated with each of the grammatical lenses I have identified, I would like to preface this discussion with a brief look at grammar from the point of view of cognitive linguistics. The arguments I will be developing in this chapter do not require acceptance of a particular theory of grammar, but I recommend the cognitive linguistic model for its emphases on embodiment and empirical inquiry, which are consistent with the postmetaphysical commitments of integral theory.

A Postmetaphysical Prolegomenon

The cognitive theory of grammar, rooted in second-generation cognitive science, rejects earlier formalist and Cartesian models of grammar as unempirical and as at odds with current neuroscientific evidence for the embodiment of mind. As Lakoff and Johnson (1999) argue in their seminal text, *Philosophy in the Flesh*, the formalist and Cartesian assumptions behind Chomsky's influential theory of grammar, for instance, are evident in its positing of an autonomous, generative syntactical mechanism that exists independently of meaning, memory, perception, communication, culture, and embodied enactment or behavior—i.e., as a neurally instantiated, but otherwise autonomous, purely formal or rational site of cognition. From a neuroscientific perspective, however, such an autonomous mechanism in the brain is a neural impossibility:

> [A] completely autonomous Chomskyan "syntax" cannot take any causally effective input from outside the syntax itself. Such a "syntax" would have to be instantiated in the brain within a neural module, localized or distributed, *with no neural input* to the module. But this is physically impossible. There is no neural

> subnetwork in the brain that does not have a neural input from other parts of the brain that do very different kinds of things. (Lakoff and Johnson, 1999, p. 480)

In contrast to the above, the cognitive neuroscientific understanding of consciousness sees cognition—and therefore conceptuality, syntax, and grammar—as inherently embodied, neurally instantiated, and nonautonomous, i.e., as arising interdependently with other neural mechanisms, in and through embodied interaction with the world[2] Francisco Varela (2000) has summarized this orientation, sometimes described as the enactive model of cognition, with four key points: Cognition is *enactively embodied*, *enactively emergent*, *generatively enactive*, and *ontologically complex*. In brief, what these points entail, respectively, is that 1) cognition is not a product of isolated, autonomous mechanisms in the brain (as modern Cartesian or formalist theories contend), and is not merely "in the head," but rather arises through, and embodies, our embodied coping with the world; 2) the global cognitive subject and the local neural structures of the brain are co-arising and co-determining; 3) cognition is intersubjectively enacted, meaning self and other are also to some degree co-arising and co-determining; and finally, 4) our understanding of consciousness is not reducible to either first- or third-person descriptions, but must involve both, in constant, co-informing circulation.

One implication of the above is that thought is not identical to "language," as some grammarians might have it, especially if we mean by language a disembodied, purely formal symbol system. Extensive empirical research has demonstrated the inseparability of cognition from sensorimotor systems of the brain, for instance, which are repurposed and deployed, via metaphorical and other extensions, to generate and support more "abstract" modes of cognition, from everyday reflection to formal philosophical thought (Lakoff and Johnson, 1999). From this perspective, then, grammar must be understood, at least in part, as an enactively embodied and emergent neural system. As Lakoff and Johnson (1999) put it,

> The grammar of a language consists of the highly structured neural connections linking the conceptual and expressive (phonological) aspects of the brain. This includes grammatical categories, grammatical structures, and lexical items. Since both semantics and phonology are grounded in the sensorimotor system, such a view of grammar makes good sense from the neural perspective. Far

> from being autonomous, grammar links these bodily-grounded systems. (pp. 498–499)

A key point of the above argument is that conceptual and phonological systems are both potentiated and constrained by embodiment, and grammar is the means by which we conjoin and coordinate these systems. Grammatical categories themselves are rooted in and grow (metaphorically) out of sensorimotor and broader social experiences, rather than being self-existing, ideal forms.

I have emphasized these points here for two reasons. First, I do not want my focus on grammar in this chapter to be understood merely as a continuation of the important, but typically disembodied and ontologically enervating, "linguistic turn" in postmodern philosophy. As I have written elsewhere (Alderman, 2012), I believe the postmetaphysical, enactive orientation of integral theory is consistent with the pragmatist "reversal" of the linguistic turn, which escapes the epistemological cul-de-sac of much postmodern theorizing by seeing language itself in ontic terms, as a performance of the real. In such a view, language becomes not simply an abstract, free-floating, strictly epistemological symbol system without any ontological depth of its own, but a living performance of, and thus also a means of transformative, participatory engagement with, the world in its ontic fullness. Grammar, understood here as embodied and enactive, can be seen as ontologically resonant and potentially revelatory.

Second, as I will discuss in more detail in the sections ahead, the cognitive grammatical descriptions of the parts of speech—namely, as radial structures consisting of core concepts with various metaphorical extensions of increasing subtlety or abstraction—will be useful in our reflections on the types of metaphysical systems that have been built upon and around the six grammatical terms I have chosen to highlight. As I noted above, the cognitive theory of grammar is not the only one that could support or guide this exploration, but I believe it is the theory most consistent with the postmetaphysical commitments of the current phase of integral thought, and in some cases, especially where there is not a clear philosophical precedent, Lakoff and Johnson's (1999) descriptions of grammatical terms will help me to justify the philosophical associations I have made with one or another of these terms.

Although pronouns are not the most common of the grammatical-philosophical roots or elements I will be discussing, I will start with them, given their prominence in integral theory. In the brief survey that follows, I will focus primarily on personal pronouns.[3]

Pronounal Philosophy: Being-as-Perspective

A pronoun, in popular understanding, is a word that *stands for* or *takes the place of* a noun. This understanding is reinforced both by the etymology of the word itself—the Latin *pro*, meaning "in place of"—and by the fact that pronouns grammatically mirror nouns, carrying similar number, gender, and case distinctions. In practice, a pronoun may function *anaphorically*, referring back to a noun that precedes it in a sentence; or *deictically*, in which case the meaning of the pronoun depends, in part, upon the extra-linguistic context in which it is uttered (such as when we point to "that" or "there," or make reference to "I" or "you"). In both cases, it is commonly understood that the pronoun, whether personal or demonstrative, is a dependent or secondary term that *substitutes for* a noun.

Philosophically, however, Charles S. Peirce (1998) has challenged this view, arguing that pronouns take precedence over nouns because they carry meaning more directly:

> There is no reason for saying that I, thou, that, this, stand in place of nouns; they indicate things in the directest possible way. It is impossible to express what an assertion refers to except by means of an index. A pronoun is an index. A noun, on the other hand, does not indicate the object it denotes; and when a noun is used to show what one is talking about, the experience of the hearer is relied upon to make up for the incapacity of the noun for doing what the pronoun does at once. Thus, a noun is an imperfect substitute for a pronoun. (p. 15)

For Peirce, then, nouns are secondary in that they always require a supplement (namely, the prior experience of the hearer). Pronouns point directly, and then nouns fill in and come to stand for what is revealed in this pointing. Wilber (2003b), perhaps following Peirce, has made a similar argument, suggesting that pronouns are best understood as *pre-nouns*, as "something prior to nouns that all nouns must follow" (p. 137). For both Peirce and Wilber, in their respective philosophical systems, *personal* pronouns in particular represent some of the most fundamental perspectives available to sentient beings: Firstness (I), Secondness (It), and Thirdness (Thou), in Peirce's early metaphysics; and the first-, second-, and third-person perspectives, or the four quadrants (I, We, It, and Its), in the later phases of Wilber's work.

Philosophically, the personal pronouns mark a space or clearing for perspectival enactment—for the manifestation and experience of first-, second-, or third-person objects. They are, as Peirce and Wilber contend, universal elements of the semiotic field, defining the space in which any encounter whatsoever must take place. As Wilber (2003b) puts it, "The relations among pronouns are relations among sentient beings wherever they arise" (p. 138).

For Martin Buber, a seminal figure in the field of pronoun philosophy, the pronouns I, Thou, and It are actually fragments of, or abstractions from, two more fundamental terms or *primary words*: I-Thou and I-It. These word-pairs denote the two basic relations available to, and constitutive of,

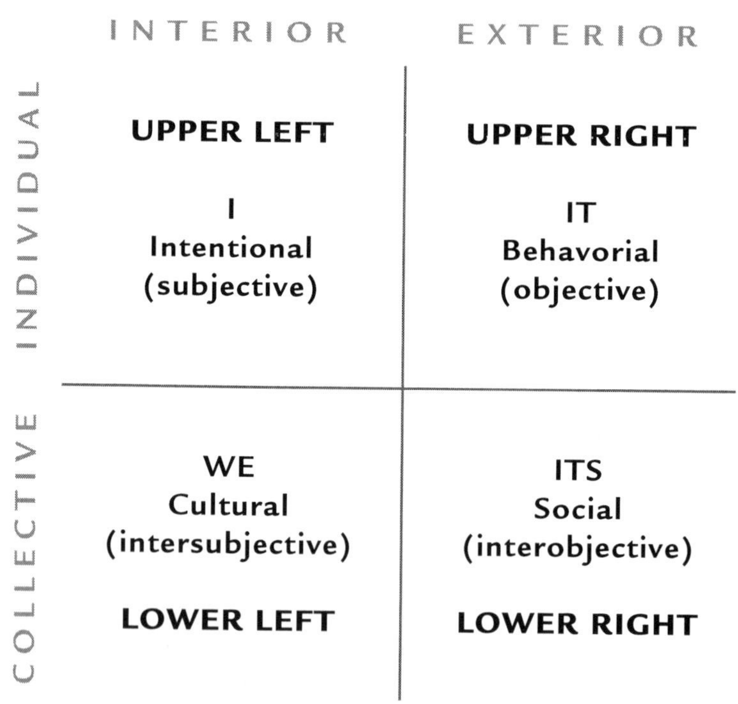

Figure 13.1. The four quadrants. *Source:* author.

human being—primary ontological and epistemological relations in which the pronominal elements are mutually defining. As Buber (1958) argues, when we say, "I," we never say the word alone, but always in relation to a "Thou" or an "It." The "I" in each case is different; the "I" that is spoken in relation to a "Thou," to the open, unbounded presence of another (or God), is of a different character to the "I" that is spoken in relation to an "It." The former relationship summons us to love and care, and is fundamentally dialogical, whereas the latter tends toward distancing and objectification and is essentially monological.

Buber's model has been critiqued as reductionist and lopsided, in that it only admits two fundamental human perspectives, and it presents the second of these (I-It) as intrinsically limited and distorting—a "cripple," as Franz Rosenzweig puts it (Batnitzky, 2000). Rosenzweig advocates instead, and at minimum[4]for a tripartite model of interdependent pronoun relations: He-It, I-Thou, and We-It (Cohen, 1994). These additional pronominal distinctions are necessary to invoke the existential and metaphysical richness of intersubjective relations, which he believes Buber inadequately represents. But Rosenzweig nevertheless joins Buber in his emphasis on intersubjectivity and the grammar of relationship as primary sites of philosophical reflection.

Of note for our discussion here, the hyphenated pronouns of Buber and Rosenzweig do double duty, philosophically, both evoking a relational *ontology of persons*, and foregrounding constitutive or co-constructive *modes of knowing*. The former emphasis on persons places their work, as both acknowledge, in the long and sprawling metaphysical lineage of *personalism*, a philosophical tradition with ancient roots in the thought of Aristotle, Aquinas, and Gregory of Nyssa, but which came to fuller flower in Europe and America in the writings of Schleiermacher, Schelling, Kierkegaard, Mournier, Maritain, Marcel, Alcott, Browne, James, and Hartshorne, among others.[5] The latter emphasis on co-constitutive modes of knowing, or perspective, anticipates the postmodern turn (as evident, for instance, in Levinas's critical engagement with, and further development of, both Buber's and Rosenzweig's models of intersubjectivity). As we will see, both emphases find echoes in Wilber's philosophy, particularly in Wilber-IV and Wilber-V.

Detailed discussion of personalist ontology is better reserved for the next section on nounal philosophy (nouns conventionally referring to persons, places, or things), so I mention it here only briefly to highlight a tension that appears in several versions of pronounal metaphysics. On the one hand, as discussed above, the abstract deictic or indexical function of pronouns has led to a philosophical focus on person-perspectives or epistemological domains, which Peirce and others have argued actually stand *prior to* nouns. On the other hand, those who philosophize about perspectives and personal pronouns typically presuppose the same underlying thing, the same ontological basis: *persons*, i.e., those *real beings* who hold perspectives and enter into relations. A personalist insists, then—typically in resistance to impersonal or idealist philosophical systems—on the irreducible ontological status and value of persons. While "I" and "you," as pronouns, are reversible abstractions or demi-abstractions—I can be a you; you are also an I—the personalist argues that these pronouns represent, are employed by, and necessarily presuppose real, ontologically distinct persons or sentient beings.

The divergent understanding of the grammatical nature of pronouns I noted at the beginning of this section—i.e., the question of whether pronouns are in some way prior to nouns, or whether they come after and substitute for them—finds expression also in pronounal philosophy, sometimes within the same philosophical system. In Wilber's (2006) postmetaphysical philosophy, for instance, he emphasizes the priority of person-perspectives, arguing that each thing *is* a perspective before it is anything else (p. 253). By this, he means that *whatever else* we might argue that something metaphysically is—whether a feeling, a dialogical relation, a perception, a material object or process, etc.—it is first, or always already, a first-, second-, or third-person perspective. To speak of, or encounter, a feeling or an atom, for example, is already to inhabit a first- or third-person relationship to reality. The emphasis, here, is on epistemology, with the personal pronouns encoding some of the most common epistemological domains. At the same time, however, Wilber (2003b) also makes the following claim:

> [A] universe comes into being, not when an inside is marked from an outside, or a before is marked from an after, but a group of sentient holons arise. Even quarks have prehension, which means, the first quark is not a first particle but a first person. And whatever that quark registers is not a second particle but a second person. (p. 141)

In arguing for the primordiality of *persons*, or sentient holons, Wilber also appears to embrace a form of personalist metaphysics, albeit more broadly conceived or globally applied than is common in most traditional personalist thought. I will discuss Wilber's personalism in more detail in the next section—and will suggest that it has, in fact, much in common with the current conception of "objects" in object-oriented ontology (OOO)—but for now I wanted just to note this dual emphasis in pronounal philosophy. While pronouns in philosophy might function as *pre*-nouns, epistemologically, they also function *for* nouns ontologically: They articulate a relational metaphysics *of* and *for* persons or sentient beings.[6]

In the remainder of this section, I will focus on Wilber's epistemological use of the pronouns, as well as several recent critiques and elaborations upon it. In contrast to Buber and Rosenzweig, who primarily explored the existential, ethical, and theological implications of pronounal relations from a Judeo-Christian point of view, Wilber aims with his four-quadrant model at more broadly philosophical and metatheoretical ends. Following Plato, Kant, and Habermas, among others, Wilber identifies three major value spheres, three major areas of knowledge and practice, which he associates with the first-, second-, and third-person perspectives (or I, We, and It).

In his four-quadrant model (see Figure 13.1 on page 398), Wilber further differentiates the exterior domain into individual and collective expressions, giving four major perspectives or dimensions of reality (subjective, intersubjective, objective, and interobjective; or I, We, It, and Its).

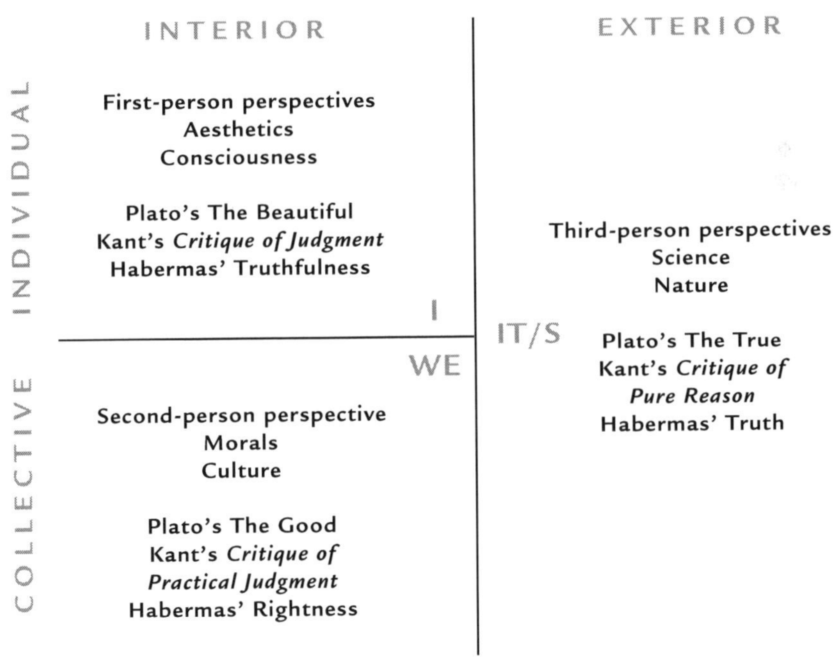

Figure 13.2. The big three. *Source:* author.

Each of these quadrant-perspectives is associated in Wilber's work with major domains of experience, knowledge disciplines, methods of inquiry, value spheres, validity claims, modes of communication, and so on, allowing for a broadly comprehensive, meta-paradigmatic map of the major modes of understanding and interfacing with reality. Assuming most readers will be familiar with the details of Wilber's quadrant model and at least a number of its more significant applications, I will not dwell on those details here, but will just note it for the particular way it employs its four personal pronoun distinctions: as elemental lenses which, taken together, disclose a complex, integrative vision of the Kosmos.

However, while Wilber's model is indeed quite comprehensive, several critics have argued 1) that it does not adequately represent all of the major socially and theoretically significant pronoun-perspectives found in human speech; and 2) that its association of pronouns or person perspectives with the quadrants is inconsistent or problematic. For instance, the observant reader will note that the lower left (interior-collective) quadrant in the figure above is associated both with the pronoun "We" and with the second-person perspective. Wilber has justified the pairing of the first-person plural pronoun, We, with the second-person perspective by pointing out that "We" includes "I" and "You" and therefore enfolds a second-person perspective within itself. Mark Edwards (2003) argues, however, that Wilber's convention of subsuming the "you" into the "we" fails to make room for second-person alterity—for You as Other. This is a distinction with significant ethical weight, as Levinas might remind us, and should not be left out of a comprehensive pronounal philosophy.[7] Similarly, the convention of representing the third person only with the pronoun, It, is equally problematic for a viable ethical or social theory, as Edwards (2003) and Dean (1996) both argue. Edwards (2003) points out the obvious ethical issues that arise from identifying foreigners or those outside our cultural or communicative circles as Its (which is an identification Wilber [2003b] has made). Along similar lines, Dean (1996) critiques Habermas's use of the pronoun, It, to represent his "neutral third" observer in a communicative situation, since the third-person observer's gender is seldom a negligible, value-neutral factor in social encounters. Both argue that inclusion of the additional third-person pronouns, He and She, is essential for any robust, ethically sensitive model of human relations.

Edwards (2003) suggests several amendments to Wilber's pronoun model: First, separating the personal pronouns from their fixed associations with the four quadrants of Wilber's integral holon, so that each can stand alone as its own holon; and second, expanding the number of personal pronouns to include You and He/She. He achieves the former, in part, by reinterpreting the quadrants, replacing the singular and plural dimensions of the map with agency and communion, and then treating singular and plural holons separately. With these moves, Edwards proposes a six-pronoun model (I, You, He/She/It, in singular and plural forms), where each pronoun can be rendered in quadratic/holonic form, as follows:

From this base, he outlines a model of forty-two common perspectives or pronominal relations. While offering a number of useful new distinctions and analytical tools, however, Edwards's model has not been widely adopted, likely because it involves a significant reinterpretation of the quadrant map. His quadratic rendering of the pronoun perspectives also appears to slide inconsistently between objective and possessive forms of the pronouns for the right-hand quadrants (using "Me" or "Us" for the upper-right quadrant

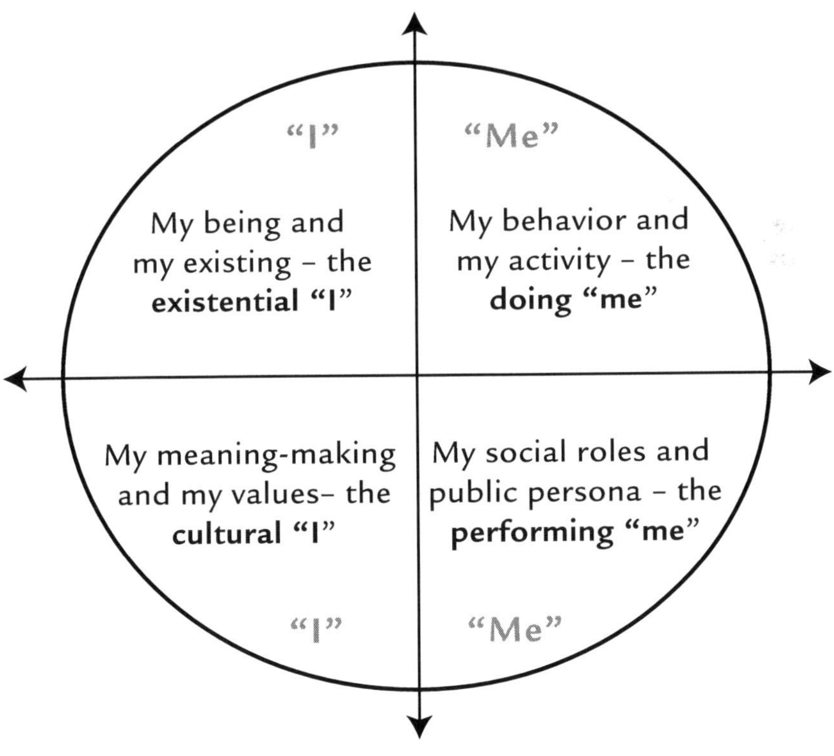

Figure 13.3. Edwards's quadratic pronouns. *Source:* Mark Edwards.

of the I and We holonic pronouns, respectively, but "Your" or "His/Her/Its" for the upper-right quadrant of the You and He/She/It holonic pronouns).

An alternative amendment to the integral pronoun model, which is more consistent with the current integral map, and also more internally consistent grammatically than Edwards's appears to be, has been proposed by Daniel J. O'Connor. Like Edwards, O'Connor (2012) separates the pronouns from their association with specific quadrants, arguing that the person perspectives and the quadrant map represent two distinct models which, while related, have been problematically conflated in integral thought.[8] Each of the personal pronouns or person-perspectives, O'Connor (2012) points out, already contains within itself all of Wilber's four domains as common grammatical distinctions, so it is problematic to identify the first-person

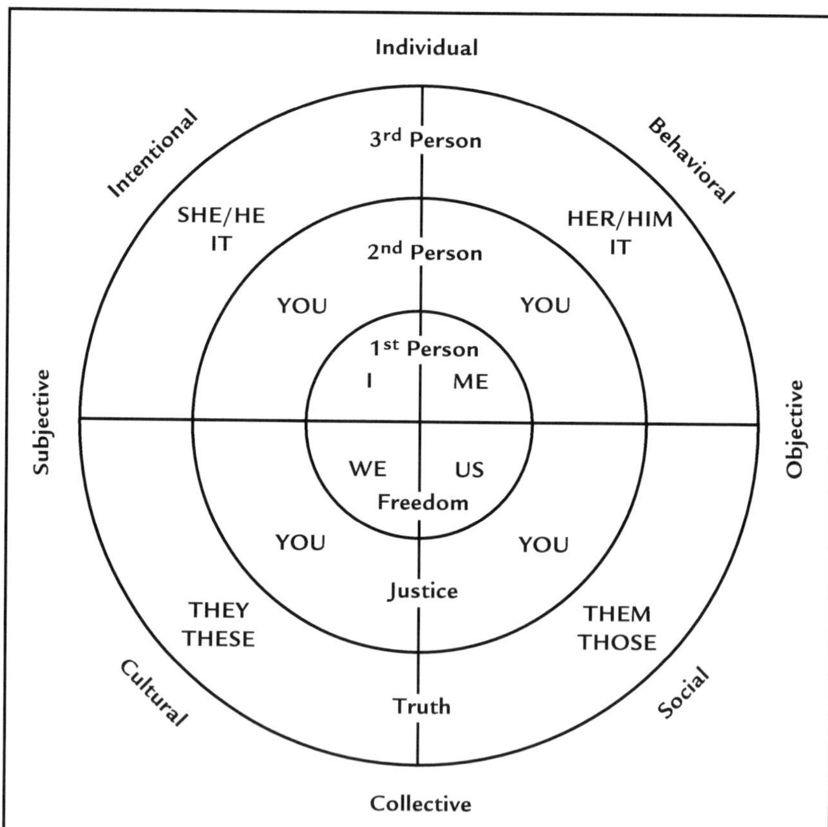

Figure 13.4. O'Connor's triadic perspectives. *Source:* Daniel O'Connor.

perspective, for example, with just two of the four quadrants. The personal pronouns include subjective and objective (Left/Right) distinctions as well as singular and plural (Upper/Lower) ones: I, Me, We, Us; He, Him, They, Them; etc. O'Connor (2012) thus recommends a quadratic mapping of all person perspectives, in effect interfacing the Big Three and the quadrants in a more consistent way.

As the illustration above makes clear, the three perspectival lenses are overlaid on the quadrants rather than being identified with particular quadrants. Several different, fractally iterative versions of this model—in which each of the persons is conceived as its own first person, able to take second- and third-person perspectives—yield a large number of interactive and enactive perspectives, which O'Connor (2012) argues are implicit in most situations. O'Connor (2012) uses this reformulation of the quadrant map to support an integral theory of human action. By placing "action" at the center of the revised quadrant map, O'Connor, in fact, presents an integration, or the beginning of an integration, of pronounal and verbal metaphysics.[9] I cannot discuss his model in detail in this brief survey of representative approaches, however; I introduce it here, along with Edwards's work, as an example of further ways the pronounal system at the center of the integral model can be expanded or further developed.

To this end, one further approach worth mentioning briefly is Lexi Neale's model of the AQAL Cube. Neale's (2011) model is predicated on a mixture of quantum theory and an idealist metaphysics of consciousness, which is controversial and not accepted by all integral theorists, but his AQAL Cube merits inclusion here for its expansion of Wilber's quadrant model to include possessive and non-possessive forms of the pronouns, in addition to the subjective, objective, singular, and plural forms discussed above. He interprets the possessive and non-possessive distinctions as relating to empirical/local and intuitive/nonlocal forms of knowing or identity, respectively.

Like Edwards (2003), Neale (2011) uses separate diagrams for each of the pronouns, so his model is complex and lacks the parsimony of O'Connor's, but it allows for an additional level of granularity in metatheoretical mapping that integral theorists may find useful in certain contexts. For instance, in identifying the possessive and non-possessive forms of the pronouns with the "inside" and "outside" views of each quadrant that Wilber employs in his model of integral methodological pluralism, Neale (2011) is able to cross-correlate the eight pronouns of his AQAL Cube diagram with the eight methodological territories of the IMP map, as well as eight related perspectives on personal identity.

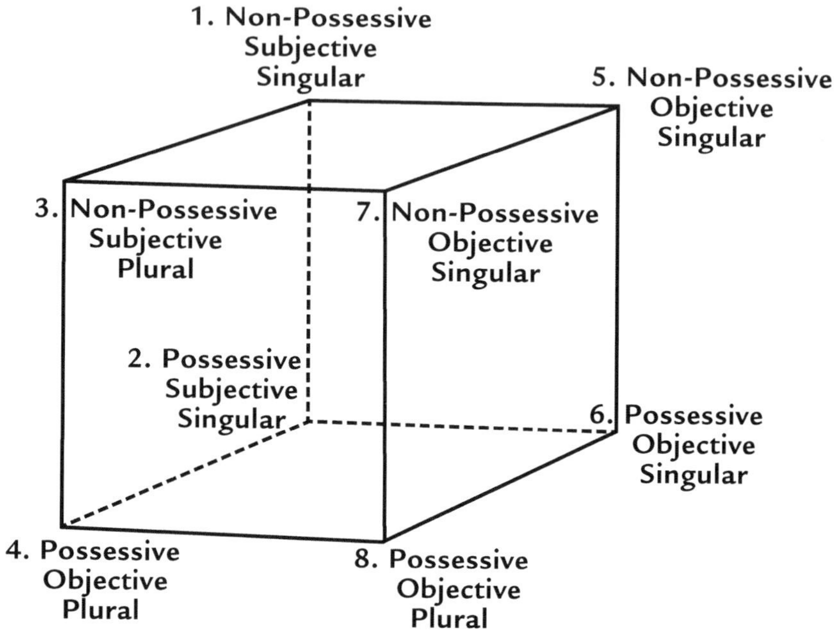

Figure 13.5. Neale's AQAL cube of personal perspectives. *Source:* Lexi Neale.

As the above brief illustrations indicate, and as I suggested at the beginning of this discussion, a significant focus in recent integral philosophizing has been on the use, and further development, of pronouns or person-perspectives as metatheoretical lenses. In several instances, the pronouns have been further supplemented with other grammatical terms, such as Edwards's (2008) combined use of the interrogative adverbs *how*, *when*, and *where* with the interrogative pronouns, *who* and *what*, or Esbjörn-Hargens and Zimmerman's (2011) use of *who*, *how*, and *what*, to form more comprehensive suites of metatheoretical lenses.

Related to these efforts, and as a central thrust of contemporary integral scholarship, the pronouns or person-perspectives have been used to support the recent turn in integral theory towards postmetaphysics, or *post-ontology*, as it is sometimes called (Rentschler, 2006). As postmetaphysical or meta-metaphysical lenses, the person-perspectives are understood as enactive operators, both giving rise to, and helping to identify and integrate, subjectivist and objectivist metaphysical systems and worldviews, for instance. Although beyond the scope of this chapter to review in any detail, the perspectival mathematics first introduced by Wilber (2003b) and further developed by Fuhs (2010), is worth mentioning in this regard. Using a simple notational system to depict the interplay of persons or sentient holons (1p, 2p, 3p) and person-perspectives (1-p, 2-p, 3-p) in various chains of perspectival relation, from the simple to the exceedingly complex (e.g., from **1p(1p) x 2p(1/p)** to **1p(1p) x 1p(1-p) x 3p(1p) x 3p(1-p) x 2p(1p) x 2p(1-p) x 3p(1-p) x 3p(3/p)**), integral mathematics aims to represent the contextual enactment of all possible worldspaces and ontological domains. As Wilber (2003b) maintains, such a notional system is useful, at the very least, to remind us that our ontological models are not simple representations of reality as *given*—i.e., the view from nowhere—but rather are always already perspective-dependent enactments.

Further, in arguing both for the ubiquity of, and the inseparable relationship among, the person-perspectives as organizing and generative epistemological lenses or structures, integral theory aims to redress past forms of metaphysical absolutism, which typically have privileged one perspective-domain over all others. But while the integral approach has been effective in identifying and countering various forms of absolutism *within* the epistemic domain, several critics maintain that it runs the risk of another error. In privileging the epistemic to the exclusion of the ontic, or else conflating the two, it may commit another, more general form of absolutism, which speculative realist and object-oriented philosophers, following Bhaskar, would call the "epistemic fallacy" (Bhaskar, 2008; Bryant, 2011a). Regarding this latter error, Bryant (2011a) writes:

> A critique of the epistemic fallacy and how it operates in philosophy does not amount to the claim that epistemology or questions of the nature of inquiry and knowledge are a fallacy. What the epistemic fallacy identifies is the fallacy of reducing ontological questions to epistemological questions, or conflating questions of how we know with questions of what beings are. In short, the epistemic fallacy occurs wherever being is reduced to our access to being. Thus, for example, wherever beings are reduced to our impressions or sensations of being, wherever being is reduced to our talk about being, wherever being is reduced to discourses about being, wherever being is reduced to signs through which being is manifest, the epistemic fallacy has been committed. (p. 60)

Does integral theory commit the epistemic fallacy? When Wilber (2006) writes, in *Integral Spirituality*, that "all things are perspectives before they are anything else" (p. 253), this might appear to be the case. It suggests that the *being* of an object is identical with one's *mode of access* to it. We will explore this question in more depth in coming sections. To anticipate that discussion: I believe integral theory can, and in some of its fuller or more robust expressions, *does*, avoid this fallacy, particularly when it employs or allies itself with a broad, speculative metaphysical palette. One of the primary aims of this chapter, in fact, is to support the further development of such a palette.

To this end, then, let us turn now to the second of the grammatical-philosophical orientations we will be reviewing: nounal metaphysics.

Nounal Philosophy: Being-as-Substance

The infant, reaching to touch her mother's face or grasp the dangling mobile overhead, learns quite early that the world consists of bounded things. Before she is a year old, she will have begun to encode this knowledge in language—to speak the names of the important people and objects in her life. From a cognitive linguistic perspective, this primitive, embodied apprehension of discrete objects forms the basis, grammatically, for the category of nouns; and philosophically, for various metaphysical systems concerned with substance or related terms (to be discussed below).

As most grammar texts inform us, a noun names a person, place, or thing, or other syntactically related terms. In many languages, the noun is the part of speech that serves as the subject or object of a verb, or the object of a preposition, among other functions. In addition to physical entities, nouns may name subjective or abstract realities, such as ideas, states, or qualities, but these latter are regarded in cognitive linguistics as radial, often metaphorical extensions of the early perceptual-motor category of discrete objects—i.e., persons, places, or things (Lakoff and Johnson, 1999). For instance, as Lakoff and Johnson (1999) illustrate, "ideas" in English are conceived metaphorically as *objects*, which can be *grasped* (understood); and similar examples are given for many other abstract nouns.

A noun-centered metaphysics, then, would be a metaphysics broadly concerned with *things*—with bounded entities, both in concrete and more abstract forms. Aristotle's metaphysics of substance is a classical example of such thinking. Philosophically, substance may be regarded in general as referring to that aspect of reality that underlies and foundationally supports or constitutes all other forms of being, such as atoms, consciousness, or the five elements (Sallis, 2000); and in a more restricted sense, substance may be understood as referring specifically to *individual objects*, which carry predicates but are not predicated of anything else (Robinson, 2004). For Aristotle, primary substances are those individual things that support, provide the ground for, and persist underneath changing qualities, actions, properties, or other predicates. In other words, primary substances are the subjects to which other forms of being are predicated, and upon which they depend. An individual person, for instance, may change her body shape, may be active or at rest, may be sick or well, and so on; but these qualities, properties, and processes cannot exist in isolation, apart from any individual substance or object (Aristotle, 1984). This characteristic of substances correlates quite closely with one of the primary grammatical functions of nouns, as discussed above; indeed, in some languages, *substantive* is the grammatical term for nouns or words that function as nouns in certain contexts.

Aristotle distinguishes between primary and secondary substances, the latter referring both to the general *kinds* of being to which individual things categorically belong, and to the various qualities or properties of being which may be predicated of individual objects (Robinson, 2004). As Levi Bryant (2011a) points out in *The Democracy of Objects*, while Aristotle defines being in multiple ways, and focuses quite a bit in his works on the question of *kinds* or categories, his ultimate view is that the *being* of beings is individual—that reality consists most basically of discrete substances or things. Some forms of substance metaphysics identify one or a relatively small number of entities as the foundational elements of being, but Aristotle's conception of substance lends itself, as I will discuss momentarily, to a more democratic, broadly pluralistic conception of being.

Concerning the former, there have been many such models, often taking one of two major forms: Ontologies that posit a single, unbroken substance, a primal whole or divine being underneath all separate appearances, and ontologies that posit eternal or indestructible elemental components that combine to make the objects of everyday life. In ancient Greek and Indian traditions, for instance, a number of philosophers concerned themselves with identifying the basic constituent element or elements of reality, from the monistic, single-element systems of Thales (water), Anaximenes (air), Anaximander (the *apeiron*, an undefined infinite thing), Plotinus (the One), or Shankara (Brahman); to the multi-element systems of Empedocles (fire, air, earth, water) or the Indian Nyaya-Vaisesika school (earth, water, fire, air, ether, time, space, self, and mind) (Ambuel, 2000; Sallis, 2000). Other ontological models, ancient and modern, have argued that earth, water, air, and other elements are themselves composed of even deeper, more fundamental constituent parts, from the atoms of Leucippus and Democritus, to the corpuscles of Descartes, the impenetrable particles of Newton, and the atoms, quarks, and strings of contemporary physics.

While there are many significant differences among these various models, they are alike in locating the foundational being of being either in one entity or a small, selective set of them, underneath or behind the world of ordinary objects. For the early atomistic models, the fundamental component was a tiny, super-dense version of familiar physical objects (noun as *concrete thing*). But from the perspective of a neurocognitive theory of grammar, the infinite, ungraspable, primal substance of certain of the monistic metaphysical systems represents a highly abstract, rarefied extension or inversion of the ordinary object: A radial, metaphorical extension of nominal thing-thinking.

Another strategy within nounal metaphysics, adopted by Aristotle and more recently by object-oriented philosophers, is simply to take *individual things* (including persons) as basic, without attempting to limit being exclusively to a single privileged object or particular set of objects (Robinson, 2004; Bryant, 2011a; Harman, 2011c). From this point of view, individual particles, molecules, trees, horses, people, planets, and so on, are equally substances, with equal ontological standing. Reality does not consist of a certain *kind* of noun, in other words, such as atoms or the five elements, but rather reality itself is *nounal*: Populated throughout by individual beings, at multiple scales. In this brief and necessarily cursory discussion of nounal metaphysics, I will not dwell further on Aristotelian or other ancient systems, but will focus for the remainder of this section on two contemporary models, namely object-oriented ontology (OOO) and Speculative Realism.

Graham Harman, the founder of modern object-oriented philosophy, defends the Aristotelian thesis that reality consists of individual substances. He does so, in part, by differentiating this view from some of the other nounal metaphysical systems discussed above, which he critiques as reductionist and compromising of the integrity of individual entities (Harman, 2011a). Noting that many metaphysical systems, ancient and modern, have tended to dismiss ordinary objects as unsophisticated and unworthy of philosophical attention, Harman (2011a) coins two terms to describe the array of reductive strategies that have most frequently been adopted to dispense with the commonsense entities of everyday experience: undermining and overmining. As indicated above, *undermining* is the approach preferred by many of the alternative nounal approaches, whereas *overmining* has typically been employed by those metaphysical systems that I am labeling pronounal, verbal, and adjectival.

In brief, undermining and overmining are philosophical strategies that seek to explain the appearance or manifestation of ordinary objects through metaphysical appeals to *more real* entities, processes, or relations (Harman, 2011a, 2011c). Specifically, an undermining approach suggests, reductively, that objects are simply surface manifestations, and that their true reality is located in their atomic or elemental subcomponents, for instance, or in some deeper substance or primal Oneness (Being, God, the apeiron). By contrast, an overmining approach denies that individual objects or entities really exist outside of perception, locating reality instead in dynamic processes or events, the qualitative play of experience, an ever-shifting field of relationships, mathematical laws,[10] and so on. Both strategies effectively put ordinary objects or entities "under erasure," undermining their reality in favor of some preferred metaphysical strata of being.

Harman and other object-oriented philosophers, such as Levi Bryant (2011a), Tim Morton (2011), and Ian Bogost (2012), reject these reductive strategies in favor of a more Aristotelian view: A "democracy of objects" (Bryant, 2011a), which regards objects at all conceivable scales as worthy of the philosophical designation, *substance*. In embracing the reality and substantiality of even everyday objects of common experience, however, Harman and his philosophical compatriots are not advocating for a naive, precritical realism. As a philosophical movement, OOO arises in the wake of (among other things):

- the post-Kantian, frequently anthropocentric subordination of objects to the structures of the subject;
- the related philosophical elevation of epistemology over ontology;
- the postmodern critique of onto-theology and the metaphysics of presence;
- various systems-theoretical critiques of the "naive billiard balls" of classical, Newtonian physics; and
- Quentin Meillassoux's (2008) critique of correlationism, the thesis that "we only ever have access to the correlation between thinking and being, and never to either term considered apart from the other" (p. 5).

Concerning the first two points, I already addressed them to some extent in the pronoun section when I described the notion of the epistemic fallacy. OOO recognizes as valid the postmodern critique of the metaphysics of presence, which I will discuss more fully in a moment, but cries foul when ontological questions are subordinated to, or conflated with, epistemological ones (Bryant, 2011a). As I noted previously, the epistemic fallacy typically involves treating the *being* of things as identical to, or somehow dependent upon, our *mode of access* to them. In other words, and in brief, OOO accepts the idea that we partly construct or "translate" the objects of our perception, as Kantians and postmodern philosophers maintain. But it rejects the frequently accompanying correlationist claims that 1) objects are *nothing more than*, or at least cannot be meaningfully discussed as *anything but*, human constructions; 2) that serious *ontological* reflection is therefore fundamentally naive; and 3) that the locus of discussion should be shifted to the fields of linguistics, sociology, psychology, or other nonphilosophical domains (Bryant, 2008). Against such assertions, object-oriented philosophers maintain that the metaphysical question of *what beings are* remains an important and valid one that can be considered, both *in spite of* and *in light of*, our epistemological limitations.

Discussion of the philosophical justification for a metaphysical system such as Object Oriented Ontology, which is multipronged and complex, is beyond the scope of this short summary; I refer interested readers to the texts by Harman and Bryant referenced in this section for further information. For our immediate purposes, it is more relevant to discuss one of the primary *strategies* OOO has adopted for advancing a critical object ontology in the wake of the postmodern critiques of onto-theology and the metaphysics of presence. According to these critiques, particularly as argued by Heidegger (1962) and Derrida (1976), traditional Western metaphysics has erred in privileging presence over absence. This has resulted in, among other things, the philosophical equation of the *being* of an entity with its perfect (self-)presence; belief in the immediacy of meaning; various forms of the philosophy of consciousness (Habermas, 1981); and empirical and representational theories of knowledge, which aim to objectively depict things as they are in themselves. For Derrida, this bias toward presence has influenced much of Western philosophy and theology, including many ontological theories of substance (whether of individual things, or of an onto-theological supreme being or foundational One) (Desilet, 2005). Wilber (2006) has identified such orientations under the broad heading of the *myth of the given*—the myth that consciousness has "direct access" to things-in-themselves—and advocates instead for a pronounal, perspective-based model of enactment.[11] OOO acknowledges these critiques and develops its own models of enactment (as I will discuss below), but it also considers the postmodern banishment of ontology, or its subordination of ontology to epistemology, to be a significant mistake. OOO's strategy, then, is to clearly differentiate epistemological and ontological philosophical discourses, and then to fold many of the postmodern insights *into* its model of ontology[12] (Bryant, 2011a).

According to OOO, the nature of objects as substances is to withdraw from relations, both to other objects, but also to themselves. While some metaphysical models hold that objects or beings are fundamentally relational, meaning they are essentially *constituted by* their relations, as we will discuss later in the chapter, Harman (2011a) contends that such models are incapable of explaining change: If an object is wholly constituted by its present relations, it would have no reason to change. Without any hidden reserve, the universe would be a frozen tableau, the being of its objects exhausted in the immediate relational field. In contrast to these exclusively relational ontologies, and to the metaphysics of presence, OOO argues that it is the nature of substance "to withdraw from presence and to be in excess of all actuality" (Bryant, 2011a). Bryant's (2011b) distinction between epistemological and ontological realism is useful here. Epistemological realism, a variant of the metaphysics of presence, is the claim that our maps of reality are objective representations of things-in-themselves. Rejecting such an understanding, OOO argues instead for ontological realism, which is "the thesis that entities are irreducible to our representations of them" (Bryant, 2011b). But this knowledge gap is not only located between humans and the objects we apprehend. OOO maintains it is the nature of *all* objects to withdraw from one another, to exceed any relationships into which they may enter at a given time.

In Bryant's (2011a) scheme, which draws on the autopoietic systems theories of Maturana and Luhmann, objects do not perceive each other nakedly; they *translate* each other, and even parts of themselves, according to their unique autopoietic regimes. For Harman (2011a), objects exhibit a fourfold nature, split within by tensions between real and sensual objects, and real and sensual qualities. Harman's model differs in several important ways from Bryant's, but it shares the claim that objects do not directly touch in simple presence. They always encounter each other as sensual objects, and sensual objects exist only on the interior of real objects. Objects or substances at all scales are equally real, irreducible entities, Harman (2011a) argues, capable of affecting and translating one another, yet also withdrawing from one another. As Bryant (2011a) puts it,

> the very essence or structure of substance lies in *self-othering* and *withdrawal.* Insofar as objects or substances alienate themselves, as it were, in qualities, they are self-othering. They generate differences in the world. However, insofar as objects are never identical to their qualities, insofar as they always harbor a volcanic reserve in excess of their qualities, they perpetually withdraw from their qualities such that they never directly manifest themselves in the world. (p. 85)

Importantly, for Harman as well as Bryant, these distinctions apply equally to so-called insentient objects, such as molecules, diamonds, or cotton balls, as they do to living organisms. In these ways, both philosophers uniquely enfold quasi-panpsychic, perspectival models into their realist object ontologies. Both contend that, while objects cannot be reduced to perspectives or representations—there is always an ontological excess, withdrawn from immediate relation—they nevertheless always only encounter each other *as* perspectives or translations,[13] i.e., *as they are for each other.*

This depiction of objects may be somewhat reminiscent of Wilber's (2003b) panpsychic model of sentient holons. Wilber (2003b) maintains that even quarks or atoms must be regarded, in some minimal sense, as first persons—specifically, as neo-Whiteheadian first-person occasions arising amid second- and third-person occasions. For this reason, I argued in the pronoun section that Wilber's cosmology could be regarded as a form of personalism, at least with regard to its implicit ontological commitments. As nouns are defined as *persons* as well as things, nounal metaphysical systems will typically identify either persons or things as the elemental constituents of existence. In Wilber's case, his epistemological emphasis on pronouns or person-perspectives appears to be closely attended by, and perhaps even inseparable from, a nounal ontology of persons. Unlike most traditional models of personalism, however, Wilber's category of person or sentient holon embraces many types of entity beyond the human (or the Godly)—from atoms to bacteria, and from ants to beluga whales.

Thus, while traditional personalism might be criticized by Harman (2011a) as undermining—locating the *being* of being exclusively in human beings or, more commonly, the Person(s) of God—Wilber's nounal metaphysics is closer in spirit to that of Aristotle or OOO, granting the dignity of "being" to a very broad range of individual entities. Between Wilber's sentient holons and OOO's withdrawn, translating objects, however, *object* is arguably the more basic concept, as it encompasses even those items Wilber would include under the categories of artifact or heap,[14] such as a cup or a stone. From an OOO perspective, Wilber's holons, artifacts, and heaps would be different *kinds* of object, but all would be equally objects, with all of the hallmarks of objects: Emergent realities that manifest as individual entities or units; which withdraw from themselves and from other objects; and which contribute and translate real differences in the world.

A fuller comparative analysis of OOO's objects and Wilber's holons must await a future publication. For now, it is sufficient to note that both OOO and integral theory have complex, well-developed models of their preferred nounal categories, whether objects or persons (sentient holons). Based on the central, even foundational, role that person perspectives play in Wilber's (2006) most recent work, I introduced integral theory at the beginning of this chapter as an exemplar of pronounal philosophy. But as I believe the above discussion also makes clear, an ontology of persons or sentient beings is an equally indispensable part of Wilber's overall model. Conversely, OOO places the nounal category, *object*, at the center of its philosophical system, but this is not the dull, inert object of past dualist and materialist metaphysics. It is an object that enfolds and embodies the epistemological insights of postmodernity—a strange, inscrutable entity that withdraws from and exceeds all relation, and which self-others in translation.

The inseparability of ontology and epistemology, of body and perspective, is notable in both approaches. From the perspective of a cognitive theory of grammar, *being embodied* and *having a perspective* appear to be equiprimordial, at least with regard to the acquisition of language. While nouns are typically among the first types of words learned, often well before pronouns, they are apparently always acquired from at least one of three perspectives: That of the *agent*, the *undergoer*, or the *observer* (Feldman, 2006). Each perspective expresses an aspect of, and arises *as* and *by virtue of*, the learner's embodied coping with the world. In the context of the panpsychic or pansemiotic visions of integral theory and OOO, this embodied perspectivity and perspectival embodiment is extended to objects and holons of all kinds and at all scales. Thus, while the being of objects cannot be reduced to or merely identified with perspective, as OOO contends, the emergence of individual substances nevertheless always entails the emergence of perspective. In Wilber's (2003b) framing, particularly the nounal inflection of it discussed here, every actual occasion or emergent holon is a four-quadrant affair.

Before concluding this section, I would like to briefly mention two recent proposals for integrative, trans-disciplinary models of research based on the principles of object-oriented ontology. Specifically, Levi Bryant's (2012) *alethetics* and Graham Harman's (2011a) fourfold model of objects both aim to provide philosophical foundation for inclusive, meta-paradigmatic approaches to knowledge generation. As they have been articulated thus far, neither Bryant's nor Harman's proposals are as comprehensive as Wilber's (2003b, 2006) integral methodological pluralism, nor are they as well-developed, but both nevertheless lay promising groundwork for future development.

Bryant's (2012) model, based loosely on the Lacanian Borromean Knot, conceives of three interlocking (but separable) orders—the Real, the Symbolic, and the Imaginary—which may be related to each other in various ways and synthetically linked in various assemblages, graphically represented by a fourth ring, the sinthome. In brief, the Real, the Symbolic, and the Imaginary represent three properties of objects that may be correlated with different knowledge disciplines or areas of philosophical focus (similar, in

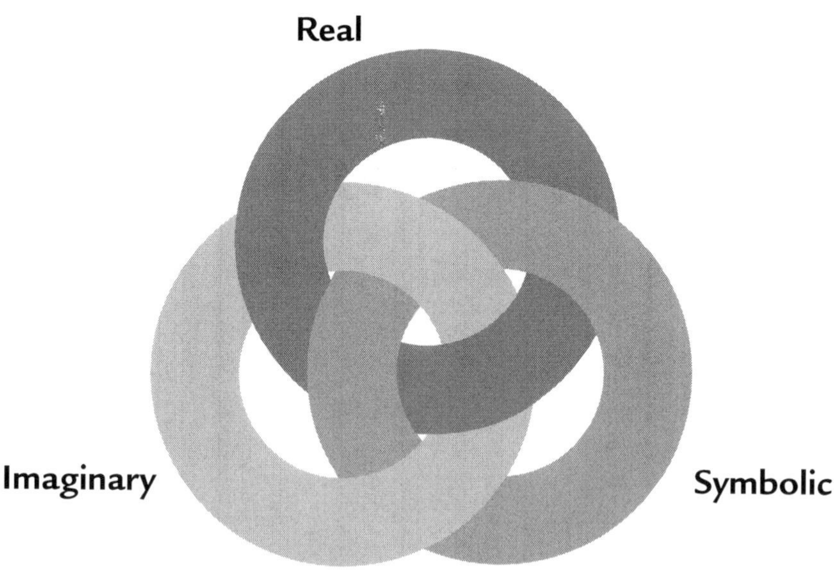

Figure 13.6. Bryant's borromean rings. *Source:* author/open source image.

some regards, to the big three of integral theory: the It, We, and I, respectively). The Real represents the ontic domain, i.e., the irreducibility of objects, entities, cultures, traditions, and so on, to our representations of them; the Symbolic encompasses the semiotic and the ecological domains, including (the study of) both the systems of signs that entities use to communicate with each other and the various modes of structural coupling that comprise ecological systems; and the Imaginary is the domain of "interiority" for all objects or entities—the unique phenomenal ways in which they encounter one another—including for knowledge disciplines and cultures (Bryant, 2012). Regarding the latter, Bryant (2012) correlates this domain at the meta-paradigmatic level with various disciplines, which Wilber (2006) would describe as Zone-5 modes of inquiry, and which Bryant, following Bogost (2012), calls alien phenomenology.

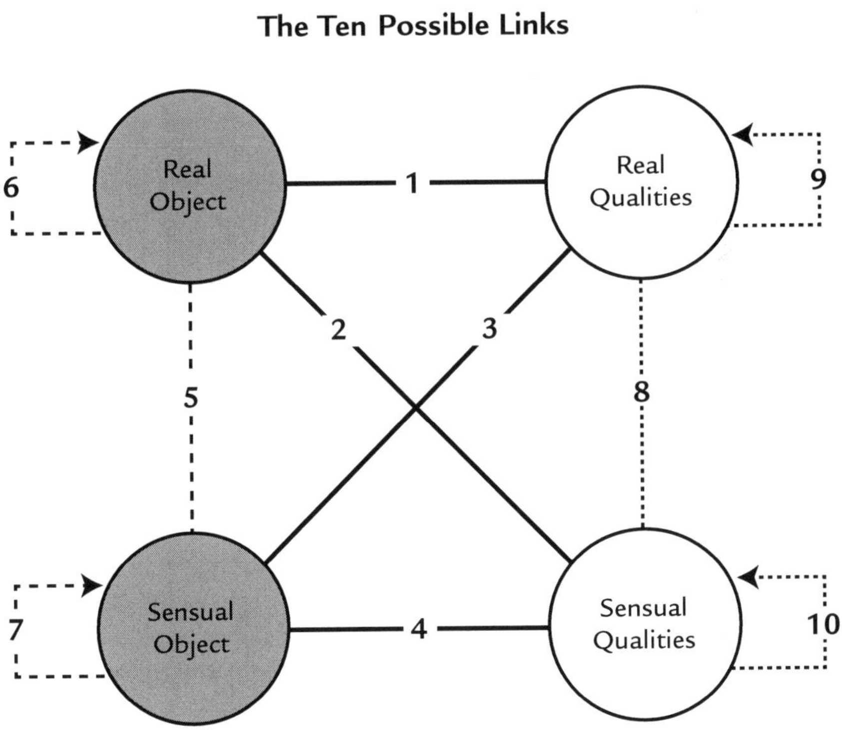

Figure 13.7. Harman's quadruple object. *Source:* Graham Harman.

Harman's (2011a) proposal thus far has only been sketchily introduced. Based on his notion of the quadruple object (consisting of real and sensual objects and qualities), his fourfold lens is similar in some respects to Wilber's quadrant model, but it presents the four "poles" or quadrants as marked by ten different generative tensions and attractions, which at the meta-paradigmatic level may allow for a more dynamic conceptualization of interdisciplinary relations. Harman (2011a) does not yet spell out how he would correlate the various dimensions of his model—the multiple types of objects with their different qualities and relations—to specific disciplines, but he suggests generally that an object-oriented philosophy, which insists on the irreducibility of emergent objects or entities, can provide a foundation for a democratic, non-reductive approach to our many knowledge practices and fields of inquiry.

With this brief summary of several representative expressions of nounal metaphysics and their metatheoretical outgrowths, I would like to turn now to a discussion of a few important philosophical movements that build, I suggest, upon a grammatical form closely related to the noun: the adjective.

Adjectival Philosophy: Being-as-Appearance

Sometimes, upon awakening in the early morning hours on a trip away from home, we may find ourselves confronted, not by immediately recognizable objects, but by various shades of light and dark, and by alien shapes that take a disconcerting second or two to organize themselves into the familiar jacket, chair, or open suitcase on the table that we had left the night before. The world, for this brief and soon forgotten moment, consists only of vague qualities or properties in chaotic flux. This is the condition, also, which has confronted congenitally blind patients who have had their vision restored through surgical intervention: The naive eye, with cataracts removed, does not immediately yield a world of objects, but a bewildering flux of dim, inchoate qualities (Zajonc, 1993).

Such experiences may give rise to philosophical reflection on the proper relation of qualities and objects. Which come first? Do individual objects (nouns) form the ontological ground for qualities (adjectives), or are objects but convenient summary terms for various patterns of qualitative conjunction that we have learned to discern? For Aristotle, as we discussed in the last section, qualities such as bright or dark, red or green, rough or smooth, were considered *secondary substances*—necessarily *dependent* forms of being that only ever manifest within primary substances or individual objects. Such a perspective appears consonant with everyday experience. An Aristotelian or object-oriented thinker might ask: How could a quality such as *fast* or *intelligent* possibly stand alone, unassociated with any individual entity?

This intuition is reflected in the structure of grammar, as well, where adjectives in most major languages play a dependent role, as *modifiers* of nouns or noun phrases. In traditional grammar, adjectives have been defined as words that describe a thing's qualities, or indicate a thing's quantity or extent, or distinguish one thing from another. In more recent grammatical models, however, the latter two functions—specifying quantity or distinctness—have been reassigned to a new part of speech, the determiner, leaving the denotation of quality as the primary function of adjectives. Syntactically, adjectives frequently appear either in an attributive position, before or after nouns or noun phrases, or as predicates. In all cases, though, the function is a dependent one; the adjective cannot stand alone.[15]

However, while qualities for Aristotle are *secondary* substances, it is only through their respective qualities that objects or entities encounter one another. Primary substances, as the ground or support for qualities, are themselves never directly perceived. When we experience the sun, it is only in its adjectival expression that we apprehend it: yellow, round, radiant, warm, mobile, distant, skyborne. In one sense, then, from the point of view of experience, qualities may also be regarded as primary: They are more immediately given than Aristotle's primary substances, which can only be inferred.

This split between accessible, empirically given qualities and inaccessible, non-empirical substances eventually leads John Locke and a number of subsequent philosophers to challenge and ultimately reject the notion of substance. As Bryant (2011c) summarizes Locke's critique, when we imagine substance as fundamentally non-qualitative or pre-qualitative—as distinct from all accidents or properties—we find that we are unable to think substance at all: It becomes, at best, a blank, featureless *whatsit* underneath all qualitative displays. Conceived as a bare substratum, substance ironically loses the capacity to serve its primary metaphysical purpose: To confer individuality to objects or entities. This is so because individual substances, being without quality in their essence, must therefore be indistinguishable from one another (Bryant, 2011a). If objects differ at all from each other, then, it is apparently only in terms of their secondary qualities or accidents.

Following this line of thinking, David Hume dispenses with the notion of substance as an unnecessary metaphysical ghost. In his analysis of the nature of the self, he finds there is no abiding substance at the center; only a bundle of passing sensations and perceptions, with the appearance of individuality or an underlying, singular essence nothing more than a product of the mind's habits of association. As Hume (1978) writes,

> I may venture to affirm of the rest of mankind, that they are nothing but a bundle or collection of different perceptions, which succeed each other with an inconceivable rapidity, and are in a perpetual flux and movement. Our eyes cannot turn in their sockets without varying our perceptions. Our thought is still more variable than our sight; and all our other senses and faculties contribute to this change; nor is there any single power of the soul, which remains unalterably the same, perhaps for one moment . . . There is properly no *simplicity* in [the Mind] at one time, nor *identity* in different; whatever natural propension we may have to imagine that simplicity and identity. (pp. 252–253)

The self is a summary term for the passing flux of perceptions, upon which the mind imposes order and unity. This same reasoning is applied to the ordinary objects of the world. As Harman (2011b) notes, "For Hume there are no objects, only 'bundles of qualities.' Here, the object is nothing more than a nickname for our habitual linking of red, sweet, cold, hard, and juicy under the single term 'apple' " (p. 23).

I am here describing such an orientation as adjectival: It places perceptual qualities at the center of the philosophical model. In doing so, it inverts the typical relationship between adjectives and nouns, either by seeing the latter as merely conceptual, secondarily derived summary terms for habitual groupings of the former; or by placing primary focus on the phenomenal play of qualities and bracketing out inaccessible "things-in-themselves" as beyond the scope of legitimate philosophical inquiry. Kant, as is well known, adopted the latter strategy. He recognized the possible existence of mind-independent things-in-themselves, but he felt we could say nothing meaningful about them and focused instead on the manifold of perceptions and their lawful ordering by the a priori categories of the mind. Other philosophers following Hume, however, have adopted a more radical approach, rejecting hidden metaphysical substrates altogether and developing elaborate "bundle theories" of objects. For bundle theorists, there are no substances or bare substrata in which qualities inhere; rather, objects and entities consist entirely of conjunctions or collocations of qualities, relations, or tropes (Újvári, 2012). Some forms of bundle theory adopt a Neoplatonic model of universals, regarding each appearance of "red" as the appearance of the same universal quality; but in other forms of bundle theory, namely trope-bundle theory, each qualitative manifestation is immanent and particular (Újvári, 2012; Bensusan and Carvalho, 2011). Under the latter theory, each instantiation of "red" is particular to the occasion of its appearance, bearing similarity to, but not identity with, other instantiations.

Bundle theories have occasionally been compared with some Buddhist schools of thought. Hume rejects the metaphysical duality of mind and world, and regards the self as nothing more than a bundling of transient qualities, without essence or substance (Brown, 2011). This perspective arguably bears some similarity to the Cittamātra or Mind-Only tradition in Buddhism. Cittamātra posits one truly existent thing: The *abhūtaparikalpa*, the *imagination of the non-existent*, a non-dual flow of perceptions that can manifest itself either in deluded, subject-object experience or in enlightened, non-dual experience (Williams, 1989). As Williams (1989) summarizes the Cittamātra perspective,

> Apparently external objects are constituted by consciousness and do not exist apart from it. Vasubhandu begins his *Viṃśatikā*: "All this is only perception [*vijñaptimātra*], since consciousness manifests itself in the form of nonexistent objects." There is only the flow of perceptions. (p. 87)

Said otherwise, there is only the qualitative flow of appearances, with no underlying, self-existent objects or subjects. Dualistic experience, separating the world into interiors and exteriors, arises through the deluded reification of various aspects of the empty play of qualia.

While it would be limiting and inaccurate to portray Cittamātra (or most Western bundle theories, for that matter) as *exclusively* adjectival in their metaphysical commitments, I feel justified in appealing to these schools as exemplars of this particular grammatical-metaphysical orientation for the following two reasons:

1. their novel inversion of the conventional noun/adjective relation, and
2. their predilection to describe reality primarily in terms of the play of qualitative appearances or perceptions.

It should be noted, however, that while such traditions may liberate qualitative appearances from their conventional metaphysical anchoring in substances or things-in-themselves, an adjectival orientation will tend more often than not to be complemented by other grammatical perspectives. In the case of integral theory, for instance, which has strong affinities both with Buddhist and Hindu non-dualist metaphysics, and with the German Idealism of Schelling and Hegel, an adjectival focus on the empty or groundless play of perceptions is recognized and embraced as valid, up to a point, but it is subordinated to the pronounal person-perspective lens. A qualitative perception is always already a first-, second-, or third-person perspectival occasion. Similarly, in those Eastern and Western traditions that focus on the adjectival play of appearances while bracketing out, or denying the validity of, nounal metaphysics, one will nevertheless frequently find an accompanying emphasis on verbal metaphysics. In other words, in those traditions that emphasize adjectives over nouns, regarding the latter as either convenient summary terms for, or naive reifications of, the impersonal play of appearances, there is often a concurrent focus on the generative *how* of appearance (a process or verbal orientation). This is certainly true in Buddhism, where in the Yogacara and Dzogchen traditions, for instance, one finds a strong, subtly conceived process view that accompanies all discussion of the illusory play of appearance. It is to an exploration of such process orientations that we now turn.

Verbal Philosophy: Being-as-Process

A verb is a word that names an act, occurrence, or mode of being. In English, the verb forms the grammatical center of a predicate, which, to be complete, must also include a subject, or a subject and object. The subject-verb-object structure of English and similar grammars assigns the verb necessarily to an agent or experiencer: All actions or modes of being must be communicated as the actions or experiences of a subject. This pertains, as David Bohm (1980) points out, even in the case of a general process such as a rainstorm: We say, “It is raining,” attributing the action of raining to a subject (“it”), even when there is no discernible agent or “rainer” involved.

In more verb-based grammars, however, such as in Japanese or some American Indian languages, the verb or action situation receives the primary emphasis, with the subject often not indicated at all. In such grammatical systems, subjects, when they *are* included, are typically presented as associated elements of an overall, dynamic or relational situation rather than as independent causal agents initiating an action. For instance, as Ken Sakai (2013) notes in an essay comparing Japanese and English sentence structure,

> In Japanese, it is preferable to express situational relationships, as if things turned out naturally. In English, human behavior is logically grasped as its center, and the word order of "Subject (as an agent) + Transitive Verb + Object" is preferred. So then, in English, what the people are doing with the situation is emphasized, while in Japanese what the situation is doing with the people is emphasized.

But in many verb-based languages, as I noted above, it is sometimes not necessary to indicate a subject or an object at all. In the Hopi language, for example, *rehpi*, meaning "flashed" (for the occurrence of light or lightning), is considered a complete sentence; there is no agent that flashes, but only the flashing (Whorf, 1956). Similarly, in Japanese, the sentence, "I am going shopping," would be translated as *Kaimono ni ikimasu*, literally meaning "Shopping (to) going" (Sakai, 2013). No subject is indicated; the semantic content of the sentence is carried entirely by verb forms and a particle.

These differences in grammatical emphasis parallel longstanding philosophical tensions between (nounal) substance- and (verbal) process-based metaphysical systems. As early as the sixth century BC, Heraclitus argued for the primacy of motion and change, declaring that "all entities move and nothing remains still." He conceived of multiple forces in balanced strife, driving the manifestation and transformation of all things. But this early form of process thinking was soon eclipsed in Western thought by the metaphysical doctrines of atomism and substance, which give primacy (as we discussed above) to individual objects or entities, and that frequently locate reality in that which is unchanging or eternal. Over the past two millennia, several other thinkers, such as Plotinus, Patrizzi, and Leibniz, have contributed to the development of the otherwise long-marginalized field of process thinking within the Western tradition, but it wasn't until the emergence of the concept of evolution and the development of various systems sciences that process metaphysics attracted wide and sustained philosophical attention (Seibt, 2012; Macy, 1991). Some of the most prominent modern contributors to process thought include Schelling, Hegel, Peirce, Bergson, Whitehead, Hartshorne, and Heidegger.

The fundamental distinction between noun- and verb-based grammars—the question of whether nouns or verbs are primary, and consequently whether verbs must be associated with an agent—finds a philosophical echo in the process reducibility thesis. According to this thesis, all processes are *owned* processes, meaning they are necessarily and always the expressions of agents or things (Rescher, 1996). On such a view, processes are real, but they are subordinate to, and ontologically dependent upon, process-transcendent substances. By contrast, while process theorists acknowledge that some processes are indeed helpfully understood as the activities or doings of an agent, they argue that 1) there are also processes that are *not* owned by any particular agent; 2) agents themselves are dependent upon, and only come into being in and through, dynamic processes; and 3) therefore processes are ontologically more fundamental than substances or things. Rescher (1996) names temperature changes or magnetic fluctuations as examples of non-owned processes, and Bohm's (1980) rainstorm provides another illustration. But the more radical claim of process philosophers, indicated in points 2 and 3 above, is that the nature of so-called substances or agents is itself processual. Individual entities or objects are, in actuality, not just the *initiators* of actions, but are themselves the products of the ceaseless and generative flow of becoming. Bohm (1980) offers the metaphor of an eddy in a stream: It has a constant, relatively stable form, but it is inseparable from the flowing movement of the water. In this view, the noun, *eddy*, refers to a stable, invariant-seeming group of processes or patterns that is isolated or abstracted (itself a process) out of a larger processual field.

In privileging process and becoming over substance, process philosophy is challenged to account for the intuition of abiding identity or sameness in the midst of change. Bohm's example of the eddy, while a suggestive metaphor for the concept of object-as-process, may nevertheless feel inadequate or incomplete as an explanation for the deeply felt intuition of ongoing subjective identity. The Buddhist process-account of the self, which sees "self" as an illusion generated by the flow of impersonal psycho-physical processes, attributes the sense of self-continuity to several related factors: the speed with which the processes take place, normally opaque to untrained awareness; the capacity of the mind to recollect past experiences or events; and the fact that momentary experiences of "sense consciousness" are always immediately followed by moments of "mind consciousness," appearing to link them and thus giving them the feel of similarity and continuity (Brahmavamso, 2005). In Western process thought, one of the most sophisticated accounts of the intuition of self-continuity was developed by A.N. Whitehead. In Whitehead's view, the immediately given sense of self-identity is related, not to the existence of underlying, unchanging substances or essences, but to the dynamic sameness of recurrent integrative processes that are fundamentally experiential in character. Because Whitehead's philosophy has been so influential in the modern development of process thought, and because aspects of his model also inform Wilber's recent work, I will spend a little time reviewing a few of its salient features.

For Whitehead (1978), reality is atomic or individual in nature, but the atoms from which it is composed are experiential events, which he calls *actual occasions*, rather than the material objects or particles of conventional scientific understanding. An actual occasion is an exceedingly transient event, perishing as soon as it arises. In its momentary arising, an actual occasion or entity reaches into the past and the future at once: It *relationally prehends* the immediately preceding moments, grasping and integrating past occasions as concrete forms that contribute to its present internal constitution; and it *creatively generates* novel, emergent features in the process of its self-realization through prehensive unification. Whitehead describes this process as *concrescence*, which is the process by which entities become what they are through their relationships to other entities, while also contributing novelty through the unique ways in which those relations are integrated. While many process thinkers prior to Whitehead have conceived of process in terms of flow and continuity, taking continuity or unbroken wholeness as a pre-given feature of processual reality, Whitehead (1978) argues, instead, for the metaphysical primacy of atomism and for the *becoming* of continuity (as opposed to the continuity of becoming). With each quantized occasion of prehensive unification, in other words, continuity is *achieved*: The present occasion enfolds the past as an aspect of its own creative self-constitution, and then passes on this achievement as an inheritance to the actual occasions that follow. This, then, is how Whitehead accounts in process terms for the feeling or intuition of continuous self-identity.[16] It is not given but realized, experientially and ontologically, through recurrent occasions of prehensive unification. The process is more complex for a human being, which is a rich nexus or society of actual occasions, than it is for a simple entity such as an electron or an atom, but it is alike in kind.

Given the historical tension that has existed between process and substantialist or atomistic forms of metaphysics, it is worth saying a little more here about Whitehead's experiential atomism. As should be apparent from the above, Whitehead's "atoms," actual occasions, are thoroughly relational in nature. In *Process and Reality*, Whitehead (1978) argues several related points that underscore this fact: 1) there is no deeper reality than actual occasions; 2) an actual occasion is wholly constituted by, and wholly analyzable in terms of, its prehensions of other actual entities; and 3) an actual occasion cannot be completely abstracted from the universe and considered in isolation, since its relations are in essence coextensive with the universe. This picture of atomic actual occasions, which are internally related and complexly interdependent, differs significantly from the classical notion of wholly discrete, externally related atoms moving through space. The latter suggests to Whitehead (1967) a vacuous, alienated "universe . . . shivered into a multitude of disconnected substantial things" (p. 133)—a model he rejects as being incapable of accounting for the actual (processual, co-constitutive, causal, communicative) relations that obtain among entities.

In embracing an ontology of individuals (and societies of individuals), as opposed to the various ontologies of pre-individual flux or dynamism preferred by process theorists such as Bergson, Deleuze, or Bohm, Whitehead would *appear* to have more in common, metaphysically, with the object-oriented ontologists than with many of his process-oriented brethren. And Harman (2011c) and Bryant (2010; 2011a), indeed, have both cited Whitehead as an important influence on their own work. Bryant, for instance, is similar to Whitehead in his willingness to think of objects in process terms—as an ongoing synthetic process of self-constitution, not an extra-processual, unchanging essence or substance. But Whitehead's actual occasions differ from OOO's objects in the thoroughly relational way that actual occasions are defined. As noted above, Whitehead contends that an actual occasion is comprised entirely of its prehensions, i.e., of its relations to other entities. Indeed, Whitehead regards it as misguided to attempt to conceive of or define an entity apart from its relations. But this is exactly what Harman (2005) and Bryant (2011a) argue must be done: For perception to be possible—indeed, for change or process to be possible—an entity must exceed all perceptions or prehensions of it; it must be irreducible to its relations to other entities. I have already reviewed some of Harman's thoughts on this issue in the section on nounal philosophy, so I will focus here on Bryant's perspective.

In a blog entry on the affinities and differences between Whitehead's process ontology and OOO, Bryant (2010) comments that he finds Whitehead's threefold model of prehension—namely, that prehension involves a *prehending subject*, a *prehended datum*, and a *subjective form* of prehension (the *way* an actual entity prehends another entity)—fully consonant with an object-oriented understanding of "inter-object relations," including the related concepts of withdrawal and translation. Bryant (2010) interprets the third point, the subjective form of prehension, in terms of the second-order cybernetics of Bateson and Luhmann: Information is always internal to autopoietic (or allopoietic) systems, intimately related to their distinctive structures, rather than a "message" that is transmitted, intact, between systems. But since information here is understood in terms of difference—a "difference that makes a difference," selecting unique system states within prehending entities—then the prehending entity cannot be identical with its prehensions; it must withdraw from or exceed its relations to other entities.

This is where OOO differs with process ontology, Bryant argues, and why OOO would suggest, instead, a fourfold model of prehension. Whitehead defines an actual entity as nothing other than the concrescence of its prehensions, in effect identifying the subject with its perceptions or experiences. But if an object is *nothing other* than its perceptions, then it is nothing in itself. It has nothing it can bring to its perceptions—no structure—and therefore no "how" or subjective form of prehension. Bryant (2010a) argues that further differentiation is needed to make for a coherent model of inter-entity relations: "the subject/substance that does the prehending (the real object), the datum prehended (another real object), the subjective-form under which the datum is prehended (the organization or endo-structure of the real object), and the sensuous object (Harman) or system-state (me) produced in the prehending" (para. 8). When the prehending entity is defined as consisting only of its previous prehensions, Bryant maintains, this misses the withdrawn, mediating endo-structure of the entity that translates and gives subjective form to its emergent prehensions.

In his more recent work, Wilber has offered his own critique and fourfold amendment of Whitehead's process model. As I intimated above, aspects of Whitehead's work have come to play an increasingly important role in Wilber's model. Specifically, Wilber (2001, 2003a, 2003b) has embraced the Whiteheadian concepts of prehension, concrescence, and the creative advance into novelty in his own accounts of the microgenesis and developmental unfolding of subject-object (or I-It) experience, the formative or causal inheritance of the past, and the interior dimensions of holarchical development. These concepts highlight and help to flesh out certain processual features of the integral model. Nevertheless, Wilber regards Whitehead's process model as limited in several important ways. It inadequately takes account of intersubjectivity (the lower left quadrant), for instance, and it does not address and cannot explain the non-prehensive causal processes and dynamics of the objective (upper right) and interobjective (lower right) domains of reality (Wilber, 2001, 2003a).

Instead of taking Whitehead's model of prehension, then, as a metaphysical foundation, Wilber situates it in his own Four Quadrant account of cosmogenesis. For Wilber (2001, 2003a), the Four Quadrants "go all the way down:" Every actual occasion involves subjective, objective, intersubjective, and interobjective dimensions. What this means with regard to Whitehead's model of prehension, in part, is that every momentary prehension of an object by a subject must be understood as necessarily situated in an intersubjective context or background that influences and gives form to the prehensive occasion. Similarly to Bryant above, Wilber (2001) argues that some mediating structures have *never* been past objects for the subject; they structure experience, and are "part" of the subject,[17] but they exceed *reduction* to either the subject or its prehensions. This is because subject-object prehension is, in Wilber's view, only part of the larger fourfold process or mesh of processes he calls *tetra-enaction*, in which intersubjectivity and interobjectivity are irreducible aspects of any occasion.

With this note, and in anticipation of bringing this section to a close, I would like to shift focus now back to the broader discussion of process metaphysics (which certainly includes, but is not limited to or defined by, Whitehead's philosophy). Although there is no unanimity on this point among process metaphysicians, several types of fundamental processes are generally recognized. Besides owned and unowned processes, which we discussed at the beginning of this section, Rescher (1996) identifies state-transformative processes, generative or product-productive processes, purposive or teleological processes, cognitive or epistemic processes, and communicative or informational processes. Anthony Kenny (2003) classifies processes according to three basic action types: activities, performances, and states of being (notably similar to the terms used in the definition of "verb" at the beginning of this section). More recently, Roy and Trudel (2011) have identified five generative processes—namely, construction, development, evolution, emergence, and autopoiesis—which they define as those processes that set up or generate structures.

Regarding the latter, Roy (2006, 2010, 2011) has proposed a generative process–based reformulation of integral theory, which I will explore here only briefly. As I discussed at the beginning of the chapter, Roy (2006) believes that, while integral theory is certainly not averse to a processual view, and includes important process-oriented concepts within it (some of which I touched on above), it nevertheless subtly privileges a structuralist orientation. The quadrant map tends to highlight discrete structures, for instance, rather than the dynamic processes that generate them. Drawing on the process insights of Whitehead (1978), David Bohm (1980), Jean Gebser (1986), Christopher Alexander (2003, 2004, 2006), Jason Brown

(1991, 1996, 1997, 1998, 2000, 2002), and Bon and Buddhist Dzogchen thinkers (Klein and Wangyal Rinpoche, 2006; Guenther, 1984, 1989), among others, Roy (2006, 2010) shows how a process model can account for the generation of the quadrants as relatively stable relational structures out of a dynamic, processual field, and can generate new super-integrative methodological zones in a Gebserian, process-oriented version of integral methodological pluralism (IMP).

Although not indicated on the image above, Roy (2006) elsewhere labels the central lines of the quadrant map as *unfolding movements* in the directions of interiority and exteriority, or singularity and plurality, out of an anterior holistic field. Related to the above approach, Roy (2010) similarly arrives at several new, super-integrative methodologies—from process eidetics, to mixed discourse, to enactive naturalism, to isomorphic field theory—by teasing out and articulating the anterior wholes that give rise

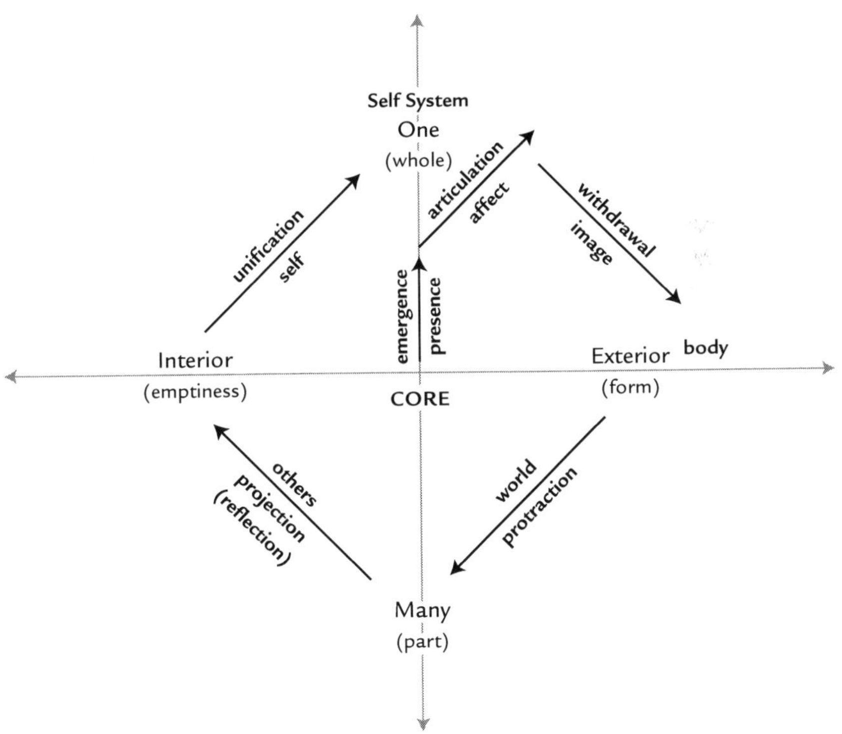

Figure 13.8. Roy's integral processual map of the self system. *Source:* Bonnie Roy.

to the inside/outside distinctions and the corresponding eight zones of IMP. Specifically, each of her methodologies is derived from exploring the nature of the anterior "space" from which we switch between our conventional methodological views, such as when we switch between phenomenological and structuralist approaches. I do not have the space here to discuss Roy's process model, which she calls *onto-logics*, in any further detail, but I have included it here as a suggestive example of a more explicitly verb-centered integrative metatheory.

In most cases, the generative and other types of processes mentioned above can be identified with various types of verbs: dynamic verbs, stative verbs, causative verbs, and so on. A number of process models, including those of Roy, Rescher, and Kenny, among others, posit and explore multiple discrete processes, in effect outlining a pluralist landscape of verbal metaphysics. But another strategy within process thought is to focus on various *modifications* or *modes* of a more generalized process or set of processes. This is the province of adverbial metaphysics.

Adverbial Philosophy: Modes of Being

An adverb is a word that modifies or qualifies a verb, verb phrase, adjective, or other adverb, among other functions. It is typically used to indicate the manner, time, location, or extent of an action, process, or a quality. In many languages, adverbs are formed (if they do not stand as independent words in their own right) by adding a suffix to, or otherwise modifying, an adjective. For the purposes of this discussion, I will focus primarily on the adverb's role as a modifier of verbs or other adverbs, since in the adverbial process models we will explore here, adjectives are typically replaced with adverbial expressions, as we will see.

The relationship of adverbial to verbal metaphysical models differs somewhat from the relationship between adjective and nounal approaches discussed previously. Grammatically, of course, both adverbs and adjectives play dependent roles, modifying their respective parts of speech. But in the case of the various empiricist/adjectival metaphysical systems I reviewed, adjectives were typically privileged *at the expense* of nouns, in *repudiation* of the metaphysical category of substance. In the adverbial models of which I am aware, this tends not to be the case. An adverbial orientation is typically used, not to repudiate or replace the verbal category of process, but to complement or complete it. For this reason, I will present adverbial philosophy itself in an adverbial manner: as either a *complement to* or a *mode of* process metaphysics, rather than a fundamentally different orientation.

In the previous section, Heidegger, as the author of *Being and Time*, may have appeared conspicuously absent from my sampling of influential process philosophers. He certainly could have been included in that discussion; as Harman (2011c) notes, he stands as one of the towering thinkers of the last century, and has generally received more recognition for his contributions to process thought than Whitehead or his descendants. (He also could have been included in the noun section, incidentally, considering the influence of his equipment analysis and his 1919 concept of the fourfold on Harman's nounal philosophy.) I have included him here, however, because much of his work on the nature and process of Being is a meditation on the various *ways* or *modes* in which Being manifests. As Joanna Seibt (2012) writes:

> Martin Heidegger's early and late philosophy also presents an analytic-interpretive contribution to process philosophy, without speculative formulations of metaphysical "laws of development," but with a view to the metaphilosophical and practical implications of process metaphysics. In *Sein und Zeit* (1927) Heidegger presents what could be called an "adverbial model" of process metaphysics; based on an analysis of human existence ("Dasein") Heidegger shows that what the metaphysical tradition understood as entities or factors standing in relational constellations—e.g., space, world, self, others, possibility, matter, function, meaning, time—can be viewed as "adverbial modifications" of Dasein, as modes and ways in which Dasein occurs, while Dasein itself is the interactivity of "disclosure" or "taking as."

In his later writings, Heidegger's focus shifts from human Being (Dasein) and its modifications, to Dasein itself as a dimension or mode—a "how"—of Being's unfolding. Related to this, Heidegger presents the history of being as a series of modes of *Ereignis*, the process of the sending and withdrawal of be-ing that has marked each epoch's understanding of Dasein's relation to reality (Guignon, 2005). Heidegger characterizes these modes of be-ing as *physis*, *poiesis*, *techne*, production, *ens creatum*, and technology: Each a unique, emergent structuring of be-ing that transforms our understanding of what is and what matters (Dreyfus, 1996). These moves further develop and extend the adverbial strategy introduced earlier in his work.

Similarly, Whitehead's (1978) eternal objects inhabit an adverbial relationship to the verbal center of his model, creativity or the creative unfolding of actual occasions. In Whitehead's system, eternal objects include abstract things such as color, form, pattern, number, space, time, gravity, and so on. They are those features of reality that distinctly characterize and inform an actual entity's qualities and relations. In that regard, eternal objects are similar to the universals of conventional metaphysics: The qualities or properties of reality, physical or abstract, which can be conceptualized independently of specific actual entities or concrete occasions, but which lend entities their "definiteness" (Whitehead, 1978), such as the redness and juiciness of an apple. In Whitehead's model, however, these qualities are conceptualized adverbially rather than as the adjectival attributes of subjects. In other words, eternal objects both characterize and inform the *how* of becoming-events in and through prehensive occasions: sun-eventuating *brightly*, *warmly*, *spherically*, *gravitationally*.

Another way of saying this is that eternal objects represent the recurrent potential for the actualization of entities along a nearly infinite number of adverbial pathways or modal expressions: manifesting *thusly* and *thusly* and *thusly*. As Steven Shaviro (2009) puts it, eternal objects adverbially "determine and express how actual entities relate to one another, take one another up, and 'enter into each others' constitutions.' Like Kantian and Deleuzian ideas, eternal objects work regulatively, or problematically" (p. 37). As such, they represent the many modal possibilities for becoming.

There is a Platonic cast to Whitehead's discussion of eternal objects, but Shaviro (2009) argues this is best understood as an *empirico-idealism*, since Whitehead maintains that eternal objects cannot be conceived apart from their concrete instantiations and do not manifest outside of individual experience. As Whitehead (1978) writes:

> An actual entity cannot be described, even inadequately, by universals; because other actual entities do enter into the description of any one actual entity. Thus every so-called "universal" is particular in the sense of being what it is, diverse from everything else; and every so-called "particular" is universal in the sense of entering into the constitution of other actual entities (p. 48).

Despite these qualifications, however, the concept of eternal object remains somewhat controversial among Whiteheadian scholars. While Shaviro (2009) attempts to give it a Deleuzian reading, Charles Hartshorne (1979) finds the concept (and the related notion of the *ingression* of eternal objects into particulars) still to be too close to Platonism, and advocates for a more nominalist interpretation.

An earlier example of adverbial process metaphysics is arguably found in Spinoza's philosophy, particularly in his concept of substance and its modes. While *substance* is normally conceptualized as a noun, it functions in Spinoza's system more like a verb (or, more properly, a gerund) (Williams, 1986). For Spinoza, substance is that one, infinite, indivisible (because infinitely divisible) Being, self-caused and eternal, of and for which all other beings are but its modes (Della Rocca, 2008; Morrison, 2007). And if all beings are necessarily dependent modes or modifications of the one infinite Substance or Being, then this relationship is best conceptualized as an adverb-verb relation, rather than the adjective-noun relation typically associated with classical substance views.

This monist version of adverbial metaphysics is in contrast to Whitehead's ontology, as well as to several Eastern non-dual ontologies. For Spinoza, all beings are but accidental (non-necessary) adverbial modes or modifications of the one substance (which Deleuze reads as the "virtual") (Shaviro, 2010). For Whitehead, however, these "modes" are instead actual entities, each a site of (verbal) creativity, each capable of its own adverbial modification. Whitehead (1978) rejects Spinoza's notion of a transcendent substance, which exists on a higher or deeper plane behind all actual entities, and argues instead for a non-dualist interpretation:

> God and the World stand over against each other, expressing the final metaphysical truth that appetitive vision and physical enjoyment have equal claim to priority in creation. But no two actual entities can be torn apart: each is all in all. Thus each temporal occasion embodies God, and is embodied in God. In God's nature, permanence is primordial and flux is derivative from the World: in the World's nature, flux is primordial and permanence is derivative from God. Also the World's nature is a primordial datum for God; and God's nature is a primordial datum for the World. Creation achieves the reconciliation of permanence and flux when it has reached its final terms which is everlastingness—the Apotheosis of the World. (p. 529)

In the non-dualist traditions of Dzogchen or Kashmiri Shaivism, a similar view is expressed: Each concrete individual is, at once, the creative (verbal) activity and the delightful (adverbial) self-ornamentation and self-determination of the supreme reality.

In each of the ontologies reviewed here, an adverbial focus on modes *complements*, rather than undermines, the central concern with (verbal) process, whether process is conceived in pluralistic, monistic, or non-dualistic terms. Adverbs give definiteness to processes, tracing infinitely varied paths toward actualization. Noting the strength of this pairing for a process approach, Rescher (1996) proposes a process semantics in which verbs and adverbs serve as the primary operators, "accomplishing whatever a semantics of individuals can manage to do with properties and relations" (p. 178). Instead of saying, *The sky is blue* or *The sun is in-the-sky*, one would say, *The sky radiates bluely* and *The sun sits in-the-skyly*, replacing a "substance and property" construction with an adverbially modified verb phrase. As Rescher (1996) notes, this approach allows for a more democratic treatment of entities, as both existent and nonexistent beings can be rendered in the same way (akin to the treatment of real and imaginary objects by OOO and actor network theory[18]).

In the second sentence example above, a prepositional phrase is rendered adverbially. In recent years, a small but growing number of philosophers have emerged who resist the long-standing tendency to hurry past prepositions on the way to substances or processes, but who prefer instead to linger with them and listen to what they have to say about being. This is the last of the grammatical-philosophical orientations we will review in this chapter.

Prepositional Philosophy: Being-as-Relation

In *Principles of Psychology*, as Bruno Latour (2011) notes, William James remarked humorously on the tendency among empiricist philosophers to limit their attention to perceptions of color and various other sensations as the essence of what is truly given in experience, and then to have to appeal to the machinations of thought to fill in the rest of the picture. But this has the effect, among other things, of rendering relations and intentional vectors as unreal—as impositions of human thought upon the world. For James (1983), this is a failure of traditional empiricism, and he calls for a more radical approach, one that recognizes that *of* and *to*, *because* and *for*, *and* and *the*, also each have their own distinct feels, their own claims to reality.

Among the parts of speech James names as meriting greater empirical and philosophical attention, he lists conjunctions, determiners, and prepositions. It is the last of these parts of speech that has captured the interest of the handful of (primarily French) philosophers we will explore here. Specifically, Bruno Latour, Étienne Souriau, Jean-Luc Nancy, Michel Serres, and Peter Sloterdijk, have appealed to prepositions as opening a field of ontological inquiry that eludes the paths normally followed by traditional empiricist and substantialist metaphysical systems.

Grammatically, a preposition is a linking word, connecting nouns, pronouns, or noun phrases to other words or phrases. Prepositions are typically used to express temporal, spatial, or logical relationships, and in so doing, often function adverbially or adjectivally within a sentence. In some languages, words with this function show up elsewhere in relation to their complement, and thus may be called *postposition*s or *circumpositions* (or simply adpositions for a position-neutral determination). In this section, I will refer to them as prepositions, as that is the grammatical term used by the authors we will be discussing.

From the perspective of the cognitive theory of grammar, prepositions are semi-complex constructions composed of several image schemes, and therefore are themselves relational. For instance, the preposition "on" consists of the embodied image schemas for CONTACT and SUPPORT. This lends support to James's claim that prepositions have their own distinct feel and reality.

With the adverbial role that prepositional phrases often play, prepositional philosophy could be considered an adjunct or a special subset of adverbial metaphysics. Indeed, Bruno Latour (2011) considers the primary domain of concern opened by prepositional reflection to be the *modes of existence* that beings might occupy in relation to one another. But since prepositional phrases also function adjectivally, a prepositional orientation cannot be considered to be exclusively dedicated to a process orientation. Instead, it moves in zones of concern that touch on substances and processes equally, without absolutizing either narrative. As Latour (2011) writes:

> The essential point is that the ontology of prepositions immediately takes us away from the all-too-familiar sorts of inquiry in the philosophies of being. Here, the preposition indicates neither an ontological domain, nor a region, territory, sphere, or material. The *if* or the *and* has no region. But as its name perfectly suggests, the preposition prepares the position that has to be given to what follows, giving the search for meaning a definite inflection that allows one to judge its direction or vector. (pp. 308–309)

Latour makes these remarks in the context of a discussion of the work of Étienne Souriau. Like some of the adverbial philosophers, Souriau wants to think being in a plurality of modes—to escape the metaphysical deadlock that attempts to restrict reality to just one form or mode of being, whether subject or object (or their dialectical integration) (Latour, 2011, pp. 306–307). To approach this, he proposes that we reflect, not on *being as being* for itself, as a singular underlying substance, but on being in and as otherness, as alteration, genuinely multiple or *plurimodal*. Prepositions, here, evoke for him, not accidental or secondary rearrangements of the one being, but genuinely different modes or ways of being. The actual modes of existence Souriau goes on to explore, however, are only abstractly related to prepositions, so I will turn to several other writers who address the prepositions more directly.

William James (1983) has reflected on the abundance of words prefixed with co-, com-, and syn-, among several others, as testament to the fundamental intuition of relationship and togetherness in human existence, and these reflections find a new echo in the work of Jean-Luc Nancy. In an extraordinary and somewhat enigmatically languaged little text, Nancy (2000) proposes a reformulation of ontology in the Western tradition by thinking being in the form of *being singular plural*. This is a philosophy, as we will see, that dances in and around the preposition *with*. In juxtaposing the three terms, *being singular plural*, as he does, Nancy means to communicate their absolute co-immediacy, without remainder, and without any suggestion of the priority of one over the other. Being-one is only ever being-with-many; or, as he puts it, "A singular being is a contradiction in terms" (p. 12).

For Nancy, there is no preexistence, no originary state other than being singular plural, which itself, in every plurisingular instance, *is* the origin. Here is how Nancy (2000) puts it:

> *Being singular plural* means the essence of Being is only as coessence. In turn, coessence, or *being-with* (being-with-many), designates the essence of the *co-*, or even more so, the *co-* (the *cum*) itself in the position or guise of an essence. In fact, coessentiality cannot consist in an assemblage of essences, where the essence of this assemblage as such remains to be determined. In relation to such an assemblage, the assembled essences would become [mere] accidents. Coessentiality signifies the essential sharing of essentiality, sharing in the guise of assembling, as it were. This could also be put in the following way: if Being is

> being-with, then it is, in its being-with, the "with" that constitutes Being . . . Therefore, it is not the case that the "with" is an addition to some prior Being; instead, the "with" is at the heart of Being. (pp. 30–31)

In pronouncing "with" to be the essence of Being, in other words, Nancy distances himself from metaphysical narratives that posit a process of rupture or unification of originary being, but also from narratives that would posit a simple dialectical swinging between oneness and multiplicity. Being is immediately and non-dually co-being, co-essence, singular plural.

In speaking [of] the singular plural of being, Nancy has found a way to give voice, as I hear him, to the integral concept of tetra-enaction. In speaking this way, he asks us to think the four quadrants at once, to appreciate their radical co-implication and co-origination. There aren't individuals over here and collectives over there. There is the being singular plural of every blooming object or occasion, and *with* is both the essence and the fragrance of these blooms.

Nancy pursues this ontological line of flight because he feels the crises and challenges of our age call for the discovery of new ways of being-together and being-in-the-world. In this, he has close company with the other prepositional philosophers considered here; all are concerned by the ecological, political, and social challenges of our time, and are seeking new forms of vision that will allow us to adequately address our destructive or inattentive modes of relating to each other and to the environment.

One way of understanding Peter Sloterdijk's (2011a) *Spheres* trilogy, for instance, is as a meditation upon several related prepositions—*with*, *in*, and *between*—in the interest of moving beyond the metaphysics of individualism and substance, which Sloterdijk (2011b) contends is no longer responsive to the challenges of our age. Thus, in *Bubbles*, the first book in the trilogy, Sloterdijk (2011a) critiques the individualist cast of modern subjectivity, and sets up in its place—starting within the fragile, charged spheres of wombs, mother-child relations, lovers' bonds, therapeutic circles, and the divine Trinitarian perichoresis—an alternate psychology of intimacy, relation, and co-being. In his subsequent texts, he charts the historical rise and collapse of traditional monospheric metaphysics, lays the groundwork for a theory of globalization, and (following Jakob von Uexküll, among others) articulates a pluralist topology of fragile, interdependent, overlapping and intersecting lived spaces and relations, which he calls foam. Sounding a little like Nancy, Sloterdijk (2009) says:

> All being-in-the-world possesses the traits of coexistence. The question of being so hotly debated by philosophers can be asked here in terms of the coexistence of people and things in connective spaces. That implies a quadruple relationship: Being means someone (1) being together with someone else (2) and with something else (3) in something (4). This formula describes the minimum complexity you need to construct in order to arrive at an appropriate concept of world. (p. 7)

The prepositions in his description—*in* and *with*—are not merely incidental to it; they are words he stops and lingers over throughout his works. When he says that being means someone being *together with* someone else, he is pronouncing the *with*, the *being singular plural*, of Nancy; but when he adds "with something else" and "in something," he moves beyond the intimate dyads of the womb or the intersubjective "bubbles" of his first book, to a more explicit acknowledgement of the nonhuman and the fact of our inescapable situatedness in concrete spaces that have their own demands. The preposition "in" is enigmatic, he suggests, because it illuminates a paradox: We are always both "in" and "outside" at once, both dependent on having a supportive space for our own existence, and never finally established in any one space or another[19] (Sloterdijk, 2009). We are fond of the freedom of openness, of being unbound, but the "in" (and here he means something concrete: a womb, a family, a house, a language, a culture, a biome, a planet) is essential: It provides immunity against the all-devouring void, the threat of nonexistence, an unbounded ecstasy that would be our own undoing.

But in acknowledging our need for supportive wombs and shelters, he never wants us to forget the impermanent, provisional nature of the walls that encase and define us, and which make possible our adventures and relations in the world:

> In placing the image of the bubble at the center of my reflections, I wish to underline my serious intention to further the revision of substance fetishism and metaphysical individualism. This means beginning with the most fragile, with what we have in common: that is, beginning in the breathiest space, in a thin-walled structure, which, owing to its fragile form and transparent appearance, already gives us to understand that we are supported neither by a security in foundation, and less still by an *inconcussum* or some other rocky base, whether outside or inside. It

> implies that we accept the suggestion to follow a movement of flight in suspension, like a child blowing soap bubbles in the air with a straw, his/her gaze following enthusiastically its works of art until the point that these colored things burst. (Sloterdijk, 2011b, pp. 139–140)

The sentiment here is almost Buddhist: All that we see, all that defines us, all *with* and *in* and *towards which* we move, is like a bubble, a dream, a flash of summer lightning. In positing the "with," it also takes it away; the bubble of our being-together quivers only thinly on the edge of existence. And, as we will see, in its evocation of transiency, of a life in suspended flight, it echoes, both in mood and form, the richly poetic work of Michel Serres, the final prepositional thinker on our list.

Michel Serres has arguably done more to develop and advance a prepositional metaphysics than any other thinker before him. Almost every one of his books takes a preposition as its central theme: *between*, *with*, *across*, *beside*; each of which highlights a different type of relation. Like the other thinkers we have discussed in this section, Serres is dissatisfied with, and wishes to eschew, the traditional metaphysical focus on substance or process, noun or verb. Like Sloterdijk, he prefers topology to geometry.

Serres (1995) is ultimately concerned, he says, with a philosophy of angels: A philosophy that meditates upon those fleeting, subtle mediators that link subjects with other subjects or objects, and that dwell in the thick midst of becoming, drawing depth and integration out of the teeming flux of things. He is concerned to tell a grand narrative, in a sense, but not the kind afforded by ontotheology or monospheric metaphysics (here, he is akin to Sloterdijk). He finds the metaphysical narratives built upon a central substantive or verb to be too static and inflexible. Instead, he prefers to trace out a skyborne, transient topography of relations—a shifting choreography of passages and intermixtures, tendencies and co-implications, adjacencies and rapports.

Summarizing his approach in a discussion with Bruno Latour, Serres (1995) says:

> Instead of creating an abstraction based on substantives—that is, on concepts or verbs (meaning on operations) or even from adverbs or adjectives modifying the substantive or the verb, I abstract *toward*, *by*, *for*, *from*, and so on, down the list of prepositions. I follow them the way one follows a direction: one takes

> it and then one abandons it. It's as though the wise grammarian who named them "prepositions" knew that they preceded any possible position. Once I have worked out the maritime map of these spaces and times that precede any thesis (meaning position), I can die. I will have done my work. (p. 106)

Of all the prepositions, he believes *on*, *in*, and *under* have received the most philosophical attention, in the form of the many metaphysics of transcendence, immanence, and substance, respectively. Serres's approach is to proceed differently, attending as well to the tracings and messages of *to, with, towards, across, through*, and *between*. Like Latour, for instance, he is interested in the ways that beings, animate and inanimate, human and nonhuman, translate and impact and reconfigure each other, *across* their various boundaries and domains; and like Nancy and Sloterdijk, he is interested in the *with* of our greater being-together, meditating on the "natural contracts" we have formed and broken with the other (human and nonhuman) inhabitants of our planet.

Rather than establishing anything once and for all, Serres (1995) observes, prepositions play the facilitative role of mathematical variables, proliferating everywhere, providing points of departure and possibilities for contact and relation. True to the nature of their angelic personifiers, prepositions are, in a sense, heralds or premediators of the many projects of becoming. As Steven Connor (2008) notes, prepositions, in inhabiting a non-place or a pre-position, traffic in between the potential and the actual, sustained attention to which allows for deeper integration of both, as we learn to intimate, discern, and (where appropriate) invite or forestall, what is "in the wings."

In Serres's writings, such work is entertained at many levels at once: A visionary task that he thinks is essential for our age. In following the flight of his angels, which can alight anywhere, and that can initiate unexpected encounters or alliances at any moment, Serres (1995, 2003) allows the shuttling of his gaze over vast terrains and scales of being to slowly kindle, or incandesce, an integral vision of the teeming relations of things.

Of Heno-Ontology and Onto-Choreography

And now we come full circle. We have completed our circuit past six of the shrines that hug the sides of Mt. Sophia at the center of the world. There are more shrines here, to be sure, but these six are popular and make for a good day's walk. Most have been attracting pilgrims for centuries. Each has its own priests and priestesses, some of whom we've met; its own rhetoric and art; its own inviting view. Not all are equal in power or prominence, and some have made allegiances of affinity or convenience with their neighbors. Occasionally sectarian violence breaks out, resulting in a flurry of speeches and papers. But for the most part, over the years, each has found its own way to thrive on the sides of its gracious host.

And how could they not? Who would want to do without nouns, or without pronouns? I know, because I have tried. Over twenty-five years ago, inspired by the work of David Bohm (particularly, his verbal experiment, the *rheomode*), I attempted to create a language without any nouns or pronouns. And I was moderately successful. I found out how well I could get by with just verbs, adverbs, particles, and a few forms of grammatical inflection (including for person-perspective). It was a worthy (if impractical) exercise, and it shifted my perspective on the scope of possibility for alternate forms of meaning-making. But in the end, I abandoned the project; I came to appreciate the beauty of nouns, and no longer felt it was important to renounce them.

In this chapter, like a good henotheist, I have attempted to pay my due respects at the shrines of each of the parts of speech. And as the guide for this pilgrimage, I have tried to give fair voice to the metaphysical visions each discloses. In my heart of hearts, I do not regard them all as equal, it is true. But when I have stepped through the gates of each shrine during the course of this journey, and have listened to the songs and stories intoned therein, I must admit I have more often than not found myself beguiled, inspired, invited in.

As I noted at the beginning of this discussion, the task I have set out for myself here is a meta-metaphysical one: The invocation of multiple worldviews, multiple ontologies; not in the interest of arriving at one final synthesis, but rather of exploring and accommodating multiple possible arrangements and integrations. In a sense, my strategy in this project is similar to the one that Wilber adopted at the beginning of his career. Noticing an abundance of competing psychological and spiritual worldviews and practices, each vying with the other for ultimacy, Wilber (1977) proposed the metaphor of the spectrum of consciousness as a means of making room for them all. This was Wilber's first enactment of the principle of non-exclusion, of *anekantavada*. In my case, I decided to explore the parts of speech as metaphoric lenses for various ontological and epistemological systems when

I began following a long, and seemingly intractable, debate among several Whiteheadian and object-oriented philosophers. I could see that they were arguing at roughly the same level of sophistication and depth, but their views were fundamentally different. One side privileged verbs, the other nouns, even though they could think in each other's terms. This insight, and a later encounter with an essay by Latour (2011) on prepositions, inspired me to explore this topic in earnest.

So, where has this journey brought us? What ground have we covered thus far? The following table lists the major metaphysical systems associated with each of the parts of speech, as well as some of their prominent representatives. For a shorthand designation, I will refer to the basic grammatical-metaphysical orientations we have covered as the Six Views.

Unlike Wilber's spectrum model, which integrated traditions by ordering them along a developmental continuum, I am not presenting the parts of speech in a fixed hierarchical relationship. Several of the parts of speech, it is true, have been regarded as naturally subordinate, but as we have seen, a number of the ontological systems that derive from them have been created by inverting such relationships. Further, although we can recognize certain hierarchical relationships among several of the approaches explored in this chapter—Whitehead's (verbal) process philosophy and Wilber's (pronounal) perspectival postmetaphysics, for instance, can both be regarded as philosophical advances over the classical (nounal) metaphysics of the thing-in-itself or the (adjectival) metaphysics of appearance—this picture is complicated by the fact that many of the different grammatical-philosophical lineages appear to exhibit their own lines of development and forms of integral organization. As I have discussed in the preceding sections, pronounal, nounal, verbal, and prepositional views have each been used to develop new trans-disciplinary, integrative models of their own. For these reasons, the table above is better compared to the quadrant map, with the various components treated as interactive elements that may be variously privileged or emphasized according to the philosophical tradition.

It is important also to note here that the list of philosophers in the chart above primarily reflects the use to which I have put them in this discussion: As instructive exemplars of one of the six grammatical-metaphysical orientations explored in this chapter. This does not mean, however, that any of these thinkers should be regarded as worshipping exclusively at the shrine(s) to which I have assigned them. For instance, as we have seen, although Heidegger's philosophy is an excellent example of an adverbial approach, it is not exclusively so: It has also inspired and informed various

Table 13.1. The Six Views: The Parts of Speech as Metaphysical Lenses

Part of Speech	*Sign*[20]	*Metaphysical Orientation*	*Representative Thinkers*	*Semantic Form*[21]
Pronoun	⌖	Being-as-Perspective Dialogical and Perspectival Epistemologies and Ontologies	Buber, Rosenzweig, Peirce, Habermas, Wilber	**3p:** The sun is shining in the sky. **2p:** O sun in the sky, how you shine! **1p:** I, Sun, am shining in the sky.
Noun	●	Being-as-Substance Substance Metaphysics, Object-Oriented Ontology	Democritus, Aristotle, Descartes, Newton, Harman, Bryant, Wilber	The Sun is shining in the Sky.
Adjective	☼	Being-as-Appearance Idealism, Bundle Theory, Trope Theory, Cittamātra	Berkeley, Hume, Modern Bundle & Trope Theorists, Vasubandhu	Round-bright-yellow in great blue.
Verb	⬆	Being-as-Process Process Metaphysics (Ancient and Modern)	Heraclitus, Plotinus, Hegel, Bergson, Whitehead, Hartshorne, Rescher, Roy	Sunshining where sky-manifesting.
Adverb	↺	Modes of Being Modal Process Metaphysics	Heidegger, Whitehead, Spinoza, Dzogchen, Kashmiri Shaivism	Sunly shining in-the-skyly.
Preposition	◈	Being-as-Relation Relational Metaphysics, Modal Metaphysics, Spherology	Latour, Souriau, Nancy, Serres, Sloterdijk	Sun-in-the-sky, shining-throughout.

Source: author.

verbal and nounal metaphysics. Similarly, while Wilber has made pronouns the centerpiece of his integrative approach, his model encompasses nounal, verbal, and (via tetra-enaction) even adverbial and prepositional elements. A further distinction then suggests itself: The parts of speech may function philosophically, not only as primary metaphysical orientations, but as philosophical elements or philosophemes. I have used the terms somewhat interchangeably in the preceding discussion, but now a clearer definition becomes possible. When we take the parts of speech individually, as the primary guiding ontological orientations or commitments of various philosophical systems, we can refer to them as the Six Views. When we take them collectively, as constitutive *elements* in any overall philosophical system, we can refer to them as philosphemes.

Regarding the former, there is no question that those metaphysical systems that do orient around a particular view will nevertheless incorporate and hierarchically arrange many of the other elements according to their preferences—either by showing how one part derives from the other, or how one is perhaps even only an illusion or appearance generated by the other. A verbal approach may demonstrate how nouns are derivative from verbs, for instance, and may take adverbs for a close partner; or a nounal approach may do the reverse, subordinating the verb and taking the adjective as its helper or its shadow. For the prepositionalists, subject and object are both derivative, and verbs must follow the flows that prepositions make available. This is why I have spoken of heno-ontology: Most of these systems acknowledge the *existence* of the other grammatical "gods" (denying or ignoring one or two of the others, perhaps, but never all), but they ultimately exalt and pledge allegiance to only one among them. This is why I have also introduced the word *onto-choreography*: Each approach uniquely choreographs these different elements or modes of being, letting one part take the lead in this model, another in that one.[22]

To summarize, then, and starting at the most general level first, I believe the model we have explored in this chapter can be approached from four closely related angles. First, the parts of speech can be used as metaphorical lenses to identify and analyze the central ontological or metaphysical commitments of various worldviews, and to classify and situate these worldviews in relation to each other. This is the most basic orientation I have presented here, which I am referring to as the Six Views. Second, as the six parts of speech considered here are constitutive elements in most of the grammars of the world, the metaphysical concepts to which they correspond may be similarly regarded as universal intuitions—each one an important element of an overall understanding of reality. While most metaphysical traditions tend to privilege one or more of the grammatical-metaphysical elements above the others, as we have already discussed, the other elements are nevertheless recognized and find some place in the overall economy of the worldview. I am referring to these as the Six Elements or the Six Philosophemes. Third, considering that most metaphysical traditions do tend to privilege a particular grammatical-metaphysical element over others, it is likely that they will have enacted it and unfolded it with a greater degree of sophistication and subtlety than those traditions for which that element is secondary or tertiary. From an integral viewpoint, then, we would likely benefit by adopting a meta-metaphysical orientation and learning to move in and out of these worldspaces, mastering the various languages, models, modes of analysis, and so on, unique to each one (including, and even especially, those that have developed metaphysical orientations that we tend to under-privilege in our own traditions). Lastly, the different grammatical ordering of these elements within the various metaphysical traditions, where one part of speech might be a central organizing lens in one case and merely an adjunct feature of another, suggests a practice of reflexive circulation of the elements—turning the kaleidoscope to see what is yielded when this piece is central, or that. Onto-choreography is the practice of circulating and coordinating these elements.

How do these reflections bear on integral theory? What do we have to gain from interfacing a model such as this with the integral map? I will review several of the possibilities here, and will save a fuller discussion for a future publication.

Firstly, following Bonnitta Roy's (2006) insight, the primary lenses upon which integral theory relies—the person-perspectives—are not sufficient in themselves to disclose the metaphysical underpinnings of the views that inform our perspective-taking. Our enactive frameworks and modes of interface with the world are not person-perspectival alone. This is not news to an integralist, of course. But I believe the grammatical-philosophical lenses outlined here constitute modes of meaning-making and perceptual organization, even of implicit, embodied ontological commitment, which are important to name and to highlight.

For instance, as discussed previously, the quadrant map can be conceptualized and employed from either a structural or processual—nounal or verbal—orientation. In light of the model of the Six Views introduced here, however, we might further consider how the quadrant model could be informed by, and used in relation with, any one of the parts of speech we have reviewed in this chapter.

For ease of reference, I am using the signs introduced in Table 1 above to represent the Six Views and their corresponding ontological elements or categories. The sign at the center of the map represents the primary

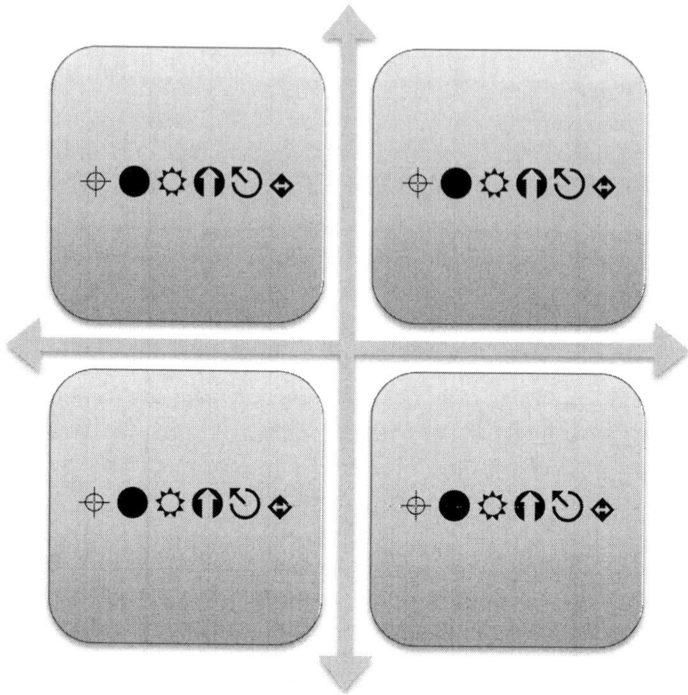

Figure 13.9. AQAL and the six views or elements. *Source:* author.

ontological view or orientation within which the person-perspectives are being enacted, whether verbal (as above), nounal, prepositional, or otherwise. And the series of signs in each quadrant is intended to indicate various aspects of being—perspectives, objects, phenomenal experiences, processes, and so on—that can be viewed or investigated from each of the four person-perspectives. In this way, the parts of speech can be interfaced with the integral map either in the form of *primary orienting view*, informing the enactment of the model itself, or as *constitutive aspects or elements of being* that can be investigated within each perspectival enactment. This would be one example of the practice of an integral onto-choreography.[23]

As a simple illustration of what this might look like in practice, let's consider a prepositional version of the quadrant map. As Serres (1995) has noted, prepositions are like mathematical variables. One immediately promising application of the prepositional orientation would be to interface it with AQAL and the integral pronouns. As we currently use the quadrant map, it is as if the I, We, It, and Its arise in neutral, empty space together. Buber's hyphen suggests the same. But when the person-perspectives—whether I-and-Thou or I-We-It-and-Its—arise, they arise already in a kind of relation, a space of vectors, flows, inclinations, pressures, gaps. What is the nature of their togetherness? This can be explored and evoked with the use of prepositions: I *with* Thou, I *under* Thou, I *over* It, I *into* It, We *over* I, I *for* (or *against*) Me, and so on. Each clearly different. The figure below graphically represents the relations and vectors among several first-person perspectives in an actual occasion.

The configuration of perspectives here suggests an occasion, or series of occasions, in which the I experiences itself as subordinate to the We, but in a way that is *for* or *in the service of* the self (as "Me"). By changing the "for" to "against," however, we can model an instance of shaming, or the experience of an oppressive pressure to conform. If we would like to map more complex relational configurations across multiple perspectival domains, we could use the prepositions in conjunction with the AQAL cube model or O'Connor's Triadic Quadratic Perspectives.

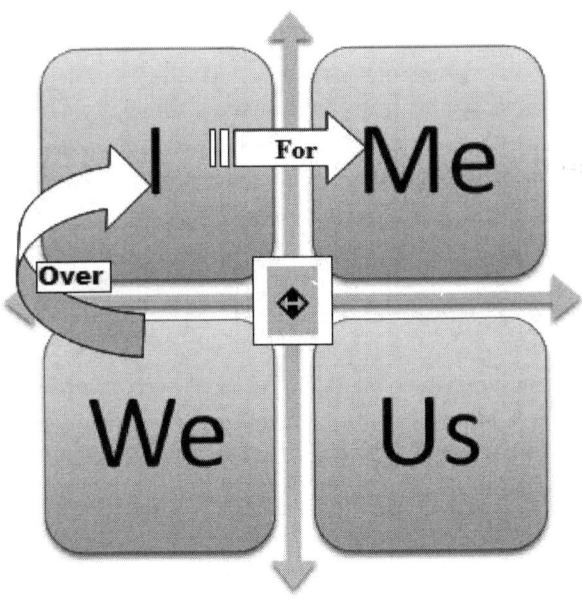

Figure 13.10. Prepositional analysis of the four quadrants. *Source:* author.

Secondly, although integral theory is not *exclusively* a pronounal or perspectival system, as I have discussed above, I believe the integral model will nevertheless be enriched by more explicitly acknowledging its place in the history of pronounal philosophy, ancient and modern. Doing so will provide integral thinkers with a deepened sense of lineage, and will encourage integral practitioners to draw more frequently from the rich well of philosophical and theological thought on this topic. The current quadrant model is useful and elegant in its simplicity, but there are a number of ways it could be made more robust, more logically consistent, more ethically sensitive, and even more deeply rooted theologically or spiritually, as I suggested above.

Lastly, at the level of metatheory, we have seen that a number of the philosophical movements associated with one or another of the parts of speech have developed, or are in the process of developing, integrative metatheories of their own. The emergence of a diversity of integral-stage philosophical models is, in fact, something integral theory itself leads us to expect, with its postmetaphysical embrace of ontological pluralism and its inclusion of "All Types" in the AQAL model. The types ensure a diversity of forms of expression and modes of being at any stage. The approach taken in this chapter is consonant with, and builds upon, these aspects of integral theory, with the Six Views model providing one means of conceptualizing a pluralist ontological typology. Work remains to be done to demonstrate more precisely how each of the philosophemes explored here manifests across multiple stages of development, and how some elements may even converge and become "entangled" at higher stages of expression. For the purposes of the suggestion I am making here, however, it is sufficient to acknowledge simply that they do so—that nounal, verbal, and other grammatically based philosophical models find expression across multiple stages of development (from Aristotle to OOO; from Heraclitus to Whitehead, etc). At postmodern and integral stages, this takes the form of various trans-disciplinary, integrative, and meta-paradigmatic projects—alternately flowering, as we have seen, in pronounal, nounal, verbal, or prepositional soils. The Six Views model provides a means, not only to classify and compare metaphysical systems, but to encourage and support an integral pluralist orientation toward such integrative metatheories, and to bring these systems into greater generative dialogue, creative tension, and potential collaboration.

To the extent that we allow this to happen, I believe we are attending well to the voice of Sophia.

Notes

1. Traditional grammar identifies eight parts of speech in English, but modern grammarians tend to regard this classification system as inadequate. Recently, an expanded model of the English parts of speech has been proposed: nouns, verbs, pronouns, adjectives, adverbs, determiners, prepositions (or adpositions), conjunctions, subordinators, complementizers, sentence connectors, degree modifiers, particles, and interjections. For this chapter, I am using only six of the major parts of speech, partly for the purposes of parsimony, but also because the six grammatical functions I have selected are common to most major languages (with a few exceptions, which I will discuss) and they are also the ones most commonly associated with major philosophical approaches.

2. Chomsky himself, in a paper published several years after *Philosophy in the Flesh*, appears now to embrace a view similar to the one argued by Lakoff and Johnson, i.e., that the faculty of language should no longer be considered as a wholly autonomous neural mechanism, but rather as interconnected with, and dependent upon, other non-linguistic systems in the brain (Hauser, Chomsky, and Fitch, 2002).

3. For a fuller discussion of pronouns in philosophy, see Tse-Wan Kwan (2010).

4 Rosenzweig also discusses four-part and five-part models of pronoun relations (which articulate various forms of relation between God, humankind, and creation). The four-part relation is He-it, I-Thou, I-Thou, and We-It, and the five-part relation is He-It, I-Thou, I-Thou, I-Thou, and We-It.

5. In Eastern philosophical traditions, one of the clearest examples of personalist metaphysics is found in Ramanuja's *vishishtadvaita*, or qualified non-dualist, philosophy (Williams and Bengtsson, 2011).

6. This dual emphasis is consistent with Wilber's (2003b, 2013) insistence on the non-duality or inseparability of epistemology and ontology.

7. See Schwartz (2010), p. 232 with notes, as well as his "Tetra Call of the Good" in the present volume.

8. Wilber also acknowledges that the quadrants and the person-perspectives are independent, so O'Connor's critique should be read as applying primarily to the shorthand identifications that Wilber has frequently and consistently made.

9. O'Connor (2012) mentions in an endnote, in fact, that a full enactive map would include not only verbs and pronouns, but nouns, adjectives, and adverbs as well.

10. See Edward Berge's (2010) extensive discussion and critique of certain mathematically based models of hierarchical development, which he argues appear to rely, per Lakoff (2010), on false (disembodied, abstract, objectivist) reasoning, and thus to perpetuate the metaphysics of presence (which we will discuss in detail later in this section).

11. As Desilet (2005) and others have argued, however, while Wilber rightly criticizes the myth of the given underlying perennial philosophical and other

metaphysical models, Wilber's notion of the causal ground of being, as the originary one lying behind, giving rise to, and pervading all apparent forms and perspectival enactments, still appears to be a form of onto-theology.

12. See Bryant's (2011d) "The Time of the Object" for a discussion of how Derrida's notion of *différance* can provide conceptual resources for rethinking substance in terms of radical withdrawal and temporality.

13. See Bryant (2010—"Even More Vitale") for his thoughts on why he prefers the word *translation* to *perspective.*

14. See Wilber (1995) for a discussion of the distinction between holons and heaps, and Bryant (2011a) for a discussion of autopoietic and allopoietic objects.

15. An archaic, nongrammatical definition of the word, adjective, is dependent or unable to stand alone; as in: "The queen's lapdog is an adjective creature; it wouldn't survive two weeks on its own."

16. There is some debate among Whitehead scholars as to whether Whitehead would count societies or nexūs of actual occasions—such as complex organisms that consist of many microscopic actual occasions—as actual entities in themselves; I am here following F. Bradford Wallack's interpretation, which holds that Whitehead applies the term "actual entity" as much to the midsized objects of ordinary experience as he does to atoms or particles.

17. Wilber and Bryant also both agree that such mediating structures, whether understood intersubjectively or as an object's endo-structure, can be influenced and changed by the experience of the subject, without necessarily ever becoming "object" for the subject.

18. See Graham Harman's (2009) *The Prince of Networks.*

19. This can be related to OOO's notion of withdrawal, which holds that no entity is ever wholly determined by or bound to its relations with other objects (including ecologies, cultures, etc).

20. A brief explanation of the six signs: I have selected the circle with a cross for pronoun because it is evocative both of the four quadrants and of a targeting site, both of which are associated with "perspective." The black circle for the noun is intended to suggest the withdrawn or subterranean substance of beings. The image for adjective, the sun, represents the radiant self-othering of beings in the form of perceptual qualities and phenomenal appearances. The symbol for process is intended to evoke dynamism or creativity arising into form. The sign for adverb is a little more complex: the marked circular space suggests a mode, pattern, or archetypal form informing the patterned unfolding of becoming or action, in the form of the emerging arrow. Finally, the sign for preposition, the two arrows within the diamond, represents relationality.

21. Following Nicholas Rescher's (1996) recommendation for a process semantics built on verbs and adverbs, which I discussed in the section on adverbial philosophy, I have offered (in a playful spirit) examples of semantic forms for each of the Six Views. I intend for these examples to be taken primarily as poetic evocations

of implicit metaphysical sensibilities, rather than as recommendations for new forms of philosophical languaging. The reader may note that the third-person pronounal expression and the nounal expression are the same. This was for convenience of expression, however. The 3p expression should not be regarded as being restricted to a nounal formulation, as the three pronounal person-perspectives could be used, in fact, to frame any of the other semantic forms (a 123p of nounal, verbal, adverbial, or other expressions). In this way, both pronouns and prepositions seem to occupy a special role, as prepositions also can be used to pre-position (or relationally inform) any of the other constructions.

22. A Serres-inspired prepositional model could be used to discern and trace out the onto-choreography of the parts of speech within a metaphysical system—how the parts of speech constellate and coordinate within each visionary space.

23. Following a familiar convention in integral theory, we could conceive of an alternative form of 3-2-1 practice: The 3-2-1 of integral onto-choreography. This would entail the coordinated practice of several of the possibilities discussed above: 1) using the distinctions and concepts introduced in this chapter to engage in third-person classification, comparison, analysis, and/or construction of various metaphysical and integrative systems; 2) using the Six Views model and language to facilitate second-person dialogue and debate with and among existing philosophical systems, whether classical, modern, or postmodern/integral; and 3) engaging in first-person experiential or contemplative exploration of the enactive potential of each of the models and worldviews with which we interact.

References

Alderman, B. 2012. "Opening Space for Translineage Practice: Some Ontological Speculations." *Journal of Integral Theory and Practice* 7(2): 49–71.

Alexander, Christopher. 2003. *The Nature of Order (Book 4): The Luminous Ground.* Berkeley, CA: The Center for Environmental Structure.

Alexander, Christopher. 2004. *The Nature of Order (Book 1): The Phenomenon of Life.* Berkeley, CA: The Center for Environmental Structure.

Alexander, Christopher. 2006. *The Nature of Order (Book 2): The Process of Creating Life.* Berkeley, CA: The Center for Environmental Structure.

Ambuel, D. 2000. "Ontology in Indian Philosophy." In *Concise Routledge Encyclopaedia of Philosophy*, ed. Edward Craig, 1918–1919. New York: Routledge.

Aristotle. 1984. *The Complete Works of Aristotle*, vol. 1 and 2, ed. J. Barnes. Princeton, NJ: Princeton University Press.

Batnitzky, Leora. 2000. *Idolatry and Representation: The Philosophy of Franz Rosenzweig Reconsidered.* Princeton, NJ: Princeton University Press.

Bensusan, Hilan, and Eros Carvalho. 2011. "Qualia Qua Qualitons: Mental Qualities as Abstract Particulars." *Acta Analytica* 26(2): 155–163.

Berge, E. 2010. "Real and False Reason." Retrieved from http://integralpostmetaphysics.ning.com/forum/topics/real-and-false-reason.

Bhaskar, Roy. 2008. *A Realist Theory of Science*. New York: Routledge.

Bogost, Ian. 2012. *Alien Phenomenology, or What It's Like to Be a Thing*. Minneapolis, MN: University of Minnesota Press.

Bohm, David. 1980. *Wholeness and the Implicate Order*. New York: Routledge.

Brahmavamso, Ajahn. 2005. "Anatta (non-self)." Retrieved from http://www.dhammatalks.net/Books3/Ajahn_Brahm_ANATTA.htm.

Brown, Anderson. 2011. "Hume on Qualia." Retrieved from http://andersonbrown-philosophy.blogspot.com/2011/03/hume-on-qualia.html.

Brown, Jason. 1996. *Time, Will, and Mental Process*. New York: Plenum Press.

Brown, Jason. 1997. *Mind, Brain, and Consciousness: The Neuropsychology of Cognition*. New York: Academic Press.

Brown, Jason. 1998. *The Life of the Mind*. Hillsdale, NJ: Lawrence Erlbaum Associates.

Brown, Jason. 2000. *Mind and Nature: Essays on Time and Subjectivity*. London: Whurr Publishers.

Brown, Jason. 2002. *The Self-Embodying Mind: Process, Brain Dynamics and the Conscious Present*. Barrytown, NY: Barrytown/Station Hill.

Bryant, Levi. 2008. "Correlationism and the Fate of Philosophy." Retrieved from http://larvalsubjects.wordpress.com/2008/06/13/correlationism-and-the-fate-of-philosophy/.

Bryant, Levi. 2010a. "Whitehead's Prehensions and Onticology." Retrieved from http://larvalsubjects.wordpress.com/2010/06/27/whiteheads-prehensions-and-onticology/.

Bryant, Levi. 2010b. "Even More Vitale: Translations, Perspectives, and Truth." Retrieved from http://larvalsubjects.wordpress.com/2010/07/01/even-more-vitale-translations-perspectives-and-truth/.

Bryant, Levi. 2011a. *The Democracy of Objects*. Ann Arbor, MI: MPublishing.

Bryant, Levi. 2011b. "OOO Realism and Epistemology." Retrieved from http://larvalsubjects.wordpress.com/2011/04/12/ooo-realism-and-epistemology/.

Bryant, Levi. 2011c. "The Ontic Principle: Outline of an Object-Oriented Philosophy." In *The Speculative Turn: Continental Materialism and Realism*, eds. Levi Bryant, Nick Srnicek, and Graham Harman. Melbourne, AU: re.press.

Bryant, Levi. 2011d. "The Time of the Object: Toward the Ontological Grounds of Withdrawal." Retrieved from http://larvalsubjects.files.wordpress.com/2010/12/timeofobject-10-tex-1.pdf.

Bryant, Levi. 2012. "Alethetics." Retrieved from http://larvalsubjects.wordpress.com/2012/03/14/alethetics/.

Buber, Martin. 1958. *I and Thou*, trans. R.G. Smith. New York: Scribner.

Cohen, Richard A. 1994. *Elevations: The Height of the Good in Rosenzweig and Levinas*. Chicago: University of Chicago Press.

Connor, Steven. 2008. "Wherever: The Ecstasies of Michel Serres." Retrieved from http://www.stevenconnor.com/wherever/.

Dean, Jodi. 1996. *Solidarity of Strangers: Feminism After Identity Politics.* Berkeley, CA: University of California Press.

Della Rocca, Michael. 2008. *Spinoza.* New York: Routledge.

Derrida, Jacques. 1976. *Of Grammatology,* trans.G.C. Spivak. Baltimore, MD: Johns Hopkins University Press.

Dreyfus, H.L. 1996. "Being and Power: Heidegger and Foucault." *International Journal of Philosophical Studies* 4(1): 1–16.

Edwards, M. 2003. "Through AQAL Eyes, part 7: 'I' and 'Me' and 'We' and 'Us' and 'You' and 'Yous.'" Retrieved February 27, 2013, from http://www.integralworld.net/edwards11.html.

Esbjörn-Hargens, Sean, and Michael Zimmerman. 2011. *Integral Ecology: Uniting Multiple Perspectives on the Natural World.* Boston: Integral Books.

Feldman, Jerome. 2006. *From Molecule to Metaphor: A Neural Theory of Language.* Cambridge, MA: MIT Press.

Fuhs, Clint. 2010. "An Integral Map of Perspective-Taking." In *Integral Theory in Action: Applied, Theoretical, and Constructive Perspectives on the AQAL Model,* ed. Sean Esbjörn-Hargens. Albany, NY: SUNY Press.

Gebser, Jean. 1986. *The Ever-Present Origin,* trans. Noel Barstad with Algis Mickunas. Athens, OH: Ohio University Press.

Guenther, Herbert V. 1984. *Matrix of Mystery: Scientific and Humanistic Aspects of rDzogs-chen Thought.* Boulder, CO: Shambhala.

Guenther, Herbert V. 1989. *From Reductionism to Creativity: rDzogs-chen and the New Sciences of Mind.* Boulder, CO: Shambhala.

Guignon, C. 2005. "The History of Being." In *A Companion to Heidegger,* eds. H.L. Dreyfus and M.A. Wrathall, 392–406. Malden, MA: Blackwell Publishing.

Habermas, Jürgen. 1981. *The Theory of Communicative Action (Vol. 1): Reason and the Rationalization of Society,* trans. Thomas McCarthy. Boston: Beacon Press.

Hanlon, Robert E. (ed.). 1991. *Cognitive Microgenesis: A Neuropsychological Perspective.* Berlin: Springer-Verlag.

Harman, Graham. 2005. *Guerilla Metaphysics: Phenomenology and the Carpentry of Things.* Chicago: Open Court.

Harman, Graham. 2009. *Prince of Networks: Bruno Latour and Metaphysics.* Melbourne, AU: re.press.

Harman, Graham. 2011a. *The Quadruple Object.* Winchester, UK: Zero Books.

Harman, Graham. 2011b. "On the Undermining of Objects: Grant, Bruno, and Radical Philosophy." In *The Speculative Turn: Continental Materialism and Realism,* eds. Levi Bryant, Nick Srnicek, and Graham Harman. Melbourne, AU: re.press.

Harman, Graham. 2011c. "Response to Shaviro." In *The Speculative Turn: Continental Materialism and Realism,* eds. Levi Bryant, Nick Srnicek, and Graham Harman. Melbourne, AU: re.press.

Harman, Graham. 2011d. "The Road to Objects." *Continent* 1(3): 171–179.

Hartshorne, C. 1979. "Whitehead's Revolutionary Concept of Prehension." *International Philosophical Quarterly* 19(3): 253–263.

Hauser, Marc D., Noam Chomsky, and W. Tecumseh Fitch. 2002. "The Faculty of Language: What Is It, Who Has It, and How Did It Evolve?" *Science* 298(5598): 1569–1579.

Heidegger, Martin. 1962. *Being and Time*, trans. John MacQuarrie and Edward Robinson. New York: Harper & Row.

Hume, David. 1739–1740. *A Treatise of Human Nature*. Retrieved from http://www.davidhume.org/texts/thn.html.

James, William. 1983. *The Principles of Psychology*. Cambridge, MA: Harvard University Press.

Kenny, Anthony. 2003. *Action, Emotion and Will*. New York: Routledge.

Klein, A.C., and T. Wangyal Rinpoche. 2006. *Unbounded Wholeness: Dzogchen, Bon, and the Logic of the Nonconceptual*. New York: Oxford University Press.

Kwan, T.W. 2010. "Towards a Phenomenology of Pronouns." In *Identity and Alterity: Phenomenology and Cultural Traditions*, eds. K.Y. Lau, C.F. Cheung, and T.W. Kwan, 259–280. Würzburg, GER: Königshausen & Neumann.

Lakoff, George, and Mark Johnson. 1999. *Philosophy in the Flesh*. New York: Basic Books.

Latour, Bruno. 2011. "Reflections on Etienne Souriau's Les differents modes d'existence," trans. Stephen Muecke. In *The Speculative Turn: Continental Materialism and Realism*, eds. Levi Bryant, Nick Srnicek, and Graham Harman. Melbourne, AU: re.press.

Macy, Joanna. 1991. *Mutual Causality in Buddhism and General Systems Theory: The Dharma of Natural Systems*. Albany, NY: SUNY Press.

Meillassoux, Quentin. 2008. *After Finitude: An Essay on the Necessity of Contingency*, trans. Ray Brassier. London: Continuum.

Morrison, J.D. 2007. *SpinbitZ: Interface Philosophy, Mathematics and Nondual Rational-Empiricism*. Retrieved March 11, 2013, from http://www.spinbitz.net/.

Morton, T. 2011. "Here Comes Everything: The Promise of Object-Oriented ontology." *Qui Parle* 19(2)163–190.

Nancy, Jean-Luc. 2000. *Being Singular Plural*, trans. R.D. Richardson and A.E. O'Byrne. Stanford, CA: Stanford University Press.

Neil, L. 2011. "The AQAL Cube: A Second-tier Differentiation of Ken Wilber's AQAL Square." Retrieved February 28, 2013, from http://www.integralworld.net/neale1.html.

O'Connor, D.J. 2012. "Awareness-in-action: A Critical Integralism for the Challenges of Our Time." Bainbridge Island, WA: Catallaxis. Retrieved from http://integralventures.typepad.com/articles/OConnor-Awareness-in-Action.pdf.

Peirce, C.S. 1998. *The Essential Peirce: Selected Philosophical Writings, 1893–1913, Volume 2*, ed. Peirce Edition Project. Bloomington, IN: Indiana University Press.

Rentschler, M. 2006. "AQAL Glossary." *AQAL: Journal of Integral Theory and Practice* 1(3): 1–39.

Rescher, Nicholas. 1996. *Process Metaphysics: An Introduction to Process Philosophy.* Albany, NY: SUNY Press.

Robinson, H. 2004. "Substance." In *The Stanford Encyclopedia of Philosophy*, ed. E.N. Zalta. Retrieved from http://plato.stanford.edu/archives/win2009/entries/substance/.

Roy, Bonnitta. 2006. "A Process Model of Integral Theory." *Integral Review* 3: 118–152. Retrieved March 1, 2012, from http://integral-review.org/back_issues/backissue3/index.htm.

Roy, Bonnitta. 2010. AQAL 2210: "A Tentative Cartology of the Future, or How Do We Get From AQAL to A-perspectival?" Paper presented at the biannual Integral Theory Conference, Pleasant Hill, CA. Retrieved from http://integraltheoryconference.org/sites/default/files/itc-2010-papers/Roy_ITC%20 2010.doc.pdf.

Roy, Bonnitta, and J. Trudel. 2011. "Leading the 21st Century: The Conception-Wware, Object-Oriented Organization." *Integral Leadership Review*. Retrieved February 27, 2012, from http://integralleadershipreview.com/3199-leading-the-21stcentury-the-conception-aware-object-orientedorganization.

Sakai 2005. "Japanese and English Sentence Structures." *Multilingual Computing and Technology* 16(8). http://www.multilingual.com/articleDetail.php?id=1089.

Sallis, John. 2000. *Force of Imagination: The Sense of the Elemental.* Bloomington, IN: Indiana University Press.

Schwartz, Michael. 2010. "Frames of AQAL, Integral Critical Theory, and the Emerging Integral Arts." In *Integral Theory in Action: Applied, Theoretical, and Constructive Perspectives on the AQAL Model*, ed. Sean Esbjörn-Hargens. Albany, NY: SUNY Press.

Seibt, J. 2012. "Process Philosophy." In *The Stanford Encyclopedia of Philosophy*, ed. E.N. Zalta. Retrieved from http://plato.stanford.edu/archives/win2012/entries/process-philosophy/.

Serres, Michel. 2003. *L'Incandescent*. Paris: Le Pommier.

Serres, Michel. 1995. *Angels: A Modern Myth*. Paris: Flammarion.

Shaviro, Steven. 2009. *Without Criteria: Kant, Whitehead, Deleuze, and Aesthetics.* Cambridge, MA: MIT Press.

Shaviro, Steven. 2010. "Whitehead vs. Spinoza & Deleuze on the Virtual." Retrieved from http://www.shaviro.com/Blog/?p=909.

Sloterdijk, Peter. 2009. "Spheres Theory: Talking to Myself About the Poetics of Space." *Harvard Design Magazine* 30. http://www.gsd.harvard.edu/images/content/5/5/553631/30.Sloterdijk.pdf.

Sloterdijk, Peter. 2011a. *Bubbles: Microspherology*, trans. W. Hoban. Los Angeles: Semiotext(e).

Sloterdijk, Peter. 2011b. *Neither Sun Nor Death*, trans.S. Corcoran. Los Angeles: Semiotext(e).

Újvári, Márta. 2012. *The Trope Bundle Theory of Substance: Change, Individuation, and Individual Essence*. Heusenstamm, GER: Ontos Verlag.

Varela, F.J. 2000. "Steps to a Science of Inter-being: Unfolding the Dharma Implicit in Modern Cognitive Science." In *The Psychology of Awakening: Buddhism, Science, and Our Day-to-Day Lives*, eds. Gay Watson, Stephen Batchelor, and Guy Claxton, 71–89. York Beach, ME: Samuel Weiser.

Whitehead, Alfred North. 1967. *Adventures of Ideas*. New York: Free Press.

Whitehead, Alfred North. 1978. *Process and Reality*. New York: Free Press.

Whorf, Benjamin. 1956. *Language, Thought, and Reality: Selected Writings of Benjamin Lee Whorf*. Cambridge, MA: MIT Press.

Wilber, Ken. 1977. *The Spectrum of Consciousness*. Wheaton, IL: Quest Books.

Wilber, Ken. 1995. *Sex, Ecology, Spirituality: The Spirit of Evolution*. Boston: Shambhala.

Wilber, Ken. 2001. "Do Critics Misrepresent My Position? A Test Case From a Recent Academic Journal." Retrieved from http://www.kenwilber.com/writings/read_pdf/2.

Wilber, Ken. 2003a. "Excerpt A: An Integral Age at the Leading Edge." Retrieved from http://www.kenwilber.com/Writings/PDF/ExcerptC_KOSMOS_2003.pdf.

Wilber, Ken. 2003b. "Excerpt C: The Ways We Are In This Together: Intersubjectivity and Interobjectivity in the Holonic Kosmos." Retrieved from http://www.kenwilber.com/Writings/PDF/ExcerptC_KOSMOS_2003.pdf.

Wilber, Ken. 2006. *Integral Spirituality: A Startling New Role for Religion in the Modern and Postmodern World*. Boston: Integral Books.

Wilber, Ken. 2013. "Response to Critical Realism in Defense of Integral Theory." Retrieved from http://integrallife.com/integral-post/response-critical-realism-defense-integral-theory.

Williams, F. 1986. "Some Reflections on Spinoza's Ethics as Edifying Ontology." In *The Life of the Transcendental Ego: Essays in Honor of William Earle*, eds. E.S. Casey and D.V. Morano. Albany, NY: SUNY Press.

Williams, Paul. 1989. *Mahayana Buddhism: The Doctrinal Foundations*. New York: Routledge.

Zajonc, Arthur. 1993. *Catching the Light: The Entwined History of Light and Mind*. New York: Oxford University Press.

Afterword

Realism and Idealism in Integral Theory

Ken Wilber

In addition to the volume's chapters, we include as an afterword a fresh piece by Ken Wilber, the principle inaugurator of integral theory: The written version of his keynote address at the Fourth International Integral Theory Conference, July 2015, in Sonoma, CA. In the essay, Wilber responds to the recent dialogues between critical realism and integral theory (cited in the introduction of this volume), evoking his concept of integral methodological pluralism (IMP) that involves the interfolding of eight primordial perspectives. This scheme extends that of the quadrants, as constituted by four perspectives, those of the individual interior (UL), the individual exterior (UR), the collective interior (LL), and the collective exterior (LR). IMP goes further by discerning each of the four quadrant-perspectives as having both an inside feel and an outside look, constituting the eightfold perspectival scheme. To give an example of this inside/outside distinction, with regard to the individual interior, the inside feel is the immediate sense of one's experience, which can be methodologically investigated via techniques like those of Husserlian phenomenology; while the outside look is the measurable structures of mind that in part pattern such experience, but escape direct introspection, and can be methodological investigated by disciplines like Piagetian developmental psychology. Wilber redeploys IMP to recast some of critical realism's own concepts like those of the epistemic and ontic fallacies.

—the Editors

What we "see out there" is a product, not just of a given ontology of the item seen, but of the methodology and epistemology we bring to see it. Again, this is not saying that the characteristics of the known object are fully created by the knowing subject (this is *not* subjective idealism); simply that the characteristics of the object that are disclosed depend in part upon the means of disclosure. If we have an iron rod, and we start heating that rod, there is no way to know that the rod is becoming hot by simply looking at it. Vision does not disclose the hotness (until, at any rate, the rod begins to glow). Touching, however, does—touch it (change your methodology) and you will see the "hotness" is disclosed. Even more, if we look at the rod through an infrared detecting device, we will see the rod lit up and radiating in all directions—those radiating fields cannot be detected by any human visual sense; but change the methodology (in this case, with an infrared detecting device), and those fields are disclosed. Saying that there is "just a single rod in existence" is to privilege one or more detecting methodologies (or types of epistemologies). We could say "the single" rod is what is disclosed by the sum total of detecting devices used on it, and that would be fine—as long as we include human epistemology in the equation of detecting devices, and then realize that the epistemological subject itself grows through upwards of a dozen different real levels, and each of those levels will see something different about the rod and its surroundings—so we have a magenta rod (an elemental spirit), a red rod (tool of a PowerGod), an amber rod (creation of an almighty Creator), an orange rod (made of atoms and crystals), a green rod (made of multiple quarks), a turquoise rod (made of eleventh-dimensional strings), and so on indefinitely. Every rod that we know is the product of the ontology of the rod (endlessly expanding) and the methodology used to detect it and the epistemology used to know it—all three of those are inseparable aspects of the single Wholeness of whatever the rod actually is. There is no such thing as "*the* rod." (The closest thing to it would be the rod "at the end of time," when all known methodologies would have been discovered and used, and the highest level of evolution would have been reached for epistemology, and the sum total of all those would be "the" rod—and if we say that, then (of course) we never have anything resembling any sort of truth, ever, because until "ultimate truth" is reached at the end of time, everything we know is shot through with some sort of falsehood. Far from anchoring our ontology—as virtually all realist schools attempt to do in this fashion, by postulating "the rod"—we have actually destroyed ontology, destroyed any hope of ever having any truth at all.) Rather, each Whole rod (a phenomenon consisting of [a particular epistemology] X [a particular methodology] X [the ontology thus disclosed]) is a *true* version of the rod *at that particular level* if all the given phenomena at that level are fully taken into account and then the best possible view of the rod is determined given the actual realities of that particular AQAL address. Less than that, is a false view of the rod (and ontology and epistemology). More than that, is not possible. Similar (but not identical) to the way Hegel put it—"Every level is adequate, every higher level is more adequate"—we have: "Every level is true, every higher level is more true." Thus, truth is on a sliding evolutionary scale, with each level capable of truth, and each higher level capable of a wider truth. Any other option—from realist to idealist to materialist to positivist—unconvincingly privileges a component of this overall process.

Another way to look at all of this is that the above is an integral overview of the results of taking all of the methodologies generated in all eight zones and including all their central features, in order to arrive at the "most correct" view of epistemology and ontology possible (or the view "most likely" true at that stage of history/evolution). In particular, we note that each zone is especially delimited by being an "inside" or an "outside" view of a prior perspective already chosen as especially real—that is, the inside or outside view of a holon "in" the upper right (i.e., zones #5 and #6); or the inside or outside of the lower right (i.e., zones 7 and 8); or the inside and outside of the upper left (i.e., zones 1 and 2); or the inside and outside of the lower left (i.e., zones 3 and 4). These zones appear in quadrants where, in most cases, it has already been decided which quadrant is the "ultimate reality," and once one has decided on what quadrant is "really real" (e.g., material objects are what is "really real"—the upper right; or social systems—the lower right; or inner empiricism/constructivism—the upper left; or cultural constructivism—the lower left, etc.)—after one has made that fundamental selection, then one will generally further select the zone—the inside-view or the outside-view—of that "really real quadrant." One doesn't even necessarily have to choose a quadrant; but one will still very likely—and almost all existing epistemologies do—select either an *inside view* (subjective, enactive, phenomenological, autopoietic, cognitive [meaning the view "from within" as the organism's own cognition sees it, compared to a "rational" scientific view "from without" as the scientists themselves see it]), or select that *outside view* (objective, "totalistic" or some form of third-person "holism," "rational" [meaning, as the scientists themselves see the overall reality], etc.). These two basic views—inside/subjective and outside/objective—are also behind the major "competing" epistemologies in history, such as materialism/realism vs. idealism (outside/objective vs. inside/subjective); body vs. mind (outside/objective vs. inside/subjective); matter vs. spirit (outside/objective vs. inside/subjective); and so on.

The point is that, since the perspective "inside/outside" is universally available (all the way up, all the way down—it's what creates the "zones" in each quadrant), it fits into the typical human inclination of choosing one side of a duality and proclaiming it real, while denying reality to its opposite—and then basing its entire methodology on the "really real" zone (inside or outside) in whatever quadrant (or quadrants) that has already been chosen as the ultimately "really real" reality there is.

Some examples will show the importance (and reality) of this distinction between the "inside-view" and the "outside-view." Two of the most important theorists in postmodern theory are Heidegger and Foucault—and while both of them acknowledged the reality of the intersubjective (lower-left) view, they did so from exactly the inside vs. the outside views. Dreyfus and Rabinow do an excellent job of summarizing Foucault's approach and differentiating it from Heidegger's:

> Foucault's devotion to the description of concrete structures understood as conditions of existence bears a striking similarity to what Heidegger, in *Being and Time*, calls an existential analytic. But there is an important difference. For although both Heidegger and Foucault attempt to . . . relate the "factical" principles which structure the space governing the emergence of objects and subjects [i.e., enact a world], Heidegger's method is hermeneutic or *internal*, whereas Foucault's is archaeological or *external*. Foucault is explicitly rejecting both Husserlian phenomenology and Heideggerian hermeneutics when he opposes to the exegetical account the *exteriority* of the archaeological attitude. (*Michel Foucault: Beyond Structuralism and Hermeneutics*, 1983, p. 57, n. 5).

It could hardly be put plainer. Heidegger is focusing on zone 3 (inside or "internal" of the collective interior); Foucault, on zone 4 (outside or "external" of the collective interior).

We can see precisely the same thing in today's battles between the different schools of systems theory. Virtually all of them make the prior judgment that the "ultimately really real" reality is the lower-right quadrant (the sum total or Whole or collective of all objective interwoven dynamic "its"), but then they split—almost down the middle—as to which view within the lower right is the truly ultimately real perspective—the inside (cognitive, enactive, autopoietic, relative) vs. the outside (objective, rational, universal, realist).

Those who choose the *inside view* will put a great deal of emphasis—sometimes, a total emphasis—on the creative power of the interior, cognitive, subjective, enactive capacity of the organism to create or co-create its own reality/environment. Thus, well-respected systems evolutionary researcher Dereck Bickerton maintains that what any organism "sees"—including humans—depends upon its evolutionary history, and therefore all knowing is "species-specific" (i.e., subjective/inside); there simply is no "objectively single and real" view of a reality that is "out there." As he puts it, "It is meaningless to talk about a 'true view of the world.' To attain such a view, a minimum prerequisite would be for the viewer not to belong to any particular species . . . It is absurd to speak about a 'true view of the world' because it is not true for any creature that what it perceives is the world itself. What constitutes any creature's view is essentially a system of categories" (*Language and Species*, 1990, pp. 82, 86; cited in Bausch, p. 52) (In other words, an enacted/co-created/inside view.) As Kenneth Bausch summarizes this view in *The Emerging Consensus in Social Systems*:

> Our representations have no reality independent of our minds and languages. They do not re-present an existing reality that is present to us. In the course of evolution and ontogeny, we have fabricated these representations, imposed them on our experience, justified them, and come to rely upon them. With all these representations, however, and all our refinements of self-observation, self-description, reflection, and theories of reflection, we never achieve a privileged access to knowledge. We remain bound to self-observation. (2001, p. 374)

In short, there is (*from this perspective*—zone 7) no single, pre-given, true "outside view" because there is no single pregiven "outside"—there are only the ways that the organism co-creates its "outside" reality/environment according to its own systems of autopoietic cognitions. This perspective is the way reality *actually looks* to somebody emphasizing a collective "inside-view" (i.e., somebody viewing reality via zone 7) and—especially given the impact of autopoiesis theory—it is a very common view in modern systems theories and evolutionary theories. This means that individuals who emphasize one or more of zones 1, 3, 5, or 7—the "inside views"—will have a great affinity with each other, with all of them maintaining, in their own ways, that the structure of the knowing subject is fundamental in creating/enacting the ontology of the given object, and, indeed, there is no "pregiven single reality" that is simply "out there" awaiting perception by all and sundry. What we call "reality" is primarily co-enacted by the perceiving organism (and its culture), and otherwise has no substantial, characterizable existence. Recall that generally a theorist will have previously selected one quadrant as being the "really real" quadrant, and so only one zone—either the inside zone or the outside zone of that quadrant—will generally be postulated as being the "really real" zone; so it's not required that all of the "inside" zones are included in any single theory—usually just one zone, which is a zone in the preselected "really real" quadrant, will be selected, and then the opposite zone in that quadrant—if the inside view is selected, then the outside view, and vice versa—will be argued to be unreal or mistaken or just plain wrong (not to mention the similar view from all the other already rejected quadrants). If two quadrants are felt to be "really real," then both inside—or both outside—views will be the "really real" ones, and so on.

Critics of this "inside view" [such as Critical Realists] typically charge it with "the epistemic fallacy," the putatitve fallacy being the idea that the structure of the subject has a substantial hand in the formation of the ontology of any object it knows. The view charging and criticizing this "epistemic fallacy" is generally held by all those who adopt the opposite stance—that is, the outside, rational, realist, objective view. (For integral theory, both are "true but partial," depending primarily on the perspective/view that one takes. So we do acknowledge a "real ontology"—*but this is the way reality looks only from the outside views*—the inside views instead tend to see autopoietic, co-enactive, co-creative realities. *Both* of those are real, and integral theory refuses to choose just one and reject the others. Doing that is just a perspective-absolutism. And that can be seen as false: All you have to do is adopt the perspective—the particular quadrant and zone—and look at reality the way the proponents of that view are looking at it, and you will see just what they are seeing—your claim of "wrongness" comes, not from the perspective itself, but from your preselection of just one of them to be the only true one—the "wrongness" is in your narrow and limited viewpoint, not in the viewpoint itself, which is perfectly "true but partial.")

And, indeed, as Bausch himself points out clearly, almost exactly half of the other systems theorists (i.e., the half other than the inside, co-creative, enactive, autopoietic views) do indeed adopt a given "objective reality" view—giving us the two major views on the nature of systems themselves—inside/enactive and outside/realist (we just saw these two views—inside and outside—in the lower left with Heidegger and Foucault; now we see them in the lower right with the two main schools of overall systems theory). As Bausch, in his full summary of systems thinking, points out: There are today "two grand unifying theories of present-day systems thinking: 1) complexity/bifurcation/components systems and 2) autopoiesis"—which he also points out are exactly the outside/realist/objective reality view and the inside/enactive/co-creative autopoietic view.

Here is a brief summary of these two major approaches by a widely acknowledged expert in the field [Bausch, p. 16]:

> These two strands of thinking advance systems theory beyond the bounds of mechanical (closed) models and organic (open) models and move it into the arena of emergent models. Component-systems thinking, which is propounded by Csanyi, Kampis, and (to some extent) Goertzel, is an outgrowth of Bertalanffy's General Systems Theory (GST). GST "enabled one to interrelate the theory of the organism, thermodynamics, and evolutionary theory" (Luhmann). Component-system theory loosely includes the bifurcation thinking of Prigogine, the molecular biology of Eigen, the complexity thinking of Kauffman and Gell-Mann, the physics of information theory, and the sociology of cognitive maps. It describes the processes that generate increasing unity and complexity in specific details that are alleged to have universal application (external, objective, realist, universal; ontology favoring).
>
> Autopoiesis in its biological form, proposed by Maturana and Varela, considers organisms as systems that are closed in their internal organization, but open on the level of their structural composition and metabolism. Autopoiesis in its sociological form, proposed by Luhmann, focuses on the difference between system and environment and identifies autopoietic systems with the unity of contradiction that derives from their being simultaneously autonomous from their environment and totally dependent upon

> it. In our thinking about autopoietic and component-systems, we discover vistas of new and possibly fruitful explanations of physical, organic, social, and cultural processes. It turns out that these ideas [component-systems and autopoiesis—the outside view and the inside view of the Lower-Right quadrant] comprise the bulk of the ideas that are considered and evaluated in this research.

The first approach is the more standard *dynamic systems theory*, which (for this simple classification) includes a wide variety of items such as general systems theory, cybernetics, dissipative structures, component-systems, chaos theories, complexity theories, and so on. As we will see, dynamic systems theory is often actually called the *outside* (or *rational*) view, because it attempts to give the overall view seen from the outside: "detached, objective, systemic, reconstructive, universal, realist."

The second major approach attempts to give an account, not of the system seen from without by a detached (scientific) observer, but the inner choices made by an individual organism as it actively participates with (and enacts) its environment—this is the *autopoietic* perspective, also specifically called the *inside* (or *cognitive*) view.

(By the way, all of those terms—*autopoietic, cognitive, inside, systems, rational, outside*—are the terms used *by the theorists themselves*—including *inside* and *outside*—as ample quotes will show. At this point, I am not giving my own interpretation of these schools, simply reporting how they see themselves. I will eventually maintain, of course, that they are respectively and actually focusing on different zones—the inside vs. the outside zones—or, for systems [LR quadrant], zone 7 and zone 8, respectively, *with both being true when addressing their own zone.*)

So we have a systems/rational/objective/outside view, and an autopoietic/enactive, cognitive/inside view. And virtually all of present-day systems theory is divided almost equally between those two major views. Some people are confused at the use of *rational* and *cognitive* in that scheme, because often those two words mean the same thing; so why in this case are they diametrically opposed to each other? As employed by the theorists themselves, *cognition* is used not to specifically mean *rational* or *intellectual*, but in its wider and more inclusive meaning, which is any organism's attempt to register its environment (e.g., an amoeba reacts to light, so it has a rudimentary cognition of light—but it does not, of course, have a "rational" view of light). In this sense, if I take a "cognitive" view of biology (à la Varela and Maturana), then I will try to explain, *from the inside view of the organism*, the types of reactions, behaviors, and cognitions that the organism itself makes as it encounters, enacts, and brings forth its world. This is also sometimes called *biological phenomenology* (a phrase Maturana and Varela themselves use), because it attempts to describe the phenomenal world of the organism itself. This is what the autopoietic approaches, pioneered by Maturana and Varela, attempt to do (and Maturana and Varela actually call their approach "biological phenomenology" and "the view from within"; and they explicitly exclude any form of standard dynamic systems theory from their view, since no biological organism actually has that view [except the human scientific organism]). Therefore: the autopoietic, cognitive, enactive, co-creative, inside view.

This view accuses the outside/objective/realist schools of committing the "ontic fallacy," the belief that the entire structure of the knowing process is created by (or dependent upon) the object as it is reflected on or known by the knowing subject—that the object is "really real," pregiven, single, intransitive, and universal—it may be interpreted in different ways, but it is, underneath all that, one and the same object, and the aim of all true knowledge is to accurately reflect or represent this pregiven ontology—and that is exactly what is denied by virtually every inside-view approach. The inside/autopoietic view also charges this realist/objectivist view with "the myth of the given"—the myth that there is, in fact, only a single pregiven world, just waiting to be known by one and all (that pregiven world might be confused, misinterpreted, covered up, or denied, but it is still the same, single, pregiven world or ontology. The realist schools claim to be plugged into this ontology).

"Rational" is merely one type (or level) of cognition; as used by these theorists, it means the rational activity of the scientists themselves as they attempt to explain phenomena in terms of, say, complex dynamic systems of mutual interaction. In this general systems approach—the "rational/outside" approach—the attempt is not made to "get inside" the organism, but to stand back and try to see the whole picture, the total system or web of relationships as they mutually interact with and influence each other. This "rational" view is not saying that the Web of Life is merely a rational entity, but simply that scientists attempt rationally to study that Web. This "rational," third-person view is only taken by the scientists themselves; only a scientist sees a "big picture systems view"—it is definitely not the cognition of, say, a frog (and thus is a view that is "outside" of the frog's view). Thus: The system's, rational, universal, objective, realist, outside view.

This is the view that charges the inside/subjective/autopoietic view with the "epistemic fallacy"—the putative fallacy that substantial aspects of the known object are imposed/enacted/co-created by the structure of the knowing subject (instead of there being one, fundamentally real ontology, which, no matter how many different ways it might be interpreted, is basically the same single, invariant, universal, intransitive reality).

So what we see are these two basic, historically dominant, fundamental views of epistemology and ontology—and the integral claim is that they are both right to the extent they are adequately describing whichever of the zones they have focused on (with, of course, the inside/autopoietic/subjective views focusing on zones such as 5 and 7; and the realist/objective/outside views focusing on zones such as 6 and 8). Each view is *right* or *correct* when it is focusing on its particular views or zones (and assuming it is doing it correctly, of course); and if so, then it has a "true but partial" reality (and this needs to be included in an overall integral approach). And possible views are *false* or *incorrect* when, among other possibles, they violate the exclusion principle and criticize other views for what they are supposedly "doing wrong." In other words, the integral view rejects both the epistemic and the ontic fallacy in principle (unless, of course, they are actually being committed, which means—for integral theory—that either specific characteristics of the subject [epistemic fallacy] or object [ontic fallacy] are being illicitly imported onto [or ascribed to] the correlated subject or object—in ways that are truly wrong and largely fabricated.) What integral theory rejects is that one or the other of these fallacies is simply *always* the case in every process of knowing—in other words, that the subject never enacts/co-creates objects, or objects never impact/co-create the structure of knowing itself. For integral theory, the epistemic fallacy applies to any overapplication of the inside view, which occurs when the substantive (subsisting) aspects of the outside/objective reality are denied entirely (or made to totally depend upon human knowing). In other words, the epistemic fallacy is the idea that there is *only* the inside/subjective/enactive world (and all objects are nothing but enacted), which is simply not true (every quadrant, after all, has an inside *and* an outside—how much clearer could that be?). And the ontic fallacy, for integral theory, applies to any overapplication of the outside view, when the significant additions/creations/enactions of the structure of the knowing subject are totally denied and their enactive impacts glibly charged with an "epistemic fallacy." Either of those fallacies can assume that, taken in themselves, they are always correct (i.e., some critical realists charge integral theory with *always* committing the epistemic fallacy, simply because integral maintains that all four quadrants are tetra-enacted—and that means that all four of them have a contributing reality, and not just one, as the epistemic fallacy stunningly maintains). That "epistemic view" of all of integral simply involves broken, partial, fragmented aspects of the real and Whole world, which has both *subsistence* ("objectively real ontological realities") and "ex-istence" ("subjectively real and enacted phenomenal realities")—*both equally real and equally important dimensions of an underlying Whole reality.*

These two stances (subsistence and ex-istence) are integrated via the notion that the best understanding of any reality's subsistence ("real ontological being"—which is indeed *real,* and apart from any particular human knowing [unless the object in question is part of a particular human knowing itself, and then of course it's involved]), but it is best given by the highest level of consciousness development at any given time in history/evolution (e.g., the "actual nature" or "subsistence" of an atom is best given, not by magenta or red or amber or orange, but by turquoise, the highest expectable level of development in today's world—that is our closest chance of getting at the *real* subsistence of an atom today). Hence, the *outside/objective view* is fully included.

At the same time, the highest view today (generally, that of turquoise) is itself involved in the enaction or co-creation of whatever it is that it happens to know—a structure can only know what will actually impact or influence that structure, and thus all knowing is, in part, an interpretation (one of the partial truths we take from postmodernism). That is, any item that appears in consciousness is something that "ex-ists" or stands out in consciousness, and does so with the imprints of that structure of consciousness. For example, although atoms had a subsistence during tribal times, no atom ex-isted in the mind of any tribal individual, and, for all intents and purposes, the atom did not ex-ist for tribal people—this is the autopoietic/inside view—although we acknowledge that, nonetheless, during tribal times, atoms did indeed subsist (they subsisted in reality, they just did not "ex-ist" in human reality; this is the outside/realist view, fully included). And, as soon as we are asked to describe exactly what these atoms were that *subsisted* in tribal times, we will actually use whatever views of the atom that *ex-ist* in the finest turquoise minds today—ubsistence and ex-istence are always linked (and outsides and insides are always correlative/united). For us of today, what we believe is the *subsistence* of an atom (i.e., its "real existence" both today and all the way back to tribal times and before) is actually the *ex-istence* of the atom as it appears to turquoise (in today's accepted science). Each higher level of development will get us closer to the "truth," but this is a sliding scale—again, as Hegel said, "Each level is adequate; each higher level is more adequate"—and this is the same for truth:"Each level has truth; each higher level has more truth."

This does not undercut ontology; it actually saves it. Otherwise, believing that there is indeed only "one pregiven intransitive reality"—coupled with the fact of ongoing evolution, each stage of which sees reality "more clearly" or "with more truth" (the way each higher level of consciousness has seen atoms more accurately and more clearly over time, from orange little "planetary systems" to green quarks to teal unified quark theory to turquoise strings—the "most real" truth of atoms today is given by the highest structure to evolution today; that is, turquoise strings). But that being the case, if there is only one, single, pregiven reality—seen more and more clearly with every higher developmental stage—that would actually mean that we would never know any truth at all. If there is only one pregiven intransitive reality, and each level of evolution sees it more and more clearly—*and* evolution never ends—then we will never know real or final truth at all—we would have to wait until the very end of evolution in order to see "final truth"—in the meantime, we will always and only know partial falsehoods for all time (because evolution never ends, and we will never have "ultimately real truth"). But by recognizing that this integral unity of inside/subjective and outside/objective views gives us a sliding scale of truth ("Each level is true, each higher level is more true"), then each level is allowed to know a *real* truth—*as true as true can be* (as best as it can, at its time, with its given tools and techniques, be adequately known—that is "truth" as far as it can have any actual or real meaning at all)—and all of these can be expected to grow and evolve and make "more truth" at each higher level—which does not deny truth as it presents itself at any lower level, but simply situates it within a total Wholeness of reality in which epistemology and ontology (inside and outside) are two aspects of the same underlying, unfolding Wholeness. In this way—and this way only—can we escape the epistemic and ontic fallacies. And in this way only can those two archetypal enemies—idealism vs. realism, spiritualism vs. materialism, subjective vs. objective, empirical vs. rational, epistemic vs. ontic—both be fully acknowledged and fully integrated.

This view comes from a sustained look at developmental studies—which is one of critical realism's weaknesses—as they acknowledge. But the first thing you learn in developmental studies is that every level has a different world. And there are basically only two ways you can handle that. You can say there is one, given, intransitive, "realist" ontology, and each higher level of development sees that ontology more and more clearly. That definitely puts ontology front and center, and allows Karl Popper to ask, essentially, "How can science put a person on the moon?" "Because," he basically answered, "there is one real ontology and science gives us access to that"—and that is the outside/rational/realist/objective ontology that guides all "outside" views. The only problem with that is that you haven't saved ontology: You've deleted it, destroyed it. By acknowledging that every higher level of development and consciousness and cognitive sees that pregiven ontology more clearly—and sees that what was taken for truth at the previous stage is actually seen as false or very limited from a higher stage/view—then you realize you will *never* see this full ontology in a complete and adequate way—because only the highest level of evolution will ever see that, and evolution never ends—knowledge of ontology is *never*, but *never*, really known. All we know are various falsehoods and illusions, and humanity is removed from ever being able to know any genuine reality. Ontology is not saved; it is utterly destroyed. Anchoring truth in just outside/objective/ontological/realist/universal/intransitive views does exactly that.

If, on the other hand, we adopt a developmental, "sliding," "evolutionary" view of truth, then every level has a degree of truth judged by the reality and the phenomena of that level—if all phenomena are brought together carefully and adequately, and all worked together into a hypothesis that accounts for all known facts and truths *at that level*, then that is as close to truth as truth can possibly mean at that point in evolution. But this also means that we stop claiming that there is only one, single, given truth, which is known by items such as science (because even if so, those truths keep changing with every new developmental level—and we will still *never* get an adequate truth). As for "every level is adequate, but every higher level is more adequate," and likewise "every level is true, every higher level is more true"—we already know that that is true for consciousness, ethics, love, awareness, cognition, morals, aesthetics—and on and on (i.e., "Each level has consciousness, each higher level has more consciousness;" "each level has ethics, each higher level has greater ethics;" "each level has love, each higher level has more love")—we have research on all that almost ad infinitum. But that means each level is helping to enact and co-create the phenomena at its level (all four quadrants tetra-arise). Both epistemology and ontology play together in a mutually unified and unifying Wholeness in this endeavor. Charging just one or the other with either the "epistemic" or "ontic" fallacy is pure idiocy, if you'll excuse my French.

In my own presentations—and largely just for space considerations—I will often argue for the reality of either the inside view or the outside view, without always taking time to argue for their unity (which is simply assumed, anyway, to be a fairly obvious assumption of integral theory).

But when emphasizing the inside view, I usually focus on the realities of enaction (usually identified as "tetra-enaction" to emphasize the important role of all four quadrants and all zones), as well as the fact that phenomena are co-created by the subject (epistemology) and the paradigm/exemplar/injunction (methodology), which together bring forth a real and different world at each level of development/evolution (overall, multiple epistemologies, multiple methodologies, and multiple ontologies—integrated in AQAL)—and *that* is the overall view of integral theory. I'll often especially focus on the importance of perspectives in the whole epistemic/ontic process: The fact that the meaning of a statement is the injunction (perspectival action) of its enaction ("The world is built of sentient beings with perspectives" is a typical shorthand of the view as integral summarizes it).

On the other hand, when I focus on the outside ("ontological") view, I focus on the actually existing elements of the AQAL Framework (quadrants, levels, line, states, types, etc.), the twenty tenets [first presented in *Sex, Ecology, Spirituality*, 1995] (such as that "reality is composed of holons;" when emphasizing their unity, I'll often say "reality is composed of holons with perspectives")—and will not mention that, for example, AQAL is a summary view of reality as explained via vision-logic at the turquoise or indigo level/perspective, is grounded in a non-dual state, and is in part an interpretation co-created by those structures/states of consciousness.

As I generally present them, the inside view emphasizes the centrality of epistemology and methodology (Who and How), and the outside view focuses on ontology (the What). The When and Where are likewise inherent in the AQAL Framework, inasmuch as one cannot fully give all the elements of the AQAL Framework without indicating the temporal When (with the overall evolutionary/developmental component being a part of that temporal dimension) and the Where (with items such as the entire lower-right quadrant dependent upon the systematic physical/material location of the overall occasion with a particular Kosmic Address). What I will never do is suggest that any of those five elements (Who, What, When, Where, How) can exist without the others; *Integral* means exactly what the word says.

And finally—briefly—these two major views—the inside/enactive/autopoietic/co-creative and the outside/rational/universal/realist—are present, as I did mention, in all four quadrants, although we focused on the lower-left and lower-right examples of that. But in the upper right, this is the quadrant where Varela and Maturana first made their breakthrough discoveries on autopoiesis and the enaction paradigm (working primarily from the inside of the UR—or "biological phenomenology" or the "view from within"). This was primarily a pure zone 5. This was contrasted, in their writings, with the outside views of the UR (namely, zone 6), such as positivism, realism, materialism, empiricism, and rationalism; as well as with the outside views of the LR, including systems theory in general (inside or outside); a biological organism did *not* see the world as a Web of Life as general system theory did, and that is one of the first items they rejected in their "biological phenomenology." Luhmann picked this enactive paradigm up and applied it to social systems in the LR (as we extensively noted). So the inside/outside dialectic "battle" we have been tracing is at work in the upper right as well.

And likewise in the upper left. The inside/enactive view (the view from zone 1) is often characterized as "prehension," and this means that each subject, emerging and coming to be, feels or prehends the previous subject, making it object—and thus co-uniting ontology (object) and epistemology (subjective) in each interactive action. Neither is privileged; reality is a co-creation of the present subject and previous subject now made object—the unity of ontology and epistemology could hardly be clearer. And as for the outside/objective/universal structuralism of zone 2, this is indeed an objective/universal view, but what it discloses is a series of developmental structures or levels, with each one presenting a different given/universal/worldview. So it is true to the outside/universal/given realities; the structures disclosed are "real entities," real ontologies; but their ongoing sequences discloses that each new level brings a new world; so the actual practice of structuralism provides that ontological/objective/universal structures (which we have always claimed are actual and real components of the Kosmos); but their ongong sequential unfolding shows a different world after a different world after a different world indefinitely—if we're careful with what we mean here, disclosed a co-enacted world after co-enactive world, a co-created reality after each co-created reality. So this zone 2 view is indeed an outside view, an objective/real/ontological/universal view; but taken over time, demonstrates as powerfully as any methodology available, the co-created, enacted, autopoietic, tetra-enacted nature of reality.

Integral-metatheory combines the inside and outside views from all four quadrants (which also gives us levels, lines, states, and types)—and we have seen that each of the quadrants has an inside and outside view (and not only that, but that the inside and outside views are often the predominant views available at that quadrant). This is the general meaning of *integral* itself.

Contributors

Bruce Alderman is adjunct faculty in the College of Graduate and Professional Studies at John F. Kennedy University (JFKU). He received his master's degree in integral psychology, with an emphasis on counseling psychology, from JFKU in 2005. He has published several articles on integral religion and spirituality in the *Journal of Integral Theory and Practice*, *Consciousness Journal*, and *Integral Review*, and has several additional essays on integral metatheory scheduled to appear in anthologies toward the end of 2019. His current areas of interest include integral theory and practice, transpersonal psychology, integral postmetaphysical spirituality, critical realism, cognitive linguistics, the time-space-knowledge vision, interfaith dialogue, composing music, and writing fiction.

Zayin Cabot is a lecturer in the philosophy department at California State University, East Bay. His work focuses on the need for nonmodern and decolonial approaches to the history and philosophy of religions. Trained as a process philosopher and initiated as a West African diviner in the Dagara tradition from Burkina Faso, his work defends the roles of scholar-practitioners in the field, and is deeply comparative in nature. Zayin has published several journal articles and book chapters, most recently a chapter on "African Beliefs" for the Routledge Companion to Death and Dying. His first book, *Ecologies of Participation: Agents, Shamans, Mystics, and Diviners* was published in 2018.

Gregory Desilet is an unaffiliated independent scholar whose academic training focused on rhetoric, communication, and language philosophy at the University of California at Santa Barbara and the University of Colorado at Boulder. This training provided the foundation for the expansion of interests into metaphysics, postmodern philosophy, cultural criticism, new spirituality, and film and television analysis and commentary. Published books include *Cult of the Kill: Traditional Metaphysics of Rhetoric, Truth, and Violence in a Postmodern World* (2002, 2006 rev.), *Our Faith in Evil: Melodrama and the Effects of Entertainment Violence* (2006), *Burning Banks and Roasting Marshmallows: The Education of Daniel Marleau* (2009), *Radical Atheism and New Spirituality: Contesting the Metaphysical Ground of Spiritual Life* (2011), and *Screens of Blood: A Critical Approach to Film and Television Violence* (2014). Current writing includes a book-length project contrasting the language philosophies of Wittgenstein and Derrida.

Sean Esbjörn-Hargens is the founder of MetaIntegral, a social-enterprise company dedicated to the professional application of integral principles. He is one of the world's leading experts on integrative metatheories (e.g., Wilber's Integral Theory, Bhaskar's Critical Realism, and Morin's Complex Thought) and their application. Building on the vision of American philosopher Ken Wilber, he has played a significant role in creating the fields of integral ecology, integral research, integral education, and integral business. Sean's articles have appeared in academic journals such as the *Journal of Consciousness Studies, World Futures, ReVision*, and the *Journal of Humanistic Psychology*. Sean coedited Ken Wilber's book *The Simple Feeling of Being* (2004) and coauthored an 830-page book with environmental philosopher Michael Zimmerman, *Integral Ecology: Uniting Multiple Perspectives on the Natural World* (2009). He has coedited an anthology on integral education (SUNY Press, 2010) and edited an anthology on integral theory (SUNY Press, 2010). Recently, he coedited a groundbreaking two-volume set on integrative metatheory and its application: *Metatheory for the Twenty-first Century* (2016) and *Metatheory for the Anthropocene*. These two volumes are the outcomes of a five-year dialogical engagement between the leading scholar-practitioners of integral theory and critical realism. He is editor of the SUNY Press series in integral theory.

Cameron Stewart Rees Freeman completed his Ph.D. in philosophy from the Flinders University of South Australia (2007) and is currently an independent researcher who does casual teaching at the University of South Australia in the School of Psychology, Social Work, and Social Policy, and the Global Center for Advanced Studies within the Institute of Critical Theology. Cameron has previously worked in the United States as a content editor for *Integral Life* and in 2011 received funding to complete the Jesus Database Project (with John Dominic Crossan) as a researcher for the Centre for Public and Contextual Theology at Charles Sturt University. Cameron's first book was *Post-Metaphysics and the Paradoxical Teachings of Jesus* (2010), and he is currently completing a new manuscript on critical-historical Jesus scholarship, radical theology, and the post-metaphysical turn in Schelling.

Nicholas Hedlund is founding director of the Eudaimonia Institute, a think tank and social innovations lab, and a Ph.D. researcher at University College London in philosophy and social sciences. Nick was an exchange scholar at Yale University, served as executive director of the Integral Research Center, and was organizer of the International Critical Realism & Integral Theory Symposia Series, held in London and San Francisco. His articles have appeared in peer-reviewed journals such as *Environmental Science & Policy* and the *Journal of Integral Theory and Practice.* He is coeditor, along with Roy Bhaskar, Sean Esbjörn-Hargens, and Mervyn Hartwig, of *Metatheory for the Twenty-First Century: Critical Realism and Integral Theory in Dialogue* (2016) and *Metatheory for the Anthropocene: Emancipatory Praxis for Planetary Flourishing.*

Martin Beck Matuštík is Lincoln professor of ethics and religion at Arizona State University. He joined the New College of Interdisciplinary Arts and Sciences at ASUW in fall 2008. After earning his Ph.D. from Fordham University in 1991, he has been on the faculty in the Department of Philosophy at Purdue University. He published seven single-author books, edited two collections, and co-edited the series New Critical Theory. Among his publications are *Postnational Identity: Critical Theory and Existential Philosophy in Habermas, Kierkegaard, and Havel* (1993), *Specters of Liberation: Great Refusals in the New World Order* (1998), *Jurgen Habermas: A Philosophical-Political Profile* (2001), *Radical Evil and the Scarcity of Hope: Postsecular Meditations* (2008), and *Out of Silence: Repair across Generations* (2015). He co-edited with Merold Westphal *Kierkegaard in Post/Modernity* (1995), and with William L. McBride *Calving O. Schrag and The Task of Philosophy after Postmodernity* (2002). His research and teaching specialties range from critical theory, continental philosophy, phenomenology, and existentialism to post-Holocaust and reparative ethics, comparative philosophy of religion, and East-Central European thought.

Sam Mickey is an adjunct professor in the theology and religious studies department and the environmental studies program at the University of San Francisco, California. Sam has worked as a researcher for the *Journey of the Universe* project and the Forum on Religion and Ecology at Yale.

His recent research focuses on ethical and theological implications of new materialism, posthumanism, and object-oriented ontology. He is the author of several books that present cross-disciplinary perspectives in ecological thought, including *Coexistentialism and the Unbearable Intimacy of Ecological Emergency* (2016), *Whole Earth Thinking and Planetary Coexistence* (2015), and *On the Verge of a Planetary Civilization* (2014). He is a coeditor of both *The Variety of Integral Ecologies* (SUNY Press, 2017) and *Women and Nature? Beyond Dualism in Gender, Body, and Environment* (2017). Sam blogs regularly at BecomingIntegral.com.

Tom Murray works part-time as a senior research fellow at the University of Massachusetts School of Computer Science, and is chief visionary and instigator at Open Way Solutions. Murray's projects include research on using text analytics to estimate developmental levels, using artificial intelligence methods to create responsive learning environments, and supporting social-deliberative skills and deep, reflective dialogue in online contexts. He is an associate editor for the journal *Integral Review*, and has published articles on integral theory as it relates to education, contemplative dialogue, leadership, ethics, knowledge-building communities, epistemology, and post-metaphysics. He has also published extensively in the field of intelligent tutoring systems.

Brian Schroeder is professor and chair of philosophy and director of religious studies at Rochester Institute of Technology (RIT). He is coeditor of the SUNY Press series in contemporary Italian philosophy, executive committee member of the Comparative and Continental Philosophy Circle, and executive committee member of the Society for Italian Philosophy. He has formerly served as codirector of the Society for Phenomenology and Existential Philosophy, codirector and chair of the board of directors of the International Association for Environmental Philosophy, director of the Colleguium Phaenomenologicum, and executive committee member of the Nietzsche Society. Schroeder has published extensively on contemporary European philosophy, the history of philosophy, Buddhist philosophy, the Kyoto School, environmental philosophy, and philosophical theology. An ordained Sōtō Zen priest, he is the Buddhist chaplain at RIT and guiding director of the Idunno Zen Community.

Michael Schwartz is professor in the Department of Art and Design at Augusta University, Augusta, Georgia, where he teaches a sequence of transdisciplinary based academic classes to students in studio art. He is cofounding executive officer of the Comparative and Continental Philosophy Circle, an international professional philosophy organization with both a peer-reviewed journal and book series (of which he is founding associate editor of both). Michael has published in the areas of art history, art criticism, art education, continental philosophy, comparative philosophy, critical social theory, integral theory, critical realism, comparative metatheory, and religious studies. Coauthor/coeditor of a number of books in philosophy and critical theory, he also curated the international art exhibition and authored the book catalog *In the Spirit of Wholeness: Integral Art and its Enchantment Aesthetic.*

Zachary Stein was educated at Hampshire College and Harvard University. Zak cofounded Lectica Inc, a nonprofit dedicated to using the learning sciences to transform educational testing. He sits on the board of the Society for Consciousness Studies and works as a scientific advisor for various technology companies seeking to impact human evolution. He is the author of *Social Justice and Educational Measurement: John Rawls, The History of Testing, and the Future of Education* (2016) and *Education in a Time Between Worlds* (2019). Most of his articles can be found at zakstein.org.

David E. Storey is currently associate professor of the practice in the philosophy department at Boston College, where he teaches courses on the history of philosophy, ethics, environmental ethics, and climate change. His research and teaching interests are in phenomenology, environmental ethics, comparative philosophy, contemplative pedagogy, and integral theory. He is the author of *Naturalizing Heidegger: His Confrontation with Nietzsche, His Contributions to Environmental Philosophy* (SUNY Press, 2015), and he has published essays in journals such as *Environmental Ethics*, *Epoche*, and *Comparative and Continental Philosophy*. David is the host of the podcast *Wisdom at Work: Philosophy Beyond the Ivory Tower*, which interviews people who have successfully translated their philosophical training into careers outside the academy. He received his Ph.D. in philosophy in 2011 from Fordham University.

Ken Wilber is the founder of the Integral Institute and the cofounder of Integral Life. He is an internationally acknowledged leader and the preeminent scholar of the integral stage of human development. He is the chief architect of integral theory and is the author of more than twenty books, including *Integral Meditation*, *A Theory of Everything*, *Integral Spirituality*, *No Boundary*, *Grace and Grit*, *The Religion of Tomorrow*, and *Sex, Ecology, Spirituality*.

Jason M. Wirth is professor of philosophy at Seattle University, and works and teaches in the areas of continental philosophy, Buddhist philosophy, aesthetics, environmental philosophy, and Africana philosophy. His recent books include *Nietzsche and Other Buddhas: Philosophy after Comparative Philosophy* (2019), *Mountains, Rivers, and the Great Earth: Reading Gary Snyder and Dōgen in an Age of Ecological Crisis* (SUNY Press, 2017), a monograph on Milan Kundera (*Commiserating with Devastated Things*, 2015), *Schelling's Practice of the Wild* (SUNY Press, 2015), and the coedited volumes (with Bret Davis and Brian Schroeder) *Japanese and Continental Philosophy: Conversations with the Kyoto School* (2011) and *Engaging Dōgen's Zen* (2016). He is the associate editor and book review editor of the journal *Comparative and Continental Philosophy*. He is currently working on a study of the cinema of Terrence Malick.

Michael E. Zimmerman, until retiring in 2015, was professor of philosophy at the University of Colorado Boulder. After receiving his Ph.D. in 1974, Zimmerman taught at Tulane University where he served three terms as department chair and codirected the environmental studies program for ten years. Zimmerman has won many teaching awards. In 2006, he was appointed to a four-year stint as director of CU Boulder's Center for Humanities and the Arts, and also joined CU's philosophy department. In addition to authoring more than one hundred academic articles and book chapters, Zimmerman has published four books: *Eclipse of the Self: The Development of Heidegger's Concept of Authenticity* (1981); *Heidegger's Confrontation with Modernity* (1990); *Contesting Earth's Future: Radical Ecology and Postmodernity* (2004); and *Integral Ecology: Uniting Multiple Perspectives on the Natural World*, coauthored with Sean Esbjörn-Hargens (2009).

Index

Note: Entries with a *t* indicate tables, entries with an *f* indicate figures.